BED A
STOPS 1997

Hotels, Guest Houses, Farmhouses,
Private Homes, for food and accommodation
throughout Britain.   Includes Campus Holidays.

FHG

FOREWORD

BED AND BREAKFAST STOPS 1997

This 1997 edition of *BED AND BREAKFAST STOPS* has more entries than ever before with over 400 pages of accommodation from which to choose. Should you desire to stay at a family run guest house *'on the fringes of Dartmoor'* or a large hotel *'close to London's West End'* you can be sure to find your requirements within these pages.

The main aim of *BED AND BREAKFAST STOPS* is to provide you, our readers, with all the details necessary for making your own direct bookings and you will find that the entries in this publication include full descriptions of each property and its facilities and, usually, an indication of what you can expect to pay.

You'll find full contact details with all the entries in the Main Sections and in the Special Welcome Supplements of *BED AND BREAKFAST STOPS* and you may find the following points helpful when you use them.

Enquiries and Bookings: The Contents page will lead you through the book in detail. Sections and counties are shown clearly at the top of each page. Make sure that you are using the section you want. Once you have seen what is suitable, contact the advertiser or advertisers by letter or telephone for further information or to make a booking. Give full details of dates, numbers etc. and any special requirements. If you write, enclose a stamped, addressed envelope for the reply. If booking by telephone, make sure that everything is confirmed in writing.

Complaints: FHG Publications Ltd. do not inspect or recommend accommodation. We accept our entries in good faith and we ask our advertisers to agree to adhere to our aims of clean and comfortable accommodation, wholesome and well-cooked food and courtesy and consideration towards guests. They are also subject to the Trades Description Act. Although we cannot accept responsibility for any of the services or accommodation advertised here, we do follow up complaints from our readers. Regretfully we cannot act as intermediaries but we invite you to let us know if you have problems or complaints. Please note, you should always try to speak to your host at the time about any complaints.

Holiday Insurance: Don't forget that as a guest or host you can insure against cancellation or other risks. There are many reputable brokers and companies who issue such policies. If you have trouble finding one let us know.

The FHG Diploma: If you have a particularly good holiday, let us know. You may help your host to win one of our annual FHG Diplomas for outstanding service and/or accommodation. The names of our 1996 Diploma winners are listed in this book and we will be happy to receive your recommendations for 1997.

It's not always necessary to book Bed and Breakfast in advance but in popular areas at holiday times it's obviously advisable, as it is in more remote parts. If you do book in advance and you change your plans, please tell your hosts that you've had to cancel. You may then be helping someone else who is looking for accommodation at short notice and your thoughtfulness will be appreciated in any case.

Please mention *BED AND BREAKFAST STOPS* when you are making enquiries or bookings and don't forget to use our Readers' Offer Voucher/Coupons if you're near any of the attractions which are kindly participating.

FHG

Other FHG Publications 1997

Recommended Short Break Holidays
Recommended Country Hotels of Britain
Recommended Wayside & Country Inns of Britain
Pets Welcome!
Bed and Breakfast in Britain
The Golf Guide: Where to Play/Where to Stay
Farm Holiday Guide England, Wales, Ireland & Channel Islands
Farm Holiday Guide Scotland
Self-Catering Holidays in Britain
Britain's Best Holidays
Guide to Caravan and Camping Holidays
Children Welcome! Family Holiday & Attractions Guide
Scottish Welcome

Please note: owing to recent boundary changes
the following counties no longer exist:

England

Avon — see under Gloucestershire and Somerset
Cleveland — see under Durham
Humberside — see under Yorkshire (East) and Lincolnshire

Scotland

Banffshire — see under Moray and Aberdeenshire
Kincardineshire — see under Aberdeenshire
Kinross-shire — see under Perth and Kinross

In **Wales** the changes have been more extensive
and we have arranged that section as follows:
North Wales — formerly Clwyd and Gwynedd
Dyfed
Powys
South Wales — formerly Glamorgan and Gwent

ISBN 1 85055 215 0 © FHG Publications Ltd. 1997
Cover picture: supplied by Mirror Syndication International.
Design by Cyan Creative Consultants, Glasgow.

Typeset by RD Composition Ltd., Glasgow.
Printed and bound by Bemrose Ltd., Derby.

Distribution – **Book Trade**: WLM, Downing Road, West Meadows Industrial Estate, Derby DE21 6HA.
(Tel: 01332 343332. Fax: 01332 340464).
News Trade: USM Distribution Ltd, 86 Newman Street, London W1P 3LD
(Tel: 0171-396 8000. Fax: 0171-396 8002).
E-mail:usm.co.uk

Published by FHG Publications Ltd.,
Abbey Mill Business Centre, Seedhill, Paisley PA1 1TJ (0141-887 0428. Fax: 0141-889 7204).

US ISBN 1-55650-760-7
Distributed in the United States by
Hunter Publishing Inc., 300 Raritan Center Parkway CN94,
Edison, N.J., 08818, USA

CONTENTS

FHG

CONTENTS

SCOTLAND

WALES

NORTHERN IRELAND

REPUBLIC OF IRELAND

Special Welcome Supplements

FHG

ORKNEY ISLANDS

SHETLAND ISLANDS

WESTERN ISLES

HIGHLAND

MORAY

ABERDEENSHIRE

CITY OF ABERDEEN

Great Britain

Counties, unitary authorities and council areas

ANGUS

PERTH AND KINROSS

FIFE

ARGYLL AND BUTE

STIRLING

EAST LOTHIAN

SCOTTISH BORDERS

NORTH AYRSHIRE

SOUTH LANARKSHIRE

EAST AYRSHIRE

SOUTH AYRSHIRE

DUMFRIES AND GALLOWAY

NORTHUMBERLAND

TYNE & WEAR

DURHAM

CUMBRIA

ISLE OF MAN

NORTH YORKSHIRE

1. CITY OF DUNDEE
2. CLACKMANNANSHIRE
3. FALKIRK
4. EAST DUNBARTONSHIRE
5. WEST DUNBARTONSHIRE
6. INVERCLYDE
7. RENFREWSHIRE
8. CITY OF GLASGOW
9. NORTH LANARKSHIRE
10. WEST LOTHIAN
11. CITY OF EDINBURGH
12. MIDLOTHIAN
13. EAST RENFREWSHIRE
14. STOCKTON-ON-TEES
15. MIDDLESBROUGH
16. HARTLEPOOL
17. REDCAR & CLEVELAND
18. NORTH LINCOLNSHIRE
19. KINGSTON UPON HULL
20. NORTH EAST LINCOLNSHIRE

21. ABERCONWY & COLWYN
22. DENBIGHSHIRE
23. FLINTSHIRE
24. WREXHAM
25. SWANSEA
26. NEATH & PORT TALBOT
27. RHONDDA CYNON TAFF
28. MERTHYR TYDFIL
29. BLAENAU GWENT
30. TORFAEN
31. MONMOUTHSHIRE
32. BRIDGEND
33. VALE OF GLAMORGAN
34. CARDIFF
35. CAERPHILLY
36. NEWPORT
37. NORTH WEST SOMERSET
38. BRISTOL
39. SOUTH GLOUCESTERSHIRE
40. BATH & NORTH EAST SOMERSET

YORK

EAST RIDING OF YORKSHIRE

LANCASHIRE

WEST YORKSHIRE

GREATER MANCHESTER

SOUTH YORKSHIRE

ANGLESEY

MERSEYSIDE

CHESHIRE

DERBYSHIRE

NOTTS.

LINCOLNSHIRE

GWYNEDD

STAFFS.

SHROPSHIRE

LEICESTERSHIRE

NORFOLK

WEST MIDLANDS

WARKS.

CARDIGANSHIRE

POWYS

HEREFORD AND WORCESTER

NORTHANTS.

CAMBRIDGE-SHIRE

SUFFOLK

BEDS

PEMBROKESHIRE

CARMARTHEN-SHIRE

GLOUCESTER-SHIRE

OXFORD-SHIRE

BUCKS

HERTS.

ESSEX

GREATER LONDON

CHANNEL ISLANDS

WILTSHIRE

BERKSHIRE

SURREY

KENT

SOMERSET

HAMPSHIRE

WEST SUSSEX

EAST SUSSEX

DEVON

DORSET

ISLE OF WIGHT

CORNWALL

SCILLY ISLES

© GEOprojects (UK) Ltd
© Crown Copyright

READERS' OFFER 1997 VALID during 1997

Sacrewell Farm and Country Centre

Thornhaugh, Peterborough, Cambridgeshire PE8 6HJ Tel: (01780) 782254

GROUP RATE ADMISSION for all members of party

NOT TO BE USED IN CONJUNCTION WITH ANY OTHER OFFER

READERS' OFFER 1997 VALID during 1997

DAIRYLAND FARM WORLD

Summercourt, Near Newquay, Cornwall TR8 5AA Tel: 01872 510246

One child **FREE** when accompanied by adult paying full admission price

NOT TO BE USED IN CONJUNCTION WITH ANY OTHER OFFER

READERS' OFFER 1997 VALID Easter to October 1997

Tamar Valley Donkey Park

St Anns Chapel, Gunnislake, Cornwall PL18 9HW Tel: 01822 834072

10% OFF admission price for up to 6 people, free donkey ride for children included

NOT TO BE USED IN CONJUNCTION WITH ANY OTHER OFFER

READERS' OFFER 1997 VALID during 1997

COARSE FISHING AT CROSSFIELD

Crossfield, Staffield, Kirkoswald, Cumbria CA10 1EU Tel: 01768 898711

ADMIT two children for the price of one; three adults for the price of two

NOT TO BE USED IN CONJUNCTION WITH ANY OTHER OFFER

READERS' OFFER 1997 VALID during 1997

THE CUMBERLAND TOY AND MODEL MUSEUM

Banks Court, Market Place, Cockermouth, Cumbria CA13 9NG Tel: 01900 827606

One person **FREE** per full paying adult

NOT TO BE USED IN CONJUNCTION WITH ANY OTHER OFFER

The fascinating story of farming and country life with working watermill, gardens, collections of bygones, farm and nature trails. Excellent for young children. Campers and Caravanners welcome.

DIRECTIONS: Junction A1/A47, 8 miles west of Peterborough.

OPEN: daily all year.

FHG PUBLICATIONS, ABBEY MILL BUSINESS CENTRE, PAISLEY PA1 1TJ

Britain's premier farm attraction - milking parlour, Heritage Centre, Farmpark and playground. Daily events include bottle feeding, "Pat-a-Pet" and rally karts.

DIRECTIONS: 4 miles from Newquay on the A3058 Newquay to St Austell road.

OPEN: from early April to end October 10.30am to 5pm. Also open from early December to Christmas Eve 12-5pm daily.

FHG PUBLICATIONS, ABBEY MILL BUSINESS CENTRE, PAISLEY PA1 1TJ

Donkey and donkey cart rides for children. Feed and cuddle tame lambs, goats, rabbits and donkeys. Playgrounds, cafe, gifts.

DIRECTIONS: just off A390 Tavistock to Callington road at village of St Anns Chapel

OPEN: Easter to end October 10am to 5pm

FHG PUBLICATIONS, ABBEY MILL BUSINESS CENTRE, PAISLEY PA1 1TJ

Relax, escape and enjoy a great day out - Carp, Rudd, Tench, Bream, Crucians, Ide, Roach and (for fly) Rainbow and Brown Trout

DIRECTIONS: from Kirkoswald follow signs for Staffield, turn right (signposted Dale/Blunderfield); Crossfield is 200m up narrow road via cattle grid.

OPEN: flexible — please telephone to book your fishing

FHG PUBLICATIONS, ABBEY MILL BUSINESS CENTRE, PAISLEY PA1 1TJ

Winner of the 1995 National Heritage Shoestring Award. 100 years of mainly British toys including working tinplate Hornby trains, Scalextric cars, Lego etc. Free quiz.

DIRECTIONS: just off the market place in Cockermouth

OPEN: daily 10am to 5pm from 1st February to 30th November

FHG PUBLICATIONS, ABBEY MILL BUSINESS CENTRE, PAISLEY PA1 1TJ

FHG

READERS' OFFER 1997

VALID Easter to end Oct. 1997

Dorset Heavy Horse Centre

Edmondsham, Verwood, Dorset BH21 5RJ Telephone: 01202 824040

Admit one adult **FREE** when accompanied by one full-paying adult

NOT TO BE USED IN CONJUNCTION WITH ANY OTHER OFFER

FHG

READERS' OFFER 1997

VALID April to October 1997

Killhope Lead Mining Centre

Cowshill, Upper Weardale, Co. Durham DL13 1AR Tel: 01388 537505

Admit one child **FREE** with full-paying adult (not valid for Park Level Mine)

NOT TO BE USED IN CONJUNCTION WITH ANY OTHER OFFER

FHG

READERS' OFFER 1997

VALID during 1997

Cotswold Farm Park

Guiting Power, Near Stow-on-the-Wold, Gloucestershire GL54 5UG Tel: 01451 850307

Admit one child **FREE** with an adult paying full entrance fee

NOT TO BE USED IN CONJUNCTION WITH ANY OTHER OFFER

FHG

READERS' OFFER 1997

VALID during 1997

NATIONAL WATERWAYS MUSEUM

Llanthony Warehouse, Gloucester Docks, Gloucester GL1 2EH Tel: 01452 318054

20% off all tickets (Single or Family)

NOT TO BE USED IN CONJUNCTION WITH ANY OTHER OFFER

FHG

READERS' OFFER 1997

VALID during 1997

BEAULIEU

Near Brockenhurst, Hampshire SO42 7ZN Tel: 01590 612345

£4.00 off adult ticket when accompanied by adult paying full admission.
(Not valid on Bank Holidays or for special events; not valid in conjunction with Family Ticket)

NOT TO BE USED IN CONJUNCTION WITH ANY OTHER OFFER

Heavy horse and pony centre, also Icelandic riding stables. Cafe, gift shop.
Facilities for disabled visitors.

DIRECTIONS: signposted from the centre of Verwood, which is on the B3081

OPEN: Easter to end October 10am to 5pm

FHG PUBLICATIONS, ABBEY MILL BUSINESS CENTRE, PAISLEY PA1 1TJ

Britain's best preserved lead mining site — and a great day out for all the family,
with lots to see and do. Underground Experience — Park Level Mine now open.

DIRECTIONS: alongside A689, midway between Stanhope and Alston
in the heart of the North Pennines.

OPEN: April 1st to October 31st 10.30am to 5pm daily

FHG PUBLICATIONS, ABBEY MILL BUSINESS CENTRE, PAISLEY PA1 1TJ

The home of rare breeds conservation, with over 50 breeding flocks and herds of rare
farm animals. Adventure playground, pets' corners, picnic area, farm nature trail,
Touch barn, Woodland Walk and viewing tower
DIRECTIONS: M5 Junction 9, off B4077 Stow-on-the-Wold road.
5 miles from Bourton-on-the-Water.
OPEN: daily 10.30am to 5pm April to September (to 6pm Sundays, Bank Holidays
and daily in July and August).

FHG PUBLICATIONS, ABBEY MILL BUSINESS CENTRE, PAISLEY PA1 1TJ

---

3 floors of a Listed 7-storey Victorian warehouse telling 200 years of inland waterway
history by means of video film, working exhibits with 2 quaysides of floating exhibits.
Special school holiday activities.
DIRECTIONS: Junction 11 or 12 off M5 — follow brown signs for Historic Docks.
Railway and bus station 10 minute walk. Free coach parking.
OPEN: Summer 10am to 6pm; Winter 10am to 5pm. Closed Christmas Day.

FHG PUBLICATIONS, ABBEY MILL BUSINESS CENTRE, PAISLEY PA1 1TJ

Beaulieu offers a fascinating day out for all the family. In the National Motor Museum there
are over 250 vehicles from the earliest days of motoring; within the Palace House many
Montagu family treasures can be viewed. Plus a host of rides and drives to enjoy.

DIRECTIONS: off Junction 2 of M27, then follow brown tourist signs.

OPEN: daily 10am to 5pm (Easter to September to 6pm). Closed Christmas Day

FHG PUBLICATIONS, ABBEY MILL BUSINESS CENTRE, PAISLEY PA1 1TJ

11

FHG **READERS' OFFER 1997** VALID during 1997

Isle of Wight Rare Breeds and Waterfowl Park
St Lawrence, Ventnor, Isle of Wight PO38 1UW Tel: 01983 852582

Admit one child **FREE** with full-paying adult

NOT TO BE USED IN CONJUNCTION WITH ANY OTHER OFFER

FHG **READERS' OFFER 1997** VALID from Easter to end 1997

White Cliffs Experience
Market Square, Dover, Kent CT16 1PB Tel: 01304 210101

One adult/child **FREE** with one full paying adult

NOT TO BE USED IN CONJUNCTION WITH ANY OTHER OFFER

FHG **READERS' OFFER 1997** VALID during 1997

SNIBSTON DISCOVERY PARK
Ashby Road, Coalville, Leicestershire LE67 3LN Telephone: 01530 510851

Admit one child **FREE** with full-paying adult

NOT TO BE USED IN CONJUNCTION WITH ANY OTHER OFFER

FHG **READERS' OFFER 1997** VALID during 1997

The Incredibly Fantastic Old Toy Show
26 Westgate, Lincoln, Lincs LN1 3ED Tel: 01522 520534

One child **FREE** (age 5-16 incl) with accompanying adult

NOT TO BE USED IN CONJUNCTION WITH ANY OTHER OFFER

FHG **READERS' OFFER 1997** VALID during 1997 except Bank Holidays

Southport Zoo and Conservation Trust
Princes Park, Southport, Merseyside PR8 1RX Telephone: 01704 538102

Admit one child **FREE** with two full paying adults

NOT TO BE USED IN CONJUNCTION WITH ANY OTHER OFFER

One of the UK's largest collections of rare farm animals, plus deer, llamas, miniature horses, waterfowl and poultry in 30 beautiful coastal acres.

DIRECTIONS: on main south coast road A3055 between Ventnor and Niton.

OPEN: Easter to end October open daily 10am to 5.30pm;
Winter open weekends only 10am to 4pm

FHG PUBLICATIONS, ABBEY MILL BUSINESS CENTRE, PAISLEY PA1 1TJ

Over 2000 years of Britain's history is vividly re-created
at this award-winning attraction

DIRECTIONS: signposted on entry into Dover from M20/A20 and M2/A2

OPEN: Easter to end October 10am to 5pm;
November to end December 10am to3pm. Closed Christmas and Boxing Day.

FHG PUBLICATIONS, ABBEY MILL BUSINESS CENTRE, PAISLEY PA1 1TJ

Award-winning science and industry museum. Fascinating colliery tours and "hands-on" displays including holograms, tornado and virtual reality.

DIRECTIONS: 10 minutes from Junction 22 M1 and Junction 13 M42/A42.
Well signposted along the A50.

OPEN: April to Oct.10am to 6pm; Nov. to March 10am to 5pm. Closed 25/26 Dec.

FHG PUBLICATIONS, ABBEY MILL BUSINESS CENTRE, PAISLEY PA1 1TJ

A marvellous collection of toys dating from the 1780s. Nostalgia and fun for all ages, with push-buttons, old pier-end machines, silly mirrors, videos of moving toys, music and lights

DIRECTIONS: approach Lincoln via A46, A15, A57 or A158. Opposite large car park at foot of castle walls

OPEN: Easter to end Sep: daily except Mon (unless Bank Hol); Oct to Christmas weekends and school holidays only. Groups by arrangement.

FHG PUBLICATIONS, ABBEY MILL BUSINESS CENTRE, PAISLEY PA1 1TJ

Lions, snow leopards, chimpanzees, penguins, reptiles, aquarium and lots more, set amidst landscaped gardens.

DIRECTIONS: on the coast 16 miles north of Liverpool; follow the brown tourist signs.

OPEN: daily except Christmas Day. Summer 10am to 6pm; Winter 10am to 4pm.

FHG PUBLICATIONS, ABBEY MILL BUSINESS CENTRE, PAISLEY PA1 1TJ

Beautiful walled garden with nearly 900 types of herbs, woodland walk, nursery, shop.
Guide dogs only.

DIRECTIONS: 6 miles north of Hexham, next to Chesters Roman Fort.

OPEN: daily March to October/November.

FHG PUBLICATIONS, ABBEY MILL BUSINESS CENTRE, PAISLEY PA1 1TJ

A modern working farm with over 3000 animals including ducklings, deer, bees, rheas, piglets, snails, lambs (all year). New pet centre.

DIRECTIONS: off the A614 at Farnsfield, 12 miles north of Nottingham.
From M1 Junction 27 follow "Robin Hood" signs for 10 miles.

OPEN: daily all year round.

FHG PUBLICATIONS, ABBEY MILL BUSINESS CENTRE, PAISLEY PA1 1TJ

Leading naval aviation museum with over 40 aircraft on display
— Concorde 002 and "Carrier". Based on an operational naval air station.

DIRECTIONS: just off A303/A37 on B3151 at Ilchester.
Yeovil rail station 10 miles.

OPEN: April to October 10am to 5.30pm; November to March 10am to 4.30pm

FHG PUBLICATIONS, ABBEY MILL BUSINESS CENTRE, PAISLEY PA1 1TJ

---

* Britain's most spectacular caves * Traditional paper-making * Fairground Memories *
* Penny Arcade * Magical Mirror Maze *

DIRECTIONS: from M5 Junction 22 follow brown-and-white signs via A38 and A371.
Wookey Hole is just 2 miles from Wells.

OPEN: Summer 9.30am to 5.30pm; Winter 10.30am to 4.30pm. Closed 17-25 Dec.

FHG PUBLICATIONS, ABBEY MILL BUSINESS CENTRE, PAISLEY PA1 1TJ

Planet Earth and Dinosaur Museum, Botanic Garden, model village, playland park,
garden centre and coffee shop

DIRECTIONS: signposted "Garden Paradise" off A26 and A259

OPEN: all year, except Christmas Day and Boxing Day.

FHG PUBLICATIONS, ABBEY MILL BUSINESS CENTRE, PAISLEY PA1 1TJ

READERS' OFFER 1997
VALID during 1997

Wilderness Wood

Hadlow Down, Near Uckfield, East Sussex TN22 4HJ Tel: 01825 830509

One **FREE** entry with full-paying adult (only one voucher per group)

Not valid Bank Holidays or special events

NOT TO BE USED IN CONJUNCTION WITH ANY OTHER OFFER

READERS' OFFER 1997
VALID during 1997

Cadeby Steam and Brass Rubbing Centre

Nuneaton, Warwickshire CV13 0AS Telephone: 01455 290462

Train ride for **TWO**, and **TWO** cream teas or similar

NOT TO BE USED IN CONJUNCTION WITH ANY OTHER OFFER

READERS' OFFER 1997
VALID during 1997

HATTON COUNTRY WORLD

Dark Lane, Hatton, Near Warwick, Warwickshire CV35 8XA Tel: 01926 843411

Admit **TWO** for the price of one (not valid weekends or Bank Holidays)

NOT TO BE USED IN CONJUNCTION WITH ANY OTHER OFFER

READERS' OFFER 1997
VALID until 31/12/1997

Eureka! The Museum for Children

Discovery Road, Halifax, West Yorkshire HX1 2NE Tel: 01422 330069

One child **FREE** with two adults paying full price

NOT TO BE USED IN CONJUNCTION WITH ANY OTHER OFFER

READERS' OFFER 1997
VALID during 1997

Furever Feline

Windhill Manor, Leeds Road, Shipley, West Yorkshire BD18 1BP Tel: 01274 531122

One child **FREE** with two full paying adults (not valid Bank Holidays)

NOT TO BE USED IN CONJUNCTION WITH ANY OTHER OFFER

See woodland with new eyes at this family-run working wood — fascinating and fun for all the family. Trails, adventure playground, exhibition, picnic areas, BBQs for hire, teas.

DIRECTIONS: on main A272 in Hadlow Down village, 5 miles north east of Uckfield

OPEN: daily all year

FHG PUBLICATIONS, ABBEY MILL BUSINESS CENTRE, PAISLEY PA1 1TJ

Working narrow gauge steam railway, railway museum and over 70 replica brasses to rub.

DIRECTIONS: on the A447 six miles north of Hinckley.

OPEN: second Saturday each month

FHG PUBLICATIONS, ABBEY MILL BUSINESS CENTRE, PAISLEY PA1 1TJ

England's largest craft village, factory shops, butcher's and farm shops, antiques centre; restaurant, cafe and bar (no entrance charge). Rare breeds farm, pets' corner, nature trail, guinea pig village, falconry and farming displays and soft play centre

DIRECTIONS: 3 miles north of Warwick, 5 miles south of Knowle, just off Junction 15 of M40 via A46 (Coventry), A4177

OPEN: daily 10am to 5.30pm

FHG PUBLICATIONS, ABBEY MILL BUSINESS CENTRE, PAISLEY PA1 1TJ

Britain's first hands-on museum designed specifically for children 4-12 years old, where they can make hundreds of fascinating discoveries about themselves and the world around them.

DIRECTIONS: next to Halifax railway Station 5 minutes from Junction 24 M62

OPEN: daily 10am to 5pm (closed 24-26 December)

FHG PUBLICATIONS, ABBEY MILL BUSINESS CENTRE, PAISLEY PA1 1TJ

An unusual attraction of animated cat characters in log cabins. Humorous repartee and educational scripts; meet "Robbie" the singing bobcat.

DIRECTIONS: on the A657 500 yards from Shipley centre on left side of road.

OPEN: weekdays 12.30pm to 4pm; weekends and school holidays 11am to 4.30pm.

FHG PUBLICATIONS, ABBEY MILL BUSINESS CENTRE, PAISLEY PA1 1TJ

READERS' OFFER 1997

VALID during 1997

The Arctic Penguin Maritime Museum

The Pier, Inveraray, Argyll PA32 8UY Tel: 01499 302213

One child **FREE** with each full-paying adult

NOT TO BE USED IN CONJUNCTION WITH ANY OTHER OFFER

READERS' OFFER 1997

VALID April 1997 to April 1998

EDINBURGH CRYSTAL VISITOR CENTRE

Eastfield, Penicuik, Midlothian EH26 8HB Telephone: 01968 675128

OFFER: Two for the price of one (higher ticket price applies).

NOT TO BE USED IN CONJUNCTION WITH ANY OTHER OFFER

READERS' OFFER 1997

VALID during 1997

MYRETON MOTOR MUSEUM

Aberlady, East Lothian EH32 0PZ Telephone: 01875 870288

One child **FREE** with each paying adult

NOT TO BE USED IN CONJUNCTION WITH ANY OTHER OFFER

READERS' OFFER 1997

VALID during 1997

Highland Folk Museum
Am Fasgadh

Duke Street, Kingussie, Inverness-shire PH21 1JG Tel: 01540 661307

One **FREE** child with accompanying adult paying full admission price

NOT TO BE USED IN CONJUNCTION WITH ANY OTHER OFFER

READERS' OFFER 1997

VALID during 1997

SPEYSIDE HEATHER CENTRE

Skye of Curr, Dulnain Bridge, Inverness-shire PH26 3PA Tel: 01479 851359

FREE entry to "Heather Story" exhibitions for two persons

NOT TO BE USED IN CONJUNCTION WITH ANY OTHER OFFER

A fascinating collection of Clyde maritime displays, memorabilia, stunning archive film and entertaining hands-on activities on board a unique three-masted schooner

DIRECTIONS: at Inveraray on the A83

OPEN: daily 10am to 6pm April to October, 10am to 5pm November toMarch

FHG PUBLICATIONS, ABBEY MILL BUSINESS CENTRE, PAISLEY PA1 1TJ

Visitor Centre with Exhibition Room, factory tours (children over 8 years only), Crystal Shop, gift shop, coffee shop. Facilities for disabled visitors.

DIRECTIONS: 10 miles south of Edinburgh on the A701 Peebles road; signposted a few miles from the city centre.

OPEN: Visitor Centre open daily; Factory Tours weekdays (9am-3.30pm) all year, plus weekends (11am-2.30pm) April to October.

FHG PUBLICATIONS, ABBEY MILL BUSINESS CENTRE, PAISLEY PA1 1TJ

Motor cars from 1896, motorcycles from 1902, commercial vehicles from 1919, cycles from 1880, British WWII military vehicles, ephemera, period advertising etc

DIRECTIONS: off the A198 near Aberlady, 2 miles from A1

OPEN: daily October to Easter 10am to 5pm; Easter to October 10am to 6pm. Closed Christmas Day and New Year's Day.

FHG PUBLICATIONS, ABBEY MILL BUSINESS CENTRE, PAISLEY PA1 1TJ

One of the oldest open air museums in Britain! A treasure trove of Highland life and culture. Live events June to September.

DIRECTIONS: Easily reached via the A9, 68 miles north of Perth and 42 miles south of Inverness.

OPEN: Easter to October: open daily. November to March: open weekdays. Closed Christmas and New Year.

FHG PUBLICATIONS, ABBEY MILL BUSINESS CENTRE, PAISLEY PA1 1TJ

Multi-award winning centre, "Heather Story" exhibition, gift shop/boutique, over 300 varieties of heather, gardens, trail.
Famous Clootie Dumpling Restaurant - "21 ways to have your dumpling"!

DIRECTIONS: signposted on A95 between Aviemore and Grantown-on-Spey

OPEN: daily 9am to 6pm (10am to 6pm Sun). Please check opening times in winter

FHG PUBLICATIONS, ABBEY MILL BUSINESS CENTRE, PAISLEY PA1 1TJ

READERS' OFFER 1997 VALID during 1997

Alice in Wonderland Centre
3/4 Trinity Square, Llandudno, North Wales LL30 2PY Tel: 01492 860082

One child **FREE** with two paying adults

NOT TO BE USED IN CONJUNCTION WITH ANY OTHER OFFER

READERS' OFFER 1997 VALID during 1997

Llanberis Lake Railway
Llanberis, Gwynedd LL55 4TY Telephone: 01286 870549

One child travels **FREE** with two full fare-paying adults

NOT TO BE USED IN CONJUNCTION WITH ANY OTHER OFFER

READERS' OFFER 1997 VALID March to October 1997

PILI PALAS – BUTTERFLY PALACE
Menai Bridge, Isle of Anglesey LL59 5RP Tel: 01248 712474

One child **FREE** with two adults paying full entry price

NOT TO BE USED IN CONJUNCTION WITH ANY OTHER OFFER

READERS' OFFER 1997 VALID during 1997

CENTRE FOR ALTERNATIVE TECHNOLOGY
Machynlleth, Powys SY20 9AZ Telephone: 01654 702400

One child **FREE** when accompanied by paying adult (one per party only)

NOT TO BE USED IN CONJUNCTION WITH ANY OTHER OFFER

READERS' OFFER 1997 VALID July to Dec 1997

Techniquest
Stuart Street, Cardiff Bay, South Wales CF1 6BW Tel: 01222 475475

One child **FREE** with full-paying adult

NOT TO BE USED IN CONJUNCTION WITH ANY OTHER OFFER

Walk through the Rabbit Hole to the colourful scenes of Lewis Carroll's classic story set in beautiful life-size displays. Recorded commentaries and transcripts available in several languages.

DIRECTIONS: situated just off the main street, 250 yards from coach and rail stations

OPEN: 10am to 5pm daily Easter to November; closed Sundays November to Easter

FHG PUBLICATIONS, ABBEY MILL BUSINESS CENTRE, PAISLEY PA1 1TJ

A 40-minute ride on a quaint historic steam train along the shore of Llyn Padarn. Spectacular views of the mountains of Snowdonia.

DIRECTIONS: just off the A4086 Caernarfon to Capel Curig road. Follow the "Padarn Country Park" signs.

OPEN: most days Easter to October. Free timetable available from Railway.

FHG PUBLICATIONS, ABBEY MILL BUSINESS CENTRE, PAISLEY PA1 1TJ

Visit Wales' top Butterfly House, with Bird House, Snake House, Ant Avenue, Creepy Crawly Cavern, shop, cafe, adventure playground, picnic area, nature trail etc.

DIRECTIONS: follow brown-and-white signs when crossing to Anglesey; one-and-a-half miles from the Bridge.

OPEN: March to end October 10am to 5pm daily; November/December 11am to 3pm.

FHG PUBLICATIONS, ABBEY MILL BUSINESS CENTRE, PAISLEY PA1 1TJ

Europe's leading Eco-Centre. Water-powered cliff railway, interactive renewable energy displays, beautiful organic gardens, animals; vegetarian restaurant.

DIRECTIONS: three miles north of Machynlleth on the A487 towards Dolgellau.

OPEN: from 10am every day all year (last entry 5pm); times may vary when cliff railway closed ie November to Easter.

FHG PUBLICATIONS, ABBEY MILL BUSINESS CENTRE, PAISLEY PA1 1TJ

Science Discovery Centre with 160 interactive exhibits, Planetarium, Science Theatre and Discovery Room. Fun for all!

DIRECTIONS: A4232 from Juntion 33 of M4. Follow brown tourist signs to Cardiff Bay and Techiquest (10 minutes)

OPEN: weekdays 9.30am to 4.30pm; weekends and Bank Holidays 10.30am to 5pm

FHG PUBLICATIONS, ABBEY MILL BUSINESS CENTRE, PAISLEY PA1 1TJ

ENGLAND

LONDON

HAMPTON COURT. Bushy Park Lodge, Sandy Lane, Teddington TW11 0DR (0181-977 4924; Fax: 0181-943 1917). ❦❦ Situated overlooking Bushy Park, close to Kingston town centre and the bridge over the River Thames. Hampton Court can be reached with a direct walk of 20 minutes through the park. Hampton Wick railway station is a seven minute walk where central London can be reached via Waterloo in 30 minutes. Bushy Park Lodge is a purpose-built six double-bedroomed property. All bedrooms have bathrooms en-suite, remote control colour TV, tea/coffee making facilities, hair dryers and trouser presses. There are mini bars and direct dial telephones in all rooms. Car parking exists for 10 cars. Single accommodation is £45, double £55; prices include VAT and Continental breakfast.

HARROW. The Crescent Hotel, 58-62 Welldon Crescent, Harrow, Middlesex HA1 1QR (0181-863 5491; Fax: 0181-427 5965; E-mail JIVRAJ@crsnthtl. demon.co.uk). ❦❦❦ COMMENDED. The Crescent Hotel is a modern friendly hotel in a quiet crescent in the heart of Harrow, yet only a short drive to Wembley and the West End with Heathrow easily accessible. The 21 guest rooms are comfortable and well furnished, all with colour TV, video and satellite, fridge, direct-dial telephone and tea/coffee making facilities. Our aim is to please and make your stay with us "from home to home".

HARROW. Mrs P. Giles, Oak Lodge, Brookshill, Harrow Weald, Middlesex HA3 6RY (0181-954 9257). If you are looking for Ghoulies and Ghosties I'm afraid you won't find them in this lovely 200 year old lodge, or in the large garden. But you will find a warm welcome and pleasant surroundings and a genuine piece of old England. Rooms have TV, tea/coffee facilities and central heating. Car ideal, we have car park, but we are also on bus route. A short drive to Harrow, Watford, Wembley, or train journey to London very easy; six miles M25, four miles M1. Single from £16.50, double from £33 including full English breakfast. Non smoking guests appreciated.

HARROW. Mrs M. Fitzgerald, 47 Hindes Road, Harrow HA1 1SQ (0181-861 1248). Private family guest house built at the turn of the century, offering very clean, comfortable accommodation. Situated within five minutes of Harrow town centre, Harrow bus and train stations. Wembley Stadium and Conference Centre six minutes away. Central London 17 minutes. 20 minutes M1, M25 and M40 motorways. Accommodation comprises single, double, twin and family rooms, all with central heating, washbasins, tea/coffee making facilities and colour television. Sorry, no pets. Terms £16 per person, per night.

HIGHGATE/CROUCH END. Penny and Laurence Solomons, The Parkland Walk Guest House, 12 Hornsey Rise Gardens, London N19 3PR (0171-263 3228; Fax: 0171-831 9489; email: parkwalk.demon. co.uk). London Tourist Board Listed COMMENDED.  Prize Winner of Best Small Hotel in London. Easy access M1/A1, Central London, Kings Cross and Euston; ideal base for Alexandra Palace, Muswell Hill and Islington. Small, friendly Bed and Breakfast accommodation in pretty, comfortable, Victorian family house. Wide choice of cooked breakfasts plus home made jams, fresh fruit and wholemeal bread. Singles and doubles available, most en suite or private. Tea/coffee making, TV and radio in all rooms. Close to many restaurants. Children welcome. Sorry, no pets. Smoking banned throughout. From £25 nightly, weekly rates available. Brochure (including map) on request.

KENSINGTON. Mowbray Court Hotel, 28-30 Penywern Road, Earls Court, London SW5 9SU (0171-370 3690; Fax: 0171-370 5693). Listed Bed and Breakfast Tourist Class Hotel with nearly all the services of a four star Hotel. Majority of rooms with bath/WC, direct-dial phone, hairdryer, trouser press, iron and colour satellite TV. Non-smoking rooms available. There is a comfortable residents' bar and a lift to all floors. Babysitting service on request. The hotel is close to all the major shopping areas and tourist sights and is situated in a residential tree-lined street. We are open 24 hours a day all year round. We accept well behaved pets. Family rooms for four/six persons with or without facilities available. Frommers recommended. All credit cards accepted.

KEW GARDENS. Mrs L. Gray, 1 Chelwood Gardens, Kew TW9 4JG (0181-876 8733). Situated in quiet cul-de-sac, private newly renovated luxury bed and breakfast accommodation in friendly family home. Seven minutes' walk to underground station with easy access by bus or tube to all parts of London, museums, theatres, shopping, etc. Convenient for Twickenham, Wembley, Heathrow Airport, M3 and M4, Hampton Court, Kew Gardens, Public Records Office, Wimbledon, Windsor Castle, Chessington World of Adventure and River Thameside walks. Comfortable, friendly house with TV, central heating, tea and coffee facilities. Varied selection of English pubs and restaurants nearby. Unrestricted street parking. Regret no pets. We welcome tourists and business people looking for an economical alternative to hotel life in relaxed informal surroundings. Open all year.

LONDON. King's Campus Vacation Bureau, Box No. 97/8, King's College London, 127 Stamford Street, Waterloo, London SE1 9NQ (0171-928 3777; Fax: 0171-928 5777). Affordable accommodation with some en suite and some parking in Halls of Residence in central and inner London for individuals, families and groups during College vacations. Bed and Breakfast from £17 per person; Room only from £12.50 per person per night.

LONDON. Mrs Anne Scott, Holiday Hosts, 59 Cromwell Road, Wimbledon, London SW19 8LF (0181-540 7942; Fax: 0181-540 2827). Tourist Board Listed. We offer Bed and Breakfast accommodation in selected friendly private homes. Our homes are chosen for their comfort and location in good residential areas of Central, South and West London. They are convenient for transport, restaurants, museums, art galleries, theatres, shopping; Wimbledon Tennis, Hampton Court, Kew Gardens and Public Records Office, Windsor Castle, Heathrow and Gatwick Airports, M3/M4, A3, River Thames boat trips and interesting riverside walks — an ideal and economical alternative for business people and tourists and an excellent base for touring Southern England. TV and tea/coffee facilities. Parking no problem. £14 to £35 each per night. Reservations by post or telephone/Fax. Brochure on request. Tourist Board Member.

LONDON. Mr Steven Poulacheris, Five Kings Guest House, 59 Anson Road, Tufnell Park, London N7 0AR (0171-607 6466/3996). A well-maintained friendly guest house offering personal attention. Quietly situated yet only 15 minutes from Central London tourist attractions and London Zoo. Central heating, washbasins and shaving points in all rooms. Lounge with colour TV; bathroom, showers, toilets on all floors. No parking restrictions in Anson Road. Bed and Breakfast from £18 to £20 single; from £28 to £32 double/twin. Children from £8 to £10. En-suite rooms £2 extra per person.

LONDON. Rose Court Hotel, 1 Talbot Square, London W2 1TR (0171-723 5128; Fax: 0171-723 1855). ♛♛♛ The Rose Court Hotel is located close to Hyde Park, Park Lane and the major shopping street of London, Oxford Street. Other famous attractions such as Madame Tussauds, Buckingham Palace, museums and theatres are within easy reach. Pleasantly situated in a quiet garden square the hotel is privately run and offers comfort, courteous service, friendliness and hospitality. The bedrooms have en suite facilities, satellite TV, telephone and fridge. Hairdryer and ironing facilities are also available. Single room £30 to £48, double/twin rooms £45 to £68, triple rooms £66 to £78, family rooms £72 to £90. Credit cards are accepted. Rates are inclusive of taxes and English breakfast.

LONDON. More House, 53 Cromwell Road, South Kensington, London SW7 2EH (0171-584 2040; Fax: 0171-581 5748). Large Victorian building in Kensington close to museums, Hyde Park and other attractions. The accommodation is available during the months of JULY and AUGUST only. Bedrooms: 38 single, 20 twin, four triple. 15 public bathrooms/showers. Bed and Breakfast single £23, twin £38, triple £43 and dormitory £14. Stay with us while you enjoy the Proms. We are just a five minute walk from the Albert Hall.

LONDON. Jill and Eric Seal, "Lakeside", 51 Snaresbrook Road, London E11 1PQ (0181-989 6100).
Visiting London? Be our guest. We are proud of being one of the few Bed and Breakfast establishments to be awarded AA QQQQQ Premier Selected Classification. Our bedrooms are beautifully decorated as is our elegant dining room and garden terrace. All bedrooms are en suite with tea/coffee making facilities, colour TV and hair dryers. We are in a unique position located directly opposite a lake yet just two minutes' walk from the Central Line tube station giving direct access to all the sights of London. The exit of the M11 motorway is nearby, making both Heathrow and Gatwick Airports within one hour's drive. Airport pickup can be arranged at competitive rates; we have free parking. Bed and Breakfast from £20 to £22 per person per night, minimum stay two nights.

Aaron House Hotel

TEL: 0171-370 3991
FAX: 0171-373 2303
ETB ♛

17 Courtfield Gardens, London SW5 0PD

Originally a family home, Aaron House Hotel now has 23 rooms of character, most en suite and with TV and tea/coffee-making facilities. Centrally located but in a quiet residential area facing a garden Square, Aaron House is only 5 minutes walk from Earls Court Road underground and from there to Heathrow Airport or the West End. An ideal base at modest price with a personal welcome from our friendly staff.

Bed & Breakfast Single Room from £29.00,
Double from £40.00 inclusive.

WHITE LODGE HOTEL   ♛♛♛

White Lodge Hotel is situated in a pleasant North London suburb, with easy access via tube and bus to all parts of London. Alexandra Palace is the closest landmark and buses pass the front door. Prices are kept as low as possible for people on low budget holidays, whilst maintaining a high standard of service and cleanliness. Many guests return year after year which is a good recommendation. Six single, ten double bedrooms, four family bedrooms (eight rooms ensuite), all with washbasins; three showers, six toilets; sittingroom; diningroom. Cot, high chair, babysitting and reduced rates for children.

No pets, please. Open all year for Bed and Breakfast from £26 single, from £36 double, from £42 double ensuite.

Mrs Nancy Neocleous, White Lodge Hotel, No. 1 Church Lane, Hornsey, London N8. Tel: 0181-348 9765 Fax: 0181-340 7851

LONDON. Mrs B. Merchant, 562 Caledonian Road, Holloway, London N7 9SD (0171-607 0930).
Comfortable well furnished rooms in small private home, full central heating. Two double and one single rooms. Extra single beds for double rooms available. Eight bus routes; one minute for Trafalgar Square, Westminster, St Paul's. Piccadilly Line underground few minutes' walk. Direct Piccadilly and Heathrow. One-and-a-half miles King's Cross, Euston and St. Pancras Main Line Stations. Four and a half miles Piccadilly, three miles London Zoo and Hampstead Heath. Central for all tourist attractions. Unrestricted street parking. Full English Breakfast. Terms: £16.50 per person per night. Children under 10 years £14.50 per night. Minimum stay two nights. SAE, please.

LONDON. Kirness House, 29 Belgrave Road, Victoria SW1V 1RB (0171-834 0030). A small friendly guest house, please try us. Situated close to Victoria Station. All European languages spoken. Satisfaction guaranteed. Six rooms available for Bed and Breakfast. Competitive rates: £25 single, £35 double.

LONDON (Borough of Sutton). Mrs J. Dixon, 17 Osmond Gardens, Wallington, London SM6 8SX (0181-647 1943). Comfortable family home in quiet road offers friendly welcome to guests. Double/family room (sleeps maximum four) with own colour TV, en suite shower/washbasin and tea/coffee making facilities; twin room also available. London approximately 30 minutes by train from local British Rail station within a few minutes' walk. Gatwick 45 minutes' drive and local bus to Hampton Court, Kingston, Croydon, Sutton, etc. Bed and full English Breakfast from £18. Reductions for children. Sorry, no singles accepted.

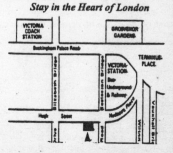

LONDON. Mrs A. Louis, 18 Silver Crescent, Chiswick, London W4 5SE (0181-994 6265). Stay at my Bed and Breakfast and experience the high quality and friendly service I offer in my well maintained Edwardian home which retains all its original features. Situated in a quiet tree-lined street two minutes from Gunnersbury underground station, M4 and A4. Five minutes Kew Gardens and River Thames. 15 minutes Heathrow Airport and 20 minutes to central London and Theatreland. Pubs and restaurants within walking distance. Central heating and colour TV in all rooms. Non-smokers preferred. Free street parking.

BEDFORDSHIRE

PULLOXHILL. Phil and Judy Tookey, Pond Farm, 7 High Street, Pulloxhill MK45 5HA (01525 712316). ETB Listed. Pond Farm is situated opposite the village green in Pulloxhill. Three miles from the A6 and five miles from the M1 Junction 12. We are within easy reach of Woburn Abbey and Safari Park, Whipsnade Zoo, The Shuttleworth Collection of Historic Aircraft at Old Warden and 11 miles from Luton Airport. Flitwick mainline station is only three miles away and 45 minutes by train to London. Pond Farm, built in the 17th century, is mainly arable although we have horses grazing on the meadow land. We also have a resident Great Dane. All bedrooms have tea/coffee facilities, washbasins and colour TV as no guest lounge is available. One WC and washbasin, one shower room with toilet and washbasin, one bathroom. Price from £15. Evening Meals at local inn.

SANDY. Mrs Joan M. Strong, Orchard Cottage, 1 High Street, Wrestlingworth, Near Sandy SG19 2EW (01767 631355). ☙ COMMENDED. Orchard Cottage is a picturesque 16th century thatched cottage with modern extension, formerly the village bakery. Comfortable accommodation includes one family and one twin bedrooms (both with washbasin), one single room; bathroom, shower, two toilets; diningroom and TV lounge. Centrally heated and no smoking throughout. Large, secluded garden. Ample parking. Cottage is situated in a quiet, country location on the Bedford/Cambridgeshire border convenient for visiting the Shuttleworth Collection of Historic Aeroplanes, RSPB, Wimpole Hall, Cambridge and Duxford. A1 and M11 nearby — convenient for travelling to London. Bed and Breakfast from £16, reductions for children.

SANDY. Mrs M. Codd, Highfield Farm, Great North Road, Sandy SG19 2AQ (01767 682332). ♛ ♛

HIGHLY COMMENDED. Tranquil welcoming atmosphere on attractive arable farm. Set well back off A1 giving quiet, peaceful seclusion yet within easy reach of the RSPB, the Shuttleworth Collection, the Greensand Ridge Walk, Grafham Water and Woburn Abbey. Cambridge 22 miles, London 50 miles. All rooms have tea/coffee facilities, most have bathrooms en suite and two are on the ground floor. There is a separate guests' sitting room with TV. Family room. Dogs welcome by arrangement. No smoking. Guestaccom "Good Room" Award. Most guests return! Prices from £17.50 per person per night.

STAGSDEN. Mrs Pam Hutcheon, Firs Farm, Stagsden MK43 8TB (01234 822344). ♛ ♛ *COMMEN-*

DED. Firs Farm is a family-run arable farm set in quiet surroundings quarter of a mile south of A422. The farmhouse is timber-framed and set in a large garden with swimming pool. Accommodation comprises double or twin (one en suite) rooms with tea/coffee making facilities and guests' lounge with colour TV. Many local tourist attractions. Children and pets welcome. Open all year. Bed and Breakfast from £16 to £22.

BERKSHIRE

HENLEY-ON-THAMES near. Mrs H. Carver, Windy Brow, 204 Victoria Road, Wargrave RG10 8AJ

(01734 403336). Detached Victorian family house in one third of an acre of garden. Ideal for touring the Thames valley, Windsor and Oxford; 30 minutes from Heathrow; 40 minutes from London by fast bus/train. Wargrave is a picturesque Thames-side village with excellent pubs. Accommodation consists of twin, family and single rooms all with colour TV; one double/twin (en-suite) on the ground floor available. Separate shower room and bathroom. Plenty of off-road parking. Children welcome. Coffee/tea facilities in rooms and hair dryer. Tourist Board Listed and graded. Please phone for more details.

NEWBURY. Mrs Kathleen Jones, Hillside Farm, Ashford Hill Road, Headley, Thatcham RG19 8AJ

(01635 268301). Large renovated Victorian farmhouse with garden in rural setting. A warm welcome in comfortable homely accommodation for tourists and businessmen alike; children and pets welcome. All rooms have colour TV, tea/coffee making facilities and central heating. Village pub serving food within walking distance. Bed and Breakfast from £17 each double, children half price sharing family room, cot free; £19 single; en suite also available. Directions: south of Newbury on A34, take A339 towards Basingstoke, in Headley take Ashford Hill Road, Hillside Farm is half a mile down on right.

**Terms quoted in this publication may be subject to increase
if rises in costs necessitate**

READING, Three Mile Cross. Mrs M.S. Erdwin, Orchard House, Church Lane, Three Mile Cross, Reading RG8 1HD (01734 884457). Orchard House is well situated close to M4 Motorway, Heathrow 30 minutes away, Gatwick 45 minutes; Oxford 30 miles and London 35 miles (just 29 minutes by train); five minutes from Arborfield Garrison. Wealth of holiday interest to suit all tastes in the area. Ideal halt for that long journey to Cornwall or Wales. Accommodation all year round in this modern, large, homely house close to the Chilterns and Berkshire Downs. Children welcome. Babysitting can be arranged; high chair available. Evening drink; English or Continental Breakfast; Evening Meal/Light Supper available; Packed Lunches on request. Pets permitted at extra charge. Close to Thames, Kennet and Avon Canal/River for coarse fishing. Also close to Digital and Racal training centres. Tourist Board registered. Terms from £16.50 for Bed and Breakfast. Taxi service at moderate rates. SAE, please.

WINDSOR. Karen Jackson, Suffolk Lodge, 4 Bolton Avenue, Windsor SL4 3JB (01753 864186; Fax: 01753 862640). ❦ ❦ A large detached Victorian house, situated in a quiet tree-lined avenue with private parking, large heated indoor swimming pool, full-size snooker table, steam room, sunbed and other leisure facilities. Near castle, river, both railway stations and Legoland. Run by a family and highly recommended world-wide. All rooms have private facilities, direct-dial telephones, Cable colour TV, clock radio, coffee/tea making facilities, shaver points, trouser press and hairdryer, also ironing facilities. Price includes full English Breakfast. Heathrow: 10 miles, Central London: 25 miles, M4: 2 miles.

WINDSOR. Netherton Hotel, 96 St. Leonards Road, Windsor SL4 3DA (01753 855508). This recently refurbished hotel offers a comfortable and friendly atmosphere. All rooms are en suite, with colour TV and tea/coffee making facilities. Also available are hairdryers and ironing facilities. There is a TV lounge for guests' use. Full English breakfast. We have a private car park and are only five minutes' walk from the town centre, train station, Castle, gardens, etc.

BUCKINGHAMSHIRE

AYLESBURY. Mrs B. Pickford, New Farm, Oxford Road, Oakley, Near Aylesbury HP18 9UR (01844 237360). Working farm. ETB Listed *COMMENDED.* A warm friendly atmosphere in fully modernised farmhouse. Lounge with colour TV and open log fire plus full central heating. Enjoy a cup of tea or coffee with biscuits on arrival. Comfortable beds in two double and one twin bedrooms. Large garden and patio with views over 163 acres of fields and oak trees. Working farm with suckler herd and arable land. Situated on the Oxfordshire/Bucks border in peaceful surroundings with walks in the adjacent Bernwood Forest Nature Reserve. Seven miles Oxford and 13 miles Aylesbury. Close to Waterperry Gardens, Waddesdon Manor and M40 to Windsor and London, approximately one mile Oxford side of Oakley; golf one and a quarter miles. Bed and Breakfast from £18 per person. Children over six years welcome. Reductions for under 10 years. Good food in pubs and restaurants in nearby villages. Sorry, no pets. Member of FHB.

HIGH WYCOMBE. Mrs Jane Vaughan, White House, North Road, Widmer End, High Wycombe HP15 6ND (01494 712221). Built as three adjoining brick and flint cottages in the early 1700s, the White House was later extended and provides a restful, self contained suite to which many of our guests return time and time again. Fully modernised, it contains three rooms — a large restful bedroom, separate bathroom and toilet which remain apart from the rest of the house. The bedroom looks out onto the large garden and paddocks where ponies and sheep often graze during the year. A traditional or Continental breakfast is served. Accommodation consists of en suite twin room and en suite family room, (sleeps four). Bed and Breakfast from £17. Open all year.

CAMBRIDGESHIRE

CAMBRIDGE. Mrs M.R. Jewitt, Blakemere, Old Mill Close, Barrington, Cambridge CB2 5SD (01223 871006). A warm welcome awaits you in our comfortable family house quietly situated in a picturesque village with 22 acres of village green surrounded by thatched cottages. Barrington, easily located just off the A10 between Cambridge and Royston and four miles from M11, is ideal for Cambridge, Duxford War Museum, Wimpole Hall and many other places of interest. Good train service for London sightseeing. One twin room and two single rooms, all with colour TV, central heating and tea/coffee making facilities. Bed and Breakfast from £18. No smoking in bedrooms. No evening meal. Open all year, except Christmas period. Tourist Board registered.

CAMBRIDGE. Mrs Jean Wright, White Horse Cottage, 28 West Street, Comberton, Cambridge CB3 7DS (01223 262914). A 17th century cottage with all modern conveniences situated in a charming village four miles south west of Cambridge. Junction 12 off M11 — A603 from Cambridge, or A428 turn off at Hardwick Turning. Accommodation includes one double room, twin and family rooms. Own sitting room with colour TV; tea/coffee making facilities. Full central heating; parking. Excellent touring centre for many interesting places including Cambridge colleges, Wimpole Hall, Anglesey Abbey, Ely Cathedral, Imperial War Museum at Duxford and many more. Bed and Breakfast from £17 per person. Children welcome.

CAMBRIDGE. Cristina's Guest House, 47 St. Andrews Road, Cambridge CB4 1DL (01223 365855/ 327700). 🌷🌷 Guests are assured of a warm welcome at Cristina's Guest House, quietly located in the beautiful city of Cambridge, only 15 minutes' walk from the City Centre and colleges. There are many places of cultural and historic interest to visit, as well as shops and leisure facilities. All rooms have colour TV and tea/coffee making equipment, some rooms are available with private shower and toilet. The house is centrally heated, and there is a comfortable TV lounge. Private car park. AA QQ, RAC Listed. Further details on application.

CAMBRIDGE. Paul and Alison Tweddell, Dykelands Guest House, 157 Mowbray Road, Cambridge CB1 4SP (01223 244300; Fax: 01223 566746). 🌷🌷 Enjoy your visit to Cambridge by staying at our lovely detached guesthouse. Ideally located for city centre and for touring the secrets of the Cambridgeshire countryside. Easy access from M11 Junction 11, but only one and a half miles from the city centre, on a direct bus route. Near Addenbrookes Hospital. All bedrooms have colour TV, clock radio, tea/coffee making facilities; heating and double glazing; most with private shower or en-suite facilities; ground floor rooms available. Garden with children's play area for guests' use. Bed and full English Breakfast from £19.75 singles, £33 doubles. Licensed. Ample car parking. Access and Visa welcome. AA QQ. Open all year. Brochure on request.

CAMBRIDGE near. Vicki Hatley, Manor Farm, Landbeach, Cambridge CB4 4ED (01223 860165).

COMMENDED. Five miles from Cambridge and 10 miles from Ely. Vicki welcomes you to her carefully modernised Grade II Listed farmhouse, which is located next to the church in this attractive village. All rooms are either en suite or have private bathroom and are individually decorated. TV, clock radios and tea/coffee making facilties are provided in double, twin or family rooms. There is ample parking and guests are welcome to enjoy the secluded walled gardens. Bed and Breakfast from £17.50 per person double, and £22 single.

CAXTON. Mrs Pauline Benson, The Old Bricklayers Arms, Ermine Street, Caxton CB3 8PQ (01954 719228).

COMMENDED. Conveniently situated for Cambridge, Huntingdon and Royston (M11, A10, A45). 16th century Grade II Listed cottage with double, twin and single rooms. Dining and sitting rooms with inglenook, oak beams and log fires. Traditional furnishings. Friendly and comfortable. Home cooking. Overnight Bed and Breakfast from £38 double, £28 single. Dinner available from £13.50 (vegetarians £10). Longer stay terms on request. Dogs accepted by arrangement.

ELY. Margaret Sicard, The Laurels, 104 Victoria Street, Littleport, Ely CB6 1LZ (01353 861972; 0850 199299 Mobile).

A large attractive Victorian house in a quiet location, offering excellent accommodation and farmhouse breakfast. Set in pretty, old-fashioned garden, 200 yards from riverside pub. Situated on the Norfolk/Suffolk/Cambridge borders. Four miles from Ely Cathedral, Wildfowl and Wetlands Trust. Cambridge's ornate colleges and famous Backs 30 minutes. Sandringham one hour. Superior twin and double en-suite rooms. One suitable for partially disabled guests. Tea/coffee facilities, radio, colour TV, easy chairs, door locks and central heating. Dining room leading to sub-tropical garden room. Evening Meal available. Cot/high chair, Z-bed. Private parking with security lights. Non-smoking guests only. Bed with en suite and Breakfast from £16.

HEMINGFORD GREY. Maureen and Tony Webster, The Willow Guest House, 45 High Street, Hemingford Grey, St. Ives (Cambs.) PE18 9BJ (01480 494748).

Large private house in the centre of this picturesque village. 100 yards from a much photographed section of the Great Ouse River, and oldest (1150) inhabited house in England. One mile from 15th century bridge west of St. Ives, 15 minutes' drive from Cambridge City Centre. Family rooms, twin rooms, doubles and singles. All bedrooms are en suite and have colour TV, tea/coffee making facilities, hairdryers, clock radios, central heating. Private parking. Guest phone. Bed and Breakfast from £19 including VAT (full English Breakfast). Sorry no pets or smoking. Ideally situated for north/south and east/west travel being only one mile from A14 dual carriageway connecting M1-A1 and M11.

CAMBRIDGESHIRE – FENLANDS AND CHALK HILLS!

Never is it easier to relax than when you are in Cambridgeshire. The flat fens in the north and gentle chalk hills in the south combine to create a unique ambience. Cambridge, a beautiful university town, is the final contribution to this county's perfection. Make sure you visit the twin villages of Hemingford Grey and Hemingford Abbots, Grafham Water, the Ouse Wash Reserves and Wicken Fen.

HOUGHTON. Robin and Marion Seaman, The Elms, Banks End, Wyton, Houghton PE17 2AA

(01480 453523). 👑 👑 COMMENDED. Rambling Edwardian house close to picturesque village of Houghton and Wyton, off the A1123 two miles between historic market towns of Huntingdon and St. Ives; five minutes from A1 and A14; M11 15 minutes. One double en suite room, one twin en suite room, and two single rooms with washbasins and private bathroom. All have tea/coffee making facilities and colour TV. Guests' sittingroom. Central heating. Bed and Breakfast from £19.00 per person. Non smoking. No pets. Friendly personal service and a warm welcome assured.

HUNTINGDON. Mrs Betty Burdell, 18 Marsh Lane, Hemingford Grey, Huntingdon PE18 9EN (01480 394045). Situated in the picturesque village of Hemingford Grey twinned with Hemingford Abbots, which is Cromwell country. Close to Cambridge, Ely and the fens, also ideal for visiting many historic houses. Minutes from A14 which leads to A1, M1 and M11. Tea and coffee making equipment; bathroom and shower. TV in rooms. Children and dogs welcomed. Bed and English Breakfast. Terms from £16. Telephone or write for further details.

HUNTINGDON. Phil and Sandra Sturgeon, Sandwich Villas Guest House, 16 George Street, Huntingdon PE18 6BD (01480 458484). Close to the centre of town and railway station, two miles from A1 and A14 (M11). Ideal for touring fens/Ely and Cambridge or breaking north/south journey. Large Victorian house built by the Earl of Sandwich in mid 19th century. All bedrooms have colour TV, tea/coffee and washbasins. One large en-suite double/family room, one large twin, one double and one single. Parking. Full English Breakfast. Comfortable surroundings. Friendly atmosphere. Riverside walks. Bed and Breakfast from £16. A non-smoking establishment.

MILTON. Mrs V. Logan, Ambassador Lodge, 37 High Street, Milton, Cambridge CB4 6DF (01223

860168). Georgian House situated in village two miles from city centre; regular bus service close by. Easy access to A14, M11, A11, A1(M). Country park and River Cam within walking distance. Also close to renowned Cambridge Science Park and Regional College. En suite rooms available. TV and tea-making facilities in all rooms. Limited use of outdoor swimming pool. Off road enclosed parking. Please write or telephone for further details.

OVER. David and Julia Warren, Charter Cottage, Horse Ware, Over CB4 5NX (01954 230056; Fax:

01954 231062). A warm welcome and a friendly atmosphere await you in our peaceful cottage accommodation in an interesting corner of the village. Open all year, we offer two ground floor, centrally heated bedrooms, one twin bedded and one double, both with hot and cold water, tea/coffee making facilities and TV. Fully equipped bathroom also adjacent. Full English breakfast. Ample off-road parking, pleasant country garden with patio. Easy reach of Cambridge, Ely and St. Ives. Bed and Breakfast £17 single, £30 double. Directions: A14 Cambridge to Huntingdon, follow signs to Over, then first left immediately after Over Church.

SANDY. Mrs S. Barlow, Model Farm, Little Gransden, Sandy, Bedfordshire SG19 3EA (01767

677361). A warm welcome awaits visitors to this traditional 1870s farmhouse situated on a working family farm. The farmhouse, providing comfortable and quiet accommodation with lovely views, is set in open countryside between the villages of Little Gransden and Longstowe. Guests are welcome to walk around the farm and garden. Model Farm is an ideal base for visiting Cambridge, Ely, Duxford Imperial War Museum, Shuttleworth (vintage aircraft and cars), Wimpole Hall and Farm (National Trust) and the RSPB at Sandy. M11, A1, A14 are all within 20 minutes' drive.

ST. NEOTS. Mrs Eileen Raggatt, The Ferns, Berkley Street, Eynesbury, St. Neots PE19 2NE (01480

213884). An 18th century house (private family home) in large garden situated on Eynesbury Green. Two rooms available with double bed plus single bed, one with private bathroom, the other with washbasin. Central heating. Charges from £17 per person for Bed and Breakfast, reduced rates for children under 10. St. Neots is a market town on the River Ouse just off the A1; one and a half hours north of London, 16 miles west of Cambridge.

WELNEY. Mrs C.H. Bennett, Stockyard Farm, Wisbech Road, Welney, Wisbech PE14 9RQ (01354

610433). A warm welcome awaits you at this cosy former farmhouse in the heart of the Fens. Equidistant from Ely and Wisbech it makes an ideal base from which to explore the numerous historic sites, watch wildlife at the nearby nature reserves or fish the famous fenland waters. Whatever your interests Cindy and Tim can offer advice and information. Both the double bedroom and the twin have washbasins and hot drinks facilities. Breakfast is served in the conservatory adjoining the guests' TV lounge. Full central heating. Private parking. Non-smokers only. Pets by arrangement. Prices range from £13 to £20 per person, depending on length of stay and choice of breakfast (full English or Continental).

WICKEN. Mrs Valerie Fuller, Spinney Abbey, Wicken, Ely CB7 5XQ (01353 720971). ♥ ♥

COMMENDED. **Working farm.** Spinney Abbey is a spacious Georgian farmhouse. A Grade II Listed building of historical interest, rebuilt from the former priory in 1775, it stands in a large garden with tennis court adjacent to our dairy farm which borders the National Trust Nature Reserve "Wicken Fen". The accommodation comprises two double en suite rooms and a twin-bedded room with private bathroom, all with TV and tea/coffee tray. Guests' sitting room. Central heating and electric blankets for colder months. Regret no pets and no smoking upstairs. Bed and Breakfast from £19 per person. Situated just off the A1123 half a mile west of Wicken. Open all year.

CHESHIRE

BALTERLEY (near Crewe). Mrs Joanne Hollins, Green Farm, Deans Lane, Balterley, Near Crewe

CW2 5QJ (01270 820214). ♥ ♥ **Working farm, join in.** Jo and Pete Hollins offer guests a friendly welcome to their home on a 145-acre dairy farm in quiet and peaceful surroundings. Green Farm is situated on the Cheshire/Staffordshire border and is within easy reach of Junction 16 on the M6. An excellent stop-over place for travellers journeying between north and south of the country. We also offer a pets' corner and pony rides for young children. One family room en suite, one single and one twin-bedded room on ground floor suitable for disabled guests. Tea making facilities and TV in all rooms. Children welcome — cot provided. This area offers many attractions; we are within easy reach of historic Chester, Alton Towers and the famous Potteries of Staffordshire. Open all year. Bed and Breakfast from £15 per person.

CHESTER. Mrs Anne Arden, Newton Hall, Tattenhall, Chester CH3 9AY (01829 770153). ♛ ♛

HIGHLY COMMENDED. Part 16th century oak-beamed farmhouse set in large well kept grounds, with fine views of historic Beeston and Peckforton Castles and close to the Sandstone Trail. Six miles south of Chester off A41 and ideal for Welsh Hills. Rooms are en suite or have adjacent bathroom. Colour TV in double rooms; guests' own TV lounge. Fully centrally heated. See our rare Shropshire Down sheep and Pedigree Cattle. Bed and Breakfast from £15. Children and pets welcome. Open all year.

CHESTER. Mrs Sally-Ann Chesters, Millmoor Farm, Nomansheath, Malpas SY14 8ED (01948 820304). ETB Listed.

Set amongst the green valleys of South Cheshire the 18th century farmhouse at Millmoor is a beautiful setting where you may escape the hurly-burly of modern life. The house has recently been refurbished, is fully centrally heated and boasts an exquisite en suite four-poster double bedroom, one double with brass bed en suite and one twin-bedded room, all with magnificent Welsh Border views. Millmoor Farm is a working dairy and beef farm and there are excellent walks and coarse fishing available for guests with its position making it an ideal base to explore Chester and the Welsh Marches area. Prices are from £15 per night Bed and Breakfast with child reductions. Non-smoking. AA Listed, Farm Holiday Bureau Member.

CHESTER. Mrs Helen Mitchell, Mitchell's of Chester, Green Gables, 28 Hough Green, Chester CH4 8JQ (01244 679004). ♛ ♛ *HIGHLY COMMENDED.*

Relax in this tastefully restored Victorian residence set in compact landscaped gardens and secluded forecourt.The tall well appointed corniced rooms are complemented by a sweeping staircase and antique furniture. This small family run guest house has all en suite rooms with hospitality tray, alarm clock, hair dryer and many other comforts. It is within walking distance of the ancient Roman walled city with its wealth of historic buildings and its famous race course. It is also the gateway to North Wales. Guests have the convenience of a pay phone, off street parking, local golf course and being on a main bus route. We are situated on the south side of Chester on the A5104. Bed and Breakfast from £19 per person.

CHESTER. Mrs Janet Miller, City Walls Hotel, City Walls Road, Chester CH1 2LU (01244 313416; Fax: 01244 313417). ♛ ♛ ♛

A peacefully situated small, friendly, licensed Hotel nestling on the historic Roman Walls, minutes' walk from town centre. All rooms are well appointed with modern facilities. Guest accommodation comprises double, twin, single and family rooms, all with en suite bath and shower, central heating, TV, direct dial telephone and courtesy tray. Rooms from £32. Relax and enjoy our bar and restaurant where good food and wine are served.

CHESTER. Audrey Charmley, Ford Farm, Nenton Lane, Tattenhall, Chester CH3 9NE (01829 770307). ETB Listed *COMMENDED.*

A friendly welcome to our dairy farm set in beautiful countryside with views of Beeston and Peckforton Castles. Close to ice cream farm and Cheshire workshops and many tourist attractions. Chester seven miles, Oulton Park eight miles. Guests' own lounge and dining room with TV. One double and one twin room, tea/coffee making facilities; bathroom with shower. Open all year. Children and pets welcome. Bed and Breakfast from £14 to £15.

CHESTER. Mr D.R. Bawn, The Gables Guest House, 5 Vicarage Road, Hoole, Chester CH2 3HZ (01244 323969). ♛ Guests are welcomed to this pleasant Victorian family house situated in a quiet residential area just off the main bus route. Near park and tennis courts. Makes an ideal base for touring with easy access to all major roads. AA and RAC Listed, the guest house offers accommodation in family, double and twin bedrooms; hot and cold, central heating throughout, remote control colour TV and tea-making facilities; bathroom, shower room facilities. Television lounge. Open from January to December. Open parking. Bed and Breakfast from £14 per person; weekly terms available. Reductions for children.

CHESTER CITY. Mrs M. Gregory, "Holly House", 41 Liverpool Road, Chester CH2 1AB (01244 383484). Holly House is a Victorian townhouse on the A5116, offering a friendly welcome in quiet elegant surroundings. Comfort and high standards are our priority. Only six minutes' walk from the famous Roman walls which encircle this historic city with its 14th century Cathedral, castle, Museum of Roman artifacts, buildings of architectural interest, Amphitheatre, walks by the river, shopping in "The Rows". Spacious accommodation comprises double room with en-suite bathroom, twin with private shower; both available as family rooms. Tea/coffee facilities, own keys, diningroom/TV lounge; central heating. Parking. Bed and Breakfast from £16 per person, or as family rooms at £11 per additional person supplement. Vegetarians catered for. Non-smoking.

CHURCH MINSHULL. Brian and Mary Charlesworth, Higher Elms Farm, Minshull Vernon, Crewe CW1 4RG (01270 522252). ♛♛ EN SUITE AVAILABLE. A 400 year old farmhouse on working farm. Oak-beamed comfort in dining and sitting rooms, overlooking Shropshire Union Canal. No dinners served but four pubs within two miles. Interesting wildlife around. Convenient for M6 but tucked away in the countryside; from M6 Junction 18, off A530 towards Nantwich. Family room, double, twin and single rooms all have colour TV, washbasin and tea/coffee facilities. Well behaved pets welcome. Within 15 miles of Jodrell Bank, Oulton Park, Bridgemere Garden World, Stapeley Water Gardens, Nantwich and Chester. Bed and Breakfast from £17. Half price for children under 12 years.

CONGLETON. Mrs Sheila Kidd, Yew Tree Farm, North Rode, Congleton CW12 2PF (01260 223569). ETB Listed *COMMENDED.* This working farm has a peaceful village setting with scenic country walks on our doorstep. It is central for the Peak District, Potteries, Alton Towers and the historic houses of Cheshire. Just 20 minutes from the M6. You can be assured of a warm welcome, a cosy atmosphere and good food. One double en suite room and two twin rooms. Lounge with open log fire. Children are welcome and guests are invited to look around the farm and get to know the animals and wide range of pets. Bed and substantial cooked Breakfast from £17; optional Evening Meal £10. Write or phone for brochure.

FRODSHAM. Mrs Susan Ward, Long Croft, Dark Lane, Kingsley WA6 8BW (01928 787193). In a delightful secluded country lane and standing in an acre of woodland, Long Croft offers a wealth of charm and character together with modern conveniences. Double and twin-bedded rooms, both with en suite, TV and tea/coffee making facilities; guests' own sitting room with private dining room overlooking secluded patio. Plenty of good pubs in the area and reasonably priced restaurants in Frodsham, a pretty market town just two miles away. Within striking distance of Chester, Manchester, Liverpool and North Wales and on the doorstep of Oulton Park racing circuit and Delamere Forest. Children welcome. Home cooked traditional English breakfast with own free range eggs. Evening meals specially prepared as requested. From £18 per person; reductions for children.

WHEN MAKING ENQUIRIES PLEASE MENTION
THIS *FHG* PUBLICATION

HYDE, near Manchester. Mrs Charlotte R. Walsh, Needhams Farm, Uplands Road, Werneth Low, Gee Cross, Near Hyde SK14 3AQ (0161-368 4610).

🌸 🌸 🌸 COMMENDED. **Working farm.** A cosy 16th century farmhouse set in peaceful, picturesque surroundings by Werneth Low Country Park and the Etherow Valley, which lie between Glossop and Manchester. The farm is ideally situated for holidaymakers and businessmen, especially those who enjoy peace and quiet, walking and rambling, golfing and riding, as these activities are all close by. At Needhams Farm everyone, including children and pets, receives a warm welcome. Good wholesome meals available in the evenings. Residential licence and Fire Certificate held. Open all year. Bed and Breakfast from £18 single minimum to £32 double maximum; Evening Meal £7. AA Listed, RAC Acclaimed.

KINGSLEY. Mrs Susan Klin, Charnwood, Hollow Lane, Kingsley WA6 8EF (01928 787097). AA

Recommended QQQ. Charnwood provides spacious accommodation, set in its own landscaped grounds in the delightful village of Kingsley. Close by are Oulton Park and Delamere Forest. Also ideally situated for historic Chester just 20 minutes away, Granada Studios at Manchester, and Albert Docks in Liverpool 30 minutes away by car. A wide range of luxury accommodation is available from £20 per person, including a private suite sleeping up to five people. Each room adjoins a private comfortable sittingroom with TV. All rooms have colour TV, tea/coffee making facilities and hair dryers. Fax and photocopying services are available. Full traditional English breakfast is served in a comfortable dining room overlooking the garden. Secure parking provided.

KNUTSFORD. Virginia Brown, Pickmere House, Park Lane, Pickmere, Knutsford WA16 0JX (Tel & Fax: 01565 733433; Mobile 0831 384460). 🌸 🌸 AA

QQQ, RAC Highly Acclaimed. A Listed Georgian farmhouse in rural hamlet close to Arley Hall and Tatton Park, two miles west of M6 Junction 19 on B5391 giving swift access to airport and all major north west towns and tourist attractions. Spacious en suite rooms with TV, tea/coffee trays and hairdryers, overlooking farmlands. Parking at rear. No smoking policy. Bed and Breakfast £19.50 to £29.50 single, £42 to £44 double/twin; Evening Meal/Dinner £9.50. Minibus groups by negotiation. AA Approved. Also Mews Cottage (two bedrooms, two bathrooms) available for self catering lets.

MACCLESFIELD. Mrs P.O. Worth, Rough Hey Farm, Leek Road, Gawsworth, Macclesfield SK11 0JQ (01260 252296). 🌸 🌸 Delightfully situated overlook-

ing the Cheshire Plain and on the edge of the Peak National Park, Rough Hey is an historic former hunting lodge dating from before the 16th century. Tastefully modernised yet retaining its old world character, this 300 acre sheep farm consists of wooded valleys and hills with plenty of wildlife and lovely walks. In the locality there are numerous old halls and villages to visit. Double room and twin room en suite and two single rooms, all with washbasins, TV and tea/coffee making facilities. Large comfortable lounge with TV. A warm and friendly welcome is assured. Terms from £18.

MACCLESFIELD. Ann and Owen Thomas, Moorhayes House Hotel, 27 Manchester Road, Tytherington, Macclesfield SK10 2JJ (01625 433228).

🌸 🌸 🌸 COMMENDED. We welcome you and your children to Moorhayes House Hotel, situated half a mile north of Macclesfield town centre on the A538 at Tytherington, 20 minutes east of Junction 17 on the M6. Standing well back from the road surrounded by a large, quiet, mature garden, our 1930's house has nine comfortably furnished bedrooms, some ground floor, many with en suite facilities and garden views. Hostess trays and colour TV are in all rooms. Ample parking in grounds. Dogs welcome by prior arrangement. Excellent reasonably priced restaurant and pubs provide good food and atmosphere nearby. Situated between Chester and Buxton on the edge of the Peak National Park and only 25 minutes from Manchester and the airport, we are ideally placed for exploring the city, historic houses and the beautiful countryside of Cheshire and Derbyshire. Bed and Breakfast from £19.50 to £36 per person per night; Evening Meal from £6.50 to £9.

MALPAS. Chris and Angela Smith, Mill House, Higher Wych, Malpas SY14 7JR (01948 780362; Fax: 01948 780566). ♛♛♛ *HIGHLY COMMENDED.*

Modernised mill house on the Cheshire/Clwyd border in a quiet valley convenient for visiting Chester, Shrewsbury and North Wales. The house is centrally heated and has an open log fire in the lounge. Bedrooms have washbasins, radios and tea-making facilities. One bedroom has an en suite shower and WC. Reductions for children and Senior Citizens. Open January to November. Bed and Brakfast from £16; Evening Meal from £8.

MIDDLEWICH. Mrs Susan Moss, Forge Mill Farm, Forge Mill Lane, Warmingham, Middlewich CW10 0HQ (01270 526204). ♛♛ Spacious and comfortable Country House in peaceful location. Friendly welcome and hospitality assured. Good position for Manchester Airport and touring the North West. Close to Exits 17 and 18 on M6 and A530 for Chester and North Wales. Delightful dining room, sitting room with colour TV and hot drinks trolley. Accommodation is in twin and double bedrooms. Bed and Breakfast from £16 per person per night.

SANDBACH. Mrs Helen Wood, Arclid Grange, Arclid Green, Sandbach CW11 0SZ (01270 764750; Fax: 01270 759255). Set in the lovely Cheshire countryside, yet within one mile of Junction 17 M6, Arclid Grange offers six attractive double/twin-bedded rooms. All rooms have en-suite bathrooms, colour TV, tea/coffee making facilities, direct dial telephones. Delicious home-cooked meals are served in the beamed diningroom. Cosy log fires in winter. Residential licence. Ample private car parking. Standing in its own mature gardens, this recently extended Cheshire farmhouse has all the charm and character of an old house, combined with comfortable, modern accommodation — rated Category 3 for disabled facilities. Bed and Breakfast from £22.50 per person, Dinner from £14.

TARPORLEY. Mrs Sutcliffe, Roughlow Farm, Willington, Tarporley CW6 0PG (Tel & Fax: 01829 751199). ♛♛ *COMMENDED.* 18th century sandstone farmhouse in outstanding position with magnificent views to Shropshire and Wales. Friendly family home, elegantly furnished to a very high standard. Three comfortable bedrooms, all en suite, one with own sitting room. Attractive garden with cobbled courtyard. Tennis court. Dinner by prior arrangement (minimum four persons). A superb home in a very peaceful rural situation only 15 minutes east of Chester. Ideal location for exploring Cheshire, The Potteries and North Wales. Recommended by Which? Good B&B Guide, The Best B&B, Staying off the Beaten Track.

CHESHIRE

Salt and silk, cheese and canals, trains and telescopes – just some of the intriguing features of this picturesque county. Make time to visit Chester Zoo, Stapeley Water Gardens, Jodrell Bank Science Centre, Port Sunlight Heritage Centre and Tatton Park – all a great day out and easily accessible from the motorway network.

CORNWALL

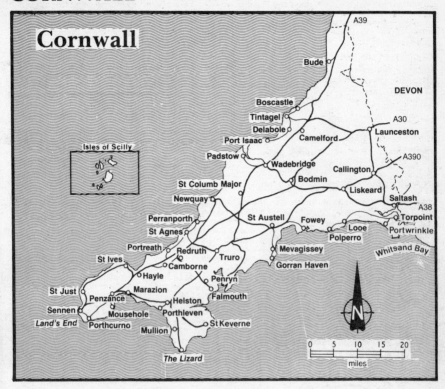

Cornwall

BODMIN. Mrs Jenny Bass, Trehannick Farm, St. Teath, Bodmin PL30 3JW (01208 850312).

Working farm. First mentioned in the Domesday Book in 1086, Trehannick is a 180 acre family farm situated in the beautiful Allen Valley. Safe sandy beaches, coastal walks, golf, sailing, surfing and fishing are all within easy reach of this peaceful farmhouse. Two double rooms, one with en suite bathroom, one with washbasin plus family room, with double and twin beds, washbasin; bathroom; lounge with colour TV (log fires when needed). Car essential. Sorry no pets. Reductions for children. "Glorious views" — "lovely peaceful atmosphere" — "a very happy stopover" — "magical" some of the comments made by our 1996 guests. Come and see and enjoy yourselves in the relaxing surroundings. Please telephone for further details.

BODMIN. Mrs S. Menhinick, Loskeyle Farm, St. Tudy, Bodmin PL30 3PW (01208 851005). ♥

COMMENDED. Loskeyle is a working dairy farm in the Duchy of Cornwall where a warm welcome awaits you. Relax and enjoy the peace and tranquillity of farm life here where you can watch the milking, feed the hens, collect eggs or enjoy leisurely walks through open fields. Children especially welcome with reduced rates. Delicious farmhouse cooking using fresh local produce. Pretty bedrooms with tea/coffee facilities and vanity units. Ideal base for north/south coasts. Golf, Camel Trail nearby, also pony trekking over the moors only a stone's throw away. Bed and Breakfast from £15; Evening Meal £8.

BODMIN. Mrs R. McNary, 26 Berrycombe Hill, Bodmin PL31 2PW (01208 75939). Bodmin is pleasantly situated midway between the north and south coasts, each being a 20 minute drive away. The accommodation makes a comfortable and friendly base from which to explore Cornwall on foot, or by car or bicycle. Bikes can be hired at reasonable cost to enable you to explore the beautiful Camel Trails leading to the coast and moors (26 miles in total). Each room has tea/coffee making facilities, also colour TV. Private parking. Bed and Breakfast from £13.50 per night, reduced rates for children. If telephoning best time to ring is after 6pm.

BOSCASTLE. Sue and Allan Miller, The Old Coach House, Tintagel Road, Boscastle PL35 0AS

(01840 250 398; Fax: 01840 250 346). 👑👑 AA and RAC Listed. Relax in a 300 year old former coach house now tastefully equipped to meet the needs of the 1990's with all rooms en-suite, colour TVs, radios, tea/coffee makers and central heating. Accessible for disabled guests. Good cooking. This picturesque village is a haven for walkers with its dramatic coastal scenery, a photographer's dream, and an ideal base to tour both the north and south coasts. The area is famed for its sandy beaches and surfing whilst King Arthur's Tintagel is only three miles away. Come and enjoy a friendly holiday with people who care. Brochure on request. Bed and Breakfast from £17 to £25.

BOSCASTLE. Mrs Sheila M. Smith, Glenthorne, Penally Hill, Boscastle PL35 0HH (01840 250502).

Glenthorne is set in its own grounds with ample parking area. Within five minutes' walk of the picturesque village with its quaint little harbour, a photographer's paradise. If you like walking there is the beautiful Valency Valley which leads to St. Juliot Church for the Thomas Hardy fans, also spectacular coastal walks. It's an ideal base for touring. Accommodation — one double with washbasin and one twin room, both with tea/coffee making facilities. Own lounge with colour TV. Pets welcome if well behaved. Own front door key. Bed and Breakfast from £14.

BOSCASTLE. Mrs Cheryl Nicholls, Trerosewill Farm, Paradise, Boscastle PL35 0DL (01840

250545). Working farm. 👑👑👑 *HIGHLY COMMENDED.* AA QQQQ Selected. Bed and Breakfast accommodation in modern farmhouse on working farm, only a short walk from the picturesque village of Boscastle. Rooms have spectacular coastal and rural views; all en suite, with tea making facilities. Colour TV and telephone available if required. Four-posters, mineral water and bath robes provided. Licensed. Centrally heated. Seasonal log fires. Large gardens. Traditional farmhouse fayre. Feed the calves. Superb coastal and countryside walks. Specially negotiated rates for nearby golf and pony trekking. One way walks arranged. Packed lunches available. Spring and Autumn breaks. Bed and Breakfast from £16. Strictly no smoking. FHG Diploma Award 1995.

BOSCASTLE. Graham and Hazel Mee, Bottreaux House Hotel, Boscastle PL35 0BG (01840

250231). Boscastle is the Jewel of North Cornwall, a beautiful village stretching from the old harbour up the sides of the Jordan and Valency Valleys. The Bottreaux Hotel which overlooks the village and surrounding hills is privately owned; seven en suite bedrooms, lounge, romantic candlelit restaurant. Car parking. When you stay with us you can be sure of a welcoming and relaxed atmosphere. Meal times are flexible and you have the freedom to use the key at any time of the day. Pets and children welcome by arrangement. Free use of mountain bikes. Bed and Breakfast from £13 low season, £18 high season.

BOSCASTLE. Mr J. Perfili, Trefoil Farm, New Road, Boscastle PL35 0AD (01840 250606). Trefoil Farm is situated on the boundary of Boscastle, overlooking the harbour, valley and ocean. On the farm we breed and show pedigree Suffolk sheep and we have large gardens to sit and relax in. Accommodation comprises family and double rooms, fully en suite, and having colour TV and tea/coffee making facilities. Full central heating, TV, lounge, seasonal log fires. Full English breakfast. Evening meal optional, traditional farmhouse fare. There are superb coastal and countryside walks, and one way walks can be arranged. Leisure facilities, sandy beaches nearby. Spring and Autumn Breaks. No pets. No smoking in the house. Bed and Breakfast from £15 to £18.

BUDE. Mrs Angela Mary Grills, Trelay, Marhamchurch, Bude EX23 0HP (01288 361218). Working dairy farm for you to enjoy. Trelay has a large farmhouse and garden and is situated in the centre of a 360 acre dairy and arable farm where you may relax at your leisure. Although we are situated in the middle of the countryside, Widemouth Bay, a large surfing beach, is within approximately two miles and Bude is only three miles away. Our local village of Marhamchurch with its pub is only one mile. Market towns and Bodmin and Dartmoor are within easy reach. Bedrooms have washbasins and tea-making facilities. A good farmhouse breakfast is served. Children welcome. Lounge with colour TV. Terms from £14 to £16.

Stamford Hill Hotel
"A Country House Hotel"

Set in five acres of gardens and woodland overlooking open countryside yet only a mile from the sandy beaches of Bude. Our spacious Georgian Manor House with 15 en-suite bedrooms with TV and tea/coffee making facilities, outdoor heated pool, tennis court, badminton court, games room and sauna is the ideal place for a relaxing holiday or short break. Daily Bed and Breakfast from £23.50; Three-day Break Dinner, Bed and Breakfast from £95.00. Pets welcome. ♥♥♥

Contact: Ian and Joy McFeat, Stamford Hill Hotel, Stratton, Bude EX23 9AY Tel: (01288) 352709.

BUDE. Mrs Rosina Joyner, "Penrose", Dizzard, St. Gennys, Bude EX23 0NX (01840 230318). Penrose is a delightful 17th century cottage with beamed ceilings and inglenook fireplaces. Tastefully modernised, yet retaining all its Olde Worlde charm. Set in one and a half acres of lawns and gardens within the National Trust area, close to the coastal path. It is ideal for those seeking peace and quiet. Nearby is the beautiful beach of Widemouth Bay. The views from the cottage are extensive. All bedrooms have washbasins, TV and tea/coffee making facilities; two rooms have double four-poster beds (one with shower). One bedroom with king-size bed with canopy, en suite and with sea views; ground floor en suite room suitable for disabled guests. Good English Breakfast, optional Evening Meal. Also available is a mobile home and cottage annexe for self catering; both sleep six from £150 low season to £375 high season. SAE, or phone, for booking form, brochure. Bed and Breakfast from £17.50 per night per person.

BUDE. Mrs S.A. Trewin, Lower Northcott Farm, Poughill, Bude EX23 7EL (01288 352350). ♥♥ *COMMENDED.* **Working farm.** Lower Northcott is built of stone in Georgian design and is situated one mile north of Bude. Set on the side of a secluded valley with outstanding views of the rugged Heritage coastline. All rooms are en suite and spacious with very comfortable furnishings. Tea/coffee facilities. Home cooking is our speciality. Children welcome. Open all year. Central heating. Bed and Breakfast from £17 per person.

Lower Northcott Farm

BUDE. Mrs Christine Nancekivell, Dolsdon Farm, Boyton, Launceston PL15 8NT (01288 341264).

Dolsdon was once a 17th century coaching inn, now modernised, situated on the Launceston to Bude road within easy reach of sandy beaches, surfing, Tamar Otter Park, leisure centre with heated swimming pool, golf courses, fishing, tennis and horse riding and is ideal for touring Cornwall and Devon. Guests are welcome to wander around the 260 acre working farm. All bedrooms have washbasins and tea making facilities (en suite family room available). Comfortably furnished lounge has colour TV. Plenty of good home cooking assured — full English breakfast, four-course evening dinner (optional). Parking. Bed and Breakfast from £13; reductions for children. Brochure available.

BUDE. Eric and Lorna Hatch, Seaview, 51 Killerton Road, Bude EX23 8EN (01288 352665). We

welcome you to Seaview situated in this lovely unspoilt seaside town of Bude. We are central for all amenities, shops, beaches and many recreational facilities including the canal and cliff top walks. Our rooms all have vanity units, tea/coffee making facilities and TV. Lounge. Garden. Private parking. Open all year. Bed and Breakfast £15. Reduced rates for children.

BUDE. Michael and Pearl Hopper, West Nethercott Farm, Whitstone, Holsworthy (Devon) EX22 6LD (01288 341394). Working farm, join in. A warm

welcome awaits you on this dairy and sheep farm. Watch the cows being milked, help with the animals. Free pony rides, scenic farm walks. Short distance from sandy beaches, surfing and the rugged North Cornwall coast. Ideal base for visiting any part of Devon or Cornwall. We are located in Cornwall though our postal address is Devon. The traditional farmhouse has washbasins and TVs in bedrooms; dining-room and separate lounge with colour TV. Plenty of traditional home cooking. Access to the house at anytime. Bed and Breakfast from £11, four course Evening Meal available. Children under 12 years reduced rates. Weekly terms available.

CALLINGTON. Brenda Crago, Cadson Manor Farm, Callington PL17 7HW (Tel & Fax: 01579 383969). The friendliest welcome awaits you at Cadson.

True Cornish hospitality guaranteed to make your stay extra special. Traditional furnishings tastefully blended with modern conveniences, sitting peacefully beneath Cadson Bury, affording unspoilt views of this ancient monument set in the beautiful Lynher Valley, secluded yet close to all main towns, riding, golf, beaches all within easy reach. Open all year. Bed and Breakfast (en suite) from £18. Farm Holiday Bureau and Cream of Cornwall Farm Holiday Group members. Brochure on request.

CAMBORNE. Mrs Christine Peerless, Highdowns, Blackrock, Praze-an-Beeble, Camborne TR14 9PD (01209 831442). Highdowns is a comfortable, quiet

and ideally situated base from which to explore the beautiful Cornish countryside and magnificent coastline. Set on a south-west facing hillside with extensive views towards St. Ives Bay. We offer traditional home-made and varied meals using fresh home grown and local produce whenever available with special and vegetarian diets catered for. All bedrooms en suite with tea/coffee making facilities. TV lounge. Easy parking. Fire Certificate. No smoking. Bed and Breakfast £16 per night; Evening Meal £8.

FALMOUTH. Mrs Jean Eustice, Trevu House Hotel, 45 Melvill Road, Falmouth TR11 4DG (01326

312852). Trevu House is a small family-run hotel with a friendly home-from-home atmosphere, with special emphasis on comfort, cleanliness and personal service. The situation is ideal for a seaside holiday, being only about two minutes' walk from Gyllyngvase Beach and within easy reach of the town, harbour and local railway station. Spacious accommodation is tastefully furnished with bright modern decor. Large comfortable lounge and reading room. Bedrooms are en-suite and have modern divan beds, colour TVs, tea/coffee making facilities and central heating. We pride ourselves on our high standard of cuisine which is well presented and served at separate tables complemented, if required, by a variety of wines. Bed and Breakfast from £15. No single room supplement. Full Fire Certificate held. Car parking. Brochure available on request.

FALMOUTH. Terry & Alison Trezise, Selwood Cottage, 38 Melvill Road, Falmouth TR11 4DQ

(01326 314135). Selwood Cottage is one of the loveliest detached houses in the whole of Falmouth, situated down a private drive in a large peaceful prize-winning garden, being the "Britain in Bloom" champion for three consecutive years. Both ITV and the Garden News have featured the garden and many subtropical plants, shrubs and trees can be seen. The sea and beaches are only 200 metres away and the picturesque town, harbour and gardens are only a few minutes' walk. The tastefully decorated accommodation offers bedrooms (some en suite) equipped with colour TV, central heating, shaver points and tea/coffee making facilities. A comfortable lounge and dining room look directly onto the garden. Access is available at all times. Plenty of car parking in private drive. Children over five years welcome. No smoking in the dining room. Highly recommended by various organisations. An ideal base for touring Cornwall. You can be assured of good food and a warm welcome. Bed and Breakfast from £15 to £18. Brochure available. AA QQQ Recommended, Which Books Good Bed and Breakfast Guide, Falmouth District Hotel Association.

FOWEY. Bob and Jill Bullock, Trevanion Guest House, 70 Lostwithiel Street, Fowey PL23 1BQ (01726 832602). ETB Listed *COMMENDED.* AA QQQ. A warm and friendly welcome awaits you at this comfortable and spacious 16th century merchant's house. Situated in the historic estuary town of Fowey in the heart of Daphne Du Maurier country, it is an ideal base from which to walk the South West Coastal Path, visit the lost gardens of Heligan and local National Trust houses and gardens or explore the Cornish Riviera. En suite facilities available and all rooms are well furnished and have washbasins, colour TV and tea/coffee making facilities. Non-smoking. From £15 per person per night.

FOWEY. Mrs Moss, Trenant Guest House, Fowey PL23 1JU (01726 833477; Fax: 01726 832192).

Trenant is a family-run guest house set well away from the road in a quiet valley. We are situated between Fowey and Par. The large extensive garden includes a kiddies play area. Families are welcome, a cot and high chair available on request. All bedrooms have tea and coffee making facilities, razor points and washbasins. We have a comfortable lounge with colour TV and Sky. There are rural views from most of the rooms and ample parking space. Fowey, itself, is an enchanting town together with the superb estuary looking across to Bodinnick and Polruan.

HELSTON. Mrs Margaret Jenkin, Boderloggan Farm, Wendron, Helston TR13 0ES (01326 572148). Working farm. "Boderloggan" is a 120 acre dairy farm, ideally situated for touring the main towns and beauty spots of South and West Cornwall. Within easy reach of the coast, Newquay, Falmouth, St. Ives, Penzance, Truro; Helston three miles. Also well situated for visiting holiday attractions and National Trust properties and gardens in the area. Two double (family) bedrooms with washbasins and tea/coffee making facilities; bathroom; beamed dining room/lounge with colour TV. Mrs Jenkin will give her guests a value-for-money holiday with plenty of fresh vegetables, clotted cream, with a three-course evening meal. English breakfast. Friendly homely atmosphere, children welcome. Food Hygiene Certificate. FHG Diploma Winner. Bed and Breakfast or Bed, Breakfast and Evening Meal.

HELSTON. Mrs P. Roberts, Hendra Farm, Wendron, Helston TR13 0NR (01326 340470). Hendra

Farm, just off the main Helston/Falmouth road, is an ideal centre for touring Cornwall; three miles to Helston, eight to both Redruth and Falmouth. Safe sandy beaches within easy reach — five miles to the sea. Beautiful views from the farmhouse of the 60 acre beef farm. Two double, one single, and one family bedrooms; bathroom and toilets; sitting room and two dining rooms. Cot, babysitting and reduced rates offered for children. No objection to pets. Car necessary, parking space. Enjoy good cooking with roast beef, pork, lamb, chicken, genuine Cornish pasties, fish and delicious sweets and cream. Open all year except Christmas. Evening Dinner, Bed and Breakfast from £110 per week which includes cooked breakfast, three course evening dinner, tea and home made cake before bed. Bed and Breakfast only from £12 per night also available.

HELSTON near. Mrs D.J. Hill, "Rocklands", The Lizard, Near Helston TR12 7NX (01326 290339).

"Rocklands" is situated overlooking part of Cornwall's superb coastline and enjoys uninterrupted sea views. The Lizard is well known for its lovely picturesque scenery, coastal walks and enchanting coves and beaches, as well as the famous Serpentine Stone which is quarried and sold locally. Open Easter to October. The Hill family have been catering for visitors on the Lizard since the 1850's. Three bedrooms with sea views, tea/coffee making facilities and electric heaters; sittingroom with TV and video; sun lounge; dining room with separate tables. Bed and Breakfast weekly terms from £126 per person. NO VAT. Children and well trained pets welcome.

LAUNCESTON. Mary Rich, "Nathania", Altarnun, Launceston PL15 7SL (01566 86426). Christian couple offer Bed, Breakfast and Evening Meal accommodation on a small farm on Bodmin Moor within easy reach of coast, moors, towns, lakes and fishing. Visit King Arthur country — Tintagel, Dozmary Pool, famous Jamaica Inn, Wesley Cottage and cathedral of the moors. Double and twin rooms with en suite bathroom and tea making facilities. Conservatory and lounge for quiet relaxation. Please telephone, or write, for details — SAE, thank you.

LISKEARD. Mrs S. Rowe, Tregondale Farm, Menheniot, Liskeard PL14 3RG (Tel & Fax: 01579

342407). ✤ ✤ *HIGHLY COMMENDED.* Feeling like a break near the coast? Come and relax, join our family with the peace of the countryside, breathtaking in Spring, on a 200 acre mixed farm situated near Looe between the A38 and A390. See pedigree South Devon cattle and sheep naturally reared, explore the new woodland farm trail amidst wildlife and flowers. This stylish characteristic farmhouse which dates back to the Domesday Book, as featured in the Daily Telegraph, Cream of Cornwall, provides exceptional comfort with quality en suite bedrooms, all with colour TV and tea/coffee making facilities; lounge, dining room, log fires. A conservatory to enjoy each day's warmth, capturing a beautiful view over the farm. Set in an original walled garden including picnic table, tennis court and play area. Special activities can be arranged, e.g., golf, fishing, cycling and walking. Home produce a speciality, full English breakfast, four course optional evening meal. Bed and Breakfast from £18.00; Evening Meal £10.00. Open all year. AA QQQQ. Self catering character cottage also available graded 4 KEYS HIGHLY COMMENDED.

LOOE. Mrs Angela Eastley, Little Larnick Farm, Pelynt, Looe PL13 2NB (01503 262837). ✤ ✤ Get

away from it all at Little Larnick, a dairy, beef and sheep farm in the beautiful Looe Valley, four miles from picturesque Looe and Polperro where we welcome guests from February to November. The character farmhouse offers twin, double and family rooms all with en-suite facilities. The rooms are spacious and have comfy armchairs, colour TV, tea/coffee facilities, electric blankets and heating. The family room is in a downstairs annexe overlooking the garden. There is a sittingroom with colour TV and log fires on cold evenings and the beamed diningroom has separate tables. Bed and Breakfast from £17. No smoking.

The Old Rectory Country House Hotel

**St. Keyne, Near Liskeard
Cornwall PL14 4RL
Tel: 01579 342617**

English Tourist Board
COMMENDED

Peacefully secluded in our own 3 acres of gardens, we are ideally situated for touring Cornwall and South-west Devon and its multitude of attractions. Enjoy the warm welcoming ambience of a family-run country house, we offer full English Breakfast and à la carte Dinners, comfortable, ensuite bedrooms (all with colour televisions & tea/coffee-making facilities). Bed and Breakfast from £27-£35 per person per night, Dinner from £16. Short Breaks (minimum 2 nights – October to March) from £38 p.p. per night Dinner, Bed and Breakfast. A comfortable lounge with open fires during cooler evenings and an "Honesty" Bar are also available for our guests' enjoyment.

No smoking in Dining Room. Pets Welcome.

LOOE. Mrs Lynda Wills, Polgover Farm, Widegates, Looe PL13 1PY (01503 240248). Working farm. Polgover Farm is situated in picturesque countryside, four miles from Looe on the B3252 and ideally situated to explore Cornwall and South Devon. Local attractions include horse riding, golf, fishing, water sports, Monkey Sanctuary and many beaches. There is always a warm welcome at Polgover's spacious 16th century Listed farmhouse, where you can have a peaceful and relaxing holiday. There are three tastefully decorated bedrooms, all with washbasins and tea/coffee facilities. Guests' bathroom. Lounge with colour TV incorporating breakfast room with separate tables. Sorry, no pets. Open Easter to October. Ample parking. Bed and Breakfast from £14. Weekly and child reductions. Brochure available.

LOOE. Mrs Jean Henly, Bucklawren Farm, St. Martin-by-Looe PL13 1NZ (01503 240738; Fax: 01503 240481). ♥ ♥ ♥ HIGHLY COMMENDED. Working farm. Bucklawren is situated deep in unspoilt countryside, yet only one mile from the beach, two and a half miles from Looe, and one mile from the Woolly Monkey Sanctuary. It is mentioned in the Domesday Book but the Manor House is now replaced by a 19th century spacious farmhouse which has a large garden and beautiful sea views. We offer excellent accommodation with television lounge, family and ensuite rooms and farmhouse cooking in a friendly and relaxed atmosphere. There is ample parking. Open March to October. Reduced rates for children. Bed and Breakfast from £18 to £20; Evening Meal £9.50 to £10. Brochure on request. Member of Farm Holiday Bureau.

LOOE. John and Hazel Storer, Kantara Licensed Guesthouse, 7 Trelawney Terrace, West Looe PL13 2AG (01503 262093). ♥ COMMENDED. AA QQ Recommended. Small but well appointed, licensed guesthouse situated near the centre of this picturesque resort and convenient for shops, restaurants, beach and watersports. The atmosphere is friendly and informal; guests have access to facilities at any reasonable time and 24 hour access to rooms. All bedrooms have washbasins, colour TV with satellite and video link, radio alarms, cordless kettles and beverages. A range of utilities is available on request; bar lounge with 28" colour TV. Kantara is very popular with anglers, many booking trips on "Valency", our charter vessel, licensed for twelve fishermen or passengers. Cold storage is available for your catch. Bed and Breakfast from £13. Children and well behaved pets welcome. Frommers Recommended.

LOOE near. Jane and Barry Wynn, Harescombe Lodge, Watergate, Near Looe PL13 2NE (01503 263158). Harescombe Lodge is a country guest house situated 'twixt Looe and Polperro in the secluded picturesque hamlet of Watergate. Once the shooting lodge of the Trelawne Estate, home of the Trelawney family. Beautiful river views and walks with interesting wildlife. Peaceful surroundings, idyllic location appealing to the discerning visitor to South East Cornwall. Ideal as a stopover or a base for a short break. All bedrooms comfortably furnished with en suite and tea/coffee making facilities. Ample off-road parking. Open all year for Bed and Breakfast; optional evening meal. Unsuitable for children under 12 years. Sorry no pets. Bed and Breakfast from £17.

MARAZION near. Jenny Birchall, Mount View House, Varfell, Ludgvan, Penzance TR20 8AW (01736 710179). Mount View House is a Victorian former farmhouse standing in half an acre of gardens overlooking St. Michael's Mount. The house is furnished in traditional style and offers one room with sea views and another with rural views. Rooms have washbasins, central heating and tea/coffee making facilities. Guests' WC and shower room; sitting/dining room with open fire. Children welcome, cot available. Situated approximately three miles from Penzance and five miles from St. Ives. We are the ideal touring stopover. Our close proximity to the heliport (one mile) makes us an ideal stopover en route to the Scilly Isles. Bed and Breakfast from £14 per person per night. Self catering accommodation also available, please telephone for details.

MARAZION (West Cornwall). Mrs Susan Barlow, "Rostherne", Feliskirk Lane, Marazion TR17 0HA (01736 711522 or 710766). Rostherne is situated in the ancient town of Marazion and enjoys spectacular views of St. Michael's Mount and Mount's Bay. The house, whilst secluded, is only 400 yards from the beach and forms an ideal base for touring West Cornwall, Land's End and The Lizard. Each of the large bedrooms affords excellent sea views and all have colour TV. Ample car parking. Sorry no pets. Open all year. Terms from £16 per night.

MEVAGISSEY. Harbour Lights Hotel, Polkirt Hill, Mevagissey PL26 6UR (01726 843249). This family-run freehouse/Hotel is situated on one of the finest cliff top positions in Cornwall, overlooking Mevagissey harbour and St. Austell Bay. All the public rooms and most of the bedrooms enjoy ever changing sea views. En suite rooms are available with TVs and tea/coffee making facilities. Bed and Breakfast from £19 per person per night. Enjoy a meal in the newly opened restaurant which is only a stone's throw from the water, or watch the fishing boats come in whilst having a drink in the bar. We have our own large car park. Ring or write for brochure.

MEVAGISSEY. Martin and Nicki Perrin, Lavorrick Orchard Hotel, Vicarage Hill, Mevagissey PL26 6SZ (01726 842265). 🐦🐦 A friendly family-run licensed Hotel situated within private grounds on a south facing hillside overlooking this picturesque fishing village. The Hotel offers excellent food and comfortable accommodation in mostly en suite rooms with colour TV, tea/coffee making facilities and central heating. The Hotel's situation means it can be easily reached from St. Austell without having to negotiate the narrow village streets. Ample private parking is available. Well behaved pets are welcome. Discounts available for children. Bed and Breakfast from £18 per person; Bed, Breakfast and Evening Meal from £25 per person. Colour brochure on request.

STEEP HOUSE 🛏🛏

Portmellon Cove, Mevagissey, Cornwall PL26 2PH
Telephone: (01726) 843732

Steep House stands in an acre of ground by the sea, in a natural cove with a safe, sandy beach 20 yards from the large garden. Comfortable, centrally heated double bedrooms with washbasins and Sea or Beach views, colour TV and tea/coffee maker; some are ensuite. Generous English breakfast served. Covered summertime swimming pool. Guests welcome all year. Modest prices, special weekly and winter break rates. Licensed. Free private parking. Fire Certificate. Colour brochure.

MEVAGISSEY. Mrs Anne Hennah, Treleaven Farm, Mevagissey PL26 6RZ (01726 842413). Working farm. Treleaven Farm is situated in quiet, pleasant surroundings overlooking the village and the sea. The 200 acre mixed farm is well placed for visitors to enjoy the many attractions of Mevagissey with its quaint narrow streets and lovely shops. Fishing and boat trips are available and very popular. The house offers a warm and friendly welcome with the emphasis on comfort, cleanliness and good food using local produce. A licensed bar and solar heated swimming pool add to your holiday enjoyment, together with a games room and putting green. Tastefully furnished throughout, with central heating, there are five double bedrooms and one family bedroom, all en suite with tea/coffee making facilities and TV; bathroom, two toilets. Sittingroom and diningroom. Open February to November for Evening Dinner, Bed and Breakfast from £28 or Bed and Breakfast from £17. Sorry, no pets. SAE, please, for particulars or telephone.

MEVAGISSEY. Mrs Dawn Rundle, Lancallan Farm, Mevagissey, St. Austell PL26 6EW (01726 842284). Lancallan is a large 17th century farmhouse on a working 200 acre dairy and beef farm in beautiful rural setting, one mile from Mevagissey and surrounded by lovely coastal walks and sandy beaches. We are well situated for day trips throughout Cornwall. Enjoy a traditional farmhouse breakfast in a warm and friendly atmosphere. Accommodation comprises one family room, one double room; bathroom; lounge with colour TV and tea-making facilities. Terms available on request, reductions for children. SAE please.

MITCHELL FARM

MITCHELL. Mitchell Farm, Mitchell TR8 5AX (01872 510657). Mitchell Farm is a smallholding specialising in organic growing with Soil Association Symbol. Situated in the attractive village of Mitchell, within close reach of the main A30. Centrally located midway between Newquay and the delightful Cathedral city of Truro, the Farmhouse is a 19th century stonebuilt Grade II Listed building. There are tea-making facilities and washbasins in all rooms; guest diningroom and lounge with colour TV. Access to the house at all times via separate guest entrance with key supplied. Pub in the village within easy walking distance. Full central heating. Ample parking. Open all year except Christmas. Bed and Breakfast £14 per night, weekly Bed and Breakfast £88. Individual family quotes. Self catering also available, details on request.

Terms quoted in this publication may be subject to increase if rises in costs necessitate

MORWENSTOW. Little Bryaton, Morwenstow, Near Bude EX23 9SU (01288 331755). Period

cottage in secluded setting, close to Heritage coastal footpath. Accommodation comprises one double and one twin bedroom, both with colour TV, tea/coffee facilities, central heating. Bathroom with shower, guests' conservatory, private dining room. Ample parking. Bed and Breakfast from £14.50 to £16.50; Dinner £8. Reduction for mini breaks, weekly bookings and children. Cot and high chair available. Open all year. Close to surfing beaches, rocky coves, impressive cliffs, seaside resort of Bude, Clovelly village, Hartland Quay, Exmoor, Dartmoor and Bodmin Moor. Five minutes' drive from A39. Ring for further information.

MULLION. Margaret Hobday, Gweal an Drea Guesthouse, Polrurrian Cove, Mullion, Near Helston

TR12 7HB (01326 240341; Fax: 01326 240039). Mullion is a pretty village on the unspoilt picturesque Lizard Peninsula, the warmest, most southerly point on mainland Britain. Recommended guesthouse next to secluded sandy beach and within walking distance of village and pubs. Surrounded by beautiful National Trust coastline. Tea/coffee facilities and TV in spacious en suite rooms. Large comfortable lounge with open fire. Separate lounge with video and book library. Pets welcome. Non-smoking. Bed and Breakfast £17 to £22 per day. Reduced rates October to March. Breakfast served from 8.30am to 10am. Evening meals available. Lizard Peninsula Tourist Association recommended. "Wonderful — a real find!" "Great hospitality and perfect location".

NEWQUAY. Mr and Mrs John and Vera Connolly, "Stanford", 91a Henver Road, Newquay TR7

3DJ (01637 875474). Luxury Guest Bungalow, open March to end October, ideally situated for all beaches, with lovely sea view and near to town. Five bedrooms (double and family), some with sea views; all with heating, hot and cold water, razor points, vanitory units, divan beds, modern furniture; some with showers and TV. Bathroom, two toilets. Attractive lounge; delightful diningroom; all home-made cooking at its best. Children welcome. Sorry, no pets. Car not essential, but plenty of parking space; buses stop by door. Fire Certificate. Everything for your comfort provided for a happy and restful holiday — evening snacks and morning tea on request at moderate charges. Bed, Breakfast and four-course Evening Dinner with tea or coffee from £115 per week. Reduced rates for Senior Citizens early and late season. Stamp, please, for brochure or telephone for a quick booking.

NEWQUAY near. Mr and Mrs Rowlands, Crantock Plains Farm, Near Newquay TR8 5PH (01637

830253). Charming character farmhouse in peaceful countryside. Comfort, home cooking and personal service combine to make an enjoyable, relaxing holiday. Crantock Plains Farm is situated two and a half miles from Newquay and half a mile off the A3075 Newquay to Redruth Road. One and a half miles to the village of Crantock with Post Office, village stores, tea rooms, two pubs and beautiful sandy beach. Riding stables and many sporting activities nearby. Choice of four doubles (one twin en suite), two family bedrooms; ground floor bedrooms are available; shower room, toilets. Electric blankets for your comfort on chilly nights. Sitting room and dining room. Home grown vegetables where available. Table licence. Sorry no pets. Bed, Breakfast and Evening Meal or Bed and Breakfast. Terms and brochure on request with SAE please. Non-smoking establishment. Cream Tea Award. Award winners of "Newquay in Bloom" 1990, 1991 and 1992.

CORNISH CUISINE!

The traditional Cornish Pasty was originally the tin-miners' portable lunch — shaped like a torpedo to fit in his pocket! The filling is usually mutton mixed with potatoes and swedes, and is enclosed in pastry pinched high along its entire length. Another Cornish speciality is Stargazey Pie, where pilchards are arranged in a dish like the spokes of a wheel, the pastry cover being cut to allow the eyes to gaze out. And to finish off — a clotted cream tea with scones and strawberry jam!

NEWQUAY. Mike and Doris Mortimer, Pensalda, 98 Henver Road, Newquay TR7 3BL (01637 874601).Tourist Board Listed. Take a break in the "heart of Cornwall". An ideal location from which to explore and enjoy the finest coastline and beaches in Europe. A warm and friendly welcome awaits you at our family-run guest house, situated on the main A3058 approximately half a mile from the town and close to beaches and amenities. Accommodation available in one twin, one single, four double and two family bedrooms including two chalets situated in pleasant and peaceful garden surroundings. En suite rooms available. All have colour TV, tea making facilities. We have an excellent reputation for serving good freshly prepared food with choice of menu. Hot and cold snacks and packed lunches available on request. Licensed bar. Central heating. Parking on premises. Fire Certificate. Bed and Breakfast from £13; Bed, Breakfast and Evening Dinner from £17 per day. Special weekly terms, Bargain Breaks and reduced rates for Senior Citizens available early and late season. Brochure on request or phone for details.

NEWQUAY. Porth Enodoc Hotel, 4 Esplanade Road, Pentire, Newquay TR7 1PY (01637 872372). 🏵🏵🏵 Standing in its own grounds overlooking Fistral Beach and Newquay Golf Course this delightful hotel offers a warm friendly welcome. Family owned and managed. Delicious home cooking. There are 15 well appointed bedrooms, most with sea views, all with en suite facilities, colour TV, radio/intercom/child listening, tea/coffee making facilities and central heating. There is a comfortable bar and the lounge and dining room have panoramic views over the Bay. Parking space for all within the hotel grounds. Bed and Breakfast from £15 daily. Dinner, Bed and Breakfast from £119 to £189 per week including VAT. Special terms for Short Breaks available throughout the year. AA QQQQ, RAC Highly Acclaimed. Self catering cottage also available.

AA ★★

Tregurrian Hotel

ETB 🏵🏵🏵

Watergate Bay, near Newquay, Cornwall TR8 4AB
Telephone: (01637) 860280

★ 27 rooms with radio/listening, tea-makers, heaters, most ensuite, TV in all rooms ★ Car park ★ Heated pool and sun patio, games room, solarium, sauna, jacuzzi ★ Parties and coaches by arrangement ★ Spring and Autumn Breaks ★ Family run: children welcome at reduced rates (some free offers) ★ Licensed bar ★ Central for touring all of Cornwall ★ Open Easter to November ★ Dinner, bed and breakfast £144 to £230 inclusive of VAT

Brochure from resident proprietors Marian and Derrick Molloy

ETB ♛♛ Approved

White Lodge Hotel

Mawgan Porth Bay, Near Newquay, Cornwall TR8 4BN
Tel: St. Mawgan (STD 01637) 860512
Les Routiers   AA & RAC Listed

Give yourselves and your dogs a quality holiday break at our family-run White Lodge Hotel overlooking beautiful Mawgan Porth Bay, near Newquay, Cornwall.

★ Dogs most welcome – FREE OF CHARGE.
★ Your dogs sleep with you in your bedroom.
★ Direct access to sandy beach & coastal path.
★ Dog loving proprietors with 12 years' experience in catering for dog owners on holiday with their dogs.
★ All bedrooms with colour TVs with video and satellite TV channels, tea/coffee makers, alarm clocks, radios, intercoms, heaters etc.
★ Some en-suite bedrooms.
★ Fantastic sea views from most rooms.
★ Well-stocked residents' lounge bar, dining room & sun patio with outstanding views across the bay.
★ Games room with pool table and dart board etc.
★ Large free car park within hotel grounds.

SPECIAL 6 DAYS (5 NIGHTS) CHRISTMAS HOUSE PARTY ONLY £215 FULL BOARD

SPECIAL 6 DAYS (5 NIGHTS) NEW YEAR (HOGMANAY) BREAK ONLY £190 HALF BOARD

SPECIAL 6 DAYS (5 NIGHTS) BREAKS ONLY £135 to £155 D.B. & B.

WEEKLY TERMS FROM £175 TO £205 FOR 5-COURSE EVENING DINNER, BED & 4-COURSE BREAKFAST WITH MENU CHOICE.

ALL PRICES INCLUDE VAT AT 17½%.

PHONE 01637 860512 JOHN OR DIANE PARRY FOR FREE COLOUR BROCHURE
Proprietors: John & Diane Parry

THE WHITE HERON

This well established, friendly, family-run hotel offers colour co-ordinated bedrooms, all with tea/coffee making facilities, TV, en-suite available. Cosy Satellite TV lounge. Come and go as you please. Ample car parking. Close to many North Cornwall attractions and surrounded by excellent surfing beaches (Polzeath 500 yards, Daymer Bay 700 yards). Courses galore for golfers, and walkers will enjoy the National Trust Coastal Path. Our popular licensed restaurant offers delicious homemade meals, reasonably priced. Bed and English Breakfast from £12. For details on bargain breaks and June specials call

Paul and Margaret Mark, The White Heron, Old Polzeath PL27 6TJ. Telephone: (01208) 863623 ₩₩

PADSTOW. The Old Mill Country House, Little Petherick, Padstow PL27 7QT (01841 540388).

₩₩₩ COMMENDED. AA QQQ Recommended, RAC Acclaimed. This is a 16th century Grade II Listed corn mill complete with waterwheel. Set in its own streamside gardens at the head of Little Petherick Creek just two miles from Padstow and in a designated area of outstanding natural beauty. The Old Mill is furnished throughout with antiques and collections of genuine artifacts to complement the exposed beams, original fireplaces and slate floors. This ensures that the Old Mill's original character and charm is retained. We regret the minimum age for children is 14 years. Licensed. En suite. Bed and Breakfast from £26.

PADSTOW. Mrs A. Woosnam-Mills, Mother Ivey Cottage, Trevose Head, Padstow PL28 8SL (Tel & Fax: 01841 520329).

Mother Ivey Cottage is an old traditionally built Cornish house, furnished with antiques and having stunning sea views. The area is renowned for swimming, fishing and surfing. There is also a Championship Golf Course nearby. Bedrooms have en suite bathrooms and twin beds. There is a TV and sitting room for guests' use and evening meals are available with notice. There is easy access for many National Trust properties, historic fishing villages and the working harbour at Padstow. Car essential, ample parking. Bed and Breakfast from £20.

PENZANCE. Mr and Mrs R.B. Hilder, Carnson House, East Terrace, Penzance TR18 2TD (01736 65589/365589).

₩₩ A friendly welcome awaits you in our centrally situated, licensed Private Hotel. We specially cater for rail and coach travellers being only yards from the station. A high standard of comfort is maintained together with a reputation for excellent food. We have a comfortable lounge, attractive dining room with separate dining tables, and eight bedrooms, all with heating, tea-makers and colour TV and some with en suite facilities. Penzance is a lively and interesting town with plenty of shops, gardens and promenade, and is the natural centre for exploring the Land's End Peninsula with its beaches, cliffs, coves and villages. We arrange many local excursions, including some to the Isles of Scilly as well as coach tours and car hire. RAC Listed. Bed and Breakfast from £16 daily.

PENZANCE. Mrs Monica Olds, Mulfra Farm, Newmill, Penzance TR20 8XP (01736 63940). Superb accommodation is offered on this 50 acre hill farm high on the Penwith moors. The 17th century stone built farmhouse has far reaching views, is attractively furnished and offers two double en suite bedrooms with tea/coffee trays and TV. The comfortable lounge with inglenook fireplace and Cornish stone oven has good selections of books and TV. Dining room with separate tables, sun lounge and good food. Car essential, ample parking. Ideal centre for exploring West Cornwall's beaches and places of historic interest. We even have our own Iron Age village, as well as cows, calves and horses. Warm, friendly atmosphere. Beautiful walking country. Penzance three miles, St. Ives nine miles. Bed and Breakfast and Evening Meal from £125 per week. Further details sent with pleasure.

PENZANCE. John and Andrea Leggatt, "Cornerways", 5 Leskinnick Street, Penzance TR18 2HA (01736 364645).

A small, friendly guest house conveniently situated close to coach/rail stations and car parks. All rooms offer good, clean basic amenities, hot and cold, tea/coffee facilities, colour TV, en suite also available. Cornerways provides good home cooked meals, and vegetarians can be catered for; packed lunches are available if required, since Penzance is ideally situated for trips to Isles of Scilly or just touring West Cornwall. Bed and Breakfast from £14 per person per night, £17.50 per person en suite. Evening Meal £5.50 per person or Bed, Breakfast and Evening Meal one week £125 per person, en suite £140 per person.

EDNOVEAN HOUSE

Perranuthnoe, Near Penzance TR20 9LZ ♨♨♨
Arthur & Val Compton Tel. 01736 711071

A beautifully situated family-run 160 year old Victorian house offering nine delightful, comfortable rooms, most having en suite facilities and panoramic sea views. Situated in one acre of gardens and overlooking St. Michael's Mount and Mount's Bay, it has one of the finest views in the whole of Cornwall. Relax in an extremely comfortable lounge, Library or informal bar, and enjoy fine food and wines in the candlelit dining room, catering also for vegetarians. Pets welcome. Car park. Bed & Breakfast from £19 to £24 per person; Evening Meal £14.50. Ideal for coastal walks and exploring from the Lizard to Land's End.

PENZANCE near. Linda and Alan Sunderland, Kerris Manor Farm, Kerris, Penzance TR19 6UY (01736 731198).

Relax and unwind in our friendly old farmhouse. You're assured of a warm welcome and peaceful surroundings on our working farm which is three miles from Penzance at the end of a country lane one mile from the main B3315. Enjoy farm and woodland walks, birdwatching, etc. (picnics provided if required). Explore Newlyn, Penzance, Lamorna Cove and Mousehole. Marvellous scenery, inviting beaches, the Minack Open Air Theatre all within easy reach. One comfy double room with TV, radio, hot drinks facilities and several extras. Lounge/dining room with colour TV and woodburner. Parking. Terms on request. Sorry no smoking.

PENZANCE near. Janet Harrison, Relubbus House, Relubbus, Penzance TR20 9EL (01736 762929). Relubbus House is a 17th century converted barn in the quiet village of Relubbus near the River Hayle. It is a spacious comfortable home offering good food and a warm welcome with full central heating and log fires. All bedrooms have en suite or private bathroom. Four-poster beds. Relax in the garden and outdoor swimming pool. Bed and Breakfast; Evening Meals by prior arrangement. Non-smoking.

PENZANCE near. Mrs Eileen Lawry, "Llawnnroc", Truthwall Villa, Botallack, St. Just, Penzance TR19 7QL (01736 788814).

Enjoy a friendly welcome in a small guest house situated on the beautiful north coast, just five miles from Land's End, 10 miles from St. Ives, seven miles from Penzance. Ideal for walking, horse riding, golf and lovely sandy beaches. Family, twin and double rooms available, good home cooking. Non smoking accommodation available. Bed and Breakfast £13; optional Evening Meal £7. Reductions for three nights or more. Children under 12 years half price. Parking space.

PENZANCE. Mr & Mrs G.W. Buswell, Penalva Private Hotel, Alexandra Road, Penzance TR18 4LZ (01736 69060). ✿✿✿ *APPROVED.* AA QQQ. The hotel is TOTALLY NON-SMOKING, offering full central heating, fresh immaculate interior, en-suite facilities, excellent food and a real welcome with courteous service. Penalva is a well positioned imposing late Victorian hotel set in a wide tree-lined boulevard with ample parking, close to promenade and shops. Perfect centre for enjoying the wealth of beautiful sandy coves, historical remains and magnificent walks. Large guest lounge and separate dining room. Colour TV and tea/coffee making facilities in bedrooms. Open all year. Special diets by prior arrangement. Sorry, no pets. Bed and Breakfast from £11 to £17. Weekly reductions for children 6 to 12 half price if sharing family rooms. Highly recommended. SAE, please, for brochure.

PERRANPORTH. Chyan Kerensa Hotel, Cliff Road, Perranporth TR6 0DR (01872 572470). ETB

✿✿ *COMMENDED.* Our small licensed hotel directly overlooks Perranporth's three miles of golden sands, rugged coastline, dunes and heathland. Only two minutes' walk from the town centre, which has various restaurants, shops and pubs to suit all tastes and ages. Also golf, horse riding, tennis and bowls. Wetsuit and surfboard hire. Our comfortable bedrooms, some en suite, have colour TV, controllable central heating and tea/coffee making facilities, many have panoramic sea views, as do our lounge and dining room. Bed and Breakfast from £15 to £22.50 per person. Reductions for room only, weekly rates. One-nighters, children and pets welcome. A warm welcome from Wendy and Will all year. Please write or telephone for our brochure.

PERRANPORTH. Richard and Ann Snow, "Gull Rock", 25 Tywarnhayle Road, Perranporth TR6 0DX (01872 573289). A large stone built Victorian property enjoying panoramic sea/cliff views. Gull Rock is one of Perranporth's "four big houses" built by a mining captain at the turn of the century. Perranporth is centrally situated for touring Cornwall, and is an ideal surfing centre. The large and comfortable double bed and breakfast room has an en suite bathroom. A bed-settee enables a further two persons to be accommodated in the same room. There is central heating, colour TV, tea/coffee making facilities and on-street parking available. We are open all the year round. Tariff from £14 per person per night.

Gull Rock

POLPERRO. Mrs Ruth Puckey, Cornerways, Landaviddy Lane, Polperro PL13 2RT (01503 272324). Homely accommodation in an elevated position only 400 yards from the harbour. Cornerways overlooks the picturesque village of Polperro. Accommodation comprises family, twin and single bedrooms, all centrally heated. Shower room with washbasins, WC, shaver point, second bathroom with WC. Colour TV, hot and cold water and tea/coffee making facilities in rooms. Parking space. Full English breakfast. Bed and Breakfast from £14 to £15. We also have a holiday cottage with fantastic views of the sea, cliffs and harbour; terms from £100 to £300 per week. SAE, please.

POLPERRO. Christine Kay, Penryn House Hotel, Polperro PL13 2RG (01503 272157; Fax: 01503 273055). ✿✿✿ Set in its own grounds, Penryn House is a country house style property in the heart of Cornwall's most photographed and painted fishing village. Offering delightfully appointed en suite bedrooms with colour TV, telephone, courtesey trays, central heating and a comfortable lounge with log fires on cooler evenings. Enjoy the warmth and ambience of our candlelit restaurant where our speciality chef offers a wide selection of freshly prepared dishes with local produce in season and fresh local fish. Nearby attractions include many National Trust properties, peaceful gardens and a lovely variety of walks for serious and casual walkers. MURDER MYSTERY WEEKENDS March and October. Dinner, Bed and Breakfast from £30 to £38; Bed and Breakfast from £19 to £26. Bargain Breaks available.

CORNWALL

There's much more to Cornwall than just sand and sea. Take time to explore the traces of the past at Chysauster Ancient Village, near Penzance, a collection of huge stone houses dating from prehistoric times, and Pendennis Castle, Falmouth, built by Henry VIII to guard against invasion. The legend of King Arthur lives on at Tintagel Castle and at Dozmary Pool, Bodmin Moor, reputed to be where he threw back the sword, Excalibur.

POLZEATH. Mrs P. White, Seaways, Polzeath PL27 6SU (0120886 2382). Seaways is a small family guest house, 250 yards from safe, sandy beach. Surfing, riding, sailing, tennis, squash, golf all nearby. All bedrooms with en suite or private bathrooms, comprising one family, two double, two twin and a single room. Sittingroom; dining-room. Children welcome (reduced price for under 10's). Cot, high chair available. Comfortable family holiday assured with plenty of good home cooking. Lovely cliff walks nearby. Padstow a short distance by ferry. Other places of interest include Tintagel, Boscastle and Port Isaac. SAE, please. Open all year round. Bed and Breakfast from £13.50; Evening Meal £7.50.

PORT ISAAC. Mrs E.R. Hawken, Poltreworgey Farm, Port Isaac PL29 3SZ (01208 880275). Poltreworgey Farm has a very old Grade II Listed house with sea and country views. It adjoins the main road to the fishing village of Port Isaac one and a half miles away. The house is comfortable with tea/coffee making facilities in all rooms; the two larger rooms also have washbasins. Bathroom and shower room; sittingroom with colour TV. Plenty of parking space. Bed and Breakfast only. Very interesting pubs within a few miles of the farm; local dishes include fish, etc. Surfing beaches, hidden coves, Camel Trail, bike rides (bikes available for hire nearby) along the river to Padstow. Cornish Tourist Board registered.

PORT ISAAC. David and Dorothy Crawford, Long Cross Hotel and Victorian Gardens, Trelights, Near Port Isaac PL29 3TF (01208 880243). One of Cornwall's most unusual hotels, situated as it is in magnificent and very popular public gardens and with its own Tavern attached. The Hotel boasts one of Cornwall's finest Tea/Beer Gardens, where Cornish cream teas are served daily. Children love the Maze, the Adventure Play Area and the Pets' Corner with pygmy goats to feed. Hotel rooms are spacious, en suite, with colour TV, etc. An excellent base for walking, beach or touring. Food is served in the Tavern both lunchtime and evening, and also in the Restaurant at night. Special three day Breaks at £48 per person for Bed and Breakfast, September to June. Full details on request.

ROSELAND PENINSULA. Mrs Shirley E. Pascoe, Court Farm, Philleigh, Truro TR2 5NB (01872 580313). Working farm, join in. Situated in the heart of the Roseland Peninsula at Philleigh, with its lovely Norman church and 17th century Roseland Inn, this spacious and attractive old farmhouse set in over an acre of garden offers Bed and Breakfast accommodation. There are double, single and family bedrooms with washbasins and tea making facilities; bathroom, separate toilet; large comfortable lounge with colour TV. Enjoy a full English breakfast in the traditional farmhouse kitchen. Children welcome, cot, high chair, baby-sitting available. Sorry, no pets indoors. Car essential — ample parking. The family livestock and arable farm includes 50 acres of woodlands which border the beautiful Fal Estuary providing superb walking, picnic areas and bird watching opportunites, while the nearest beaches are just over two miles away. Please write or telephone for brochure and terms.

SALTASH. Peter and Violet Batten, Burcombe Farm, St. Dominick, Saltash PL12 6SH (01579 350217; Fax: 01579 350105). 🌸🌸 *APPROVED.* Burcombe Farm extends to 160 acres, mainly arable, corn and beef cattle with a history that dates back to 1722. It is an ideal spot for a quiet holiday with many walks in this scenic area of Cornwall. The farmhouse is large with wonderful views across the River Tamar to Plymouth and as far as the eye can see. Bedrooms are en suite and have colour TV and hot drink making facilities; lounge with colour TV, dining room. Car parking space. Sorry no children. Bed and full English Breakfast £20 per person per night, two or more nights £17.50. Brochure giving full details available on request.

ST. AGNES. Ted and Jeanie Ellis, Cleaderscroft Hotel, 16 British Road, St. Agnes TR5 0TZ (01872 552349). This small, detached, family-run Victorian hotel stands in the heart of the picturesque village of St. Agnes, convenient for many outstanding country and coastal walks. Set in mature gardens and having a separate children's play area we can offer peace and relaxation after the beach, which is approximately half a mile away. Accommodation is provided in generous sized rooms, mostly en suite with colour TV, and there is also a self contained flat; public rooms comprise lounge, bar, dining rooms and games room. Non-smoking and smoking areas. Private parking. Bed and Breakfast from £20 with discounts for children sharing. Evening set menu.

ST. AGNES. Dorothy Gill-Carey, Penkerris, Penwinnick Road, St. Agnes TR5 0PA (01872 552262).

PENKERRIS

🌺🌺 An enchanting Edwardian residence in garden with large lawn in unspoilt Cornish village. AA, RAC and Les Routiers Recommended. Penkerris has fields on one side yet there are pubs, shops, etc only 150 yards away on the other side. Attractive dining room, lounge with colour TV, video, piano and log fires in winter. Bedrooms with washbasins, TV, kettles, shaver points, radios; en suite if required. There is a shower room as well as bathrooms. Delicious meals, traditional roasts, fresh vegetables and home made fruit tarts. Beaches, swimming, surfing, gliding and magnificent cliff walks nearby. From £15 per night Bed and Breakfast and from £22.50 with Dinner. Open all year.

ST. AUSTELL. Mrs Collins, Rose Cottage, St. Ewe, St. Austell PL26 6EY (01726 842797). Bed and Breakfast at Rose Cottage. Two rooms, each with one double bed and one single bed, radio, tea/coffee making facilities and electric blankets. Sittingroom with colour TV. Full English breakfast. Situated in St. Ewe, a small, quiet, unspoilt country village with busy pub which serves good food. Several sandy beaches with safe bathing within four miles, fishing village of Mevagissey with numerous eating places about three miles away. Please write or telephone for further details.

ST. AUSTELL. Mr and Mrs Berryman, Polgreen Farm, London Apprentice, St. Austell PL26 7AP (01726 75151). Polgreen is a family run dairy farm nestling in the Pentewan Valley in an Area of Outstanding Natural Beauty. One mile from the coast and four miles from the picturesque fishing village of Mevagissey. A perfect location for a relaxing holiday in the glorious Cornish countryside. Centrally situated, Polgreen is ideally placed for touring all of Cornwall's many attractions. Pentewan Valley Leisure Trail adjoining, Lost Gardens of Heligan three miles. Bed and Breakfast accommodation includes en suite rooms, colour TV in bedrooms, tea/coffee facilities. Guests lounge. Children welcome. Terms from £15 per night; £98 per week.

CORNWALL — FROM COAST TO COAST

Stretching for some 300 miles, Cornwall's north and south coastlines are equally spectacular in different ways. The North is a paradise for those who enjoy watersports, with the Atlantic Ocean crashing onto long stretches of beautiful beach, while the more sheltered South Coast, with its picturesque fishing villages and sheltered coves, is ideal for a break at any time of year. Stretch your legs along the South West Coast Path and see for yourself!

MANOR FARM

Farmhouse Bed & Breakfast

Come and stay on our family-run Dairy Farm set amidst 450 acres of Cornish countryside. Our Grade II Listed Georgian farmhouse offers en suite and family en suite facilities with colour TV, tea/coffee in all rooms. Relax in the spacious gardens with camelias and rhododendrons, or roam around the fields and nearby woodland. Manor Farm is centrally located for exploring the character of Cornwall's unique countryside and coastline. Tariff from £17. Please contact:

**Suzanne Manuell, Manor Farm,
Burngullow, St. Austell PL26 7TQ.
Telephone/Fax: 01726 72242**

ST. BURYAN. Mrs Julia Hosking, Boskenna Home Farm, St. Buryan, Penzance TR19 6DQ (Tel & Fax: 01736 810705). ETB Listed *APPROVED.* A warm welcome awaits you at Boskenna Home Farm, a working dairy farm situated on the south coast five miles from Land's End. Why not relax on one of the many beautiful beaches, visit the legendary picturesque coves or take advantage of the striking coastal walks? Enjoy the friendly atmosphere and excellent farmhouse breakfast; Bed and Breakfast from £15 per person with reductions for children. Two double rooms and one twin-bedded room with tea/coffee facilities, wash-basins and heating. Lounge with colour TV; separate dining room. Large garden to relax. Please ask for brochure. Sorry, no smoking.

ST. IVES. Mrs C. Verney, Chy Lelan, Bunkers Hill, St. Ives TR26 1LJ (01736 797560). Chy Lelan is a quaint 17th century Cottage Guest House. Two fishermen's cottages have been restored yet still retain the original charm of the popular fishing quarter of St. Ives. We are in a pretty cobbled street literally 50 metres from the harbour, shops and car park and only 100 metres away from Porthmeor surfing beach and Tate Gallery. All bedrooms have colour TV, tea-making facilities, fitted carpets, washbasins, shaver points; access at all times, en suite available. Open all year. Children are very welcome at reduced rates. Tariff from £15. Brochure on request.

PLEASE SEND A STAMPED ADDRESSED ENVELOPE WITH ENQUIRIES

ST. IVES. Mrs N.I. Mann, Trewey Farm, Zennor, St. Ives TR26 3DA (01736 796936). Working farm.
On the main St. Ives to Land's End road, this attractive granite-built farmhouse stands among gorse and heather-clad hills, half-a-mile from the sea and five miles from St. Ives. The mixed farm covers 300 acres, with Guernsey cattle and fine views of the sea; lovely cliff and hill walks. Guests will be warmly welcomed and find a friendly atmosphere. Five double, one single and three family bedrooms (all with washbasins); bathroom, toilets; sittingroom, dining room. Cot, high chair and babysitting available. Pets allowed. Car essential, parking. Open all year. Electric heating. Bed and Breakfast only. SAE for terms, please.

ST. IVES. Miss B. Delbridge, Bella Vista Guest House, St. Ives Road, Carbis Bay, St. Ives TR26 2SF

(01736 796063). ✿ First class accommodation, highly recommended, satisfaction guaranteed. Extensive views of sea and coastline. Washbasins in all rooms. Colour TV. Central heating. Own key to rooms. Free parking on premises. Personal supervision. Fresh farm produce. Radio intercom and baby listening service in all rooms. Fire Certificate held. Bed and Breakfast from £15. Open all year. Non-smokers welcome. SAE for brochure.

ST. JUST-IN-PENWITH. Alison & Bob Hartley, Bosavern House, St. Just-in-Penwith, Penzance TR19 7RD (01736 788301). ✿ ✿ Modernised 17th century country house in two acres of garden, one mile from the coast, four miles from sandy beach, Penzance six miles, near Land's End. Convenient for airport. An ideal walking and touring centre. The house is well appointed, double glazed and several rooms have their own showers and toilets. Home cooking, log fires and friendly personal service ensure your comfort. Open March to mid-November. Bed and Breakfast from £14.75. Write or phone for brochure.

TINTAGEL. Kate and Peter West, Chilcotts, Bossiney, Tintagel PL34 0AY (Tel & Fax: 01840 770324). Without stepping onto a road, slip through the

side gate of this 16th Century listed cottage into a landscape owned by the National Trust and designated as an Area of Outstanding Natural Beauty. Closest cottage to nearby Bossiney beach for rock pools, surfing, safe swimming and caves to explore. Walk the airy cliff path north to nearby Rocky Valley or on to picturesque Boscastle Harbour. Southwards takes you to the ruins of King Arthur's Castle and onwards to busy Trebarwith Strand. Notice you have not stepped onto a road yet? Detached traditional country cottage ideal for a small number of guests. Home cooking, warm informal atmosphere, large bright double/family bedrooms with beamed ceilings and olde worlde feel. All rooms have TV, tea/coffee makers. Self catering annexe available. May we send you a brochure? Bed and Breakfast from £14.50. Directions: Bossiney adjoins Tintagel on the B3263 (coast road), Chilcotts adjoins large lay-by with telephone box.

TINTAGEL. Mrs R.J. de Boyer, Rosebud Cottage, Bossiney, Tintagel PL34 0AX (01840 770861).

Picturesque stone cottage with secluded garden half a mile from Tintagel off B3263 and only 10 minutes' headland walk from nearest beach at Bossiney Haven. Surfing and swimming on sandy beach. Close by North Cornwall Coastal Path. Excellent walking and touring centre. Open all the year. One family, one double and one twin room with washbasins, TVs and tea/coffee makers. Dining room and lounge with TV. Bed and Breakfast with optional Evening Meal. Good home cooking. Off road parking. Pets welcome. From £14 per night. SAE for brochure.

TREBARWITH STRAND. Mr Vickers, The Mill House Inn, Trebarwith Strand, Tintagel PL34 0HD (01840 770932 or 01840 770200). Tourist Board *APPROVED.* Formerly a corn mill The Mill House Inn now provides accommodation throughout the year. It is situated in the dramtic Trebarwirth Valley in seven acres of unspoilt woodland with small trout stream flowing past. The Inn has seven letting bedrooms, most en suite, all with tea/coffee making facilities, hair dryer and TV. Restaurant with full à la carte menu, beer garden and patio. Central heating. Families and pets welcome. Winter Breaks are especially popular. Self catering cottage also available. Please write or telephone for our information leaflet.

AA**RAC   Approved

Bossiney House Hotel

TINTAGEL, CORNWALL PL34 0AX
Telephone: 01840-770240 or Fax: 01840-770501

Peaceful haven in the historic hamlet of Bossiney, half a mile from Tintagel overlooking one of the finest stretches of coastline in Gt. Britain. Ideally located for exploring the whole of North Cornwall and personally supervised by the resident proprietors to ensure comfort, good food and friendly service.

- 19 Bedrooms – pleasant sea or country views, central heating, most en-suite; all with TV, hairdryer and tea/coffee making facilities
- Spacious dining room with views over front and rear lawns to coast or country;
- Indoor Heated Pool – Sauna – Solarium;
- 2½ acres of Garden;
- Residents' Lounge Bar;
- Magnificent cliff walks;
- Riding, Surfing & Golf nearby.

Ashley Courtenay Highly Recommended

TREGONY. Mrs Sandra R. Collins, Tregonan, Tregony, Truro TR2 5SN (01872 530249). ✿

COMMENDED. **Working farm.** Discover Tregonan, tucked away down a half mile private lane. This comfortable, spacious farmhouse is set in a secluded garden at the centre of a 300 acre sheep and arable farm. On the threshold of the renowned Roseland Peninsula, six miles west of Mevagissey. Two beaches within 3 miles, St. Austell 7 miles, Truro 12 miles and St. Mawes and Fowey 14 miles. Car essential, ample parking. Bedrooms with washbasin, radio and beverage making facilities. TV lounge. Limited to six guests. Regret no pets. Bed and full English Breakfast from £15. A good selection of eating places locally. OS Ref: SW 955 452.

TRURO. Mrs Shirley Wakeling, Rock Cottage, Blackwater, Truro TR4 8EU (01872 560252). ✿ ✿ ✿

Rock Cottage

HIGHLY COMMENDED. 18th century beamed cottage, formerly the village schoolmaster's home. A haven for non-smokers. Two double and one twin en suite rooms with beverage facilities, toiletries, clock/radio, colour TV, hairdryer and shaver point. Centrally heated. Attractive guest sittingroom with colour TV. Cosy dining room with antique Cornish range. Separate tables. Optional dinner by prior arrangement, from à la carte menu. Private parking. Village location three miles from sea and six miles from Truro. We cannot accommodate children or pets. Open all year. Bed and Breakfast from £20.50. AA QQQQ Selected. RAC Acclaimed. Telephone for brochure and menu.

TRURO. Marcorrie Hotel, 20 Falmouth Road, Truro TR1 2HX (01872 77374; Fax: 01872 41666). ✿ ✿ ✿ *APPROVED.* Victorian town house in conservation area, five minutes' walk from the city centre and cathedral. Centrally situated for visiting country houses, gardens and coastal resorts. All rooms are en suite and have central heating, colour TV, telephone, tea-making facilities. Ample parking. Outdoor swimming pool. Credit Cards: Visa, Access, Amex. Open all year. Bed and Breakfast from £19.50 per person per night.

TRURO. Mrs Diane Dymond, Great Hewas Farm, Grampound Road, Truro TR2 4EP (01726 882218; mobile 0860 117572). ETB ⚘ ⚘ Great Hewas is ideally situated in central Cornwall, just two miles from the main A30. This spacious centrally heated farm guesthouse has extensive views from all bedrooms and is ideal for touring or relaxing. Personal attention and good home cooking assured. Double, twin, single and family rooms, three en suite, all with TV and tea/coffee facilities. Public WC. Comfortable lounge, dining room with separate tables. Fire Certificate/Food and Hygiene Certificate. Traditional breakfast or fresh fruit and yoghurt. Bed and Breakfast £16.50 to £18 nightly. Three course Evening Dinner £7 to £8. Family room and weekly terms available on request. Pets by arrangement. Open Easter to October. Car essential. From A30 take exit to Grampound Road. Please telephone for brochure, without obligation.

TRURO. Mrs Maltwood, Old Inn Cottage, Mingoose, Mount Hawke, Truro TR4 8BX (01209 890545). 16th/17th century cottage in pretty hamlet near St. Agnes. A short walk leads through lovely National Trust valley to Chapelporth beach. Old Inn Cottage has two bedrooms, each with four-poster bed, one twin-bedded room and one single room; bathroom, toilet; large cosy sitting room with colour TV, books and open granite fireplace; oak beamed dining room. Self catering facilities available on request. Off road parking. Regret no smokers or pets. Bed and Breakfast from £15 per person.

TRURO. Mrs Sue Lutey, Penhale Farm, Grampound Road, Truro TR2 4ER (01726 882324). A warm welcome awaits you at our 240 acre mixed farm set in peaceful countryside. Central for touring, beaches, National Trust properties. The spacious farmhouse offers tastefully decorated family, double and twin bedrooms, all with washbasins; dining room with separate tables; lounge with colour TV. Tea/coffee facilities. Health and Hygiene Certificate held. Reductions for children; cot, high chair, games. Sorry no pets. Car essential, ample parking. Comfort, cleanliness and excellent food guaranteed. Bed and Breakfast from £15; optional Evening Meal £8. Open Easter to October.

Terms quoted in this publication may be subject to increase if rises in costs necessitate

TRURO. Mrs Margaret Retallack, Treberrick Farm, Tregony, Truro TR2 5SP (01872 530247).

Working farm. Treberrick is a 250 acre working farm situated on the edge of the Roseland Peninsula and two miles from unspoilt beaches at Carhays and Portholland and six miles from Mevagissey. Most parts of Cornwall reached by car within one hour. Guests are welcome to walk around the farm. Spacious house, bedrooms have washbasins and tea making facilities. Dining room with separate tables, lounge with TV always available. Guests can expect traditional home cooked food using own produce where possible. Maximum number of guests six. Sorry no smoking. Bed and Breakfast from £15; Evening Meal available. Near Heligon Manor Gardens — Restoration Project. Please telephone or write for brochure.

TRURO. Mrs J.C. Gartner, Laniley House, Near Trispen, Truro TR4 9AU (01872 75201). Laniley

House, a Gentleman's Residence built in 1830, stands in two acres of gardens amidst beautiful, unspoilt countryside, yet only three miles from the Cathedral City of Truro. Ideally situated for discovering Cornwall and close to major towns, beaches and National Trust properties, Laniley offers unequalled privacy and peace. Our aim is to make you feel at home, giving each person individual attention; only six guests at any one time. Accommodation consists of three large double bedrooms, two with washbasins, one with en-suite bathroom; separate breakfast room; lounge with colour TV. All rooms with TV, radio and Teasmaid. Regret, unable to accommodate children under 13 years, also no pets. Bed and Breakfast from £17 per person. SAE, please. Highly recommended accommodation.

TRURO. Andrew and Catherine Webb, Tregony House, 15 Fore Street, Tregony, Truro TR2 5RN

(01872 530671). Grade II Listed building on main street of Tregony, nine miles Truro, many beaches close by. Ideally situated for exploring all of Cornwall. Accommodation comprises one single, two double, three twin bedrooms; two form a suite along with own bathroom overlooking the garden. Front double room has en suite facilities. All have tea/coffee making facilities. Guests' sitting room with colour TV and open fire. Breakfast and dinner served in low beamed 18th century dining room. Private or off-road parking available. Access and Visa cards accepted. Terms from £18.75 Bed and Breakfast, £11 for four-course Dinner. Brochure available.

TRURO/ST. MAWES. Mrs Ann Palmer, Trenestrall Farm, Ruan High Lanes, Truro TR2 5LX (01872

501259). Working farm, join in. A family run farm offers accommodation in 200-year-old stone built barn. Centrally situated in the beautiful and peaceful Roseland Peninsula close to St. Mawes. Accommodation comprises one double and one twin-bedded rooms with washbasin and one further twin room, all with tea making facilities; bathrooms and shower rooms for guests' use only; sittingroom with TV. Children welcome. A friendly personal service assured. Pets welcome by arrangement. Bed and Breakfast from £14 per person per night.

TRENESTRALL FARM

CORNWALL – LAND'S END AND THE ISLES OF SCILLY

Britain's most westerly point, Land's End, is now under private ownership and offers multi-sensory exhibitions, craft workshops and play areas to the many thousands of visitors who are attracted by its unique, breathtaking views.

The 200-odd Isles of Scilly lie 22 miles south-west of Land's End (access by plane, ferry or helicopter). The temperate climate allows visitors to enjoy exotic flowers, palm trees and tropical gardens, and the islands are a bird-watcher's paradise (May and June are the best months).

WADEBRIDGE. Mrs A. Wills, "Tredavice", Trevelver Farm, St. Minver, Wadebridge PL27 6RJ

(01208 863290). A warm welcome awaits you at "Tredavice", a superior modern bungalow overlooking our own grounds to the banks of the Camel Estuary in beautiful North Cornwall. Our uninterrupted views are some of the most delightful in the Duchy. Our bungalow is very spacious and designed to suit all requirements. Double and twin rooms with separate bathroom and toilet. Bed and Breakfast is our main service, but an Evening Meal is available with good home cooking. Bed and Breakfast £14 to £16 per person; Evening Meal from £7 per person. Personal attention.

WADEBRIDGE. Mrs Estelle Hodge, Pengelly Farm, Burlawn, Wadebridge PL27 7LA (01208

814217). Working farm, join in. A Listed Georgian farmhouse situated in a quiet location on a 150 acre mixed farm overlooking wooded valleys, approximately one and a half miles Wadebridge, country walks. Easy access to the start of the Camel Trail, coast with a number of beaches and activities six miles. Guests are welcome to roam the farm and see the variety of animals. Large garden where children can play. Prettily decorated bedrooms with own washbasins and tea/coffee making facilities. Guests' bath/shower room, WC. Traditional English breakfast served or special requests by prior arrangement. Lounge with colour TV. Children welcome, cot, high chair available and babysitting on request. Bed and Breakfast £14. Cornwall Registered Accommodation.

WADEBRIDGE. Susan and David Old, "Elba", Whitecross, Wadebridge PL27 7JB (01208 812007). Bed and Breakfast in a friendly and quiet family home. One twin, one family double plus single; an adjoining shower/toilet is shared, for guests' use only. Both rooms have pleasant views, are centrally heated and are provided with washbasins, colour TV and shaving points. Tea or coffee tray provided. Near the Royal Cornwall Showground, two miles from Wadebridge and 100 yards from the A39 road, and well-placed for beaches, golf courses and many Cornish tourist attractions. Parking. Regret no pets. Pub meals within walking distance. Full English breakfast. Our 1996 all-year inclusive price is £13, reductions for children.

WADEBRIDGE near. Mr W. R. Veall, Roskarnon House Hotel, Rock, Near Wadebridge PL27 6LD (01208 862785 or 862329). 🌸🌸🌸 The golden sands of Rock and the Camel Estuary offer a glorious holiday to the visitor to Roskarnon House Hotel, an ideal place in which to enjoy to the full the delights of a visit to Cornwall. Under the personal supervision of the Resident Hosts, the highest standard of comfort is offered. Ten double bedrooms, two single bedrooms and four family rooms, some with private bath; all have spring interior mattresses, razor points, bed lights; most have sea views, colour TV and tea/coffee making facilities. Ample conveniences. Well-appointed lounge and diningroom overlook lawns and beach. Open March to October, the house is suitable for the disabled. Car essential; parking for 12 cars. Sorry, no pets. Bed and Breakfast from £19.50; Evening Meal from £12.50. Reduced rates for children sharing parents' room. AAQQ, RAC Two Stars. Also self-catering cottage fully equipped for four persons.

FOR THE MUTUAL GUIDANCE OF GUEST AND HOST

Every year literally thousands of holidays, short-breaks and overnight stops are arranged through our guides, the vast majority without any problems at all. In a handful of cases, however, difficulties do arise about bookings, which often could have been prevented from the outset.

It is important to remember that when accommodation has been booked, both parties — guests and hosts — have entered into a form of contract. We hope that the following points will provide helpful guidance.

GUESTS: When enquiring about accommodation, be as precise as possible. Give exact dates, numbers in your party and the ages of any children. State the number and type of rooms wanted and also what catering you require — bed and breakfast, full board, etc. Make sure that the position about evening meals is clear — and about pets, reductions for children or any other special points.

Read our reviews carefully to ensure that the proprietors you are going to contact can supply what you want. Ask for a letter confirming all arrangements, if possible.

If you have to cancel, do so as soon as possible. Proprietors do have the right to retain deposits and under certain circumstances to charge for cancelled holidays if adequate notice is not given and they cannot re-let the accommodation.

HOSTS: Give details about your facilities and about any special conditions. Explain your deposit system clearly and arrangements for cancellations, charges, etc, and whether or not your terms include VAT.

If for any reason you are unable to fulfil an agreed booking without adequate notice, you may be under an obligation to arrange alternative suitable accommodation or to make some form of compensation.

While every effort is made to ensure accuracy, we regret that FHG Publications cannot accept responsibility for errors, omissions or misrepresentation in our entries or any consequences thereof. Prices in particular should be checked because we go to press early. We will follow up complaints but cannot act as arbiters or agents for either party.

CUMBRIA — including "The Lakes"

ALSTON. Mrs Susan Younger, "Harbut Law", Alston CA9 3BD (01434 381950), Set in some of the

most beautiful countryside, Harbut Law is a large Victorian stone built former farm house set high in the North Pennines. We are one mile out of Alston with Hadrian's Wall, Lake District and the Scottish Borders all within 45 miles — there is plenty to see and do. Our large comfortable rooms all have central heating, tea/coffee making facilities; some are en suite. You can relax in our comfortable lounge with colour TV. Bed and Breakfast from £13 to £17 with reductions for children. Packed lunches available as the house is situated on the Pennine Way.

AMBLESIDE. Linda and Alan Bleasdale, Borwick Lodge, Outgate, Hawkshead, Ambleside LA22

0PU (015394 36332). ♛ ♛ *HIGHLY COMMENDED.* Three times Winners of the Award for "Accommodation of the Highest Standards". A leafy driveway entices you to the most enchantingly situated house in the Lake District, a very special 17th century lodge with magnificent panoramic lake and mountain views, quietly secluded in beautiful gardens. Ideally placed in the heart of the Lakes and close to Hawkshead village with its good choice of restaurants and inns. Beautiful en suite bedrooms with colour TV and tea/coffee facilities, including "Special Occasions" and "Romantic Breaks", two king-size four-poster rooms. Linda and Alan welcome you to their "haven of peace and tranquillity" in this most beautiful corner of England. Ample parking. NON SMOKING THROUGHOUT. Bed and Breakfast from £18. May we send our brochure?

AMBLESIDE. Peter and Anne Hart, Bracken Fell, Outgate, Ambleside LA22 0NH (015394 36289).

Bracken Fell

♛ ♛ *COMMENDED.* Bracken Fell is situated in beautiful open countryside between Ambleside and Hawkshead in the picturesque hamlet of Outgate. Ideally positioned for exploring the Lake District and within easy reach of Coniston, Windermere, Ambleside, Grasmere and Keswick. All major outdoor activities are catered for nearby including wind surfing, sailing, fishing, pony trekking, etc. All six bedrooms have private facilities, complimentary tea/coffee making and outstanding views. There is central heating throughout, a comfortable lounge and dining room, together with ample private parking and two acres of gardens. Fire Certificate. Open all year. Bed and Breakfast from £20. Non-smoking. Self catering accommodation also available. Write or phone for brochure and tariff.

AMBLESIDE. Mr and Mrs Russ, Croyden House, Church Street, Ambleside LA22 0BU (015394

32209). Croyden House offers warm, friendly welcome — comfortable tastefully furnished rooms (some en suite), all with colour TV, tea/coffee tray and washbasin. Its central location with private car park makes it an ideal base for all the places of interest, outdoor activities and eating establishments that the Lake District offers. Open all year for Bed and generous English Breakfast from £16.50 to £21 with special rates for children; very good terms for winter and mid-week breaks. Each year we enjoy the company of thousands of guests, many paying return visits and many who have been recommended. We hope that you become one of our regular guests.

AMBLESIDE. Mrs E. Peers, Fisherbeck Farmhouse, Old Lake Road, Ambleside LA22 0DH (015394 32523). ♛ ♛ This charming 16th century farmhouse is situated in a quiet side lane at the foot of Wansfell to the south of the village. Not a working farm. Warm, comfortable rooms with washbasins. Single, double, twin and family rooms. Lounge with television. Separate morning/breakfast room. Tea/coffee making facilities. Adequate parking on own ground, road and free car park. Car not essential as village is only five minutes' level walk away. Only one minute's walk to the bus stop. Bed and Breakfast from £14 to £18. SAE for terms and more details.

AMBLESIDE. Jim and Joyce Ormesher, Rothay House, Rothay Road, Ambleside LA22 0EE (015394 32434). Rothay House is an attractive detached guest house set in pleasant gardens with views of the surrounding fells. There is ample space for parking in the grounds. All bedrooms are en suite, comfortable and well furnished with colour TV and tea/coffee trays. Our visitors are assured of warm and friendly service in pleasant surroundings. Children welcome. We are within easy walking distance of Ambleside village centre which has a variety of interesting shops and commendable restaurants, and makes an ideal base for walking, touring or enjoying sailing, watersports and angling on Lake Windermere. Bed and Breakfast from £18 to £22. We are open all year round and offer special rates for out-of-season breaks.

AMBLESIDE. Liz, May and Craig, Wanslea Guest House, Lake Road, Ambleside LA22 0DB (015394 33884). ✿ ✿ ✿ Wanslea is a spacious family-run Victorian guest house with fine views, situated just a stroll from the village and Lake shore with walks beginning at the door. We offer a friendly welcome and comfortable rooms, all of which have colour TV and tea/coffee trays; most rooms are en suite. A good breakfast will start your day before enjoying a fell walk or maybe a more leisurely stroll by the lake. Relax in our licensed residents' lounge with a real fire on winter evenings. Children are welcome and pets accepted by arrangement. Bed and Breakfast from £16 per person. Evening Meal also available. Autumn, Winter, Spring Breaks at reduced rates. Brochure on request.

AMBLESIDE. Helen and Chris Green, Lyndhurst Hotel, Wansfell Road, Ambleside LA22 0EG (015394 32421). ✿ ✿ *COMMENDED.* RAC Acclaimed, AA Listed. Attractive Victorian Lakeland stone family-run small hotel with private car park, quietly situated in its own garden. Lovely bedrooms, all en suite and with colour TV, tea/coffee trays. Four-poster bedroom for that special occasion. Scrumptious food, friendly service. Full central heating for all-year comfort. Cosy bar. Winter and Summer Breaks. A delightful base from which to explore the Lakes either by car or as a walker. Bed and Breakfast from £17.50. Phone or write for colour brochure, please.

AMBLESIDE. Mrs Elizabeth Culbert, Kingswood, Old Lake Road, Ambleside LA22 0AE (015394 34081). Kingswood is ideally situated near the town centre, yet off the main road. Ample car parking. Well-equipped and comfortable bedrooms with hot and cold water, and tea/coffee making facilities. Colour TV. Central heating. Single, double, twin and family rooms. Pets welcome. Open most of the year, with special bargain breaks off season. No smoking. Write or phone for rates and details.

FERNDALE HOTEL
Lake Road, Ambleside LA22 0DB

This friendly, family-run hotel at the heart of the popular Lakeland village of Ambleside is renowned for exceptional value for money accommodation. Our guests are assured of a warm welcome and excellent service throughout their stay. The nine comfortable, en suite rooms have colour television and tea/coffee facilities. Private car park, residential licence, magnificent views onto Loughrigg, Wansfell and the Horseshoe Range. Within easy walking distance of the lake, boat trips and some of the most beautiful scenery in Britain. Open all year. Bed and Breakfast from £17.00 to £21.00.

Telephone: 015394 32207

AMBLESIDE. Anthony Marsden, Betty Fold, Hawkshead Hill, Ambleside LA22 0PS (015394 36611). *HIGHLY COMMENDED.* Betty Fold is a large country house in its own spacious grounds, rich in fauna and flora with magnificent views and set in the heart of the Lake District National Park. Hawkshead, Coniston and Ambleside are all within easy reach and the beauty spot Tarn Hows is 20 minutes' walk away. This privately licensed guest house, run by the resident owner, offers Bed, Breakfast, Evening Meals and Packed Lunches. All bedrooms are en suite. Children are welcome, cots available and babysitting can be arranged. Parties are particularly welcome from November to Easter. We regret no pets in the guest house. Open all year. Terms approximately £34 per night for Bed, Breakfast and Evening Dinner. See also advertisement in SELF CATERING section of the guide.

AMBLESIDE. Mr and Mrs Bob and Anne Jeffrey, The Anchorage, Rydal Road, Ambleside LA22 9AY (015394 32046). *COMMENDED.* RAC Acclaimed. The Anchorage is situated within a two minute level walk from the centre of Ambleside. We have our own large car park. The house has a comfortable lounge; all our bedrooms have pleasant views and are well furnished with colour TV and tea/coffee facilities; en suite rooms available. A warm welcome awaits you and you are assured of an excellent breakfast. Sorry, no pets. Reductions for four or more nights. Open February to October. Bed and Breakfast from £17 to £22.50.

AMBLESIDE. Mike and Gill Dixon, The Howes, Stockghyll Brow, Ambleside LA22 0QZ (015394 32444). ETB Listed *COMMENDED.* The Howes is a modern detached house situated in a very quiet and peaceful area of Ambleside with ample parking. Two minutes from Stockghyll waterfalls and five minutes from village centre. The rooms are all on the ground floor, purpose built and of a very high standard. En-suite, colour TV, tea/coffee making facilities and, as an added luxury, your breakfast will be served in your room. The Howes is an ideal centre for walkers and touring guests, We know you will appreciate the comfort and friendly service provided. Bed and Breakfast £17.50 to £22.50. Non-smoking.

AMBLESIDE. Mrs Margaret Rigg, The Dower House, Wray Castle, Ambleside LA22 0JA (015394 33211). ♛ *COMMENDED.* Lovely old house, quiet and peaceful, stands on an elevation overlooking Lake Windermere, with one of the most beautiful views in all Lakeland. Its setting within the 100-acre Wray Castle estate (National Trust), with direct access to the Lake, makes it an ideal base for walking and touring. Hawkshead and Ambleside are about ten minutes' drive and have numerous old inns and restaurants. Ample car parking; prefer dogs to sleep in the car. Children over five years welcome, reduced rates if under 12 years. Bed and Breakfast from £18.95; optional Evening Meal from £10.50. Open all year round.

- The Dower House, Wray Castle, Ambleside -

AMBLESIDE. Mrs Sheila Briggs, High Wray Farm, High Wray, Ambleside LA22 0JE (015394 32280). ETB Listed *COMMENDED.* Charming 17th century olde worlde farmhouse once owned by Beatrix Potter. Original oak beams, cosy lounge with log burning fire. Pretty colour co-ordinated bedrooms, one with en suite facilities. Heating and tea/coffee trays are in all rooms. Situated in a quiet unspoilt location, panoramic views and lake shore walks close by. A warm welcome awaits all who visit us where comfort, cleanliness and personal attention are assured. Follow the B5286 from Ambleside towards Hawkshead, turn left for Wray. Follow road to High Wray, the farm is on the right. Families welcome. Terms from £15.50. FHG Diploma Winner.

AMBLESIDE. Mr D. Sowerbutts, 2 Swiss Villas, Vicarage Road, Ambleside LA22 9AE (015394 32691). A small Victorian terrace house set just off the main road in the centre of Ambleside, near the church, in a slightly elevated position overlooking Wansfell. There is immediate access to the cinema and shops and the wide variety of restaurants and cafes in the town. There are three double bedrooms (one with twin beds) recently refurbished in the traditional style. Each room has central heating, tea making facilities and colour TV. A full English Breakfast or vegetarian meal available. We are open all year round and you are sure of a friendly welcome and good home cooking. Bed and Breakfast from £17 per person.

APPLEBY. Mrs Diana Dakin, Morningside, Morland, Penrith CA10 3AZ (01931 714393). Morningside is idyllically situated in the pretty village of Morland, midway between Appleby and Penrith, in the beautiful Eden Valley. Convenient for touring all of Cumbria and only 10 miles from Ullswater, it is perfect for a relaxing break. Friendly, personal service is assured in the beautifully appointed ground floor twin-bedded room with en suite shower room, colour TV, hot drinks facilities plus the advantage of own entrance from private patio. A delicious breakfast is served in the bedroom overlooking the garden and village views. Central heating. Parking. Bed and Breakfast from £16 per person. No smoking please.

CUMBRIA – LAKELAND SPLENDOUR!

The Lake District has for long been a popular tourist destination; however, the Fells and Pennine areas are also worth exploring. The many attractions of Cumbria include the Ennerdale Forest, St. Bees Head, Langdale Pikes, Bowness-on-Solway, the market town of Alston, Lanercost Priory, Scafell Pike – England's highest mountain – and the Wordsworth country around Ambleside, Grasmere and Cockermouth.

APPLEBY. Mrs K.M. Coward, Limnerslease, Bongate, Appleby CA16 6UE (017683 51578).

Limnerslease is a family run Guest House five minutes' walk from the town centre. A good half-way stopping place on the way to Scotland. There is a good golf course and an indoor heated swimming pool. Many lovely walks are all part of the charm of Appleby. Two double and one twin bedrooms, all with washbasin, colour TV, tea/coffee making facilities at no extra charge; bathroom, toilet; diningroom. Open January to November with gas heating. Ample parking. Bed and Breakfast from £15.

APPLEBY-IN-WESTMORLAND. Mrs Edith Stockdale, Croft House, Bolton, Appleby-in-Westmorland CA16 6AW (017683 61264).

Croft House is situated in Bolton, an unspoilt village of sandstone houses and an inn on the banks of the River Eden. Three miles north of Appleby off A66. This is an excellent base for exploring Eden Valley, Lakes, Dales and Border Country or as a midway break from Scotland. This historic town of Appleby welcomes visitors to its ancient castles and churches and to the country's oldest Gypsy Fair, which is held annually in June. Local attractions include pony trekking, golf, fishing and swimming. The comfortable farmhouse offers traditional farmhouse breakfast, and guest accommodation comprises sittingroom with colour TV, diningroom, one twin and two double bedrooms with washbasins. Separate bathroom and shower. Children welcome at reduced rates, cot and babysitting available. Pets welcome by arrangement. Open all year (except Christmas). Rates from £15.

BOWNESS-ON-WINDERMERE. Vivien and Howard Newham, Whitegates, Middle Entrance Drive, Storrs Park, Bowness-on-Windermere LA23 3JZ (015394 43509). Opening March 1997, Whitegates is beautifully situated in tranquil surroundings close to lake and Bowness. Our accommodation is all ground floor with spacious double and twin en suite rooms complete with TV and furnished to a high standard. Our breakfasts are excellent, hospitality warm and sincere with private parking and delightful situation, pleasant walks, and within a short drive of some of the best restaurants, pubs, boating and golf in Lakeland. Sorry, no pets or smoking. Directions leaving Bowness half a mile past ferry and Windermere Marina on the left hand side of A592. Bed and Breakfast from £20 to £25. Open February to November.

BOWNESS-ON-WINDERMERE. Beech Tops, Meadowcroft Lane, Storrs Park, Bowness-on-Windermere LA23 3JJ (015394 45453).

Quiet secluded modern detached house near lake offers first class spacious accommodation in serviced double/twin/family suites. All with en suite facilities, central heating, tea/coffee trays, colour TV and lounge. We are ideally positioned for exploring Lakeland; Bowness village, boats, ferry, public slipway only half a mile. Ample off street car/boat parking. Daily terms from £17.50; child reductions. Weekly terms on request. Sorry no smoking.

BRAMPTON. Mrs I. Roberts, Windyhaugh, Station Road, Brampton CA8 1EZ (016977 3248).

Tourist Board Listed. Windyhaugh Bed and Breakfast is situated just off the A69, the Gateway to Hadrian's Wall. Near Gretna Green, Carlisle, Naworth Castle, Lanacost Priory, Gelt Woods. Local attractions include golf, horse/pony trekking, fishing, delightful walks, or just a restful break in this market town. By prior arrangement you can travel on horse and trap through our beautiful countryside. One double, one twin, one single, with tea/coffee making facilities. TV. Lounge-cum-playroom, with countless games to while away the evenings. Breakfast room. Ample parking. Lovely garden with pond. £16 per night. Food Hygiene Certificate held.

BRAMPTON. Mrs Una Armstrong, Town Head Farm, Walton, Brampton CA8 2DJ (016977 2730).

Tourist Board Listed *COMMENDED.* Town Head offers comfortable and pleasant accommodation. Our 100 acre dairy/sheep farm is situated in the peaceful village of Walton overlooking the village green commanding scenic views of the Pennines and Lakeland hills. An ideal base for touring the Lakes, Hadrian's Wall and Scottish Borders; three miles from Brampton, 10 miles from Carlisle — leave M6 at Junction 43. One double, one twin or family bedrooms with tea making facilities and TV lounge/dining room. Children welcome. Open all year except Christmas and New Year. Bed and Breakfast from £14. Cheap rate for children and Short Breaks.

CALDBECK. Mr and Mrs A. Savage, Swaledale Watch, Whelpo, Caldbeck CA7 8HQ (016974

78409). ☙ *HIGHLY COMMENDED.* Ours is a mixed farm of 300 acres situated in beautiful countryside within the Lake District National Park. Easy reach of Scottish Borders, Roman Wall, Eden Valley. Primarily a sheep farm (everyone loves lambing time), with 60 dairy cattle. Visitors are welcome to see farm animals and activities. Many interesting walks nearby or roam the peaceful fells where John Peel hunted. Enjoyed by many Cumbrian Way walkers. Very comfortable accommodation with excellent home cooking. All rooms have private facilities. Central heating. Tea making facilities. Bed and Breakfast from £17 to £18; Evening Meal £10. AA QQQQ Selected.

CARLISLE. Graham Arms Hotel, English Street, Longtown, Near Carlisle CA6 5SE (Tel & Fax:

01228 791213). Comfortable former Coaching Inn of character situated six miles from motorway on the A7, scenic route to and from Scotland and five miles from Gretna Green, ideal for that special occasion or overnight stop. Perfect base for touring Carisle and Borders, Hadrian's Wall, Pennines and Lake District. 14 comfortable bedrooms including four poster-room, all rooms have colour TV and tea/coffee making facilities. En suite family and standard rooms available. Good traditional food served at lunchtime and evenings, excellent range of Real Ales and Whiskies. Secure vehicle park for cars, cycles and motorcycles, padlocked at night. Room and full traditional breakfast from just £18. Brochure available.

CARLISLE. Mr Kilpatrick, The Beeches, Wood Street, Carlisle CA1 2SF (01228 511962). The Beeches is a Grade II Listed house (1767) situated in a quiet conservation area one mile from city centre and one mile from the M6 Exit 43. "The Times" describes The Beeches as "a little Georgian Gem". Blue and white plates and other family treasures add atmosphere to the oak-beamed dining room. The three country-style bedrooms are furnished to a high standard with coffee/tea making facilities, colour TV and other thoughtful items for your comfort. There is a private car park and many local restaurants and inns nearby. Dinner by previous arrangement. From £16 to £18.50 per person per night.

CARLISLE. Jean and Dennis Martin, The Hill Cottage, Blackford, Carlisle CA6 4DU (01228 74739).

☙ *HIGHLY COMMENDED.* One minute from M6/A74 Junction 44, three miles north of City Centre, a 19th century cottage recently modernised and extended. Spacious, centrally heated rooms (most on ground floor) and a high standard of furnishings and decor. Enjoying a rural setting in farm country, ideal base for Solway coasts, Lakes, Scottish Borders, Hadrian's Wall and historic Carlisle (expert historical/tourism advice) or for Scottish and Northern Ireland stopover. Golf, fishing, bird watching nearby. Accommodation in single, twin, double or family rooms with washbasins, shaver points, tea-making facilities, Yale locks and really comfortable beds. Bathroom/shower, two toilets. Visitors' lounge with colour TV; dining room. Excellent Cumbrian breakfasts. Sorry, no pets. Ample parking, though car not essential, convenient public transport. Special weekly or short break terms, out of season bookings etc. Non smoking. SAE for details.

CARLISLE. Eric and Daphne Houghton, Corner House, Carlisle CA1 2AW (Tel & Fax: 01228 41942). AA QQQ Recommended. Situated on the corner of Warwick Road and Petteril Street, one mile from M6 Junction 43, five minutes' walk from Carlisle city centre. Eric and Daphne offer a very homely run guest house with en suite or private bathrooms, which are fully centrally heated. All have colour TV, hair dryer, welcome tray, radio alarms. Choice of double, single, twin and family accommodation available. A substantial English breakfast is included, vegetarian and special diets catered for whenever possible. If arriving by coach or train a courtesy car will be provided upon request. Prices from £16 per person.

CARLISLE. Pam and John Smith, Craighead, 6 Hartington Place, Carlisle CA1 1HL (01228 596767). ✿✿ *COMMENDED.* We would like to welcome you to Craighead, a spacious Listed Victorian town house with many original features and a warm and friendly atmosphere. There is a colour TV and welcome tray in all the rooms which consist of one large family (one double and two single beds), one twin, one single and two double (one en suite). All are on the first floor. Craighead is only minutes' walk from city centre, bus and rail stations, cathedral, castle, heritage centre and award-winning Lanes Shopping Centre. You can visit Gretna Green (nine miles), one of Scotland's premier visitor attractions, the beautiful Lake District (25 miles) and Roman Wall (15 miles) — a world Heritage Site. Easy access M6 Junction 43. Breakfasts are delicious (so our guests tell us). Eat as much as you like with a wide choice available. Prices start at £15.50.

CARLISLE. Mrs G. Elwen, New Pallyards, Hethersgill, Carlisle CA6 6HZ (01228 577308). ✿✿✿ *COMMENDED.* **GOLD AWARD WINNER. Working farm, join in.** AA, HWFH, FHB. Relax and see beautiful North Cumbria and the Borders. A warm welcome awaits you on our 65-acre livestock farm tucked away in the Cumbrian countryside, yet easily accessible from M6 Junction 44. In addition to the surrounding attractions there is plenty to enjoy including hill walking, peaceful forests and sea trout/salmon fishing or just nestle down and relax with nature. Two double en-suite, two family en-suite and one twin/single bedrooms, all with tea/coffee making equipment. Menu choice. Filmed for BBC TV. Best Breakfast in Britain Competition Winner. Bed and Breakfast from £20 to £21; Dinner £13. Dinner, Bed and Breakfast £160 to £170 per week. Self-catering cottages also available.

CARLISLE. Mrs C.M. Murray, Parkland Guest House, 136 Petteril Street, Carlisle CA1 2AW (01228 48331). ✿✿✿ *COMMENDED.* AA QQQ. A warm welcome awaits you at Parklands, just off M6 (Junction 43). Ideal for an overnight stop en route to Scotland and Ireland. Also an ideal base to tour Scotland and the Lake District with a short drive to Hadrian's Wall. In walking distance of Carlisle town centre, the Lanes Shopping, the Cathedral and Castle. Also award-winning golf course close by. All rooms en suite and tastefully decorated with colour TV and welcome tray. Relax in our lounge bar with a quiet drink after a tiring day (satellite TV). Meals available. Ground floor rooms and family rooms, doubles, twins. Open all year round. Private parking. Colour brochure available.

CARLISLE. Royal Hotel, 9 Lowther Street, Carlisle CA3 8ES (01228 22103; Fax: 01228 23904). ✿✿✿ The Royal Hotel has been owned by the Ridley family for most of this century and they do their best to ensure that guests have a comfortable and enjoyable stay. Centrally situated, it is within a few minutes' walk from both bus and railway stations making it ideal for enjoying the numerous activities and places of interest in the area. The hotel has 23 bedrooms all with central heating, telephones and colour TV; 15 rooms have en suite facilities. Lounge with Sky TV. Sauna available to soothe away tension and fatigue. Breakfast, bar lunches and evening meals served daily in the dining room and there is a small well-stock bar. Coach parties welcome. RAC Acclaimed. Winter Special Breaks available. Terms on application.

CARLISLE. Mrs Jennifer Bainbridge, Beech House, Whitrigg, Kirkbride, Carlisle CA5 5AA (016973 51249).

Beech House is situated on the Solway Firth and overlooks the Lake District Hills from the front and the Scottish Hills from the rear. This is an ideal place for a quiet holiday and a birdwatcher's paradise. Guests are assured of a friendly welcome at the house which is surrounded by lawns and flower gardens. Excellent home cooking using fresh garden produce and Solway-caught salmon. Two family and one double rooms; two bathrooms, two toilets; lounge and diningroom. Children welcome and cot and babysitting available. Open all year except Christmas for Evening Dinner, Bed and Breakfast from £20 or Bed and Breakfast from £14. Welcome cup of tea at bedtime (inclusive). Reductions for children. Car essential — parking.

CARLISLE. Mrs Dorothy Nicholson, Gill Farm, Blackford, Carlisle (01228 75326). 🐾 In a delightful

setting on a beef and sheep farm, this Georgian style farmhouse, dated 1740, offers a friendly welcome to all guests breaking their journey to or from Scotland or having a holiday in our beautiful countryside near Hadrian's Wall, Borders and Lake District. Golf, fishing, swimming and large agricultural auction marts all nearby. Accommodation in one double, one family and one twin or single bedroom, all with washbasins, shaver points and tea/coffee facilities; two bathrooms, shower; lounge with colour TV and separate diningroom. Open all year. Reductions for children. Cot and babysitting available. Central heating. Car essential, good parking. Pets permitted. SAE please, or telephone for further details.

CARLISLE. Mrs Croskery, Whitelea Guest House, 191 Warwick Road, Carlisle CA1 1LP (01228 33139 or 32353). 🐾 COMMENDED. Feel at home in this

small family-run guest house extending a warm welcome to all our guests. Accommodation offered in two double rooms (one en suite), two twin rooms, one family room and a single room. Carlisle is the gateway to the Lake District and Scotland. You only have a short walk to the city centre where you will find the award-winning Lanes Shopping Centre, the beautiful Cathedral, the Castle and Tullie House Museum. There are two golf courses close to hand with beautiful parkland. Directions: Find us on M6 Junction 43. Bed and Breakfast from £15 to £18; Evening Meal £5 to £7.

CARLISLE. Mrs Jane Lawson, Craigburn Farm, Catlowdy, Penton, Carlisle CA6 5QP (Tel & Fax: 01228 577214). 🐾 🐾 🐾 COMMENDED. Enjoy the delights

of beautiful Cumbrian countryside and life on our 250 acre working farm, some rare breeds of animals, one of the Best Farmhouse for Meals, a distinction in cookery held. Lovely bedrooms, some four-poster beds; all are en suite and have TV and tea making facilities. Central heating throughout. Residential licence. Short break discounts 20% off weekly bookings. Stop here to and from Scotland and Northern Ireland.

CARLISLE. Mrs M.N. Nichol, Croft End, Hurst, Ivegill, Carlisle CA4 0NL (017684 84362). Working farm. Comfortable Bed and Breakfast midway between Carlisle and Penrith, three miles west of Southwaite Service Area; M6 Junctions 41 and 42 just 10 minutes. Two double bedrooms. Children welcome. Sorry no pets. Bed and Breakfast from £14 to £15.

CARLISLE. James and Elaine Knox, The Steadings, Townhead, Houghton, Carlisle CA6 4JB (01228 23019). We offer you a warm welcome to our new self-contained barn conversion adjoining our Grade II Listed Georgian house circa 1700. Exposed beams, tastefully decorated. Eight rooms, six en suite, two standard, all are centrally heated, double glazed and with colour TV and tea/coffee making facilities. Private parking. Excellent breakfasts. Tearoom on site. Situated minutes from M6 Junction 44; rural location yet only three miles from Carlisle City Centre. Extremely easy to find. Ideal location for visiting historic Carlisle, Lake District, Roman Wall, Scottish Borders. To find us leave Junction 44, take A689 Hexham Road for three-quarters of a mile, first on right. Bed and Breakfast £15 to £16.50 double/twin, £18 to £20 single.

CARLISLE. Ronnie and Jackie Fisher, Cornerways Guest House, 107 Warwick Road, Carlisle CA1

1EA (01228 21733). Ronnie and Jackie welcome you to their family-run Guest House. A Grade II Listed building situated in the heart of historic Carlisle just two minutes' walk from city centre with castle, cathedral, bus and railway stations. An ideal base for visiting the Lake District, Hadrian's Wall and Gretna Green. Colour TV, welcome tray, shaver points and central heating in all rooms; en suite rooms available. Payphone and off-street parking. Reasonable rates from £13 per person with reductions for children. Home cooked meals available by arrangement. To reach us by car turn off M6 at Junction 43.

CARLISLE. Mrs Ellen McLaughlin, The Warren Guest House, 368 Warwick Road, Carlisle CA1 2RU

(01228 33663). 🏆🏆🏆 *COMMENDED.* AA QQQ, RAC Listed. A warm welcome awaits you at The Warren, just off Junction 43 M6. Ideal base for Scotland, Lake District, Hadrian's Wall and all the attractions Carlisle offers. Six en suite bedrooms available with central heating, telephone, colour TV, tea/coffee making, hair dryers and bathrobes: everything to make your stay comfy. Four-poster bedroom and large family room, both on ground floor leading out into large conservatory and patio area. Come and see our large chamber pot collection. Bed and Breakfast from £17. Ellen and John look forward to seeing you all.

CARLISLE. Mr M.J. Potts, Greysteads Private Hotel, 43 Norfolk Road, Carlisle CA2 5PQ (01228

22175). Greysteads is a family-run hotel on the outskirts of Carlisle but still within easy walking distance of the town centre. The Lake District is only 30 minutes' drive and Scotland four miles away. Offering spacious, comfortable rooms with washbasins, TV, tea/coffee making facilities, radio clock/alarm in all single, double and family rooms. Separate toilets, two shower/bathrooms. Cot and high chair available. A warm welcome and wholesome home cooking ensure a happy stay; evening dinner available if booked in advance. Mature gardens and adequate car parking. Brochure on request.

CARLISLE. Marchmain Guest House, 151 Warwick Road, Carlisle CA1 2LU (01228 29551). 🏆

COMMENDED. A lovely Victorian house of character offering comfort and warm hospitality, central heating, vanity suite, shaver point, colour TV, hair dryer and welcome tray in every room. Choice of single, double, twin and family accommodation. All guests have their own key for access at all times. Within easy reach of beautiful Lake District and only a few minutes' walk from Carlisle's historic city centre and cathedral; sports facilities available at the Sands Leisure Centre and shopping in the picturesque Lanes. Easy access from M6 Junction 43. Full English breakfast, home cooked evening meals by arrangement. Well recommended by guests. From £16 per person per night.

CARLISLE. Mrs Elizabeth Woodmass, Howard House Farm, Gilsland, Carlisle CA6 7AJ (016977

47285). 🏆🏆 *HIGHLY COMMENDED.* **Working farm, join in.** A 250 acre mixed farm with a 19th century stone-built farmhouse situated in a rural area overlooking the Irthing Valley on the Cumbria/Northumbria border. Half a mile from Gilsland village and Roman Wall; Haltwhistle five miles and the M6 at Carlisle, 18 miles. Good base for touring — Roman Wall, Lakes and Scottish Borders. Trout fishing on farm. Guests' lounge with colour TV where you can relax anytime in comfort. Dining room. One double room en suite, one twin and one family room with washbasins, bath or shower. All bedrooms have tea/coffee making facilities. Bathroom with shower, toilet. Children welcome at reduced rates. Sorry no pets. Car essential, parking . Open January to December. Bed and Breakfast from £17 to £20; Evening Meal optional. Weekly terms available. SAE or telephone for brochure.

CHAPEL STILE. Mrs Jackie Rowand, Baysbrown Farm, Chapel Stile, Great Langdale, Ambleside LA22 9JZ (015394 37300). Working farm, join in. Bays-

brown Farm is set at the beginning of the Langdale Valley. It has Herdwick sheep and beef cows, with 835 acres of land. It is a good "stopping off" place for Cumbrian Way walkers and within easy reach of Ambleside (five miles), Windermere (nine miles), Coniston (six miles) and Hawkshead (nine miles). Enjoy a relaxing evening in front of an open log fire after a home cooked meal. Accommodation comprises one family, one twin room, one double room, all with tea/coffee making facilities. Reductions for children, cot provided. Non-smoking accommodation available. Pets welcome. Open February to October. Bed and Breakfast from £17.50; Evening Meal £9. ELDHCA Award.

COCKERMOUTH. Mrs Dorothy E. Richardson, Pardshaw Hall, Cockermouth CA13 0SP (01900 822607). Old farmhouse in a small, quiet village three and a half miles from Cockermouth with views to the Fells. Children most welcome — cot, high chair and babysitting available, and a large garden to play in. Pardshaw Hall is ideally situated for touring the Lakes; children delight in the miniature railway at Ravenglass and there are some lovely walks. Accommodation is in one double, one single and one family or twin room, most with washbasins. Good home cooking with fresh produce. Log fires. Open all year. Sorry, no pets in house. Car essential, parking. Bed and Breakfast from £14; Evening Meal optional. Reduced rates for children.

COCKERMOUTH. The Rook Guesthouse, 9 Castlegate, Cockermouth CA13 9EU (01900 828496). Interesting 17th century town house, adjacent to historic castle, we offer comfortable accommodation with full English, vegetarian and Continental breakfast served in rooms which are equipped with washbasin, colour TV, tea/coffee facilities and central heating. En suite and standard rooms available. Cockermouth is an unspoilt market town located at the North Western edge of the Lake District within easy reach of the Lakes, Cumbrian Coast and Border country. We are ideally situated as a base for walkers, cyclists and holiday-makers. Bed and Breakfast from £15 per person sharing room, single occupancy £20. Open all year.

COCKERMOUTH. Mrs M.E. Chester, Birk Bank Farm, Brandlingill, Cockermouth CA13 0RB (01900 822326). Comfortable farmhouse accommodation on a 125-acre beef and sheep farm pleasantly situated four miles from Cockermouth (the birthplace of Wordsworth). Within easy reach of Loweswater Lake, Crummock Water, Buttermere and the picturesque coast. Ideal holiday location with lovely walks, hill climbing, fishing and trekking easily accessible. Embleton Golf Course five miles. Guests are given a warm welcome and accommodated in three double bedrooms (electric blankets on beds); bathroom, toilet, shower room with toilet; lounge with colour TV; diningroom. Good home cooking using own fruit and vegetables, home-made bread rolls. Children over five years welcome at reduced rates. Sorry no pets. Car essential — parking. Evening Dinner, Bed and Breakfast from £23; Bed and Breakfast from £15. Bedtime drink with home-made biscuits included in terms. Weekly rates available. Open Easter to October.

CONISTON. Mr and Mrs R. Newport, Brigg House, Torver, Coniston LA21 8AY (015394 41592).

🌑🌑 *HIGHLY COMMENDED.* Explore the Lake District from our tranquil early 19th century house set in its own wooded grounds at the foot of Coniston Old Man. All our comfortable rooms have been recently refurbished and have en suite facilities, colour TV, radio, tea/coffee. Excellent views over fields and hills. Varied breakfast menu catering for the traditional or the more adventurous! Guests' lounge. Private parking. Splendid walks start from our door and there are opportunities for riding, sailing, birdwatching, etc nearby or simply relax and enjoy the scenery. Two pubs within five minutes' walk serve good food. Bed and Breakfast from £20 to £21 per person. Pets welcome. No smoking.

CRUACHAN

Cruachan is a modern detached house situated in a quiet cul-de-sac in the centre of Coniston village. The bedrooms are spacious and comfortable, all are en-suite and have TV and tea/coffee making facilities. The lounge has a log stove. Bed and Breakfast from £19 to £24. Vegetarian and special diets catered for. Car parking. Non smokers. No pets. Coniston is an attractive Lakeland village, renowned for its breathtaking views of the Fells and Coniston Water. It is a fine central base for visiting other parts of the Lake District.

♛♛ Commended

Mrs Lilian Grant, Cruachan, Collingwood Close, Coniston, Cumbria LA21 8DZ. Telephone: 015394 41628.

CONISTON. Mrs Diana Munton, Piper Croft, Haws Bank, Coniston LA21 8AR (015394 41778). Small friendly Bed and Breakfast, "home from home", warm welcome assured. Ideally situated for walking and touring South Lakeland. Coniston Water Yachting Club and Cumbrian Way five minutes' walk. Two double rooms, one twin with washbasins and central heating. Lounge with TV. Private parking. No smoking. Double £32 per night. Open all year.

ENNERDALE. Mrs Elizabeth Loxham, Beckfoot, Ennerdale, Cleator CA23 3AU (01946 861235).

Jim and Liz would like to welcome you to their homely, comfortable, NO-SMOKING guest house which stands on the northern shore of Ennerdale Lake, in one of Lakeland's quiet and spectacular valleys. Guests' lounge with colour TV, guide books, games and tea/coffee making facilities. Two double bedrooms and one twin bedroom, all with washbasins. Lake and mountain views from all bedrooms. Beds have continental quilts and electric underblankets. Central heating. Superb home cooking with quality, variety and quantity being our aim. Bed and BIG Breakfast (with choice of menu) £15.50 to £17.50. Three-course candlelit Evening Dinner plus coffee and mints and complimentary glass of wine £10.50. Please telephone for further details or a leaflet.

ESKMEALS. Ms. Yvonne Stewart, Eskmeals House, Ravenglass LA19 5YA (01229 717151). A

lovely old Listed Georgian house in idyllic wooded setting close to picturesque estuary and beach. Step back in time and enjoy the old world charm. Excellent Cumbrian breakfast and evening meals served. Delightful bedrooms. Situated on Coastal Way, Cycle Way and near Coast to Coast and Furness Way. Free transport to and from station. Also excellent walking and touring area. Self catering cottage available.

GRANGE-OVER-SANDS. Corner Beech, Kents Bank Road, Grange-over-Sands LA11 7DP (015395

33088). ♛♛ *COMMENDED.* John and Linda Bradshaw offer a home from home in their spacious Victorian house. Good generous home cooking, stylish comfort and personal attention. Most rooms en suite, all with tea/coffee facilities, thermostatically controlled heating and colour TV. Overlooking Morecambe Bay, close to Promenade. Grange is a quiet genteel haven, an ideal walking and touring location for South Lakeland. Bed and Breakfast from £15.50 per person, weekly from £105; Dinner, Bed and Breakfast from £21.50 per person, weekly from £145. Reduced rates for children. Phone or write for brochure.

PLEASE SEND A STAMPED ADDRESSED ENVELOPE WITH ENQUIRIES

GRANGE-OVER-SANDS. Bill Lambert, Prospect House, Kents Bank Road, Grange-over-Sands LA11 7DJ (015395 32116). 🏵🏵🏵

A warm welcome awaits you at Prospect House. En suite rooms with TV, radio, tea/coffee making facilities. Car parking. Residents' bar. Noted for our cuisine using fresh produce and definitely no junk food. Open all year. There are no single rooms but we will take singles. Our best advertisement is the many return visits we receive. Bed and Breakfast from £22; Dinner (served at 7pm) £10.50. Vegetarians welcome.

GRANGE-OVER-SANDS. Mrs Jean Jackson, Templand Farm, Allithwaite, Grange-over-Sands LA11 7QX (015395 33129). Working farm, join in. Though built in 1687, Templand offers comfortable and quiet accommodation with all modern conveniences. This 100 acre mixed farm is close to the Grange-over-Sands/Cartmel road and is within easy reach of the Lake District. Under two miles to the sea. Fishing and hill walking, swimming pool, golf and tennis at Grange. Superb 12th century Priory at Cartmel. One double, one single and one family bedrooms; bathroom, toilet; lounge and dining room. Children welcome — cot, high chair and babysitting available. Car not essential but parking provided. Open 1st March to 31st October. SAE brings prompt reply. Terms for Evening Dinner/Meal, Bed and Breakfast from £17 or Bed and Breakfast from £10. Half price for children. No pets.

Bridge House Hotel

🏵🏵🏵 Commended   RAC Highly Acclaimed

Bridge House is situated in the centre of Grasmere enjoying a quiet secluded position just off the main road. There are two acres of mature gardens beside the River Rothay, with fine views of the surrounding fells. The twelve tastefully furnished bedrooms have private facilities, television, tea trays, telephone and hairdryer. Splendid food completes your holiday, a full English breakfast to start the day and an excellent five course evening meal, with coffee served by the fire, to round it off. You are ensured a warm, friendly welcome, your comfort and enjoyment being our prime concern. Open throughout the year. Bed & Breakfast from £23 per person per night; Evening Meal from £10.

Mr & Mrs M. Rushton, Bridge House Hotel, Stock Lane, Grasmere, Cumbria LA22 9SN
Tel: 015394 35425   Fax: 015394 35523

GRASMERE. Dunmail House, Keswick Road, Grasmere LA22 9RE (015394 35256). 🏵🏵 COMMEN-DED.

A traditional Lakeland stone house on the edge of the village and set in spacious gardens with outstanding views. Ideally located for all the activities for which this area of Lakeland is noted. Personally run by Trevor and Lesley Bulcock who aim to provide a friendly family atmosphere. Guest lounge with TV. All rooms have tea/coffee facilities, central heating, double glazing and beautiful views. Some en suite. Non smoking. Ample parking. No pets. Easily accessible by public transport. Bed and Breakfast from £17.50 per person per night. Weekly rates and special winter breaks available.

Dunmail House

CUMBRIA – THE GREAT OUTDOORS

Lakes, rivers, mountains and moors (and a mild climate) make Cumbria a paradise for the outdoor enthusiast — with something to suit every age group and every level of ability. Practically every kind of watersport can be enjoyed — if you haven't tried water ski-ing, canoeing, windsurfing or yachting, then now's your chance! Climbing, abseiling, walking, cycling, mountain biking, pony trekking, fishing, orienteering . . . the list is endless!

HAWESWATER/ULLSWATER. Anne and Rob Hunt, Holywell Country Guest House, Helton, Penrith CA10 2QA (01931 712231). Fed up? Tired? Need a break?

Look no further, we have the perfect tonic — so we warmly invite you to sample Cumbrian hospitality in our superbly situated non-smoking country house in the least discovered part of the National Park. Guests are amazed at the commanding views from all rooms and appreciative of the peace and quiet that surrounds them. Tastefully furnished throughout. Own cosy sitting room and dining room. En suite, private facilities. Central heating. Convenient en route to and from Scotland. Hearty breakfast. Enthusiastic advice on pursuits and activities. No pets. Good pubs locally. Bed and Breakfast from £20 per person. Open February to November. Brochure.

HAWKSHEAD. Peter and Anne Hart, Bracken Fell, Outgate, Ambleside LA22 0NH (015394 36289).

♛♛ COMMENDED. Bracken Fell is situated in beautiful open countryside between Ambleside and Hawkshead, in the picturesque hamlet of Outgate. Ideally positioned for exploring the Lake District and within easy reach of Coniston, Windermere, Ambleside, Grasmere and Keswick. All major outdoor activities are catered for nearby including wind surfing, sailing, fishing, pony trekking, etc. All six bedrooms have private facilities, complimentary tea/coffee making and outstanding views. There is central heating throughout, a comfortable lounge and dining room, together with ample private parking and two acres of gardens. Fire Certificate. Open all year. Bed and Breakfast from £20. Non-smoking. Self catering accommodation also available. Write or phone for brochure and tariff.

Bracken Fell

Linda & Alan Bleasdale

Borwick Lodge

Outgate, Hawkshead, Ambleside
Cumbria LA22 0PU
Tel: Hawkshead (015394) 36332

Three times winners of the AWARD for 'Accommodation of the Highest Standards'. A leafy driveway entices you to the most enchantingly situated house in the Lake District, a very special 17th century country lodge with magnificent panoramic lake and mountain views, quietly secluded in beautiful gardens. Ideally placed in the heart of the Lakes and close to Hawkshead village with its good choice of restaurants and inns. Beautiful ensuite bedrooms with colour televisions and tea/coffee facilities including 'Special Occasions' and 'Romantic Breaks', two king-size four-poster rooms. Prize-winning homemade breads. Tourist Board 'Two Crown Highly Commended'. Linda and Alan welcome you to their 'haven of peace and tranquillity' in this most beautiful corner of England. Ample parking. NON-SMOKING THROUGHOUT. Bed and Breakfast from £18. May we send our brochure?

HAWKSHEAD. Lynda and James Johnson, Borwick Fold, Outgate, Near Ambleside LA22 0PU (015394 36742). Tourist Board Listed. 17th century farmhouse on the edge of the fell. Glorious views over the Hawkshead Valley and the High Fells. Large garden, orchard, walks from the door. We have three friendly Elkhounds, two aloof cats and geese roaming in the field. A house of character and comfort with lovely old furniture. Delightful sitting room full of books/pictures for unwinding, log fire for chilly evenings; central heating. Bedrooms have TV and tea/coffee facilities. Cooking is a pleasure — full English breakfast or freshly baked fruit muffins, etc., homemade bread/marmalade. A haven of tranquillity one mile from picturesque Hawkshead and country inns for bar meals/dinner. Ample parking. A warm welcome to all our guests. Bed and Breakfast £22 per person from Easter 1997. Brochure.

WHEN MAKING ENQUIRIES PLEASE MENTION
FARM HOLIDAY GUIDES

HAWKSHEAD. Mrs Diane Dean, Balla Wray Cottage, High Wray, Ambleside LA22 0JQ (015394

32401). Set in a quiet secluded position, amongst the trees and wildlife, this 19th century Lakeland stone cottage overlooks Lake Windermere with direct access to the unspoilt west shore. There are two well appointed bedrooms, one with double bed and the other with twin beds. Both are of a very high standard with en suite facilities, colour TV and tea/coffee trays. In the morning there is a choice of full English breakfast or vegetarian on request, served in the lovely sunny dining room or, on fine days, on the terrace overlooking a beautiful garden. Sorry no smoking. Pets welcome by arrangement but sorry, no children under 10 years. Bed and Breakfast from £20. Brochure available.

KENDAL. The Jolly Anglers, Burneside, Kendal LA9 6QS (01539 732552). Cumbria Tourist Board

Listed. Situated in the village of Burneside, a mile north of the market town of Kendal and within six miles of Lake Windermere. This old traditional Lakeland inn offers Bed and Breakfast accommodation in Taylors Cottages (attached to the inn and once the village smithy) and Strickland Ketel Guest House situated in a quieter position at the rear. Some rooms have en suite facilities, all have colour TV and tea/coffee making facilities. Guests are offered good home cooking in the ground floor rooms of Taylors Cottages. Real ale is served in the bars, which have low beamed ceiling and log fires. Moderate rates with special bargain breaks. Children and pets welcome. Bed and Breakfast from £14 per person. Free fishing is available, and there is an 18 hole golf course close by. RAC Listed.

KENDAL. Mrs Jean Bindloss, Grayrigg Hall, Grayrigg, Near Kendal LA8 9BU (01539 824689).

Working farm. Comfortable, peaceful 18th century farmhouse set in a beautiful country location, ideal for touring the Lakes and famous Yorkshire Dales. We run a beef and sheep farm only four and a half miles from Kendal and with easy access to M6 motorway, Junction 38. Guests are assured of the finest accommodation and a friendly welcome. One spacious family room and one double bedroom; tasteful lounge/dining room with colour TV; bathroom. Children most welcome, cot, babysitting if required. Open March to November. Bed and Breakfast from £15 per person; Evening Meal available. Further information gladly supplied.

KENDAL. Mrs Joan Carrington-Birch, Birslack Grange, Hutton Lane, Levens, Kendal LA8 8PA

(015395 60989). AA Listed. A conversion of an old Westmorland farmhouse incorporating the original barns and milking sheds. The conversion has been aimed at providing warm, comfortable and relaxing accommodation situated within an area of outstanding natural beauty. Our large comfortable residents' lounge enjoys panoramic views across the Lyth Valley in addition to colour TV and a wide variety of reading matter. One of our bedrooms is located at ground floor level and all are en suite with tea/coffee making facilities. Levens village has been a frequent winner of Cumbria's "Best Kept Village" award and still retains its traditional village store, sub post office and local inn. Non-smoking, full terms on request.

KENDAL. Mrs A. Taylor, Russell Farm, Burton-in-Kendal, Carnforth, Lancs. LA6 1NN (01524 781334; Fax: 01524 782511). Why not spend a few days

at Russell Farm? The proprietors pride themselves on trying to give guests an enjoyable holiday with good food, friendly atmosphere, relaxing surroundings away from the hustle and bustle. The 150-acre dairy farm is set in a quiet hamlet one mile from the village of Burton-in-Kendal, and five miles from the old market town of Kirkby Lonsdale. An ideal centre for touring Lakes and Yorkshire Dales, or going to the coast. Ideal stopover for people travelling south or to Scotland, only five minutes from M6 Motorway. One double, one single and one family bedrooms; bathroom, toilet; sittingroom and diningroom. Children welcome; cot, high chair and babysitting offered. Pets accepted, if well-behaved. Open from March to November for Evening Dinner, Bed and Breakfast or Bed and Breakfast. Reductions for children. Car essential, parking. Send large SAE, please, for terms and brochure.

KENDAL. Mrs Anne Knowles, Myers Farm, Docker, Grayrigg, Kendal LA8 0DF (01539 824610). A

mixed farm of 220 acres with sheep and dairy cows. Children are welcome to see the working of the farm. The house is over 250 years old with oak beams and a beautiful partition in the lounge/dining room where a log fire burns. Two double rooms and one twin room; bathroom, shower and toilet, all providing homely and friendly accommodation. Peaceful, scenic countryside, beautiful area for walking locally and further afield, yet close to Kendal amenities. Two and a half miles from Junction 37 on the M6 motorway, good half way stop en route to Scotland and within easy reach of the Lake District and Dales National Park and the coast. Central heating. Reduced rates for children under 11 years with high chair and babysitting available. Open from March to November for Bed and Breakfast from £15.50. Car essential, parking. SAE, please.

KENDAL. Mrs A.E. Bell, Hill Fold Farm, Burneside, Kendal LA8 9AU (01539 722574). Working farm. Situated three miles north of Kendal close to rolling

hills of Potter Fell, with many quiet walks and within easy reach of lakes and sea. Genuine working farm of over 1000 acres carrying beef and sheep. Guests are accommodated in three double rooms with washbasins, tea-making facilities, heaters, TV and shaving points. Sittingroom; diningroom; bathroom, toilet. Cot and babysitting; reduced rates for children under 12 years. Wholesome meals served. Car essential, parking. Open January to December (including Christmas and New Year). Sorry, no pets. Terms on request.

KENDAL. Mrs Val Sunter, Higher House Farm, Oxenholme Lane, Natland, Kendal LA9 7QH (015395 61177; Fax: 015315 61520). 🌑🌑🌑

COMMENDED. In a peaceful village south of Kendal, this 17th century beamed farmhouse offers comfortable accommodation wth delicious breakfast. Two double and one twin rooms, each with private bathroom. Four-poster bed. TV, hair dryer and coffee/tea making facilities in all bedrooms. Residents' lounge with colour TV. Central heating throughout. Pay phone in hall. Overlooking the Lakeland Fells, convenient for the M6 and Oxenholme station. Golf, riding, historic visits nearby. Bed and Breakfast from £18 to £22. Pets welcome. AA QQQQ Selected. Self catering accommodation also available.

KENDAL.Mrs June Ellis, Gateside Farm, Windermere Road, Kendal LA9 5SE (01539 722036). ETB Listed COMMENDED. **Working farm.** AA/RAC Acclaimed.

Traditional Lakeland Farm, two miles north of Kendal on A591 main tourist route through Lakes. Easily accessible from M6 junction 36. Ideally situated for touring all Lakes and Yorkshire Dales. All bedrooms have colour TV, tea/coffee making facilities and heating, some en suite. Short or weekly stays welcome. Good home cooked breakfasts and evening meals served at separate tables. Good parking facilities. Children and pets welcome. Open all year (closed Christmas and New Year). Bed and Breakfast from £15 to £19; Evening Meal £7.50.

KENDAL. Mrs S. Beaty, Garnett House Farm, Burneside, Kendal LA9 5SF (01539 724542). 🐦🐦

COMMENDED. **Working farm.** This is an AA/RAC Acclaimed 15th century farmhouse on large dairy/sheep farm, situated a half mile from the A591 Kendal/Windermere road. Accommodation comprises double, twin and family rooms (some en suite), all with washbasins, colour TV, clock/radio and tea making facilities. Lovely oak panelling, beams, door and spice cupboard. Full English breakfast and five course dinners served at separate tables; all prepared in the farmhouse kitchen including homemade soups, lamb and beef from the farm and delicious sweets. Children welcome at reduced rates if sharing with two adults. Good private parking. Near village and public transport. Special offer November to mid-March — three nights Bed and Breakfast £45, en suite £50. AA QQQ.

KENDAL. Mrs Judith Keep, West Mount, 39 Milnthorpe Road, Kendal LA9 5QG (01539 724621).

Friendly, non-smoking, centrally heated Victorian guest house on southern outskirts of Kendal. Easy access Junction 36, M6. One double, one family room both en suite have colour TV, clock radio alarms, hair dryers. Private parking. Open all year. Terms from £16 to £18 per person per night.

KENDAL. Pat and Bill Evans, Field End, Brigsteer LA8 8AN (015395 68570).

Set on the hillside overlooking the Lyth Valley, renowned for its Damson Blossom in spring, enjoy our delightful terraced garden, fountain and waterfall with afternoon tea included in price of stay. Brigsteer is a peaceful village with beautiful walks in surrounding area. Market town of Kendal three miles, Windermere and South Lakes 12 miles, Yorkshire Dales 15 miles. Located five miles west of M6 Junction 36 on the A591. One double and one twin-bedded rooms, spacious bathroom adjacent includes separate shower. Central heating, radio, beverage facilities. Lounge with colour TV and open fire. Sorry no pets, young children or smokers. Bed and Breakfast £15. Packed lunches available. Private parking.

KENDAL. Sundial House, 51 Milnthorpe Road, Kendal LA9 5QG (01539 724468). 🐦 *APPROVED.* Sundial House is on the A6, quarter of a mile from Kendal town centre, directly opposite the College. Known as "The Gateway to the Lakes" Kendal is a charming and historic market town and is the perfect base for a visit to the Lake District. Whatever your pastime — walking, golfing, fishing or sightseeing — Kendal has it all. We offer you a homely and warm welcome here at Sundial House; Bed and Breakfast from £15. The cosy bedrooms all have tea/coffee making facilities and colour TVs. There is a reading lounge and ample parking. Follow the Kendal signs from Junction 36. We are 10 minutes from the M6.

KENDAL. Eileen and Brian Kettle, Holmfield, 41 Kendal Green, Kendal LA9 5PP (Tel & Fax: 01539

720790). ETB Listed *DE LUXE.* Holmfield is an elegant Edwardian house set in quiet gardens with swimming pool, croquet and panoramic views. We have double, twin and four-poster bedrooms, with adjacent spacious bathrooms. All rooms are pretty, with every comfort, TV, radio and beverage making facilities. Elegant dining room and lounge with lovely views. Central heating. Private parking. Within walking distance of Kendal's many amenities and excellent restaurants. Ideal base from which to enjoy the Lake District. Sorry, no smokers, pets or young children. Enjoy genuine hospitality. Bed and Breakfast from £19 per person. Short listed for ETB B&B of the Year.

KENDAL near. Mrs Olive M. Knowles, Cragg Farm, New Hutton, Near Kendal LA8 0BA (01539

721760). Working farm. Tourist Board Listed. Cragg Farm is a delightful 17th century oak beamed farmhouse which retains its character yet has all the modern comforts. This 280 acre working dairy/sheep farm is set in peaceful countryside and ideally positioned for exploring the Lake District and Yorkshire Dales. Located four miles from Kendal on A684 road and three miles M6 Junction 37. This makes an ideal stopover between England and Scotland. We have one double, one family and one single bedrooms, all with tea/coffee facilities; bathroom with shower and toilet; lounge/dining room with colour TV. Full central heating. Full English breakfast served. Families are welcome, reduced rates for children. Weekly terms and Short Breaks available. Open March to November for Bed and Breakfast from £15 per person. Self catering caravan also available; weekly terms.

KESWICK. Mrs M. Roper, Grasslees, Rickerby Lane, Portinscale, Keswick CA12 5RH (017687

79632). Luxurious Bed and Breakfast accommodation built in the late 20s on a scale that is seldom now achieved. Grasslees is a house of spacious and generous proportions furnished and equipped to a very high standard. Set in its own attractive and well tended gardens with a pleasant outlook toward Barrow and Grizedale Horseshoe. Situated in the heart of the pretty little village of Portinscale it offers the delights of the countryside with the convenience of Keswick three-quarters of a mile away. Colour brochure available.

KESWICK. The Swan, Thornthwaite, Keswick CA12 5SQ (017687 78256). This fully licensed, attractive 17th century former coaching inn is situated in the heart of the countryside just off the main A66 overlooking Bassenthwaite and Skiddaw. All rooms have colour TV and the majority have en suite facilities. Enjoy a pre-dinner drink before dining in the restaurant which is noted for its quality and variety of menu. The panoramic view is one of the finest in the Lake District. The Swan offers a warm and friendly atmosphere under the personal supervision of the resident directors, Vivienne and Allan Cairns. AA/RAC Two Stars; RAC Restaurant Award and Merit Award. Terms on application.

KESWICK. Brienz Guest House, 3 Greta Street, Keswick CA12 4HS (017687 71049). Cumbria Tourist Board Listed *COMMENDED.* Small friendly guest house comprising two double rooms with showers and one twin room. All have central heating, washbasins, colour TV and tea/coffee making facilities. High standards of comfort and cuisine. Dinner with a choice of menu is optional. Licensed. Special diets catered for with prior notice. Situated just off Penrith Road about five minutes' walk from town centre and within easy reach of all Lake District amenities. No smoking. Open February to mid-December. Bed and Breakfast from £14 per person; Dinner from £9.

KESWICK. Mrs M. E. Harrison, Shundraw Farm, St. Johns-in-the-Vale, Keswick CA12 4RR (017687 79227). This lovely old farmhouse, built in 1712, is situated in the beautiful valley of St. Johns-in-the-Vale. All rooms look on to the Helvellyn Mountain range, an ideal spot for those seeking peace and quiet in country surroundings. Three double bedrooms; bathroom and toilet are separate. A car is an advantage, but not essential. Keswick is only three miles away and makes an excellent touring centre. A warm welcome and good breakfast assured. Open Easter to October. Bed and Breakfast from £13 per person per night including a bedtime drink. No smoking. SAE please.

KESWICK. Mrs Elizabeth Scott, Woodside, Penrith Road, Keswick CA12 4LJ (017687 73522).

Situated on the outskirts of Keswick, "Woodside" is an ideal centre for sightseeing in the picturesque Lake District. This is a family-run bed and breakfast establishment offering the very highest of standards. Bedrooms with ensuite, TV, tea making facilities and central heating. Large car park and lovely gardens. Many local attractions and country walks. Open all year round. Full English Breakfast. Bed and Breakfast from £16. Reduced rates in winter.

ALLERDALE HOUSE

RELAIS ROUTIERS APPROVED
1 Eskin Street, Keswick
Cumbria CA12 4DH
Tel: (017687) 73891

IN THE HEART OF THE ENGLISH LAKES

👑👑👑 COMMENDED   AA Approved, RAC Highly Acclaimed

Personally run by us for the last 19 years, we are quietly situated, yet close to town, parks, lake and fells. We have a relaxed friendly atmosphere where you can be at ease. Comfortably furnished, all bedrooms are ensuite and have colour TV, hairdryer, telephone and radio. We have a drying room for the occasional wet day! Car park for all our guests' cars. We specialise in generous portions of quality home-cooked food in our licensed dining room, and for the additional comfort of our guests we are a NO SMOKING house. Bed & Breakfast £23.00; Dinner, Bed and Breakfast £34.00. Child reductions. Write or phone now for your colour brochure (a stamp would be appreciated).

KESWICK. I. and M. Atkinson, "Dancing Beck", Underskiddaw, Keswick CA12 4PY (017687 73800).

Large Lakeland country house two and a half miles from Keswick just off A591 Carlisle road, signposted Millbeck. Situated in its own elevated, spacious grounds with summerhouse. Magnificent views of Derwent Valley and surrounding mountains. Walks onto Skiddaw Mountain are possible from the grounds of "Dancing Beck". All rooms are centrally heated. All bedrooms have private facilities and tea/coffee making. Children welcome. Car essential. Bed and Breakfast from £19. Weekly terms available. Open Spring to November. A pleasant welcome assured. A self catering cottage also available.

KESWICK. Chris and Anne Wood, Lonnin Garth, Portinscale, Keswick CA12 5RS (017687 74095).

👑👑 COMMENDED. Ideally situated at a gateway to Borrowdale and Newlands valleys, yet within easy walking distance of Keswick. A comfortable relaxing base for exploring the surrounding lakes and fells. Lonnin Garth is an interesting house with character, having a large guests' lounge with magnificent views of the fells. It stands in an acre of gardens and there is ample parking. There are three double and two twin-bedded rooms, all tastefully decorated and furnished. Four rooms offer private facilities; all have tea making facilities, central heating and colour TV. Bed and Breakfast from £18.50 per person per night.

KESWICK. Alan and Jean Redfern, Heatherlea, 26 Blencathra Street, Keswick CA12 4HP (017687 72430). Tourist Board Listed COMMENDED. This charming and friendly guest house is personally run by the owners. A full and varied breakfast menu is served (8am to 9am) in our delightful dining room with its views of the Skiddaw Fells. The house is centrally heated and each room offers every comfort, with en suite facilities, remote control colour TVs, electric blankets, hair dryers and tea/coffee facilities. Heatherlea is close to the town centre and an ideal place from which to tour and walk this wonderful part of the Lake District. Residential licence. Non-smokers only. Bed and Breakfast £17 to £18.50. AA QQQ.

KESWICK. Bay Tree, Wordsworth Street, Keswick CA12 4HU (017687 73313). ♥♥ Small, family-run, licensed, non-smoking Guest House situated just three minutes' walk from the town centre on the Penrith road. Most rooms have lovely views over River Greta and Fitz Park to the mountains. All rooms have washbasins, central heating, double glazing, tea/coffee making facilities; some rooms en suite. Home cooking, residents' lounge. Fire Certificate. Own key. Excellent location for touring Lake District and, for those who enjoy walking, we are near many of the well-known mountains. Lake, museums, leisure pool, etc only a short distance away. Bed and Breakfast from £15; Evening Meal; packed lunches by arrangement.

KESWICK. AnneMarie and Ian Townsend, Latrigg House, St. Herbert Street, Keswick CA12 4DF (017687 73068). ♥♥ An attractive detached Victorian house in a quiet area, only a few minutes' walk from the town centre and Lake, providing an excellent base for visiting the Lake District. We promise a very warm welcome, good food, comfort and hospitality (vegetarian and vegan meals provided if required). We offer a no-smoking environment for the well being and safety of guests, comfortable rooms (some with en suite facilities), all with colour TVs and tea/coffee facilities and heating. Comfortable residents lounge with TV. Bed and Breakfast from £14 to £18 (evening meals available). Children under 12 special rate if sharing adult room. Sorry no pets.

KESWICK. Mr and Mrs P.H. Smith, Goodwin House, 29 Southey Street, Keswick CA12 4EE (017687 74634). ♥♥ Goodwin House is an imposing detached three storey residence with central hall and staircase of solid pine with verandah on first landing. It affords easy access to parks and town shopping centre and is an ideal base for walks and drives to fells and lakes. All rooms have central heating, washbasin, tea making facilities and colour TV. There are en-suite rooms and guests have own front door keys. Delicious home cooking. Bed and Breakfast from £15. Weekly terms by arrangement. Reduced rates for children. Open all year. Non smoking. AA Approved.

KESWICK. J.W. and S. Miller, Acorn House Hotel, Ambleside Road, Keswick CA12 4DL (017687 72553). ♥♥ *HIGHLY COMMENDED.* Georgian house situated in gardens with private car parks yet only a few minutes from town centre, ideal for touring the Lake District. Traditional furniture enhances the character of each of the 10 spacious bedrooms complemented by the co-ordinated decor. All have ensuite bath/shower rooms, colour TV and tea/coffee making facilities; four poster beds also available. The generous full English breakfast will set you up for the day whether walking, climbing or sightseeing, and after the day's exertions you can relax in the large, comfortable, elegant lounge. The Hotel is open most of the year and you can be sure of a warm welcome. Bed and Breakfast from £23 per person. Reduced rates for children. Directions, from M6 take A66 to Keswick. AA Listed, RAC Highly Acclaimed.

KESWICK. Gladys and David Birtwistle, Kalgurli Guest House, 33 Helvellyn Street, Keswick CA12 4EP (017687 72935). ♥♥ *COMMENDED.* Be assured of a warm and friendly welcome at this comfortable non-smoking four bedroomed guest house. Excellent grilled breakfast, served between 8am and 9am. Menu choice. Vegetarians catered for. Packed lunches available. Kalgurli is an ideal location for touring and walking, plenty of on-street parking. Rooms accessible all day. Own key. Accommodation comprises one large en suite family room/twin, one en suite double room and two standard rooms, all with colour TV and tea/coffee making facilities. Standard rooms £15; en suite £17 to £18. Special rates for children.

KESWICK. Mr and Mrs J. McMullan, Jenkin Hill Cottage, Thornthwaite, Keswick CA12 5SG (017687 78443). 🏵🏵 HIGHLY COMMENDED. Situated in

a quiet village, nestled between Bassenthwaite Lake and Thornthwaite Forest, some four miles from Keswick; within 20 minutes of M6 Junction 40 this is an ideal base for a Lakeland holiday or stopover when travelling north or south. There are award-winning gardens on all sides of the cottage giving all the bedrooms a garden view. Each room is tastefully decorated and furnished with matching en suite bath and shower rooms. Tea/coffee making facilities, colour TV, central heating available in all rooms. Full four-course English breakfast offered and diets will be catered for whenever possible. Highly recommended bar meals available at local Hotel. We have a non-smoking policy throughout the premises. Private parking with security lighting. Terms from £20 to £23 per person. Open all year except Christmas.

KESWICK. Mrs Sharon Helling, Beckside Guest House, 5 Wordsworth Street, Keswick CA12 4HU (017687 73093). 🏵🏵 COMMENDED. Beckside is a small, very comfortable guest house for non-smokers. We are situated close to the town centre and are convenient for the shops, Fitz Park, pool, lake, walking and touring. Our bedrooms are tastefully decorated and furnished; all have en suite facilities, colour TV, hospitality tray and central heating. We offer full English breakfast (or vegetarian alternative). Packed lunches are also available by arrangement. Bed and Breakfast £18.50 per person per night. AA QQQ, RAC Highly Acclaimed.

KESWICK. David and Margaret Raine, Clarence House, 14 Eskin Street, Keswick CA12 4DQ (017687 73186). 🏵🏵🏵 COMMENDED. AA QQQ. A lovely

Victorian house ideally situated for the Lake, parks and market square. Bedrooms are decorated to a high standard, have full en suite facilities, colour TVs, hospitality trays and central heating. A four-poster room and ground floor room are available. A warm welcome and hearty breakfast await you. Bed and Breakfast from £18 per person. Non smoking. Brochure sent with pleasure on request.

KESWICK. Mr & Mrs J.M. Pepper, Beckstones Farm, Thornthwaite, Keswick CA12 5SQ (017687 78510). 🏵🏵 COMMENDED. Keswick three-and-a-half

Beckstones Farm
Thornthwaite, Keswick, Cumbria.

miles, near the head of Bassenthwaite Lake. Beckstones is a homely and comfortable converted Georgian farmhouse built in 1726. Set in peaceful surroundings and enjoying superb views of Skiddaw and Helvellyn ranges, yet an excellent touring centre for the motorist. Run as a small-holding; all modern amenities along with traditional comfort in our cosy oak-beamed diningroom and in the TV lounge; all bedrooms are centrally heated with full en-suite facilities and tea/coffee making. Ample private parking. Dogs welcome by arrangement. Bed and Breakfast from £19.

KESWICK near. Mrs Val Bradley, North Mount, North Row, Bassenthwaite, Near Keswick CA12 4RJ (017687 76044). Picturesque small village near north

end of Bassenthwaite Lake, in an area with a large variety of activities, lovely walks, fishing and horse riding all nearby. North Mount is delightfully situated in the Lake District National Park enjoying spectacular views over the village and Skiddaw. There is a 15th century inn serving excellent food within 100 yards. Val Bradley offers a warm welcome to all who visit; single, double, family or twin rooms have tea/coffee making facilities and colour TV. Guests' own bathroom. Available all year. Private parking. From £15 per person per night. Special children's rates.

KESWICK (Lake District). Tony and Ann Atkin, Glencoe Guest House, 21 Helvellyn Street, Keswick CA12 4EN (017687 71016). Cycling, walking or touring, a warm welcome is guaranteed. Our renovated Victorian Guest House is conveniently situated only five minutes' stroll from centre of Keswick and all amenities. Glencoe offers spacious en suite and standard rooms, all decorated and furnished to a high standard, each with their own colour TV and hospitality tray. Double, twin and single rooms available. This is a totally non-smoking guest house with full central heating and Fire Certificate. Local knowledge and maps are available to those wishing to explore the Northern Lakes and Fells. Cycle storage also available. Bed and Breakfast from £15 per person.

KESWICK. Ian and Janice Picken, Lynwood House Licensed Guest House, 35 Helvellyn Street, Keswick CA12 4EP (017687 72398). 🐝 *COMMENDED.*

Fantastic scenery, fabulous fell walking; five minutes from town centre, 10 minutes to Lake Derwentwater. Free from smoke. Full Fire Certificate. Full breakfast menu. Finest cuisine — optional four-course evening meal. Facilities for tea/coffee making, heating; TV; washbasins and shaver points. Furnished distinctively. Friendly welcome. In short . . . absolutely fabulous!! Bed and Breakfast from £15 per person per night.

KESWICK near. Muriel Bond, Thornthwaite Hall, Thornthwaite, Near Keswick CA12 5SA (Tel & Fax: 017687 78424). 🐝🐝🐝 *APPROVED.*

Thornthwaite Hall is a traditional 17th century farmhouse, modernised and converted into a very comfortable guesthouse. All rooms are en suite with TV, tea/coffee making facilities. Catering includes good home cooking, residential licence. The Hall lies in an acre of grounds complete with a lovely garden. Thornthwaite is a lovely hamlet three miles west of Keswick. There are numerous walks from Thornthwaite, with a different feel to other parts of the Lake District. Climbing in pine forest locations on the numerous paths and forest trails, spectacular views rewarding those who climb to the tops of Barf, Lords Seat, Seat How. Dogs and children most welcome. Open all year except Christmas. Bed and Breakfast from £21 to £24; Dinner, Bed and Breakfast from £30.50. Send for brochure, please.

KESWICK (Newlands). Mrs Christine Simpson, Uzzicar Farm, Newlands, Keswick CA12 5TS (017687 78367).

A warm welcome awaits you at Uzzicar Farm, situated in the peaceful Newlands Valley, only three miles from Keswick with magnificent views of the surrounding Fells. Being within 30 minutes of the M6 Junction 40 makes this the ideal place for a holiday in the Lake District or a break in your journey when travelling north or south. Well located for touring by car and the comfortable farmhouse makes a particularly good base for fell walking and sailing. Fishing, swimming, golf and pony trekking are all relatively close. All bedrooms have washbasins, central heating, tea/coffee making facilities and shaver points. There is a separate sitting room, dining room, toilet and bathroom with toilet. Sorry no smoking. Open February to December. Ample parking. Bed and Breakfast from £14 to £16 per person. Please write or phone for further details.

KESWICK/BORROWDALE. Mrs S. Bland, Thorneythwaite Farm, Borrowdale, Keswick CA12 5XQ (017687 77237). Thoneythwaite Farm has a beautiful, peaceful position in the Borrowdale Valley standing half a mile off the road. The 220 acre sheep farm is seven miles from Keswick and half a mile from Seatoller. The 18th century farmhouse has great character inside and out, several rooms having oak beams and panelling and being furnished to suit. Two double and one family bedrooms, all with tea/coffee making facilities; sitting room with open or electric fire; dining room; bathroom and toilet, Cot, high chair and reduced rates for children. Sorry no pets. Open from April to November, mid-week bookings accepted. A perfect base for a honeymoon or for those who enjoy fell walking. Bed and Breakfast from £16.

KESWICK/BORROWDALE. Mrs S.A. Roscamp, Stable Rigg, Grange-in-Borrowdale, Keswick CA12 5UQ (017687 77605).

Stable Rigg is situated in the village of Grange in the Borrowdale Valley which is renowned for splendid scenery, Derwentwater, a wealth of walks and places of interest and four miles from Keswick town. Comfortable accommodation offered in this small cottage converted from a stable, is one double and one single room with tea/coffee tray, private facilities. Sitting room with TV for guests' use. An open log fire burns early/late season. Easy off road parking. Choice of good eating places nearby for evening meal. Open Easter to end October, then by request. Bed and full Breakfast £17.

FREE and REDUCED RATE Holiday Visits!
See our READERS' OFFER VOUCHER for details!

KIRKBY LONSDALE. Mrs M.V. Eglin, Hole House, Casterton, Kirkby Lonsdale, Carnforth LA6 2LF (015242 76374). Converted farmhouse two miles from Kirkby Lonsdale situated in the Lune Valley. We offer comfortable accommodation comprising one double en suite, one double, one twin and one single bedded rooms; bathroom with shower. Snooker and games room. Central heating, double glazing. We serve traditional English breakfast. Close by are two golf courses, fishing and ample opportunities for fellwalking from the garden gate. Six miles away is Ingleton with many walks around waterfalls and caves and the Yorkshire Dales are within easy driving distance. Bed and Breakfast from £15 to £18.

KIRKBY LONSDALE near. Pat Nicholson, Green Lane End Farm, Lupton, Kirkby Lonsdale, Carnforth LA6 2PP (015395 67236). Working farm. Three miles from M6 Junction 36. Excellent stopover when travelling to and from Scotland. 17th century farmhouse with oak beams and fine old staircase in quiet unspoilt area of South Lakeland. Ideally situated for touring Lakes and Dales. Tea/coffee making facilities. Pets by arrangement. Terms from £15. Directions: From M6 take A65 to Kirkby Lonsdale, first right after Plough Inn, follow Farm B&B signs. From Kirkby Lonsdale, fourth left after Kirkby Motors follow signs.

KIRKBY STEPHEN. Mrs Sylvia Capstick, Duckintree House, Kaber, Kirkby Stephen CA17 4ER (017683 71073). Duckintree is a working family farm set in the quiet Eden Valley countryside just off the A685 Kirkby Stephen to Brough road. Easy access to the Lakes and Yorkshire Dales or ideal for breaking your journey from the south of England/Midlands to Scotland. Car essential, ample parking. The rooms comprise family, double and twin (cot available) with tea/coffee making facilities. Lounge/dining room with colour TV. All rooms overlook a large garden and countryside. Bed and Breakfast from £15. Reductions for children under 12 years. Pets welcome by arrangement. Evening meal can be provided. Open from March to October. Write or phone for details.

KIRKBY STEPHEN near. Mrs B.M. Boustead, Tranna Hill, Newbiggin-on-Lune, Near Kirkby Stephen CA17 4NY (015396 23227). Tranna Hill offers a relaxing and friendly atmosphere in a non-smoking environment. Five miles from M6 (Junction 38), beautifully situated on fringe of Newbiggin-on-Lune village, ideal base for country lovers and walkers with nature reserve and Sunbiggin Tarn nearby. Well placed for touring the Lake District, Yorkshire, Durham Dales and for breaking your journey. Relax in guests' lounge with TV and then have a good night's sleep in en suite rooms with tea making facilities, central heating and beautiful views, followed by a delicious breakfast. RIPHH Certificate. Bed and Breakfast from £16.

LAKESIDE/NEWBY BRIDGE. Brian and Sylvia Slingsby, Landing Cottage, Lakeside, Newby Bridge, Ulverston LA12 8AS (015395 31719). ✿✿ Traditional Lakeland stone cottage built about 1870, situated at the southern tip of Lake Windermere about 100 yards from the Lake Steamer and Lakeside/Haverthwaite Steam Railway terminals. Conveniently located as a touring base to all the Lakes, places of interest and the Morecambe Bay coast. The cottage has en suite, standard double and family bedrooms with pretty, colour co-ordinated decor, tea/coffee making facilities. The whole of the ground floor is non-smoking which includes an en suite bedroom. Just starting our 13th year, we shall be extending a warm welcome to all our new and returning guests. Good home cooking, packed lunches available on request. Complimentary pot of tea/coffee on arrival. Car parking. Open all year. Bed and Breakfast £17 to £19.50. Brochure on request.

LOWICK (near Coniston). Garth Row, Lowick Green, Ulverston LA12 8EB (01229 885633). Tourist

Board Listed. Traditional, beamed cottage only three miles from Coniston Water in this beautiful and little-known corner of the National Park. The house stands alone amidst farmland and common with lovely valley and mountain views. We offer quality accommodation with two attractive rooms for guests. Our super family room with its gallery (children love it!) can also serve as a double or twin. Comfortable lounge with books, TV and a real fire on cold nights. Good food, tea/coffee in rooms, dogs welcome, wonderful walking, drying room, no smoking. Super quiet holiday spot or overnight stay. Bed and Breakfast from £14. Brochure.

MIDDLETON. Mrs Pauline Bainbridge, Tossbeck Farm, Middleton, Kirkby Lonsdale, via Carnforth,

Lancs. LA6 2LZ (015242 76214). Tossbeck Farm is a 110 acre dairy and sheep farm situated in the beautiful unspoilt countryside of the Lune Valley midway between the market towns of Kirkby Lonsdale and Sedbergh. The farmhouse is a 16th century listed building featuring oak panelling. Ideally situated for visiting both the Lake District and the Yorkshire Dales. One family room and one double room, both spacious with washbasins and tea/coffee making facilities. Lounge with TV, dining room, visitors' bathroom and central heating. Bed and full English Breakfast from £12.50 with reductions for children and weekly stays. No smoking please.

MILNTHORPE. Mrs Carey, Homestead, Ackenswaithe, Milnthorpe LA7 7DH (015395 63708).

Small, friendly, non-smoking guest house situated in South Lakeland. Approximately 10 minutes by car from Kendal and conveniently positioned between the Lakes, Dales and Lancashire Border making an ideal base for walking and touring; we are close enough to the A6 and M6 motorway to be convenient for your overnight stop to and from Scotland. The small but busy market town of Milnthorpe is within strolling distance and the Nature Reserves at Leighton Moss and Silverdale are close by. En suite double, family, twin or standard single/twin rooms available. Bed and Breakfast from £16. Evening Meals by arrangement.

MILNTHORPE. Mrs Lynn Green, "Springlea", Heversham, Milnthorpe LA7 7EE (015395 64026).

Situated in South Lakeland, Springlea faces rolling farmland framed by woods and stone walls with the Kent estuary glinting between the trees. It is ideally positioned for the Lakes, Yorkshire Dales and the Morecambe Bay resorts. Historic houses, nature reserves and many other centres of attraction are within easy reach. Local pubs and restaurants serve good food at reasonable prices. There are twin and double en-suite rooms with central heating, TV and tea/coffee making facilities. A lounge, sunroom and terrace are available, as is safe off-road parking. Bed and Breakfast or Bed, Breakfast with Evening Meal. Open all year. Terms from £14.50 per person per night. AA QQQ Recommended.

CUMBRIA – THE LAKES (AND SO MUCH MORE!)

The magnificent Lakeland scenery attracts thousands of visitors each year, but there are many other unspoiled areas of the county well worth a visit. The Eden Valley is a walkers' and anglers' paradise, while the North Pennines (an Area of Outstanding Natural Beauty) is a haven for wildlife. Don't forget the county town of Carlisle, where traces of a rich history dating from pre-Roman times blend with excellent shopping and leisure facilities.

BANNERDALE VIEW
Mungrisdale, Near Penrith, Cumbria CA11 0XR
Tel: 017687 79691   Mike & Penny Sutton

If you love the Lakes, but prefer to avoid the crowds, welcome to our centrally-heated 17th century Lakeland cottage. Surrounded on three sides by Fells and with a river running through the 2 acres of garden, a more peaceful and idyllic location would be hard to imagine. Though we have a double and a twin-bedded room, each with beverage making facilities, we only accept one booking at a time, for up to 4 people, so that the adjoining bathroom is for the exclusive use of that booking. There is also a toilet and wash basin on the ground floor, as well as a guests' lounge with colour TV. As retired hoteliers, we are renowned for good food and breakfasts to satisfy the heartiest appetites, although we provide a Continental Breakfast if you insist! Mountain or low level walks can be made from the Cottage and any part of the Lakes can easily be explored in the day by car. Well-behaved dogs are welcomed. We are a non-smoking establishment. Rates from £18. Dinner (pre-booking essential) £13.50. Brochure.

NEWBY BRIDGE. "Lakes End", Newby Bridge, Ulverston LA12 8ND (015395 31260). 🐾 *COMMEN-*

DED. AA QQQ. This very friendly Bed and Breakfast accommodation, ideally situated for touring Lake District, is located within 200 yards of the southern outfall of Lake Windermere. It is a lovely 1920's gentleman's residence within substantial terraced gardens and woods, which guests are encouraged to enjoy. A great place as a centre for sightseeing, walking, golf, etc. The spacious, tastefully furnished bedrooms are all en suite, each with tea/coffee making facilities and colour TV; central heating. Lots of free parking. Plenty of good eating places nearby. Free use of superb local Leisure Club. Bed and Breakfast from £17.50 per person per night.

NEWLANDS. Mrs M.A. Relph, Littletown Farm, Newlands, Keswick CA12 5TU (017687 78353).

Working farm. Littletown has all the facilities of a small hotel and most bedrooms are en suite. Situated in a peaceful part of the beautiful Newlands Valley, with surrounding hills providing excellent walking and climbing. Market towns of Keswick and Cockermouth, Lakes Derwentwater and Bassenthwaite all within easy distance. Farmhouse, though fully modernised, still retains a traditional character with comfortable lounge, dining room and cosy licensed bar. All bedrooms have tea-making facilities, heating and washbasins. Traditional four-course dinner (roast beef, lamb, etc) served six nights a week; full English breakfast every morning. Littletown Farm is featured in Beatrix Potter's "Mrs Tiggy Winkle". Ample parking. Dinner, Bed and Breakfast from £35 to £39 per person; Bed and Breakfast from £24 to £29 per person. SAE please.

Littletown farm

PENRITH. Mrs Mary Harris, Whitbarrow Farm, Penrith CA11 0XB (017684 83366). 🐾🐾 *COMMEN-*

DED. **Working farm.** A warm friendly welcome is extended to guests on our 255 acre dairy farm set in an attractive hilltop position with superb views of the Lakeland hills and over looks the Eden Valley. The accommodation consists of double/twin en suite rooms and a standard family room, all tastefully decorated to a high standard and with tea/coffee facilities and TV. Full central heating. Comfortable guests' lounge with open fire. Penrith and M6 seven miles, Ullswater five miles making the farm an ideal centre for touring the Lake District and Scottish Borders. Tariffs from £18.50 per person per day Bed and Breakfast. Mid week bookings accepted. SAE for brochure.

PENRITH. Mrs Jean Raynor, Blue Swallow Guest House, 11 Victoria Road, Penrith CA11 8HR (01768 866335). 🐾🐾 *COMMENDED.* A comfortable Victorian house set in the attractive market town of Penrith, ideally situated to explore the delightful Eden Valley, the wonderful scenery of the Lake District and the Yorkshire Dales National Park. For the golfing enthusiast Penrith boasts an 18 hole course and there are several more within easy driving distance. Resident proprietors Jean and Mel Raynor look forward to welcoming you whether you are on holiday, just breaking a long journey or in the area for business — you'll be made to feel at home. All rooms have colour TV, tea trays and central heating. Full and varied English breakfast served. Bed and Breakfast from £15 to £19 per person.

PENRITH. Mrs Eileen Lamond, Prospect House, Piper Lane, Kirkby Thore, Penrith CA10 1UP (017683 61672). Prospect House is situated in a quiet location on the edge of Kirkby Thore village in an elevated position with beautiful views of the Lake District hills to the west and the Pennines to the East. We are situated in the Eden Valley, nine miles south of Penrith and four miles north of Appleby on the A66. Ideal for walking and touring with easy access to Lakes, Yorkshire Dales and Scottish Borders. A special welcome awaits you in our Victorian farmhouse, with comfortable and friendly accommodation and a hearty English breakfast to start the day.

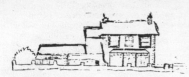

PENRITH. Mrs Mary Milburn, Park House Farm, Dalemain, Penrith CA11 0HB (017684 86212). *COMMENDED.* **Working farm.** Enjoy countryside tranquillity, relax in comfort taking in the stunning views of our Lakeland Fells. Three miles from Lake Ullswater or M6 Junction 40 or A592, entering via Dalemain Mansion (historic house) ignoring the "no cars" sign into the courtyard, then bear right along road. Cumbrian hospitality is assured with a welcome cup, home baking and a generous breakfast. Good evening meal available locally. Two family bedrooms (one en suite), electric blanket, heater, tea/coffee facilities, wash-basin; bathroom and shower room. TV lounge with open fire. Open April to October. Sorry no pets in house. Bed and Breakfast from £16 per person. Farm Holiday Bureau Member, Welcome Host Certificate.

PENRITH. Mr S.E. Bray, Norcroft Guest House, Graham Street, Penrith CA11 9LQ (Tel & Fax: 01768 862365). *COMMENDED.* Spacious Victorian house in a quiet area. Large and comfortable ensuite bedrooms with colour TV and beverage making facilities. We have two family suites, with main bedroom and separate connecting children's bedrooms. We have a very pleasant dining room. Residential licence. Private car park. Penrith is an ideal centre for touring the Lake District, the Eden Valley, Hadrian's Wall and the Borders. It is an ideal stopover for travellers going north to Scotland or south to holiday in England or the Continent. Bed and Breakfast from £16, Dinner from £10.50. A warm welcome awaits you. Children welcome. Directions: Leave M6 at Junction 40 into one way system, left at town hall opposite R.C. Church.

PENRITH. Tim and Jane Metcalfe, Home Farm, Edenhall, Penrith CA11 8SS (01768 881203). **Working farm.** A warm welcome awaits you at Home Farm, situated on the outskirts of the peaceful village of Edenhall three miles east of Penrith. We are ideally situated for seeing the Eden Valley, North Pennines, Hadrian's Wall and are conveniently located for the Lake District or en route to/from Scotland. Full English Breakfast, evening meals obtainable locally. Accommodation comprises double, family or twin rooms. Reduced rates for children. Bed and Breakfast from £16 per person.

PENRITH. Mrs C. Blundell, Albany House, 5 Portland Place, Penrith CA11 7QN (01768 863072). ETB *COMMENDED.* AA QQQ. Close to town centre, Albany House is a large mid-Victorian terraced house. A high standard of cleanliness, comfort and personal friendly attention is assured at all times. Five spacious nicely decorated bedrooms (one double, three triple, all with washbasins; one family en-suite). All have central heating, colour/satellite TV and tea/coffee making facilities. Situated close to M6, A6 and A66, ideal base for touring Lake District, Eden Valley, Hadrian's Wall, Scottish Borders and an excellent stopover between England and Scotland. Within easy reach are Lowther Leisure Park, sailing, wind surfing, fell walking, pony trekking, golf and swimming. Bed and Breakfast from £15.50.

PENRITH. Mrs Brenda Preston, Pallet Hill Farm, Penrith CA11 0BY (017684 83247). Pallet Hill Farm is pleasantly situated two miles from Penrith on the Penrith-Greystoke-Keswick road (B5288). It is four miles from Ullswater and has easy access to the Lake District, Scottish Borders and Yorkshire Dales. There are several sports facilities in the area — golf club, swimming pool, pony trekking; places to visit such as Lowther Leisure Park and the Miniature Railway at Ravenglass. Good farmhouse food and hospitality with personal attention. Double, single, family rooms; dining/sitting room. Children welcome, cot, high chair. Sorry no pets. Car essential, parking. Open Easter to November. Bed and Breakfast from £9.50 (reduced weekly rates). Reduced rates for children.

PENRITH. Mrs Jean Ashburner, Lattendales Farm, Berrier Road, Greystoke, Penrith CA11 0UE (017684 83474). Working farm, join in. Comfortable 17th century farmhouse in quiet attractive village five miles from Penrith. Ideal for touring the Northern Lakes. Accommodation comprises one twin room and two double rooms; lounge with colour TV. Children and pets welcome; reductions for children. Non-smoking. Bed and Breakfast from £14.50 to £15.50 per person. Directions, follow B5288 from Penrith and Lattendales Farm is first B&B on left in Berrier Road.

PENRITH. Angela and Ivor Davies, Woodland House Hotel, Wordsworth Street, Penrith CA11 7QY (01768 864177; Fax: 01768 890152; E-mail idavies a@cix.compulink.co.uk). 🏵🏵🏵 *COMMENDED.* Small, friendly and elegant licensed private hotel situated at the foot of Beacon Hill, and only five minutes' walk from the centre of the town. Large car park. All rooms are en-suite and have tea/coffee making facilities and colour TV. We serve delicious food using the best fresh local produce and, with notice, will gladly meet any special dietary requirements. Whether on business or pleasure an ideal base for exploring Lakes, Borders, Pennines, Eden Valley or stopover to/from Scotland. Library of maps and books for walkers, nature lovers and sightseers. Open all year. Sorry, no pets. The Hotel is NO SMOKING throughout. Bed and Breakfast from £26; Dinner from £9.50. AA QQQ, RAC Acclaimed. Brochure.

PENRITH. Mrs Ann Toppin, Gale Hall, Melmerby, Penrith CA10 1HN (01768 881254). Working farm. Mrs Ann Toppin welcomes guests to her home on a working beef/sheep farm 10 miles east of Penrith and the M6, a mile and a half from the peaceful village of Melmerby. Beautiful setting at the foot of the Pennines and with extensive views of the Lakeland Fells. Ideal for walking, convenient for the Lake District. Single, double, twin or family rooms available; cot and babysitting. Residents' lounge. Pets welcome by arrangement. Bed and Breakfast from £14; reductions for children under 12 years. Special diets catered for. Full English or Vegetarian Breakfast served. Excellent bar meals available locally.

PENRITH. Mrs C. Tully, Brandelhow Guest House, 1 Portland Place, Penrith CA11 7QN (01768 864470). A warm welcome assured at this AA Listed QQQ guest house offering a high standard of comfort and cleanliness. Five spacious, tastefully decorated bedrooms, all with hot and cold water, central heating, double glazing, colour TV and tea/coffee making facilities. Twin, double and family rooms available, including one excellent family room for five. Ideally situated, close to M6, A6 and A66, for touring the Lake District, Scottish Borders, Hadrian's Wall and for overnight stops en route to and from Scotland. Local amenities include Lowther Fun Park, golf, sailing and pony trekking. Bed and Breakfast from £15 double, £18 single inclusive. Weekly terms available.

SEDBERGH. Mrs Susan Sharrocks, Holmecroft, Station Road, Sedbergh LA10 5DW (015396 20754). Holmecroft nestles at the foot of the Howgill Fells on the edge of Sedbergh, a quaint old market town situated within the Yorkshire Dales National Park. 'Twixt Lakes and Dales, Holmecroft is an ideal base for walking or touring, also for breaking the journey to and from Scotland. We offer friendly hospitality in bright comfortable accommodation comprising one twin and two double rooms each with washbasins, and views to the fells. Guests have their own sitting room with television. Private parking. Pets by arrangement. No-smoking please. Open all year. Bed and Breakfast £16. Arrive as a stranger, leave as a friend.

Terms quoted in this publication may be subject to increase if rises in costs necessitate

SHAP. Mr and Mrs D. L. and M. Brunskill, Brookfield, Shap, Penrith CA10 3PZ (01931 716397). AA Listed. Fire Certificate granted. Situated one mile from M6 Motorway (turn off at Shap interchange No. 39), first accommodation off motorway. Excellent position for touring Lakeland, or overnight accommodation for travelling north or south. Central heating throughout, renowned for good food, comfort and personal attention. All bedrooms are well appointed and have colour TV and tea/coffee making facilities; en suite available. Diningroom where delicious home cooking is a speciality. Well-stocked bar. Residents' lounge. Sorry, no pets. Open from February to December. Terms sent on request. Car essential — ample parking.

TROUTBECK. Gwen and Peter Parfitt, Hill Crest, Troutbeck, Penrith CA11 0SH (017684 83935). Gwen and Peter assure you of a warm and friendly welcome at Hill Crest, their unique Lakeland home which offers two en suite double/family rooms, one twin room. Home cooking, choice of menu including vegetarian; non smoking lounge/dining room, early morning tea, bedtime drinks; packed lunches. Panoramic mountain views. Aira Force waterfalls, Ullswater 10 minutes, Keswick 15 minutes, a good base for walking, boating, touring, Lakes, Hadrian's Wall and the Borders. Books, maps and hints from Gwen on what to see. Walkers, children and dogs welcome. Bed and Breakfast £14 per person twin room, £16 per person en suite rooms. Children half price sharing. Dinner from £5 (optional). Weekly rates. 10 minutes Junction 40 M6. At Hill Crest we aim to create a relaxed and informal atmosphere where guests are treated as part of the family. Highly recommended by previous guests.

TROUTBECK. Mrs Anne Ross, Greenah Crag Farm, Troutbeck, Penrith CA11 0SQ (017684 83233). Ron and Anne welcome you to their lovely 17th century farmhouse. Ideal for touring the Northern Lakes, Ullswater five miles. Accommodation comprises one double en suite, one double and one twin-bedded rooms, all with tea making facilities. Lounge with colour TV. Non-smoking only. Sorry, no pets. Bed and Breakfast from £15. Self catering units also available.

ULLSWATER. Mrs S. Hunter, Grove Foot Farm, Watermillock, Penrith CA11 0NA (017684 86416). **Working farm.** Grove Foot is a 90 acre dairy farm just off the A66 and two miles from Lake Ullswater. The house, built around 1650, has oak beams and open fires and sleeps six guests. Close by are historic houses and gardens, fishing, swimming pools, golf and pony trekking. Open March to October. Children welcome. Sorry, no pets. Bed and Breakfast from £14.

ULLSWATER (3 miles). Mrs Julia Thompson, Gill House, Stainton, Penrith CA11 0ES (01768 890785). ♥♥ *COMMENDED.* Lovely house in own grounds situated in pretty village. Good bar meals just five minutes' walk. Central heating, TV lounge, twin and double bedrooms with washbasins, TV and tea/coffee making facilities. One room en-suite. All home comforts with personal attention. Ideal base for touring Lakes or stop-off for Scotland. Open March to October. Two miles from M6 (Exit 40); on A66 Keswick road. Bed and Breakfast from £16 per person. Reductions for children.

UNDERBARROW. Mrs D.M. Swindlehurst, Tranthwaite Hall, Underbarrow, Near Kendal LA8 8HG (015395 68285). Working farm. Commended and AA Selected for excellent standards of Comfort and Quality.

Tranthwaite Hall is said to date back to 1186, a charming olde world farmhouse with beautiful oak beams, doors and rare black iron fire range. This working dairy/sheep farm has an idyllic setting half a mile up an unspoilt country lane where deer can be seen, herons fish in the stream and there are lots of wild flowers. This is a very peaceful and quiet retreat yet only minutes from all Lakes and local attractions. Attractive bedrooms, all en suite with tea/coffee making facilities, hair dryer and radio. Full central heating. Lounge with colour TV. Full English breakfast is served with milk and eggs from our farm, plus home made jam and marmalade. We like guests to enjoy our home and garden as much as we do. Walking, pony trekking and many good country pubs and inns nearby. Bed and Breakfast from £18 to £20.

WIGTON NEAR. Derek E. Knight, Fiddleback Farm, Westwoodside, Near Wigton CA7 8BA (016973 42653). Fiddleback, originally called "The Folly", dates back to the 1600's with alterations being completed in 1709.

Situated in its own grounds Fiddleback offers the discerning traveller a comfortable and peaceful stay. Amidst its old world charm is the well stocked pine and curio shop plus tea rooms. Positioned just off the A595 six miles west of Carlisle, makes us the ideal base for the Lakes, Hadrian's Wall and the Scottish Borders. Accommodation consists of three family rooms of which one is en suite. Open all year round with prices starting from £15 for Bed and Breakfast. Evening Meals are available in our licensed dining room. AA QQQ Recommended.

WINDERMERE. Gill and Barry Pearson, Broadlands Guest House, 19 Broad Street, Windermere LA23 2AB (Tel & Fax: 015394 46532). ♥ ♥ *COMMENDED.* AA Listed. A warm welcome awaits you at Broadlands

overlooking Elterthwaite Gardens in the centre of Windermere. It is close to all amenities and is an ideal base for the Lake District, being only 300 yards from train/coach station and convenient for the Lakes, walks, tours, etc. Car not essential though public parking is available. Double, twin and family rooms en suite and have colour TV, central heating and tea/coffee making facilities. Substantial full English breakfast or vegetarian breakfast provided. Bed and Breakfast from £15 to £20. Reductions for children. Small dogs by arrangement. Open all year. All major credit cards accepted.

WINDERMERE. Mr P. Whitton, Glenville Hotel, Lake Road, Windermere LA23 2EQ (015394 43371; E-mail: Clg Hse@aol.Com). ♥ ♥ *COMMENDED.* AA/RAC

Highly Acclaimed. "Glenville" stands comfortably in its own grounds perfectly positioned for access to all amenities. The hotel retains a host of original features and is full of character with a genuine country house atmosphere and a high standard of comfort and cleanliness. En suite bedrooms have colour TV, tea/coffee making facilities. Licensed, with comfortable lounge. Superb car park. Bed and Breakfast from £17 to £24 per person. Reductions for children. Mid-week bookings welcome. Please telephone for room availability.

OUT AND ABOUT IN CUMBRIA

Take a trip back in time on a narrow-gauge railway: The Lakeside and Haverthwaite runs through the beautiful Leven Valley, Ravenglass and Eskdale travels 7 miles from the coast up into the fells, and the South Tynedale Railway offers a journey through a beautiful North Pennine Valley.

The perfect way to appreciate the magnificent Lakeland scenery is on a leisurely Lake cruiser — Ullswater, Coniston, Derwentwater all have scheduled services daily in season.

WINDERMERE. College House, College Road, Windermere LA23 1BU (015394 45767). A non-smoking, spacious Victorian family home offering a warm and friendly welcome, in a quiet area close to village centre and railway station. Some rooms have superb mountain views, all are either en suite or have private bathroom, colour TV, tea/coffee making facilities and full central heating. We have plenty of interesting local guides, maps, books, pictures and fresh flowers plus a small private garden with furniture for guests' use. We can pre-arrange local minibus tours, hire of mountain bikes or horse riding facilities. Bed and Breakfast from £17 to £24. Vegetarians welcome. Private car spaces and garage for bikes.

WINDERMERE. Mrs Sandra Garside, Boston House, 4 The Terrace, Windermere LA23 1AJ (015394 43654). 👑👑👑 *COMMENDED.* A delightful Victorian Gothic building dating from 1849. Situated in a peaceful cul-de-sac on the edge of the village with panoramic views of the lake and surrounding fells, yet close to village centre, train and coach stations (collection by arrangement). Five spacious double/twin/family en suite rooms with tea trays, hairdryers, radio alarms and colour TV; two have four-poster beds and another has an oak half-tester bed — very romantic! Choose hearty breakfasts from an extensive menu; superb home cooked dinners are also available. Restaurant/residential licence. No smoking please. Private parking. Bed and Breakfast from £20 to £26 per person. Brochure on request. RAC Highly Acclaimed.

WINDERMERE. Mr and Mrs R. Tyson, Holly-Wood Guest House, Holly Road, Windermere LA23 2AF (015394 42219). Comfortable accommodation in elegant stone-built Lakeland guest house. Situated in quiet position away from the main road but within easy walking distance of buses, trains and local amenities. An ideal central base for touring the Lake District. Also within easy reach of Morecambe Bay and the Dales. Single, double, twin and family rooms are available (some en-suite). Central heating, tea/coffee makers, colour TV. Reductions for children and long stays. Low Season Mini Breaks. Open March to November. Bed and Breakfast from £14 per person. RAC Acclaimed. Sorry no pets. SAE please for brochure and tariff.

WINDERMERE. Firgarth Private Hotel, Ambleside Road, Windermere LA23 1EU (015394 46974). Elegant Victorian house on Windermere to Ambleside Road with a Lake viewpoint nearby. The front rooms overlook a tree lined paddock, the rear rooms overlook Wynlass Beck where ducks, rabbits and the occasional deer can be seen. We have a private lounge for guests to relax in. All bedrooms have colour TV and tea/coffee making facilities. Non smoking rooms available. Ample private parking. A good selection of restaurants available nearby. Rooms are available from £16.50 per person all with en-suite facilities. Ring Mary or Brian who will be happy to discuss your requirements.

WINDERMERE. Mrs R. Phelps, Winbrook House, 30 Ellerthwaite Road, Windermere LA23 2AH (015394 44932). 👑👑 *COMMENDED.*

A friendly welcome awaits you at Winbrook House which is convenient for village and lake. Ideal touring centre. We offer personal service, together with excellent English cooking, under the personal supervision of the proprietors. All rooms are decorated to a high standard; residents' lounge with colour TV; full central heating. All bedrooms have private showers/baths, colour TV, tea/coffee making facilities, and most have private toilets. Access to rooms at all times. Private parking. Full Fire Certificate. AA Listed, RAC Acclaimed. Open all year. Bed and Breakfast from £16 to £21.

WINDERMERE. Greenriggs Guest House, 8 Upper Oak Street, Windermere LA23 2LB (015394 42265). 👑👑 *COMMENDED.*

A small family-run guest house situated in a quiet cul-de-sac off the main Windermere to Bowness road close to a park and all other amenities including trains and buses. All our bedrooms have tea making facilities and colour TV and the majority are en suite. Also available is a TV lounge where you may relax at your leisure. We aim to make sure you feel at home whatever time of year you wish to visit. Our hearty full English breakfast is sure to set you up for the day. Bed and Breakfast from £14 to £21; Evening Meal from £9.75 to £10.50. Brochure available.

Key to
Tourist Board Ratings

The Crown Scheme
(England, Scotland & Wales)

Covering hotels, motels, private hotels, guesthouses, inns, bed & breakfast, farmhouses. Every Crown classified place to stay is inspected annually. *The classification:* Listed then 1-5 Crown indicates the range of facilities and services. Higher quality standards are indicated by the terms APPROVED, COMMENDED, HIGHLY COMMENDED and DELUXE.

The Key Scheme
(also operates in Scotland using a Crown symbol)

Covering self-catering in cottages, bungalows, flats, houseboats, houses, chalets, etc. Every Key classified holiday home is inspected annually. *The classification:* 1-5 Key indicates the range of facilities and equipment. Higher quality standards are indicated by the terms APPROVED, COMMENDED, HIGHLY COMMENDED and DELUXE.

The Q Scheme
(England, Scotland & Wales)

Covering holiday, caravan, chalet and camping parks. Every Q rated park is inspected annually for its quality standards. The more √ in the Q – up to 5 – the higher the standard of what is provided.

WINDERMERE. Mrs P. Wood, The Haven Guest House, Birch Street, Windermere LA23 1EG (015394 44017). The Haven is a comfortable Victorian Guest House conveniently located in the attractive lakeside village of Windermere, a short walk from the railway station, restaurants, shops and all local amenities. Sports such as walking, mountaineering, pony trekking and water ski-ing can be enjoyed in the area. All rooms have TV and tea/coffee making facilities. Open all year. Bed and Breakfast from £15. Vegetarians catered for. Reductions for children. No smoking. Parking. Brochure on request. AA QQ.

WINDERMERE. St. John's Lodge, Lake Road, Windermere LA23 2EQ (015394 43078). ♣♣♣ *COMMENDED.* A private hotel situated midway between Windermere and the Lake, close to all amenities. AA, RAC Highly Acclaimed, Les Routiers. All 14 bedrooms have en suite facilities and are comfortably furnished with colour TV and tea/coffee making facilities. Centrally heated throughout. There is a comfortable lounge for residents, and a friendly bar, where you may take an aperitif before enjoying a four course dinner which has been personally prepared by the chef/proprietor. Bed and Breakfast from £18.50 to £23; Evening Meal £10.50. Bargain Breaks available.

WINDERMERE. John and Liz Christopherson, Villa Lodge, Cross Street, Windermere LA23 1AE (Tel & Fax: 015394 43318). ♣♣ *COMMENDED.* Friendliness and cleanliness guaranteed. Extremely comfortable accommodation in peaceful area overlooking Windermere village, yet two minutes from station. All seven bedrooms are tastefully decorated, mostly en-suite (some four-posters), with colour TV, tea/coffee making facilities and full central heating. Most have magnificent views of the Lake and mountains. Access to rooms at all times. Superb English Breakfast served in our delightful dining room. Vegetarian and special diets catered for. Open all year. Special offers November-March. Safe, private parking for six cars. An excellent base for exploring the whole of the Lake District. Bed and Breakfast from £16. AA QQQ. Ring John and Liz Christopherson for details.

WINDERMERE. Mick and Angela Brown, Haisthorpe Guest House, Holly Road, Windermere LA23 2AF (Tel & Fax: 015394 43445). ♣♣ *COMMENDED.* RAC Highly Acclaimed and AA QQQ family-run Victorian guest house concentrating on high standards of accommodation and service at reasonable prices. We are situated in a quiet central area of Windermere and convenient for the local train/coach station (free collection by arrangement). All rooms have colour TV with satellite channel, tea/coffee facilities and hair dryers. Five rooms are en suite and one has private bathroom. No smoking in bedrooms. Pets by prior arrangement. Private off-street parking. Credit cards accepted. Bed and Breakfast from £13 to £19, with reductions for long stays, reductions for children when sharing. Evening Meal available from £7.50.

WINDERMERE. Mr and Mrs J.N. Fowles, Rockside Guest House, Ambleside Road, Windermere

LA23 1AQ (Tel & Fax: 015394 45343). ❦ ❦ A Lakeland Guest House, full of character, Rockside is RAC Acclaimed. Centrally situated two minutes from the railway station, shops and restaurants of Windermere. Parking for 12 cars. All bedrooms have washbasins, central heating, colour TV, clock, radio and telephone. Most rooms en-suite with tea/coffee making facilities. A choice of Breakfast is served from 8.30am to 9.15am. Open all year for singles, twins, doubles and families to enjoy "the most beautiful corner of England". Car routes and walks arranged if required. Bed and Breakfast from £14.50 to £22.50. Reductions for children. Visa, Mastercard and Access accepted.

WINDERMERE. Mrs B.J. Butterworth, Orrest Head House, Windermere LA23 1JG (015394 44315).

This beautiful house is part 17th century, located in three acres of lush garden and woodland. Nestling above Windermere village it enjoys superb views of the Lake and mountains. From February to December guests are assured of comfortable Bed and Breakfast accommodation in five en-suite rooms, three double and two twin, all non-smoking and with washbasins, central heating, tea-making facilities. Separate dining room. Private parking for up to 10 cars. The ideal choice for a really relaxing holiday. Terms from £19.50 Bed and Breakfast.

WINDERMERE. Brian and Margaret Fear, Cambridge House, 9 Oak Street, Windermere LA23 1EN

(015394 43846). ETB Listed *COMMENDED.* Cambridge House is a traditional, family run Lakeland guesthouse situated in the middle of Windermere village convenient for all amenities including buses and trains. It is also central for all South Lakes beauty spots. One hour to Keswick and the Northern Lakes and only 20 minutes from M6 Junction 36. Double, single, twin and family rooms are available; all are modern and comfortable and include en suite facilities, colour TV and tea/coffee making. A full English, Continental or vegetarian breakfast is provided. Centrally heated throughout. Bed and Breakfast from £15. Open all year.

WINDERMERE. Roger Wallis and James Peters, Holly Park House, 1 Park Road, Windermere LA23

2AW (015394 42107). ❦ ❦ *COMMENDED.* An elegant stone-built house which has retained all its Victorian character but offers every comfort and is furnished to a high standard. All the spacious bedrooms have a private bathroom or shower room, colour TV and tea/coffee making facilities. Licensed bar. Holly Park House is situated in a quiet district but is convenient for shops, train, bus and tour services and restaurants. A warm welcome is assured from the resident proprietors. Bed and Breakfast from £17. Credit cards welcomed. AA QQQQ, RAC Highly Acclaimed.

PUBLISHER'S NOTE

DERBYSHIRE

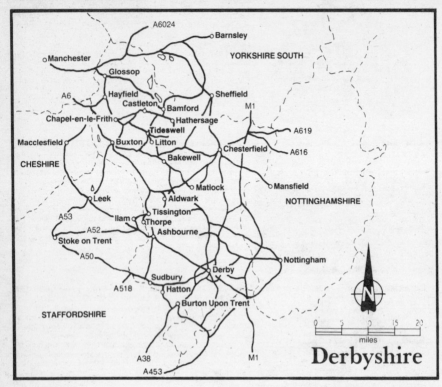

Derbyshire

AMBERGATE. Mrs Carol Oulton, Lawn Farm, Whitewells Lane, off Holly Lane, Ambergate DE56 2DN (01773 852352). 🐄 **Working farm, join in.** Enjoy comfortable bed and breakfast accommodation on a working beef and sheep farm, one mile from the A6 at Ambergate. Ambergate has many woodland walks and a picturesque canal which leads to nearby Cromford, home of the Arkwright Mill. Matlock Bath is 10 miles away and offers many attractions including the Cable Cars. Within easy travelling distance of Haddon Hall, Chatsworth House and Gardens, the Peak District National Park and the National Tramway Museum at Crich. Accommodation comprises double en-suite room and family room with handbasin. Terms on request from £15 per night. Children welcome at reduced rates. Pets welcome by arrangement. Non-smokers preferred.

ASHBOURNE. Mrs Paula Catlin, Jinglers Inn/The Fox & Hounds, Belper Road, Bradley, Ashbourne DE6 3EN (01335 370855). ETB Listed. Character Country Inn famous for having two names, set adjacent to 18 acres. Pub food is served together with Real Ale and the menu ranges from filled cobs to steaks. Pool/family room, public/lounge bar, pool and darts. Six letting bedrooms for Bed and Breakfast; some en suite, all have separate entrances and tea/coffee making facilities. Children and pets are most welcome. Conveniently placed for Derbyshire Dales, Alton Towers, Chatsworth House, Dovedale, American Adventure and several golf courses. Carsington Water is only two miles where sailing, wind surfing, cycle hire and fishing are available. Clay pigeon shooting. Everybody welcome. Licensed site for 34 caravans with hook-ups and hard standings.

ASHBOURNE near. Mrs Dot Barker, Waterkeepers Cottage, Mappleton, Near Ashbourne DE6 2AB (01335 350444). Tourist Board Listed. Cosy cottage in the Dove Valley village of Mappleton with small patio and garden for visitors. It lies to the right of the "Okeover Arms", the village pub. Visitors have use of car park. Everyone is sure of a friendly welcome. Reduced prices for under 12 years. Dogs welcomed by prior arrangement. Excellent food, nicely presented. Special diets catered for by prior arrangement. Bed and Breakfast from £16 per person per night; four night breaks £60 per person.

ASHBOURNE. Alan and Liz Kingston, Old Boothby Farm, The Green, Ashbourne DE6 1EE (01335 342044).

The converted Hayloft and Stables of our 17th century farmhouse are an idyllic location for your stay in the "Gateway to the Peak District". Just a five minute level walk to the centre of Ashbourne with its historic pubs and wide variety of restaurants. Handy for visiting Alton Towers, Dovedale, Buxton, Matlock and numerous stately homes. Excellent walking country. The Hayloft with its verandah, exposed beams, log fire, fully equipped kitchen, lounge with colour TV, two double bedrooms and one twin bunk bedroom is ideal for party or family bookings; cot and high chair available. The Stables studio flat with en suite facilities, king-size bed, colour TV and kitchen is the perfect setting for that romantic break away from it all. Bed and full English, or alternative, Breakfast from £17.50 per person per night. Also let as self catering accommodation from £15 per person per night low season.

ASHBOURNE. Mrs E.J. Harrison, Little Park Farm, Mappleton, Ashbourne DE6 2BR (01335 350 341). *COMMENDED.* **Working farm.**

This 125 acre dairy farm is situated in the peaceful Dove Valley, ideally placed for the Derbyshire Dales, National Trust properties and Alton Towers. Nearby cycle hire, five minutes' ride from Ashbourne, and in walking distance of the village local, where bar meals are served. Plenty of wildlife and beautiful walks, ideal place for unwinding. The oak beamed listed farmhouse is over 300 years old and is tastefully furnished with lounge (colour TV), diningroom (separate tables, tea making facilities); two double and one twin-bedded rooms with washbasins; bathroom and toilet. Sorry no pets. Open March to end of October. Bed and Breakfast from £15. Non smoking establishment.

ASHBOURNE. Mrs Paula Coker Mayes, The Coach House, The Firs, Ashbourne DE6 1HF (01335 300145). ETB Listed *HIGHLY COMMENDED.*

A private house, formerly a Victorian Coach House, now offering its guests luxurious accommodation and warm hospitality in a quiet location near Ashbourne town centre. We have three ground floor double rooms ranging from small and cosy to sumptuously panelled with en suite and a handcrafted four-poster bed. All the usual facilities are offered. Rooms include TV, tea and coffee tray, central heating and a few little extras to make your stay memorable. Breakfast is cooked individually to order from our menu and evening meals and packed lunches are available by arrangement. Bed and Breakfast from £16.50 to £25 per person per night, discounts for longer stays. Off road parking. Open all year. Children and pets welcome. Non-smoking. Brochure available.

ASHBOURNE. Mrs Catherine Brandrick, Sidesmill Farm, Snelston, Ashbourne DE6 2GQ (01335 342710). Tourist Board Listed *COMMENDED.*

Peaceful dairy farm located on the banks of the River Dove. A rippling mill stream flows quietly past the 18th century stone-built farmhouse. Delicious English breakfast and the warmest of welcomes are guaranteed. Comfortable accommodation; guests' own lounge, diningroom; bathroom; TV in lounge. Ideal base for touring: within easy reach of Dovedale, Alton Towers, stately homes and many other places of interest. Open Easter-October. Car necessary, parking available. Bed and Breakfast from £15 per person. A non-smoking establishment.

ASHBOURNE. Mrs A.M. Whittle, Stone Cottage, Green Lane, Clifton, Ashbourne DE6 2BL (01335 343377). ♥♥ *COMMENDED.*

This accommodation is in a charming 19th century cottage near to the quiet village of Clifton. It is not far from the National Trust property of Dovedale and within easy reach of Alton Towers and the historic houses of Chatsworth and Haddon Hall. Also close to Carsington Waters Leisure Centre. A warm welcome awaits guests in this Bed and Breakfast accommodation which comprises one double, one family and one twin rooms (all en suite); bathroom, toilet; sitting room; dining room. Large garden to relax in. Open all year with central heating. Pets by prior arrangement. Bed and Breakfast from £18; optional Dinner £9. Reductions for children under 10 years. Directions: leave Ashbourne on the A52 Leek-Uttoxeter road, travel one mile, turn left at signpost for Clifton, second house on the right.

ASHBOURNE near. Mrs Heathcote, Yerley Farm, Oakeover, Near Ashbourne DE6 2BR (01335 350244). Working farm.

Working farm set in 180 acres of beautiful countryside situated two miles north of Ashbourne. Ideal for walking in the Dales and visiting historic houses. Five miles from Alton Towers and within easy reach of the American Adventure Park. Lounge tastefully decorated. Cosy dining room with good wholesome cooking. One twin, two double rooms with washbasins. Central heating, log fires, colour TV. Bed and Breakfast from £15. Reductions for children. Non-smoking establishment.

ASHBOURNE near. Tony and Linda Stoddart, Cornpark Cottage, Swinscoe, Near Ashbourne DE6 2HR (01335 345041).

If you want tea and coffee making facilities in your room, we don't have them. We like to make it for you. No colour TV in your room either, we like to see you in the large lounge drinking coffee, watching TV and putting logs on the fire. How else can we make you feel at home? We have got beds, duvets, pillows and hot and cold water in the bathroom. We can pronounce "en suite" but we haven't got it. We have got en suite tennis court and a multi gym. We are 10 minutes from Dovedale or Alton Towers. So if you require friendliness, charm and wit send for a brochure or book direct — How much? £15 adult, £10 children. Also available, self catering in either cottage or static van. Brochures on request.

FREE entry offer for children on visits to HEIGHTS OF ABRAHAM, Matlock Bath when using our READERS' OFFER VOUCHER.

ASHBOURNE near. Mrs Carole Eastwood, The Old Kennels, Birdsgrove Lane, Mayfield, Near Ashbourne DE6 2BP (01335 344418). Tourist Board Listed. Set away from the road in a quiet and peaceful location with lovely views, the Old Kennels is only two miles from Ashbourne and its many surrounding attractions (Alton Towers eight miles). The accommodation comprises guests' dining room with colour TV, guests' bathroom with shower, and two roomy bedrooms, one with a double bed and one with a double and two single beds. Each bedroom has a colour TV and tea/coffee making facilities. Ample parking. Bed and Breakfast from £16. Open March to October. Further details on request.

ASHBOURNE near. Mrs H. Leason, Overdale, Lode Lane, Alstonefield, Near Ashbourne DE6 2FZ (01335 310206). Overdale is a beautiful, spacious house situated in one and a half acres of landscaped gardens, including shaded walks, orchard and lily pond. Alstonefield is a quiet, extremely pretty village adjacent to Dovedale, the spa towns of Buxton and Matlock, Chatsworth House and Haddon Hall. The guest house has full central heating, two family and five double bedrooms, all equipped with wash-basins; three toilets, bathroom. A charming sitting room and pleasant dining room complete this perfect holiday home in its exclusive setting. Bed and Breakfast including drink from £15. Open all year.

ASHBOURNE near. Mrs Mary Hollingsworth, Collycroft Farm, Near Ashbourne DE6 2GN (01335 342187). Tourist Board Listed COMMENDED. **Working farm.** AA QQQ Recommended. This is a 260-acre mixed farm located two miles south of Ashbourne on the A515, within easy reach of Alton Towers, Peak District and Carsington Water. Accommodation includes double room en suite, twin-bedded room and a family room; colour TV, tea/coffee making facilities and full central heating. All rooms overlook beautiful country views. A warm welcome awaits you at Collycroft Farm which is open all the year round for Bed and Breakfast from £17 to £19 per person including bedtime drink. Reductions for children.

ASHOVER. The Red Lion Inn, Butts Road, Ashover, Chesterfield S45 0EW (01246 590271). A picturesque Tudor Inn, in the very historic, pretty village of Ashover. Recently refurbished, with an extensive menu of home cooked foods. Activities nearby include fishing, shooting (clays), riding and country walks. Bed and Breakfast from £30 double, £45 en suite; Evening Meals available. Please write or telephone for further details.

BAKEWELL. Mrs Sheila Gilbert, Castle Cliffe Private Hotel, Monsal Head, Bakewell DE45 1NL (01629 640258). ✹✹ COMMENDED. Monsal Head is a popular beauty spot in the heart of the Derbyshire Dales. There are superb views from all the bedrooms in Castle Cliffe Hotel, some overlooking Monsal Dale and the famous via-duct. It is an ideal centre for visiting the dales, caverns and historic houses. Some of the hotel's three double, two family and four twin rooms have en suite shower/WC, all have tea making facilities. Centrally heated plus open fires in the lounge and bar. Food is home cooked with the emphasis on British dishes from old traditional recipes. Children welcome. Sorry, no pets. Christmas and New Year and Special mini Breaks available. Licensed. Bed and Breakfast from £24 to £27.50. AA Listed QQQ.

BAKEWELL. Mrs Julia Finney, Mandale House, Haddon Grove, Bakewell DE45 1JF (01629 812416). 🏵🏵 Relax in the warm and friendly atmosphere of our peaceful farmhouse situated on the edge of Lathkill Dale, now a nature reserve managed by English Nature. Our rooms have en suite facilities, colour TV and tea making equipment, and are on the ground floor making them suitable for disabled visitors. A varied breakfast menu is offered and packed lunches are available. Excellent local inns and restaurants a short drive away. Bed and Breakfast from £18 to £20. 10% reductions for weekly bookings. Three night Bargain Breaks available in March, April and October. No smoking in the house. Telephone for brochure.

BAKEWELL. Mrs Jenny Spafford, Barleycorn Croft, Sheldon, Near Bakewell DE45 1QS (01629 813636). A well converted small attached barn with private bathroom and TV lounge. Accommodates two, three or four people in a twin and/or double room with washbasins, shaver points, thermostatically controlled heaters and tea/coffee making facilities, creating a pleasant private apartment. Also provided: full English or vegetarian breakfast, ironing facilities, hairdryer; independent access with own key and private parking. Sheldon is a unique, unspoilt farming village with no through traffic, only three miles from Bakewell and ideal for visiting Chatsworth House, Haddon Hall, Matlock, Buxton and all parts of the Peak District. Open all year. Non-Smokers only please. Bed and Breakfast from £15 to £17.50. AA QQ Recommended.

BAKEWELL. Gayle and Hugh Tyler, Sheldon House, Chapel Street, Monyash, Near Bakewell DE45 1JJ (01629 813067). 🏵 *HIGHLY COMMENDED.* An 18th century listed building in the picturesque village of Monyash (five miles from Bakewell), in the heart of the Peak National Park. Recently renovated to a high standard, we offer comfortable accommodation and a friendly atmosphere. Three doubles with en-suite facilities (two with colour TV), guests' sittingroom. All rooms have central heating and tea/coffee making facilities. Ideal base for visits to Chatsworth House, Haddon Hall, Hardwick Hall and excellent for cycling and walking. Open all year round except Christmas. No smoking. Bed and Breakfast from £19.

BAKEWELL. Mrs P. Stanley, 'Wheel Cottage', Fennel Street, Ashford-in-the-Water, Near Bakewell (01629 814339). 'Wheel Cottage' is a delightful 18th century cottage in the unspoilt village of Ashford nestling by the River Wye just one and a half miles from the market town of Bakewell. Ashford is situated in the Peak National Park a few miles from attractions such as Chatsworth House and Haddon Hall. The village is famous for its Well Dressing and Sheep Wash Bridge and is surrounded by glorious walking country. Accommodation in two double and one single bedrooms with colour TV and tea/coffee making facilities. Children and pets welcome. Bed and Breakfast from £12.50, en suite from £17.50. Evening Meal by arrangement. Special diets catered for. Reductions off season from October to March. Open all year.

BAKEWELL near. Mr and Mrs Clarke, Upperdale House, Monsal Dale, Buxton SK17 8SZ (01629 640536). Tourist Board Listed. Idyllic riverside guesthouse enjoying a unique setting in the prettiest of Derbyshire Dales. Accommodation includes two double and two twin-bedded rooms, all en suite (one with private bathroom), with colour TV, tea/coffee facilities, full central heating and river views. Splendid local walks, numerous outdoor activities including trout fishing available. Closed Christmas and New Year. No pets. Sorry no smoking in the bedrooms. Monsal Dale signposted from A6 near Bakewell. Bed and Breakfast from £21 per person. Special off-peak Breaks available. Vegetarians/medical diets catered for.

BAMFORD. Pioneer House, Station Road, Bamford S30 2BN (01433 650638). 👑👑 *COMMENDED.* A warm welcome awaits you in our friendly and comfortable Edwardian home in the Hope Valley area of the Peak District. All our bedrooms have en suite/private facilities, colour TV, hair dryers, beverage tray, etc. Hearty breakfasts, including vegetarian are provided with packed lunches on request. We are open all year and have central heating and drying facilities. Off-road parking and secure cycle facilities, if required. Bamford is a tranquil village set in spectacular scenery, ideal for walking, sightseeing and just relaxing. We are a non-smoking establishment. Please telephone for further details.

BASLOW. Mrs Jean White, Rose Hill Farm, Over End, Baslow, Bakewell DE45 1SG (01246 583280). Tourist Board Listed. Working farm, join in. Modern farm house offering comfortable Bed and Breakfast. Full English breakfast; diets can be catered for. Accommodation comprises one double and one twin rooms with tea/coffee making facilities, TV; shared bathroom, shower and toilet, two washbasins. Views over Chatsworth Park and situated within walking distance of Chatsworth House, the village of Baslow and excellent bar food. Private parking for four cars. Good walking and climbing area. Children welcome. Bed and Breakfast from £13 to £15.

THE CHARLES COTTON HOTEL

The Charles Cotton is a small, comfortable hotel with 3 Crowns. The hotel lies in the heart of the Derbyshire Dales, pleasantly situated in the village square of Hartington, with nearby shops catering for all needs. It is renowned throughout the area for its hospitality and good home cooking. Pets and children welcome, and special diets catered for. The Charles Cotton makes the perfect centre to relax and enjoy the area, whether walking, cycling, pony trekking, brass rubbing or even hang gliding. Open Christmas and New Year.

**Hartington, near Buxton, Derbyshire SK17 0AL
Tel: 01298 84229; Fax: 01335 42742**

BUXTON. Mr Andrew McKerrow, Cotesfield Farm, Parsley Hay, Buxton SK17 0BD (01298 83256). A quiet, easily accessible, Listed farmhouse on a working farm overlooking the High Peak Trail and Upper Long Dale and less than one mile to the cycle hire centre. Guests have the benefit of accommodation separate from the farmhouse allowing guests to go "free range" yet still have the use of TV lounge, bathroom with shower and tea making facilities. The farm is central to some of the main natural attractions of the Peak District — Hartington Dale two miles, Bakewell eight miles, Lathkill six miles, Dovedale four miles, the Roaches eight miles, Monsal Dale 11 miles, Buxton eight miles; the High Peak Trail is 100 yards and accessible from the farm.

BUXTON. Mrs Ann Oliver, "Westlands", Bishop's Lane, St. John's Road, Buxton SK17 6UN (01298 23242). ETB Listed. Close to Staffordshire and Cheshire borders, this well established Bed and Breakfast is for non-smokers. Situated on country lane one mile from town centre and Opera House, Westlands offers three rooms with central heating, washbasins, TV and drinks making facilities. Full English Breakfast provided. Ample off-road parking available. Very convenient for Chatsworth House, the Potteries, etc. An excellent centre for walking in the Peak District. Golf facilities available locally. Rates from £15 per person for Bed and Breakfast. Weekly reductions. Special diets catered for by arrangement.

BUXTON. Jill and Bernard Harrison, Overglen Guest House, 4 White Knowle Road, Buxton SK17 9NH (01298 23004). ❦❦ *COMMENDED.*

A warm welcome awaits you at our comfortable Victorian home overlooking Buxton Country Park, just off the A515 Buxton to Ashbourne road on the southern edge of town. Buxton strides the hills of the High Peak District in this spectacular part of the country, and is a popular destination all year round for tourists. Accommodation comprises one double and one twin-bedded room, each with private bathroom and tea-making facilities. The house is centrally heated throughout, and there is a charming guest lounge with colour TV. Parking. No smoking. Good food freshly prepared. Hearty breakfast served. Bed and Breakfast £17.50; Dinner from £9.50.

BUXTON. Maria and Roger Hyde, Braemar, 10 Compton Road, Buxton SK17 9DN (01298 78050).

Guests are warmly welcomed all the year round into the friendly atmosphere of Braemar, situated in a quiet residential part of this spa town. Within five minutes' walk of all the town's many and varied attractions i.e., Pavilion Gardens, Opera House, swimming pool; golf courses, horse riding, walking, fishing, etc are all within easy reach in this area renowned for its scenic beauty. Many of the Peak District's famous beauty spots including Chatsworth, Haddon Hall, Bakewell, Matlock, Dovedale and Castleton are nearby. Accommodation comprises comfortable double and twin bedded rooms fully en suite with colour TV and hospitality trays, etc. Full English Breakfast served and diets catered for. Non-smokers preferred. Terms £18.95 inclusive for Bed and Breakfast. Weekly terms available.

BUXTON. Buxton View, 74 Corbar Road, Buxton SK17 6RJ (Tel & Fax: 01298 79222). ❦❦❦ *COMMENDED.* A friendly welcome awaits you at this stone built guesthouse with its pleasing garden and splendid views over Buxton and the surrounding hills. Only a short walk from this spa town's Georgian centre, the Peak National Park surrounds you with its glorious scenery and a host of varied attractions. Comfortable en suite rooms are provided with every thoughtful touch and a spacious guest lounge is stocked with maps and guide books. Delicious English breakfasts are served in the conservatory and you will be warmed by the interest we take in our guests; you will leave wishing you had stayed longer! Bed and Breakfast from £16 per person per night; Evening Meal available. Children and pets welcome. AA QQQ Recommended.

BUXTON near. P. Kneller, Candlemas Cottage, Damside Lane, Peak Forest, Near Buxton SK17 8EH (01298 24853). ETB Listed. Candlemas Cottage is peacefully situated in the heart of the Peak District National Park with its great variety of beautiful scenery, close to the borders of Yorkshire, Lancashire, Cheshire and Staffordshire; five miles from Buxton. Fabulous walking country, wild flowers and birds; within easy reach of the Pennine Way, Chatsworth, the Caverns, Derbyshire Dales and many other attractions. Welcoming hospitality, sumptuous breakfasts, lots of choice. Excellent evening meals available locally. Cosy lounge with log fire. The bedrooms have TV, electric blankets, bedside lights and tea/coffee making facilities. Drying facilities. Special diets by prior arrangement. Well behaved children and pets welcome. Directions: 200 yards off A623. Turn opposite Devonshire Arms, then sharp right by US Mail box. Bed and Breakfast from £14.50. Open all year.

CASTLETON. Mrs P.J. Webster, Hillside House, Pindale Road, Castleton S30 2WU (01433 620312). ❦❦ A large country house in landscaped gardens with panoramic views located on quiet outskirts of this historic village. Come and relax in a friendly atmosphere, emphasis on quality, comfort and good food. We offer clean, spacious twin and double rooms, also de luxe en suite, all have TV, radio and tea-making facilities. Start your day with hearty English or vegetarian breakfasts. Ample parking. Cycle lock up. Children welcome but no pets please. A central base for outdoor pursuits like walking, touring or cycling. Look at our caves or castle, visit our market towns or sit in the garden. A non-smoking establishment. Closed Christmas. From £17.50 per night. Brochure available.

CASTLETON. Mrs B. Johnson, Myrtle Cottage, Market Place, Castleton, Near Sheffield S30 2WQ (01433 620787). Myrtle Cottage is pleasantly situated near the village green in the picturesque village of Castleton, famous for its castle and caverns. It is an ideal base for walking, caving, hang-gliding or touring the Peak District and Derbyshire Dales. Buxton, Bakewell, Chatsworth House and the plague village of Eyam are within 20 minutes' drive. The guest accommodation comprises family, twin and double bedrooms all with private shower/toilet, colour TV and tea/coffee making facilities; sittingroom with TV and diningroom. One en suite ground floor room suitable for disabled guests. Central heating. Fire Certificate held. Parking. Regret no pets. Open all year (except Christmas) for Bed and Breakfast only.

Stoney Ridge
Granby Road, Bradwell, Derbyshire S30 2HU
Telephone: 01433 620538

Situated in a small village in the beautiful Hope Valley close to Castleton, this split-level bungalow has good views, established gardens and an indoor heated pool. Accommodation in three double and one twin bedrooms, three with private facilities. All have colour TV, tea/coffee making facilities, hairdryer, etc. Children over 10 years only. Pets welcome. Bed and Breakfast from £22 to £28 per person per night. Access/Visa/Switch/Delta accepted.

ETB ♕♕ Highly Commended   AA QQQQ Selected

CASTLETON. D. Broome and L. Garside, Kelseys Swiss House Hotel and Restaurant, How Lane, Castleton S30 2WJ (01433 621098). ♕ ♕ ♕ *COMMEN-*

DED. Situated in a historic village in the heart of the Peak District. Ideal centre for all beauty spots (Chatsworth House, Dovedale, Derwent Dams, Monsal Dale, Buxton, Bakewell, Tissington Trail, local caverns and castles, Matlock and many others). Stay with us in our family-run licensed restaurant and guest house with clean, comfortable accommodation. All rooms en-suite with colour TVs and tea-making facilities. You will be assured of excellent and interesting food — all diets catered for — with friendly service and hopefully good weather! Bed and Breakfast from £22.50; Evening Meal optional. Fire Certificate held. Private parking. Access to rooms all day. Please telephone or SAE for brochure.

CHAPEL-EN-LE-FRITH. Mrs Maureen Howarth, The Forge, Top o' th' Plane, Ashbourne Lane, Chapel-en-le-Frith SK12 6UG (01298 815172). The

Forge is on the south edge of town, half a mile from A6 old road. Above the residential area overlooking the moors, this unique Listed building (c. 1797) is in a peaceful garden setting. Ideal for walking and touring the Dales and Peak National Park and visiting stately homes and many places of interest including Stockport and Manchester. The accommodation comprises three double (one en suite), one twin-bedded room; bathroom includes shower and WC, plus separate WC; breakfast/sitting room with TV. Central heating. Parking. Open all year. Directions: from Buxton on approaching bypass take slip road for Chapel-en-le-Frith, take third turning on left into Ashbourne Lane. After white cottage at bottom of hill take third driveway on left, signposted Top o' th' Plane. Forward through courtyard. Bed and Breakfast from £15.

CHESTERFIELD. Mrs Hopkinson, South View, 95 Church Lane, North Wingfield, Chesterfield S42 5HR (01246 850091). Tourist Board Listed *COMMEN-*

DED. Spacious late Victorian farmhouse standing in one acre of land on the edge of village three miles from M1 Junction 29. Easy access to Hardwick Hall, Chesterfield, Matlock, Crich, etc. Guests welcome to watch TV in family lounge. Central heating. Children over eight years welcome. Off road parking. Open all year. No smoking. Terms: £30 double, £15 single.

CHESTERFIELD. Abigails Guest House, 62 Brockwell Lane, Chesterfield S40 4EE (01246 279391).

👑👑 *COMMENDED.* Abigails offers accommodation in seven en suite bedrooms all having TVs, tea/coffee making facilities and central heating; ground floor rooms available. Relax taking breakfast in the conservatory overlooking our garden with pond and waterfall. Rooms available for the sole use of non-smokers. Extensive views of Chesterfield and surrounding moorlands. Children welcome, cot available. Dogs accepted by prior arrangement. Special diets catered for. Car park. Open over Christmas and New Year. Weekly rates available. Terms from £19.50.

DERBY.Mr and Mrs J. Richardson, Rangemoor Park Hotel, 67 Macklin Street, Derby DE1 1LF (01332 347252; Fax: 01332 369319).

👑 Long established family-run Hotel. Privately owned and run by the present owners since the late 70s. The hotel is modern with traditional standards offering outstanding hospitality and comfort. All 24 bedrooms have colour TV and tea/coffee making with 13 also having en suite facilities, direct-dial telephone and hair dryer. Ideally situated just a few minutes' walk from the centre of Derby. For your convenience there is ample free car parking, own front door key and night porter. Whether for business or holiday the proprietors pride themselves on personal and attentive service.

EDALE. Sue and Tony Favell, Skinners' Hall, Edale S30 2ZE (01433 670281; Fax: 01433 670481).

Attractive 18th century home standing in a delightful country garden with grounds bordering the River Noe, small lake, ducks and fish! The spacious bedrooms enjoy spectacular views and offer en suite bathrooms, colour TV and tea/coffee making facilities, hair dryers, etc. Edale, one of the most beautiful valleys in Britain, lies at the foot of the Pennine Way and is an ideal base for other beauty spots and places of interest in the Peak National Park. Local activities include walking, golf, pony trekking, hang gliding, potholing, tennis, rock climbing, cross-country ski-ing and fishing on the famous Ladybower Reservoir. Bed and Breakfast £22.50 per person per day; £125 per week. Please send for our brochure.

GLOSSOP. Margaret Child, Rock Farm, Glossop SK13 9JZ (01457 861086). Peace and quiet, friendly service and even a few farmyard pets. Situated in the hills above Glossop, with beautiful scenery in every direction. Looking out over Kinder Scout, the highest peak in the National Park, we are well placed for touring both Dark and White Peak areas. Walks from the doorstep, and plenty of pubs nearby offering good food. Though remote, our central location provides an attractive stopover as well as access to all major cities of the North West. We offer a double and a twin-bedded room, both with beamed ceilings, colour TV, radio and tea/coffee facilities. Guest bathroom with shower, and guest lounge. Bed and Breakfast from £15. Please send for colour leaflet.

BED & BREAKFAST
ROCK FARM
IN THE PEAK DISTRICT

DERBYSHIRE

The major portion of the Peak District, England's first National Park, lies within the county, high wind-swept heather moors and gritstone outcrops providing a vivid contrast to the softer rural landscapes of the south. Derbyshire's rich industrial heritage can be traced at Arkwright's Mill, Cromford; National Tramway Museum, Crich; Peak District Mining Museum, Matlock Bath; Royal Crown Derby Works, Derby, plus a host of other fascinating exhibitions and museums.

HARTINGTON. The Manifold Inn, Hulme End, Hartington SK17 0EX (01298 84537). ✿✿✿ The Manifold Inn is a 200 year old coaching inn now owned by Frank and Bridgette Lipp. It offers warm hospitality and good "pub food" at sensible prices. This lovely mellow stone inn nestles on the banks of the River Manifold opposite the old toll house that once served the turnpike and river ford. All guests' accommodation is in the converted old stone blacksmith's shop in the secluded rear courtyard of the inn. The bedrooms have en suite shower, colour TV, tea/coffee facilities and telephones. Bed and Breakfast £20 to £30. Brochure available.

HATHERSAGE. Mrs Jean Wilcockson, Hillfoot Farm, Castleton Road, Hathersage, Near Sheffield S30 1AH (01433 651673). Tourist Board Listed *COMMENDED.* Welcome Host, East Midlands Tourist Board Member. Newly built accommodation onto existing farmhouse offering comfortable, well appointed, en suite rooms. All with central heating, colour TV, tea/coffee making, hair dryer and comfortable easy chairs. We have a large car park and public telephone for guests' use. Excellent home cooked food including vegetarian meals. Bed and Breakfast from £17 to £20 per person. We are situated in the heart of the Peak District, ideal for walking or visiting Chatsworth House, Bakewell, Castleton, Edale and many more places of interest. Current Fire Certificate held. Open all year. Non-smokers.

HATHERSAGE. Mrs M.K. Venning, 'The Old Vicarage', Church Bank, Hathersage, Via Sheffield S30 1AB (01433 651099). ✿✿ The Old Vicarage, dating back to 1700, is situated on a hill, five minutes' walk from the village, with glorious views of the Hope Valley. Charlotte Bronte stayed here in 1845 and based her novel 'Jane Eyre' on the village and vicarage. Little John's Grave is in the local churchyard and Robin Hood's Cave nearby. Hathersage is a delightful village and conveniently situated for Chatsworth House and Adventure Playground, the Derwent Valley Reservoir, the Pennine Way, Castleton caves and castle. There is trout fishing on the reservoir and excellent walking all around. Superb bird-watching. Bed and Breakfast from £18 to £22, reductions for children.

ILAM. Mrs M. Richardson, Throwley Hall Farm, Ilam, Ashbourne DE6 2BB (01538 308202 or 308243). ✿✿ *COMMENDED.* Situated on a working beef and sheep farm in quiet countryside near the Manifold Valley, on the public road from Ilam to Calton. Within easy reach of Dovedale and Alton Towers, also stately homes. Accommodation comprises two double and two twin rooms, two rooms en suite, all with washbasins and TVs. Dining/sitting room with colour TV. Full central heating, also open fire. Tea/coffee making facilities. Bed and Breakfast from £17. Reduced rates for children, cot and high chair available.

MATLOCK. Mrs Lynda Buxton, Winstaff Guest House, Derwent Avenue, Matlock DE4 3LX (01629 582593). ✿✿ *APPROVED.* Winstall is a large late Victorian semi, standing in a quiet cul-de-sac with the garden going down to the River Derwent. Fishing can be enjoyed in this quiet conservation area and on the opposite side of river there is a park. At the same time Winstall is only five minutes' walk from town centre and bus and train stations. Accommodation comprises five double rooms, three with washbasins and two en suite; one en suite family room which sleeps four, and one twin room with washbasin. All are centrally heated and have colour TV and tea/coffee making facilities. Parking available. Open all year. Bed and Breakfast from £18 per person.

MATLOCK BATH. Mrs P. Clayton, Woodlands View, 226 Dale Road, Matlock Bath DE4 3RT (01629 55762). ✿ Ideal for tourists and only three minutes from the railway station. Close to shops and restaurants and beautiful scenery around. Two double, one family and one twin-bedded rooms; two bathrooms and three toilets. Open from January to December with Bed and Breakfast from £12.50 per person per night. Children half price. Tea making facilities in all rooms. Central heating. Children are welcome and pets permitted. Only one minute to the new tourist attraction "The Heights of Abraham Cable Car". Telephone for further details.

MATLOCK. Mrs Barbara Martin, Tuckers Guest House, 48 Dale Road, Matlock DE4 3NB (01629

583018). A large Victorian home where you can feel most relaxed. Spacious, well equipped rooms. Pets welcome. Close to rail and bus stations. You can be assured of a jolly good English or Vegetarian breakfast and your hosts will make every effort to help you discover the wonderful Peak District. Marvel at the glorious rugged scenery, enjoy splendid walks, visit the famous stately homes of Chatsworth, Haddon and Hardwick; ride on trams, steam trains, cable cars and carriages; visit caves, mills and mines; canoe, cycle, climb, sail (or just relax!). Something for everyone. Bed and Breakfast from £17; Evening Meal by arrangement.

MATLOCK. Mrs S. Elliott, "Glendon", Knowleston Place, Matlock DE4 3BU (01629 584732). 🐾

Warm hospitality and comfortable accommodation in this Grade II Listed building. Conveniently situated by the Hall Leys Park and River Derwent, it is only a short level walk to Matlock town centre. Large private car park available. Rooms are centrally heated and have washbasins, colour TV and tea/coffee making facilities. No smoking in the dining room. An ideal base for exploring the beautiful Peak District of Derbyshire, with easy access to many places of interest including Chatsworth House, Haddon Hall, National Tramway Museum and Heights of Abraham cable car. Bed and Breakfast from £16.50 per person.

MATLOCK. Mr and Mrs O.J. Allen, "Edgemount", 16 Edge Road, Matlock DE4 3NH (01629

584787). ETB Listed *APPROVED.* "Edgemount" is a private house situated in a peaceful position overlooking surrounding countryside. Five minutes' walk to shops, swimming pool, tennis and golf, bus/rail stations. Convenient for touring stately homes — Chatsworth, Haddon, Hardwick — or the tourist attractions of Carsington Water, Alton Towers, Matlock Bath, mining caverns, mills; organised walks in the area. We offer our visitors a warm welcome with individual care and comfort assured. Good English breakfast, special diets catered for. TV lounge. Tea/coffee provided. Central heating. Toilets, bath/shower/handbasins for guests' use. Children welcome, reduced rates. Pets welcome by arrangement. One double/family, twin, single rooms. Non-smoking only. From £13. Ring for details.

MATLOCK near. Ray and Pauline Sanders, Sycamore Guest House, Town Head, Bonsall, Near

Matlock DE4 2AR (01629 823903). 🐾🐾 A lovely 18th century family guest house in the village of Bonsall, nestling high on Masson Hill on the edge of the Peak District National Park. Easy access to Matlock Bath (for cable cars), Chatsworth House, Haddon Hall, Dovedale, Alton Towers and Carsington Water. Five very comfortable en suite rooms equipped with tea/coffee makers, colour TV, hair dryers and alarm clocks. Guest lounge. Full central heating. Residential licence. Own off street car park. AA QQQ Recommended. Bed and Breakfast from £21; Evening Meal from £12. Open all year with special breaks from November to March. Ring or write for details.

If you've found
FARM HOLIDAY GUIDES
of service please tell your friends

MONYASH/BAKEWELL. Mr Mycock, Cheney Lodge, Rowson House Farm, Monyash, Bakewell DE45 1JH (01629 815336/813521). Located at the heart of the Peak District National Park, Monyash nestles at the head of Lathkill Dale (a National Nature Reserve) at almost 1000ft. The village is surrounded by the beautiful scenery of the White Peak. The limestone farm lodge offers friendly comfortable accommodation; rooms have TV, radio, tea/coffee, en suite facilities and lovely views. Aga cooked breakfasts. Oak beamed lounge with log fires for the chilly evenings. The lodge is situated on 180 acres of quiet farmland looking to the moors. Children and pets welcome. Bed and Breakfast from £14 to £25.

Ye Olde Cheshire Cheese Inn

How Lane, Castleton, Sheffield, Derbyshire S30 2WJ
Telephone: 01433 620330 Fax: 01433 621847

A delightful 17th century Freehouse situated in Castleton, Derbyshire, the heart of the Peak District National Park. Family run with the atmosphere of yesteryear. Two heavily beamed traditional lounge bars, **NO** machines, **NO** pool, **NO** juke-box. A roaring log fire, full central heating. Accommodation has 6 bedrooms, prettily decorated with ensuite, colour TV, tea & coffee, hairdryers. *Good home cooking, good ale, good company.*

PEAK FOREST. Mrs T.H. Warburton, Pedlicote Farm, Peak Forest, Near Buxton SK17 8EG (01298 22241). ❀ ❀ Situated within a few miles of Chatsworth, Haddon Hall, Bakewell, and Castleton's famous Blue John Caverns, Pedlicote Farm is a charming 17th century farmhouse conversion with oak beams, an open log fire and relaxed atmosphere. Standing in its own gardens and grounds of two acres within the Peak National Park, it offers glorious views of the surrounding hills. This is magnificent walking country and the farm itself sits 1100 feet above sea level. Accommodation comprises three simply but pleasantly furnished twin-bedded or double-bedded rooms with TV in each. Terms: Bed and Breakfast from £15 per person; Bed, Breakfast and Evening Meal from £22 per person.

REPTON. Bulls Head, 84 High Street, Repton DE65 6GF (01283 703297). 18th century coach house tastefully converted to pub/restaurant set in rural village five minutes from main A38 (Burton-on-Trent/Derby), 15 minutes to East Midlands Airport. Ample parking. All rooms are comfortable and have TV, tea/coffee making facilities; twin and single rooms available. Function room for private parties. Patio and garden with children's play equipment. Lunches from £3; Dinner from £5. Home cooked traditional fayre. Quality cask ales.

Terms quoted in this publication may be subject to increase if rises in costs necessitate

TIDESWELL. Mrs J. Bell, Laburnum House, Sherwood Road, Tideswell SK17 8LH (01298 872317).

Tideswell is a picturesque village situated in the heart of the Peak District. An ideal centre for touring, walking, cycling and sightseeing, it is only 15 minutes' drive to Buxton, Bakewell, Castleton and Chatsworth House. A 19th century house set in a quiet location in this attractive village offering a homely atmosphere, accommodation of the highest standards, residents' lounge with TV. Bed and full English Breakfast from £14.50 per person. Rooms: two double, one single, all with tea/coffee making facilities; guests' bathroom. No smoking. Off street parking.

TIDESWELL. Mr D.C. Pinnegar, "Poppies", Bank Square, Tideswell, Buxton SK17 8LA (01298

871083). Tourist Board Listed. "Poppies" is situated in the centre of an attractive Derbyshire village in the Peak District. Ideal walking country and within easy reach of Castleton, Bakewell, Matlock and Buxton. Accommodation comprises one family room and twin room with washbasins, one double room en-suite, all with TV and tea/coffee making facilities. Bathroom and two toilets. Restaurant with interesting menu which always includes good selection of vegetarian dishes. Children welcome. Bed and Breakfast from £14.50; Evening Meal from £10.

TIDESWELL. Pat and David Harris, Laurel House, The Green, Litton, Tideswell, Near Buxton SK17

8QP (01298 871971). ❤❤ *COMMENDED.* A warm welcome awaits you in this elegant Victorian House overlooking the green in the pretty village of Litton. There are many lovely dales and rivers virtually on the doorstep, yet Tideswell is only one mile away. We are ideally situated for discovering all Derbyshire has to offer. One double with en-suite facilities and a twin with washbasin and private use of bathroom and toilet; tea/coffee making facilities in both rooms. A lounge with colour TV is available. Bed and Breakfast from £16. Non-smoking establishment. Directions: Off A623 at Tideswell. We look forward to seeing you.

Laurel House, Litton, Derbys.

FOR THE MUTUAL GUIDANCE OF GUEST AND HOST

Every year literally thousands of holidays, short-breaks and overnight stops are arranged through our guides, the vast majority without any problems at all. In a handful of cases, however, difficulties do arise about bookings, which often could have been prevented from the outset.

It is important to remember that when accommodation has been booked, both parties — guests and hosts — have entered into a form of contract. We hope that the following points will provide helpful guidance.

GUESTS: When enquiring about accommodation, be as precise as possible. Give exact dates, numbers in your party and the ages of any children. State the number and type of rooms wanted and also what catering you require — bed and breakfast, full board, etc. Make sure that the position about evening meals is clear — and about pets, reductions for children or any other special points.

Read our reviews carefully to ensure that the proprietors you are going to contact can supply what you want. Ask for a letter confirming all arrangements, if possible.

If you have to cancel, do so as soon as possible. Proprietors do have the right to retain deposits and under certain circumstances to charge for cancelled holidays if adequate notice is not given and they cannot re-let the accommodation.

HOSTS: Give details about your facilities and about any special conditions. Explain your deposit system clearly and arrangements for cancellations, charges, etc., and whether or not your terms include VAT.

If for any reason you are unable to fulfil an agreed booking without adequate notice, you may be under an obligation to arrange alternative suitable accommodation or to make some form of compensation.

While every effort is made to ensure accuracy, we regret that FHG Publications cannot accept responsibility for errors, omissions or misrepresentation in our entries or any consequences thereof. Prices in particular should be checked because we go to press early. We will follow up complaints but cannot act as arbiters or agents for either party.

DEVON

ASHBURTON. The Old Coffee House, 27/29 West Street, Ashburton TQ13 7DT (01364 652539). 🏵

Beautifully situated next to the 15th century church of St. Andrews in the ancient stannary town of Ashburton, this charming 16th century Grade II Listed home offers guests all the creature comforts plus a cosy guest lounge to relax in. Centrally located for magnificent Dartmoor, the beaches of South Devon, cathedral city of Exeter and historic Plymouth. We are also a licensed Tearoom/lunchtime restaurant open daily (except Mondays), serving traditional lunch every Sunday. There are many excellent eating places in and around Ashburton for evening meals and we keep menus from those recommended in our guest lounge. Open most of the year. Bed and Breakfast double room, own bathroom and lounge £35, two persons sharing and £25 single. We are a NON-SMOKING establishment.

ASHBURTON. Margaret Phipps, New Cott Farm, Poundsgate, Newton Abbot TQ13 7PD (01364 631421; Fax: 01364 631338). 🏵 🏵 *COMMENDED.* A

friendly welcome, beautiful views, pleasing accommodation await you at New Cott in the Dartmoor National Park. Enjoy the freedom, peace and quiet of open moorland and the Dart Valley. Farm trail, birds and animals on the farm. Riding, golf, leisure centre locally. Bedrooms en suite, tea/coffee/chocolate, central heating. Ideal for less able guests, special diets catered for — lots of lovely homemade food. Bed and Breakfast from £17; Evening Dinner £10. Weekly reductions, short breaks welcome. Open all year. AA QQQQ.

ASHBURTON. Chris and Annie Moore, Gages Mill, Buckfastleigh Road, Ashburton TQ13 7JW (01364 652391). 🏵 🏵 🏵 *COMMENDED.*

Relax in the warm and friendly atmosphere of our lovely 14th century former wool mill, set in an acre of gardens on the edge of Dartmoor National Park. Eight delightful en suite bedrooms, one on the ground floor, all with tea-making facilities, central heating, hair dryers, radio and alarm clocks. We have a large comfortable lounge with corner bar and granite archways leading to the dining room, and a cosy sittingroom with colour TV. Home cooking of a very high standard. Licensed. Ample car parking. Being one mile from the centre of Ashburton, this is an ideal base for touring South Devon or visiting Exeter, Plymouth, Dartmouth, the many National Trust properties and other places of interest. Children over five years welcome. Sorry no pets. Bed, Breakfast and Evening Meal or Bed and Breakfast only. AA QQQQ Selected, RAC Acclaimed.

ASHBURTON (Dartmoor). Mrs Anne Torr, Middle Leat, Holne, Near Ashburton TQ13 7SJ (01364 631413).

Middle Leat, set in three acres, offers very comfortable accommodation with wonderful views, in the picturesque village of Holne, three and a half miles west of Ashburton in the Dartmoor National Park. We have one large ground floor bedroom with a double bed, bunk beds and a single bed, private bathroom and full facilities; available as a double or family room. Full English Breakfast. Vegetarians welcome. Large garden, free range rare breed chickens and ducks, cows and calves, horse and pets. Visitors are welcome to join in, feeding chicks and ducklings, collecting eggs, etc. A warm welcome and relaxed friendly atmosphere assured in very peaceful surroundings. Sorry, no smoking in the house. Bed and Breakfast from £17. SAE for details or telephone for brochure.

AXMINSTER. Ms C.M. Putt, Highridge Guest House, Lyme Road, Axminster EX13 5BQ (01297 34037). Let me make you feel at home, pamper you with good food and make you comfortable in pretty, clean rooms, all with vanity units, colour TV and tea/coffee facilities. Take tea in our beautiful gardens with ponds and ornamental ducks. Nearby there are six lovely beaches and several golf courses and a wild life park are easily accessible. We can provide maps and details of no less than 15 fishing venues, encompassing sea fishing, fly fishing, coarse fishing. Enjoy a day on Dartmoor or a trip to Exeter, Taunton or Yeovil for shopping, or walk the Coastal Path from Lyme Regis to Seaton. End your day with a well cooked three-course meal for only £6.50. Bed and Breakfast £14.50. Reduced rates for under 10 year olds. Pets welcome.

BAMPTON. Elaine Goodwin, Lodfin Farm, Morebath, Tiverton EX16 9DD (Tel & Fax: 01398 331400).

The calming ambience of this beautiful 17th century Devon farmhouse offers everything to relax and unwind. Lodfin Farm is situated on the edge of Exmoor, one mile north of the historic floral town of Bampton and nestles in a secluded valley of which five acres ia a natural woodland habitat with a stream and lake for our guests to enjoy. A vast inglenook fireplace forms the heart of the house and original features spread to the log fired guests lounge and all bedrooms which include tea/coffee and TV. We welcome children and pets. Open all year. Bed and Breakfast from £16.50 per person.

BAMPTON. Mrs Lindy Head, Harton Farm, Oakford, Tiverton EX16 9HH (01398 351209). 🏵

Working farm, join in. Real farm breaks for country lovers. A unique rural experience for children and the chance to meet the animals on our traditional non-intensive farm near Exmoor. Tranquil 17th century stone farmhouse, secluded but accessible, ideal touring centre. Comfortable accommodation in three double bedrooms with washbasins and tea making facilities; luxury bathroom with a view; dining room serving real country cooking with farm-produced additive-free meat and organic vegetables; home baking a speciality; guests' lounge with colour TV. Home spun wool. Garden. Children over four welcome. Pets accepted. Car essential, parking. Open for Evening Meal, Bed and Breakfast from £19; Bed and Breakfast from £13. Reductions for children. Farm walks. Fishing, shooting, riding can be arranged. Vegetarian meals available on request.

FREE and REDUCED RATE Holiday Visits!
See our READERS' OFFER VOUCHER for details!

BARNSTAPLE. Mrs B. Isaac, Alscott Barton, Alverdiscott, Near Barnstaple EX31 3PT (01271 858336). Our family-run traditional Devonshire farmhouse offers a delightful holiday base within easy reach of coast and moors. Situated in tiny rural village commanding panoramic views, there are acres of farmland to enjoy incorporating three private lakes for trout and coarse fishing, recreation barn, landscaped gardens and ample parking. Charming accommodation with visitors' lounge, dining room, family and double bedrooms with washbasins, also single and twin rooms. Bathroom and shower room facilities. Cots, high chairs provided. Pony available. Pets welcome out of season at our discretion. Bed and Breakfast £15.50 per day; Bed, Breakfast and Evening Meal £21.50 per day. Reductions for children. Brochure available.

BARNSTAPLE. Mrs Sheelagh Darling, Lee House, Marwood, Barnstaple EX31 4DZ (01271 74345). Stone-built Elizabethan Manor House dating back to 1256, standing in its own secluded gardens and grounds with magnificent views over rolling Devon countryside. James II ceilings, an Adam fireplace, antiques and the work of resident artist add interest. Easy access to coast and moor. Family-run, friendly and relaxing atmosphere. Walking distance to local pub with excellent food. Open April to October. One double, one twin room and one four-poster room, all en suite with colour TV and tea/coffee making facilities. Bed and Breakfast from £18.

BARNSTAPLE. Mrs V.M. Chugg, "Valley View", Guineaford, Marwood, Barnstaple EX31 4EA (01271 43458). Working farm. "Valley View" is a bungalow set in 320 acres of farmland which visitors are free to enjoy. It is near Marwood Hill Gardens and Arlington Court, properties renowned for their beauty, and which are open from March to December. Situated three and a half miles from Barnstaple, the Market Town. Accommodation comprises two bedrooms each containing a double and single bed. Dining/sittingroom with colour TV and video. Bathroom/toilet. Good English Breakfast. Bed and Breakfast from £13. Evening Meal supplied if required from £6. Children are welcomed, half price for those under 12 years. Babysitting free of charge. Pets by arrangement. Car essential — parking. Open all year.

BARNSTAPLE. Mr and Mrs D. Woodman, The Old Rectory, Challacombe, Barnstaple EX31 4TS (01598 763342). Within the Exmoor National Park, easily accessible on a good road, The Old Rectory is tucked away peacefully on the edge of Challacombe. A glance at the map of North Devon will show how excellently the house is placed, either for touring the spectacular coastline or for walking on Exmoor. Superbly furnished bedrooms, with tea/coffee making equipment, washbasins and heating. Ample bathroom, toilet, shower facilities. Comfortable diningroom, lounge with colour TV. Bed and Breakfast from £15.50 per night, from £105 per week. No VAT charge. Further particulars on request.

DEVON – ENDLESS CHOICES!

People never tire of visiting Devon. There's so much to do, like visiting Alscott Farm Museum, Berry Head Country Park, Bickleigh Mill Farm, Farway Countryside Park, Haytor Granite Railway, Kent's Cavern, Dartmoor National Park, Exmoor National Park and of course Plymouth and its Hoe.

BARNSTAPLE near. Mrs J. Ley, West Barton, Alverdiscott, Near Barnstaple EX31 3PT (01271

858230). Working farm. West Barton is a mixed family-run farm of 210 acres with a pedigree Friesian herd and sheep. An ideal touring point, with Dartington Glass, RHS Rosemoor Gardens, Clovelly, Hartland Point, many other beauty spots and golf courses nearby. Pleasantly situated beside the B3232 Barnstaple to Torrington road with Bideford only five miles away. Sandy beach only six miles. Children welcome. Regret no pets. One twin-bedded room with washbasin, one family room and one single room. Lounge with colour TV. Bed and Breakfast from £14; Evening Meal optional.

BEER. Mr and Mrs Les Andrews, The Mullions, New Road, Beer, Seaton EX12 3EB (01297 21377).

The Mullions is situated overlooking the old fishing village of Beer and the sea. Most rooms are large, with private facilities. Evening Meals are available in the Summer months (March to October). The Mullions has a residential licence, with a bar situated in the conservatory overlooking the village. Children are welcome at reduced rates. Bed and Breakfast from £18; Evening Meal £8. Special weekly rates from £160 for Bed, Breakfast and Evening Meal.

BEER. Nikki and Richard Oswald, Bay View Guest House, Fore Street, Beer EX12 3EE (01297 20489). Beer is a charming uncommercialised fishing village on the East Devon Heritage Coast, ideally situated for walking, fishing or simply relaxing on the beach. Bay View is beautifully placed right on the sea front with stunning views of the headland and sea. There are three en suite bedrooms and six bedrooms with shared bathrooms. All are centrally heated and have colour TV, tea/coffee facilities and attractive furnishings. Bed and Breakfast from £15. For evening meals Beer has a good selection of reasonably priced restaurants. Open March to November. We look forward to welcoming you to Bay View and Beer. AA Recommended.

BERE FERRERS. Mrs Margaret Willmott, The Lanterna, Bere Ferrers, Yelverton PL20 7JL (01822

840380). A family-run guest house in the centre of a quiet village. An ideal area for bird watching and walking. Bere Ferrers is beside the River Tavy with the River Tamar two miles away, eight miles from the market town of Tavistock, 15 miles from Plymouth. Railway station with trains daily to Plymouth and Gunnislake. One family and one double bedrooms en suite and a twin-bedded room with washbasin; all have tea/coffee facilities and are centrally heated. TV lounge. Bed and Breakfast from £15. Sorry no pets. Own car park at rear. Open all year.

BIDEFORD. Jenny and Barry Jones, The Pines at Eastleigh, Near Bideford EX39 4PA (01271

860561; E-mail Barry@barpines.demon.co.uk). ♛♛♛ *HIGHLY COMMENDED.* RAC Highly Acclaimed, AA QQQQ Selected. Jenny and Barry offer a warm welcome and a peaceful, relaxing time at their home set in seven acres. Distant views from the grounds of Bideford and beyond to Lundy and Hartland Point. En suite rooms have colour TV and complimentary tea and coffee. King-size beds and ground floor rooms available. Generous farmhouse style cooking, catering for all diets. Licensed. Pets and children welcome. Wood-burning stove in lounge. Open all year. Bed and Breakfast from £29. set meal £14. Weekly terms and weekend breaks in winter. Telephone for colour brochure. Credit cards. No smoking.

FREE ENTRY offers on visits to THE BIG SHEEP, Bideford –
see our READERS' OFFER VOUCHER for details.

BIDEFORD. Mrs Chris Leonard, Lane Mill Farm, Woolfardisworthy, Bideford EX39 5PZ (01237 431254).

Lane Mill Farm is situated three miles off the A39, south of Clovelly and three-quarters of a mile from Woolfardisworthy village. Bed and Breakfast accommodation is offered at nightly or weekly rates. Evening meals are available at our own restaurant and inn, The Manor, in the village. The spacious farmhouse offers double and family bedrooms each with shower en suite; tea/coffee making facilities are available. Guests have their own lounge/diner with colour TV and use of the indoor heated swimming pool. There are many local places of interest to visit including Dartington Glass, Rosemoor Gardens, The Milky Way, Big Sheep, The Tarka Trail and coastal walks. Bed and Breakfast £15.

BIDEFORD. Chris and Keith Merton, Ford Mill, Woolfardisworthy, Near Bideford EX39 5RF (Tel & Fax: 01409 241289).

16th century farmhouse mentioned in the Domesday Book, set in nine acre meadow with duck pond, all bordering Torridge River. Midway between Bideford and Bude with picturesque Clovelly only five miles away. One family room, one double room, two single rooms, one with bunks. All rooms have TV and drink facilities, with en suite showers in main rooms. Separate toilets and bathroom available. Relaxed dining room with versatile cuisine and daily home-made bread served from our range. Bed and Breakfast from £14; Evening Meals from £10. Reductions for children. Pets welcome. Three bedroomed self contained annexe with inglenook fireplace and woodburner also available.

BIDEFORD. Sunset Hotel, Landcross, Bideford EX39 5JA (01237 472962).

SOMEWHERE SPECIAL in North Devon. Small country hotel in quiet peaceful location, overlooking spectacular scenery in an area of outstanding natural beauty, one and a half miles from Bideford town. Beautifully decorated and spotlessly clean. Highly recommended quality accommodation. All en suite with colour TV, tea/coffee facilities. Superb cooking, everything homemade with all fresh produce. Vegetarians and special needs catered for. Excellent reputation. Book with confidence in a NON SMOKING ESTABLISHMENT. Licensed. Private parking. AA QQQ. Bed and Breakfast £22.50 to £23.50; Bed, Breakfast and Evening Meal £32.50 to £33.50 daily, £217.50 to £220 weekly. Mr and Mrs C.M. Lamb, resident proprietors since 1971.

BIDEFORD. Richard & Hilarie Wilson, Marchwood House, Limers Lane, Northam, Bideford EX39 2RG (01237 477627).

Marchwood House is between Bideford and Westward Ho! conveniently close to the North Devon link road (A361/A39). It is an unusual house built about 125 years ago, down a quiet lane leading to the River Torridge. Extensive estuary and country views. Picturesque walk along river to Appledore on National Trust land. The sea is one and a half miles away. Clovelly and unspoilt coastal villages nearby. Spacious accommodation, rooms with private bathrooms; TV, tea/coffee making facilities. Country Breakfast — Bed and Breakfast from £15, or self catering flats available. Parking in grounds. Reductions for children. Pets welcome. Please write for brochure. Open all year.

BIDEFORD. Mrs C. Colwill, Welsford Farm, Hartland EX39 6EQ (01237 441296). Working farm, join in. Relax, enjoy the peaceful countryside yet be within easy reach of towns, interesting places and picturesque beaches with miles of scenic cliff walks. This 360 acre dairy farm is situated two miles from Hartland Village; four miles from cobblestoned Clovelly and the rugged Hartland coastline. Comfortably furnished farmhouse with colour TV lounge and washbasins in bedrooms. Children welcome at reduced rates. Wander around the farm and "pets' corner". Babysitting always available. Good country food using home grown produce. Car essential. Bed and Breakfast from £13 per night, Evening Meal £8. Bed, Breakfast and four-course Evening Meal from £135 weekly. Warm welcome. Regret no pets. Open April to October.

The Bulstone Hotel
THE HOTEL FOR FAMILIES WITH YOUNG CHILDREN

ENGLISH
TOURIST BOARD
COMMENDED
♥♥

*Holiday
Which*

Higher Bulstone, Branscombe, Near Sidmouth, Devon EX12 3BL
Telephone & Fax: Branscombe 01297 680446

A message from Judith & Kevin Monaghan of the Bulstone Hotel.

Where children are especially welcomed, not just catered for!

We offer a relaxed and pleasant stay all year round including Christmas and New Year. There are facilities for Mum and Dad to have a holiday with their children without the worries of daily life. The Bulstone is fully equipped to cope with children from as young as one week and our facilities include:

● Baby alarms; ● Family rooms and suites; ● Parents kitchen with fridge, microwave, steriliser, iron and spin drier; ● A large play room and three acres of garden with play area; ● We provide cots and bedding including spares; ● High chairs and much much more to make the whole family's stay comfortable and relaxed

Children enjoy a high tea together in a group and parents can enjoy a relaxed candlelit dinner followed by coffee in the lounge in front of a log fire.

No smoking and no pets!   Open all year
Why not come along and try us out for a week or even a couple of nights?

Available from most bookshops, the 1997 edition of THE GOLF GUIDE covers details of every UK golf course – well over 2000 entries – for holiday or business golf. Hundreds of hotel entries offer convenient accommodation, accompanying details of the courses – the 'pro', par score, length etc.

Endorsed by The Professional Golfers' Association (PGA) and including Holiday Golf in Ireland, France, Portugal, Spain and the USA.

£8.99 from bookshops or £9.80 including postage (UK only) from FHG Publications, Abbey Mill Business Centre, Paisley PA1 1TJ.

BRAUNTON. Christine and Roy Gardner, Hillside Gardens, Heddon Mill, Knowle, Near Braunton EX33 2NG (01271 815721).

Hillside Gardens, in six acres of gardens and grounds, is ideally situated for exploring the beautiful coastline and countryside of North Devon and Exmoor. Nearby are the gardens of Marwood Hill and Rosemoor and Braunton Burrows Nature Reserve. Ideal location for surfing, riding, golf, bird watching and walking. Barnstaple market town is seven miles away. Comfortable accommodation consists of two double rooms (one en suite) and one single. Tea/coffee making facilities. Guests' lounge with TV. Bed and Breakfast £14.50. Evening Meals by arrangement using fresh garden produce. Ample space for parking.

BRAUNTON. Mrs Roselyn Bradford, "St. Merryn", Higher Park Road, Braunton EX33 2LG (01271 813805).

Set in beautiful, sheltered garden of approximately one acre, with many peaceful sun traps, Ros extends a warm welcome to her guests. Rooms (£15-£17 per person) include single, double and family rooms, with washbasins, central heating, colour TV and tea/coffee facilities. Two bathrooms plus separate toilets. Evening meal (£8) may be served indoors or out. Guests may bring own wine. Guest lounge with colour TV, patio door access to garden. Swimming pool, fish ponds, hens and thatched summerhouse plus excellent parking. Please send for brochure.

BRIXHAM. Graham and Yvonne Glass, Raddicombe Lodge, 112 Kingswear Road, Brixham TQ5 0EX (01803 882125).

The Lodge lies midway between the picturesque coastal harbour towns of Brixham and Dartmouth, overlooking sea and country, with National Trust land between us and the sea. The Lodge is reached by a short drive off the B3205, in a quarter acre garden with the charm and character of pitched ceilings, lattice windows and cosy open log fires for the winter months. Scrumptious traditional English Breakfast with locally baked crusty bread or Continental Breakfast with Batons and Croissants, light/vegetarian breakfast also available. Colour TV and tea/coffee making facilities in all bedrooms. Come and go as you please, make the Lodge your home from home. Smoking restricted to the lounge area only. Ample parking. Open all year. Children welcome. Sorry no pets. Offering room and breakfast only from £15.40 to £18.70 per night each. En suite rooms £3.20 per night each extra. Popular carvery restaurant just 400 yards away. MasterCard/Access/Visa/DinersClub cards accepted.

BRIXHAM. Angela and Peter Ellis, "Westbury", 51 New Road, Brixham TQ5 8NL (01803 851684).

Brixham, a quaint harbour town with winding streets and steps leading to steep terraced slopes, an ideal base for exploring the beautiful Devon countryside. Westbury is a short level walk from the harbour (approximately 5-10 minutes) and has six bedrooms, most en suite. All bedrooms have washbasins, colour TV and tea making facilities. Private parking is to the front, but a car is not essential as there are frequent buses, also boats to Paignton, Torquay and Dartmouth. Courtesy car from stations provided. Children over seven years welcome. Pets by arrangement. Bed and Breakfast from £16 per person.

DEVON – LAND OF DOONE AND DRAKE

Exmoor is the setting of R.D. Blackmore's "Lorna Doone", and visitors today can still soak in the romantic atmosphere of Doone Valley where the outlaws lived, and Oare Church, near Lynmouth, the scene of Lorna's wedding. Devon's most famous son is undoubtedly Sir Francis Drake, born at Crowndale, near Tavistock. It was to Plymouth he returned after sailing round the world in 1580 and on Plymouth Hoe he reputedly finished his game of bowls before tackling the Spanish Armada in 1588.

BRIXHAM. Ian and Carol Hayhurst, Richmond House Hotel, Higher Manor Road, Brixham TQ5 8HA (01803 882391). ⚘⚘ *COMMENDED.* Victorian Hotel of character, central for historic harbour, shops and restaurants yet quietly located with residents' car park and south-facing sun terrace. Spacious rooms all with hot drink facilities, TVs, pleasant views and either en suite or vanity units. There are all types of rooms available including family size, twin and ground floor. Well appointed lounge with colour TV, video and games. Excellent base for touring South Hams and Dartmoor; also the area is ideal for sea fishing, boating, painting, walking and golf. Bed and full English Breakfast from £16 to £20 per person per night. Visa and Access are accepted.

BUCKFASTLEIGH. Mrs Rosie Palmer, Wellpark Farm, Dean Prior, Buckfastleigh TQ11 0LY (01364 643775). ETB Listed *HIGHLY COMMENDED.* Set on the edge of Dartmoor near Buckfast Abbey. A warm and friendly welcome is extended to all our guests. Very comfortable rooms available with colour TV, tea/coffee facilities and clock radio. Relaxing lounge with log fire and colour TV. Delicious farmhouse breakfasts are served. Enclosed garden with slide and swings. Excellent local 11th century inn is well worth a visit. Bed and Breakfast from £15 to £18. Reductions for children and weekly bookings.

CHAGFORD. Mrs Elizabeth Law, Lawn House, Mill Street, Chagford TQ13 8AW (01647 433329). On the edge of Dartmoor within the National Park, Chagford is a beautiful unspoilt former stannary town dating back to the Middle Ages. In the centre of Chagford stands Lawn House, a small but elegant 18th century listed thatched house providing an ideal base for walking expeditions onto the moor. Lawn House offers friendly, comfortable, en suite Bed and Breakfast accommodation in spacious rooms with tea/coffee making facilities; TV lounge. Open all year round. Prices are from £14 per person. Discounts are available for stays of five nights and over; reductions for children. Packed lunches available.

CHERITON BISHOP. Mrs N.M. Stephens, Horselake Farm, Cheriton Bishop, Exeter EX6 6HD (Tel & Fax: 01647 24220). Horselake Farm offers unique accommodation in a lovely 16th century Grade II Listed Tudor farmhouse. Set in beautiful gardens with outside heated swimming pool. Owner runs an Arabian horse stud and fruit farm. The accommodation comprises three rooms — one four-poster, one en suite and a twin room, all have washbasin, TV and tea/coffee making facilities. Central heating, log fires in winter. Children welcome. Bed and Breakfast from £15 to £21 per person; Evening Meal £10 per person.

Terms quoted in this publication may be subject to increase if rises in costs necessitate

CHUDLEIGH. Jill Shears, Glen Cottage, Rock Road, Chudleigh TQ13 0JJ (01626 852209). FHG

Diploma Award. Just a few minutes' drive from the A38 at Chudleigh can be found a delightful old cottage nestling in a quiet and secluded glen, surrounded by 10 acres of woodland garden complete with small lake, waterfall and ducks! Open air sheltered swimming pool available. Glen Cottage provides comfortable centrally heated accommodation comprising family, double and twin bedrooms, all with washbasins and tea/coffee making facilities. There is a separate guest lounge with colour TV. We offer good home cooking with traditional full English breakfast and optional Evening Meal. Children welcome. Brochure available. Bed and Breakfast from £14.

CLOVELLY. R.C. and C.M. Beck, Stroxworthy Farm, Woolfardisworthy, Near Clovelly EX39 5QB (01237 431333). ♛ ♛ *COMMENDED.* Stroxworthy Farm is

family-run with a herd of pedigree Guernsey cattle. The picturesque village of Clovelly with its cobbled street leading down to its small harbour and the sea is four and a half miles distant. The area is well known for its scenic beauty and unspoilt coastline, where there are several quiet little beaches between the resorts of Westward Ho! and Bude. Exmoor and Dartmoor are within easy reach. Horse riding, fishing and golf locally. All rooms including family suite (two rooms), have duvets, en-suite bathrooms, colour TV and tea/coffee making facilities. Large comfortable lounge. Ample parking. Terms: £17.50 Bed and Breakfast. SAE for colour brochure.

CLOVELLY. Mrs J. Johns, Dyke Green Farm, Clovelly, Near Bideford EX39 5RU (01237 431699 or 431279). Situated on the edge of the ancient Roman Dyke at

the entrance of famous Clovelly. The tastefully converted barn offers beautiful accommodation furbished to a high standard throughout. All three bedrooms have washbasins, (one en suite and one with private WC), colour TV and tea/coffee making facilities. Ideal base for Devon and Cornwall especially lovely Dartmoor and Exmoor. Close to Coastal Path on South West Way. Amenities close by include golf, tennis, fishing, swimming; perfect for walks and sandy beaches. This lovely home offers you first class Bed and Breakfast from £15 with a warm friendly welcome all year. Evening Meal can be provided from £6. Special rates for children. Please apply for full details.

CLOVELLY. Mrs P.M. Vanstone, The Old Smithy, Slerra Hill, Clovelly, Bideford EX39 5ST (01237 431202). The Old Smithy is a 16th century cottage and

converted forge, situated one mile from the sea and the unspoilt picturesque village of Clovelly. Open all year. Three family or double rooms, all with colour TV and tea/coffee making facilities. Children welcome. Dogs allowed (except in the dining room). Large car park. This is an excellent base for touring Exmoor, Dartmoor and Cornwall. Also beautiful coastal walks on the South West Way. Bed and Breakfast from £14.50 standard, £17.50 en suite. Reductions for children in family room.

CLOVELLY near. Mrs Caroline May, Lower Waytown, Horns Cross, Bideford EX39 5DN (01237 451787). This delightful, unique Roundhouse offers

excellent accommodation in beautiful surroundings. Extensive grounds with ornamental waterfowl and black swans on the stream-fed ponds create the perfect ambience in which to relax and unwind. Situated five miles from Clovelly and with the coastal footpath nearby, Lower Waytown makes an ideal centre for walking, touring and beaches. Tastefully furnished accommodation comprises three en-suite bedrooms; two double (one on ground floor), and one round twin-bedded room, all with tea/coffee making facilities, hair dryers and colour TV. Spacious dining room, round sitting room with beams and inglenook. Central heating. Private parking. Children over 12 years welcome. Sorry no smoking. Bed and Breakfast from £21. AA QQQQQ Premier Selected. Also thatched self catering cottages available.

COLEBROOKE. Mrs V. Hill, Birchmans Farm, Colebrook, Crediton EX17 5DN (01363 82393). ♕ ♕ COMMENDED. **Working farm.** We are situated seven miles from Crediton in a peaceful part of the countryside with unspoilt views. Two double and one twin bedrooms, all en suite and have tea/coffee making facilities. Children welcome. Bed and Breakfast from £15. Evening meal available if required.

COLYTON. Mrs Joy Selway, Mossbank, Southleigh, Near Colyton EX13 6JB (01404 871358). You

are sure of a warm welcome at Mossbank, which is a lovely house, recently restored, and situated in a very quiet small village with beautiful views. About one and a half miles from the main A3052 coastal road from Lyme Regis to Exeter. This is an ideal place from which to visit various places of interest within easy daily driving distance — Farway Countryside Park, Beer Caves, Bicton Park, Model Trains at Beer, Cricket St. Thomas Countryside Park, horse riding and many more. Plenty of good eating places nearby. Private parking. Accommodation in one family, one double and one single room. Optional Evening Meal.

COLYTON. Mrs Norma Rich, Sunnyacre, Northleigh, Colyton EX13 6DA (01404 871422). Need a

quiet and peaceful break? A warm welcome, with a relaxing atmosphere, is what we aim to provide at Sunnyacre which is on a working farm situated centrally between Honiton and Exeter (A30) and Lyme Regis to Exeter (A3052) in a beautiful valley with glorious views. This very scenic area provides plenty of attractions including golf courses, country parks, lovely quaint villages and coves. Accommodation comprises one family, one double and one twin bedrooms with washbasins. Children welcome at reduced rates; cot and high chair available. Bed and Breakfast from £12 per person per night. Traditional home cooked evening meals available using fresh and home-grown produce.

CREDITON. Mr and Mrs R. Barrie-Smith, Great Leigh Farm, Crediton EX17 3QQ (01647 24297).

Delightfully set in the mid-Devon hills between Cheriton Bishop and Crediton, two miles off the A30, Great Leigh Farm is ideally situated for a quiet holiday or for touring Devon and Cornwall. Guests are free to wander over the farmland and may also join in farm activities. The outstandingly comfortable accommodation, comprising one family, one double and two single rooms, is fully centrally heated, and two rooms have bathroom en suite. Children welcome at half price, babysitting available. Bed and Breakfast £15; Bed, Breakfast and Evening Dinner £21. Children half price.

CROYDE BAY. Chris and Roslyn Gedling, West Winds Guest House, Moor Lane, Croyde Bay EX33

1PA (Tel & Fax: 01271 890489; Mobile: 0831 211247). ♕ ♕ ♕ COMMENDED. Small guest house located picturesquely by the water's edge overlooking Croyde Bay beach adjacent to Baggy Point National Trust coastal path. Private steps onto the beach. En-suite rooms available, all with TV, radio, tea/coffee making facilities; some rooms have sea view. Dogs welcomed. Ample car parking. Residential bar and separate sun lounge overlooking sea. Fire Certificate. Situated in an ideal position for surfing, touring Exmoor National Park and surrounding countryside with Saunton Golf Club only two miles away. Comfortable and relaxing atmosphere. Open all year. Bed and Breakfast from £21 per person. Write for brochure or telephone. AA QQQ Recommended.

FUN FOR ALL THE FAMILY IN DEVON

Arlington Court, near Barnstaple; Bygones Victoria Street, Torquay; Clovelly Village, near Bideford; Dartington Crystal, Great Torrington; Dartmoor Wildlife Park, Sparkwell; English Riviera Leisure Centre, Torquay; Exeter Maritime Museum; Exmoor Bird Gardens, Bratton Fleming; Kents Cavern Show Caves, Torquay; Babbacombe Model Village, Torquay; National Shire Horse Centre, Yealmpton; Paignton Zoo and Botanical Gardens; Plymouth Dome; Plym Valley Railway Steam Centre, Plymouth; Woodland Leisure Park, Blackawton.

CULLOMPTON. Mrs B. Hill, Sunnyside Farm, Butterleigh, Near Cullompton, Tiverton EX15 1PP

(01884 855322). Working farm. Here at Sunnyside Farm everything is done to give guests a happy holiday. Conveniently situated three and a half miles from the M5, it makes an ideal overnight stop and is three miles from the lovely village of Bickleigh, a great tourist attraction with a craft centre, etc. There is a spacious garden for children to play on the lawn. Trout fishing nearby and many places of interest. Comfortable accommodation has three rooms en suite, family and double/twin rooms with tea/coffee making facilities; bathroom, two toilets. Sittingroom has log fire and colour TV; dining room with separate tables; sun lounge with panoramic views. Cot, high chair, babysitting and reduced rates for children. Pets allowed. Car essential, parking. Open all year except Christmas. Traditional farmhouse food and plenty of it! Evening Meal, Bed and Breakfast from £24 daily, £150 weekly; Bed and Breakfast from £16. Short Breaks catered for. Fire Certificate. Essential Food Hygiene Certificate held.

CULLOMPTON. Mr and Mrs T. Coleman, Town Tenement Farm, Clyst Hydon, Cullompton EX15 2NB (01884 277230). A recommended Bed and Breakfast stop in 16th century farmhouse in quiet village, four miles from M5 Junction 28. Guests are accommodated in one double and one family room with bathroom, and one double en suite with kitchen (ground floor). All rooms have tea making facilities. The guests' lounge has inglenook fireplace, exposed beams and panelled screen and is comfortably furnished. A farmhouse breakfast is served and a home cooked evening meal can be provided or guests may visit the "Five Bells" in the village. Open all year. Bed and Breakfast from £14. Reduced rates for children, cots available.

CULLOMPTON. Mrs Sylvia Baker, Wishay Farm, Trinity, Cullompton EX15 1PE (01884 33223).

👑👑 COMMENDED. **Working farm.** Wishay Farm is a 200 acre working farm with a recently modernised Grade II Listed farmhouse with some interesting features. It is situated in a quiet and peaceful area with scenic views, yet is central for touring the many attractions Devon has to offer. Comfortable and spacious accommodation in family room with en suite bathroom, double room with washbasin and private bathroom, both with colour TV, fridge, tea/coffee making facilities. Central heating, log fire when cold. Children welcome, cot and high chair available. Bed and Breakfast from £15. Reduced rates for children.

CULLOMPTON. Mrs Margaret Chumbley, Fig Tree Farm, Butterleigh, Cullompton EX15 1PQ

(01884 855463). Treat yourself to a "special break" and enjoy our welcoming friendly family atmosphere. Set in a magnificent position overlooking the beautiful Burn Valley, Fig Tree Farm is an idyllic rural retreat for that peaceful relaxing holiday. There are many lovely walks in the area with the coast, Exmoor, Dartmoor and several National Trust properties all within easy reach; Cullompton (M5) four miles. Coarse fishing available. Generous farmhouse hospitality, full menu, delicious four course evening meals using organically grown produce, special diets welcome. Comfortable guest lounge with colour TV, video. Charming double and family rooms, some with verandah, shower and tea/coffee facilities. Bed and Breakfast £14.50; Bed, Breakfast and Evening Meal £132 per week. Phone now, many special offers, "free wine", "free children", "free cycle hire". Open all year.

DARTMOOR. Ladymede, Throwleigh, Near Okehampton EX20 2HU (01647 231492). Delightful

detached bungalow situated on the edge of the very popular village of Throwleigh which nestles in the tranquillity of Dartmoor foothills. The area is popular for walking and riding. Built before the war, the bungalow is set in one acre of gardens with views to the moors. Friendly atmosphere with children and pets welcome. Tea-making facilities. Ample parking. Bed and Breakfast from £16 per person. Directions: from A30 at Whiddon Down pick up signs for Throwleigh and on entering the village turn right, bungalow on left. Write or phone for further information. Tourist Board registered.

DARTMOUTH. Jill and Michael Fell, Victoria Cote, 105 Victoria Road, Dartmouth TQ6 9DY (01803 832997). Victoria Cote is a comfortable Victorian house set in a lovely garden, within easy walking distance of the town centre. Bedrooms are spacious and attractively decorated, all with tea/coffee making facilities and colour TV. Accommodation comprises three double rooms with bath or shower rooms en suite. There is private parking for several cars — a must in this town! Open all year. Prices from £20 per person per night for Bed and Breakfast. Dinners are available, if booked. Children and dogs are also welcome.

EXETER. Mrs N. Easterbrook, Drakes Farm House, Ide, Near Exeter EX2 9RQ (01392 256814/495564). Drakes Farm House is a Listed old farmhouse with a large garden, situated in centre of quiet village, with Listed public house and one of the longest road fords in the country. Situated just two miles from M5 and Cathedral City of Exeter. Convenient for coast and moors. Two restaurants within five minutes' walking distance. Tea/coffee facilities. One family room en suite, one double en suite and one twin-bedded room with separate facilities. Two bathrooms. Lounge/separate TV lounge. Laundry facilities. Full central heating. Parking. Bed and Breakfast from £15.

EXETER. Janet Bragg, Marianne Pool Farm, Clyst St. George, Exeter EX3 0NZ (01392 874939). Tourist Board Listed. Situated in peaceful rural location two miles from M5 Junction 30, and midway between the seaside town of Exmouth and the historic city of Exeter. This thatched Devon Longhouse offers spacious family and twin-bedded rooms with washbasins, tea/coffee making facilities; comfortable lounge with colour TV and a dining room in which a full English Breakfast is served. Large lawned garden, ideal for children. Car essential. Open March to November. Bed and Breakfast from £16.50.

EXETER. Mrs L.A. Branfield, Willhayes Farm, Longdown, Exeter EX6 7BN (01392 832636). ♥♥ COMMENDED. Standing some 700 feet high at the edge of Exeter Forest, the house has extensive views over the Teign Valley and Dartmoor. An ideal touring centre with the moors, coast, golfing and fishing facilities within easy reach. Accommodation comprises three double rooms each with en suite facilities. All rooms enjoy valley and moor views. Tea/coffee making facilities are provided. Strictly non-smoking. Terms: January to June and September to December (except Christmas) £16.50 per person per night Bed and Breakfast; July and August £20 per person per night Bed and Breakfast. Brochure available.

EXETER. Mrs Dudley, Culm Vale Guest House, Stoke Canon, Exeter EX5 4EG (01392 841615). ♥♥ A fine old country house of great charm and character, giving the best of both worlds as we are only three miles to the north of the Cathedral city of Exeter, with its antique shops, yet situated in the heart of Devon's beautiful countryside on the edge of the pretty village of Stoke Canon. An ideal touring centre. Our spacious comfortable Bed and Breakfast accommodation includes full English breakfast, there is a lounge with a colour TV, tea/coffee facilities, washbasins and razor points in all rooms, some with bathrooms en suite. Full central heating. Our lovely gardens boast a beautiful swimming pool and there is ample free parking. Bed and Breakfast £17.50 per person per night. Brochure on request.

EXETER. Mrs M.A. Glanvill, Higher Bagmores Farm, Woodbury, Exeter EX5 1LA (01395 232261). A

working beef, sheep and arable farm, set in delightful Devon countryside approximately three miles from M5. Exmouth five miles with sandy beaches and sailing facilities. Exeter, the Cathedral city of Devon, is seven miles away and has an excellent shopping centre. Bedrooms are equipped with tea/coffee facilities, washbasins and shaver points. Central heating. Lounge with colour TV. A full English breakfast is served. Local inns and restaurants nearby. Ample parking, car essential. Children welcome. Bed and Breakfast from £14 to £16.

EXETER. Mr Derek Sercombe, "Rhona" Guest House, 15 Blackall Road, Exeter EX4 4HE (01392

77791). A small family guest house situated within seven minutes' walk from the centre of historic Exeter, making an ideal base for touring the National Parks of Dartmoor and Exmoor. Luxury en suite accommodation. Colour TV, also tea/coffee making facilities in all rooms. Golf and riding parties catered for. Open all year. Private car park. Single rooms from £11; twin/family rooms from £21 with full English Breakfast. Dinner available on request.

EXETER near. The Royal Oak Inn, Dunsford, Near Exeter EX6 7DA (01647 252256). ETB Listed

APPROVED. Traditional Victorian country pub offering relaxation with six Real Ales, home-made food and the friendliest landlord you could find. Accommodation comprises eight bedrooms, five en suite. Bed and Breakfast from £20.

EXETER. Mrs Sally Glanvill, Rydon Farm, Woodbury, Exeter EX5 1LB (Tel & Fax: 01395 232341).

HIGHLY COMMENDED. Come, relax and enjoy yourself in our lovely 16th century Devon Longhouse. We offer a warm and friendly family welcome at this peaceful dairy farm. Ideally situated for exploring the coast, moors and the historic city of Exeter. Only 10 minutes' drive from the coast. Inglenook fireplace and oak beams. All bedrooms have private or en suite bathrooms, central heating, hair dryers and tea/coffee making facilities; one room with romantic four-poster. A traditional farmhouse breakfast is served with our own free range eggs and there are several excellent pubs and restaurants close by. Pets by arrangement. Open all year. Bed and Breakfast from £18 to £24. AA QQQQ Selected.

EXETER. Mrs Gillian Howard, Ebford Court, Ebford, Exeter EX3 0RA (01392 875353; Fax: 01392

876776). 15th century thatched farmhouse set in quiet surroundings yet only five minutes from Junction 30, M5. The house stands in pleasant gardens and is one mile from the attractive Exe Estuary. The coast and moors are a short drive away and it is an ideal centre for touring and birdwatching. The two double bedrooms have washbasins and tea/coffee facilities; sitting/dining room with colour TV. Non smoking accommodation. Open all year. Ample parking. Bed and Breakfast from £15 per night; £90 weekly.

EXETER. Mr Chris Morris, Clock Tower Hotel, 16 New North Road, Exeter EX4 4HF (01392 424545; Fax: 01392 218445). The greatest care and comfort offered by caring resident proprietors of this Grade II Listed historically interesting city centre hotel with its award-winning patio/garden and the modern facilities expected of large hotels at a fraction of their cost. En suite rooms with baths and Satellite TV. Licensed bar. All major credit cards accepted. Bed and Breakfast from £15 per person per night; Evening Meal from £7.50. Send for colour brochure with details of free holiday insurance.

EXMOUTH. Annis Matthews, Carlton Guest House, 110 St. Andrews Road, Exmouth EX8 1AT (01395 265940). Small family guest house close to town centre, 100 yards from sandy beach. Full English breakfast, front door keys, access to rooms at all times. Washbasins, shaver points, colour TV and tea making in all rooms. Private car park. Fire Certificate. Children and pets welcome. Bed and Breakfast £14.

HOLSWORTHY. Mrs L.A. Cole, The Barton, Pancrasweek, Holsworthy EX22 7JT (01288 381315). ♥ ♥ **Working farm, join in.** A peaceful holiday awaits you on our 200 acre working dairy farm on the Devon/Cornwall border, six miles from Cornish coast with quaint fishing villages, beautiful beaches and famous Clovelly. Fishing, sailing, sailboarding at Tamar Lakes, also close to leisure pool and sports centre. Historic Dartmoor and Bodmin Moor within easy reach. The 16th century farmhouse has three bedrooms for guests — two double rooms and one twin, all en suite with tea making facilities. Games room, lounge with TV, separate dining room. Traditional farmhouse cooking with home grown produce when available. Open Easter to end September. Bed and Breakfast from £15; Evening Meal £8. Reductions for children. Brochure on request.

HONITON. Mrs June Ann Tucker, Yard Farm, Upottery, Honiton EX14 9QP (01404 861680). ♥ A most attractively situated working farm. The house is very old traditional Devon farmhouse located just three miles east of Honiton and enjoying a superb outlook across the Otter Valley. Enjoy a stroll down by the River Otter which runs through the farmland. Try a spot of trout fishing. Children will love to make friends with Honey, our pony. Lovely seaside resorts 12 miles, swimming pool three miles. Traditional English breakfast, colour TV, washbasin, heating, tea/coffee facilities in all rooms. Bed and Breakfast £15; Dinner (if requested) £8. Reductions for children.

HONITON. Mrs K. Manley, Birds Farm, Awliscombe, Near Honiton EX14 0PU (01404 841620). Comfortable 16th century beamed farmhouse situated in a peaceful hamlet. Within easy reach of Exmoor and Dartmoor; gliding club two miles; convenient for Crealy Country Adventure Park near Exeter. Honiton is known for its lacemaking. Accommodation is in two double, one family and one single bedrooms; bathroom with shower and WC, also separate shower; lounge with colour TV; dining room. Cot available. Lawned garden. Full English breakfast. Village inn two miles for evening meals. Sorry no pets. Car parking. No smoking. Bed and Breakfast from £14 to £15 per person.

HONITON. Pamela and Derek Boyland, Barn Park Farm, Stockland Hill, Cotleigh, Honiton EX14 9JA (01404 861297). ❧ *COMMENDED.* **Working farm, join in.** Working dairy farm situated off a good secondary road one and a half miles south of the A30/A303 Junction, in peaceful countryside, ideal for bird watching and rambling. Within easy reach of many beauty spots, coast 12 miles. Traditional English breakfast (collect your own eggs from our free range hens), home grown produce used. Barn Park is a house brimming with character and has a home-from-home atmosphere. Accommodation comprises a twin or double room, family room on request. Open all year except Christmas Day. Bed and Breakfast £15; Evening Meal, if required, from £9. No smoking in the house please. West Country Tourist Board Member.

HONITON/LYME REGIS. Mrs Susan Turpin, Ham Farmhouse, Ham, Dalwood, Axminster EX13 7HL (Tel & Fax: 01404 831697). Situated in an area of outstanding natural beauty, Ham Farmhouse is a thatched non-working farm in a quiet rural hamlet. Twin-bedded rooms overlook a small tranquil walled garden. We offer en suite shower and basin and large bathroom. Tea/coffee and radio in each room. TV is available. Continental or traditional breakfasts are served in a separate dining room or in the garden. Children over 12 years welcome. We have an outside, dry and secure area for dogs. Good local pubs serving excellent food are within walking distance. Just 10 minutes from the A30/A303. Non-smoking house. Prices from £15 per person per night.

ILFRACOMBE. Jill Rapley, Two Ways, St. Brannocks Road, Ilfracombe EX34 8EP (01271 864017). ❧ ❧ For non-smokers. Two Ways is a late Victorian house offering old fashioned service with every modern comfort. All rooms have tea/coffee making, clock/radio, electric blankets, and individually controlled heating. Some have TV and are en suite. Full English breakfast is served at 8.30am, and we also offer a choice of healthy options. The TV lounge has a variety of games and books. Licensed bar. Two Ways, situated on the main A361 and Bicclescombe Park Road, has easy level parking for every room. An ideal point from which to tour all the North Devon attractions including beautiful Exmoor, and stroll around appealing Ilfracombe. Bed and Breakfast £13 to £17 (PRICES HELD). The longer the stay the lower the tariff.

ILFRACOMBE. Sunnymeade Country House Hotel, Dean Cross, West Down, Ilfracombe EX34 8NT (01271 863668). ❧ ❧ ❧ A charming country house hotel in its own large gardens set in the rolling Devonshire countryside. Every effort is made to ensure that guests feel welcome and relaxed from the moment they arrive, a feeling which is enhanced by the standard of food and accommodation. Most of the 10 pretty bedrooms are en suite and all have tea making facilities, phones, radios, alarms and colour TV; some of the rooms are on the ground floor. Fresh local ingredients are used in the traditional English cooking which has a regional flavour. There is always a vegetarian choice and any special diets can be accommodated. Clothes drying facilities for walkers and garage for cycles. Sunnymeade is close to Woolacombe, Exmoor and Ilfracombe. Access and Visa accepted. AA. Bed and Breakfast from £20.50 en suite daily; Dinner, Bed and Breakfast from £179 en suite weekly.

FREE and REDUCED RATE Holiday Visits!
See our READERS' OFFER VOUCHER for details!

ILFRACOMBE. St. Brannocks House Hotel, St. Brannocks Road, Ilfracombe EX34 8EQ (01271 863873).

🌸 🌸 🌸 A detached Victorian hotel set in its own grounds and close to the beautiful Bicclescombe Park, Cairn Nature Reserve, town centre and seafront. The cosy well stocked bar is an ideal place to relax and socialise, while the dining room offers generous portions of good home cooked food and a selection of table wines. Choice of bedrooms, most en suite. An ideal base for a perfect family holiday or special break. Children and pets welcome. Bed and Breakfast from £18.50; Evening Meal from £8.50. RAC Acclaimed, Les Routiers.

KINGSBRIDGE. Colin and Betty Fowles, West Charleton Grange, Church Lane, West Charleton, Kingsbridge TQ7 2AD (01548 531779; Fax: 01548 531100). Approached by a tree-lined private drive, surrounded by its own 10 acres of woodland, fields and lake, this family-owned 16th/18th century country house and small exclusive holiday complex is cunningly hidden in its own quiet valley, two miles from centre of Kingsbridge. Centrally placed and only short distance from towns, beaches, country walks and most holiday activities. A very good centre for touring. Two en suite bedrooms, tea/coffee trays, clock alarm radios. Large breakfast room, colour TV, central heating. Full English breakfast. Use of 10 metre indoor heated pool, short tennis court, games room, laundry room. Fax/telephone. Parking. All NON SMOKING. No pets. Children over 10 years welcome.

KINGSBRIDGE. Mrs C. Lloyd, Lower Norton, East Allington, Totnes TQ9 7RL (01548 521246).

Come and enjoy a quiet holiday at Lower Norton, a stone built farmhouse now run as a guest house within a two acre holding providing eggs, milk, etc. The house is surrounded by farmland and is situated approximately five miles from Kingsbridge and eight miles from Dartmouth; the nearest beach is Slapton and Torbay, Plymouth and Dartmoor are all within 20 miles. Four double/family rooms, two bathrooms, separate lounge/dining rooms, utility room and tea making facilities. Children welcome. No smoking. Car essential. Open April to October for Bed and Breakfast only, £105 per week. Reduction for children. Stamp only please for brochure.

KINGSBRIDGE. Mrs M. Darke, Coleridge Farm, Chillington, Kingsbridge TQ7 2JG (01548 580274).

Coleridge Farm is a 600 acre working farm situated half a mile from Chillington village, midway between Kingsbridge and Dartmouth. Many safe and beautiful beaches are within easy reach, the nearest being Slapton Sands and Slapton Ley just two miles away. Plymouth, Torquay and the Dartmoor National Park are only an hour's drive. Visitors are assured of comfortable accommodation in a choice of one double and one twin-bedded rooms; private shower; toilet; shaver points and tea/coffee making facilities. Spacious lounge with TV. A variety of eating establishments in the locality will ensure a good value Evening Meal. Children welcome. Terms on request.

KINGSBRIDGE. Woodland View Guest House, Stokenham, Kingsbridge TQ7 2SQ (01548 580542).

👑 👑 *COMMENDED.* Set in a picturesque village one mile from Slapton Sands and the Field Centre, also many other beaches; Dartmouth and Kingsbridge nearby. Superb coastal and country walks. Comfortable rooms, some ground floor; en suite available. Tea/coffee making facilities. As animal lovers we hope you will bring your pets and enjoy our hospitality. No guard dogs. Children welcome. Short Breaks available.

KINGSBRIDGE. Yvonne Helps, Hillside, Ashford, Kingsbridge TQ7 4NB (01548 550752). Character

house set in acre of orchard garden surrounded by lovely countryside, in quiet hamlet just off the A379 Plymouth to Kingsbridge road. Superb beaches and sandy coves nearby. Dartmoor 20 minutes' drive. Very comfortable accommodation with washbasins, shaver points, tea/coffee making facilities in all bedrooms. Two bathrooms. Colour TV in lounge. Diningroom with separate tables. Car parking. Visitors find a friendly, relaxed atmosphere with own keys. Full central heating. No dogs in the house please. Bed and Full English Breakfast from £15. Evening Meal optional. Open all year. Booking any day of the week. Write or phone for brochure.

KINGSBRIDGE near. Mrs M.E. Lonsdale, Fern Lodge, Hope Cove, Near Kingsbridge TQ7 3HF

(01548 561326). 👑 👑 This friendly guesthouse welcomes pets, and children over five years. Offers good home cooking, comfort and cleanliness. All rooms en suite with beverage making facilities, colour TV and own keys; TV lounge and separate lounge. Fern Lodge is three minutes' walk from sandy beaches and is situated in a small uncommercialised fishing village with miles of National Trust coastline, offering beautiful cliff and country walks. Bed and Breakfast £22 to £23 daily; Bed, Breakfast and Evening Meal £27.80 daily, £185 weekly. Please send SAE for a colour brochure.

KINGSBRIDGE near. Mrs M. Newsham, Marsh Mills, Aveton Gifford, Near Kingsbridge TQ7 4JW

(01548 550549). Former Mill House, overlooking the River Avon, with gardens, mill leat and duck pond. Small farm with friendly animals. Peaceful and secluded, just off A379. Kingsbridge four miles, Plymouth 17 miles, Bigbury and Bantham with their beautiful beaches nearby, or enjoy a walk along our unspoilt river estuary. Salcombe seven miles, Dartmoor eight miles. A warm welcome awaits our guests, who have access to the house at any time. Bedrooms have washbasins, tea/coffee making and room heaters. Guest bathroom, WC; lounge/dining room with colour TV. Car essential, ample parking. Bed and Breakfast from £15 per person. SAE for brochure, or telephone.

LYNMOUTH. Mrs J. Parker, Tregonwell Riverside Guest House, 1 Tors Road, Lynmouth, Exmoor National Park EX35 6ET (01598 753369). 👑 👑

COMMENDED. Truly paradise, our outstandingly elegant Victorian riverside stone-built house is snuggled into the sunny side of tranquil Lynmouth's deep wooded valleys, alongside beaches, waterfalls, cascades, England's highest cliff tops, enchanting harbour, all steeped in history! A wonderful walking area, where Exmoor meets the sea. Exceptionally dramatic scenery around our Olde Worlde smugglers village. Wordsworth, Shelley and Coleridge all kept returning here. An all year resort, each season unveiling its own spectacle. Pretty bedrooms, luxury en suites with breathtaking views. Guests' drawing room with open log fires in cooler seasons. Garage, parking. Bed and Breakfast from £18.50. Come as a resident then return again as our friend!

LYNMOUTH. Tricia and Alan Francis, Glenville House, 2 Tors Road, Lynmouth EX35 6ET (01598

752202). Charming licensed Victorian house in sunny position overlooking East Lyn River at the beginning of Watersmeet Valley. Picturesque village and tranquil harbour a short stroll away. Ideally situated for touring/walking this beautiful part of Exmoor with its breathtaking scenery and spectacular coastline. Some bedrooms have private facilities and all have tea/coffee making. Comfortable TV lounge and attractive dining room offering a four course breakfast. Our guests will be assured a warm welcome, good food and friendly hospitality for their stay. Non-smoking. Bed and Breakfast from £17 to £20 per person per night. Dinner (optional) £11.50 per person. Open March to November.

LYNMOUTH. Mrs P.M. Pile, Oakleigh, 4 Tors Road, Lynmouth EX35 6ET (01598 752220). A small comfortable guest house under the personal supervision of the proprietors, situated at the entrance to the famous Watersmeet Valley and enjoying a central sunny position. The surrounding countryside is ideal for walking and convenient for Exmoor, the sea and the Doone Valley. Dinner is provided if required. Five double, two single and two family bedrooms, all with washbasins, razor points and tea/coffee making facilities. Bathroom, two toilets; sitting room and dining room. Pets permitted. Reduced rates for children (if sharing parents' room). Open all year. Car useful, parking. Bed and Breakfast from £16.50; Evening Dinner, Bed and Breakfast from £25.50.

LYNTON. Mrs R. Pile, Coombe Farm, Countisbury, Lynton EX35 6NF (01598 741236). 🐾🐾

Working farm. Coombe Farm, set amid 370 acres of beautiful hill farming country, dates back to the 17th century. Ideal holiday base from which to visit lovely Doone Valley and Exmoor countryside. Two double rooms with en-suite shower rooms; one twin and two family rooms with washbasins, and all with hot drinks facilities. Bathroom, shower, two toilets; lounge; diningroom. Central heating. Children welcome, cot, high chair and occasional babysitting. Dogs by arrangement. Car essential, parking space. Guests enjoy watching farm animals, including Exmoor Horn sheep and horses. Pony trekking, tennis, fishing, golf nearby. Open March to end October. Fire Certificate held. Excellent country fare served. Bed and Breakfast from £17 to £22 per night. Reductions for children 11 years and under sharing family room. Stamp, please, for brochure. Residential licence. No smoking.

LYNTON. Nigel and Denise Hill, The Denes Guesthouse, Longmead, Lynton EX35 6DQ (01598

753573). A comfortable, friendly guest house situated on the outskirts of Lynton at the entrance to the Valley of the Rocks, a well known beauty spot. There are numerous walks over Exmoor National Park with magnificent views over the moors, sea and woodland. The cliff railway to Lynmouth is only a short walk away. All rooms have washbasins and tea making facilities and a log fire burns in the lounge during the colder evenings. We welcome children but sorry, no pets. Ample car parking. Bed and Breakfast from £15 per person. Evening Meals on request. Open all year. Please telephone for brochure.

LYNTON. Ben and Jane Bennett, Victoria Lodge, Lee Road, Lynton EX35 6BS (Tel & Fax: 01598

753203; Freephone 0500 303026). 🐾🐾🐾 *HIGHLY COMMENDED.* Elegant Victorian family-run, non-smoking hotel. Awarded 1996 RAC Best Small Hotel in South West England and one of only five in North Devon to be awarded AA Premier Selected for its comfort, hospitality and outstanding cuisine. All our en suite bedrooms are beautifully decorated, with colour TV, radios and tea/coffee making facilities; some are de luxe with four-poster beds or original brass beds, with lounge areas. Enjoy a candlelit dinner, which combines an imaginative blend of English and Continental cuisine complemented by fine wines. We are ideally situated for exploring Exmoor and its spectacular coastline. Full central heating, private car park and secluded gardens. Bed and Breakfast from £21 to £32 per person; Dinner £14. Special offers. Children welcome. No pets. Please write or telephone for free brochure.

LYNTON. Don and Jenny Bowman, Gable Lodge Hotel, Lee Road, Lynton EX35 6BS (Tel & Fax: 01598 752367). You can be sure of a warm welcome at our Victorian Grade II Listed hotel situated in a level part of Lynton. Nestling at the foot of Hollerday Hill with views over Countisbury Hill, the East Lyn Valley and Exmoor National Park. Comfortable and pretty bedrooms, both standard and en suite. Family, double and twin rooms, all with TV, beverage facilities and central heating. The cosy lounge is warmed by an open fire in winter. Car parking at rear. Bed and Breakfast from £15. Evening Meals are available. Special offers for out of season Short Breaks.

LYNTON. Sylvia House, Lydiate Lane, Lynton EX35 6HE (01598 752391). ♛♛♛ *COMMENDED.* A delightful Listed Georgian House in the "Little Switzerland" of England where Exmoor meets the sea. Offering delightful pretty rooms, most en suite, some with four-poster beds at no extra cost. All rooms with TV, tea/coffee making facilities. Scrumptious home cooked dinner served by candlelight in our elegant dining room. Guests have use of a lounge with a large TV and a wide range of books to read. Pets welcome free of charge. Bed and Breakfast from £15 to £18 per person. Dinner with choice of menu £10 per person. We also have a varied light snack menu available every evening for guests preferring a lighter meal. Children welcome. Special tariff for weekly stays and Short Breaks. Ideally situated for exploring Exmoor and its spectacular coastline and surrounding countryside. Open all year. We offer high standards of comfort and hospitality at Sylvia House and you are assured of a very warm welcome. Telephone for your FREE brochure.

LYNTON. Woodlands, Lynbridge Road, Lynton EX35 6AX (01598 752324). ♛♛♛ *COMMENDED.* AA QQQ. Peacefully located yet only a few minutes' walk from the centre of Lynton, Woodlands overlooks Summerhouse Hill and the unspoilt wooded valley of the West Lyn River. There is a choice of single, double and twin rooms, all with colour TV, radio and tea/coffee making facilities. Most rooms are very spacious, fully en suite and have glorious views across the valley. Delicious home cooking using fresh produce. Choice of menu including vegetarian option. Private parking, licensed, cosy lounge, log fire and central heating. Non-smoking. Ideal base for exploring Exmoor and the stunning coastal scenery. Bed and Breakfast £16 to £22; Evening Meals £12.

LYNTON. Mrs V.A. Ashby, Rodwell, 21 Lee Road, Lynton EX35 6BP (01598 753324). Rodwell is a small, friendly guest house situated in the most level part of Lynton facing south with lovely views of the surrounding hills and close to all amenities. Many beautiful walks start at our door and the famous Valley of Rocks and the unique cliff railway to Lynmouth are a short walk away. Comfortable lounge with colour TV, double and twin bedrooms, some en suite, all with colour TV, washbasins and tea/coffee making facilities. Parking. Bed and Breakfast from £14. Directions: opposite Cottage Hospital on the main road through Lynton.

LYNTON. Highcliffe House, Sinai Hill, Lynton EX35 6AR (Tel & Fax: 01598 752235). 🏵🏵🏵

HIGHLY COMMENDED. AA Red Star Hotel. Small luxury Victorian gentleman's summer residence 800ft above picturesque bay, commanding panoramic views of Exmoor and its finest coastline. Antiques, fine furnishings, beautifully decorated spacious en suite rooms with all modern comforts one could wish for. Roaring log fires throughout the cooler months. Our cuisine embodies the best of Victorian values, assembled with love, presented with panache. Elegant candlelit dining room. Come share our unique house. We'd like to pamper you. Totally non-smoking. Licensed. Bed and Breakfast from £35 to £38 per night; Dinner £18.50. Special Breaks. Open all year.

LYNTON. South View Guest House, 23 Lee Road, Lynton EX35 6BP (01598 752289). South View is a

small friendly guest house in the heart of the picturesque Exmoor village of Lynton. Open all year, our aim is to provide a comfortable base from which to explore this beautiful coastal region. We have five rooms, all fully en suite with colour TV, tea/coffee making facilities, hair dryer, alarm clock and individually controlled heating. We serve a full breakfast with choice of menu. Our comfortable guests' lounge is always open. Private parking is available at the rear. Overnight guests welcome. Bed and Breakfast from £14 to £18 per person per night.

LYNTON near. Glen Doone, The Old Rectory at Oare, Near Lynton EX35 6NU (01598 741202). A

house of character and tranquillity set in the heart of Doone Country in the most beautiful rolling countryside in an area steeped in history. On Exmoor and within a few minutes' walk of the quaint old church of Lorna Doone fame. Superb walking, riding and fishing are available and pets are welcome. We have stabling and a paddock as well as a lovely garden. Children over 12 years welcome. Bed and Breakfast from £20 per person per night, £128 per week. Special mid-week Breaks available. Please send for further details and our brochure.

MORTEHOE. Lundy House Hotel, Chapel Hill, Mortehoe EX34 7DZ (01271 870372). 🏵🏵🏵

COMMENDED. Small, friendly hotel spectacularly situated on cliff side with gardens adjoining coastal path, access to secluded beach and magnificent sea views over Woolacombe Bay to Lundy Island. Superb food served daily, with four-course candlelit dinners and Nadine's à la carte restaurant. Well stocked licensed bar lounge. Full gas centrally heated en suite bedrooms. Satellite TV lounge and separate colour TV and video lounge for non-smokers. Ideal base for local award-winning beaches, rambling and exploring Exmoor. Les Routiers Commended. Fully furnished holiday cottage, sleeps six, in magnificent position also available. Colour brochure on request. Short Breaks available.

NEWTON ABBOT. Mrs Dawn Cleave, Mill Leat Farm, Holne, Ashburton, Newton Abbot TQ13 7RZ

(01364 631283). A friendly welcome awaits you at Mill Leat, a family-run working farm tucked away into the foothills of Dartmoor. There is a peaceful atmosphere where you can relax and unwind and enjoy the birds and wildlife. Plenty of good walks to take in with National Trust woodlands adjoining the farm. The A38 is only three miles and Buckfast Abbey even closer. En suite is available and tea/coffee facilities are in all bedrooms. Lots of lovely homemade food. Bed and Breakfast from £16 to £17; Evening Meal from £8. Weekly reductions. Open all year except Christmas.

NEWTON ABBOT. Nigel Bell, Sampsons Farm & Lower Teign Barn, Preston, Newton Abbot TQ12

3PP (01626 54913). Thatched 14th century longhouse with oak beams, panelling and inglenook fireplaces. Sampsons is a Grade II Listed building, featuring low beams, creaky floors and is hidden away in the hamlet of Preston with lovely walks along River Teign. Always a warm welcome and a cheerful atmosphere. All rooms (three double, two family) have tea/coffee making facilities and colour TV; two en suite. New for 1997 three superb en suite rooms in converted barn (two four posters). The restaurant has an excellent reputation with only the finest produce being used. There is a licensed bar and cellar containing wines from around the world. Sampsons is well placed to explore Devon and Cornwall. Bed and Breakfast from £15; Dinner from £10.95. Open all year.

NEWTON ABBOT near. Mrs Angela Dallyn, Bulleigh Park, Ipplepen, Near Newton Abbot TQ12 5UA

Bulleigh Park

Bed & Breakfast
FARMHOUSE ACCOMMODATION
Evening Meal if required

(01803 872254). 🏆🏆 Small family farm with friendly atmosphere and extensive views over surrounding Devon countryside but within easy reach of Dartmoor; three miles from the coast and within three miles of the English Riviera. Numerous local attractions nearby, including the historic town of Totnes, four miles away, and Compton Castle half-a-mile; golf one mile. Comfortable, spacious, centrally heated accommodation. Twin/family room with en-suite facilities, double room also available; tea/coffee making facilities and colour TV in both rooms; guests' bathroom, toilet; lounge with colour TV and open fire; diningroom with separate tables. Plenty of home cooking. Special diets catered for. Reduced rates for children under 12. Cot, highchair and babysitting available. Reduced out of season rates for Senior Citizens. Car essential, ample parking. Large secluded garden with conservatory and patio. Traditional country pub within walking distance. Bed and Breakfast from £14 (Full English Breakfast). Evening Meal by arrangement.

NEWTON FERRERS. Slade Barn and Netton Farm Holiday Cottages, Noss Mayo, Near Plymouth PL8 1HA (Tel & Fax: 01752 872235). Tourist Board Listed *COMMENDED.* Coastal South Devon beside the beautiful Yealm estuary. Sandy Cherrington assures you of a warm welcome to Slade Barn. Only three bedrooms — one twin, one double and one with shower en suite. All rooms have central heating, TV/radio and hairdryers. Tea/coffee on request. Full English breakfast naturally! Lovely indoor pool, games room, tennis court and private gardens. Easy access to fabulous National Trust cliff walks; nearby sandy beaches, golf, fishing, riding. Ideal base for day trips to Cornwall or the Moors. Plenty of parking. Non smoking. Open all year. Bed and Breakfast from £17.50; Evening Meal on request. SPECIAL INTEREST: professional Reflexology/Aromatherapy Massage by appointment.

NEWTON FERRERS, near PLYMOUTH. Pat and John Urry, "Barnicott", Parsonage Road, Newton Ferrers, River Yealm, Plymouth PL8 1AS (01752 872843). 16th century thatched cottage situated in an area of outstanding natural beauty on a river valley. Facilities nearby for sailing, rowing, fishing, south Devon Heritage coastal path walks, short drives to beaches, Dartmoor National Park and historic Plymouth departure point of the Pilgrim Fathers. Accommodation comprises two double, one twin bedrooms, all with shaving points, heating, colour TV, washbasin, hospitality tray and rural views. Guests' bathroom. Full English breakfast or menu to suit. Three local inns and a Bistro serving Evening Meals all within walking distance. Private parking. Bed and Breakfast from £17 single; £28 double.

NORTH TAWTON. John and Gill Russell, Kayden House Hotel, High Street, North Tawton EX20 2HF (01837 82242). ♛♛♛ Family-run hotel in mid Devon. All rooms en suite with TV and tea making facilities. Our à la carte restaurant has an extensive menu and a comprehensive wine list, and is open from Tuesday to Saturday 7pm, last orders 9.30pm. Our traditional Sunday lunch proves very popular and is good value. We have a full bar menu, and family celebrations are catered for. Bed and Breakfast from £16. Open all year.

NORTH TAWTON. Mrs Pam Jordan, Higher Nichols Nymett, North Tawton EX20 2BP (01837 82181). A warm welcome and friendly atmosphere await you in our 15th century thatched hall house with its wealth of beams and old world charm. Situated between Okehampton and Crediton close to Dartmoor, ideal for touring Devon countryside and coast. Enjoy the moors with their lovely walks, good coarse and fly fishing or local sporting facilities just 10 minutes away. We have three bedrooms, one double and one twin together with a further double downstairs, all en suite and with tea making facilities and colour TV. Ample private parking. Bed and Breakfast from £17; optional Evening Meal available. Traditional cooking using garden produce.

OKEHAMPTON. Mrs E.G. Arney, The Old Rectory, Bratton Clovelly, Okehampton EX20 4LA (01837 871382). An ideal centre for a visit to Devon and Cornwall. With two acres of lawns, gardens and a paddock the Old Rectory is a beautifully quiet spot to spend a relaxing holiday. Thoroughly modernised property, so the visitor can be assured of comfortable accommodation and good food. Sandy beaches, beautiful countryside, rugged Dartmoor, a lake with prime fishing and water sports, all within a car journey. Three large double rooms, all with washbasins, one with shower. A warm welcome, friendly atmosphere and personal attention encourages visitors to return again and again. Pets welcome. Bed and Breakfast from £16; Evening Meal available.

OTTERY ST MARY. Mrs Susan Hansford, Pitt Farm, Fairmile, Ottery St. Mary EX11 1NL (01404 812439). ♛♛ COMMENDED. Bed and Breakfast at this most attractive thatched farmhouse, with 190 acres, situated in peaceful village of Fairmile, quarter of a mile off the A30 on the B3176. Enjoying picturesque views of the surrounding countryside it is an ideal base for touring moors, East Devon, South Devon, Exeter. Double, twin and family rooms, some en suite; three bathrooms; lounge with colour TV; dining room. Regret no pets. Car essential — ample parking. Fire Certificate held. Bed and Breakfast from £17. SAE, or phone for terms; prompt reply.

DEVON – FROM COAST TO COAST

Dramatic cliffs, hidden coves, rolling surf and traditional family holiday resorts are some of the attractions which make holidaymakers return year after year to the unspoiled coastline of North Devon. There are unparalleled opportunities for watersports of all kinds, and, for the less energetic, picturesque fishing villages to explore and hidden coves for sunbathing.

The sheltered South Coast has been dubbed the "English Riviera", with an exceptionally mild climate and lively resorts offering amenities and attractions for all the family.

PAIGNTON. Freda Dwane and Steve Bamford, Clifton Hotel, 9/10 Kernou Road, Paignton TQ4 6BA (01803 556545). Ideally located, friendly, relaxed, licensed small hotel with excellent food, open Easter to November plus Christmas Breaks. A short level walk to sea, theatre, shops, rail and coach stations. Perfect spot for leaving the car and relaxing by exploring on foot or using the plentiful public transport. All bedrooms are non smoking with TV and tea/coffee making facilities and are double glazed and centrally heated with radiator thermostats. All bedrooms are en suite or have private shower/bathroom. Bed and Breakfast from £16. Spring and Autumn breaks in en suite rooms (minimum two nights) £46 per night two persons Dinner, Bed and Breakfast.

PAIGNTON (Torbay). Mrs Mandy Tooze, Elberry Farm, Broadsands, Paignton TQ4 6HJ (01803 842939). Working farm. Elberry Farm is a working farm uniquely situated close to Broadsands Beach, Elberry Cove and a pitch and putt golf course. Close to many of Torbay's tourist attractions. Warm welcome and good hearty meals (using local and home grown produce) are guaranteed. The comfortable rooms (three family and one twin) all have tea/coffee making facilities. Baby listening, cot and high chair available. Pets by arrangement. Restricted smoking. Open January to November. Bed and Breakfast from £12.50 per person; Evening Meals £5.50. Reductions for children.

PLYMOUTH. Mayflower Guest House, 209 Citadel Road East, The Hoe, Plymouth (01752 202727; Fax: 01752 667496). Family-run guest house, opposite Hoe Park, close to shops, marinas, restaurants, bus station, theatres. Most rooms en suite, shower and toilet, colour TV, tea and coffee making facilities, central heating. Own keys, payphone, full Fire Certificate. All major credit cards accepted. Directions — leave expressway (A38) follow city centre signs, bear left at Hoe, seafront sign, 100 metres by third traffic lights, by sign turn left for Hoe, seafront, turn into Hoegate Street, top of road, turn right, we are in the middle cul-de-sac opposite Hoe Park.

PLYMOUTH. Irvine's, 50 Grand Parade, West Hoe, Plymouth PL1 3DJ (01752 227739). Victorian town house offering comfortable Bed and Breakfast accommodation. Traditional English breakfast served, special diets catered for. Accommodation comprises one double and one twin bedroom, both with colour TV, washbasins, tea/coffee making facilities, central heating and double glazing. Other facilities include bathroom, separate shower room and private parking. The house overlooks Drake's Island and Plymouth Sound and is within walking distance of town centre, Plymouth Pavilion's Leisure and Conference Centre, theatre, the Barbican and all other local amenities including Ferry Port, rail and bus stations. Bed and Breakfast from £14 per person. Brittany Ferries recommended.

PLYMOUTH. Lynn and Ralph Whitworth, Four Seasons Guest House, 207 Citadel Road East, The Hoe, Plymouth PL1 2JF (01752 223591). A friendly, long established guest house situated in a quiet position opposite Hoe Park and near to historic Barbican sea front, town centre, ferry port. Most rooms en suite, all have free colour TV and tea/coffee making facilities. Central heating, payphone, own keys giving access at all times. Vegetarians catered for; recommended by Independent Caterer Magazine. AA QQQ Recommended. Please write or phone for further details.

PLYMOUTH. Caraneal Hotel, 12 & 14 Pier Street, West Hoe, Plymouth PL1 3BS (01752 663589). Caraneal is a friendly family-run licensed Hotel offering a warm atmosphere and personal service. All nine bedrooms have full en suite facilities with remote control colour TV and complimentary tea and coffee. Pleasantly situated just off the picturesque waterfront opposite a small park within easy walking distance of the city centre, historic Barbican, famous Plymouth Hoe, theatres and the Pavilions Leisure facilities. Even closer to Brittany Ferries' gateway to France and Spain with early full English breakfasts for ferry passengers. All major credit cards accepted. Bed and Breakfast from £17.50 per person.

PLYMOUTH. The Lamplighter Hotel, 103 Citadel Road, The Hoe, Plymouth PL1 2RN (01752 663855). Lamplighter Hotel is a family-run business situated on Plymouth Hoe, close to the sea front, Barbican and city centre. All rooms are of the highest standard and provide full English breakfast, tea/coffee and biscuits; TV, Sky, video. Car park. Reductions for children. Please telephone, or write, for further details.

PLYMOUTH. Joyce and Keith Taylor, Hotspur Guest House, 108 North Road East, Plymouth PL4 6AW (01752 663928). ETB ✿ APPROVED. Licensed family-run "home from home" guest house close to station, city centre, university, ferry port and coach station and also close to all leisure facilities. Accommodation in family rooms, doubles, singles and twins, all centrally heated with colour TV and tea/coffee making facilities. Payphone. Ironing facilities. Own keys. Fire Certificate. Families welcome at reduced rates when sharing. Mid-week bookings or single nights welcome. Early breakfasts by arrangement if required for ferry passengers etc. Further information on request.

PLYMOUTH. Drake Hotel, 1 & 2 Windsor Villas, Lockyer Street, The Hoe, Plymouth PL1 2QD (01752 229730 & 228133). Two elegant Victorian villas have been linked to form the Drake Hotel, centrally situated with all city centre amenities and the sea front within walking distance. You also have the benefit of free on-site parking. The Drake is an appointed AA and RAC One Star establishment and is a member of the prestigious Logis group. The bar and restaurant are open each evening with food prepared from locally purchased produce. Bed and Breakfast from £24.

PLYMOUTH. Allington House, 6 St. James Place East, The Hoe, Plymouth PL1 3AS (01752 221435). Situated in a secluded square between the city shopping centre and Hoe Promenade. An elegant Victorian town house which offers clean, comfortable accommodation. All bedrooms have colour TV, washbasin, central heating and beverage facilities. En suite rooms are available. Within close reach are railway and bus stations and the ferry port, the Pavilion, Theatre Royal, cinemas, Hoe seafront, Citadel and historic Barbican are within walking distance. A full English breakfast is included unless otherwise requested (vegetarians catered for). 15% discount on bookings of three days or more two adults sharing. Bed and Breakfast from £15 per person. Brittany Ferries Recommended.

Beautiful 16th Century Coaching House with log fires and brasses. Jan and John Moore will give you the warmest of welcomes and help you plan your days if you wish. Set in an area of outstanding natural beauty. Central for sea or country. Footpaths lead through woodland. Cliff walks. Wonderful wildlife. Honiton's antique shops and lace, historic Exeter, all at hand. Sidmouth is just 10 minutes away. All bedrooms are centrally heated and have tea/coffee making facilities. Traditional jazz every Saturday night in the function room, so if you want a quiet drink in the lounge bar you're not disturbed. Real ales served. Bed and Breakfast from £14. ♛♛

THREE HORSESHOES INN

On the main A3052 between Sidmouth and Seaton

**Branscombe, Seaton, Devon EX12 3BR
Telephone: 01297 680251**

SEATON. Jill and Wanley Cook, Overleas, Harepath Hill, Near Colyford, Seaton EX12 2TA (01297 20220). Peaceful country house on the side of a hill overlooking the beautiful Axe Valley. From the south-facing panorama can be seen the delightful village of Axmouth, and the picturesque town of Seaton. The house is set in approximately one acre of ornamental lawns and landscaped flower gardens. There is ample car parking space. All rooms have washbasins, central heating, shaver points and tea/coffee making facilities. Bed and Breakfast from £17.50.

WHEN MAKING ENQUIRIES PLEASE MENTION
FARM HOLIDAY GUIDES

SIDMOUTH. Mrs B.I. Tucker, Goosemoor Farm, Newton Poppleford, Sidmouth EX10 0BL (01395

568279). Goosemoor Farmhouse is an old Devon Long House with a bread oven in the dining room. The 25-acre mixed farm is on the Exeter — Lyme Regis bus route, about four miles from the sea, and has streams running through its meadows. There are many delightful walks in country lanes, or over Woodberry and Alsbeare Commons. Guests may wander freely on the farmland. Coarse fishing available also. There are four double and one family rooms, all with wash-basins; two bathrooms, three toilets; sitting room; dining room. Open all year with log fires. Central heating throughout. Car not essential, but there is parking. No children under eight years. Bed and Breakfast from £15. Cream teas also available.

Berwick House

Salcombe Road, Sidmouth, Devon EX10 8PX Tel: 01395 513621

Attractive 19th century house situated close to the River Sid and National Trust Byes and within easy level walking distance of the sea and town centre. The locality is part of the Heritage Coast, offering ideal walking, and is also well placed for visiting many other attractions. We have two twin/family rooms, two double, one self-contained, the other with private sitting room. All rooms en suite with TV and tea/coffee-making facilities. Comfortable lounge. Car park. Sorry, no pets or smoking. Open all year. Optional Evening Meal March-October. Terms from £17pp for Bed and Breakfast. *Further details from:*
Rosemary Tingley and Tony Silversides
Members of Sidmouth & District Hotels & Caterers' Association
WCTB ❦❦ COMMENDED

Bovett's Farm

Bovett's nestles amid the rolling hills of the truly breathtaking Roncombe Valley. There are many excellent walks nearby. Within easy reach of Exeter and East Devon's Heritage Coast. Guests have use of the garden and are free to come and go as they please. The comfortable lounge has a wood-burning stove, colour TV and a selection of books and games. A full English Breakfast is served in the lovely dining room. We offer a choice of three attractively furnished double/twin bedrooms all with ensuite shower room and shaver point. Bedrooms are heated and have tea/coffee making facilities. Friendly personal service. Ample parking. No smoking. *Call Bridget and Brian Hopkinson for further details.*

Bovett's Farm, Roncombe Lane, Sidbury, Sidmouth, Devon EX10 0QN   Telephone: (01395) 597456

SIDMOUTH. Mrs Betty S. Sage, Pinn Barton, Peak Hill, Sidmouth EX10 0NN (01395 514004; Fax:

01395 514004). ❦❦ *COMMENDED.* A 330-acre farm peacefully set just off the coastal road, two miles from Sidmouth and close to the village of Otterton. Safe beaches and lovely cliff walks. Pinn Barton has been highly recommended, and offers a warm welcome in comfortable surroundings with good farmhouse breakfast. All bedrooms have bathrooms en-suite; colour TV; central heating; free hot drinks facilities; electric blankets. Children very welcome. Reductions for children sharing parents' room. Open all year. Bed and Breakfast including bedtime drink from £19. Own keys provided for access at all times.

PLEASE SEND A STAMPED ADDRESSED ENVELOPE WITH ENQUIRIES

SOUTH MOLTON (6 miles). Tony and Myra Pring, The Gables, On-the-Bridge, Umberleigh EX37 9AB (01769 560461). 🌑🌑 We offer friendly personal service here at The Gables, which is situated facing the River Taw, famous for its salmon fishing and "Tarka the Otter".

You will find us ideally placed for the beautiful Exmoor National Parks, Dartington Glass, Lynton and Lynmouth and the sandy beaches of Woolacombe. The Barnstaple to Exeter railway line is within easy access for those who do not wish to drive. The accommodation is in three en-suite rooms, one twin, one double and one single, all with central heating and tea/coffee facilities. There is a quiet lounge and a TV lounge. Tea rooms available. Private parking. Sorry, no children. Open all year. Bed and Breakfast from £16.50 to £21.50.

SOUTH MOLTON (Exmoor National Park). Mary Yendell, "Crangs Heasleigh", Heasley Mill, South Molton EX36 3LE (North Molton [015984] 268). 🌑🌑 **Working farm.** Traditional Listed Devon Longhouse offering Bed and substantial Breakfast all year round. This is a mixed working farm in the Exmoor National Park area. A

beautiful situation for touring the Exmoor countryside, exploring Devon and West Somerset, lovely beaches, walking, looking at old mines or riding, indeed all country pursuits. Within easy reach of Barnstaple with its leisure centre and amenities and the coast and market towns. Tea/coffee making facilities. Bed and Breakfast. Open all year.

TAVISTOCK. Aileen Kuttschreutter, Broadacre, Gulworthy PL13 8HX (01822 832470). On the edge of Dartmoor, three miles from Tavistock on the A390 to Callington, just past the Harvest Home Pub which serves excellent meals. A comfortable bungalow comprising one double and one twin bedrooms sharing bathroom. Both rooms have colour TV and satellite, washbasins, tea/coffee facilities and central heating. Guests' sitting area. Parking. Large garden. Situated close to National Trust areas, Buckland Abbey and Cothele House. Also near "Victorian" Morwellham Quay. In summer there are art and craft markets in Tavistock. Full English or Continental breakfast available. Bed and Breakfast £15 to £17. English and Dutch spoken.

TAVISTOCK. Mrs Rose Bacon, "April Cottage", Mount Tavy Road, Tavistock PL19 9JB (01822 613280). 🌑🌑 *HIGHLY COMMENDED.* Recommended by

"Which?" Good Bed and Breakfast Guide. Lovely Victorian cottage in a unique setting on the banks of the River Tavy with flower gardens and patios overlooking the River as it tumbles along towards the Tamar Valley. We are situated within two minutes' level walk of the centre of town. Local facilities include golf, fishing, tennis, swimming, canoe or cycle hire. Dartmoor on our doorstep offers walking, climbing or horse riding in an area of outstanding beauty, a natural habitat for wildlife. "April Cottage" offers extremely comfortable accommodation with attention to detail ensuring a very pleasant stay. En-suite facilities. Colour TV, radios, tea/coffee, also comfortable TV lounge with seasonal log fire overlooking the river. The house has central heating and double glazing. Parking. Bed and Breakfast from £14 nightly.

TAVISTOCK near. Ed and Merl Stevens, The Old Coach House Hotel, Ottery, Near Tavistock PL19 8NS (01822 617515). 🌑🌑🌑 A lovely small country Hotel on edge of tiny hamlet of Ottery, close to historic Tavistock and beautiful Dartmoor. Ideal base for visiting any part of Devon or Cornwall. Peaceful setting amid rolling farmland adjacent to Tamar Valley, designated an area of outstanding beauty. Superb walking country, fishing and many National Trust houses and gardens nearby. Two golf courses within three miles and St. Mellion International Golf Club 20 minutes, or just relax in our tranquil walled garden. All rooms en suite and have colour TV, tea/coffee making facilities, telephone and clock/radios. Bargain Breaks from £62 to £90 for three nights Dinner, Bed and Breakfast. AA QQQQ.

FREE and REDUCED RATE Holiday Visits!
See our READERS' OFFER VOUCHER for details!

TEIGN VALLEY. S. and G. Harrison-Crawford, Silver Birches, Teign Valley, Trusham, Newton Abbot TQ13 0NJ (01626 852172). A warm welcome awaits you at Silver Birches, a comfortable bungalow at the edge of Dartmoor. A secluded, relaxing spot with two acre garden running down to river. Only two miles from A38 on B3193. Exeter 14 miles, sea 12 miles. Car advisable. Ample parking. Excellent pubs and restaurants nearby. Good centre for fishing, birdwatching, forest walks, golf, riding; 70 yards salmon/trout fishing free to residents. Centrally heated guest accommodation with separate entrance. Two double-bedded rooms, one twin-bedded room, all with own bath/shower, toilet. Guest lounge with colour TV. Diningroom, sun lounge overlooking river. Sorry, no children under eight. Terms include tea on arrival. Bed and full English Breakfast from £23 nightly, £154 weekly. Evening Meal optional. Open all year. Self catering caravans also available.

TIVERTON. Colin and Christine Cook, Higher Western Restaurant, Oakford, Tiverton EX16 9JE (01398 341210). Licensed small country restaurant with en-suite accommodation set in three-quarters of an acre. On the B3227 Taunton/Barnstaple Holiday Route, one-and-a-half miles west of Oakford, in an area of outstanding natural beauty. A relaxing base for touring Exmoor and the North Devon coast. Excellent food, cooked to order, specialising in imaginative menus using local and own produce, complemented by a carefully chosen wine list. We offer quality accommodation to those seeking peace and quiet. One twin-bedded and two double rooms, all en-suite. Children welcome. Car essential: ample parking. Open all year round. Terms: Bed and Breakfast from £14 per night. Caravan also available.

TIVERTON. Mrs Diana Knapton, Hole Farm, Witheridge, Tiverton EX16 8QD (01884 860265). Hole Farm is a 17th century Devon Longhouse situated in rural surroundings just outside the village of Witheridge in Mid-Devon, approximately 25 minutes' drive west of Junction 27 of the M5. The house provides comfortable family accommodation comprising lounge with inglenook fireplace, colour TV and video, dining room; double bedroom with en suite shower room, twin bedroom with en suite bathroom and connecting children's room and two single rooms with shared bathroom. All rooms have tea/coffee making facilities. Undercover parking available. Children welcome at reduced rates. Pets welcome. Bed and Breakfast from £12; Evening Meal from £8.

If you've found
FARM HOLIDAY GUIDES
of service please tell your friends

TIVERTON. Mrs Ruth Hill-King, Little Holwell, Collipriest, Tiverton EX16 4PT (01884 257590).

Little Holwell is an old Devon longhouse believed to date from the 13th century, set amidst rolling hills in the Exe Valley, just one and a half miles south of Tiverton. We offer a warm welcome with ample home cooking, homemade bread. Three guest rooms, one room with en suite facilities, all with washbasins, tea/coffee making facilities, radios and hairdryers. The house is centrally heated, with log fires in winter, and is open all year except Christmas; we are also a NON-SMOKING house. Essential Food Hygiene Certificate held. There are pleasant views from the garden over the surrounding countryside, and some interesting walks. We are in a quiet location, yet within 15 minutes you can be on the M5 motorway. There are many places to explore, and the coasts and moors are both within easy driving distance. We also have National Trust houses not far away, a museum, and plenty of other interesting things to find and do. Directions: from M5 take A361 towards Tiverton, take left junction at B3391, proceed to fourth roundabout, take left exit, follow round left, and proceed for one and a half miles, last property along lane on right. Bed and Breakfast from £16 per person per night; Bed, Breakfast and Evening Meal £24.50 per person per night.

TIVERTON. Mrs S.M. Kerslake, Landrake Farm, Chevithorne, Tiverton EX16 7QN (01398 331221).

ETB Listed. Landrake is situated in a glorious part of Devon, amidst lovely rolling hills with extensive country views and plenty of lovely walks close to the farmhouse. Within 20 minutes' drive of the M5 it offers the perfect base for a relaxing family break or touring holiday. Accommodation is available from April to October and children and well behaved pets are welcome. We have one double, one twin and one family room with washbasin, all with tea/coffee making facilities; bathroom with bath and shower; cosy sitting and dining rooms. Traditional farmhouse cooking. Cot, high chair and baby sitting available. Ample car parking. Please write or telephone for our brochure and terms.

TORQUAY. Mrs R. Wilkinson, Deane Thatch Accommodation, Stoke-in-Teignhead, Near Torquay TQ12 4QU (Tel & Fax: 01626 873724). 🐾🐾 *COMMENDED.* A charming thatched Devonshire cob cottage, and thatched cob Linhay. Situated in a secluded rural spot enjoying uninterrupted views of farmland with an atmosphere of total tranquillity. Half a mile from the village of Stoke-in-Teignhead and ideally situated for Torquay (the English Riviera) and Dartmoor National Park. All rooms have colour TV, private bathroom/shower or bidet and tea/coffee making facilities; king-size bed in Linhay. Children welcome, reduced rates and babysitting available. Open all year. Bed and Breakfast from £16; discounts for weekly rate. Brittany Ferries recommended.

TORQUAY. Mike and Silvia Young, Chelston Banks Hotel, Old Mill Road, Torquay TQ2 6HW (01803 607129). A small family-run hotel set in peaceful surroundings yet within easy reach of the beach, railway station and the Riviera Centre. The picturesque village of Cockington is also nearby. All rooms are en suite and have complimentary tea/coffee facilities and central heating; own keys with access to rooms at all times; comfortable lounge with colour TV and a selection of video films for your entertainment. Enjoy a drink in our attractive Harbourside Inn where you can enjoy the company in a friendly holiday atmosphere (pool table). Home cooking and a good choice of menu is offered. Parking. Open all year. Special Christmas and New Year programme. Visitors' comments include "Our best holiday ever" — Mrs Rachel Gorman and family. Please write, or telephone, for our colour brochure.

PLEASE SEND A STAMPED ADDRESSED ENVELOPE WITH ENQUIRIES

HEATHCLIFF HOTEL

16 Newton Road, Torquay, Devon TQ2 5BZ

Telephone: 01803 211580

This former vicarage is now a superbly appointed hotel equipped for today yet retaining its Victorian charm. All the bedrooms have full ensuite facilities, colour TV and drink making facilities. The elegant licensed bar boasts an extensive menu and unlike many hotels, the car park has sufficient space to accommodate all vehicles to eliminate roadside parking. Torquay's main beach, High Street shops, entertainment and restaurants are all nearby and with full English breakfast included, it is easy to see why guests return time after time.

Tariff for B&B ranges between £14 and £21.50 pp. Family rooms from £42 per night.

So, be it main holiday, touring or business, make the Heathcliff your 1st choice.

VISITORS	BOOK
Rick & Elaine	Best in Devon
Mr & Mrs T	Excellent !
The S Family	1st Class
Mac & June	Fantastic Hosts

TORQUAY. Clevedon Hotel, Meadfoot Sea Road, Torquay TQ1 2LQ (01803 294260). ♥♥♥ AA QQQ, RAC Acclaimed. Small licensed family run hotel ideally situated in beautiful wooded suburb, 300 yards from beach, half a mile from harbour and town centre. Business and holiday guests alike enjoy our peaceful location, delicious food and genuine home from home atmosphere. All 12 bedrooms are comfortably furnished with private facilities en-suite, colour TV and tea/coffee making. Ground floor and family rooms available. Dogs accepted by arrangement. Ample parking. Open all year including Christmas. Bed and Breakfast from £19. Evening Meal optional.

TORQUAY. West Winds, Teignmouth Road, Maidencombe, Torquay TQ1 4TH (01803 328369). Dennis and Wyvene Maisey welcome you to their family home; relaxed atmosphere, comfortably furnished, centrally heated. Attractive TV lounge, large conservatory overlooking gardens and fields. Some rooms with sea views and en-suite facilities. Tea/coffee making facilities and colour TV in all rooms. Full English Breakfast. Own key, ample parking. Bed and Breakfast from £15.50 per person. Reduced rates for weekly bookings and for children. Local beach is nearby with safe bathing from a sheltered cove and there is a Thatched Tavern within walking distance for a variety of meals and bar snacks.

Terms quoted in this publication may be subject to increase if rises in costs necessitate

BRADDON HALL HOTEL

Braddons Hill Road East, Torquay TQ1 1HF
Telephone: 01803 293908
Proprietors: Peter and Carol White

This delightful personally run hotel is situated in a peaceful yet convenient position, only a few minutes from the harbour, shopping centre and entertainments.

★ All en suite rooms are individual in character and tastefully decorated with remote control colour TVs and tea/coffee making facilities

★ Romantic four-poster bed available for that special occasion

★ Attractive well-stocked bar

★ Superb traditional food with varied menus

★ Discounts for the over 55's on weekly bookings out of season

★ Full central heating for those early and late breaks

★ Ground floor bedroom

★ Parking

★ Full Christmas programme

Bed and Breakfast from £16.00 to £20.00 per person.

TORQUAY. Hotel Fiesta, 50 St. Mary Church Road, Torquay TA1 3JE (01803 292388). An elegant neo-Georgian building in spacious grounds with large sunny garden. Good food and friendly atmosphere. All rooms have tea making facilities, washbasins and central heating. Separate tables in dining room. TV lounge, games room, pool table and children's play area. Within easy reach of beaches, shops and entertainment plus 18 hole golf course and a wide range of sporting facilities. Bed and Breakfast from £93 to £126 weekly; £14 to £18 per person per day. Colour brochure and tariff available.

Silverlands Hotel
27 Newton Road, Torquay, Devon TQ25 5DB
Telephone: 01803 292013

Situated on a main route to town and beach (approx. $\frac{1}{2}$ mile). Superb family run guest house. Eleven superior rooms furnished and decorated to a high standard, mostly ensuite. Relaxed and homely atmosphere. Satellite TV, hot and cold wash facilities, tea and coffee making, full central heating available in all rooms. Ample car parking. Full English Breakfast. Open all year. From £13 to £20 per person.

ETB COMMENDED   RAC Listed   AA QQQ

WINNER SOUTH HAMS
FOR ALL SEASONS AWARD

TOTNES. Mrs Jeannie Allnutt, The Old Forge at Totnes, Seymour Place, Totnes TQ9 5AY (01803 862174). ✿✿ *HIGHLY COMMENDED.* A charming 600-year-old stone building, delightfully converted from blacksmith and wheelwright workshops and coach houses. Traditional working forge, complete with blacksmith's prison cell. We have our own bit of "rural England" close to the town centre. Very close to the River Dart steamer quay, shops and station (also steam train rides). Ideally situated for touring most of Devon — including Dartmoor and Torbay coasts. A day trip from Exeter, Plymouth and Cornwall. May to September — Elizabethan costume worn Tuesdays. Double, twin and family rooms with all en suite. Ground floor rooms suitable for most disabled guests. All rooms have colour TV, beverage trays (fresh milk), colour co-ordinated Continental bedding, central heating. Licensed lounge and patio. No smoking indoors. New conservatory style leisure lounge with whirlpool spa. Parking, walled gardens. Excellent choice of breakfast menu including vegetarian and special diets. Children welcome but sorry, no pets. Bed and Breakfast from £25 per person (en suite). Cottage suite for two to four persons also available, suitable for disabled visitors. AA Selected (QQQQ) Award.

UMBERLEIGH. Mrs Pauline Warne, Emmett Farm, Umberleigh EX37 9AG (01769 540243). Emmett is a full working farm set in quiet countryside. You will be most welcome to browse around the farm at your own leisure. The traditional farmhouse has a beamed dining room, comfortable lounge with open log fire and colour TV. The relaxing bedrooms are equipped with tea/coffee facilities and radio/clock/alarms. Fresh home grown produce is used (whenever possible) in the farmhouse cooking, with our farm-fresh eggs for breakfast and a different four-course meal each evening if required. We are situated approximately seven miles from Barnstaple, South Molton and Torrington. There are many local places of interest to visit with the sandy beaches of the North Devon coastline in easy reach, as is scenic Exmoor with its panoramic views. Bed and Breakfast from £15; Evening Meal £8.50. Ample car parking. Sorry, no pets.

UMBERLEIGH. Lyn & David Billington, Westacott, Townsend, Chittlehampton EX37 9PU (01769 540463). This centrally heated 300 year old former bakery set on the edge of a pretty thatched village is ideally located for exploring Exmoor, Dartmoor and surrounding areas, including the market town of Barnstaple and South Molton with its many antique shops. Guests have the use of the owners' lounge. Evening Meals are always available at the local pub 300 yards away. An excellent location for an active or relaxing break. Non-smoking visitors only. Bed and Breakfast from £15 per person to £29 per couple. Self catering holiday let, two bedrooms, is also available at certain times.

WHIDDON DOWN. Mrs Elizabeth Knox, Tor View, Whiddon Down, Okehampton EX20 2PR (01647 231447). Come and relax in our friendly guesthouse on the fringe of Dartmoor National Park and enjoy the panoramic moorland view from our large garden. Accommodation is on the ground floor, centrally heated throughout, separate bath and shower in bathroom; tea/coffee making facilities, colour TV/radio in guests' lounge. Ideally located for walking, riding, fishing, golf, swimming, exploring Dartmoor and situated midway between North and South coasts. Situated one mile from main A30 Exeter to Bodmin Road and four miles from medieval stannary town of Chagford. Bed and Breakfast from £15. Sorry, no smoking, no pets. Member of Dartmoor Tourist Association.

WOOLACOMBE. Mrs C. Robbins, Springside, Mullacott Road, Woolacombe EX34 7HF (01271 870452). Springside is a seven-bedroomed detached country residence standing in two and a half acres just off the B3343 road on the outskirts of Woolacombe, three miles from Ilfracombe. All bedrooms have en suite facilities, colour TV and tea/coffee making facilities. Own keys to bedrooms. Separate tables in large dining room. Residential licence. Central heating. Ample free off road car parking. Food is of the highest quality and is always highly recommended. Sorry, no pets. Bed and Breakfast available March to October.

YELVERTON. Justine Colton, Peek Hill Farm, Dousland, Yelverton PL20 6PD (Tel & Fax: 01822 854808). ✿✿ COMMENDED. "Come up to where the buzzards fly, the air is clean, the water clear". Situated on the southern slopes of Dartmoor with sweeping views to Cornwall and adjacent to wooded Burrator Lake. Comfortable, sunny bedrooms, with en suite bathrooms. Log fire in lounge and much more. We are friendly and informal and are easily located off B3212. Open January to November. Children and pets welcome. Bed and Breakfast from £17 to £20.

FOR THE MUTUAL GUIDANCE OF GUEST AND HOST

Every year literally thousands of holidays, short-breaks and overnight stops are arranged through our guides, the vast majority without any problems at all. In a handful of cases, however, difficulties do arise about bookings, which often could have been prevented from the outset.

It is important to remember that when accommodation has been booked, both parties — guests and hosts — have entered into a form of contract. We hope that the following points will provide helpful guidance.

GUESTS: When enquiring about accommodation, be as precise as possible. Give exact dates, numbers in your party and the ages of any children. State the number and type of rooms wanted and also what catering you require — bed and breakfast, full board, etc. Make sure that the position about evening meals is clear — and about pets, reductions for children or any other special points.

Read our reviews carefully to ensure that the proprietors you are going to contact can supply what you want. Ask for a letter confirming all arrangements, if possible.

If you have to cancel, do so as soon as possible. Proprietors do have the right to retain deposits and under certain circumstances to charge for cancelled holidays if adequate notice is not given and they cannot re-let the accommodation.

HOSTS: Give details about your facilities and about any special conditions. Explain your deposit system clearly and arrangements for cancellations, charges, etc, and whether or not your terms include VAT.

If for any reason you are unable to fulfil an agreed booking without adequate notice, you may be under an obligation to arrange alternative suitable accommodation or to make some form of compensation.

While every effort is made to ensure accuracy, we regret that FHG Publications cannot accept responsibility for errors, omissions or misrepresentation in our entries or any consequences thereof. Prices in particular should be checked because we go to press early. We will follow up complaints but cannot act as arbiters or agents for either party.

DORSET

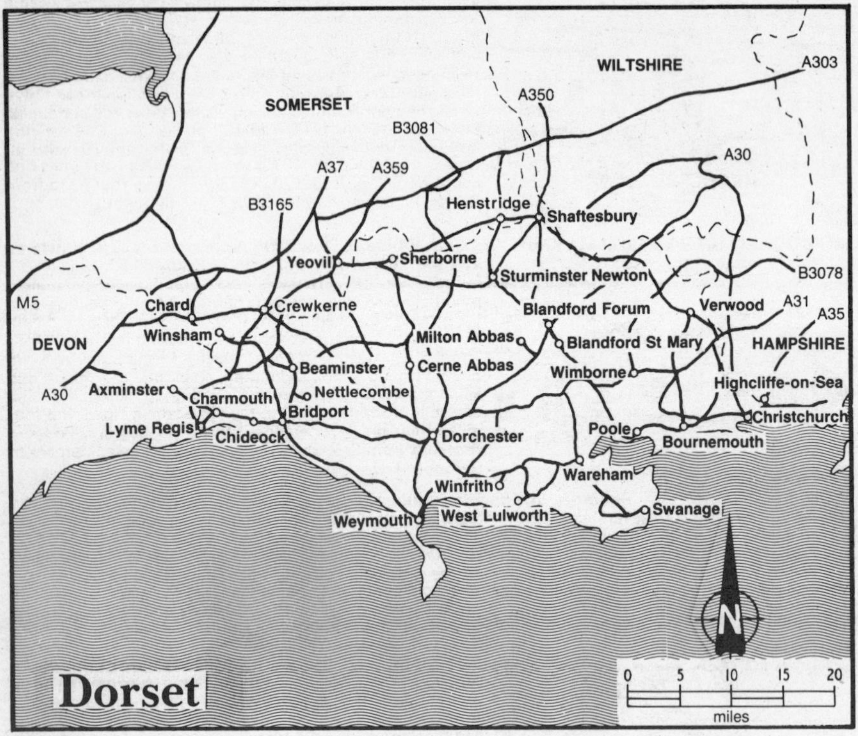

BEAMINSTER (4 miles). Mrs Pauline Wallbridge, Watermeadow House, Bridge Farm, Hooke, Beaminster DT8 3PD (01308 862619). *HIGHLY COMMENDED.* Watermeadow House is a large stone built Georgian-style country house set in a tiny West Dorset village amidst acres of beautiful countryside. Hooke is 10 miles from the sea and approximately 13 miles from Dorchester and Yeovil. Bridge Farm is a 230 acre dairy farm. The accommodation consists of one large family room with en-suite shower room and one double room with washbasin and own bathroom next to bedroom. Both rooms have tea/coffee making facilities and colour TV. A generous English breakfast is served in a beautiful sun lounge. Perfect for those seeking peace and quiet and friendly, personal service. Bed and Breakfast from £18. Special weekly terms. Children from £8.

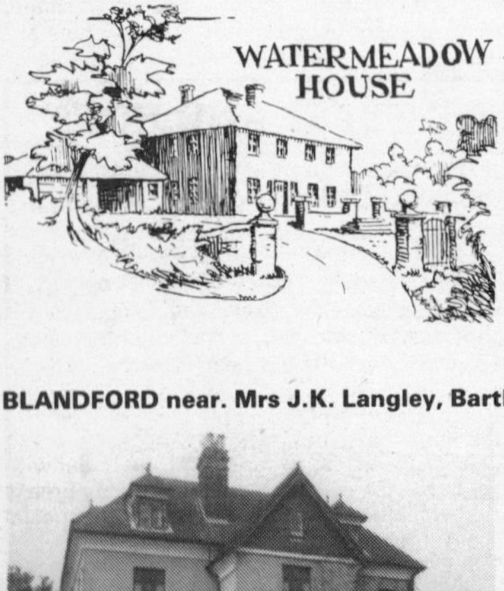

BLANDFORD near. Mrs J.K. Langley, Bartley House, Upper Street, Child Okeford, Near Blandford DT11 8EF (01258 860420). Bartley House is situated in the centre of this lovely Dorset backwater. Originally built as a Temperance Hall during Victoria's reign it later became the village Co-op shop, and then a private residence. Renovated and modernised to a very high standard of comfort by the present owners, it offers a diningroom, sittingroom with TV, two family rooms, one double and one twin. Three rooms have en-suite showers, one has en suite WC, all have vanity units, central heating, kettles for morning tea or coffee. Within easy reach of Bournemouth, Poole, Weymouth and the Blackmore Vale, this is luxury accommodation at reasonable cost. Car parking space.

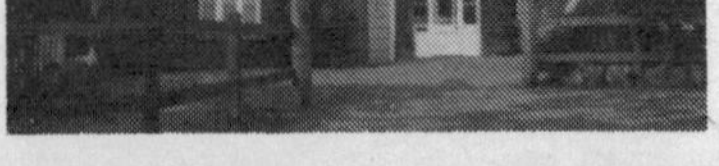

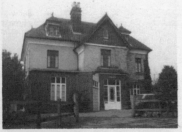

BLANDFORD. The Anvil Hotel and Restaurant, Pimperne, Blandford DT11 8UQ (01258 453431/480182). ♥ ♥ ♥ *COMMENDED.*

A long, low thatched building set in a tiny village deep in the Dorset countryside two miles from Blandford — what could be more English? And that is what visitors to the Anvil will find — a typical old English hostelry offering good, old-fashioned English hospitality. A full à la carte mouth-watering menu with delicious desserts available in the charming beamed and flagged restaurant with log fire, and a wide selection of bar meals in the attractive, fully licensed bar. All bedrooms have private facilities. Ample parking. Pets welcome. Good Food Pub Guide, Les Routiers. £110 for two persons for two nights Bed and Breakfast or from £70 per night double room and from £45 per night single room. Dogs £2.50 per night.

BLANDFORD. Mr and Mrs D.A. Selby, "Simplers Joy", Tarrant Keynston, Blandford DT3 9EJ (01258 453686).

"Simplers Joy" is a tastefully renovated cob thatched 17th century Listed cottage overlooking the Tarrant Valley. Ideally situated for visiting Poole and Bournemouth and the National Trust's Kingston Lacy House, and the surrounding lovely Dorset countryside. Accommodation comprises ground floor twin room and first floor double room, each with its own luxury en suite bathroom. Each room has colour TV and tea/coffee-making facilities. Guests' sun lounge. Access at all times. Central heating. Easy parking. Full English Breakfast served. Terms £16 per person, per night. Brochure on request.

BOURNEMOUTH. Denise and Brian Shepherd, Westbrook Private Hotel, 64 Alum Chine Road, Westbourne, Bournemouth BH4 8DZ (01202 761081).

Westbrook is a friendly, family-run private hotel offering holiday accommodation for families and couples. We are situated approximately one mile from the town centre at the top of Alum Chine. Westbourne shops are within a few minutes' walk where buses can be taken to the surrounding areas. Approximately quarter of a mile away lies a beautiful sandy beach which can be reached by a leisurely stroll down the wooded Alum Chine. Most bedrooms have en suite, all have colour TV, shaver points, tea/coffee making facilities, clock radios and hair dryers. Access at all times. Babies and children catered for. Sorry, no pets. Brochure available on request.

BOURNEMOUTH. Mayfield Private Hotel, 46 Frances Road, Bournemouth BH1 3SA (01202 551839).

Sandra and Mike Barling welcome you to this AA and ETB Two Crowns registered and regularly inspected Hotel offering a high standard of catering and comfort. It overlooks gardens, bowls, putting and tennis; sea, shops, shows, rail and coach stations are a short walk away. Residential licence. Colour TV and tea making facilities in all rooms; some rooms have shower and toilet en-suite. Other amenities include full central heating, own keys, evening refreshments, parking. Bed and Breakfast from £13 to £16 daily; Bed, full English Breakfast and four-course Dinner with tea/coffee from £110 to £130 weekly. Bargain Breaks October/April; mid-week bookings early/late season; special package for Senior Citizens during May.

BOURNEMOUTH. David and Barbara Fowler, Sea Breeze Hotel, 32 St. Catherines Road, Southbourne, Bournemouth BH6 4AB (01202 433888). A small, peaceful hotel in a delightful location opposite beach where dogs are allowed at all times of year. Close to Hengistbury Head; New Forest 10 minutes' drive. Superb sea views. Family atmosphere. Full central heating. All rooms en suite; with TV and tea making facilities. Residential licence. Children from five to 16 sharing with parents half price. Parking. Open all year excluding Christmas. Bed and Breakfast from £17; Evening Meal £8.50.

BOURNEMOUTH. Mrs Broom, Bournecliffe House, 31 Grand Avenue, Southbourne, Bournemouth BH6 3SY (01202 426455). Enjoy a happy holiday in our small family guest house pleasantly situated in a quiet tree-lined avenue, just a few minutes' walk to the cliff top with easy access to beach via slope or cable car. Shops, cafes, restaurants and pubs close by. Tea/coffee, colour TV and showers in all rooms. Central heating. Forecourt parking. Access at all times. Babysitting and children's suppers available. Bed and Breakfast from £13 per day; £84 per week. The Guest House also runs a clinic offering treatments with Herbal Medicine and Aromatherapy by qualified therapists at special rates for guests. Please telephone for further details.

BOURNEMOUTH. Freshfields Hotel, 55 Christchurch Road, Bournemouth BH1 3PA (01202 394023). Small licensed hotel, just a short walk to sandy beach through Boscombe Chine. Close to town and all Bournemouth's attractions, shops and theatres. Golf, tennis, putting and bowling are all nearby. All rooms have colour TV and tea/coffee, most are en suite. Access at all times with own keys. Front car park. BARGAIN BREAKS SEPTEMBER TO JUNE. Bed and Breakfast from £12.50. Reductions for Senior Citizens.

BOURNEMOUTH. Seacrest Lodge, 63 Alum Chine Road, Bournemouth BH4 8DU (01202 767438). A warm welcome awaits you whether you are here on business or for leisure. We are ideally situated at the head of beautiful Alum Chine, leading to miles of golden beaches. Also close to shops, restaurants and entertainments and within easy reach of the New Forest, Poole Harbour and many other attractions. Bed and Breakfast £16 to £18. Good accommodation en suite, tea/coffee making facilities, colour TV all rooms. Full English breakfast. Ample car parking. Large garden for guests' use.

BOURNEMOUTH. Cherry View Hotel, 66 Alum Chine Road, Bournemouth BH4 8DZ (01202 760910). ✿ ✿ ✿ RAC Acclaimed, AA Listed Quality Award. Family-run hotel ideally situated between shops and beaches. 11 en suite rooms with TV, radio, tea-making facilities and central heating. Non-smoking rooms available. Excellent food, choice of menu. Residents' bar. Private parking. Bed and Breakfast from £18 to £20 daily; weekly terms from £115 to £135 (based on two sharing). Room only and optional evening meal available. Two Day and Five Day Bargain Breaks available early/late season. Special tariff on request. Christmas and New Year programme. Open all year. Colour brochure available.

BOURNEMOUTH. Sandy Beach Hotel, Southbourne Overcliff Drive, Southbourne, Bournemouth

BH6 3QB (Tel/Fax: 01202 424385). ♛ ♛ ♛ *COMMENDED.* Family run hotel in superb position overlooking sea. Easy access to safe, sandy beach. Near to shops and buses. Convenient for Bournemouth, the New Forest and day trips. Panoramic sea views over Bournemouth Bay. All rooms en suite. Colour TVs. Tea/coffee making facilities. TV lounge. Pleasant dining room with separate tables. Licensed bar. Full central heating. Ample car parking. Access to hotel at all times — own keys. For brochure please write or phone resident proprietors Bryan and Caroline Channing. Terms: Bed and Breakfast from £18 per night. Evening meal optional. Special weekly rates.

BOURNEMOUTH. Ashdale Hotel, 35 Beaulieu Road, Alum Chine, Bournemouth BH4 8HY (01202

761947). Cliff and Sue Loggey welcome you and your pet to their small family hotel, within minutes' walk of beautiful Alum Chine and beach. En suite rooms with colour TV and tea/coffee facilities. Central heating. Access to hotel at all times. Residential licence. Bed and Breakfast daily from £14 to £18.50; Bed, Breakfast and Evening Meal weekly from £110 to £165. Reductions for over 55's and Senior Citizens early/late season. Dogs welcome free.

BOURNEMOUTH. Nina and Paul Covell, Grasmere Hotel, 15 Cecil Road, Boscombe, Bournemouth

BH5 1DU (Tel & Fax: 01202 303004). The Grasmere Hotel offers a warm welcome and a relaxed and friendly atmosphere. Situated close to the heart of Boscombe and is just a few minutes' walk from the golden beaches, pier, beautiful gardens, bowling and putting greens and tennis courts. We are also close to the famous cliffs and the zig-zag path to the beach. All rooms have tea/coffee making facilities and en suites and family rooms are available. Lounge with colour TV. Full English breakfast; excellent home cooking with choice of menu. Fully licensed, bar snacks. Bed and Breakfast from £11, reduced rates for children sharing and off peak rates for over 55s. Car park. Open all year.

BOURNEMOUTH. Tony and Veronica Bulpitt, Sun Haven Hotel, 39 Southern Road, Southbourne,

Bournemouth BH6 3SS (01202 427560). ♛ ♛ The Sun Haven Hotel is in a superb position being only 150 yards from the cliff top, near the cliff lift and zig-zag path to the beach yet only a few minutes' walk to Southbourne shopping area, with its variety of cafes and restaurants. Bournemouth centre short drive away. All day access. All bedrooms have colour TV, shaver point, power point, washbasin and central heating. Tea making facilities. Forecourt parking. Bed and Breakfast from £15 per night. Overall winner Bournemouth in Bloom 1992.

DORSET – RURAL SPLENDOUR!

Absorbing old towns like Dorchester and Shaftesbury, surrounded by panoramic vales, undulating chalklands and peaceful villages contribute to Dorset's great appeal. Included in any tourist's itinerary should be, Abbotsbury Village and Swannery, Ackling Dyke Roman road, Brownsea Island, Lulworth Cove and, of course, the many locations that constitute Hardy's Dorset.

BOURNEMOUTH. "La Mer" Private Hotel, 37 Southbourne Overcliff Drive, Southbourne, Bournemouth BH6 3PL (01202 422614). Small family-run hotel on seafront. Convenient for amenities including shops. En suite bedrooms with colour TV and tea/coffee making facilities; some rooms have panoramic sea views. Central heating throughout. Car parking. Access to hotel at all times. Own keys. Dining room with separate tables. Open all year. Member of Bournemouth Hotel Association. Bed and Breakfast from £15 per person; Evening Meal optional at £7.50 per person. Discount for weekly bookings. Write or phone June and Andy Cole resident proprietors for brochure.

BOURNEMOUTH. Bay View Hotel, Southbourne Overcliffe Drive, Bournemouth BH6 3QB (01202 429315 or 0585 488150 (mobile); Fax: 01202 424385). ❦❦❦ COMMENDED. 14 en suite bedrooms with colour TV and Teasmaid; key access to rooms at all times (own key). Panoramic sea views from most rooms. Personal service with maximum attention to comfort and fine foods. Sandy beaches, level cliff top walks across the road. Special Christmas programme. Bed and Breakfast from £16 per night. Special tariff for weekly terms and short breaks. Four-course scrumptious, home cooked evening meal available, special diets by arrangement. Non-smoking accommodation available. Car parking. For brochure please write or phone resident proprietors Alison and Adrian Homa.

BOURNEMOUTH. Gervis Court Hotel, 38 Gervis Road, East Cliff, Bournemouth BH1 3DH (01202 556871). ❦❦ Alan and Jackie Edwards welcome you to a friendly and relaxing stay whether for business or pleasure. Our late Victorian detached hotel of character is set in its own attractive gardens and has ample parking space. Non-smoking accommodation available. A few minutes' walk to the beautiful clean, sandy beach, shops, theatres, B.I.C and other attractions. Bed and Breakfast from £18 to £22. Please ask about our Special Activity Breaks.

BOURNEMOUTH. Joan and John Adams, Valberg Hotel, 1A Wollstonecraft Road, Boscombe, Bournemouth BH5 1JQ (01202 394644). ❦❦ Small modern hotel in superb position near Boscombe pier, two minutes' walk to cliff top. Five minutes to shopping centre. All bedrooms have shower and toilet en suite, central heating, tea/coffee making facilities and colour TVs. Lounge with colour TV; diningroom with separate tables, overlooking lovely garden. Licensed bar. Car parking. Access to hotel at all times, own key. Bed and Breakfast from £15 to £20 daily inclusive; £90 to £120 weekly. Dinner optional at £7. Please write or phone for brochure. AA QQQ, RAC Listed.

WHEN MAKING ENQUIRIES PLEASE MENTION
FARM HOLIDAY GUIDES

BRADFORD ABBAS. Wendy and Robin Dann, Heartsease Cottage, North Street, Bradford Abbas

DT9 6SA (01935 75480). Wendy and Robin have run a chalet in the French Alps for a number of years and now own Heartsease, a delightful old stone cottage in a beautiful Dorset village close to Sherborne, Somerset border, A30. They can collect from the local station only two hours from Waterloo — THE PERFECT WEEKEND BREAK, overnight or longer. Three bedrooms with different themes and tea/coffee facilities — Victoria, an en suite double, Farmhouse and Napier each a twin sharing luxury bathroom. Good food is the "heart" in Heartease — breakfasts, dinners, light suppers, even barbecues/picnics in the idyllic mature garden. Easy motoring to Sherborne, Lyme Regis, Shaftesbury, Longleat, Wells. Marvellous walks. Guests' sittingroom with log fire, TV/video. Badminton and French boules courts. Prices from £15, May to November.

BRIDPORT. Mrs Andrea Gisborne, Burton Lodge, Burton Bradstock, Bridport DT6 4PU (01308 897378; Fax: 01308 898008). Country house set in the rolling hills of West Dorset and enjoying splendid views over National Trust land to the coast. All principal rooms and bedrooms have sea views. The golf course at West Bay which is open to visitors can also be viewed from the house and garden. The area abounds in wildlife and there are several popular beaches in the locality. Enjoy Bed and Breakfast in our friendly family home. Traditional breakfast and tea/coffee available (no extra charge) at all times. Children and pets welcome. Bed and Breakfast from £15 to £20 per person per night.

BRIDPORT. Mrs D.P. Read, The Old Station, Powerstock, Bridport DT6 3ST (01308 485301).

Ex-GWR station set in two-and-a-half acres in an area of outstanding natural beauty which is especially pretty in the spring. The house dates from 1857 and the interior has been completely modernised. Our pipe-smoking ghost (no appearances, just the scent of his pipe and downstairs only!) was featured in the press and on TV. We ask guests to restrict their smoking to downstairs. All rooms have free hot drinks making facilities and tea, coffee, etc are provided free. Daytime access. Generous Breakfast. Evening Meals available locally. Tennis court, fun nine-hole golf. Very peaceful and relaxing. Two double, one single bedrooms, all with washbasins; bathroom, two toilets; sittingroom; diningroom. Central heating. Children welcome, cot, high chair and babysitting. Sorry no pets. Car essential, parking. Bed and Breakfast only from £13, reduced rates for children under 10 years.

FUN FOR ALL THE FAMILY IN DORSET
Brewers Quay, Weymouth; Deep Sea Adventure, Weymouth; Dinosaur Museum, Dorchester; Dinosaurland, Lyme Regis; Maiden Castle, Dorchester; Natural World, Poole Aquarium; Sea Life Centre, Weymouth; Upton Country Park, Poole; Waterfront Museum, Poole.

BRIDPORT. Ann and Dan Walker MHCIMA, Britmead House, West Bay Road, Bridport DT6 4EG (01308 422941). ✿✿✿ HIGHLY COMMENDED. AA QQQQ Selected, RAC Acclaimed. Guestaccom Good Room Award 1997. Delightful freshly cooked food, personal service and putting guests' comfort first means visitors return time after time. Situated between Bridport, West Bay Harbour with its beaches/golf course/walks, Chesil Beach and The Dorset Coastal Path. Full en suite rooms (one ground floor) all with colour TV, tea making facilities, hair dryers and mini bar. South-facing lounge and dining room overlooking the garden. Optional table d'hôte dinner menu, incorporating local fish and other produce. Licensed. Full central heating. Private parking. Dogs by arrangement. Children welcome. Break rates all year. Discount for two or more rooms for three or more nights. Open all year. Bed and Breakfast from £20 to £28.

CERNE ABBAS. Mrs V.I. Willis, "Lampert's Cottage," Sydling St. Nicholas, Cerne Abbas DT2 9NU (01300 341659; Fax: 01300 341699). Bed and Breakfast in unique 16th century thatched cottage in unspoilt village. The cottage has fields around and is bounded, front and back, by chalk streams. Accommodation consists of three prettily furnished double bedrooms with dormer windows, set under the eaves, and breakfast is served in the dining-room which has an enormous inglenook fireplace and original beams. The village, situated in countryside made famous by Thomas Hardy in his novels, is an excellent touring centre and beaches are 30 minutes' drive away. West Dorset is ideal walking country with footpaths over chalk hills and through hidden valleys, perfect for those wishing peace and quiet. Open all year. Terms on request.

BROADVIEW GARDENS

ETB ✿✿✿ **De Luxe &**
AA QQQQQ Premier Selected
BOTH TOP QUALITY AWARDS

Unusual Colonial bungalow built in an era of quality. Carefully furnished with antiques. En-suite rooms overlooking our beautiful 'NGS' acre of secluded, elevated gardens. Achieving top quality awards for comfort, cooking & friendliness. Quality traditional English home cooking. Rooms with easy chairs, col. T.V., Tea/Fac.C/H. Perfect touring base for country & garden lovers, antique enthusiasts, NT houses, moors & quaint old villages. Dorset coast 20 min. List of 50 places provided. A no smoking house. Open all year. B&B £23–£27. Dinner £12.50.

East Crewkerne, Nr Yeovil, Somerset
TA18 7AG (Dorset Border)
Mrs G. Swann   Tel: 01460 73424

DORCHESTER. Mr and Mrs Michael Eaton, The Dower House, Bradford Peverell, Dorchester DT2 9SF (01305 266125). Warm welcome in our relaxing village home. A Listed house, The Dower House, set in four and a half acres of partially walled and wooded garden, is an excellent base for exploring the famous Hardy countryside. Dorchester, with its interesting museum, is only three miles away and the lovely coastline is within easy reach. On arrival guests are offered tea and home-made cakes in their sitting room which has a TV. Breakfasts, in the interesting dining room, are a speciality with home-made bread. No smoking in the house please. All cotton sheets. Bed and Breakfast with private bathroom from £16.50. FHG Diploma Winner.

DORCHESTER near. Mr Howell, Appletrees, 23 Affpuddle, Dorchester DT2 7HH (01929 471300). 1960's character home on site of 16th century cottage with splendid views across farmland of rolling Dorset hills. Within easy direct reach of six towns, all of historic or Hardy interest. Thoroughly peaceful. Stop-over for Devon/Cornwall (A35 2km). Cyclists and walkers especially welcome. Transport services provided at minimum charge (BR main line 4km). Accommodation comprises one double, two single and one twin bedrooms all with TV and tea making facilities. Use of kitchen if required. Children welcome. Bed and Breakfast from £12.50 to £16; Evening Meal from £2.50 to £10.

DORCHESTER. Mrs Marian Tomblin, Lower Lewell Farmhouse, West Stafford, Dorchester DT2 8AP (01305 267169). 🐾 This old, historic house, originally a farmhouse, is situated in the Frome Valley, four miles east of Dorchester in the heart of Hardy country. It is two miles from his birthplace and is reputed to be the Talbothays Dairy in his famous novel "Tess of the d'Urbervilles". Situated as it is in quiet countryside yet so near the county town, it makes an ideal base from which to explore Dorset. There is one family bedroom and two double bedrooms, all with washbasins. Visitors' lounge with colour TV. Much appreciated by guests are the tea/coffee making facilities. Car essential, ample parking. Regret no dogs. Children welcome. Terms from £16. Open January to December.

DORCHESTER. The Poachers Inn, Piddletrenthide, Dorchester DT2 7QX (01300 348358). Country Inn set in the heart of the lovely Piddle Valley, within easy reach of all Dorset's attractions. All rooms are en suite and have colour TV, tea/coffee making facilities and telephone. Swimming pool and riverside garden. Half Board guests choose from our à la carte menu at no extra cost. Bed and Breakfast from £23 to £25 per person; Dinner, Bed and Breakfast from £33 to £35 per person. 10% discount for seven nights or more. Special offer Short Breaks 1st November to 31st March: two nights Dinner, Bed and Breakfast £66 per person, third night FREE. Send for brochure.

DORCHESTER. Michael and Jane Deller, Churchview Guest House, Winterbourne Abbas, Near Dorchester DT2 9LS (01305 889296). 🐾🐾🐾 COMMENDED. Our 300-year-old AA QQQ Guest House is set in a small village five miles west of Dorchester in an area of outstanding natural beauty. Noted for warm, friendly hospitality and delicious home cooked food, it makes an ideal base for exploring Hardy country. Churchview is a non-smoking establishment offering two comfortable lounges, attractive oak-beamed dining room and bar. Our character rooms have hospitality trays and central heating; most en suite. Your hosts will give every assistance with local information to ensure a memorable stay. Pets welcome. Parking. Bed, Breakfast and four-course Evening Meal £29.50 to £37; Bed and Breakfast from £18.50 to £25.

DORCHESTER. Mrs Martine Tree, The Old Rectory, Winterbourne Steepleton, Dorchester DT2 9LG (Tel & Fax: 01305 889468). 🐾🐾🐾 HIGHLY COMMENDED. The Old Rectory was built in 1850 on one acre of private ground and is situated in the quaint little village of Winterbourne Steepleton. The area is of outstanding natural beauty, with country walks all round, giving superb views of the valley and surrounding countryside. The five guest rooms are all individually furnished to a high standard, each with en suite or private facilities and containing a welcome basket filled with those little items you may have forgotten. Breakfast is a delight, enjoyed in The Garden Room with views of the beautiful little courtyard and a musical backdrop of a waterfall and taped birdsong. Sailing, swimming, children's attractions, walks, hiking, cycling, shooting, horse riding, visits to arts and craft shops, museums, archaeological finds and many more. Open all year except Christmas. Brochure with full details available on request.

DORCHESTER. Mrs V.A. Bradbeer, Nethercroft, Winterbourne Abbas, Dorchester DT2 9LU (01305 889337). This country house with its friendly and homely atmosphere welcomes you to the heart of Hardy's Wessex. Central for touring the many places of interest that Dorset has to offer, including Corfe Castle, Lyme Regis, Dorchester, Weymouth, Lulworth Cove, etc. Lovely country walks and many local attractions. One family room, one double and one single, all with washbasins. Separate shower. Bathroom. Three toilets. TV lounge. Dining room. Large garden. Open all year. Central heating. Car essential, ample parking. Bed and Breakfast from £15. Reduced rates for children. Take A35, we are the last house at the western end of the village.

DORCHESTER. Mrs Roffey, Coneygar, Turners Puddle, Dorchester DT2 7JA (01929 471375).

Beautiful small country house in six acres of land, lovely garden and setting. Seven miles from coast and in Thomas Hardy country. The accommodation is very comfortable and comprises two double/twin-bedded rooms, with private bathrooms, tea-making facilities and central heating; TV in one room. Children welcome; regret, no pets. Terms from £18 per person per night. All guests are made to feel at home.

HINTON ST MARY. Mrs Sally Sofield, The Old Post Office Guest House, Hinton St. Mary, Sturminster Newton DT10 1NG (01258 472366; Fax: 01258 472173). ♥♥ *COMMENDED.*

Comfortable and homely guest house, convenient for exploring the beautiful, varied scenery of unspoilt Dorset. Guests' lounge with games, TV, maps and books. Car park. Large garden backing onto fields. Footpaths and River Stour (good fishing) nearby. Village has quaint thatched houses, church, manor house and a traditional sociable Dorset village pub. No one goes hungry here with good traditional home cooked fayre using local produce where possible. We do our best to provide a warm welcome, good value and a friendly place to stay. Bed and Breakfast from £16; optional Evening Meal £7. Brochure.

LILLINGTON. Mrs M.E.G. Messenger, Ash House, Lillington, Sherborne DT9 6QX (01935 812490). Ash House is spacious, surrounded by farmland, with delightful views all round. Although so rural and peaceful it is only three miles south of the picturesque town of Sherborne, with its Abbey and other historic buildings. Easy access to Dorchester in one direction and Yeovil in the other. One double or family room (extra bed available) with washbasin, and one twin room. Two toilets, bathroom, shower room. Ample parking. Lounge, conservatory, TV, garden. Full English Breakfast and a friendly welcome. Pets by arrangement. Bed and Breakfast from £12.50 — £13. Rates reduced for children. South from Sherborne — A352 Dorchester Road.

LULWORTH COVE. Jenny and John Aldridge, The Orchard, West Road, West Lulworth, Near Wareham BH20 5RY (01929 400592).

Comfortable home in central yet quiet off-road position in old vicarage orchard. Accommodation comprises double room, twin room, and room with double and single beds. One room has large balcony. Ample parking in spacious walled garden. Mature fruit trees, lawns, barbecue and garden furniture for guests' use. Full English, vegetarian or vegan breakfasts. Home produced eggs, vegetables, etc. Central for South Dorset, Swanage, Poole, Weymouth, Dorchester; 10 minutes' walk to Lulworth Cove. Near coast path for other beaches, Durdle Door and Fossil Forest. Bed and Breakfast from £12.50 per person per night. Enquire for children's rates and low season discounts. Open all year.

LULWORTH COVE. Val and Barry Burrill, Graybank Guest House, Main Road, West Lulworth BH20 5RL (01929 400256). ETB Listed.

Victorian Guest House situated in beautiful country surroundings, five minutes' stroll from Lulworth Cove. Excellent breakfasts and friendly hosts make this an excellent base for walking the Coastal Path and surrounding countryside and touring the many places of interest in Dorset or for just relaxing. Come and enjoy excellent hospitality in this comfortable guest house. All rooms have washbasins, heating and tea/coffee making facilities; most rooms have remote control colour TVs. There is a car park for our guests' use. Bed and English Breakfast from £17.

LULWORTH COVE. Mrs Jan Ravensdale, Elads-Nevar, West Road, West Lulworth, Near Wareham BH20 5RZ (01929 400467). The house is set in the beautiful village of West Lulworth, half a mile from Lulworth Cove. The rooms are large enough for a family and all have tea/coffee making facilities and colour TV. West Lulworth is central for many towns and beaches; Weymouth 14, Swanage 18, Poole 23 miles, and there are many places of interest to visit. Reduced rates for Senior Citizens out of season and children sharing with adults; also weekly bookings. Open all year. Central heating. Bed and Breakfast from £13.

LYME REGIS. Mrs C.S. Ansell, Providence House, Lyme Road, Uplyme, Lyme Regis DT7 3TH (01297 445704). Set in the lovely village of Uplyme, one mile from Lyme Regis, our small Regency guest house has been beautifully renovated — we even have a Minstrels' Gallery! A warm welcome is extended to you from your hosts Clem and Jean Ansell. The meals are special, the beds very comfortable and as some guests recently said, "It's like being at home without the washing up". We have a small cat but your dog is welcome. There are always fresh flower arrangements around and part of our garden is upstairs where you are very welcome to sit and enjoy the sun. This is wonderful walking country. Cricket is played regularly in the village, where there are also tennis courts. All rooms are freshly decorated and are either en suite or have private facilities. Bed and Breakfast from £15.50; four-course Dinner and coffee £8.

LYME REGIS. Sheila and David Taylor, Buckland Farm, Raymonds Hill, Near Axminster EX13 5SZ (01297 33222). Situated back off the A35 in quiet and unspoilt surroundings with gardens and grounds of five acres which are ideal for guests to relax or stroll in; about three miles from the lovely coastal resort of Lyme Regis and Charmouth. A warm welcome awaits you. Accommodation mainly on the ground floor. Two family bedrooms, one double en suite shower and one twin bedded room, all with TV, washbasin, tea/coffee making facilites. Bathroom, shower in bath, separate WC. Lounge with colour TV, video and log fire. Dining area with separate tables. A good full English breakfast served, a real home from home plus our very friendly dog. Friendly pub within two minutes walk for evening meals. Payphone. No smoking in bedrooms. Bed and Breakfast from £13. Send SAE for further details. Self-catering caravan available.

LYME REGIS. Jenny and Ivan Harding, Coverdale Guesthouse, Woodmead Road, Lyme Regis DT7 3AB (01297 442882). 🖤🖤 *COMMENDED.* AA QQQ Recommended. Friendly, well established Guesthouse situated in a quiet residential area of Lyme Regis, a few minutes' walk from the sea and town centre. Fine views over Woodland Trust's land to rear and sea to front. Double, twin, family and single rooms (en suite available). Tea/coffee facilities in all rooms. Comfortable TV lounge, attractive dining room with separate tables. Good home cooking using own garden produce. Access to house all day. Private parking. No smoking please. Ideal base for exploring countryside and unspoilt scenic coastline on foot or by car. Walkers welcome — South Coast Path/Liberty Trail close by. Bed and Breakfast from £13 to £20; Dinner optional (June to September only). Weekly reductions. Write or phone for brochure.

LYME REGIS. Mrs M.J. Powell, Meadow View, Green Lane, Rousdon, Lyme Regis DT7 3XW (01297 443262). A warm welcome awaits you at this working family farm situated quarter of a mile off the A3052 road at Rousdon just three miles from Lyme Regis, four from Seaton. Ideal centre to explore the Devon and Dorset countryside, sand and shingle beaches, fossil hunting. One family/double bedroom with washbasin and one double bedroom, both with colour TV, tea/coffee making facilities, central heating. Two guest bathrooms, one with shower over bath. Lounge with colour TV. Access at all times. Full English breakfast served at separate tables. Bed and Breakfast from £13 to £15. Reductions for children sharing parents' room. Ample car parking.

DORSET – FOLLOW THE HARDY TRAIL

The life-size statue of Thomas Hardy in Dorchester, his "Casterbridge" and home for many years, bears witness to his love for this peaceful county. Hardy enthusiasts should visit his birthplace at Higher Bockhampton; Waterston Manor, east of Puddletown – Bathsheba's home in "Far From the Madding Crowd"; Bere Regis – "Kingsbere"; Puddletown – "Weatherbury". Full details can be obtained from local Tourist Information Offices.

MIDDLEMARSH. Terry and Thelma, White Horse Farm, Middlemarsh, Sherborne DT9 5QN (01963 210222). Comfortable country farmhouse within three acres of gardens, paddock and lake. Our excellent facilities include pine-furnished rooms with comfortable beds en suite or private bathroom, all with washbasin, colour TV and tea/coffee making equipment. Our breakfasts are renowned! Set in peaceful Hardy countryside near Cerne Abbas, the ancient abbey town of Sherborne and historic Dorchester. Easy travelling distance to lovely coastline including Lulworth Cove, Weymouth and Lyme Regis. Enjoy walking, fishing, horse riding, golf, etc. 100 yards local inn. Open all year except Christmas. Bed and Breakfast from £15 to £20 per person. Also four attractive self-catering cottages where pets are welcome and ideal for partially disabled guests. Brochure available.

OSMINGTON. Mrs Joyce Norman, Dingle Dell, Osmington, Near Weymouth DT3 6EW (01305 832378). Tourist Board *HIGHLY COMMENDED.* Situated down a lane on the fringe of the picturesque village of Osmington, in the centre of farming country, with safe bridle-ways and footpaths right by the gate — a beautiful rural setting with the coast only one and a half miles away. This family home of mellow local stone is set in a large garden full of roses and apple trees. The two spacious, attractively furnished bedrooms (one with full en suite facilities, both with TV), overlook garden and fields and the famous "White Horse" on the nearby hill. Regret no pets. No smoking please. This is a quiet corner of Hardy's Wessex, a peaceful and friendly base for exploring the beautiful Dorset countryside whether by car, on foot or on horseback. Open March to October. Bed and Breakfast from £18.50. Car essential, parking.

POOLE. Mrs Margaret Gregory, Ashton Lodge, 10 Oakley Hill, Wimborne BH21 1QH (01202 883423; Fax: 01202 886180). 🌼🌼 *COMMENDED.* A warm friendly greeting awaits you when you arrive at Ashton Lodge. Margaret Gregory will offer you the comforts of home, including a Full English Breakfast served in the dining room that overlooks the attractively laid out garden. Accommodation includes two en-suite bedrooms. Tour maps of the local area, guidance on what to do and see, along with packed lunches can all be supplied to make your stay a holiday you will wish to remember. Children are welcome, reduced rates if sharing, and a cot is available. Bed and Breakfast (bedtime drink inclusive) from £18.50. Take A349 — Wimborne/Poole road.

POOLE. Eileen and Michael Standhaft, Rosemount, 167 Bournemouth Road, Lower Parkstone, Poole BH14 9HT (01202 732138). Run by the same owners for the past 21 years, your comfort is a priority. We are situated on the A35 halfway between Bournemouth and Poole town centres and near many beaches — Sandbanks and Branksome Chine to name but two. Convenient for ferry to Cherbourg. All bedrooms have colour TV, tea making facilities; two are en suite and one is on the ground floor and has en suite shower. Bed and Breakfast from £15 to £18 per person. Full English breakfast served. Brochure on request.

PORTLAND. Elaine and Jim Perkins, "Lijuan", 7B Avalanche Road, Southwell, Portland DT5 2DJ (01305 820735; Fax: 01305 860032). A friendly, comfortable home situated on the English Channel coast close to the beautiful seaside resort of Weymouth. Ideal location for country walks, bird watching, horse riding, fishing, swimming, windsurfing or golf. We will gladly arrange any sporting activities or advise on places to visit locally. For visitors who want to escape the crowds — in or out of season — on foot or on horseback — there are always spectacular views to be seen and interesting wildlife, flora and fauna to be spotted in this land of superb natural beauty. Bed and Breakfast £12; Evening Meal £5. Open all year.

SHERBORNE. Mrs E. Kingman, Stowell Farm, Stowell, Near Sherborne DT9 4PE (01963 370200).

A former 15th century Manor House, now a farmhouse on a family-run dairy and beef farm, set in beautiful countryside. It is a good area for walking and cycling and has a riding stable close by. Five miles from the A303, two miles from the A30. A good area for touring Somerset and Dorset. You will receive a warm welcome and good breakfast. There are two rooms, one double and one twin, both with tea/coffee facilities; guest bathroom and lounge with colour TV and log fires. £15 per night, special weekly rates. Reductions for children under 12 years. Evening meals by arrangement. Open all year. Good local pubs close by.

SHERBORNE. Mrs Pauline Tizzard, Venn Farm, Milborne Port, Sherborne DT9 5RA (01963

250598). The perfect stop when travelling, easy to find on main A30 three miles east of historic castle and abbey town of Sherborne, 30 minute drive to coast. Our 200 acre working dairy farm is situated in beautiful wooded parkland within walking distance of local village inn. Attractively furnished accommodation includes one twin, one double and one family room, all with washbasins, colour TV, tea/coffee making facilities. Bathroom equipped with shower and separate WC. Full central heating plus guests' lounge with log fires. Children welcome. AA QQ Recommended. Bed and Breakfast from £15. Reductions for children. Open all year.

STURMINSTER NEWTON. Mrs J. Miller, Lower Fifehead Farm, Fifehead St. Quinton, Sturminster

Newton DT10 2AP (01258 817335). ❦ ❦ Come and stay with us on our 400 acre dairy farm. Our lovely Listed 17th century farmhouse with interesting mullion windows is pictured and mentioned in Dorset Books. We have three bedrooms — one double en suite, one double and one twin, each with private bathrooms, own sitting room, TV and large garden. Tea and coffee making. No evening meals but we can recommend the local places. We also have a self contained one bedroom flat with en suite bathroom, private sitting room as well as a self catering annexe sleeping four/five. Bed and Breakfast from £15 per person. Right in the heart of the Blackmore Vale and "Hardy" country; lovely walks, golfing, fishing and riding can be arranged.

SWANAGE. Mrs Linda Benfield, Solent House, Solent Road, Swanage BH19 2HW (01929 425601).

A warm welcome awaits you at our spacious tastefully furnished accommodation. Double and twin rooms are available, all en suite with TV, hair dryer and tea/coffee making facilities. A full English breakfast is served or Continental if preferred. There is ample parking for guests' cars in the enclosed driveway. Solent House is set in a peaceful location to the south of Swanage overlooking Durlston Country Park and adjacent to the coastal pathway. Ideally placed for a quiet holiday or as a base for touring the Isle of Purbeck. Short Break rates low season. Bed and Breakfast from £20 to £24. Non-smoking accommodation.

DORSET – OUTSTANDING NATURAL BEAUTY

Almost all the coastline and much of the inland county has been designated an Area of Outstanding Natural Beauty, with fine sandy beaches and sheltered coves backed by undulating chalkland and unspoiled moorland. The county retains many traces of its rich heritage e.g. Maiden Castle, the finest known example of an Iron Age hill fort, and Dorchester, rich in Roman remains. The region was immortalised by Thomas Hardy in his Wessex novels — follow the "Hardy Trail" to Bere Regis ("Kingsbere") and Bournemouth ("Sandbourne").

THE LITTLE MANOR SWANAGE

Beautiful view. Informal friendly Guest House with access at any time. Cheerful personal service. Television, tea and coffee making facilities in all rooms. Most en suite. Dogs are welcome in bedrooms. Children welcome.

s.a.e Gillian MacDermott
389 HIGH STREET,
SWANAGE, DORSET BH19 2NP
Open all year Tel/Fax: 01929 422948

TOLPUDDLE. Paul Wright, Tolpuddle Hall, Tolpuddle, Near Dorchester DT2 7EW (01305 848986).

An historic house in village centre in an area of outstanding natural beauty, not far from the coast. Convenient for Bournemouth, Poole, Dorchester, Weymouth, Isle of Purbeck and many small market towns and villages. Centre for local interests e.g., birdwatching, walking, local history, Thomas Hardy, the Tolpuddle Martyrs, etc. Two double, one twin, one family and two single bedrooms. Full English breakfast. Tea/coffee making, TV sitting room. Pets welcome except high season. From £15 per person. Weekly rate available. Open all year.

WAREHAM. Mr and Mrs Axford, Sunnyleigh, Hyde, Wareham BH20 7NT (01929 471822). Mary and Eric offer their guests a friendly welcome to their bungalow with a cup of tea. Situated in the quiet hamlet of Hyde, five miles west of Wareham, we are adjacent to East Dorset Golf Club; follow the sign from Wareham and we are the first bungalow past the golf club on the right. It is an ideal base for visiting Swanage, Poole and Bovington Tank Museum, with many interesting coastal walks, including Lulworth Cove. Accommodation consists of three double bedrooms (one with twin beds), all with tea/coffee facilities, central heating. Bathroom and separate shower room; two toilets. Visitors' lounge with colour TV and log fires in winter. Open all the year except Christmas. Car essential, ample parking. Bed and Breakfast from £14.

WAREHAM. Miss Sarah Lowman, Long Coppice, Bindon Lane, East Stoke, Wareham BH20 6AS

(01929 463123). Long Coppice is situated in a peaceful country lane one and a half miles from the A352 at Wool. We have eight acres of our own meadows, woodlands and gardens. The large bungalow provides separate guest accommodation, all rooms en suite, spacious and comfortably furnished, with TV and tea facilities. The family room has its own patio and enclosed garden, ideal for those with young children or dogs. Lulworth is four miles away and there are many good local pubs nearby. Family and twin rooms all non-smoking. Bed and English Breakfast from £17.50. Safe parking. Open all year except Christmas.

WEYMOUTH. Firtrees Guest House, 27 Rodwell Avenue, Weymouth DT4 8SH (01305 760190 daytime, 01305 772967 evenings).

Mr Stuart-Brown extends a warm welcome at Firtrees. Relax and have an enjoyable holiday. Rooms en suite with tea/coffee making facilities and colour TV. Parking. Full English breakfast or Continental. Firtrees is situated four minutes from harbour and sailing centre, 10 minutes' walk to Weymouth seafront, while Portland is a 10 minute drive. Explore Dorest's beautiful countryside with Bournemouth and Swanage approximately 30 miles away; West Bay/Lyme Regis 15-25 miles. The towns of Shaftesbury, Blandford and Yeovil are all within driving distance.

WEYMOUTH. Mrs S. Lambert, The Wessex Guest House, 128 Dorchester Road, Weymouth DT4 7LG (01305 783406).

Quality detached residence close to sea and shops. The accent here is on good food and good service. Ideally situated for Lulworth Cove, Corfe Castle and Abbotsbury Swannery. Safe bathing, fishing and riding. Three family rooms and two double, all with washbasins. Ground floor bedroom available. Free tea/coffee anytime. Children welcome. Enclosed garden, play room available. Access at all times. Open May to September for Bed and Breakfast only from £13. Secure parking in grounds. Reductions for children. In the know for local bird watching and rarities. Also self catering holiday flat to let.

WIMBORNE. Mrs Eveline Stimpson, Acacia House, 2 Oakley Road, Wimborne Minster BH21 1QJ (01202 883958; Fax: 01202 881943). ✿✿ *HIGHLY COMMENDED.*

Extensive improvements have greatly changed what was formerly Thorburn House, including the addition of a Victorian conservatory. What has not changed is the warmth of welcome with home-made cake and tea. To get there, find the A31/A349 junction and follow Wimborne signs; Oakley Road is second on the right past the Willett Arms. If you wish you will be helped to discover the beauties of the area. Rooms: one triple and one double, both with shower/WC en suite, one twin with private shower/WC if required, and one single. Each room has colour TV, tea/coffee making facilities and radio alarm. From £17 to £20 (based on two persons sharing room) including full English breakfast. NO SMOKING.

WINTERBOURNE ZELSTON. Mrs Irene Kerley, Brook Farm, Winterborne Zelston, Blandford DT11 9EU (01929 459267).

A warm welcome awaits you at Brook Farm, a friendly working farm situated in a pretty, peaceful hamlet overlooking the River Winterborne, between Wimborne and Dorchester. Central for coast and exploring the beautiful Dorset countryside, New Forest, etc. Comfortable family and twin rooms with either en suite or private facilities, TV, easy chairs, beverage tray and central heating. Access to rooms at all times. No parking problems. Hearty breakfasts are served with own free range eggs and homemade marmalade! The local country inns provide excellent food. Open all year except Christmas. Terms from £16 per person per night with favourable rates for longer stays and children sharing.

PUBLISHER'S NOTE

While every effort is made to ensure accuracy, we regret that FHG Publications cannot accept responsibility for errors, omissions or misrepresentation in our entries or any consequences thereof. Prices in particular should be checked because we go to press early. We will follow up complaints but cannot act as arbiters or agents for either party.

DURHAM (including former Cleveland)
Hartlepool, Middlesbrough, Stockton, and Redcar & Cleveland

DURHAM. Mrs J. Dartnall, Idsley House, 4 Green Lane, Spennymoor DL16 6HD (01388 814237).

HIGHLY COMMENDED. A large Victorian detached house situated in a quiet residential area close to the A167/A688 junction just eight minutes from Durham City. Direct route to Beamish, Metro Centre and the Dales. All rooms are spacious and well furnished. Double, twin and family bedrooms are all en suite and have colour TV and welcome tray. Full English or vegetarian breakfast is served in a pleasant conservatory overlooking a mature garden. Large guest lounge to relax. Safe parking on premises. Prices for a twin or double room £38. Open all year except Christmas. AA QQQ. Visa, Mastercard, Switch, Delta cards all accepted.

DURHAM. Mrs Delia Slack, Ash House, 24 The Green, Cornforth DL17 9JH (01740 654654). Ideally

situated on a lovely rural conservation village green, in the heart of "the Land of the Prince Bishops". Adjacent A1(M) motorway, 10 minutes from historic Durham, 25 minutes to Beamish Museum, Metro Centre, Newcastle and Darlington. Ash House is a beautifully appointed Victorian home lovingly restored. The elegant rooms are spacious and comfortable, equipped with washbasins, colour TV, hospitality tray, shaver point, hairdryer, clock/radio alarm and all with open views; traditional four-poster bed available. Mature trees surround the property. Hearty breakfasts are provided. Private parking. Well placed between York and Edinburgh. Excellent value from £18 — Single £20.

SALTBURN-BY-SEA. Mrs Bull, Westerlands Guesthouse, 27 East Parade, Skelton, Saltburn-by-Sea (01287 650690). This guest house is situated alongside Cleveland Way. It is a quiet, modern detached house with beautiful views of sea and countryside. An ideal base for touring Yorkshire Moors and the East Coast resorts, and there is a golf course nearby. Plenty of parking space. Bed and Breakfast £13 with packed lunches and flasks prepared and snack meals on request; Evening Meals by arrangement. Special meals available. Northumberland Tourist Board registered. Reduced rates for children and small reduction for Senior Citizens. Pets welcome free. Private bathrooms and/or showers and Teasmaid in all bedrooms. Open March till end September.

STANLEY. Mrs P. Gibson, Bushblades Farm, Harperley, Stanley DH9 9UA (01207 232722). Tourist

Board Listed COMMENDED. AA QQ. Ideal stop-over when travelling north or south. Only 10 minutes from A1M Chester-le-Street. Durham City 20 minutes, Beamish Museum two miles, Metro Centre 15 minutes, Hadrian's Wall and Northumberland coast under an hour. Comfortable Georgian farmhouse set in large garden. Twin ground floor en suite room plus two double first floor bedrooms. All rooms have tea/coffee making, colour TV and easy chairs. Ample parking. Children welcome over 12 years. Sorry, no pets. Bed and Breakfast from £16 to £18.50 per person per night, single £20 to £25.

DURHAM – MOORS, VALLEYS AND INDUSTRY!
At its western extent Durham embraces the moors and valleys of the Pennines but otherwise this is an industrial county, with a strong coal mining tradition. Places worth a visit include Barnard Castle, the Upper Teesdale Valley, the gothic church at Brancepeth and the farm and industrial museum at Beamish.

TEESDALE. Mrs M. Rabbitts, Glendale, Cotherstone, Barnard Castle DL12 9UH (01833 650384).

🌹🌹 *HIGHLY COMMENDED.* Bed and Breakfast in beautiful spacious house; three double rooms en suite, TV, tea-making, etc. Separate dining and sitting rooms. No smoking, no children under 10 years and no pets. Personal attention. We are situated in superb open countryside close to the village of Cotherstone. Splendid all round views, superb gardens and bedding displays, very large water feature with specimen fish. Our area is famous for Hannah of Yorkshire, High Force, Bowes Museum and breathtaking scenery for walking. Durham and Beamish 45 minutes. £30 to £32 double room. A warm welcome awaits. Brochure on request.

THORNLEY. Mrs Margo Farrow, Bracken Hill, Thornley, Tow Law DL13 4PQ (01388 731329). 🌹🌹

HIGHLY COMMENDED. Newly refurbished 200 year old Pennine Long House. For true romantics. Original oak beams, inglenook fire and polished wooden floors all add charm to the character in this relaxing setting. Tea making facilities, remote control TV, private bathroom for your comfort. We pride ourselves on candlelit dinners with fine cuisine. Set in 10 acres of countryside with views from every angle. An excellent base for walking and touring. 20 minutes from Durham City, 45 minutes from Newcastle. Local places of interest are Hamsterly Forest for enjoying nature at its best, Weardale open to the eastern slopes of the Pennines and Beamish Heritage Museum for a day to remember.

ESSEX

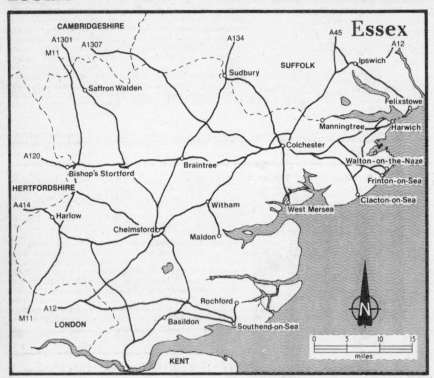

BRAINTREE. Mrs Delia Douse, Spicers Farm, Rotten End, Wethersfield, Braintree CM7 4AL (01371 851021). ♛♛ *HIGHLY COMMENDED.* **Working farm.** FHG Diploma Winner. Attractive farmhouse with large garden set in delightful, peaceful position overlooking beautiful countryside. Comfortable centrally heated bedrooms all with en suite shower or bathrooms, colour TV, tea/coffee making facilities, clock radios and lovely views. Breakfast in our sunny conservatory overlooking the large garden and picturesque countryside. There is a separate lounge for guests. Excellent base for walking or touring and convenient for Stansted, M11, Harwich, Cambridge and Constable country. Plenty of parking. Bed and Breakfast double/twin £15 to £17 per person per night.

BRAINTREE near. Mrs J. Reddington, Park Farmhouse, Bradwell, Near Braintree CM7 8EP (01376 563584). ETB Listed *COMMENDED.* Listed 16th century timber-framed family home on the outskirts of Bradwell, superb views, large secluded garden with listed dovecote, tranquil countryside setting. Well placed for Stansted Airport, M11 and A12, picturesque places and historic houses Essex/Suffolk borders and Stour Valley. Double or twin-bedded rooms (one four-poster) with tea making facilities; guests' bathroom, ground floor shower room, lavatory and basin. Continental/English breakfast. Ample parking. Children over 12 years welcome. Sorry no smoking or pets. Some French/German spoken. Bed and Breakfast from £16 to £18 single, £32 to £34 double. Take A120; in Bradwell turn off beside "Swan" public house, drive for half a mile, Park Farmhouse on right hand side. AA QQQ.

COLCHESTER. Mrs Wendy Anderson, The Old Manse, 15 Roman Road, Colchester CO1 1UR

(01206 545154). Tourist Board Listed. This spacious Victorian family home is situated in a quiet square beside the Castle Park. Only three minutes' walk from bus/coach station or through the Park to town centre. We promise a warm welcome and a friendly, informal atmosphere. All rooms have central heating, TV and tea/coffee making facilities. Ground floor double room has private facilities; two twin-bedded rooms on first floor with two bathrooms. Full, varied English Breakfast. Bed and Breakfast from £25 single, £35 double. Only 30 minutes' drive from Harwich and Felixstowe. Within easy reach of Constable country and one hour's train journey from London. Sorry, no smoking.

COLCHESTER. Mrs S.P. Cox, The Maltings, Mersea Road, Abberton, Colchester CO5 7NR (01206

735780). ♥ ♥ Attractive period house dating back to 15th century set in walled garden with swimming pool. Owned and run by proprietor and family. Guests have their own lounge with log fire and colour TV. Open all year round, the house offers one double, one single, one family room; bathroom; diningroom. Central heating. Cot and babysitting. Ample parking provided, and bus stop outside. Four miles to sea at Mersea Island and boating facilities. Near Abberton Reservoir with its bird sanctuary and nature reserve. Bed and Breakfast from £15. Reduced rates for children.

KELVEDON. Mr and Mrs R. Bunting, Highfields Farm, Kelvedon CO5 9BJ (Tel & Fax: 01376 570334). ♥ ♥ *COMMENDED.* Highfields Farm is set in a quiet area on a 700 acre arable working farm. This makes a peaceful overnight stop on the way to Harwich or a base to visit historic Colchester and Constable country. Convenient for Harwich, Felixstowe and Stansted Airport. Easy access to A12 and main line trains to London. The accommodation comprises two twin rooms en suite and one twin room with private bathroom, all with TV and tea/coffee making facilities. Residents' lounge. Good English Breakfast is served in the oak beamed diningroom. Ample parking. Bed and Breakfast from £20 single, £36 twin.

GLOUCESTERSHIRE
including South Gloucestershire, and Bristol, formerly Avon

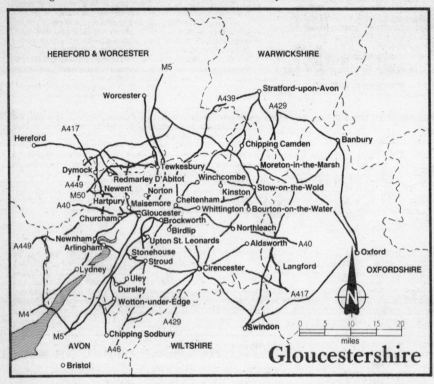

Gloucestershire

AMBERLEY, near Stroud. The Dial Cottage, Amberley, Near Stroud GL5 5AL (01453 872563). A warm welcome awaits you at our character filled Cotswold cottage. The Dial Cottage is situated within the "Royal Triangle" on 600 acres of a National Trust Common, Minchinhampton, with its picturesque views, ancient golf course and famous Five Valley Walks. Good pub food within walking distance. Well positioned to explore the Cotswolds, Sudley and Berkley Castles, Cirencester, Tetbury, Bath, world famous Westonbirt Arboretum and Slimbridge Wild Life Park. Golf, gliding, ballooning, horse riding; equestrian events at Gatcombe Park, Badminton and Cheltenham horse racing. The bedrooms with their antique beds retain their unique cottage atmosphere and all have en suite and modern facilities to add to your comfort. Non-smoking. Sorry, no pets. Bed and Breakfast from £25 per person.

BATH near. Mrs Lynn Hooper, Greenway Farm, Bath Road, Wick, Near Bristol BS15 5RL (0117 9373201). Greenway is a small working beef farm with a large early Georgian house, just a few yards off the A420 leading to Lansdown, Bath and four miles from Exit 18 on the M4. We are overlooking/adjacent to Tracy Park Golf Course. All rooms have tea/coffee making facilities, colour TV, central heating; some en suite. We also have a spacious garden with Koi pond and are surrounded by beautiful country scenery. Bath four miles, Bristol six miles. Sorry, no pets. Terms from £18 per person.

BIRDLIP. Mrs P.M. Carter, Beechmount, Birdlip GL4 8JH (01452 862262). ✿✿ *COMMENDED.* Good

central base for touring Cotswolds, conveniently situated for many interesting places and picturesque views with lovely walks, Beechmount is in the centre of Birdlip village, convenient for post office/village shop. Front door key is provided so that guests may come and go freely. Bedrooms are equipped to a high standard, all having washbasins; some en-suite facilities; bathroom, separate shower, shaver point; toilet. Children welcome at reduced rates, cot, high chair provided. Pets allowed by arrangement. Parking space. Open January to December for Bed and Breakfast, with Evening Meal by prior arrangement, using home produce when available. Choice of menu for breakfast. Small family-run guest house, Highly Recommended and with competitive rates. Terms on application.

COTSWOLD COTTAGE

Chapel Street, Bledington OX7 6XA
Tel & Fax: 01608 658996

Selected period cottage in unspoilt award-winning Cotswold village, Gloucestershire/Oxford borders, four miles from Stow-on-the-Wold. Ideally situated for fishing, horse riding and golf, and for exploring the picturesque villages of Bourton-on-the-Water, the Slaughters, Chipping Campden and Broadway. Places of historic interest such as Stratford, Blenheim Palace, Warwick Castle and Cirencester are within easy reach. Cotswold Cottage offers a very high standard of accommodation, luxurious en suite centrally heated rooms, colour TV, hairdryers, tea making facilities. 15th century inn on village green, three minutes' walk. Bed and Breakfast from £24 per person. Non-smoking establishment.

✿✿ Highly Commended   **AA QQQQQ** Premier Selected
Which 1997 County Hotel of the Year

BOURTON-ON-THE-WATER. Mrs Helen Adams, Upper Farm, Clapton-on-the-Hill, Bourton-on-the-Water, Cheltenham GL54 2LG (01451 820453). ✿✿

HIGHLY COMMENDED. If peace and tranquillity are what you require then this charming undiscovered village two miles from Bourton-on-the-Water makes an ideal holiday retreat. Clapton enjoys uninterrupted views from its hill position. Here you will find Upper Farm with its 17th century Cotswold stone farmhouse, lovingly restored and retaining a wealth of original charm. The centrally heated bedrooms have been individually designed and some are en-suite, one on ground floor. For the walker the farm gives access to numerous footpaths and bridleways, whilst the motorist is central for Oxford, Bath, Broadway and Stratford. Personal attention is assured together with fresh and hearty farmhouse fare. Please, no smoking. Brochure and tariff available.

BREDON'S NORTON. Michael and Pippa Cluer, Lampitt House, Lampitt Lane, Bredon's Norton, Tewkesbury GL20 7HB (01684 772295). ✿✿

COMMENDED. Lampitt House is situated in a large informal garden on the edge of a quiet village at the foot of Bredon Hill. Splendid views across to the Malverns. Ideal for visiting the Cotswolds, Stratford, Worcester, Cheltenham, Gloucester and the Forest of Dean. All rooms are furnished to a high standard and have private bathrooms, central heating, colour TV and tea/coffee making facilities. Ground floor room available. Children are welcome. Ample parking. No smoking. Open all year. Hill and riverside walks. Arrangements can be made for windsurfing and riding. Terms from £26 single room, £36 double room.

BRISTOL. Mrs Marilyn Collins, Box Hedge Farm, Coalpit Heath, Bristol BS17 2UW (01454 250786).

Box Hedge Farm is set in 200 acres of beautiful rural countryside on the edge of the Cotswolds. Local to M4/M5, central for Bristol and Bath and the many tourist attractions in this area. An ideal stopping point for the South West and Wales. We offer a warm, friendly atmosphere with traditional farmhouse cooking. The large spacious bedrooms (one single, one double and one family) have colour TV and tea/coffee making facilities. Adventure days or weekends can also be provided with Clay Pigeon Shooting, Quads and Pilots to name but three events. Bed and Breakfast from £15; Dinner from £7.50.

BRISTOL. Mrs Judi Hasell, Woodbarn Farm, Denny Lane, Chew Magna, Bristol BS18 8SZ (01275 332599).

Woodbarn is a working mixed farm, five minutes from Chew Valley Lake. Chew Magna is a large village with pretty cottages, Georgian houses and is central for touring. There are two bedrooms, one double and one family, both with tea trays. Guests' lounge and dining room. Cream teas Sunday June to September. Open March to December (closed Christmas). Children welcome. Bed and Breakfast from £17 to £20. Non smokers preferred. Brochure available.

BRISTOL. Mrs Doreen Keel, Valley Farm, Sandy Lane, Stanton Drew, Bristol BS18 4EL (01275 332723). *HIGHLY COMMENDED.*

1994 Award-winning Valley Farm is a modern farmhouse offering Bed and Breakfast accommodation. Pleasantly situated on the edge of an ancient village near the River Chew with Druid Stones and many footpaths to walk. It is located near the Chew Valley Lakes, renowned for trout fishing and in easy reach of Bath, Bristol, Wells and Cheddar. There are three rooms with double beds, each has washbasin and tea/coffee making facilities; there are also two rooms with en suite and another with private bathroom; all bedrooms have TV. The house is double glazed and centrally heated. We try to create a friendly relaxed atmosphere in lovely countryside and we are always pleased to give information about the area. Non-smoking. Brochure.

BRISTOL. Margaret Hasell, The Model Farm, Norton Hawkfield, Pensford, Bristol BS18 4HA (01275 832144). *COMMENDED.*

The farmhouse is a Listed building situated two miles off the A37 in a peaceful hamlet nestling under the Dundry Hills. A working arable and beef farm in easy reach of Bristol, Bath, Wells, Cheddar and many intertesting places. The accommodation consists of one family room en suite and one double room with washbasin, both with tea/coffee facilities. Guests' lounge with TV and dining room. Open all year except Christmas and New Year. I can assure you of a warm welcome and a peaceful and comfortable stay.

GLOUCESTERSHIRE – THE IDYLLIC COTSWOLDS COUNTY!

A combination of the Cotswolds and The Vale of Severn, Gloucestershire is a popular tourist destination. Visit Chipping Campden, Cirencester, The Cotswolds Farm Park, The Forest of Dean, Keynes Park and Tewkesbury and you will not be disappointed. If you are around at the right time, the Severn Bore can also be quite a spectacle.

BRISTOL near. Mrs Colin Smart, Leigh Farm, Pensford, Near Bristol BS18 4BA (01761 490281; Fax: 01761 490270). Working farm. Close to Bath, Bristol, Cheddar, Mendip Hills. Large, comfy, stone-built farmhouse with lawns. Twin, single, family, double rooms, some en suite; cot and high chair available. Guests' private lounge with night storage heating and open log fires in cold weather. Traditional farmhouse breakfasts. Tea/coffee facilities, hair dryer available. Carp and tench fishing close to the farmhouse. Floodlit car park with plenty of space. Payphone. Close to Blagdon and Chew Valley reservoirs. Fire Certificate. Sorry no pets. Bed and Breakast from £20. Also self catering accommodation available (some units with night storage heating) from £95 to £330 weekly.

CHELTENHAM. Mrs Sue Perkin, St. Michaels Guest House, 4 Montpellier Drive, Cheltenham GL50 1TX (01242 513587). Elegant Edwardian guest house offering delightful accommodation in a friendly informal atmosphere. Situated in a quiet location five minutes' walk from the town centre, restaurants and theatres. Most rooms are en suite, all have colour TV, beverage tray, clock/radio, hairdryer and central heating. The dining room is furnished in oak and offers a variety of delicious breakfasts. As a base for touring, within easy reach are Broadway, Bourton-on-the-Water, the Forest of Dean, Bath and Stratford. By car follow the A40 for through traffic, from Montpellier Terrace turn into Montpellier Parade, this becomes Montpellier Drive. Parking available. Visa accepted. .

CHELTENHAM. Mrs Lorna Seeley, Old Stables, 239A London Road, Cheltenham GL52 6YE (01242 583660). HETB Listed. Former coach house and stable, now a family home with stable block as Bed and Breakfast accommodation. One and a half miles east of town centre on A40. Easy car access and parking. Children and pets welcome. Non smoking. En suite facilities available. Bed and full Breakfast from £14 to £16. Reductions for children.

CHELTENHAM. Ann and Ian Duesbury, Lonsdale House, Montpellier Drive, Cheltenham GL50 1TX (Tel & Fax: 01242 232379). ✿✿ *COMMENDED.* AA QQ. We extend a warm welcome to visitors to our Listed Regency house which has been recently renovated and redecorated. All our rooms have tea/coffee/chocolate refreshment tray, remote-control colour TV, radio alarm and central heating. Some rooms are en suite (shower and toilet) but all floors have public bathrooms and toilets. The house is situated in a tree-lined residential road about five/seven minutes' walk from town centre including restaurants, town hall and theatres but also only yards from Junction of A40 and A46, giving easy access to M5, Cotswolds, Forest of Dean and other places of interest. Children welcome at reduced rates, but sorry no pets. Bed and Breakfast from £18.

CHELTENHAM. Mrs Helen Risborough, Wishmoor Guest House, 147 Hales Road, Cheltenham GL52 6TD (01242 238504; Fax: 01242 226090). ✿✿ *COMMENDED.* At Wishmoor Guest House you will find a warm and friendly welcome from your hosts Helen and Robin Risborough whose aim is to provide a relaxed atmosphere so that you may enjoy your stay. Wishmoor is a late Victorian residence, carefully modernised to preserve its charm and character. Situated on the eastern side of Cheltenham at the foot of the Cotswold Hills it is an ideal base for touring the Cotswold Villages, Wye Valley, Malvern Hills and the Royal Forest of Dean. The scenic towns of Hereford, Stratford and Bath are conveniently situated for day visits. Single and double bedrooms available, some ensuite. All have colour TV and tea/coffee facilities. Full central heating; adequate hot water; quiet guest lounge. Non-smoking accommodation available. Off road parking. Fire Certificate. Bed and Breakfast from £18; Evening Meal from £12. Reductions for children. AA Listed. Winner of Cheltenham Spa Award for Hygiene and Healthy Eating.

CHELTENHAM (Cotswolds). Mrs A. E. Hughes, Ham Hill Farm, Whittington, Cheltenham GL54 4EZ

(01242 584415; Fax: 01242 222535). ♛♛ *COMMEN-DED.* This 160-acre farm has farmhouse built in 1983 in true traditional style, with panoramic views. Two miles from the town of Cheltenham. Leisure activities nearby are horse riding, golf and walking the Cotswold Way. The tastefully decorated and comfortable en suite bedrooms all have colour TV, tea/coffee facilities. Two doubles, two twin, one family and one single. Two comfortable lounges, with maps and information about the area. Excellent farmhouse breakfast; non-smoking; open all year round. Bed & Breakfast from £20 to £23.50 per person. Colour brochure on request.

CHELTENHAM. Dove House, 128 Cheltenham Road, Bishops Cleeve, Cheltenham GL52 4LZ (Tel & Fax: 01242 679600). Dove House is situated on the outskirts of Cheltenham, close to the Racecourse and is ideal as a base for touring/walking the Cotswolds, Forest of Dean, Tewkesbury, Evesham. Golf courses and private fishing lakes close by. All rooms are furnished to a high standard and have central heating, colour TV and tea/coffee making facilities. Ample parking and garden for guests' use. Bed and Breakfast from £15 per person per night; en suite available. Open all year.

CHELTENHAM near. Mr and Mrs C. Rooke, Frogfurlong Cottage, Frogfurlong Lane, Down Hatherley, Near Cheltenham GL2 9QE (01452 730430).

At Frogfurlong Cottage we offer exclusive accommodation for one couple; a truly "get away on your own" break. The 18th century cottage surrounded by fields is situated on the green belt area within the triangle formed by Cheltenham, Gloucester and Tewkesbury. The accommodation, which is totally non-smoking and self-contained, consists of a double bedroom with colour TV and teamaker, luxury en suite bathroom and jacuzzi; there is direct access to the 30' indoor heated swimming pool. Local attractions include the Cotswolds, Malverns, Forest of Dean, National Waterways Museum, National Falconry Centre, Three Choirs Vineyard, Slimbridge Wildfowl Trust, Nature in Art, Cheltenham Festivals. Sorry no pets. Bed and Breakfast from £17 per person per night; Evening Meals by arrangement.

CHIPPING CAMPDEN. Mrs Gené Jeffrey, Brymbo, Honeybourne Lane, Mickleton, Chipping Campden GL55 6PU (01386 438890; Fax: 01386 438113). HETB Listed. Brymbo is a warm and spacious farm building conversion with large gardens in beautiful Cotswold countryside. Close to Stratford-upon-Avon, Broadway, Chipping Campden, with easy access to Oxford and Cheltenham. Ideal base for walking and touring in the Cotswolds. The comfortable bedrooms all have colour TV and tea/coffee making facilities; two en suite rooms available. Sittingroom has extensive views and an open log fire, whilst the breakfast room has the views and sunshine, subject to the English weather, of course! Central heating. Ground floor bedrooms. Parking. There are maps and guides to borrow, with quantities of helpful information about the area and sample menus from local hostelries to assist with your choice for meals. FREE Four-Wheel Drive Tour of the area offered to three-night guests. Bed and Breakfast from £15. Children and pets welcome. Brochure on request.

COTSWOLD COUNTRY
BED AND BREAKFAST

FREE and REDUCED RATE Holiday Visits!
See our READERS' OFFER VOUCHER for details!

CHIPPING CAMPDEN. Mrs C. Hutsby, Holly House, Ebrington, Chipping Campden GL55 6NL (01386 593213). Tourist Board Listed COMMENDED.

Holly House is set in centre of the picturesque Cotswold village of Ebrington. Ideally situated for touring the Cotswolds and Shakespeare's Stratford. Two miles from Hidcote Gardens and Chipping Campden, seven miles from Broadway and 10 miles from Stratford. All rooms are beautifully appointed with en suite facilities, TVs, tea/coffee facilities. Rooms are on ground floor with independent entrances. Private parking. Children welcome. The village inn serves lunches and evening meals. Bed and Breakfast from £17 per person. From Chipping Campden take B4035 towards Shipston, on leaving Campden take first left to Ebrington after garden centre.

CHURCHAM. Penny and Steve Stevens, Edgewood House, Churcham, Gloucester GL2 8AA (01452 750232). ♛♛ Family-run country guest house set

in two acres of lovely gardens. Ideal for visiting Forest of Dean, Wye Valley, Cotswolds and Malverns. Close to RSPB Reserve and viewpoint for Severn Bore Tidal Wave. Centrally heated double, family and single rooms decorated and furnished to a high standard. Most rooms are en suite and have tea/coffee making facilities. Spacious dining room and lounge with colour TV. Ample parking. Hearty breakfast provided. Several excellent eating places nearby. Bed and Breakfast from £18.50 to £20. Children over five years welcome with reductions if sharing with two adults. Sorry no smoking or pets. Open all year. Brochure available.

CIRENCESTER. Mrs R.J. Barton, The Coach House, Manor Farm, Middle Duntisbourne, Cirencester GL7 7AR (01285 653058). ♛♛ APPROVED. A warm

welcome at the 17th century coachhouse by the River Dunt. Centrally situated in 400 acre arable and beef farm with lovely walks and ideal for visits to Bath, Oxford, Stratford and many pretty villages in and around Cirencester area. Pretty garden with country views. TV, tea/coffee making facilities in bedrooms. Pleasant lounge with colour TV. Always a choice of breakfast including English farmhouse breakfast. Open all year except Christmas. Children over 12 years and pets welcome. Bed and Breakfast from £16 to £22.

COTSWOLDS. Mrs Alison Coldrick, Hill Barn, Clapton Road, Bourton-on-the-Water GL54 2LF (01451 810472). In the midst of beautiful rolling pastures

yet only five minutes' drive from the picturesque village of Bourton-on-the-Water, this 17th century converted barn offers high standard en suite accommodation, tea/coffee and TV in all rooms with a choice of breakfast from £17 per person. Beautiful views. Ample parking. Lovely walks directly from the property. Open all year. Sorry, no smoking or pets. Ideally situated for exploring the Cotswolds, Gloucestershire, Oxfordshire and Warwickshire.

DIDMARTON. Mrs M.T. Sayers, The Old Rectory, Didmarton GL9 1DS (01454 238233). ♛♛ HIGHLY COMMENDED. Small and comfortable, this former

Rectory, with a pleasant walled garden, is set in an attractive little south Cotswold village on A433. It has a very friendly informal atmosphere and is an ideal base for touring the Cotswolds, Severn Vale, North Wiltshire and Bath area, or as we are close to M4/5 is a convenient overnight stop. Westonbirt Arboretum is five minutes away and the antiques centre of Tetbury is less than 10. Three double/twin rooms with colour TV, hair dryers, en suite or private bathroom. Central heating. Guests' sitting room. Ample parking. Food available within walking distance. Terms: Double room from £35.

DURSLEY near. Bob & Linda Woodman and Neil Smith, Rose and Crown Inn, Nympsfield, Stonehouse GL10 3TU (Tel & Fax: 01453 860240).

🌱🌱🌱 COMMENDED. Three-hundred-year-old Cotswold stone coaching inn situated in centre of quiet, friendly, unspoilt village, half a mile from Cotswold Way; with easy access to M5/M4. Ideal base for touring, walking, cycling and gliding in the Cotswolds. Accommodation includes centrally heated, spacious, en-suite family and double rooms. Evening meals are optional and can be selected from a comprehensive bar menu. Bed and Breakfast from £26 per night. AA, RAC, Relais Routiers Listed, Logis UK. Open all year. All credit/debit cards accepted.

FALFIELD. Mrs Rosemary Blair, Whitfield Farm, Falfield GL12 8DR (01454 260334).

Ideal stopover — five minutes from Junction 14 of the M5, handy to A38 yet situated in peaceful surroundings with open views. Accommodation offered in one twin-bedded room and two single rooms; all are attractively furnished and have complimentary tea trays, radios and comprehensive tourist information. The lounge/dining room is spacious and sunny with TV. All rooms overlook mature gardens. This is a mixed working farm which is of historical interest and crops include commercially grown strawberries — delicious with locally made clotted cream. Ideally situated for touring the West Country. Well behaved pets accepted. Non-smoking accommodation. Children over 12 years welcome. Choice of local restaurants. Terms from £18.

FALFIELD. Mr and Mrs B.C. Burrell, Green Farm Guest House, Falfield, Gloucestershire GL12 8DL (01454 260319). ETB Listed.

Delightful 16th century stone farmhouse, beautifully converted into a country guest house with style and traditional charm. Open all year. Bath, Cheltenham, Cardiff, Forest of Dean, Cheddar are all approximately 35 minutes away. Easy access M4 and M5 Junction 14, AZTEC Business Park 10 minutes. The ideal touring centre. Tourist Board registered. Bed and Breakfast from £16. Excellent food always available from simple snacks to à la carte dinner. A warm welcome assured at Green Farm. Ample parking. AA QQ.

FOREST OF DEAN. Mrs Joan Thorpe, Brook House Guest House, Bridge Street, Blakeney GL15 4DY (01594 517101).

🌱🌱 COMMENDED. Enjoy a relaxing break in the Forest of Dean and Wye Valley. The area is ideal for walking, mountain hiking, fishing or simply enjoying the scenery. Brook House is an attractive 17th century building. We offer a warm welcome, personal service and comfortable accommodation. All rooms have central heating, colour TV and tea/coffee making facilities. En suite and four-poster rooms are available. Optional home cooked evening meal; supper licence. Blakeney is midway between Gloucester and Chepstow on A48. Brook House is in the centre of the village behind the Post Office. Car parking. Secure cycle storage. Bed and Breakfast from £16. Colour brochure.

FOREST OF DEAN. Symonds Yat Rock Motel, Hillersland, Coleford GL16 7NY (01594 836191).

ETB Listed. Small family-run quiet Motel in a beautiful forest setting. Restaurant with licensed bar. All rooms en suite with colour TV, tea/coffee facilities and central heating. Situated on B4432 Christchurch/Symonds Yat Rock road three quarters of a mile from the famous view point and peregrine falcon nesting area. Ideal central position for touring the Forest, the Brecons, South Wales and the Cotswolds. Special breaks available October/November, January/February/March. Brochure on request.

GLOUCESTER. Mrs S. Carter, Severn Bank, Minsterworth GL2 8JH (01452 750357). 🐦🐦

COMMENDED. Severn Bank is a fine country house standing in its own six-acre grounds on the bank of the River Severn, four miles west of Gloucester. Ideally situated for touring Cotswolds, Forest of Dean and Wye Valley, and at the recommended viewpoint for the Severn Bore tidal wave. Severn Bank has a friendly atmosphere and comfortable accommodation in spacious rooms with superb view over river and countryside. Full central heating, en-suite rooms, tea/coffee making facilities and colour TV in non-smoking bedrooms. Ample parking, with several excellent restaurants and pubs nearby. Terms: Bed and Full English Breakfast £18 to £20. Reduced rates for children.

GLOUCESTER near. S.J. Barnfield, Kilmorie Guest House, Gloucester Road, Corse, Staunton, Near Gloucester GL19 3RQ (01452 840224). Built in 1848 by the Chartists, Kilmorie is Grade II Listed in a conservation area, and is a smallholding keeping farm livestock and fruit in a lovely part of Gloucestershire. Good home cooking with own produce and eggs when available. Large garden. Children are welcome to "help" with the animals if they wish, and a child's pony is also kept. There are many places of both historic and natural interest to visit, and river trips can be

enjoyed from Tewkesbury and Upton-on-Severn. Kilmorie is situated close to the borders of Herefordshire and Worcestershire, and the Forest of Dean, the Cotswolds, Malvern Hills, the Wye Valley and four castles are all within easy reach. Four double, one twin, one single and one family bedrooms, all with washbasins and TVs, some with private facilities available; two bathrooms and two additional toilets; shower. Tea-making facilities. Lounge with colour TV; diningroom. Central heating. Fire Certificate. Children over five years welcome. Pets accepted. Ample parking. Three course Dinner, Bed and Breakfast from £20.50; Bed and Breakfast from £14. Reduced rates for children. Open all year.

GLOUCESTER near. Mrs Judith Price, "Merrivale", Tewkesbury Road, Norton, Near Gloucester GL2 9LQ (01452 730412). 🐦 COMMENDED. "Merrivale"

is a bright and cheerful house and a warm welcome is given to all guests. The house is situated on the A38, three miles north of Gloucester. Ample garden for guests' use and plenty of parking space (car advisable). Tea and coffee making equipment and TV in all rooms, much enjoyed by the weary traveller. Ideal spot for those travelling from Scotland to South West resorts of England. For a longer stay there are many interesting places to visit: The Cotswolds, Forest of Dean, Herefordshire and Welsh Border, historic Tewkesbury and Severn and Avon Rivers. Packed lunches prepared. Bed and Breakfast from £16 to £17 per person. Reductions for children under 14. Fire Certificate held.

LECHLADE near. Mrs Elizabeth Reay, Apple Tree House, Buscot, Near Faringdon SN7 8DA (01367 252592). 🐦🐦 17th century listed house situated in small interesting National Trust Village, two miles from Lechlade and four miles from Faringdon on the A417. River Thames five minutes' walk through village to Buscot lock and weirs.

Ideal touring centre for the Cotswolds, Upper Thames, Oxford, etc. Good fishing, walking and cycling area. Access at all times to the three guest bedrooms, all of which have washbasins, razor points, tea/coffee facilities and central heating when necessary. En-suite room available. Residents' TV lounge with log fire in winter. Bed and Breakfast from £17 per person per night. Choice of many restaurants, etc, within a five-mile radius of Buscot. I look forward to welcoming you to Apple Tree House.

MINCHINHAMPTON, near Stroud. Mrs Margaret Helm, Hunters Lodge, Dr Brown's Road, Minchinhampton Common, Near Stroud GL6 9BT (01453 883588; Fax: 01453 731449). 👑👑 *HIGHLY COMMENDED.* AA QQQQ Selected. Hunters Lodge is a beautiful stone built Cotswold country house set in large secluded garden adjoining 600 acres of National Trust common land at Minchinhampton. Accommodation available — one double room en suite; one family and one twin-bedded rooms both with private bathrooms. All have tea/coffee making facilities, central heating and colour TV and are furnished and decorated to a high standard. Private lounge with TV and a delightful conservatory. Car essential, ample parking space. Ideal centre for touring the Cotswolds — Bath, Cheltenham, Cirencester, with many delightful pubs and hotels in the area for meals. You are sure of a warm welcome, comfort, and help in planning excursions to local places of interest. Bed and Breakfast from £19 per person. Non-smokers preferred. SAE please for details, or telephone.

MORETON-IN-MARSH. Richard & Lorraine Carter, The Cottage, Oxford Street, Moreton-in-Marsh GL56 0LA (Tel and Fax: 01608 651740). HETB Listed. A warm and friendly greeting awaits you in this Grade II Listed Cotswold cottage with exposed beams and inglenook fireplace. Ideal touring centre for the Cotswolds, Stratford-upon-Avon and Cheltenham. Many delightful pubs and restaurants within easy walking distance. Accommodation comprises one twin room and one double room with shared bathroom, and one double room with en suite bathroom in the Wheelwright Cottage with separate entrance. Colour TV in all rooms together with tea/coffee making facilities. Pretty garden available for the use of guests. Bed and Breakfast from £18 to £22.50 per person. No smoking. Ample parking. Within easy walking distance of BR station on direct line from Paddington Station, London.

NAILSWORTH, near Stroud. Brian and Chris Butcher, Windsoredge House, Windsoredge, Nailsworth GL6 0NP (01453 833626 or 836503). 👑👑 A Cotswold stone house built about 1650 with later additions and alterations up to about 1865. Our recently added private/en suite bathrooms are to the highest standard and the subject of much comment. The house occupies a prominent position on a hillside at the junction of two valleys adjoining large areas of National Trust land and enjoys panoramic views which defy description. Many popular walks are nearby. The location is quiet and tranquil and our hospitality and home cooking are widely acclaimed. Tea/coffee making facilities in all rooms, together with TV in bedrooms or guests' lounge. No smokers. No pets.

NEWENT. Old Court, Church Street, Newent GL18 1AB (01531 820522). 👑👑👑 *COMMENDED.* Surrounded by an acre of walled gardens this magnificent 17th century Country House is an oasis of peace and seclusion. Old Court has a fascinating history and still retains an atmosphere of unhurried elegance and comfort. All bedrooms are individually styled to the highest standard with colour TV, radio, tea/coffee and direct-dial telephone. Our four-poster bedroom is particularly spacious and perfect for that special occasion! Before dinner guests may relax with a drink in the Green Drawing Room, with its fluted pillars and intricate ceiling plasterwork. Dining is a must with a new menu and wine list carefully developed by the resident owners, Ron and Sue Wood. Bed and Breakfast from £25 per person.

👑👑👑
COMMENDED

RAC
★★

NORTHLEACH. Theresa and Mike Eastman, Market House, The Square, Northleach GL54 3EJ (01451 860557). A 400-year-old house of olde worlde charm, characterised by exposed beams, inglenook fireplace yet with modern facilities. Pretty bedrooms, one double en suite, one double/twin and two singles, each with washbasin, central heating, tea/coffee making facilities and touring guides. Located in an unspoilt tiny town in the heart of the Cotswolds near the intersection of the A40 with A429, amidst a wide choice of inns and restaurants and surrounded by a variety of attractions and beautiful countryside. A delicious breakfast is cooked to order for your enjoyment, before you tour to nearby Bath, Stratford-upon-Avon or Oxford. Children over 12 years. No pets. No smoking. Packed lunches available. Bed and Breakfast from £17. "Which?" Recommended.

PAINSWICK. Jan Haslam, Culvert Cottage, Kingsmill Lane, Painswick GL6 6RT (01452 812293).

 COMMENDED. Once an old wheelwright's cottage, Culvert Cottage has been skilfully extended and is a homely guest house of unusual design. It is set in beautiful gardens of one and a half acres bordering a stream and opposite historic Kings Mill. The picturesque village of Painswick with its famous churchyard is an ideal centre for exploring the Cotswolds. Berkeley Castle, Slimbridge Wildfowl Trust, Gloucester and Cheltenham are all nearby. The Cotswold Way footpath is within half a mile. Non smoking accommodation comprises one double and one twin bedroom, both en suite with colour TV and tea making facilities. Bed and Breakfast from £16.50. Reductions for children.

PAINSWICK. Jean Hernen, Brookhouse Mill Cottage, Tibbiwell Lane, Painswick GL6 6YA (Tel & Fax: 01452 812854). Brookhouse Mill Cottage is a beautiful 17th century cottage situated in Painswick — the "Queen of the Cotswolds" in an area of outstanding natural beauty.

Bed & Breakfast

Jean Hernen
Brookhouse Mill Cottage.

The cottage was once the village forge and has been lovingly restored by the proprietors, Brian and Jean Hernen, with exposed original beams and timbers, inglenook fireplace and cast iron range. It straddles a trout stream and the two-acre garden encompasses a lake and two waterfalls. Each bedroom has en suite facilities and is furnished to a very high standard in keeping with the cottage style. The beds are covered in hand-stitched patchwork quilts designed by Jean; some are for sale together with cot quilts and cushion covers. All this is topped by the use of the beautiful indoor swimming pool. Plenty of parking space and a totally "non smoking" house. Brochure.

RANDWICK. Mr and Mrs J.E. Taylor, Court Farm, Randwick, Stroud GL6 6HH (01453 764210; Fax: 01453 766428). A 17th century beamed farmhouse on a small farm in the centre of hillside village of Randwick, on the Cotswold Escarpment. Beautiful views over Stroud Valleys. Randwick is topped by a deciduous National Trust wood. Much of our food produced organically on seven acres of meadowland. A stream divides the sloping fields, haven for wildlife. Large garden for guests to enjoy, village pub food. Leisure centre one mile. Convenient overnight stop, good base. Tourist attractions nearby include Wildfowl Trust, Gloucester Waterways, Prinknash Abbey, Berkeley Castle. London two hours A419, M5 Junction 13 five miles. Bed and Breakfast from £15 to £17; Evening Meal can be provided. Children and pets welcome.

STONEHOUSE. Mrs D.A. Hodge, Merton Lodge, 8 Ebley Road, Stonehouse GL10 2LQ (01453 822018). A former gentleman's residence situated about three miles from Stroudwater interchange on the M5 (Junction 13), on A419 (keep going on old road) just outside Stonehouse towards Stroud. Opposite side to Kennedy's Garden Centre, 300 yards from the Cotswold Way. Full central heating and washbasins in all bedrooms; one en-suite. Only cotton or linen sheets used. Two bathrooms with showers. Large sittingroom with panoramic views of Selsey Common. Well placed for Cotswold villages, Wildfowl Trust, Berkeley Castle, Westonbirt Arboretum, Bath/Bristol, Cheltenham and Gloucester ski slope and Forest of Dean. Satisfaction guaranteed. Excellent cuisine. Carvery/pub 200 yards away. Bed and Breakfast from £16 per person, en suite from £17 per person. Reductions for children. Friendly welcome. Sorry, no smoking or dogs.

STOW-ON-THE-WOLD. Graham and Helen Keyte, The Limes, Evesham Road, Stow-on-the-Wold GL54 1EN (01451 830034/831056). The centre of the Cotswolds. This is an RAC and AA Listed guest house. Large attractive garden with ornamental pond and waterfall overlooking fields. Only four minutes' walking distance to town centre. Central for places to visit like Stratford-upon-Avon, Burford, Cheltenham, Oxford, Broadway, Evesham, Chipping Campden, etc, all within 20 miles' radius. Good sized bedrooms; one four-poster, two rooms en-suite and one twin-bedded room, all with colour TV and tea/coffee making facilities; TV lounge; diningroom. Cot, high chair. Established for over 22 years, we have many guests returning each year, even from abroad, and are well recommended. Many guests book for one or two nights then stay for a week. Bed and Breakfast from £16 to £19.50. Central heating. Car park. Open all year except Christmas. Children and pets welcome.

STOW-ON-THE-WOLD. Mrs F.J. Adams, Aston House, Broadwell, Moreton-in-Marsh GL56 0TJ (01451 830475). ETB Listed *COMMENDED.*

Aston House is a chalet bungalow overlooking fields in the peaceful village of Broadwell, one and a half miles from Stow-on-the-Wold. It is centrally situated for all the Cotswold villages, while Blenheim Palace, Warwick Castle, Oxford, Stratford-upon-Avon, Cheltenham, Cirencester and Gloucester are within easy reach. Accommodation comprises a twin-bedded and a double/twin room, both en suite on the first floor and a double room with private bathroom on the ground floor. All rooms have tea/coffee making facilities, colour TV and electric blankets. Bedtime drinks and biscuits are provided. Guests and children over 10 years are welcomed to our home February to November. No smoking. Car essential, parking. Sorry, no pets. Pub within walking distance. Bed and good English Breakfast from £18.50 to £20.00 per person daily; weekly from £129.50 per person.

STOW-ON-THE-WOLD. Mrs S. Davis, Fairview Farmhouse, Bledington Road, Stow-on-the-Wold, Cheltenham GL54 1AN (01451 830279). 👑👑 *HIGHLY COMMENDED.*

You are assured of a warm welcome at Fairview Farmhouse situated one mile from Stow-on-the-Wold on a quiet B road with outstanding panoramic views of the surrounding Cotswold Hills. Ideal base for touring the pretty villages of Bourton-on-the-Water, The Slaughters, Broadway, Chipping Campden, also famous Stratford etc. The cosy bedrooms are furnished to a high standard with a king-size four-poster de luxe for that special occasion; all are en suite with colour TV and tea/coffee making equipment. Lounge and additional lounge area with books, maps, etc. Central heating. Ample parking. Open all year.

STOW-ON-THE-WOLD. Robert and Dawn Smith, Corsham Field Farmhouse, Bledington Road, Stow-on-the-Wold GL54 1JH (01451 831750). 👑👑 Homely farmhouse with traditional features and breathtaking views, one mile from Stow-on-the-Wold. Ideally situated for exploring all the picturesque Cotswold villages such as Broadway, Bourton-on-the-Water, Upper and Lower Slaughter, Chipping Campden, Snowshill, etc. Also central point for places of interest such as Blenheim Palace, Cotswold Wildlife Park, Stratford and many stately homes and castles in the area. Twin, double and family rooms available, most with en suite facilities. Other rooms have washbasins, TV and tea/coffee making equipment. Pets and children welcome. AA Listed. Bed and full English Breakfast from £13.50 to £18.50 per person. Good pub food five minutes' walk away.

STROUD. Mrs Salt, Beechcroft, Brownshill, Stroud GL6 8AG (01453 883422). 👑 *COMMENDED.*

Our Edwardian house is quietly situated in a beautiful rural area with open views, about four miles from Stroud. The house is set in an attractive garden with mature trees, shrubs and herbaceous borders. We are in the midst of good walking country, for which we can lend maps and guides. We provide a full cooked breakfast or fruit salad and rolls with home-made bread and preserves. We welcome the elderly and small children. We are within easy reach of Cheltenham, Gloucester, Cirencester and Bath, also Berkeley Castle, Slimbridge and the North Cotswolds. We are a non-smoking establishment. Evening Meal by prior arrangement. Bed and Breakfast from £16 to £20.

STROUD near. Mrs Caroline Garrett, Lamfield, Rodborough Common, Stroud GL5 5DA (01453 873452).

Delightful Cotswold stone house altered over the years from a row of cottages dating back to 1757. Situated 500ft above sea level bordering National Trust Common land two miles south east of Stroud between A46 and A419, we enjoy superb views across the valley. Lamfield offers one room with a double bed and one with twin beds. Both with washbasins. Shared bathroom. Sittingroom for guests (TV on request). Set in three-quarters of an acre of secluded garden. Ample off road parking. Excellent pubs locally for evening meals. Bed and Breakfast from £30 per room for two sharing. Come and share my home for a night or two.

TEWKESBURY. Mrs Lynn Bird, Green Gables, Ripple, Tewkesbury GL20 6EX (01684 592740).

Modern house set in beautiful quiet village of Ripple which is only three miles from Tewkesbury and Upton on Severn and one mile from Junction 1 of M50 and M5 in the heart of the Severn/Avon Valley with views of Malvern and Bredon Hills. Luxurious accommodation, all rooms en suite with tea maker and colour TV. Friendly comfortable lounge for evening relaxation. Children welcome. Sorry, no pets. Open all year. Car necessary, parking available. Bed and wonderful English Breakfast £17.50 single, £35 double/twin. Reductions for children.

TEWKESBURY. Mrs B. Williams, Abbots Court, Church End, Twyning, Tewkesbury GL20 6DA (01684 292515). ♛♛ *COMMENDED.* A large quiet com-

fortable farmhouse set in 350 acres, built on the site of a monastery between the Malverns and Cotswolds, half a mile from M5/M50 junction. Large bedrooms, five en suite, fully carpeted, with washbasins, tea making facilities and colour TV. Centrally heated. Open all year. Large lounge with open fire and colour TV, spacious dining room. Good home cooked food in large quantities, home produced where possible. Children's own TV room, games room and playroom. Play area on lawn. Cot, high chair and babysitting available. Laundry facilities. Licensed bar. Ideally situated for touring with numerous places to visit. Swimming, tennis, cinema, sauna, golf within three miles. Coarse fishing available on farm. Bed and Breakfast from £14.50 to £16.50. Reduced rates Senior Citizens and children.

ULEY. Gerald and Norma Kent, Hill House, Crawley Hill, Uley, Near Dursley GL11 5BH (01453 860267). Cotswold stone house situated on top of a hill with

beautiful views of the surrounding countryside, near the very pretty village of Uley. Ideal spot for exploring the various walks in the area including the Cotswold Way and there are many places of interest within reasonable driving distance of Uley. Choice of bedrooms with or without en suite facilities, all with washbasins, central heating, shaver points, tea/coffee making facilities and TV. Yours hosts' aim is to make your stay in the Cotswolds an enjoyable and memorable one, with comfort and hospitality of prime importance. Bed and Breakfast from £15 per person. Evening Meals are normally available if required. Please phone or write for brochure.

WICKWAR, Near Wotton-Under-Edge. Mrs Jenny Cox, Kingfisher, 84 Station Road, Wickwar, Wotton-Under-Edge GL12 8NB (01454 294753). Comfortable accommodation with en suite bathroom, colour TV, tea/coffee making facilities situated on the B4060 between Chipping Sodbury and Wotton-under-Edge overlooking valley of trees and farmland. Single room available. Ideal for country lovers, bird watchers and walkers who appreciate the advantage of easy communications. A full English or Continental breakfast is served in our garden room overlooking colourful terraced gardens. Children welcome at reduced rates. Well behaved pets accepted. Bed and Breakfast from £14 to £17 per person per night.

WINCHCOMBE. The Plaisterers Arms, Abbey Terrace, Winchcombe GL54 5LL (Tel and Fax: 01242 602358). ♛♛ *COMMENDED.* Set in historic Winchcombe,

in the North Cotswolds, this friendly old and unusual split-level Inn has five comfortable and well appointed en suite bedrooms with colour TV and tea/coffee facilities. Lunches and evening meals are available every day from an extensive menu supplemented by daily specials. Winchcombe is an ideal spot for walking or touring the Cotswolds region and Sudeley Castle is within walking distance. Broadway, Cheltenham, Evesham and Tewkesbury are all within 15 minutes' drive.

WINCHCOMBE. Mick and Sally Simmonds, Gower House, 16 North Street, Winchcombe GL54 5LH (01242 602616). 🐾 🐾 A warm welcome awaits you at this 17th century town house situated close to the town centre of Winchcombe, a small picturesque country town on the Cotswold Way. It is an ideal base for ramblers, cyclists and motorists to explore the beautiful Cotswold countryside. The three comfortable bedrooms all have TV, radio, tea/coffee making facilities, washbasins, shaver points, full central heating and are served by two bathrooms, each with shower and bath. There is a TV lounge and a large secluded garden available for guests' use. Off road car park with two garages. Children welcome but sorry, no pets. Bed and Breakfast from £17 per person.

WINCHCOMBE near. Mr and Mrs Bloom, The Homestead, Smithy Lane, Greet, Near Winchcombe GL54 5BP (01242 603808). Tourist Board Listed. The Homestead is a 16th century period country house, built in Cotswold stone and standing in one acre of lovely gardens, with commanding views of the Cotswold Hills. It is situated just one mile from the Anglo-Saxon village of Winchcombe and Sudeley Castle, and within easy reach of many Cotswold villages and Stratford-upon-Avon. There are several pubs and a restaurant nearby for evening meals. We have two double rooms, one with en-suite facilities, one family room ensuite and one twin room with washbasin. All rooms have exposed beams and lovely views. Tea making facilities in rooms. Bed and Breakfast from £16. Private parking for cars.

WOODCHESTER. Mrs Wendy Swait, Inschdene, Atcombe Road, South Woodchester, Stroud GL5 5EW (01453 873254). Inschdene is a comfortable family house with magnificent views across the valley, set in an acre of garden near the centre of a quiet village. A double room with private bathroom and a twin-bedded room are available, both being spacious with washbasin and tea/coffee making facilities. Colour TV available in the rooms. Woodchester is an attractive village with excellent local pubs renowned for their food, and all within easy walking distance. An ideal centre for the Cotswolds and close to Slimbridge, Berkeley Castle and Westonbirt Arboretum and more, including Badminton and Gatcombe Horse Trials. Guests are requested not to smoke in the house. Bed and Breakfast from £12.50 to £17.50.

WOTTON-UNDER-EDGE. Mrs K.P. Forster, Under-the-Hill House, Adey's Lane, Wotton-under-Edge GL12 7LY (01453 842557). Open Easter to October, Under-the-Hill is a fine Queen Anne Listed house on the edge of the ancient wool town of Wotton-under-Edge. We are bounded on the east by National Trust land which is let to the owners who run a breeding herd of Welsh Black cattle. The house is only a few minutes from the town centre and there are beautiful walks with views of the Severn Vale and River. Ideally situated for Bath, Berkeley Castle, Wildfowl Trust and the Cotswolds. The house is centrally heated and there are two guest bedrooms (one twin and one double) with washbasins, colour TV and tea/coffee making facilities. Shared garden for guests' use. Bed and Breakfast from £16.50 per person per night for three or more nights, £18.50 per night for one or two nights. Sorry no pets, no children under 12 years and no smoking.

WOTTON-UNDER-EDGE. Paul and Carol Cory, The Thatched Cottage, Wortley, Wotton-under-Edge GL12 7QP (01453 842776). Situated in a charming and peaceful little hamlet on the edge of the Cotswolds, surrounded by farmland and wooded hillsides. Walker's paradise. Easy distance to Gloucester, Cirencester, Bath and Bristol with numerous smaller market towns and villages well worth visiting. The Thatched Cottage dates from the 14th century and sits on land where the remains of a Roman Villa are at present being excavated. Accommodation comprises double-bedded or twin-bedded rooms with TV and tea/coffee making facilities. Private bathroom available — £5 per night. Bed and Breakfast (good English) from £17 per person per night. Reductions for four nights or more.

HAMPSHIRE

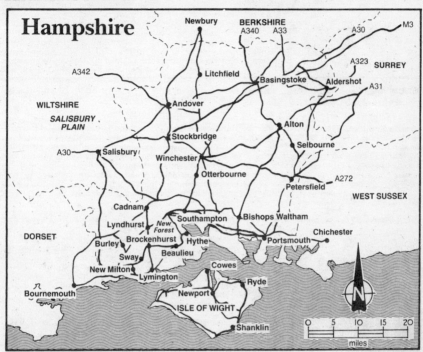

Hampshire

BARTON-ON-SEA. Mrs J. Copeland, Laurel Lodge, 48 Western Avenue, Barton-on-Sea BH25 7PZ (01425 618309). ETB 🌼🌼🌼 AA QQQQ Selected, RAC Acclaimed. A superb area in all seasons for that special break. Scenic clifftop walks, beaches, golf, sailing, riding and the delights of the nearby historic New Forest. Laurel Lodge offers every possible comfort in a cosy atmosphere, friendly, personal service, great home-cooked food. Bed and four-course Breakfast from £17 (single occupancy from £21). Special diets catered for. The centrally heated en suite double, twin and family rooms all have remote-control colour TV, tea/coffee facilities, and more . . . Ground floor bedrooms available. An ideal touring base for a holiday to remember. We are open all year.

BEAULIEU near. Mick and Alexis McEvoy, Langley Village Restaurant, Lepe Road, Langley, Southampton SO45 1XR (01703 891667). A friendly family atmosphere will greet you in this large detached property on the edge of the beautiful New Forest. Ample off road parking. Each day begins with a hearty full English breakfast. Accommodation comprises one twin, one double and two single rooms, all tastefully decorated and having washbasins, central heating, colour TV and tea-making facilities. A restaurant is attached offering meals all day. Conveniently situated for golf, fishing, horse riding and walking. Close to Exbury Gardens, Lepe Country Park and Beaulieu Motor Museum. Open all year. Bed and Breakfast from £16.50. Special diets catered for by arrangement.

BURLEY. Mrs Gina Russell, Charlwood, Longmead Road, Burley BH24 4BY (01425 403242). Charlwood is situated on the edge of Burley, a picturesque little village in the midst of the New Forest. An ideal walking and touring base with Bournemouth and Southampton only 16 miles away and Isle of Wight ferry 12 miles. Riding and golf are nearby. The bedrooms, one double, one twin, have washbasins, colour TV and tea/coffee facilities. Central heating throughout. The friendly family home stands in its own attractive grounds on a no-through Forest road offering visitors a peaceful "away from it all" break. A full traditional English Breakfast is served. Pets welcome. No smoking. Open January to November. Bed and Breakfast from £16.50.

CADNAM (New Forest). Mrs Elaine Wright, Bushfriers, Winsor Road, Winsor, Southampton SO40

2HF (01703 812552). Bushfriers is a charming cottage enclosed by a fragrant garden overlooking open countryside. Accommodation comprises two comfortable bedrooms with tea/coffee making facilities, a well appointed bathroom, TV lounge with log fire and timbered ceiling, all reflecting the warm and friendly atmosphere. Our highly rated breakfast is freshly prepared with local farm produce and home-made preserves. Bushfriers is situated in the rural village of Winsor on the edge of the beautiful New Forest off A336 and two miles to Junction 1 M27. An ideal location central for all the south's major towns. Golf, horse riding, fishing and good pubs close by. Bed and Breakfast from £15 per person per night.

FORDINGBRIDGE (New Forest). Mrs S. Harte, Alderholt Mill, Sandleheath Road, Alderholt, Fordingbridge SP6 1PU (01425 653130). Alderholt Mill stands on a tributary of the Hampshire Avon, on the Hampshire/Dorset border. The Water Mill and house are on an island formed by the mill stream and race. Open to the public, with working machinery, art gallery and craft shop. Three double rooms and one twin room, all en suite, £19 per person per night; one single room with washbasin £16 per person per night. Prices include Continental or English breakfast. Evening Meal available if required. Guests welcome to bring own wine. All rooms have colour TV, tea/coffee making facilities. Horses and dogs welcome. Rough fishing. Open all year. Car essential, parking. From M27 Cadnam take B3078 to Fordingbridge, continue to Sandleheath, left for Alderholt (half mile). Further details available from Mrs Harte.

FRITHAM (New Forest). Maureen and Barry Penfound, Primrose Cottage, Fritham, Near Lyndhurst

SO43 7HH (01703 812272). A pretty Victorian forest cottage, ideally situated in the heart of the Forest on the outskirts of the small Forest hamlet of Fritham. From our cottage you can walk for miles across the open forest, experience the freedom of Stoney Cross and Fritham Plains, and explore the surrounding ancient beech and oak woodlands with their wide variety of flora and fauna. Ideal touring location. Privacy assured in quiet comfortable accommodation which includes private shower room and TV lounge. Tea/coffee making facilities. Garage parking available. Non smoking home. Bed and full English Breakfast £16 per person. Reductions for three/five nights.

FRITHAM (New Forest). John and Penny Hankinson, Fritham Farm, Fritham, Lyndhurst SO43 7HH

(Tel & Fax: 01703 812333). 🦢🦢 *COMMENDED.* AA QQQQ Selected. Lovely farmhouse on working farm in the heart of the New Forest. Dating from the 18th century, all bedrooms have en suite facilities and provision for tea/coffee making. There is a large comfortable lounge with TV and log fire. Fritham is in a particularly beautiful part of the New Forest, still largely undiscovered and with a wealth of wildlife. It is a wonderful base for walking, riding, cycling and touring. No smoking. Children 10 years and over welcome. Come and enjoy peace and quiet in this lovely corner of England. Bed and Breakfast £17 to £19.

HOOK. Mr Field, Oaklea Guest House, London Road, Hook, Near Basingstoke RG27 9LA (01256

762673). 🦢🦢 Oaklea is a fine Victorian house one mile from Junction 5 of M3. Ideally placed for the West Country with easy access to Southampton, Reading, London, Guildford also Heathrow and Gatwick Airports. Accommodation offered in single, double and family rooms, some en suite with TV. Guest lounge. Homely atmosphere. Bed and Breakfast from £25 to £44 including VAT. Licensed. AA Listed.

Reduced rate for adult when accompanied by a full-paying adult at Beaulieu, near Brockenhurst Hampshire. Our READERS' OFFER VOUCHER gives full details.

HYTHE, near Southampton. David and Marion Robinson, Four Seasons Hotel, Hamilton Road, Hythe, Southampton SO45 3PD (01703 845151 or 846285). A warm welcome is extended to guests staying in this friendly, family run hotel. Situated on the edge of the New Forest it is ideal for touring. The picturesque market town of Hythe with its pubs and restaurants is one and a half miles distant. Here is an attractive Marina and a regular ferry service to Southampton and Isle of Wight. Golf, horse riding, wind surfing and other sports are available within five miles. Bedrooms have colour TVs and tea/coffee facilities; en suite facilities available. Highly praised for its standard of good home cooking, there is also a licensed bar, attractive garden and ample parking. Bed and Breakfast from £19; Evening Meal by arrangement.

String of Horses

This unique secluded hotel is the perfect setting for a visit to the New Forest. Experience the luxury of individually designed bedrooms, each with its own fantasy bathroom offering every facility. Savour the delights of our candlelit 'Carriages' Restaurant. Set in four acres with heated swimming pool. Close to five Golf Courses including Links course. We regret we are unable to accommodate children or pets. Terms from £40 per person Bed and Breakfast. Two days Dinner, Bed and Breakfast from £103 per person.

Mead End Road, Sway, near Lymington SO41 6EH
Telephone 01590 682631   AA★★ & Rosette

👑👑👑👑 Highly Commended

LYMINGTON. Our Bench, Lodge Road, Lymington SO41 8HH (Tel & Fax: 01590 673141). 👑👑👑 COMMENDED. Welcome Host, FHG Diploma Winner. A warm and friendly welcome awaits you in our large bungalow situated in a quiet area between the beautiful New Forest and the Coast. In the large garden stands a chalet which houses an indoor heated swimming/exercise pool, jacuzzi and sauna. We have double, twin and single rooms, all en suite. There is a separate lounge with colour TV, and a four-course breakfast is served in our dining room, where evening meals are also available if required. RAC Acclaimed, AA QQQQ Selected. For non-smokers only and sorry, no children. Tariff from £20 per person per night.

LYMINGTON. Mrs R. Sque, "Harts Lane", 242 Everton Road, Everton, Lymington SO41 0HE (01590 645902). Bungalow (non-smoking) set in three acres; large garden with wildlife pond and an abundance of bird life. Quiet location, convenient for A337, three miles west of Lymington. Friendly comfortable accommodation comprising three double bedrooms, two en suite, all with tea/coffee making facilities and colour TV. The sea and forest are five minutes away by car. Horse riding, golf, fishing and a real ale pub serving homemade meals are all nearby. Children and pets welcome. Bed and Breakfast from £17.50 per person per night.

WHEN MAKING ENQUIRIES PLEASE MENTION THIS *FHG* PUBLICATION

LYMINGTON (New Forest). Jane and Mike Finch, "Dolphins", 6 Emsworth Road, Lymington SO41 9BL (01590 676108 or 679545; Fax: 01590 688275).

"Dolphins" is a very comfortable and homely Victorian cottage offering warm hospitality and the highest standard of accommodation. Single, twin, double and family rooms all have colour TV and tea/coffee making facilities; en suite available if required. Spacious and very comfortable sitting room with open log fire (in winter) and colour TV with satellite. Choice of breakfast; traditional home-cooked evening meals available. Very quiet position, centrally located, just five minutes' walk from railway/bus stations. Beautiful Forest walks, excellent cycle rides in and around Lymington and the New Forest (maps provided, mountain bikes available). Open all year. From £16 per person per night; Evening meals optional. Children half price. Access/Visa/Mastercard accepted. Please write or telephone for brochure.

EFFORD COTTAGE
Everton, Lymington, Hampshire SO41 0JD
Tel & Fax 01590 642315

Efford Cottage is friendly, part Georgian family home, standing in an acre of garden. All rooms have full tea/coffee making facilities, colour TV, heated towel rail, hair dryer, electric blanket, trouser press and mini fridge. We offer a four course, five choice breakfast with homemade bread and preserves. Evening meals, if required, are table d'hôte and à la carte and we use home grown vegetables, when available. Honesty Bar. The cottage is an excellent centre for exploring both the New Forest and the South Coast with sports facilities, fishing, bird watching and horse riding in the near vicinity. Private parking. Dogs welcome. Bed and Breakfast from £19 per person; Evening Meal from £10.

AA QQQQ Selected   ETB ♛♛♛ Commended   RAC Acclaimed

The Penny Farthing Hotel

This cheerful private hotel offers rooms with en-suite, colour TV and tea/coffee facilities. We also provide a licensed bar, a residents lounge with satellite TV, a large car park and a lock-up bicycle store. Lyndhurst is home to the New Forest Tourist Information Centre and offers a charming variety of shops, restaurants and bistros all within a moments walk. The Penny Farthing is centrally situated and provides an excellent location from which you can enjoy some of England's most beautiful countryside.

Romsey Road, Lyndhurst, Hampshire SO43 7AA
Tel: 01703 284422 Fax: 01703 284488

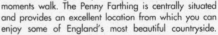

LYNDHURST. Mrs E.M. Rowland, Forest Cottage, High Street, Lyndhurst SO43 7BH (01703 283461). ETB Listed *COMMENDED*. Charming 300 year old cottage. Three bedrooms — double, twin and single, each with washbasin. The sittingroom has a library of natural history, reference books, maps and local literature. Tea/coffee and special breakfast diets available on request. The garden contains an interesting collection of plants, some unusual. Lyndhurst is the centre of the New Forest, convenient for the many inland and coastal attractions and activities provided by the area. There is a wide choice of food in the village and nearby. Private parking. No smoking please. Bed and Breakfast from £17 per person per night.

ORMONDE
H O U S E
Southampton Road, Lyndhurst,
Hampshire SO43 7BT
Telephone: 01703 282806
Fax: 01703 282004

Ormonde House, in the heart of the New Forest, offers elegant, luxury accommodation at affordable prices, all rooms ensuite, TV, phone, beverage facilities. Luxury rooms are spacious with bath and shower, sofas and remote TV. Comfort extends throughout the lounge and conservatory overlooking the flower filled gardens. Your host, Paul, who has been a leading restaurateur, offers freshly prepared traditional English dinners. Bordering the south coast and famous for its ponies, the New Forest can be reached in under $1^1/_2$ hours from London. Close to Beaulieu Motor Museum and Exbury Gardens. Special Break details on request. Rover welcome! B&B £20-£35 pppn.

NEW FOREST TOURISM   **AA QQQQ** *Selected*

LYNDHURST (New Forest). John and April Robinson, Little Hayes, 43 Romsey Road, Lyndhurst SO43 7AR (01703 283000). ❦ ❦ *HIGHLY COMMENDED.* Little Hayes is a late Victorian family home, beautifully restored and furnished, with a friendly and informal atmosphere. Three spacious and comfortable bedrooms, two double (one with private bathroom) and one twin; with tea/coffee, central heating, washbasins and colour TV. The guest lounge has TV and video. You will have a wonderful breakfast, choosing from an extensive menu. Private parking. Little Hayes is a strictly "no smoking" house. We are close to the centre of Lyndhurst village with its superb range of small shops, pubs and restaurants, yet the New Forest, where the famous ponies and other animals wander freely is only 200 yards away. Bed and Breakfast from £17 per person per night.

Little Hayes

MINSTEAD. Mrs A. Saunders, Orchard Gate, Minstead, Near Lyndhurst SO4 7FX (01703 813584). Orchard Gate is a large country house set in the picturesque village of Minstead. Facilities for riding and fishing are only a short distance away, in an area noted for fascinating New Forest walks. All the family are welcome and we offer friendly accommodation at reasonable prices, good food and comfortable beds. The popular village of Lyndhurst is only three miles down the road, with excellent shopping and above average catering establishments. Bed and Breakfast from £15 (children seven to 12 years £8, young children negotiable). Disabled guests welcome with downstairs en suite room available. Further information on application.

NEW FOREST (Brockenhurst). Mrs Pauline Harris, Little Heathers, 13 Whitemoor Road, Brockenhurst SO42 7QG (01590 623512). Little Heathers is on the edge of the village close to open forest where ponies, cattle and deer roam free. Wonderful countryside for walking, cycling (local hire available), riding (stables nearby), golf courses. Lymington Yacht Basin approximately six miles, Southampton and Bournemouth a short drive away. Family room en suite, double/twin bedroom with private shower/bathroom. TV and tea/coffee making facilities in bedrooms. Full English breakfast, special diets can be catered for. Ground floor bedrooms. No smoking. Bed and Breakfast from £18 per person, with reduced rates for three nights plus. Out of season Short Break Specials. Children accepted. Brochure available.

PLEASE SEND A STAMPED ADDRESSED ENVELOPE WITH ENQUIRIES

NEW FOREST. Mrs Valerie Rawlings, St. Lawrence, Salisbury Road, West Wellow, Near Romsey SO51 6AP (01794 322086). We are situated on the very edge of the New Forest conveniently close to Salisbury, Southampton, Portsmouth, Bournemouth, Winchester; M27 just two miles away. We offer a warm welcome to our guests in our comfortable and individual home, in one double and one twin room, both interestingly decorated and cosy. Bathroom and WC upstairs, shower room and WC on ground floor. Tea and coffee facilities. Guests lounge with TV. Ample off road parking. Ideal for ferries. Open all year. Bed and Breakfast £15. Regret no smoking.

NEW FOREST. Mrs V. Burgess, Picket Hill, Canada Road, West Wellow SO51 6DD (01794 322550).

A large country house in a quiet, secluded position with views over the New Forest. The house is set in six acres of gardens and paddocks with direct access onto the Forest for walking or riding. There is a good pub and restaurant within walking distance and Romsey, Salisbury, Southampton and Winchester are all an easy drive. Picket Hill is an ideal base for a New Forest holiday; all rooms have en suite facilities and prices are £16 per person for Bed and Breakfast with special rates for families. Horses and dogs accepted by prior arrangement.

NEW FOREST. Mrs Sandra Hocking, Southernwood, Plaitford Common, Salisbury Road, Near

Romsey (01794 323255 or 322577). Modern country family home, surrounded by farmland, on the edge of the New Forest. Two double, one family and one twin bedrooms. Terms from £14. Full English breakfast. Cots and high chairs available for babies. Four miles from M27 off A36. Salisbury, Southampton 11 miles, Stonehenge 17 miles. Portsmouth half an hour. Winchester 14 miles, Romsey five miles. Within easy reach of Continental ferries. Large garden. Ample parking. Lounge area for guests. TV. Tea/coffee always available. Horse riding, golf, fishing, swimming, walking in New Forest 10 minutes. Local inns for good food. Open all year.

NEW FOREST. Mrs J. Pearce, "St. Ursula", 30 Hobart Road, New Milton BH25 6EG (01425

613515). ✿✿✿ Large detached family home offering every comfort in a friendly relaxed atmosphere. Off Old Milton Road, New Milton. Third right past traffic lights. Ideal base for visiting New Forest with its ponies and beautiful walks; Salisbury, Bournemouth easily accessible. Sea one mile. Leisure centre with swimming pool etc, town centre and mainline railway to London minutes away. Twin (en suite), double, family, single rooms, all with handbasins and tea-making facilities. High standards maintained throughout; excellent beds. Two bathrooms, one shower, four toilets. Downstairs twin bedroom suitable for disabled persons. Children and pets welcome. Cot etc available. Pretty garden with barbecue which guests are welcome to use. Lounge with colour TV. Two dining rooms. Smoke detectors installed. Full central heating. Open all year. Bed and Breakfast from £17. AA Recommended QQQ.

NEW FOREST (near Beaulieu). Mrs M. Stone, Heathlands, Lepe Road, Langley SO45 1YT (01703 892517). A Bed and Breakfast bungalow near Beaulieu, just two miles from Lepe Beach, an unspoilt natural beach and country park opposite Isle of Wight; ferries at Lymington (half an hour's drive). Centrally situated for touring the New Forest which is especially beautiful in autumn and spring with the new-born foals; three miles to Beaulieu and Exbury Azalea Gardens (Rothschild's collection), half an hour to Southampton and one hour to Bournemouth. The bungalow offers large breakfast in comfortable bedrooms for non-smoking couples. All rooms have washbasins, central heating, tea-making facilities and colour TV. There is a shower room and WC. Bed and Breakfast Special Offer £15 per person per night. Car parking. SAE, please.

NEW FOREST (near Lyndhurst). Mrs Mavis Newell, "Storm Oaks", York Drive, Nomansland, Near Salisbury, Wiltshire SP5 2BT (01794 390259). Situated in the New Forest with a warm welcome for our guests, the house is often visited by ponies and donkeys that roam this beautiful area. Near Romsey, Winchester, Salisbury, Beaulieu and only 10 minutes from the M27. Accommodation comprises one double en suite, one double and one twin, both with washbasins, and one single room. Also public bath/shower room and downstairs cloakroom. Guests have use of TV lounge and dining room, generous English/Continental breakfast served, good choice of local inns for evening meals. Ample parking. Non-smokers only. £16 per person; £2.50 per person supplement for en suite. Open March to October.

NEW MILTON. Mrs Jelley, Angel Cottage, Angel Lane, Downton, New Milton BH25 5PT (01425 629506). Built in 1842, Angel Cottage, set in idyllic surroundings, offers a warm and friendly welcome to the whole family. Within easy reach of the New Forest, Bournemouth, Southampton and ferries for the Isle of Wight. Our accommodation is of a very high standard, offering double, twin and family en suite rooms, each with tea making facilities, TV and central heating. Pets welcome. Cot, high chair and baby-sitting available. A must for golfers with 27-hole course right on the doorstep. Pretty garden, ample parking and plenty of walks. Open all year round from £20 per person. Dinner by arrangement.

PETERSFIELD. Mrs Mary Bray, Nursted Farm, Buriton, Petersfield GU31 5RW (01730 264278). Working farm. This late 17th century farmhouse, with its large garden, is open to guests throughout most of the year. Located quarter of a mile west of the B2146 Petersfield to Chichester road, one and a half miles south of Petersfield, the house makes an ideal base for touring the scenic Hampshire and West Sussex countryside. Queen Elizabeth Country Park two miles adjoining picturesque village of Buriton at the western end of South Downs Way. Accommodation consists of three twin-bedded rooms (one with washbasin), two bathrooms/toilets; sitting room/breakfast room. Children welcome, cot provided. Sorry, no pets. Car essential, ample parking adjoining the house. Bed and Breakfast only from £16 per adult. Reductions for children under 12 years except March and April.

PORTSMOUTH. Graham and Sandra Tubb, "Hamilton House", 95 Victoria Road North, Southsea, Portsmouth PO5 1PS (Tel & Fax: 01705 823502). 🐦🐦 COMMENDED. Delightful AA Recommended/RAC Acclaimed family-run Guesthouse centrally located five minutes by car from Continental and Isle of Wight ferry terminals, M27, stations, city centre, University and sea front, tourist attractions, heritage area and museums. Bright, modern rooms, all centrally heated with colour TVs and tea-making facilities; some en suites available. Ideal touring base for Southern England. Full English, vegetarian and Continental breakfasts served from 6am (for early travellers). Nightly/weekly stays welcome all year. Bed and Breakfast £17 to £19 per person per night standard; £20.50 to £22.50 per person per night en suite.

RINGWOOD (New Forest). Mrs Yvonne Nixon, "The Nest", 10 Middle Lane, Ringwood BH24 1LE (Tel & Fax: 01425 476724; mobile 0589 854505). This lovely Victorian house is situated in a quiet residential lane within five minutes' walk of Ringwood town centre. The ancient riverside market town has many good restaurants and inns. Ample parking is provided. Beautifully decorated, very clean and well maintained. Breakfast times are flexible and the meal is served in the delightful sunny conservatory overlooking the gardens. Pretty colour-co-ordinated "Laura Ashley"-style bedrooms with pine furnishings, washbasins, colour TV and tea/coffee making facilities. Local activities include fishing, golf, riding, swimming, visiting historic houses and forest walks. This is an excellent base to explore the New Forest with Bournemouth, Poole, Salisbury, Southampton and Portsmouth nearby. AA QQQQ Selected. Highly recommended. Bed and Breakfast from £15. No smoking in the bedrooms.

HAMPSHIRE – THE NEW FOREST

One of the most extensive tracts of oak woodland in England, interspersed with heathland and modern plantations of conifers, the New Forest was used by William the Conqueror as a hunting reserve. Today it is popular with walkers and riders, and is home to deer and half-wild ponies. To find out more, call in at the Visitor Centre at Lyndhurst and learn about traditional customs.

SOUTHAMPTON. Mrs Pat Ward, Ashelee Lodge, 36 Atherley Road, Shirley, Southampton SO1 5DQ (01703 222095). Welcome extended to all our guests, including those from overseas, in friendly Bed and Breakfast accommodation with varied menus. Bright comfortable bedrooms, pleasant dining room and TV lounge. Nice garden with dip pool, weather permitting. Near town centre and an excellent touring base; ideal for visits to several places of historic interest — Romsey, Winchester, Stonehenge, Salisbury, New Forest and Portsmouth. Near Southampton Docks for liners, ferries, Sealink Stena; M27 and train station easily accessible. Terms from £14 to £15 per night. Brochures sent on receipt of enquiries.

NEW FOREST — WOODLANDS
Tel: (01703) 292272/292077
Fax: (01703) 292487
ETB ♕ ♕ ♕ ♕ Commended
Delightful family-run Country House Hotel in beautiful New Forest setting.

Bed, Breakfast and Evening Meal, with morning coffee, light lunches and afternoon teas always available. Reductions for children sharing parents' room. Extremely high standard of Personal Friendly Service. Excellent food, fully licensed, with dancing some winter weekends. All rooms ensuite with radio/telephone and colour TV, hospitality trays, hairdryers, trouser press, mini fridges. Seasonal heated swimming pool. Croquet, Putting and Mini Football pitch. Open all year. Established 1968.

AA
★★

Mr & Mrs Con Hayes, BUSKETTS LAWN HOTEL, Woodlands, Near Southampton, Hampshire SO40 7GL

RAC
★★

SOUTHAMPTON. Rose and Dick Pell, Verulam House, 181 Wilton Road, Shirley, Southampton SO1 5HY (01703 773293). Tourist Board Listed. Rose and Dick warmly welcome guests to their comfortable, warm, roomy Edwardian establishment, in a nice residential area. Good cuisine. One double or family, one twin, one single bedrooms all with TV and tea/coffee making facilities; two bathrooms — plenty of hot water. Car parking space. Five minutes by car to historic Southampton city noted for its parks; railway station 10 minutes. Airport, Cross Channel ferries and Isle of Wight within easy reach and not far from M27, M3, Portsmouth, Winchester, Bournemouth, New Forest and coast. Bed and Breakfast from £15 per person; Evening Meal from £6 per person. Half Board per person from £22 daily, from £150 weekly. Non-smokers only.

SOUTHSEA. Mr and Mrs Willett, Oakleigh Guest House, 48 Festing Grove, Southsea PO4 9QD (01705 812276). Southern Tourist Board Listed. Small family run guest house two minutes from sea. Double, twin, family or single rooms, all with colour TV, washbasins, central heating and tea/coffee making facilities. Special rates for Senior Citizens and weekly bookings. Children welcome. Bed and Breakfast from £14; Evening Meal from £6 per head. Reductions for children. Open all year including Christmas and Easter. Close by — historic ships and Navy and Marine museums. Courtesy car service from local railway/bus stations.

STOCKBRIDGE. Mr and Mrs A.P. Hooper, Carbery Guest House, Stockbridge SO20 6EZ (01264 810771). 🏵🏵🏵 *COMMENDED.* RAC Acclaimed. AA

Listed. Ann and Philip Hooper welcome you to Carbery Guest House situated on the A30, just outside the village of Stockbridge, overlooking the famous trout fishing River Test. This fine old Georgian House has one acre of landscaped gardens, with swimming pool. Stonehenge and numerous places of interest nearby; sporting and recreational facilities close at hand. Accommodation includes double, twin, family and single rooms, available with private facilities. Centrally heated with colour TV, tea and coffee making facilities, hair dryers, radio alarms. Cots, high chairs. Car essential, parking. Open January to December for Evening Dinner, Bed and Breakfast or Bed and Breakfast only. Terms on application.

WINCHESTER. Mrs Ann Regan, "Leckhampton", 62 Kilham Lane, Winchester SO22 5QD (01962 852831). AA QQQQ. "Leckhampton" is peacefully situated

along a quiet rural lane, just five minutes' drive from city centre. A warm friendly welcome is extended to all our guests, who will enjoy attractively decorated, comfortable bedrooms, all overlooking our beautiful garden. Each is well equipped, with colour TV, beverage tray, radio and either en suite or private bathroom. Start the day with our hearty full English breakfast grill or try the healthy option, served in our sunny conservatory or cosy dining room. No smoking. Bed and Breakfast from £17 per person per night in double or twin rooms, one of which is a family apartment. For Kilham Lane from city centre follow signs to Romsey, A3090, pass hospital, over roundabout and turn right at second set of traffic lights.

WINCHESTER. Richard and Susan Pell, "The Lilacs", 1 Harestock Close, off Andover Road North, Littleton, Winchester SO22 6NP (01962 884122). This

attractive Georgian-style family home offers comfortable, clean and friendly accommodation, together with excellent home cooking. Situated on the outskirts of Winchester off the B3420, overlooking beautiful countryside, yet only one and a half miles from the city centre, which is convenient for all the attractions in the area. One twin-bedded room and one double/family room, both with tea/coffee making facilities, TV and central heating. Cot, high chair, babysitting available. Ironing facilities. Full English Breakfast is served. Pets by prior arrangement. Non-smokers please. Open all year. Bed and Breakfast from £16. Reductions for children and long stays. From Winchester, on Andover Road North, take left turn after Mountbatten Court, and before Harestock Road.

WINCHESTER. Mrs S. Buchanan, "Acacia", 44 Kilham Lane, Winchester SO22 5PT (01962 852259; 0585 462993 mobile). 🏵🏵 *COMMENDED.* First

class Tourist Board inspected accommodation in a peaceful location on the edge of the countryside, yet only a five minute drive from Winchester city centre. Excellent and easy access to road and rail communications to many tourist areas, all within one hour including London (by rail), Portsmouth, the New Forest, Salisbury, Stonehenge, etc. The accommodation consists of one double and two twin bedrooms, all of which have en suite or private bathroom and tea/coffee making facilities. Charming sitting room with satellite TV. Excellent choice of breakfast. Non-smokers only. Off street parking. Leave Winchester by the Romsey road, Kilham Lane is right at the second set of traffic lights. "Acacia" is 200 metres on the right. Bed and Breakfast from £18 per person.

HAMPSHIRE – VARIED ATTRACTIONS!
Coastal resorts like Southsea, river valleys like that of the Itchen, The New Forest and the nautical centres of Southampton and Portsmouth combine to give Hampshire its reputation as a holiday destination. Also of interest in this large county are places like Bucklers Hard, a preserved 18th century ship building village; Broadlands, home of the late Lord Mountbatten; New Forest Butterfly Farm, Longdown; and Paulton's Park, a family leisure park with lots to do and see.

WINCHESTER. Mrs A. Farrell, The Farrells, 5 Ranelagh Road, Winchester SO23 9TA (01962 869555). 🌸🌸 *COMMENDED.*

Number Five is a delightful Victorian house within 15 minutes' walk of Winchester Cathedral, City Centre, the unique water meadows, and the ancient Hospital of Cross. The New Forest, Salisbury, Stonehenge, and the South Downs are within easy reach. The area is also excellent for short local walks and excursions. Single, double, family rooms, most with washbasins, two rooms en suite. We offer central heating, tea-making facilities and a TV lounge. There is a bathroom, shower room and two toilets. A splendid English Breakfast is served. Bed and Breakfast from £17 to £20.

WINCHESTER. Mrs O. Fetherston-Dilke, 85 Christchurch Road, Winchester SO23 9QY (Tel & Fax: 01962 868661). 🌸🌸 *COMMENDED.*

Comfortable centrally heated Victorian family house in St. Cross area of Winchester, near the water meadows and the beautiful Chapel and Almhouses of St. Cross, five minutes' drive from City Centre. Double and twin (en suite) or single rooms from £20 per person — all bedrooms with TV. Access to rooms at all times. Children welcome. Ideal centre for touring Hampshire, with Salisbury, Stonehenge, New Forest, Beaulieu and Portsmouth all under an hour's drive. Off-street parking. Public transport two minutes' walk. Open all year. Non-smoking.

WOODLANDS. Mrs A. Cull, Summerhayes, Bartley Road, Woodlands, Near Southampton SO40 7GN (01703 292072). Tourist Board Listed.

A lovely Tudor-type house situated in the New Forest, central to many places of interest and beauty — maritime Portsmouth, Bournemouth, Winchester, Beaulieu Motor Museum, Exbury and Furzey Gardens. Thatched villages and inns all reached by lovely drives through the Forest. Two double and one twin-bedded rooms with tea/coffee facilities; lounge with log fire and TV. No pets. Non-smokers only. Car essential. Choice of local inns for evening meals, some within walking distance. Bed and Breakfast from £14.50. Friendly welcome.

WOODLANDS, NEW FOREST. Mrs Rosemary Sawyer, Glen Rest, Bourne Road, Woodlands, Southampton SO40 7GR (01703 812156).

A warm welcome awaits in this comfortable detached house situated in quiet village on the borders of the beautiful New Forest. Two letting rooms both have TV, tea/coffee facilities and central heating. Pleasant garden with ample off road parking. Good local pub food. Glen Rest is just five minutes from Junction 1 on M27, off A336, and offers an ideal base for exploring the forest and its attractions, with south coast beaches and cities all within easy reach. Bed and Breakfast from £16 per person per night. Children under 12 years half price. Sorry no smoking.

HEREFORD & WORCESTER

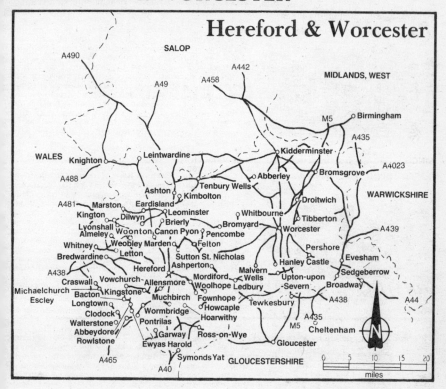

Hereford & Worcester

BROADWAY. Mr Allen, "Tudor Cottage", 56 High Street, Broadway WR12 7DT (01386 852674). This traditional 17th century Cotswold stone cottage situated on Broadway's famous High Street is an ideal base for touring the many places of beauty and interest that are the Cotswolds. Bedrooms, all en suite, have been tastefully decorated, furnished with style and equipped with modern comforts including colour TV and tea/coffee making facilities. Breakfast is served in a charming dining room with pretty soft furnishings. Prices from £22.50 per person per night for double and twin rooms; from £27.50 per person per night for a delightful four-poster room. Off street parking. AA QQQQ Selected.

BROMSGROVE. Mrs C. Gibbs, Lower Bentley Farm, Lower Bentley, Bromsgrove B60 4JB (01527 821286). An attractive Victorian farmhouse with modern comforts on a dairy and beef farm is an ideal base for a holiday, short break or business stay. Overlooking peaceful countryside, we are situated five miles from M5 and M42 between Redditch, Bromsgrove and Droitwich. The accommodation comprises spacious double, twin and family rooms with en suite or private bathroom, colour TV and tea/coffee making facilities. The comfortable lounge and separate dining room overlook the large garden. Young children are welcome. We are ideally situated for visits to Stratford-upon-Avon, Warwick, Worcester, Stourbridge, Birmingham, the Black Country, the NEC and International Convention Centre. AA QQQ.

BROMYARD. Mrs G. Williams, Littlebridge House, Norton, Bromyard HR7 4PN (Tel & Fax: 01885 482471).

Littlebridge stands in large gardens and open countryside with panoramic views to Bromyard Downs and the Malvern Hills. A Victorian gentleman's residence formerly built as the Estate Manager's home of the Saltmarshe Estate, Littlebridge has been decorated to high standards with period furniture and comfort in mind. Bedrooms have co-ordinated fabrics, en suite facilities, colour TV and hospitality trays; cots also available. Log fires burn in the lounge and dining room on cooler days, where hearty breakfasts and evening meals are served using local produce and some grown in our own walled garden. Positioned just three miles off the A44 Littlebridge is an ideal place to take a break or for touring the counties of Hereford and Worcester which contain many areas of outstanding natural beauty, are rich in black and white villages and towns, and civil war history is in abundance.

CLIFTON UPON TEME. David and Anne Blair-Gordon, The Threshing Barn, Harpley, Clifton upon Teme WR6 6HG (Tel & Fax: 01886 853578).

The Threshing Barn

Luxury period barn offering olde world charm created by a wealth of oak beams and antique furniture. Peacefully yet conveniently situated in the beautiful Teme Valley on the Hereford/Worcestershire border between the pretty award-winning village of Clifton upon Teme and the glorious Malvern Hills. Discover an unspoilt area of hidden England full of interests and history yet only an hour's drive from Shakespeare country and the Cotswolds. Alternatively why not just relax and let the world go by. Delightful bedrooms all with private facilities, colour TV, tea/coffee. Try our special interest breaks or sporting packages. Bed and Breakfast from £19.50 per person with reductions for two or more nights. This is a no smoking establishment and is unsuitable for children.

CROWLE. Mrs Lucy Harris, Green Farm, Crowle Green, Worcester WR7 4AB (01905 381807). 🏵

COMMENDED. Green Farm is a peaceful and substantial oak-beamed Geogian farmhouse, architecturally Grade II Listed set in large garden and 25 acres of farmland. Accommodation comprises twin-bedded, double or single room with own basin, private bathroom and tea/coffee making facilities and central heating. Cosy lounge with colour TV and woodburning stove. Full English breakfast included in tariff. Evening meal available on request or our local country pub within easy walking distance offers good food. Open all year. Bed and Breakfast from £18. Just off Junction 6 M5, so well situated for Worcester, Malverns, Stratford and Cotswolds.

DROITWICH. Mrs Tricia Havard, Phepson Farm, Himbleton, Droitwich WR9 7JZ (01905 391205). 🏵 🏵

COMMENDED. **Working farm.** AA QQQQ. We offer a warm welcome and a comfortable and relaxed atmosphere in our 17th century farmhouse with oak beamed lounge and dining room. Situated on peaceful stock farm just outside the unspoilt village of Himbleton where visitors may see farm animals and walk on Wychavon Way. Full English breakfast. Double, twin and family rooms, all with en suite facilities, colour TV, radio alarms and tea/coffee making. Convenient for M5, M42 and central for touring the many places of interest in the Heart of England. Featured on "Wish You Were Here". Bed and Breakfast from £19. Self catering flat also available.

HEREFORD & WORCESTERSHIRE – THE HEART OF ENGLAND!

A beautiful county which includes The Vale of Evesham and the rugged – if petite – Malvern Hills. It has been designated an "Area of Outstanding Beauty". Places of interest include The Avoncroft Museum of Buildings, Brockhampton, Ross-on-Wye, The Teme Valley and The Hereford & Worcester County Museum.

FELTON HOUSE
Felton, Near Hereford HR1 3PH
Telephone: 01432 820366

Marjorie and Brian Roby extend a warm welcome to their home, a romantic old country house in beautiful tranquil gardens in the heart of unspoilt rural England. The house combines the very best of modern centrally heated facilities with period furnishings throughout, including four-poster, half-tester and brass beds, superb diningroom, drawingroom, library and garden room. Ensuite and private bathrooms. Wide choice of traditional English and vegetarian breakfasts. Local inns serve excellent evening meals. Off A417 between A49 and A465 just eight miles north of Hereford. Children and pets welcome. B&B from £18.50. Open all year.

ETB 👑👑 Highly Commended.   AA QQQQ Selected.   Self-catering cottage in grounds.

GOLDEN VALLEY. Mrs Powell, The Old Vicarage, Vowchurch, Hereford HR2 0QD (Tel & Fax: 01981 550357). HETB 👑👑 *COMMENDED.* Warm hospitality guaranteed in this Victorian house of character, once the home of Lewis Carroll's brother. Ideal for walking/cycling through rich agricultural land, by historic churches and castles, near the Black Mountains (Welsh Border) and Offa's Dyke Path. Visit Hay-on-Wye, world famous town of books, or the Mappa Mundi. Enjoy our attractively presented quality breakfasts after restful nights in individually decorated en suite rooms (single, double, family, twin) from £19 per person; refreshment trays, fresh fruit and flowers await you. Be greeted with a freshly baked scone and homemade preserves. Dinner, including vegetarian and special diets, may be ordered in advance. Fresh local produce used. Four-course meal £13.50; lighter meals by arrangement.

HEREFORD. Mrs Diana Sinclair, Holly House Farm, Allensmore, Hereford HR2 9BH (01432 277294; mobile 0589 830223). 👑👑 *COMMENDED.* Spacious luxury farmhouse and over 10 acres of land with horses, situated in beautiful and peaceful open countryside. Bedrooms en suite or with private bathroom, central heating, TV and tea/coffee making facilities. We are only five miles south west of Hereford city centre. Ideal base for Welsh Borders, market towns, Black Mountains, Brecon and Malvern Hills and the Wye Valley. We have a happy family atmosphere and pets are welcome. Brochure on request. From £16 per person per night and with your delicious English breakfast you will be fit for the whole day!

HEREFORD. Ashgrove House, Wellington Marsh, Hereford HR4 8DU (01432 830608). 👑👑 *COMMENDED.* Mike and Sandra Fletcher welcome you to luxurious accommodation with high standard furnishings and lovely gardens. Situated in a quiet rural location, overlooking cider apple orchards, three miles north of the historic Cathedral City of Hereford. Lovely walks nearby, golf and salmon fishing 10 minutes by car. Double, twin-bedded or single rooms, all en suite with TV and tea-making facilities. Good pub food in old inns nearby. Bed and full English Breakfast £17 to £20 per person.

WHEN MAKING ENQUIRIES PLEASE MENTION
THIS *FHG* PUBLICATION

HEREFORD. Mrs R.T. Andrews, Webton Court Farmhouse, Kingstone, Hereford HR2 9NF (01981

250220). ✿ ✿ Working farm. Black and white Georgian farmhouse in the Wye Valley on a working farm. Situated midway between Hay-on-Wye, Ross-on-Wye just off the B4348, ideal for touring places of local interest. We offer a selection of bedrooms including en suite with TV, tea/coffee making facilities and washbasins. Large parties catered for. Rates £16 single, £15 per person double and £20 per person en suite; Evening Meal £8 per person by prior arrangement. Children welcome at reduced rates.

HEREFORD. Mr David Jones, Sink Green Farm, Rotherwas, Hereford HR2 6LE (01432 870223).

✿ ✿ Working farm, join in. Warm and friendly atmosphere awaits your arrival at this 16th century farmhouse, on the banks of the River Wye. Three miles south of the cathedral city of Hereford, with Ross-on-Wye, Leominster, Ledbury, Malvern and the Black Mountains within easy reach. All rooms en-suite, tea/coffee making facilities and colour TV. One room with four-poster, family room by arrangement. Guests' own lounge. Pets by arrangement. Bed and Breakfast from £18 per person. AA QQQQ.

KIMBOLTON. Mrs Jean Franks, The Fieldhouse Farm, Kimbolton, Near Leominster HR6 0EP

(01568 614789). Tourist Board Listed. Working farm. A warm friendly welcome awaits you on our working family farm three miles from the attractive market town of Leominster, and 11 miles from the historic town of Ludlow. We offer excellent accommodation in peaceful surroundings, with truly magnificent views. The comfortable and spacious bedrooms have tea-making facilities. Private bathroom available. There is an attractive guests' sitting/dining room with oak beams and inglenook fireplace. Home cooking is a speciality and delicious breakfasts are served by Mrs Franks, a former Home Economics teacher; Evening Meals on request. Personal attention and high standards are assured. Bed and Breakfast from £17 per person.

LEDBURY. Mrs Jane West, Church Farm, Coddington, Ledbury HR8 1JJ (01531 640271). Tourist

Board Listed. Working farm. This accommodation is on a working farm with a Black and White 16th century Listed farmhouse, close to the Malvern Hills in quiet hamlet four and a half miles from Ledbury. It is ideal for touring. Warm hospitality assured in happy, relaxed atmosphere. There is accommodation in three double bedrooms, two with washbasins; bathroom, toilet; sittingroom; diningroom. Log fires, television. Open all year. Car essential, parking. Situated midway between Ross-on-Wye, Hereford, Gloucester and Worcester. Bed and Breakfast from £19. SAE, please, for full details. Also available, self catering cottage in immaculate condition (4 KEYS HIGHLY COMMENDED).

LEDBURY. Mrs S.W. Born, The Coach House, Putley, Near Ledbury HR8 2QP (01531 670684). The

Coach House is an 18th century coaching stable with a cobbled courtyard. It is set in the delightful Herefordshire county of cider, hops, poetry and music. The historic and picturesque market town of Ledbury is only six miles away, with the nearest M50 motorway access just 10 miles distant. A wonderful area for walking, riding, fishing or just relaxing. The accommodation comprises two double bedded en suite rooms each having TV, payphone and tea/coffee making facilities; guests have their own sitting/dining room. The rooms are £28 and £33 per night. We regret there are no facilities for children or pets. A car is essential. No smoking in all rooms.

LEDBURY near. Mrs Elizabeth Godsall, Moor Court Farm, Stretton Grandison, Near Ledbury HR8

2TR (01531 670408). ♥♥♥ *COMMENDED.* Relax and enjoy our attractive 15th century timber-framed farmhouse with its adjoining oast-houses, whose picturesque location will ensure a peaceful stay. We are a traditional hop and livestock farm situated in the beautiful countryside of Herefordshire being central to the local market towns, with easy access to the Malverns, Wye Valley and Welsh Borders. Guests will enjoy spacious bedrooms, all with en suite facilities, their own oak-beamed lounge, dining room and the peaceful setting of the garden or walks through surrounding woods and farmland with their rural views. Fishing is available in our own pool and there are stables on the farm. Bed and Breakfast from £17.50; Evening Meal available. Residential licence.

LEOMINSTER. Mrs J.S. Connop, Broome Farm, Pembridge, Leominster HR6 9JY (01544 388324). Working farm, join in. A comfortable 17th century farmhouse situated in beautiful rural Herefordshire midway between the picturesque Black and White villages of Pembridge and Eardisland, seven miles from the market town of Kington; Leominster six miles. An excellent stopping-off place on a journey to Wales or South Coast. Two double and two twin-bedded rooms; two bathrooms, toilet; sittingroom and diningroom. Cot, babysitting and reduced rates for children. Pets permitted but not encouraged. Car essential, ample parking. Open all year. Bed and Breakfast from £15 per night including bedtime drink.

MALVERN. Barbara and Richard Rowan, The Red Gate, 32 Avenue Road, Great Malvern WR14 3BJ

(Tel & Fax: 01684 565013). ♥♥♥ *HIGHLY COMMEN-DED.* Guestaccomm, RAC Highly Acclaimed. Come, relax and be pampered in our centrally heated, beautifully restored Victorian hotel. Situated on a tree-lined road near to Great Malvern railway station, town centre and hills. Parking on the premises. Renowned for friendly informal atmosphere — ''It's like coming home''. Seven individually decorated bedrooms with en suite facilities, all non-smoking with colour TV and tea/coffee facilities. We offer a breakfast menu to suit all tastes. Vegetarians welcome. Residential licence. Enjoy a good book from a wide selection in our attractive lounge. On better days relax on the verandah or sit in the south-walled garden and forget your cares. Bed and Breakfast from £25.

MALVERN. Mrs Audrey Emuss, ''Priory Holme'', 18 Avenue Road, Great Malvern WR14 3AR

(01684 568455). ♥♥ Our Victorian house is situated in its own grounds in a quiet avenue between railway station and town centre. It is central to most amenities including Winter Gardens, theatre and leisure centre with the Three Counties Showground a few minutes away by car. Bedrooms are large and comfortable and have integral toilet facilities, with full en suite bathrooms in some. A separate guests' sitting room with TV is available and evening meals can be provided by prior arrangement. Though we discourage smoking we offer a warm welcome to ensure your stay with us, whether business or leisure, is a pleasurable one. Bed and Breakfast from £18.

Priory Holme

MALVERN. Jean and John Mobbs, Rock House, 144 West Malvern Road, Malvern WR14 4NJ

(01684 574536). ♛ *COMMENDED.* Attractive family-run Early Victorian Guest House situated high on hills in quiet peaceful atmosphere with superb views over 40 miles. Ideal rambling centre for hills or open country. Eleven comfortable bedrooms, some with showers/bathrooms; most overlooking our splendid views. TV lounge. Separate quiet room. Licensed to enhance the excellent cuisine. Groups welcome. Parking on premises. Bed and Breakfast from £18. Open all year; special Christmas package. Also available pretty cottage for self catering holidays. Stamp only please for brochure.

MALVERN near. Ann and Brian Porter, Croft Guest House, Bransford, Worcester WR6 5JD (01886

832227). ♛♛ AA QQ Listed. 16th-18th century part black and white cottage-style country house situated in the River Teme Valley, four miles from Worcester and Malvern. Croft House is central for visiting numerous attractions in Worcester, Hereford, Severn Valley and surrounding countryside. There is fishing close by and an 18 hole golf course opposite. Facilities include three en suite rooms (two double, one family) and two double rooms with washbasins, hospitality trays. Double glazing, central heating, residential licence and home cooked dinners. There is a TV lounge, sauna and large jacuzzi for guests' use. A cot and baby listening service are provided. Bed and Breakfast from £18 to £25. Festive Christmas and New Year Breaks available.

MALVERN WELLS. Mrs J.L. Morris, Brickbarns Farm, Hanley Road, Malvern Wells WR14 4HY

(016845 61775). Working farm. Brickbarns, a 200 year old mixed farm, is situated two miles from Great Malvern at the foot of the Malvern Hills, 300 yards from the bus service and one and a half miles from the train. The house, which is 300 years old, commands excellent views of the Malvern Hills and guests are accommodated in one double, one single and one family bedrooms with washbasins; two bathrooms, shower room, two toilets; sitting room and dining room. children welcome and cot and babysitting offered. Central heating. Car essential, parking. Open Easter to October for Bed and Breakfast from £15 nightly per person. Reductions for children and Senior Citizens. Birmingham 40 miles, Hereford 20, Gloucester 17, Stratford 35 and the Wye Valley is just 30 miles.

NEWNHAM BRIDGE. Mrs Gill Morgan, Deepcroft Farm House, Newnham Bridge, Tenbury Wells WR15 8JA (01584 781412). Set in the Teme Valley, off the A456, on the borders of Worcestershire, Herefordshire and Shropshire this secluded old farmhouse, with five acres of garden and orchard, offers easy access to the Severn Valley Railway, the historic towns of Ludlow and Worcester as well as to the Welsh Marches and the Shropshire Hills. Ideal for fishermen, cyclists and tourists the accommodation comprises two twin-bedded and one single room, all with hand basins, shaver points, and tea/coffee making facilities. A comfortable sitting room with colour TV is also available for guests. Bed and full English Breakfast £15.

OMBERSLEY. Mrs M. Peters, Tytchney, Boreley, Ombersley WR9 0HZ (01905 620185). 16th Century medieval Hall House cottage in peaceful country lane, two and a half miles from Ombersley. Ideal walking, touring Heart of England, fishing in River Severn and just half a mile to Ombersley Golf Course. Double, family and single rooms; cot available. Bed and Breakfast from £13.50.

PRESTON WYNNE. Rachel and Julie Rogers, New House Farm, Preston Wynne, Hereford HR1 3PE (Tel & Fax: 01432 820621). Tourist Board Listed *HIGHLY COMMENDED.* We offer you exceptional quality Bed and Breakfast in our character farmhouse with lots of beams. Antique furniture and inglenook fireplace in your private sitting room. You have your own private garden and use of a games room with pool table and lots more. For guests staying two nights or longer there is the use of a washing maching and ironing facilities. There is a TV and video in the sitting room for your enjoyment. We are situated deep in the heart of rural countryside with lovely views and central to all the historic towns in this area. Terms from £18.

ROSS-ON-WYE. Mrs Mary Savidge, Wharton Farm, Weston under Penyard, Ross-on-Wye HR9 5SX (01989 750255). 🌸 *COMMENDED.* Situated on the edge of the Royal Forest of Dean and the Wye Valley, this is an arable farm. Part 17th and 18th century farmhouse. Four miles from Ross-on-Wye, just off the A40, 14 miles from Gloucester. Easily accessible from the M50/M5 motorway, also South Wales and the M4 motorway. Excellent accommodation comprises two double rooms — one en suite, one with private bathroom and shared separate toilet, one twin room with en suite shower room and shared separate toilet. All rooms have colour TV and tea/coffee making facilities. Children by arrangement. Bed and Breakfast from £18.

ROSS-ON-WYE. The Skakes, Glewstone, Ross-on-Wye HR9 6AZ (01989 770456). 18th century former farmhouse, set in an acre of gardens and Hereford-shire's rolling and unspoilt countryside at the heart of the Wye Valley. Monmouth, Hereford and the Forest of Dean are all close, with a wealth of places to visit, charming villages, and pubs/restaurants serving excellent food. Our bedrooms are mostly en suite, and all contain colour TV, clock radios and beverage trays. Downstairs are the cosy lounges (log fires when cold) and if the day's exploring leaves you too tired to sample the local hostelries, we can, given warning, usually feed you! Children aged 10 years and over welcome and also dogs (by arrangement). Bed and Breakfast from £17.

ROSS-ON-WYE. Geoffrey and Josephine Baker, Brookfield House, Ledbury Road, Ross-on-Wye HR9 7AT (01989 562188). 🌸🌸 *APPROVED.* Large Queen Anne Georgian House close to town centre on M50 entrance into town. All rooms have TV, washbasin, central heating and tea/coffee facilities; some with bath/shower and WC. A good choice of breakfast (diets catered for). A large private car park. Ideal for overnight stop-offs. Bed and Breakfast from £18.50 per person. AA and RAC Listed, Travellers Britain Recommended.

ROSS-ON-WYE. Mrs H. Smith, Old Kilns, Howle Hill, Ross-on-Wye HR9 5SP (01989 562051). 🐦🐦
HIGHLY COMMENDED. A high quality bed and breakfast establishment in picturesque, quiet village location. Centrally heated, private parking. Easy walking distance to village inn where home-cooked meals are served. Some rooms with super king-size bed plus en suite shower, toilet; also brass king-size four-poster bed with en suite jacuzzi. Colour TV and tea/coffee making facilities in bedrooms. Lounge with log fire. Full English breakfast. Central for touring Cotswolds, Malvern, Stratford-upon-Avon, Wye Valley and Royal Forest of Dean. Open all year. Bed and Breakfast from £10 per person. Children and pets welcome (high chair and babysitting service provided). Please telephone for free brochure. Self catering cottages also available.

ROSS-ON-WYE. Mrs Berrie Lewis, Doward Cottage, Crockers Ash, Whitchurch, Ross-on-Wye HR9 6DS (01600 890389; Fax: 01600 890951). 🐦🐦 A Geor-

gian country house overlooking the A40 near Whitchurch village, and five minutes' drive from Monmouth. Great Doward Woods adjoin the property, and the situation is ideal for touring the local beauty spots. We offer a warm welcome, double and twin accommodation with private bathroom, colour TV and tea making facilities. Non-smoking. Full English breakfast. Cold supper or evening meals by arrangement. Bed and Breakfast from £18.50 to £20 per person per night; Evening Meal from £10.50. Reductions for weekly stays.

ROSS-ON-WYE. Mrs M.E. Drzymalska, Thatch Close, Llangrove, Ross-on-Wye HR9 6EL (01989 770300). 🐦🐦 *COMMENDED.* **Working farm, join in.**

Secluded Georgian farmhouse set in large colourful gardens in 13 acres of pasture situated in the beautiful Wye Valley between Ross and Monmouth. Thatch Close offers a comfortable, homely atmosphere where guests are welcome to help feed the sheep, cows, calves, or just relax and enjoy this traditionally run farm. Places of scenic beauty and historic attractions nearby include Forest of Dean, Black Mountains, Cathedral Cities, old castles and buildings. Guests have their own lounge and dining room with colour TV. Twin bedroom and one double room, both with bathrooms en suite, one double room with private bathroom; all bathrooms have showers. Central heating. Non-smokers please. Breakfast and optional evening meal are prepared using mainly home grown produce. Vegetarian and diabetic meals arranged. Bed and Breakfast from £15 to £19 with reductions for longer stays and reduced rates for children. SAE for further details.

ROSS-ON-WYE. Mrs Susan Dick, Merrivale Place, The Avenue, Ross-on-Wye HR9 5AW (01989 564929). 🐦 *COMMENDED.* Merrivale Place is a lovely big

Victorian house set in half an acre of gardens in a splendid tree-lined anvenue. Peaceful surroundings overlooking trees and hills, yet close to the old market place centre of Ross, and near the River Wye. Guest accommodation in three spacious, comfortable bedrooms (double, twin and family) with washbasins and shaver points. Three bathrooms, three toilets. TV lounge and separate dining room. Full central heating. A very warm welcome extended to all guests. Sorry, no pets. Ample parking space inside grounds. Open April to October. Bed and Breakfast £17. Weekly terms. Come and see the lovely Wye Valley, Malverns, Brecon Beacons and the Golden Valley.

ROSS-ON-WYE near. Mrs L.M. Baker, Walnut Tree Cottage Hotel, Symonds Yat West, Near Ross-on-Wye HR9 6BN (01600 890828). 🐦🐦🐦 We

offer a high standard of accommodation in a friendly and relaxing atmosphere. Walnut Tree Cottage Hotel is set high on the River Wye and enjoys outstanding panoramic alpine-style views. There are excellent river and woodland walks. Above all the area offers the quiet timelessness of the English countryside at its finest and a true escape from the pressures and bustle of everyday life. All rooms are centrally heated; tea/coffee facilities; log fires in season. Bed and Breakfast from £24 per person in en suite room. Open 1st March to 31st October. Two night half board breaks (1st March to 3rd June) £72 per person excluding Public and Bank holidays.

ROSS-ON-WYE. Jean and James Jones, The Arches Hotel, Walford Road, Ross-on-Wye HR9 5PT (01989 563348).

🐦🐦🐦 Small family-run hotel set in half an acre of lawned garden, ideally situated only 10 minutes' walk from town centre. All rooms are furnished and decorated to a high standard, have views of the lawned garden, tea/coffee making facilities and colour TV; some rooms en suite. Also one ground floor en suite room available. Full central heating. There is a delightful Victorian-style conservatory to relax in and the garden to enjoy in the summer months. Licensed. Ample parking in grounds. A warm and friendly atmosphere with personal service. Bed and Breakfast £17, en suite rooms £22; Dinner by arrangement. Generous weekly reductions. AA Listed, RAC Acclaimed, Les Routiers Award. Please telephone or send SAE for colour brochure.

UPTON-ON-SEVERN. Pauline and Ray Ellis, Madge Hill House, Severn Stoke WR8 9JN (01905 371362).

🐦🐦 Accommodation in bungalow annexe in the garden of a Georgian house in beautiful quiet setting amid Worcestershire's most glorious countryside. Halfway between Worcester and Tewkesbury and seven miles from the Malvern Hills. One double bedroom and one twin, both en suite, comfortably furnished, including colour TV, shaver point, hair dryer and tea/coffee making facilities. Centrally heated. Ideal base for touring the Heart of England. Access to rooms at all times. Open all year for bed and breakfast at £17 per person.

WINFORTON. Mrs Jackie Kingdon, Winforton Court, Winforton HR3 6EA (01544 328498). A warm

welcome and country hospitality awaits you at historic 16th century Winforton Court, former home of Roger De Mortimer, Earl of March. Unwind and enjoy spacious and elegant surroundings in the beautiful Wye Valley. Set in old world gardens with rural views, Winforton Court offers delightfully furnished bedrooms all with private bathrooms, one with four-poster bed. Luxurious drawing room, library with wealth of local guide books, etc. Enjoy a hearty breakfast (vegetarian available) in historic former court room with its magnificent early 17th century oak staircase. The house abounds in oak beams, open fires, early stencilling, interesting collections of old china, samplers and antiques. Bed and Breakfast from £20 per person per night. 10% discount for five or more nights.

WORCESTER. Eddie and Sylvia Lewis, Heathside, Worcester Road, Fernhill Heath, Worcester WR3 7UA (Tel and Fax: 01905 458245). 🐦🐦🐦 *COMMEN-*

DED. This Guest House offers accommodation in nine bedrooms, six with full en suite facilities, all with TV and tea/coffee making equipment. Situated two miles from Junction 6 of the M5, it is very near to pubs and a steak bar. Worcester itself offers a riverside racecourse, steamer trips on the River Severn, the Royal Worcester Porcelain Works and a museum. Within easy reach of Severn Valley Railway, Bewdley Safari Park, Black Country Museum, Dudley Zoo, Warwick Castle and the Royal Shakespeare Theatre. Bed and Breakfast from £21 single standard, £38 twin/double standard, en suite single £27, en suite twin £46. Reduced rates for children under 10. Open all year.

WORCESTER. Burgage House, 4 College Precincts, Worcester WR1 2LG (01905 25396). Comfort-

able Georgian house in cobbled street next to the Cathedral. Large relaxing rooms, all with TV. A hearty English or vegetarian Breakfast served in large dining room. Close by are the Royal Worcester Porcelain Works, the Commandery, cricket ground, riverside walks, shops, restaurants and just five minutes from M5 (Worcester South Junction 7). Convenient for trips to Malvern, Hereford, Cotswolds and Stratford. Bed and Breakfast from £19.

KENT

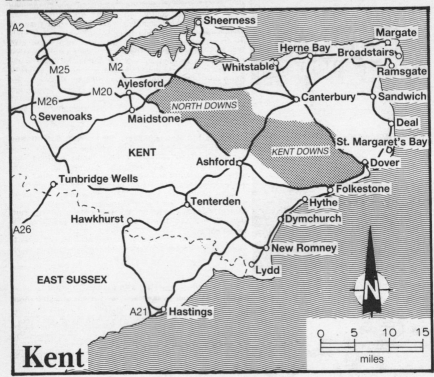

GREAT WEDDINGTON
Ash, Canterbury, Kent CT3 2AR
Tel: 01304 813407 Fax: 01304 812531

Great Weddington is situated just outside the village of Ash, near Canterbury and has been the home of Neil and Katie Gunn for over 20 years. The house, which is late Georgian, is set in two acres of attractive gardens surrounded by farmland. It is within easy reach of Canterbury, Dover and the coast. There are two double bedrooms each with their own washbasin, adjoining bathroom with a shower and single bedroom with basin. Lovely drawing room, exclusively for guests' use which leads off an elegant hallway, with garden door that opens onto pretty terrace where guests can sit for tea or drinks on a summer evening. There is also a hard tennis court. Bed and Breakfast from £25 per person per night; dinner can be provided by prior arrangement. For further information, tariff and directions please send for our brochure or telephone.

KENT – THE GARDEN OF ENGLAND!

The pleasant landscape of Kent, including The North Downs and The Weald, is the venue of many engaging places to visit. These include Chiddingstone – the half-timbered village, the sophisticated spa town of Tunbridge Wells and Swanton Mill. There are also day trips to the continent and for railway enthusiasts, The Sittingbourne & Kensley Light Railway, The Kent & East-Sussex Railway and the 'World's Smallest Public Railway' from Hythe to Dungeness.

ASHFORD. Ros and John Martin, Hogben Farm, Church Lane, Aldington, Ashford TN25 7EH (01233 720219). Tourist Board Listed. This farmhouse, dating from the 16th century, lies in a very quiet location down its own drive, set amongst extensive gardens and lawns. It is an ideal centre for visits to Canterbury, Rye, Tenterden, etc, and handy for the ferries and the Channel Tunnel. Accommodation includes one double room and two twin rooms; en suite available. A sittingroom with inglenook fireplace and colour TV is available for guests. Not only tea/coffee in your room but also good home cooking for your Evening Meal by arrangement. Open all year. Bed and Breakfast from £19.50.

ASHFORD near. Mrs Pam Mills, Cloverlea, Bethersden, Ashford TN26 3DU (01233 820353). A warm welcome awaits in spacious new country bungalow in lovely peaceful location with large garden surrounded by views of fields and woods. Patio area for breakfast (when fine). Ideal for Folkestone, Euro Tunnel (half hour), Ashford International Station (10 minutes), London (one hour), Leeds and Sissinghurst Castles and Gardens, Rye, Canterbury. Superb accommodation in two twin rooms, one en suite (family), one with private bathroom; both have colour TV, tea/coffee, biscuits. Full central heating. Excellent breakfast, home made bread everyday. Ample safe parking. Close to village pubs. Bed and Breakfast from £16.50 per person. No smoking.

BIDDENDEN. Iain and Jane Drysdale, Bishopsdale Oast, Biddenden TN27 8DR (01580 291027/ 292065 or Fax: 01580 292321). 🐦🐦🐦 *HIGHLY COMMENDED.* 18th century double kiln oast house of historical interest with original hop press. Set in four acres with magnificent views in a peaceful setting. Local to Sissinghurst, Leeds and Hever Castles and many other places of interest. 20 minutes from Rye and the coast. Large bedrooms with king size beds are en suite with colour TV, radio, tea/coffee facilities. Jane and Iain are members of "Guild of Professional Caterers" and "Guild of Master Craftsmen" so Dinner is always excellent and relaxed in our private diningroom. Try our Winter Breaks. Bed and Breakfast from £20 per person, reductions for children. Dinner from £15 on terrace or in dining room. Open all year. Midway between Cranbrook and Tenterden on the Cranbrook Road, B&B sign and post box on corner (ring for further directions).

BIRCHINGTON near. Mrs Liz Goodwin, Woodchurch Farmhouse, Woodchurch, Near Birchington CT7 0HE (01843 832468). This attractive Elizabethan/ Georgian farmhouse is situated in a quiet rural area yet only two miles from long stretches of sandy beach. Within easy reach of Canterbury, Sandwich, Rye, Chilham and the cross Channel ferries. There is ample parking, a car is essential. Very comfortable bedrooms with tea/coffee making facilities. Sitting room with TV. Bathroom and shower for guests' use only. Separate beamed dining room. A warm welcome and a comfortable stay assured at Woodchurch. Bed and Breakfast from £16. Please write or telephone for further details.

CANTERBURY. Mr and Mrs P.W. Harris, London Guest House, 14 London Road, Canterbury CT2 8LR (01227 765860). SEETB Listed *COMMENDED.* The London Guest House is a Victorian "listed" house conveniently situated within easy walking distance of cathedral, shops, theatre, university and other places of interest. The accommodation is spacious and comfortably furnished and includes two single, two twin, one double and one family rooms. All have washbasins, shaver points, TV, tea facilities and full central heating. Open all year, the London makes an ideal base from which to tour Canterbury and surrounding areas. Bed and Breakfast from £18 to £20. Home cooking.

CANTERBURY. Saint Stephens Guest House, 100 St. Stephens Road, Canterbury CT2 7JL (01227 767644). SEETB Listed COMMENDED.

Located just a few minutes' walk from the cathedral and town centre where you will find a theatre and a varied selection of restaurants. In the surrounding area there are many attractions and places of historic interest. Comfortable accommodation is provided by a residents' lounge and separate dining room. All bedrooms are equipped with a colour TV and tea/coffee making facilities; two bedrooms en suite. Private car park located to the rear. A warm welcome is offered all year round. Bed and Breakfast from £21 to £28. Brochure available.

CANTERBURY. Maria and Alistair Wilson, Chaucer Lodge Guest House, 62 New Dover Road, Canterbury CT1 3DT (01227 459141). 👑👑 HIGHLY COMMENDED.

A highly recommended friendly guest house which is elegantly decorated and immaculately clean. Fully double glazed and centrally heated. Secure parking. Seven bedrooms en suite, including family rooms, with colour TV, tea/coffee making facilities, radio/alarm and hair dryer. Open all year round. 10 minutes' walk to city centre, cathedral, bus and rail stations. Hospital and cricket ground only five minutes' walk. Ideal base for touring Kent and for trips to the Continent. Bed and Breakfast from £17 per person.

CANTERBURY. The White House, 6 St. Peters Lane, Canterbury CT1 2BP (01227 761836). 👑👑👑

A superb spacious Regency house in a quiet lane within the old city walls. All nine rooms are tastefully decorated and all are en suite with colour TV and tea/coffee making facilities. The famous Marlowe Theatre is close by as well as the Cathedral which is two minutes' walk away. A warm welcome awaits you at this lovely family-run house. Open all year. Bed and Breakfast from £45 to £65 for family room, £40 to £50 for double and £30 for single.

CANTERBURY. R. & D.J. Martin, The Tanner of Wingham, 44 High Street, Wingham, Canterbury CT3 1AB (01227 720532). Family run restaurant with bed and breakfast accommodation, situated in a 16th century building in historic and picturesque village, midway between Canterbury and Sandwich. Ideal for touring East Kent and convenient for docks and Chunnel. Relax in a friendly atmosphere and enjoy optional evening meal from our monthly-changing menu — which includes the largest vegetarian and vegan options in East Kent. Rooms are individually decorated with antique beds and furniture — some rooms heavily beamed. Families welcome, cot available. The many local attractions include historic houses and gardens, wildlife and bird parks. Don't forget your day trip to the Continent! Bed and Breakfast from £12.25 to £20; Evening Meal £11.50.

CANTERBURY. Mrs Joy Wright, Milton House, 9 South Canterbury Road, Canterbury CT1 3LH (01227 765531). Family home built in 1906 situated in residential area just off the main road to Dover (15 miles). Established in 1967 and providing one double and one twin-bedded rooms with washbasins, TV and tea/coffee making facilities. One bathroom with shower, separate toilet. Central heating. Open all year. Full English Breakfast. Prices £15 to £17 per person. Easy walking distance for East Railway Station, Bus Station, Kent Cricket Ground, Cathedral etc. Ideal base for exploring Kent, visiting London, and passport day trips to the Continent. "Very comfortable and friendly" is a typical comment in our visitors' book.

CANTERBURY near. Mrs J. Smith, 55 Guilton, Ash, Near Canterbury CT3 2HR (01304 812809). Situated in the village of Ash between Canterbury and Sandwich, a warm homely welcome awaits you. Ideal for touring and for overnight stops to and from the ferries of Ramsgate and Dover. Kent International Airport and Spitfire Museum are 10 minutes away, bird parks, castles, zoo and wine trails all within easy reach. Two double rooms both with washbasin, tea/coffee making facilities and TV. Terms from £28 per room (double). En suite available. Full English breakfast, evening meal by arrangement; own vegetables and eggs.

CANTERBURY. Mrs A. Hunt, Bower Farmhouse, Stelling Minnis, Near Canterbury CT4 6BB (01227 709430). 🏵️ 🏵️ *HIGHLY COMMENDED.*

Anne and Nick Hunt welcome you to Bower Farmhouse, a traditional 17th century Kentish farmhouse situated in the midst of Stelling Minnis, a medieval common of 125 acres of unspoilt trees, shrubs and open grassland; seven miles south of the cathedral city of Canterbury and nine miles from the coast; the countryside abounds in beauty spots and nature reserves. The house is heavily beamed and maintains its original charm. The accommodation comprises a double room and a twin-bedded room, each with private facilities. Full traditional English Breakfast is served with home-made bread, marmalade and fresh free-range eggs. Children welcome; pets by prior arrangement. Open all year (except Christmas). Car essential. Excellent pub food five minutes away. Bed and Breakfast from £18 per person.

CANTERBURY. Mrs Prudence Latham, Tenterden House, The Street, Boughton, Faversham ME13 9BL (01227 751593).

Enjoy Bed and Breakfast in the renovated gardener's cottage of this Tudor house. Close to Canterbury and the ferry ports, making an ideal base for day trips to France and for touring rural, historic and coastal Kent. Other amenities include golf (five minutes), walking and ornithology. Accommodation comprises two bedrooms (one double, one twin) with guests' own shower and toilet. Both rooms have washbasins and tea/coffee facilities. Full English breakfast is served in the main house. Open all year. Bed and Breakfast from £17.50. Excellent pub food within walking distance.

CANTERBURY. Mr and Mrs R. Linch, Upper Ansdore, Duckpit Lane, Petham, Canterbury CT4 5QB (01227 700672). ETB Listed.

English Tourist Board
Listed

Beautiful secluded Listed Tudor farmhouse with various livestock, situated in an elevated position with far-reaching views of the wooded countryside of the North Downs. The property overlooks a Kent Trust Nature Reserve, is five miles south of the cathedral city of Canterbury and only 30 minutes' drive to the ports of Dover and Folkestone. The accommodation comprises one family, three double and one twin-bedded rooms. All have shower and WC en-suite and tea-making facilities. Dining/sitting room, heavily beamed with large inglenook. Car essential. Bed and full English Breakfast from £19 per person. AA QQQ.

CANTERBURY. Raemore Guest House, 33 New Dover Road, Canterbury CT1 3AS (01227 769740; Fax: 01227 769432). SETB Listed *COMMENDED.* Family-run, ideally situated near to Canterbury city centre with private car parking facilities. Central location for touring East Kent. All rooms have TV and tea/coffee facilities. Family rooms from £12.50 per person, doubles from £18.50 per person, en suite rooms from £22.50 per person, single rooms from £20. All with full English breakfast.

CANTERBURY near. Mrs Joan Hill, Renville Oast, Bridge, Near Canterbury CT4 5AD (01227 830215).

Renville Oast is situated amongst apple orchards in beautiful Kentish countryside, only two miles from the Cathedral City of Canterbury, 10 miles from the coast and two hours' drive from London. Many interesting castles and historic houses within easy reach. Nature Reserves, golf courses and Howletts Zoo nearby. A day trip to France is a possibility. All rooms are comfortable and attractively furnished, with tea-making facilities. One family room is en suite; a twin-bedded room and a double room have washbasins and separate bathroom. Lounge/TV room. Bed and Breakfast from £21 per person includes good farmhouse breakfast. Excellent pub food nearby.

DEAL. Mr and Mrs P.S.F. Jailler, "Blencathra Country Hotel", Kingsdown Hill, Kingsdown, Deal CT14 8EA (01304 373725). 🐦🐦🐦 Blencathra is a small private hotel situated in the picturesque unspoilt village of Kingsdown. With panoramic views over the Channel and countryside, it is an ideal centre for a touring, walking or golfing holiday (close to four golf courses). Kingsdown is only five miles from the ferries at Dover and early breakfasts are available. Blencathra is a family run hotel offering eight bedrooms, personal service and attention from the proprietors. The hotel is in a private road and a peaceful stay is guaranteed. Open all year. Evening snacks available by prior arrangement. AA and RAC Listed. Bed and Breakfast from £17 per person.

BLERIOT'S
47 Park Avenue, Dover, Kent CT16 1HE   Telephone (01304) 211394

A Victorian Guest House situated in a quiet residential area, in the lee of Dover Castle. Within easy reach of trains, bus station, town centre, Hoverport and docks. Channel Tunnel terminus only 10 minutes' drive. Off-road parking. We specialise in one night 'stop-overs' and Mini Breaks. Single, Double, Twin and Family rooms with shower or full en suite available. All rooms have Colour TV, tea and coffee making facilities, washbasin with shaver points/lights and are fully centrally heated. Full English Breakfast from 7am, earlier Continental available on request. Evening snacks and meals available in our licensed restaurant. Open all year. Tourist Board 🐦🐦 rating.

Rates: Bed & Breakfast: £15 to £17 per person per night. Mini-Breaks: January-April £13, October-December £13 per person per night. Small en suite and single surcharge.
CREDIT CARDS ACCEPTED.

DOVER. Betty and Alastair Dimech, Cleveland Guest House, 2 Laureston Place, off Castle Hill Road, Dover CT16 1QX (01304 204622; Fax: 01304 211598). 🐦🐦🐦 COMMENDED. Situated in a quiet street, close to the town centre and with Dover Castle as a picturesque backdrop, this beautiful Grade II Listed building offers high standards and a warm welcome. The charming bedrooms with bay windows (two with balconies) have delightful panoramic views. In addition all the bedrooms are en suite and have a comprehensive range of facilities. Passing through or staying longer, then enjoy our hospitality and good food. Explore Dover's ancient history and visit the many surrounding places of interest. AA QQ, RAC Acclaimed.

DOVER. Mr and Mrs Christo, Elmo Guest House, 120 Folkestone Road, Dover CT17 9SP (01304 206236). 🐦 Family-run guesthouse offering friendly personal service. Ideal for overnight stops and Short Breaks. Early breakfast catered for. Conveniently situated near town centre, stations, Hoverport and docks. 10 minutes' drive to Channel Tunnel. One single, one twin, two double and two family bedrooms, all with washbasin, shaver points, colour TV and tea/coffee making facilities. Private parking, lock-up garage. Bed and Breakfast from £12 to £18 per person. RAC Listed.

DOVER. "Dover's Restover" B&B, 69 Folkestone Road, Dover CT17 9RZ (01304 206031). 🐦 A warm, friendly welcome awaits you at this clean, highly recommended guesthouse. Situated opposite Dover Priory Railway Station and three minutes to Dover's ports (a free bus runs from station to ports); Channel Tunnel 10 minutes' drive. Central for town centre and all amenities. Double, twin and family rooms, all with colour TV, tea/coffee facilities, washbasins, central heating and double glazing. Perfect for overnight stops en route to the Continent. Hearty English breakfast served from 6.30am. Private parking available. Bed and Breakfast from £13 to £19 per person. Reduced rates for Senior Citizens and children. "Room only" rates available. Members of Dover Hotel and Guesthouse Group, ETB and SEETB.

DOVER. Jean and Roger Walkden, Linden Guest House, 231 Folkestone Road, Dover CT17 9SL (01304 205449 or 367915). 🐾🐾 *COMMENDED.* AA QQQ. A highly recommended homely guest house. Fully double glazed and centrally heated, with secure light-protected car park, the Linden provides clean and comfortable accommodation and is ideally located for the town centre. Ports and ferries are just a five minute drive away and the Channel Tunnel is only 10. Comprehensive room facilities and a friendly service (including a free courtesy service to and from the bus and coach station and ferry), make the Linden an ideal base for touring this historic part of Kent, or overnight stops/weekend breaks for Continental shopping. Most rooms have either full en suite or en suite shower. Bed and Breakfast from £15 per person.

DYMCHURCH. Mrs Caroline Rasmussen, Wenvoe House, 88 Dymchurch Road, St. Mary's Bay, Romney Marsh TN29 0QR (01303 874426). Situated right on the sea front overlooking the English Channel, this family run guest house is ideal for a relaxing break. Half a mile from the smuggling village of Dymchurch on the Romney Marsh, the beach is one of the best in Kent. There is a golf course handy and the unique Romney, Hythe and Dymchurch 1/3 scale railway runs nearby. The ancient town of Rye is nearby as are the Channel Ports of Folkestone and Dover. Bed and Breakfast from £17.50. En suite chalets available from £20. Ideal for children. All bedrooms have tea/coffee facilities. TV in all rooms (satellite in family room).

EDENBRIDGE. Marjorie and Peter McEwan, "Four Oaks", Swan Lane, Edenbridge TN8 6BA (01732 863556; Fax: 01732 867022). ETB Listed. Welcome to our Bed and Breakfast establishment in homely and comfortable surroundings, half a mile from British Rail station and approximately 20 miles from Gatwick Airport (transport arranged). Four miles to Hever Castle, Chartwell, Penshurst and Lingfield Park Racecourse. Convenient for M25. One double room en suite and two single rooms; all have tea/coffee making facilities and colour TV. Secure storage for bicycles, off road parking. No smoking.

FAVERSHAM. N.J. and C.I. Scutt, Leaveland Court, Leaveland, Faversham ME13 0NP (01233 740596). 🐾🐾 *HIGHLY COMMENDED.* Guests are warmly welcomed to our enchanting timbered 15th century farmhouse which nestles between Leaveland Church and woodlands in rural tranquillity. Offering high standards of accommodation whilst retaining their original character, all bedrooms are en suite with colour TV and hot drinks trays. Traditional breakfasts, cooked on the Aga, are available with a choice of alternatives. There is a large attractive garden with heated outdoor swimming pool for guests' use and ample car parking. Ideally situated for visiting Kent's historic cities, castles, houses and gardens with Canterbury only 20 minutes by car and also easy access to Channel ports, 30 minutes. Good walking country, being close to both the Pilgrims Way and the coast. Terms from £20 for Bed and Breakfast.

Terms quoted in this publication may be subject to increase if rises in costs necessitate

FOLKESTONE. Mrs J. Young, Sunny Lodge Guest House, 85 Cheriton Road, Folkestone CT20 2QL

(01303 251498). 🏵 Sunny Lodge is an interesting Victorian Guest House surrounded by a lovely garden, noted for its high standard and recommended by the Hotel Association. All rooms have comfortable armchairs, colour televisions, tea making facilities and central heating. We are minutes from the central railway and bus stations, town centre, beach, SeaCat and Channel Tunnel. With easy access from the M20 from Junction 12. Private car park. Good value for money with choice of breakfast. Bed and Breakfast from £15 to £17 per person. Reductions for children sharing; weekly rates. We look forward to meeting you.

FOLKESTONE/ASHFORD. Duncan and Alison Taylor, Bolden's Wood, Fiddling Lane, Stowting, Near Ashford TN25 6AP (Tel & Fax: 01303 812011).

Between Ashford/Folkestone. Friendly atmosphere on a working smallholding set in unspoilt countryside. Modern centrally heated accommodation built for traditional comforts. No smoking throughout. One double, one twin, two single rooms. Log burning stove in TV lounge. Full English breakfast. Evening meals by arrangement. Children love the old-fashioned farmyard, the free range chickens and friendly sheep and cattle. Our paddocks, ponds, stream and small wood invite relaxation. Nearby, our private secluded woodland and downland allow quiet visitors to observe bird life, rabbits, foxes, badgers and occasionally deer. To round off your stay you could even book a short sightseeing or fishing trip on our Folkestone fishing boat! Bed and Breakfast £17.50 per person.

GILLINGHAM. Mrs Y. Packham, 215 Bredhurst Road, Wigmore, Gillingham ME8 0QX (01634 363275). Friendly, comfortable Bed and Breakfast accommodation situated midway between Channel ports/Tunnel and London; close to M2 and M20. Hempstead Valley Shopping Centre and restaurants nearby; close to Rochester and Leeds Castles. Open all year. Full facilities. Quiet residential area with parking available. Reduced rates for children, cots available.

Key to Tourist Board Ratings

The Crown Scheme
(England, Scotland & Wales)

Covering hotels, motels, private hotels, guesthouses, inns, bed & breakfast, farmhouses. Every Crown classified place to stay is inspected annually. *The classification:* Listed then 1-5 Crown indicates the range of facilities and services. Higher quality standards are indicated by the terms APPROVED, COMMENDED, HIGHLY COMMENDED and DELUXE.

The Key Scheme
(also operates in Scotland using a Crown symbol)

Covering self-catering in cottages, bungalows, flats, houseboats, houses, chalets, etc. Every Key classified holiday home is inspected annually. *The classification:* 1-5 Key indicates the range of facilities and equipment. Higher quality standards are indicated by the terms APPROVED, COMMENDED, HIGHLY COMMENDED and DELUXE.

The Q Scheme
(England, Scotland & Wales)

Covering holiday, caravan, chalet and camping parks. Every Q rated park is inspected annually for its quality standards. The more √ in the Q – up to 5 – the higher the standard of what is provided.

GILLINGHAM. Mrs B.L. Penn, 178 Bredhurst Road, Wigmore, Gillingham ME8 0QX (01634

233267). Wigmore is four minutes from M2 motorway via the A278. Midway between London and Channel Ports, close to the Weald of Kent, castles and countryside. Hempstead Valley Shopping Centre is also nearby. En-suite accommodation with own sittingrooms. Reasonable rates. Reductions for children. Open all year.

HAWKHURST. Susan Woodard, Southgate, Little Fowlers, Rye Road, Hawkhurst TN18 5DA

(01580 752526). ♥♥ *COMMENDED.* AA QQQ Recommended. Stay in our Listed 300-year-old former Dower House on the Kent/Sussex borders. Historic Hawkhurst, once famous for smuggling, is near Sissinghurst, Rye, Bodiam, Batemans, Scotney, Tunbridge Wells, Battle, Hever and coast. Folkestone approximately half an hour's drive. En suite twin, double, triple Georgian bedrooms furnished with antiques, all with magnificent views, TV, tea/coffee facilities. Relax in our one acre gardens. Choice of breakfast in our flower-filled original Victorian conservatory. Guests' sitting room. Excellent village restaurant and inn a few minutes' walk. Helpful and friendly family. Non-smoking. Bed and Breakfast from £20.

HEADCORN. Mrs D. Burbridge, Waterkant Guest House, Moat Road, Headcorn, Ashford TN27 9NT

(01622 890154). SEETB Listed. Waterkant is a small guest house situated in the tranquil setting of olde worlde charm of Wealdon Village. A warm and friendly welcome is assured and the relaxed and informal atmosphere is complemented by fine cuisine, excellent service and comfortable surroundings. Bedrooms have private or en suite bathrooms, tea/coffee making facilities and are centrally heated and double glazed. Lounge with colour TV. The large secluded garden bounded by a stream provides a large pond, summerhouse for visitors' use and ample parking. Fast trains to London and a wealth of historic places to visit nearby. Open all year. Visitors return year after year. Bed and Breakfast from £17, with reduced rates for children and Senior Citizens.

MAIDSTONE. Mrs Merrilyn Boorman, The White Lodge, Loddington Lane, Linton, Maidstone

ME17 4AG (01622 743129). Guests return again and again to this elegant house beautifully situated in parkland overlooking the Weald of Kent. Just 15 minutes from Leeds Castle, four miles from central Maidstone and within easy reach of Sissinghurst Castle and many other interesting places. The White Lodge is well established, with a friendly, relaxed atmosphere; guests are encouraged to enjoy the two and a half acre garden with its two ponds. Ample parking, quiet location. Terms from £21 per person per night with full English breakfast. En suite double/family room with sitting-room and kitchen available. Directions: south on A229 left on to B2163, first right Loddington Lane, nearly to bottom of hill, on right.

MARGATE. Malvern Hotel, 29 Eastern Esplanade, Cliftonville, Margate CT9 2HL (01843 290192). ETB ♥♥ *COMMENDED.* Open all year. Small seafront private hotel. All bedrooms with TV and tea/coffee making facilities — most have en suite shower and toilet. Bed and Breakfast (choice of menu). Double/twin £35 to £42 per night; family and single room prices on request. NO VAT. No coin meters. Close to Margate Winter Gardens, Indoor Bowls Complex and amenities, etc. Within easy reach of Channel ports of Ramsgate, Dover and Folkestone and the Channel Tunnel "Le Shuttle" Terminal, also ideal for visiting Canterbury and touring the area. Local coach excursions and daytrips to France and Belgium arranged. Short Breaks, weekends, midweek and stopovers. Access and Visa telephone bookings accepted. Send stamp only for details — and mention Bed and Breakfast Stops. Credit cards — Access/Visa/Amex/Diners.

SUTTON VALENCE. Mrs Stephanie Clout, Sparks Oast Farm, Forsham Lane, Sutton Valence, Maidstone ME17 3EW (01622 842213).

Sparks Oast is a characteristic converted Kentish Oasthouse, on small sheep farm in quiet country lane overlooking the Weald of Kent. Ideally situated for visiting the many attractive castles, famous gardens such as Sissinghurst, Scotney Castle, etc and other places of interest in the Garden of England, or just rambling amid orchards and hop gardens. There is a wealth of excellent pubs offering good food. A warm welcome by the family including the animals, waterfowl, barn owls, etc. Bed and Breakfast from £16.50 per person. One double room, one twin and one en suite. TV. Guests' bathroom and beverage facilities. ALSO SELF CATERING SUITE.

TONBRIDGE near. Mrs L. Tubbs, Dunsmore, Hadlow Park, Hadlow, Near Tonbridge TN11 0HX (01732 850611). Hadlow is a small village situated on the A26 between Tonbridge and Maidstone. The M25, M26 and M20 are just a few miles away, making Hadlow a convenient 'stop-over' point for Continental trips or a base for visiting the many places of interest that abound in Kent. The accommodation has its own entrance to a large ground floor twin bedded/sitting room, shower and WC. Additional children's beds available. Colour TV and tea-making facilities. Doors lead onto own patio with views of Downs. Easy parking. Bed and Breakfast from £18 per person per night. Very peaceful.

THE OLD PARSONAGE
Frant, Tunbridge Wells, Kent
Tel/Fax: 01892 750773

Quietly situated by the church in pretty Frant village, two miles south of Tunbridge Wells, this magnificent Georgian country house, built by the Marquess of Abergavenny in 1820, provides superior accommodation: luxurious en suite bedrooms, including two four-posters, antique-furnished reception rooms, plus a spacious conservatory and balustraded terrace overlooking the secluded walled garden. For evening meals, the two village pubs and restaurant are less than three minutes' walk away. Many historic houses and fine walks in the area. B&B from £29.00.

AA – Premier Selected QQQQQ   RAC Highly Acclaimed   ETB De Luxe
English Tourist Board Award Winner "Best B&B in S.E. England"
Gatwick 40 minutes, Heathrow 55 minutes, London 40 minutes by train

---

WALTHAM. Tracy Childs, Beech Bank, Duckpitt Lane, Waltham, Near Canterbury CT4 5QA (01227 700302). SEETB ✿ ✿ AA QQQ.

15th century Tudor style coach house situated on the valley downs. Surrounded by magnificent views with landscaped garden adjoining Nature Reserve. Oak king posts, minstrels' gallery and architectural features. Luxury bedrooms, three en suite, one of which has sunken bath. Four poster room. Breakfast is served in Victorian conservatory. Children welcome. Open all year except Christmas. Bed and Breakfast from £30–£45. Non-smoking.

LANCASHIRE
including Greater Manchester and Merseyside

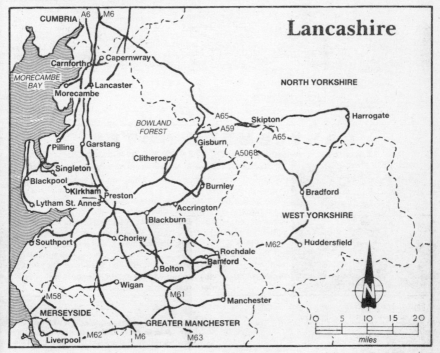

BLACKPOOL. Elsie and Ron Platt, Sunnyside and Holmesdale Guest House, 25-27 High Street, North Shore, Blackpool FY1 2BN (01253 23781). Two minutes from North Station, five minutes from Promenade, all shows and amenities. Colour TV lounge. Full central heating. No smoking. Late keys. Children welcome; high chairs and cots available. Reductions for children sharing. Senior Citizens' reductions May and June, always welcome. Handicapped guests welcome. Special diets catered for, good food and warm friendly atmosphere awaits you. Bed and Breakfast from £15; extra for optional Evening Meal. Morning tea available. Overnight guests welcome. Small parties catered for.

BLACKPOOL near. Mrs Joan Colligan, High Moor Farm, Weeton, Kirkham PR4 3JJ (Tel & Fax: 01253 836273). 🐾🐾 High Moor Farm is situated six miles from Blackpool and is within easy reach of Lytham St. Annes, Lancaster, Morecambe, the Lake District and the Dales of Yorkshire. Local attractions include sea fishing, golfing, sand yachting, riding schools, Isle of Man ferry (July/August) Fleetwood. Guest accommodation comprises one double, one family, one twin-bedded and one single rooms; the double and family rooms have central heating, colour TV and tea-making facilities. Bed and Breakfast from £15 per person. Special family room (for four) at £30. Reductions for children under 12 years. Closed January until mid February. Travellers cheques accepted.

BLACKPOOL. Proprietress: Mrs Yvonne Anne Duckworth, "Kelvin Private Hotel", 98 Reads Avenue, Blackpool FY1 4JJ (01253 20293). Welcome to our comfortable and friendly small hotel. Centrally situated between sea and Stanley Park, Lake District, Scotland, North Wales and Yorkshire. TV lounge; plenty of good food. Bed and English Breakfast; Evening Dinner optional; light snacks. Tea/coffee facilities all bedrooms. Overnight, Short Break and period stays welcome. Open most of the year. Fire Certificate. Car park. Bed and Breakfast from £11 to £14.50 per person according to season. Reduced rates for children and Senior Citizens. Weekly rates competitive. Please do not hesitate to enquire. SAE for brochure.

CASTLEMERE HOTEL

13 Shaftesbury Avenue, Blackpool FY2 9QQ Tel. 01253 352430

Proprietors: Dave & Sue Hayward FHG DIPLOMA WINNER

Castlemere is a licensed private hotel, family run and conveniently situated off Queen's Promenade in the very pleasant North Shore area of Blackpool. The busy town centre, bus and train stations are convenient and a range of entertainment opportunities for all ages and tastes are within an easy walk or a short tram ride, including golf course. Ideal for touring the Lakes and Dales, "Bronte" Country and Fylde Coast. Easy access to M55. En suite rooms; all rooms have central heating, colour TV with Sky, and tea-making facilities. The Castlemere has a bar and evening snacks are available. Open all year. Car park. Visa & Mastercard accepted.

From £18.00 per day for bed and breakfast. Dinner is optional. Winter Break terms on application.

BLACKPOOL. Mark and Claire Smith, The Old Coach House, 50 Dean Street, Blackpool FY4 1BP (01253 344330). ♥♥♥ An historic detached house surrounded by its own gardens in the heart of Blackpool. One minute from the sea and South Pier. Free car parking. All bedrooms are fully en suite with central heating, colour TV, telephone, trouser press, hair dryer, razor point, radio alarm and tea/coffee making facilities; four-poster beds available. Sun lounge. Open all year for Bed and Breakfast from £23.50. Licensed restaurant. Non-smoking dining room. Children welcome at reduced rates. Sorry, no pets. RAC Highly Acclaimed. AA QQQQ.

BLACKPOOL (North Shore). Mildred and Ken Robinson, The Birchley Hotel, 64 Holmfield Road, Blackpool FY2 9RT (01253 354174). The Birchley is situated in a pleasant select North Shore area adjacent to Queens Promenade. Open most of the year and totally no smoking. Seven bedrooms all with private shower en suite facilities, tea/coffee tray, colour TV and central heating. Lovely lounge to relax in, a cosy dining room with separate tables and a small licensed bar for residents. In our ownership since 1978 we have built up a fine reputation for excellent cuisine offering full English breakfast each day and an optional evening dinner. Bookings accepted with a minimum stay of two nights. Bed and Breakfast from £15 nightly or weekly from £100. Full week Dinner, Bed and Breakfast from £130. Open for "Festive Season" and "Illuminations". Please telephone for our brochure.

BURY. J.R. & B. Baxter, Loe Farm Country House, Redisher Lane, Hawkshaw, Bury BL8 4HX (01204 88 3668; Fax: 01204 88 8081). This 200-year-old farmhouse is situated off A676 approximately five miles east of Bolton and four miles north of Bury within four to five miles of M66, M62, M61. We have two double rooms both with en suite facilities, colour TV, radio alarm, tea/coffee making facilities and fridge freezers. The premises are centrally heated and double glazed. Both rooms have lovely views of the surrounding countryside which is renowned for its attractive walks and interesting history. Open all year round. Bed and Breakfast single from £25, double from £38.

CAPERNWRAY. Mrs Melanie Smith, Capernwray House, Capernwray, Via Carnforth LA6 1AE (Tel & Fax: 01524 732363). ETB 🏵🏵 COMMENDED. Situated in the Lower Lunesdale Valley on the North Lancashire and Cumbria borders (M6 Junction 35, off B6254) where the peace and solitude of the countryside are yours to enjoy. The house is beautifully furnished to ensure a delightful and comfortable stay for the non-smoking guest. There are three centrally heated en-suite bedrooms with tea/coffee facilities, shoe cleaning, clock radio and hair dryer. Panoramic views can be enjoyed over the Cumbrian or Pennine Hills. Superb location in five and a half acres of rolling countryside, ideal for the coast, Lakes, Dales, Lancaster bird reserves, historic houses, steam railways or a break en-route London-Scotland. Spacious lounge. Ample parking. Sorry, no pets. Children welcome. Bed and Breakfast from £17. Open all year. Brochure available. RAC Acclaimed. Also small select touring caravan park.

CARNFORTH. Mr and Mrs F. Holmes, Kiln Croft, Warton, Carnforth LA5 9NR (01524 735788). You are welcome at our small family-run hotel where we will do our best to make your stay a pleasant one. We are in the village of Warton yet only five minutes Junction 35 off M6. You can walk through our organic smallholding to beautiful Warton Crag Nature Reserve and on to Leighton Moss Bird Sanctuary. We serve our own meat and vegetables in the restaurant when available. Central for Lakes, Dales and lesser known picturesque beaches of Morecambe Bay. En suite Bed and Breakfast £18.50, single £22. Also self contained self catering two bedroomed flat £35 daily, £200 weekly fully inclusive.

CHORLEY. Mrs Val Hilton, Jepsons Farm, Moor Road, Anglezarke, Chorley PR6 9DQ (01257 481691). Jepsons Farm, formerly a 17th century inn, is a stone built farmhouse with oak beams and wood burning stoves and is situated in Anglezarke, next to Rivington in the West Pennine Moors. Non-working farm apart from horses. It boasts excellent views and is surrounded by beautiful countryside for all outdoor activities including riding, walking, climbing, abseiling, cycling and fishing or simply relaxing. Good food assured and bedrooms have colour TV and tea/coffee trays. Accommodation for horses in spacious looseboxes; bridleways in abundance for all riding requirements. Places of interest include Wigan Pier, Martin Mere, Astley Hall, Camelot and coastal resorts of Blackpool and Southport. Bed and Breakfast from £17; Evening Meal from £7.50. Reductions for children. Special rates for longer stays.

CLITHEROE. Mrs Margaret A. Berry, Lower Standen Farm, Whalley Road, Clitheroe BB7 1PP (01200 424176). 🏵🏵 This farmhouse is situated 20 minutes' walk from town centre, one mile from A59 road. Convenient for M6, 20 minutes' drive from Junction 31. There are two double rooms en suite, one twin-bedded room with washbasin only and an additional single room if required. TV and tea/coffee making facilities; cot also available. Own lounge with electric fire and TV; dining room. Full central heating. Pets and children are welcome, reduced rates for children under 12 years. Open all year except Christmas and New Year. Golf club nearby. Bed and Breakfast from £15 per person, £17 in en suite room.

WHEN MAKING ENQUIRIES PLEASE MENTION THIS *FHG* PUBLICATION

LANCASTER. Roy and Helen Domville, Three Gables, Chapel Lane, Galgate, Lancaster LA2 0NP

(01524 752222). A large detached bungalow, three miles south of Lancaster and 400 yards from Lancaster University. Access from M6 Junction 33 and A6 in Galgate village. Two double bedrooms each with shower, toilet, colour TV and tea/coffee facilities. One bedroom also has private TV lounge. Open all year with full central heating. A cot and high chair are available. Spacious parking. A good location for visiting Blackpool, Morecambe, the Lake District and Yorkshire Dales. You will be sure of a friendly welcome and a homely atmosphere. Sorry no pets. Non-smokers only please. Bed and Breakfast £15 per person.

LYTHAM ST. ANNES. Mr M.J. Doran, Willow Trees, 89 Heyhouses Lane, Lytham St. Annes FY8 3RN (01253 727235). A warm welcome awaits you in this comfortable detached house with pleasant gardens situated

between Blackpool and Lytham, one mile from the sea and backing on to open countryside. Close to all amenities and within easy reach of Lake District, Trough of Bowland and Dales. Convenient for touring, swimming, golf, horse riding, sailing, wind surfing and fishing. The house is in a quiet situation and centrally heated throughout. Guests are accommodated in two double, one twin-bedded and two single rooms, each with tea/coffee making facilities and TV. Bathroom and toilets. Ample parking. Bed and Breakfast from £14 each. Reduced rates for children. No smoking in the house please.

LYTHAM ST. ANNES. Harcourt Hotel, 21 Richmond Road, St. Annes on Sea, Lytham St. Annes FY8 1PE (01253 722299). ♥♥ Small 10 bedroomed private Hotel. Perfectly situated adjacent to town centre and 200 yards from sandy beach and Promenade. Open all year with central heating. One mile from Blackpool. Tea making facilities in all rooms. Colour TV with Sky in some bedrooms. En suite rooms available. Twin bedded and double rooms, family rooms. Free car park. Licensed. Friendly personal service from **Sue and Andy Royle.** Bed and Breakfast from £16; en suite from £18. Long and short stays available. Special reductions for Senior Citizens on weekly terms. Child reductions for up to 14 year olds, under five years FREE.

MANCHESTER. Margaret and Bernard Satterthwaite, The Albany Hotel, 21 Albany Road, Chorlton-cum-Hardy, Manchester M21 0AY (0161-881 6774; Fax: 0161-862 9405). ♥♥♥ *COMMENDED.* The Albany Hotel, having recently undergone a major refurbishment, offers luxurious and elegant period accommodation with all the comforts of a modern deluxe hotel, plus the personal attention of the owners. Facilities include Erica's Restaurant, licensed bar, games room and full conference facilities. A choice of single, double or family rooms, all with shower or en suite bathroom, direct-dial telephone, colour TV, hair dryer, radio and tea/coffee. Conveniently located being only 10 minutes from the City and Airport, five minutes Manchester United, L.C.C.C., Salford Quays, Trafford Park and Universities. Directions:- just off the A6010 (Wilbraham Road), approximately one mile from Metrolink, one mile Junction 7 M63 for M62, M61 and M6 North, two miles M56 and M6 South. AA/RAC Two Stars. Brochure and tariff on request.

MELLOR. Mrs Marj Adderley, Rose Cottage, Longsight Road (A59), Clayton-le-Dale, Ribble Valley

BB1 9EX (01254 813223; Fax: 01254 813831). A warm welcome awaits at our picturesque cottage situated at the gateway to the Ribble Valley, five miles from Junction 31 of M6 on A59. Excellent night stop travelling to and from Scotland, easy access to Yorkshire Dales, Lake District and Blackpool. Full English breakfast included in price; Singles from £20, Double from £17 per person. Three night break to include Sunday night shared occupancy £46 per person. Comfortable well equipped rooms offering tea/coffee, TV and Sky, radio alarms, heated towel rails, hair dryers, shoe cleaning, smoke detectors; all have private facilities. Phone for our brochure. Nearby coarse fishing, cycling, walking. Trace your family at Records Office, Preston.

MORECAMBE. The Warwick Hotel, 394 Marine Road East, Morecambe LA4 5AN (Tel & Fax: 01524 418151). The Warwick Hotel is a medium-sized family-run licensed hotel specialising in good service and a friendly atmosphere. We are situated on the seafront with views across Morecambe Bay to the hills of the southern Lake District. Ideal for that well deserved quiet break to "watch the world go by" or use as a base to discover the many attractive facets of this fascinating area of England. Guests are accommodated in comfortable double, twin and single rooms with en suite facilities. Since the present proprietors have taken over the Warwick Hotel has rapidly established an enviable reputation for quality of service, cleanliness and good food. No smoking. No pets. For enquiries please telephone or fax as above.

PLEASE SEND A STAMPED ADDRESSED ENVELOPE WITH ENQUIRIES

PILLING. Beryl and Peter Richardson, Bell Farm, Bradshaw Lane, Scronkey, Pilling, Preston PR3

6SN (01253 790324). Beryl and Peter welcome you to their 18th century farmhouse situated in the quiet village of Pilling, which lies between the Ribble and Lune Estuaries. The area has many public footpaths and is ideal for cycling. From the farm there is easy access to Blackpool, Lancaster, the Forest of Bowland and the Lake District. Accommodation consists of one family room with en-suite facilities, one double and one twin with private bathroom. Tea and coffee making facilities. Lounge and dining room. All centrally heated. Children and pets welcome. Full English Breakfast is served. Open all year, except Christmas and New Year. Bed and Breakfast from £15.50.

Bell Farm

PRESTON. Mrs M. Jackson, Smithy Farm, Huntingdon Hall Lane, Dutton, Near Longridge, Preston PR3 2ZT (01254 878250). Just a happy home set in the unspoilt beautiful Ribble Valley. 20 minutes from the M6 and 45 minutes to Blackpool. Just come and enjoy the friendly hospitality and good food. No rules. Children, pets and grandmas welcome! Bed and Breakfast from £12.50 per person per night; Evening Meal from £5. Reduced rates for children under 12 years.

PRESTON near. Mrs B. Brown, Wall Mill Farm, Great Eccleston, Blackpool Road, Near Preston PR3 0ZQ (01995 670334). Comfortable accommodation in farmhouse on 46 acre dairy farm. Blackpool eight miles. Two double bedrooms and one single bedroom. Bed and Breakfast from £15.

ROCHDALE/BURY. Mrs Jane Neave, Leaches Farm, Ashworth Valley, Bamford, Rochdale OL11

5UN (01706 41116/7 or 228520). Tourist Board Listed. Hill farm in the "Forgotten Valley", with magnificent views of the Roch, Irwell and Mersey river valleys; West Yorkshire, Lancashire and Derbyshire hills, Cheshire Plain, Jodrell Bank Telescope, Welsh mountains. At night there are the panoramic twinkling lights of Greater Manchester. Accommodation features oak beams, 18-inch walls, log fires and central heating. Unique rural wildlife in the heart of industrial East Lancashire. Three miles from M62 and M66, 30 miles from Manchester Airport. Ideal for holiday or business visitors. Bed and Breakfast from £18. AA Listed.

SALFORD. Beaucliffe Hotel, 254 Eccles Old Road, Salford, Greater Manchester M6 8ES (061-789 5092). ✿ ✿ ✿ Excellent Hotel that places hospitality, comfort and cleanliness as high priorities. All rooms en suite with TV, direct-dial telephone and tea/coffee making facilities. Good restaurant with market fresh produce. Quiet bar lounge. Car parking front and rear. Manchester centre and G Mex only 10 minutes away. Manchester Airport 20 minutes. Motorway network quarter of a mile. Resident proprietors. Full English Breakfast and accommodation from £25 for single. AA/RAC one star. Les Routiers.

SILVERDALE. Mrs Helen Rushworth, Havendale, 58 Emesgate Lane, Silverdale, Carnforth LA5

0RN (01524 701833). Havendale is a family home on the outskirts of Silverdale with extensive views in beautiful limestone countryside. The house is a fine centre for touring the Lakes, Dales and Blackpool, for bird watching at Leighton Moss, walking, cycling and visiting stately homes, yet is only 10 minutes from M6. Havendale features en suite rooms with beverage trays, TV and a clock/radio. Children are particularly welcome and we provide a play area, books, toys, games, cot and a high chair. Baby sitting by arrangement. Children sharing parents rooms free. We regret we cannot accommodate smokers or guests with pets. Brochure available.

LANCASHIRE – A COMBINATION OF COAST AND COUNTRY!

The choice is yours! A day on the beach or a trip to the moors – and don't forget Blackpool and Morecambe. In between all this the discerning tourist would also do well to visit the Roman fort and museum at Ribchester, the country park at Wycoller, the nature reserve at Lytham St. Annes, the Royal Empire Exhibition at Leyland and the Steamtown Railway Museum at Carnforth.

SOUTHPORT. Mrs Judith Leck, Sidbrook Hotel, 14 Talbot Street, Southport PR8 1HP (Tel: 01704 530608; Fax: 01704 531198). ❀ ❀ ❀ ❀ *COMMENDED.* A quiet hotel in the centre of this picturesque seaside town, fantastic shopping in Victorian tree-lined boulevard and arcades. We offer select accommodation at a realistic price. All our attractive bedrooms are en suite with remote control TV and satellite, tea/coffee facilities, telephone, radio alarm, hair dryer and toiletries. We have a sauna and sun bed to help you relax, together with a secluded garden and games room in basement with pool table. We have a cosy bar and two lounges. Bed and Breakfast from £17.50. RAC One Star.

LEICESTERSHIRE

BROUGHTON ASTLEY. Mrs A. Cornelius, The Old Farm House, Old Mill Road, Broughton Astley LE9 6PQ (01455 282254). Tourist Board Listed. Quietly situated but within walking distance of the village centre with good pubs and restaurants. Georgian farmhouse with easy access to M1, M69 and A14, good local walks. Children welcome but sorry no pets. Accommodation comprises two family rooms, one twin-bedded room and a single room, all with TV; two bathrooms; sitting room with TV. Bed and Breakfast from £15 to £18 per person per night. Advance booking please. Smoking discouraged!

EARL SHILTON. The Townhouse, 32 Wood Street, Earl Shilton LE9 7ND (01455 847011; Fax: 01455 851490). The Townhouse is a highly rated Two Star hotel which has 26 comfortable bedrooms sleeping a total of 42 guests. All rooms are en suite with either bath or shower and are complete with colour TV, radio alarm and beverage facilities. The Townhouse Restaurant offers à la carte menu and light meals are available in our elegant cafe bar. Free parking for up to 150 cars with a further 300 spaces opposite. The Townhouse is located in the village of Earl Shilton just minutes away from the historic city of Leicester, with easy access to the M69, M1, M6, Coventry, Birmingham and is ideal for sales meetings, seminars or full conferences and weddings. Please send for our brochure.

LUTTERWORTH. Mrs A.T. Hutchinson, The Greenway and Knaptoft House Farm, Bruntingthorpe Road, Near Shearsby, Lutterworth LE17 6PR (Tel & Fax: 01162 478388). ❀ ❀ *HIGHLY COMMENDED.* **Working farm.** AA QQQQ Selected. Ample off road parking. M1 Exit 20, M6 Exit 1, A14 Exit 1 (A50). Nine miles south of Leicester (A50 Bruntingthorpe-Saddington crossroads). Very peacefully situated with lovely views across our pretty garden to the fields where our sheep and horses graze. Warmth, comfort and good wholesome farmhouse breakfast. Twin/double/single/family rooms, some ground floor. Each room carefully and thoughtfully furnished with colour TV, either fully en suite or with shower and handbasin en suite, tea/coffee making facilities. Sunny dining and sitting room with woodburner and colour TV. Family history memorabilia. Payphone, fridge and iron. On farm coarse fishing, horses at livery in cobbled stable yard. Excellent food at local pubs. Bed and Breakfast from £18. Phone for brochure. Major credit cards accepted.

MARKET HARBOROUGH. Mrs J.A. Wainwright, Homestead House, 5 Ashley Road, Medbourne, Market Harborough LE16 8DL (Tel & Fax: 01858 565724). 🐾🐾 *HIGHLY COMMENDED.* Open all year for

Bed and Breakfast, Homestead House is situated in an elevated position overlooking the Welland Valley on the outskirts of Medbourne, a picturesque village dating back to Roman times, with a meandering brook running through the centre. Surrounded by open countryside, the village has two public houses, post office/shop, etc. Local places of interest include Foxton Locks on Grand Union Canal, Rockingham Castle, Rutland Water (sailing, fishing, windsurfing), Eyebrook Reservoir (fishing, bird watching), Naseby Battlefield, various houses and halls, gliding, riding, nature trails and many delightful picnic spots. Accommodation comprises three twin-bedded rooms, all en-suite and having TVs, telephones and tea/coffee making facilities; sitting-room, diningroom. Children welcome and pets accepted free of charge. Central heating. Car not essential, although there is parking for four cars. Bed and Breakfast from £17.50 to £20. Evening Meal available. Reductions for children.

MELTON MOWBRAY. Mr R.S. Whittard, Elms Farm, Long Clawson, Melton Mowbray LE14 4NG (Tel & Fax: 01664 822395). A very warm welcome awaits

you in a 17th century farmhouse with superb home cooking and comfortable, centrally heated rooms in the heart of Stilton cheese-making rural England. Situated in beautiful Vale of Belvoir between M1 and A1, six miles north of Melton Mowbray and 25 minutes from Grantham, Nottingham, Loughborough and Leicester. Also convenient for Belvoir Castle, Belton House, Burghley House, Caulk Abbey and Stamford. One double/family room and one single room. Separate dining room and lounge with colour TV. Bed and Breakfast £16 per adult; Double £30; self-contained suite £38 (bedtime drink included). Evening Meal by arrangement (including special diets) from £7. Longer stay terms available. Open all year except Christmas. Sorry, no smoking in the house please.

MELTON MOWBRAY (4 miles). Mrs Brenda Bailey, Church Cottage, Main Street, Holwell, Melton Mowbray LE14 4SZ (01664 444255). Church Cottage, an

18th century Listed building, is situated next to Holwell's 13th century church in the heart of the Leicestershire countryside. This is an excellent location for walkers and lovers of the rural scene. The high standard accommodation offers an en-suite double room and one twin bedroom, plus own colour TV, radio and tea-making facilities. Guests also have private use of lounge and summerhouse. Full central heating. Children and dogs welcome. Bed and Breakfast from £17 per person. No smoking.

MELTON MOWBRAY near. Mrs J.S. Goodwin, Hillside House, 27 Melton Road, Burton Lazars, Near Melton Mowbray LE14 2UR (01664 66312; mobile 0585 068956). Hillside House is a charmingly converted

19th century old farm building with views over rolling countryside situated on the outskirts of Burton Lazars. Melton Mowbray, famous for Pork Pies, is close by as is Belvoir Castle, Stamford and Rutland Water. The recently restored accommodation is spacious and very comfortable offering one double en suite, one twin en suite and one twin with own toilet and shower. Prices from £16.50. Children 10 years and over welcome.

OAKHAM near. Mrs J.H. Wilson, "Priestwells", Main Street, Greetham, Near Oakham LE15 7NU (01572 812660). A comfortable modern family house situated in three acres of gardens and paddocks. Very peaceful! The village is convenient for north/south travellers (A1 two miles) and visitors to the delightful old town of Stamford and to Burghley House (and horse trials). Also to Rutland Water which attracts naturalists, ramblers, sailors and fly fishermen and is the venue for the British Bird Watching Fair. Guests' rooms, shower room and loo are on a private landing. Bed and Breakfast from £15 with reduced rates for children. It is just a short stroll to the pub for an evening meal. Ample parking. Horses and dogs can also be accommodated.

OAKHAM. Miss J. Layton, Knebworth House, Launde, Near Tilton LE7 9DF (0116 2597257). Knebworth House was built in 1868 and has been modernised throughout, situated on the Leicestershire/ Rutland border in the heart of beautiful Leicestershire — seven miles from Oakham, 15 from Leicester, 10 from Rutland Water, 20 miles from Belvoir Castle — and is a ramblers' paradise. Comfortably furnished accommodation available (with washbasins) in one single, one double and one twin-bedded room; upstairs bath/shower/toilet facilities. Best home cooking served, fresh garden produce. Car essential, excellent parking facilities for cars and caravans. Bed and Breakfast from £15 per person per night.

UPPINGHAM. The Old Rectory, Belton-in-Rutland, Uppingham, Rutland LE15 9LE (01572 717279; Fax: 01572 717343). 😾 😾 *COMMENDED.* On the edge of the picturesque conservation village of Belton in Rutland, 10 minutes from Rutland Water, Launde Abbey, Rockingham Castle and numerous other historical and tourist landmarks. Excellent walks, cycling, golf, bird watching, fishing, water sports and riding locally. This is a relaxed atmosphere to come and go as you please, offering Bed and Breakfast in comfortable en suite rooms with TV and tea/coffee facilities. Arrange an evening meal in or visit one of the local restaurants or pubs (the best in England). More than 50% of you will return!

LINCOLNSHIRE
including North Lincolnshire, and North East Lincolnshire, formerly Humberside

GRANTHAM. Mrs Janice Standish, The Lanchester Guest House, 84 Harrowby Road, Grantham NG31 9DS (01476 74169). 😾 😾 The Lanchester is now a well established Edwardian Guest House where service and professional standards are our top priorities but we have still retained our warm and friendly atmosphere. We are situated on a pleasant, tree-lined road, yet only five minutes to town centre. Single, twin and double rooms (one en suite), all with TV, tea/coffee making facilities. Lounge, separate diningroom. Bed and Breakfast from £15. If Evening Meal is not required a supper can be provided until 9pm. Open all year. Children welcome. RAC Acclaimed.

GRANTHAM. Mrs M. Holliday, The Hawthornes Guest House, 51 Cambridge Street, Grantham NG31 6EZ (01476 573644). The Hawthornes is an attractive and comfortable family-run Victorian guest house. Centrally situated, convenient for shops, bus and train stations, local parks and leisure centre. Spacious accommodation consists of twin, double, family and single rooms, all with washbasins, shaver points, tea/coffee facilities; most rooms have TV. Large bathroom and shower, two toilets. Comfortable lounge/diner with TV. Bed and Breakfast from £16. Families welcome. Easy access from A1, excellent touring centre. Open all year. Vegetarian diets catered for.

HORNCASTLE. Michael and Jill Swan, The Old Rectory, Fulletby, Near Horncastle LN9 6JX (Tel & Fax: 01507 533533). Our lovely country house is idyllically situated nestling in the southern Wolds — an Area of Outstanding Natural Beauty. The house, with five acres of gardens and grounds, enjoys wonderful views and the whole setting is one of complete rural tranquillity. We offer Aga home cooking, fresh flowers, books, log fires and lovingly furnished accommodation. Enjoy in the locality walking, cycling, golf, fishing, riding, bird watching, local history, antiques, or just relaxing. Visit historic Lincoln or Cadwell Park. Superior Bed and Breakfast en suite with all facilities from £20 per person per night. Four-course Dinner (by prior booking) £12 per person. Guided local tour option. Come and stay with us and discover a real gem!

HORNCASTLE. Mrs C.E. Harrison, Baumber Park, Baumber, Near Horncastle LN9 5NE (01507 578235; Fax: 01507 578417). Period farmhouse in quiet parkland setting, standing in attractive gardens and on a mixed farm. Situated in the centre of the county and close to the Lincolnshire Wolds, an Area of Outstanding Natural Beauty, this rolling agricultural countryside is little-known and quite unspoilt. The Viking Way long distance footpath passes close by and there is a championship golf course near at hand. There are also a number of interesting market towns within easy reach: Horncastle, only four miles away, has become an important antiques centre for the East Midlands. The historic Cathedral City of Lincoln is 17 miles away. Bed and Breakfast £17.50 per person. Brochure available.

KIRTON IN LINDSEY. Mrs Maxine Walker, Kirton Lodge, Dunstanhill, Kirton Lindsey, Gains-borough DN21 4DU (Tel & Fax: 01652 648994). 🏵 🏵 🏵

COMMENDED. Delightful old barn lovingly converted to a four-bedroomed Hotel. All rooms are double-bedded with colour TV, clock radios, tea/coffee making facilities and en suite bathrooms. The restaurant is renowned in the area, boasting an "ACE" Award (Accolade for Catering Excellence) and a quality and service certificate from the Guild of Master Craftsmen. Kirton Lindsey is an excellent central location to explore North Lincolnshire, there is plenty to see and do. Bargain Breaks — £30 per person per night for Dinner, Bed and Breakfast, less for five nights or more. Dogs most welcome. Please ring for a brochure and fact sheet.

LINCOLN. Mr David Benson, Mayfield Guest House, 213 Yarborough Road, Lincoln LN1 3NQ (01522 533732). 🏵 🏵 *COMMENDED.* Small, friendly Victorian guest house with private enclosed parking. Panoramic

views of the Trent Valley, yet within a short level walk from the main tourist attractions including Cathedral, Castle, Windmill, Museum and Lawn Visitor Centre. All bedrooms are en-suite with colour TV, clock radio, beverage tray, central heating and double glazing. Spacious dining room with a good breakfast choice. Terms from £17. School-age children welcome at reduced rates. Access to car park at rear from Mill Road. A completely non-smoking establishment. We offer quality bed and breakfast at a comfortable price.

LINCOLN. Mr R.H. Taylor, Halfway Farm Motel, Swinderby, Lincoln LN6 9HN (01522 868749; Fax: 01522 868082). 🏵 🏵 Ideally situated for Lincoln and Newark, this Georgian House and converted Farmstead

offers 15 en suite plus two other bedrooms, furnished and equipped to a high standard of cleanliness and comfort. All rooms have welcome trays and heating under guests' control. Facilities for guests include public telephone, lounge with coal fire and beamed ceilings, unlimited parking, and pub with restaurant within walking distance. Payment by Access or Visa if desired. Excellent value from £18 per person for Bed and full Breakfast. Open all year. Prior inspection welcomed. RAC Acclaimed, AA Recommended.

LINCOLN. Edward King House, The Old Palace, Lincoln LN2 1PU (01522 528778; Fax: 01522 527308). EMTB Member. A former palace of the Bishops

EDWARD KING HOUSE

of Lincoln, Edward King House offers Bed and Breakfast accommodation in a friendly and informal atmosphere. It is in a wonderful setting at the heart of historic uphill Lincoln, next to the Cathedral and Old Palace and overlooking the modern city with views over many miles to the west and south. Single and twin-bedded rooms (non-smoking) are all centrally heated and have washbasins and tea/coffee making facilities. Prices from £18.50 single, £36 twin with Continental breakfast (full breakfast £2 extra per person).

LINCOLN near. Mrs Brenda Williams, Gallow Dale Farm, Marton Road, Sturton by Stow, Lincoln LN1 2AH (01427 788387). Situated eight miles north west of Lincoln on the A1500 road between the villages of Sturton by Stow and Marton (one mile west of Sturton by Stow village centre). Tastefully refurbished, centrally heated, Grade II Listed Georgian farmhouse set in 33 acres of grass paddocks. TV lounge with beamed ceiling, pretty bedrooms including en suite room with four-poster bed. Tea/coffee making facilities. Full English farmhouse breakfast. Lunch and evening meals available at three local public houses. Sorry, no smoking. Bed and Breakfast from £14 to £20. AA QQQQ Selected.

LINCOLN. Hilary and Tony Raley, Tinley Cottage, Broxholme, Near Saxilby LN1 2NG (01522 704001). 🐾🐾 *HIGHLY COMMENDED.* An old world beamed cottage set in a peaceful hamlet only 10 minutes' drive from the centre of the historic city of Lincoln, with its majestic 900 year old Cathedral and nearby Castle, which now houses King John's original 1215 Magna Carta. A village house has stood on the present site of Tinley Cottage since Tudor times and although changed over the years from three farm labourers' cottages to a larger family house, it has lost nothing of its character and charm. The cottage has two double rooms, one de luxe en suite and one with private bathroom, both have colour TV, tea/coffee making facilities, radio, hair dryer and central heating. Separate guests' lounge with open log fires. Bed and Breakfast from £19 to £25 per person. Wide choice of restaurants nearby. Reductions for Short Breaks. A non-smoking home.

LOUTH. Mr and Mrs Brumpton, Glebe Farm, Church Lane, Conisholme, Louth LN11 7LX (01507 358189). Detached farmhouse with grassland mainly for horses situated in the peaceful hamlet of Conisholme off A1031 road. Convenient for the Lincolnshire coast, city of Lincoln and Market Rasen. Amenities include RSPB bird nature reserve, fishing, horse racing; ideal countryside for cycling. Family accommodation includes own entrance, TV lounge, two double bedrooms (cot if required), bathroom and garden. Tea/coffee making facilities. Full English breakfast. Sorry no smoking or pets. Price £15 per adult. Reduction for children under 12 years.

LOUTH near. Bill and Ann Painter, "Wickham House", Church Lane, Conisholme (A1031), Near Louth LN11 7LX (01507 358465). 🐾🐾🐾 *HIGHLY COMMENDED.* En-suite accommodation in attractive 18th century cottage with exposed timber and brickwork. Rural location between the Wolds and the sea. Easy reach of Lincolnshire Wolds, Humber Bridge, Cadwell Park, RSPB Bird and Nature Reserves. Furnished to high standard. Bedrooms, one on ground floor, all en-suite with colour TV, tea/coffee tray. Sittingroom, library and diningroom with separate tables. Central heating throughout. Children over eight years welcome. Seating in garden. Sorry no pets. Ample car parking. No smoking please. AA QQQQ. Bed and Breakfast from £19.50.

PETERBOROUGH. Mrs S.M. Hanna, Courtyard Cottage, 2 West End, Langtoft, Peterborough, Cambridgeshire PE6 9LS (01778 348354). A warm, sincere welcome greets you at our delightful tastefully renovated 18th century stone cottage. We are situated in a small village just 50 yards off A15 at the Langtoft crossroads. We are ideally sited for visiting Peterborough, Stamford, Spalding, Bourne, Sleaford and Lincoln. Our home is maintained to high standards, has double glazing, central heating and we offer a hearty breakfast. Guests accommodated in twin room en suite or family suite; rooms have TV, tea making facilities and hair dryers. Evening meals (from £5.50) available. Bed and Breakfast from £20 per person per night. Open all year. Full details on request.

NORFOLK

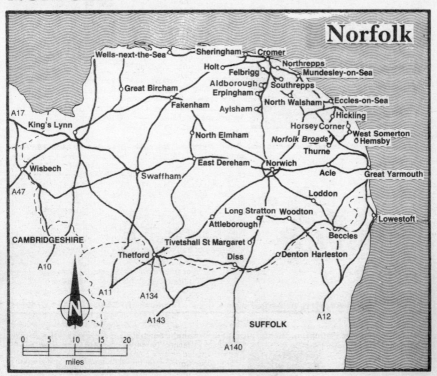

ACLE. East Norwich Inn, Old Road, Acle, Norwich NR13 3QN (01493 751112). ♥♥♥ Acle is midway between Great Yarmouth and Norwich. We are ideally situated for visiting all Heritage, National Trust and holiday attractions. The inn is situated on a quiet residential road and has a full on licence with a good "local" bar trade. All our rooms are situated well away from the bar area and comprise two twin rooms, four double rooms and three family rooms, all have en suite bathrooms, colour TV with Sky and tea/coffee making facilities. Bed and Breakfast from £17 per person per night. Three-night break prices available. Ample car parking. Pets welcome by arrangement.

ALDBOROUGH near. The Grange, Harmers Lane, Thurgarton, Near Aldborough NR11 7PF (01263 761588). A fine rural Victorian country house, former rectory, situated in secluded grounds of two acres offering peace and tranquillity in warm, friendly and comfortable surroundings. Close to Cromer and the coast and central for all the North Norfolk attractions and National Trust properties. The accommodation comprises two spacious double bedrooms with tea and coffee making facilities and private shower/bathrooms. A large guests' dining room and lounge with colour TV. Double bed and full English breakfast from £16 per person per night. Evening meals on request. Two night Short Breaks including evening meals at reduced rates. Private parking. No smoking. No pets. Open March to November. Further information on request.

AYLSHAM. Enid Parry, The Old Bank House, 3 Norwich Road, Aylsham NR11 6BN (01263

733843). 👑 👑 *HIGHLY COMMENDED.* Relax in the comfort and traditional Victorian atmosphere of Aylsham's former private Bank. We offer our guests a warm and friendly break with home cooking and spacious welcoming bedrooms with TV, tea/coffee facilities, radios and washbasins. Double with en suite Victorian bathroom; family room with half-tester bed and marble washbasin, twin room, fully panelled, use of a Victorian bathroom. Situated centrally, we are surrounded by National Trust land, lovely country walks and woodland, convenient for the coast and bird watching, yet only 10 miles from the historic city of Norwich. Lounge, games room with sauna, table tennis, darts, shower. Central heating. Evening Meals by arrangement. Bed and Breakfast £17 per person. Reductions for children. AA QQQ Recommended.

AYLSHAM. The Old Pump House, Holman Road, Aylsham, Norwich NR11 6BY (01263 733789).

👑 👑 *HIGHLY COMMENDED.* This comfortable 1750's family house, facing the thatched pump a minute from Aylsham's church and historic marketplace, has five bedrooms, three en suite, with colour TV and tea/coffee facilities. English Breakfast with free range eggs and local produce (or vegetarian Breakfast) is served in the pine-shuttered Red Sitting Room overlooking the garden. Aylsham is central for Norwich, the coast, the Broads, National Trust houses, steam railways and unspoilt countryside. Well behaved children are very welcome. Bed and Breakfast from £17 to £25. Dinner by prior arrangement from October to May. Non-smoking.

BECCLES. Mrs E. Lord, Maypole Barn, Maypole Green, Toftmonks NR34 0EY (01502 678235).

Tranquil setting just off the village green in the hamlet of Maypole Green but only four miles from Beccles and within easy reach of the market town of Bungay and the Norfolk Broads. 12 miles Yarmouth, 14 miles Lowestoft, making it an ideal centre for touring both Norfolk and Suffolk. Maypole Barn offers excellent accommodation recently converted to a very high standard. Set in three acres of grounds. Family room en suite with TV, double room en suite with TV. Lounge, table tennis room. Full central heating. Tea and coffee facilities in all rooms. Terms from £16. Child reductions.

BECCLES near. Mrs Rachel Clarke, Shrublands Farm, Burgh St. Peter, Near Beccles, Suffolk NR34

0BB (01502 677241; mobile 0468 313527). 👑 👑 *COMMENDED.* This attractive homely farmhouse offers a warm and friendly welcome and is peacefully situated in the Waveney Valley on the Norfolk/Suffolk border, surrounded by one acre of garden and lawns. The River Waveney flows through the 550 acres of mixed working farmland; opportunities for bird-watching. Ideal base for touring Norfolk and Suffolk; Beccles, Lowestoft, Great Yarmouth and Norwich are all within easy reach. The house has one double room and one family room with en suite facilities and one twin-bedded room with private bathroom, shower room and toilet. All have satellite colour TV and tea/coffee making facilities; dining room, separate lounge with colour TV. Non-smoking rooms available. Games room for snooker and darts. Tennis court available; swimming pool and food at River Centre nearby. Children over five years welcome at reduced rates. No pets. Car essential — ample parking. Open all year. Bed and Breakfast from £16.50 to £18.50 per person. SAE please.

NORFOLK – NOT JUST THE BROADS!

There's more to do in Norfolk than messing about in boats – pleasurable though that may be. Other places of interest include the gardens and steam museum at Bressingham, the Broadland Conservation Centre, the flint mines at Grimes Graves, The Norfolk Rural Life Museum, Sandringham – which is often open to the public – and of course Norwich itself.

DEREHAM. Mrs Pam Gray, Sycamore House, Yaxham Road, Mattishall NR20 3PE (01362 858213).

A guesthouse offering friendly, personal service, ideal for overnight stops and short breaks. Quiet rural location in central Norfolk within easy reach of Norwich, the Broads, beaches, country houses, etc. All rooms with colour TV, washbasins, tea/coffee making facilities. Separate WC and shower for guests' use. Traditional home cooking with fruit and vegetables from the garden in season. Early breakfasts if required, served with a smile. Village pub within walking distance. Ample off road parking. We regret no pets. Bed and Breakfast from £13.50; three-course Evening Meal £8.50.

DEREHAM. David and Annie Bartlett, Bartles Lodge, Church Street, Elsing, Dereham NR20 3EA (01362 637177). 👑👑 *COMMENDED.* If you would like a

peaceful tranquil stay in the heart of Norfolk's most beautiful countryside yet only a short drive to some of England's finest sandy beaches, then Bartles Lodge could be the place for you, with all rooms tastefully decorated in country style, with full en-suite facilities, TVs, tea/coffee making facilities, etc. Overlooking 12 acres of landscaped meadows with its own private fishing lakes. The local village inn is within 100 metres which has a restaurant and serves "pub grub". Bed and Breakfast from £20. Why not telephone David or Annie so that we can tell you about our lovely home.

DISS. Mrs Jill Potterton, Blacksmiths Cottage, Langmere Green Road, Langmere, Diss IP21 4QA (01379 740982). Friendly relaxed atmosphere in our

detached country cottage in pretty hamlet, with three and a half acre meadow, home to our collection of poultry, waterfowl and Shetland sheep. Ideal central location for touring being two and a half miles off A140, 18 miles south of Norwich. Cosy self contained accommodation with a double and single rooms with tea/coffee facilities. Guest bathroom and lounge/dining room with colour TV overlooking large lawned garden. Full English breakfast using free range eggs and home made preserves. Packed lunch and evening meals available. No dogs. Children over 10 welcome. Bed and Breakfast £15. Reductions for longer stay.

DISS. Mrs D.A. Butler, Shelfanger Hall, Shelfanger, Diss IP22 2DE (01379 642094). 👑👑

Shelfanger Hall is a 16th century Listed moated farmhouse two miles from the town of Diss and close to Bressingham Gardens and steam museum. It is tucked away from busy roads and overlooks large garden and farmland. Accommodation consists of one double and one twin-bedded room with en-suite facilities and one double room with private bathroom. All have TV and tea/coffee making facilities. A games room is available for guests including full sized snooker table. We are now in our 17th year of welcoming guests. Bed and Breakfast from £18.

DOCKING. Holland House, Chequers Street, Docking PE31 8LH (Tel & Fax: 01485 518295). Once

the Dower House to Docking Manor, Holland House is early Georgian and Grade II Listed. It retains many original features and provides spacious accommodation, en suite rooms, TV and tea/coffee facilities. Holland House is particularly suited to groups and families. Ample car parking and use of a delightful walled garden. Quiet village with good amenities: church, post office and restaurants. Bed and Breakfast from £20 per person, reductions for children. Special rates available for longer stays. Non-smoking house. Five minutes from sea, unspoilt beaches, bird and nature reserves. Minutes from picturesque Burnham Market, Titchwell, Holme and Thornham.

· The Old Shop ·

24 London Road, Downham Market, Norfolk PE38 9AW   Tel: 01366 382051   Mrs June Roberts

Charming conversion of three cottages built in 1815. Relaxed, homely atmosphere in a quiet market town approximately 12 miles from the historic towns of King's Lynn and Wisbech, bordering on Lincolnshire and Cambridgeshire. Ideally situated for walking, cycling, fishing, bird watching and touring East Anglia. Two double and one twin rooms, all en suite, with colour TV and tea/coffee making facilities. Guests' lounge. Bed and Breakfast from £16. Evening Meal available. Pets welcome. Open all year. **AA QQ.**

EAST DEREHAM. Old Hall Farm, Scarning, Dereham NR19 2LG (01362 691754). A large 16th century Grade II Listed timber frame farmhouse with one acre garden and lawns. Set amongst open countryside, two miles from Dereham town centre, one mile from A47 bypass. Norfolk offers sandy beaches, golf, sailing, riding, swimming and the Norfolk Broads. Also stately homes, museums, bird sanctuary and wildlife parks. Accommodation comprises one double room with en suite facilities, one double, one twin with separate bath/WC. Central heating, TV and tea/coffee facilities in all rooms. Guest lounge with TV and log fire. Open all year for weekly or short stays. Bed and Breakfast from £17.50 per person per day. Car essential, ample parking. Sorry, no pets.

FAKENHAM. Mrs Dorothy MacCallum, Cobblers, Front Street, South Creake, Fakenham NR21 9PF (01328 823200). A warm welcome awaits you at this charming c1800 brick and flint cottage. Situated in the heartland of the heritage coast is the attractive village of Creake with its village green, shop and local pub. Ideal for the birdwatching sanctuaries at Cley, Salthouse and Titchwell. Close to Sandringham, Holkham, the shrines at Walsingham and Nelson's birthplace. There are two bedrooms (twin/double), both en suite. Central heating. Open all year. Car essential. Bed and Breakfast from £16 depending on season. Special rates on request.

GARBOLDISHAM. Ingleneuk Lodge, Hopton Road, Garboldisham, Diss IP22 2RQ (01953 681541). 🏵🏵🏵 COMMENDED. AA QQQ, RAC Highly Acclaimed, Guestaccom Good Room Award. Our modern single level home is set in 10 acres of partly wooded rural countryside. We have seven bedrooms with a choice of single, double, twin or family with en suite facilities and one double room with private facilities. All rooms have remote-control TV, hot drink making facilities, telephone, central heating and comfortable easy chairs. Spacious lounge and bar overlooks the garden; the comfortable dining room overlooks the sheltered patio. There is a no smoking policy in the dining room and some bedrooms. Many interesting places to visit are within easy reach — take a week or stay a day or two. Special breaks available. Please send for our color brochure and full tariff listing. A warm welcome awaits.

FHG PUBLICATIONS LIMITED publish a large range of well-known accommodation guides. We will be happy to send you details or you can use the order form at the back of this book.

GILLINGHAM. Mrs Craggs, Windle Hill House, Gillingham, Beccles, Suffolk NR34 0EF (01502 677392; Fax: 01502 678293). Attractive Listed 18th century country house set in extensive gardens and paddocks. Three miles from Beccles and River Waveney, it makes an ideal base for exploring this fascinating part of Broadland. Large bedrooms, one twin, one double; en suite bathroom. Breakfast served in elegant dining room. Use of drawing room (with log fire in winter). All rooms centrally heated. No smoking in bedrooms. Children over 10 years welcome. Dogs by arrangement. Open January to December except Christmas. Prices from £18.50 per person. Reductions for longer stays.

GREAT YARMOUTH. Mr and Mrs Brian and Diana Kimber, Anglia House Hotel, 56 Wellesley Road, Great Yarmouth NR30 1EX (01493 844395). This comfortable private hotel is pleasantly situated adjacent to the sea front and near the coach station, just three minutes from pier and town centre. A warm and friendly welcome awaits you. Our reputation and good name have been built on service, a friendly atmosphere and fine food with a choice of menu. Radio, colour TV and tea making facilities in all bedrooms. Most rooms en suite. Own front door keys with access to rooms at all times. Licensed bar. Children welcome. Bed and Breakfast from £13; Bed, Breakfast and Evening Meal from £99 weekly. Open all year. For a happy holiday please send SAE or telephone.

GREAT YARMOUTH. Mrs E. Dack, 'Dacona', 120 Wellesley Road, Great Yarmouth NR30 2AP (01493 856863 or 855305). Homely guest house with own keys and access at all times. Centrally situated, it is only two/three minutes from the seafront and five minutes from shopping centre. Every amenity provided — tea making facilities in all rooms, comfortable accommodation and an ideal location. Bed and Breakfast terms from £13 to £14 nightly. Small parties (up to 24) welcomed. Children catered for (half price rates). Dogs accepted on enquiry.

GREAT YARMOUTH. Pam and Mick Eady, Shrewsbury Guest House, 9 Trafalgar Road, Great Yarmouth NR30 2LD (01493 844788). Family-run Guest House with a warmth and friendliness that makes many of our visitors return again and again. A relaxed atmosphere, comfort and cleanliness are high on the list of priorities. Each bedroom is tastefully decorated and has colour TV; some have the added luxury of being en suite. Spacious dining area enables guests to have separate tables and you'll find the hostess takes great pride in the home cooked food; only the finest produce is used and special attention given to its presentation. Comfortable lounge area has colour TV and is an excellent place to relax. Children welcome, under 12s half price. Special reductions for Senior Citizens in May and June. Open all year. Full central heating. Bed, Breakfast and Evening Meal from £106 for standard room to £150 for en suite rooms per week; daily rates available. Please send SAE for brochure and price list.

HARLESTON. Mrs June E. Holden, Weston House Farm, Mendham, Harleston IP20 0PB (01986 782206). 🐦🐦 17th century Grade II Listed farmhouse set in one acre garden overlooking pastureland on a mixed farm. Close to Norfolk/Suffolk border, it is within easy reach of Suffolk Heritage Coast, Norfolk Broads, Wild Life Parks and many stately homes. Accommodation comprises one family/double and two twin rooms, all with en suite facilities, shaver points and beverage facilities. Comfortable lounge with colour TV for guests' use, dining room with separate tables. Adequate parking space. Bed and Breakfast from £18. Discount for longer stays. AA Recommended QQQ.

HELHOUGHTON (Near Fakenham). Mrs C. Curtis, Greenlea, Raynham Road, Helhoughton, Fakenham NR21 7BH (01485 528547). Tranquillity and relaxation are assured in this friendly home in a rural setting. Ground floor bungalow accommodation consists of two double and one twin bedrooms; bathroom, two toilets and shower room. All rooms have colour TV, tea/coffee facilities and central heating. Helhoughton can be found five miles from Fakenham and is an ideal base for touring. Close to Sandringham, many attractions and beaches are within easy reach. Bed and Breakfast from £17; Evening Meal available by prior arrangement. Open all year.

HORSEY CORNER. The Old Chapel, Horsey Corner NR29 4EH (01493 393498). ETB Listed

COMMENDED. Tranquil and traditional English Bed and Breakfast from £15. A short stroll from both the wide sandy beach and Horsey Mere, an integral part of the Broads National Park. Our non-smoking accommodation offers a double, a twin and, for extra luxury, a large en suite double aspect room, all with colour TV, tea/coffee making facilities, etc. Ideal for naturalists and holidaymakers alike. The Old Chapel offers evening meals to suit any dietary requirements, central heating throughout and the warmest of welcomes; a unique location combining beach and Broads. Category Three — National Accessible Scheme for Wheelchair Users. Phone **Keith or Heather Webster** for illustrated brochure and reservation.

KING'S LYNN. Mrs Joan Bastone, Maranatha Guest House, 115 Gaywood Road, King's Lynn PE30 2PU (01553 774596). ✿✿ APPROVED. A friendly small establishment close to the town centre and Lynn Sports Centre. Sandringham House and the coast near by. Owned and run by Joan Bastone providing personal service. Accommodation comprises two double (one en suite), three twin (one en suite), two family and one single bedrooms; ground floor room available en suite. Ideal for business travellers or holiday makers alike. Children and pets welcome. Bed and Breakfast from £14 to £17; Evening Meal from £5. AA QQ, RAC.

KING'S LYNN. Mrs P. Barnes, The Lime House, The Green, East Rudham, King's Lynn (01485 528356). This family run listed Georgian house is situated

on the A148 just five and a half miles from Fakenham facing the village green near to Newsteads shops. It is an ideal base for sightseeing, birdwatching, peaceful walking or just lazing on the beach. The house comprises three well appointed rooms, one of which is en suite and one a nice sized family room. Bed and Breakfast from £18. The house is open all year and there are car parking facilities opposite.

MATTISHALL, near Dereham. Mrs Betty Jewson, Ivy House Farm, Welgate, Mattishall, Dereham NR20 3PL (01362 850208). Working farm. This architec-

turally interesting house dates from the Cromwellian period with a strong Jacobean influence and a later Georgian facade. Situated in 17 acres in the village of Mattishall, four miles from East Dereham, 12 from Norwich and within easy reach of the Coast and Norfolk Broads. Guests are accommodated in one double and two twin-bedded rooms; bathroom and toilet; guests' own dining and drawing room. We provide a full English Breakfast, a four course Evening Meal if required, and packed lunches. Bed and Breakfast from £14, Evening Meal from £6. Reductions for children. Pets welcome. Brochure available.

NORFOLK BROADS/NEATISHEAD. Alan and Sue Wrigley, Regency Guest House, The Street, Neatishead, Near Norwich NR12 8AD (01692 630233).

✿✿ COMMENDED. An 18th century guest house in picturesque, unspoilt village in the heart of Broadlands. Personal service top priority. Long established name for very generous English breakfasts. 20 minutes from medieval city of Norwich and six miles coast. Ideal base for touring East Anglia — a haven for wildlife, birdwatching, cycling and walking holidays. No. 1 centre for Broads sailing, fishing and boating. Guest house, holder of "Good Care" Award for high quality services, has five bedrooms individually Laura Ashley decorated and tastefully furnished. Rooms, including two king-size doubles, and family room, have TV and tea/coffee making facilities and most have en suite bathrooms. Two main bathrooms. Separate tables in beamed ceiling breakfast room. Guests' sitting room. Cot, babysitting, reduced rates children and all stays of more than one night. Pets welcome. Parking. Open all year. Fire Certificate held. AA QQQ. Also self catering cottage, sleeps six, available next to guest house. Bed and Breakfast from £19.50.

NORTH WALSHAM. Mr and Mrs McCarthy and Mr and Mrs Lamplugh, Hill House Country Hotel, Yarmouth Road, North Walsham NR28 9NA (01692 402151; Fax: 01692 406686).

A charming country house standing in eight acres of grounds in a quiet position just outside North Walsham. Within easy reach of the Broads, the coast and a wide range of National Trust properties, RSPB reserves and other attractions this is an ideal base for exploring North Norfolk. All bedrooms are en suite with private telephone, colour TV and tea/coffee making facilities. Licensed bar and dining room serving good home cooked food. Children and dogs welcome. Self catering cottage also available in the grounds. An informal, family-run hotel where all are welcome.

NORWICH. Mrs M.A. Hemmant, Poplar Farm, Sisland, Loddon, Norwich NR14 6EF (01508 520706). Working farm.

This 400 acre mixed farm is situated one mile off the A146, approximately nine miles south east of Norwich, close to Beccles, Bungay, Diss and Wymondham. An ideal spot for the Broads and the delightful and varied Norfolk coast. We have a Charolais X herd of cows, with calves born March-June. The River Chet runs through the farm. Accommodation comprises double, twin and family rooms, bathroom, TV sittingroom/dining room. Central heating. Tennis court. Children welcome. A peaceful, rural setting. Car essential. Open all year for Bed and Breakfast. Terms from £15 per person per night.

NORWICH. Mrs R. Thompson, Oakfield, Yelverton Road, Framingham Earl, Norwich NR14 7SD (01508 492605). ❀ ❀ HIGHLY COMMENDED. "Oakfield" is in a quiet and picturesque setting five miles from Norwich city centre with its fine shops, Norman Cathedral, Castle, Museum and cobbled streets. Close to the Norfolk Broads and coast, ideal centre for touring East Anglia. Excellent centrally heated accommodation includes one double with en-suite facilities, one twin, one single room all with washbasin, shaver point, tea/coffee making facilities. Residents' lounge with colour TV. Superb breakfasts served in dining room. Children over 10 years welcome. Ample car parking. Four acres meadowland and garden for guests' use. Several local pubs serving good food. Bed and Breakfast from £18 per person. No smoking. Directions: five miles south east of Norwich between A146 Lowestoft and B1332 Bungay roads.

NORWICH. Mr Brian and Mrs Diane Curtis, Rosedale Guest House, 145 Earlham Road, Norwich NR2 3RG (01603 453743). Tourist Board Listed. Friendly, family-run Victorian Guest House pleasantly situated within short walking distance of city centre and University, on the B1108. All rooms have colour TV, tea/coffee making facilities and own keys for your convenience. A full English breakfast is served in the diningroom and vegetarians are made very welcome. There are several good eating places nearby and once you have parked your car you can relax and enjoy Norwich. The Norfolk Broads are just seven miles away and the coast 20 miles. Full central heating. Bed and Breakfast from £15 per person.

NORWICH. John and Jean Murden, The Seafarers, North Gap Eccles Beach, Near Lessingham, Norwich NR12 0SW (01692 598218). Tourist Board Listed. The Seafarers, a former 18th century farmhouse, is set in a quiet rural area with open views over farmland and within five minutes' walk of a sandy beach. An ideal holiday retreat for exploring the Norfolk Broads, countryside and coast, nature reserves, National Trust houses, churches, museums and craft centres. There are pleasant rural walks nearby including Weavers Way. Norwich, Great Yarmouth and Cromer are with a 20 miles radius. Open all year except Christmas. Please send SAE for brochure.

NORWICH. Mrs M. Gilbert, Aberdale Lodge, 211 Earlham Road, Norwich NR2 3RQ (01603 502100). Tourist Board Listed. Visiting Norwich? Enjoy your overnight accommodation, weekend break or annual holiday at this friendly guest house close to the centre of Norwich, ideally situated for visiting all the historic places of interest for which the city is famous. Within 10 minutes you are on the Norfolk Broads, or you can visit the bird sanctuaries in the depths of the Norfolk countryside. Six bedrooms, all with hot and cold water, colour TVs, tea/coffee making facilities and central heating. There is a pleasant diningroom with separate tables; excellent food and service under the personal supervision of the proprietor. Full Fire Certificate. Guests have access at all times with keys provided. Bed and Breakfast from £15. No VAT. Reduced rates for children.

NORWICH. The Station Hotel, 5-7 Riverside Road, Norwich NR1 1SQ (01603 611064; Fax: 01603 615161). City centre hotel offering comfortable bed and breakfast accommodation, consisting of 18 rooms, having direct telephone, colour TV, radio, tea/coffee beverages and most are en suite. The hotel is called after the Yacht Station which is situated opposite on the River Wensum, this you will find on all city maps. British Rail station is one minute's walk for those travelling by rail. City centre shopping is approximately five to ten minutes' walk. We have a licensed bar and bar meals are available. Single room rates from £30, double from £55, breakfast and taxes included in these rates. Please ring reception for our descriptive brochure.

NORWICH near. Mrs Daphne Vivian-Neal, Welbeck House, Brooke, Near Norwich NR15 1AT

(01508 550292). We would like to welcome you to our quiet 300 year old farmhouse surrounded by interesting gardens and trees. Given notice, we will cater for vegetarians/vegans. Guests are accommodated in one double, one twin and one single rooms, all with tea-making facilities. Dogs welcome. Ideally placed for excellent theatre, museums, churches, shopping in new Castle Mall, Otter Trust, beaches and two fishing lakes; within easy distance of specialist nurseries and garden centres, nature reserves, National Trust properties and scenic walks. Half a mile from pub serving good food. Bed and Breakfast £16 to £20 per person, Evening Meal available if required. We are situated off the B1332 between Norwich and Bungay near Brooke Church.

RACKHEATH. Julie Simpson, Barn Court, Back Lane, Rackheath NR13 6NN (Tel & Fax: 01603

782536). Tourist Board Listed *APPROVED*. Friendly and spacious accommodation in a traditional Norfolk Barn conversion built around a courtyard. Situated five miles from the historic city of Norwich and two miles from the heart of the Norfolk Broads at Wroxham. Our accommodation consists of one double en suite room with a four-poster and two double/twin rooms. All rooms have colour TV and facilities for making tea/coffee. We are within walking distance of a very good Norfolk pub which serves reasonably priced meals. Packed lunches and dinners are available on request. Children are very welcome. Bed and Breakfast from £17 to £20.

RACKHEATH. Mr and Mrs R. Lebbell, Manor Barn House, Back Lane, Rackheath, Norwich NR13

6NN (01603 783543). 👒👒 *COMMENDED*. 17th century converted barn with a wealth of exposed beams. A family home with lovely gardens in quiet surroundings, situated just off A1151. Very convenient for Norwich (five miles), and two miles from Wroxham, heart of Broadland. Accommodation includes twin/double rooms with central heating, tea/coffee facilities, TV and own bathroom. Separate lounge area with colour TV. We are 100 yards from traditional old Norfolk pub, "The Green Man", where it is possible to eat very well and inexpensively. Open all year for Bed and Breakfast from £18 to £21 single, £34 to £38 double.

SHERINGHAM. Mrs Pat Pearce, The Birches, 27 Holway Road, Sheringham NR26 8HW (01263

823550). Small guest house conveniently situated for town and sea front. Ideal centre for touring North Norfolk. Accommodation comprises one double and one twin-bedded rooms, both with luxury bathrooms, tea/coffee making equipment and colour TV. Full central heating. Open March to November. Bed and Breakfast for two nights £37 per person; Evening Meal available on request. Special diets catered for. No children under 12 years. No pets. NON-SMOKING ESTABLISHMENT. EATB registered. Member of the North Norfolk Hotel and Guest House Association. Heartbeat Award for 1994/5 and 1996/97.

STALHAM GREEN. Mrs A. Adams, The Yews, Moor Lane, Stalham Green NR12 9QD (01692

581880). Idyllically situated in a quiet leafy lane just minutes' walk from the nearby Broads. Half an hour's drive from Norwich, Great Yarmouth and the North Norfolk Coast. Beautifully appointed kingsize double/twin bedded suites, both with luxury bathrooms. Complimentary beverage trays, plus a host of extras. Elegant lounge with deep chintzy settees. Separate dining room with choice of hearty English breakfasts. Tranquil and pretty gardens. All day access. Regretfully no children or pets. Open April to October. Illustrated details sent with pleasure.

SWAFFHAM. Mrs C. Webster, Purbeck Guest House, 46 Whitsands Road, Swaffham PE37 7BJ (01760 721805/725345). Family-run guesthouse for over 20 years. Five minutes from Norfolk's most attractive market town. Ideal for touring the Norfolk Broads and Sandringham, Peddlars Way and nearby local towns. Central heating throughout, en suite available. All rooms have colour TV, tea/coffee making facilities. Fire Certificate and video camera are installed. Ironing facilities available. Full English breakfast. Homely atmosphere. Reductions for children sharing parents' room. Large garden and parking available; undercover for cycles. Small dogs accepted by arrangement.

SWAFFHAM. Mrs Green, "Paget", Main Road, Narborough, King's Lynn PE32 1TE (01760 337734). Private house offering Bed and Breakfast. Lounge available, log fire. TV in bedrooms. Ample parking. Pleasant local river, lakes and rural walks. Situated between the old market town of Swaffham and King's Lynn. Trout and coarse fishing lakes nearby. Pets welcome. SAE please.

THETFORD/WATTON. Kevin and Yvonne Fickling, Rose Cottage, Butters Hall Lane, Thompson, Thetford IP24 1QQ (01953 488104). EATB Listed

COMMENDED. Thompson, situated 10 miles north of Thetford, three miles south of Watton off the A1075, is a quiet village on the edge of Thetford Forest in an area noted for its interesting walks, including Peddars Way. Rose Cottage is a spacious and comfortable house in an acre of ground. Excellent breakfasts and evening meals are served in the oak beamed diningroom. Bedrooms, two large double and one single, have colour TV, radio, tea/coffee facilities. There is central heating throughout. Bed and Breakfast from £18 single, £35 double. Three-course Evening Meal £10. Sorry, no smoking. Pets welcome. We are open throughout the year including Christmas. Business people are welcome.

THURSFORD. Mrs Sylvia Brangwyn, The Heathers, Hindringham Road, Thursford, Fakenham NR21 0BL (01328 878352). Very quiet country location ideal for touring, walking and visiting stately homes (ie., Sandringham, Holkham Hall, Blickling and Felbrigg), bird watching at Cley, Titchwell and Blakeney Point; Walsingham Shrine four miles. There is one ground floor double room with one twin and one double on first floor; all rooms have private en-suite with shaver points, colour TV and tea/coffee making facilities. Full central heating. Christmas and New Year Breaks. Car is essential; ample parking facilities. Bed and Breakfast from £19 to £21 per person per night; optional Evening Meals by prior arrangement.

THURSFORD, near Holt. John and Jenny Duncan, Mulberry Cottage, Green Farm Lane, Thursford Green, Fakenham NR21 0BX (01328 878968). We are situated approximately seven miles from Holt and six miles from Fakenham. The sandy beaches of the North Norfolk coast lie within easy reach. Plenty of walks for the energetic. Accommodation comprises double and single bedrooms (one on ground floor), both are en suite and have tea/coffee making facilities. Log fires in winter to relax by. Wide choice of breakfast. Ample parking. We regret our home is not suitable for children or pets and we would ask guests to kindly refrain from smoking. Bed and Breakfast from £20 per person per night.

WALSINGHAM. The Old Rectory, Waterden, Walsingham NR22 6AT (01328 823298). This charming

rectory is situated in peaceful rural surroundings on the Holkham Estate close to the village of South Creake. Ideally positioned for exploring the North Norfolk coast and countryside and for bird watching, walking, cycling, sailing, golfing and much more. A great place for gourmet restaurants and pubs. Three well appointed en suite rooms are available. A warm welcome awaits guests from your hostess Mrs Pile. Prices on application. This is a non-smoking house. Open all year.

WELLS-NEXT-THE-SEA. Mrs Wickens, The Warren, Warham Road, Wells-next-the-Sea NR23 1NE (01328 710273). Situated a few minutes' walk from the harbour and town, The Warren offers a peaceful location in its own gardens. Two light and airy, centrally heated ground floor en suite bedrooms (one double, one twin) contain the usual facilities. Guests' lounge and conservatory. Full choice of breakfast, vegetarians welcome. Non-smoking. Private parking.

NORFOLK – THE BROADS!

Formed by the flooding of medieval peat diggings, the Broads have a unique quality which attracts thousands of visitors each year. Slow moving waterways are bounded by reed and sedge, and despite the pressures of the modern world are home to rare birds, butterflies and plants. Motor boats and sailing boats can be hired in most towns and villages and there are lots of lively riverbank pubs to round off a day afloat.

WOODTON. Mrs J. Read, George's House, Woodton, Near Bungay NR35 2LZ (01508 482214). This

is a charming late 17th century cottage with a six acre free range egg unit and blacksmith on site. It is situated in the centre of the village, just off the main Norwich to Bungay road. Wonderful holiday area, ideal for touring Norfolk and Suffolk. Historic Norwich, with its castle, cathedral, theatre and good shops is only nine-and-a-half miles, and everyone should find something there to suit them. Sea 18 miles. Guest accommodation comprises three double bedrooms, with washbasins. There is a bathroom and toilet. Dining room and TV lounge. A car is essential to make the most of your holiday, and there is ample parking. The house is open to guests for Bed and Breakfast from £14 per person per night. Evening meal available. SAE please.

NORTHAMPTONSHIRE

KETTERING. Audrey Clarke, Dairy Farm, Cranford St. Andrew, Kettering NN14 4AQ (01536 330273). ❀ ❀ ❀ *COMMENDED.* Enjoy a holiday in a com-

fortable 17th century farmhouse with oak beams and inglenook fireplaces. Four-poster bed now available. Peaceful surroundings, large garden containing ancient circular dovecote. Dairy Farm is a working farm situated in a beautiful Northamptonshire village just off the A14 within easy reach of many places of interest or ideal for a restful holiday. Good farmhouse food and friendly atmosphere. Open all year except Christmas. Children welcome, pets by arrangement. Bed and Breakfast from £20 to £30; Evening Meal £12. Half price for children under 10 years.

PETERBOROUGH. Trudy Dijksterhuis, Lilford Lodge Farm, Barnwell, Oundle, Peterborough PE8 5SA (01832 272230). ❀ ❀ *COMMENDED.* Mixed farm set

in the attractive Nene Valley situated on the A605, three miles south of Oundle and five miles north of the A14. Peterborough and Stamford are within easy reach. Guests stay in the recently converted original 19th century farmhouse. All bedrooms have en suite bathrooms, central heating, radio and tea/coffee making facilities. Comfortable lounge with satellite TV and separate dining room. Coarse fishing available. Children welcome. Bed and Breakfast from £18. Reductions for children. Open all year except Christmas and New Year.

QUINTON. Mrs Margaret Turney, Quinton Green Farm, Quinton NN7 2EG (01604 863685; Fax: 01604 862230). ❀ ❀ The Turney family look forward to

welcoming you to their comfortable, rambling 17th century farmhouse only 10 minutes from Northampton, yet overlooking lovely rolling countryside. We are close to Salcey Forest with its wonderful facilities for walking. M1 Junction 15 is just five minutes away; central Milton Keynes 20 minutes. Children and pets welcome. Open all year. Bed and Breakfast from £20.

NORTHAMPTONSHIRE – WHAT TO DO AND SEE!

Rolling farmland and woods contrasted against industrial towns such as Corby and Kettering, this is what makes up Northamptonshire. The canal centre at Stoke Bruerne, the coloured stone church at Stanford-on-Avon and the country parks at Barnwell and Irchester all make for interesting visits.

THE GLOBE HOTEL

– A Countryside Inn –
Watling Street, Weedon, Northants NN7 4QD
Tel: 01327 340336   Fax: 01327 349058
👑👑👑👑 **Commended   RAC ★★**

Conveniently located three miles west of Junction 16 of the M1, this eighteenth century coaching inn offers attractively furnished and well equipped rooms, all with private bathrooms, colour TV, radio, telephones and tea/coffee making facilities. A comprehensive food operation, OPEN ALL DAY, features home fayre bar meals and value for money à la carte menus. Pies are our speciality. Weedon is centrally located for visiting the many historic places and fascinating market towns in the area also Silverstone Racing Circuit; leisure activities include golf and walking. Weekend Giveaway Breaks – bed and breakfast £21.50 per person per night sharing a double or twin room.

WELFORD. Mrs Susie Bevin, West End Farm, 5 West End, Welford NN6 6HJ (01858 575226). 👑

COMMENDED. This comfortable 1848 farmhouse is set in beautiful countryside. Twin and double rooms both have washbasins and tea-making facilities, double with en suite WC. Guests' sitting room with woodburner and TV. In a quiet village street with four local pubs. Near A50/A14 access, M1 Junction 20. Convenient for Stanford, Lamport, Althorp and Cottesbrook; Naseby Battlefield, Cold Ashby and South Kilworth Golf. On the Jurassic Way. Good holiday or business base. Open all year. Children welcome. Non-smoking. Bed and Breakfast from £16.

NORTHUMBERLAND

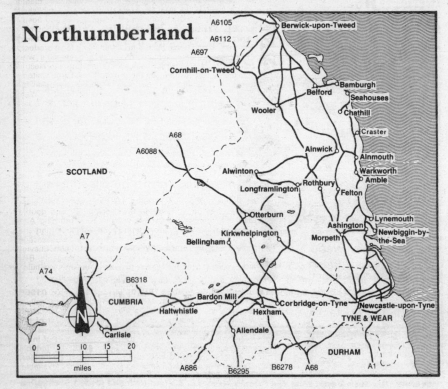

Northumberland

A6105
A6112
A697
Cornhill-on-Tweed
Berwick-upon-Tweed
Bamburgh
Belford
Seahouses
Wooler
Chathill
Craster
A68
A6088
Alnwick
Alnmouth
SCOTLAND
Alwinton
Warkworth
Amble
Rothbury
Longframlington
Felton
Otterburn
Lynemouth
A7
Kirkwhelpington
Ashington
Newbiggin-by-the-Sea
Bellingham
Morpeth
A74
B6318
Bardon Mill
CUMBRIA
Corbridge-on-Tyne
Newcastle-upon-Tyne
Haltwhistle
Hexham
TYNE & WEAR
Carlisle
Allendale
DURHAM
0 5 10 15 20
miles
A686
B6295
B6278
A68
A1

ALLENDALE. Mrs Eileen Ross Finn, Thornley House, Allendale NE47 9NH (01434 683255). ♥ ♥

HIGHLY COMMENDED. Beautiful country house in spacious grounds surrounded by field and woodland, one mile out of Allendale, 10 miles south of Hexham, near Hadrian's Wall. Two large beautifully furnished lounges, one with TV, one with Steinway Grand Piano; three bedrooms all with private facilities, tea makers and home-made biscuits. Marvellous walking country where you don't see anybody. Conducted walks sometimes available. Riding school, golf course nearby. Home baking. Bring your own wine. Packed lunches, vegetarians catered for. Christmas Breaks. Portable TV available. Ample parking. Bed and Breakfast from £18.50. Dinner £11.

ALNMOUTH. Mrs A. Stanton, Mount Pleasant Farm, Alnmouth, Alnwick NE66 3BY (01665 830215). Mount Pleasant is situated on top of a hill on the

outskirts of the seaside village of Alnmouth, with spectacular views of surrounding countryside. We offer fresh air, sea breezes, green fields and beautiful beaches, country roads and peace and quiet. There are two golf courses and a river meanders around the farm with all its bird life. There are also historic castles, Holy Island, the Farnes and the Cheviots to explore. Farmhouse has large rooms, with washbasins, TV, tea making and en suite facilities. Guest bathroom with shower. Ample parking. Terms from £17.50. Self catering accommodation can be booked. Details on request.

PLEASE SEND A STAMPED ADDRESSED ENVELOPE WITH ENQUIRIES

ALNMOUTH. Janice and Norman Edwards, "Westlea", 29 Riverside Road, Alnmouth NE66 2SD (01665 830730). 🕸🕸🕸 *COMMENDED.*

We invite you to relax in the warm, friendly atmosphere of "Westlea" situated at the side of the Aln Estuary. We have an established reputation for providing a high standard of care and hospitality. Guests start the day with a hearty breakfast of numerous choices and in the evening a varied and appetising four-course traditional meal is prepared using local produce. All bedrooms are bright, comfortable and en suite with colour TVs, hot drinks facilities, central heating and electric blankets. Two bedrooms on the ground floor. Large visitors' lounge and diningroom overlooking the estuary. Ideal for exploring castles, Farne Islands, Holy Island, Hadrian's Wall. Fishing, golf, pony trekking, etc within easy reach. Bed and Breakfast from £20; Bed, Breakfast and Evening Meal from £32. Alnwick District Council Hospitality Award 1989/1991/1992. 1994 Award for Overall Contribution to Tourism.

ALNWICK. Mrs Ann Bowden, Roseworth, Alnmouth Road, Alnwick NE66 2PR (01665 603911). 🕸🕸 *HIGHLY COMMENDED.*

A warm Northumbrian welcome awaits you at Roseworth, set in a beautiful situation covered in Virginia creeper and roses. You can enjoy sitting in our large garden. Roseworth is a very clean and comfortable house which is very tastefully decorated to the highest standards. Two en suite rooms, and one with private facilities. All bedrooms have tea trays, colour TV and double glazed windows. Comfortable lounge. Each morning Ann serves a good hearty Northumbrian breakfast to start the day. Alnwick is a good touring area with good, clean beaches four miles to the east and 17 miles north west to the Cheviot Hills. Many castles and good country walks available. Bed and Breakfast from £19. Please telephone for further details.

ALNWICK. The Hotspur Hotel, Bondgate Without, Alnwick NE66 1PR (01665 510101; Fax: 01665 605033). NTB 🕸🕸🕸 **RAC and AA Two Star.**

Originally a coaching inn, The Hotspur is located in the town centre within walking distance of Alnwick Castle, the seat of the Duke of Northumberland. Set between sandy beaches and rolling moorland, surrounded by numerous places of interest, The Hotspur offers a friendly welcome, 23 comfortable en suite bedrooms, a high standard of food and fine ales. Children welcome. Non-smoking accommodation available. Bed and Breakfast rates from £35 per person, reductions for longer stays, half board rates available, excellent rates for children sharing with adults. Telephone for brochure.

ALNWICK. Mrs J.W. Bowden, "Anvil-Kirk", 8 South Charlton Village, Alnwick NE66 2NA (01665 579324).

A very characterful cottage offering a friendly, homely atmosphere and a welcome to match. Former Smithy built in 1771, completely modernised in 1974, affording very comfortable accommodation comprising a double bedroom and one twin bedded room with washbasin, shower and shaver points. Open wood-burning fire in communal lounge. Full English Breakfast. Good value meals at local pubs. A peaceful village surrounded by farmland plus moorland walks with views of the Cheviot Hills, Bamburgh and Dunstanburgh Castles and, of course, our lovely clean beaches. Three-quarters of a mile from the A1 and very easy to locate. Pets welcome. Ample parking. Bed and Breakfast terms from £16 to £18. Also available, a 39 ft. Residential Caravan for hire weekly from £165 to £195. Please phone for details.

NORTHUMBERLAND – BORDER COUNTRY!

You cannot go any further north and remain in England! There is much outstanding scenery, both inland and on the coast, and a host of interesting places to visit. Border Forest Park has everything you would expect, plus many interesting Roman remains. There are also remains at Housesteads and other places of interest include Lindisfarne, the "conserved" village of Blanchland, Hexham, Heatherslaw Mill and Craster.

ALNWICK. Charlton House, 2 Aydon Gardens, South Road, Alnwick NE66 2NT (01665 605185).

🐦🐦🐦 *HIGHLY COMMENDED.* Beautiful Victorian town house where guests are always welcomed in a friendly, relaxed, informal atmosphere. There is a real flair for decor with antiques, home-made patchwork quilts and excellent home cooking. Two double, one twin, one family and one single bedrooms have en suite facilities and are complete with colour TV and hospitality trays. Comfortable guests' lounge with satellite TV. We offer a choice of breakfast — full English, Continental, vegetarian, "healthy option", local Craster kippers (when in season), various crepes. We also serve evening meals if required. Alnwick District Council "Lionheart Award" Winners (past three years). Bed and Breakfast from £18 per person. Information leaflet available.

ALNWICK. Mrs B. Gaines, Crosshills House, 40 Blakelaw Road, Alnwick NE66 1BA (01665 602518).

🐦🐦 *HIGHLY COMMENDED.* Come and join us at Crosshills for your stay in historic Northumberland. A friendly family-run house situated in a quiet area near golf course and only a short walk into town. We have two double rooms and one twin room, all en-suite and having colour TV and tea/coffee making facilities. Twin room has balcony with a beautiful view of coast and countryside. Parking. Sorry, no dogs. Bed and Breakfast from £19 per person. Parking available.

BELFORD. Jan and David Thompson, The Cott, Belford NE70 7HZ (01668 213233).

🐦 *COMMEN-DED.* The Cott is situated on the A1 outside the village of Warenford, 12 miles north of the market town of Alnwick. The Cott consists of two cottages, owners living in one, the other — "Etive" — converted into four comfortable bedrooms, two family/twin and two double rooms, all with washbasins, tea/coffee, central heating and double glazing. All rooms are on ground level with use of gardens and private car park. We are an ideal base for exploring the beautiful Northumberland coast or countryside, five miles from Bamburgh and Seahouses. Golf courses nearby. Pets welcome. Rates from £12 to £17 for Bed and Breakfast; Evening Meal (optional) £9.

BELSAY (3 miles). Mrs Kath Fearns, Bounder House, Belsay, Newcastle-upon-Tyne NE20 0JR (01661 881267).

Stone built farmhouse situated in beautiful Northumbrian countryside off A696 Newcastle/Edinburgh road. Half a mile north of Belsay, turn right onto B6309, follow B&B sign; 15 minutes from Newcastle Airport. Ideally situated for touring Northumberland and the Borders or convenient overnight stop en route for Scotland. Two double rooms (en suite), a family room and a twin room, all with colour TV and tea/coffee facilities. Pets welcome. Open all year round. Terms from £18 per person.

CORBRIDGE. Mr and Mrs F.J. Matthews, The Hayes, Newcastle Road, Corbridge NE45 5LP (01434 632010).

❦ Spacious, attractive stone-built guesthouse set in seven acres of grounds. Single, double, twin, family bedrooms. Lounge and dining rooms. Open 11 months of the year. Bed and Breakfast from £16. Children's reductions. Stair lift for disabled guests. Also self catering properties — three cottages, flat and caravan. Awarded two Farm Holiday Guide Diplomas. Car parking. For brochure or booking SAE/phone.

CORBRIDGE. Mrs Ann Hodgson, Clive House, Appletree Lane, Corbridge NE45 5DN (01434 632617).

❦ ❦ *HIGHLY COMMENDED.* Built in 1840 as the village school, Clive House has been tastefully converted to luxurious Bed and Breakfast accommodation. The three bedrooms all have en suite facilities, tea/coffee, colour TV and telephone. The four-poster bedroom with its own sitting area is particularly popular. In the centre of Hadrian's Wall country, historic Corbridge is an ideal base for exploring Northumberland and is a convenient break between York and Edinburgh. Clive House is two minutes' walk from the village centre with its wide range of restaurants and speciality shops. Bed and Breakfast all year from £20 per night. Car parking. No smoking.

EMBLETON. Mr and Mrs K. Robson, Brunton House, Brunton, Near Embleton, Alnwick NE66 3HQ (01665 589238).

❦ ❦ *COMMENDED.* Elegant country house set in large gardens, ideally situated close to miles of clean sandy beaches and the unspoilt and beautiful Cheviot Hills. Excellent centre for walking, golfing, fishing, birdwatching and visiting the numerous castles and stately homes in the area. The accommodation is spacious and comfortable, with twin, double and single rooms, some of which are en suite; a pleasant dining room and two lounges, one for those who wish to smoke. Guests can look forward to enjoying good home cooking and a warm welcome. Open all year, except Christmas and New Year. Bed and Breakfast from £17; Evening Meal by arrangement. Reduction for children under 12 years.

FORD VILLAGE. Mrs Maureen A. Burton, The Estate House, Ford, Berwick-upon-Tweed TD15 2QG (Tel & Fax: 01890 820414).

❦ ❦ *HIGHLY COMMENDED.* Very comfortable and peaceful accommodation for non-smoking guests in three lovely bedrooms, all with that extra personal touch and two with en suite bathrooms. Maureen and John Burton are warm, welcoming hosts who enjoy sharing their charming home with their many guests. In addition to a full breakfast, Maureen provides her speciality of homemade wholemeal and granary bread. If you are lucky John may entertain you with his superb organ playing in the drawing room. Children over 12 years welcome. Bed and Breakfast from £20 to £25 per person per night; Dinner (by arrangement) £14. Open all year.

PUBLISHER'S NOTE

HADRIAN'S WALL. Mr Mark Chaplin, Hadrian Lodge, Hindshield Moss, North Road, Haydon Bridge, Hexham NE47 6NF (01434 688688). Hadrian Lodge is a quality conversion of a stone-built hunting and fishing lodge into Bed and Breakfast and Self Catering accommodation. Set in 18 acres of idyllic Northumberland countryside, Hadrian Lodge provides a friendly social atmosphere with single, twin, double and family rooms; some en suite available. Two miles from the most popular attractions — Hadrian's Wall, Housesteads and Vindolanda Museum. Hadrian Lodge is the ideal base from which to explore the beauty and history of the Hadrian's Wall area and the North Pennines. Licensed lounge/bar. Ample parking. Trout fishing in our well stocked private lake. We offer a high standard of accommodation and service. Bed and Breakfast from £10. Find us two miles north of Haydon Bridge.

HADRIAN'S WALL. Mrs Jean Wanless, Craws Nest, East Twice Brewed, Bardon Mill, Hexham NE47 7AL (01434 344348). ❦ Converted farm house with spectacular views, situated quarter of a mile from Hadrian's Wall, very near to Housesteads and Vindolana. We are just off the B6318 road, four miles from Haltwhistle and two and a half miles from Bardon Mill. Accommodation available in one twin and two family bedrooms. Children welcome. Bed and Breakfast from £16. Customer Choice Winner 1992.

HAYDON BRIDGE. Geeswood House, Whittis Road, Haydon Bridge NE47 6AQ (01434 684220). ❦ *HIGHLY COMMENDED.* John and Doreen Easton's home, a comfortable early Victorian Country house, near to Hadrian's Wall and many other attractions, has a pleasant informal atmosphere, log fire, lovely views and garden. One double and two twin bedrooms. Good food including home made bread; dinner optional (BYO wine!). No smoking. No children under 10 years. Good touring centre for Durham, Beamish Museum, Metro Centre, Wallington, Cragside. Bed and Breakfast from £17.50; Dinner £10.50. Three-night breaks £78. Recommended by "Which?" Good B&B Guide.

HEXHAM. Mrs D.A. Theobald, Dukeslea, 32 Shaws Park, Hexham NE46 3BJ (01434 602947). ❦❦ *HIGHLY COMMENDED.* AA QQQ Recommended. Dukeslea is an unusual modern detached family home situated in a quiet position overlooking Hexham Golf Course, with private parking. High standards are maintained throughout the tasteful guest accommodation conveniently located on the ground floor. Both comfortable double en suite rooms have central heating, tea/coffee making facilities, hair dryers and radio/alarms. Relax and enjoy excellent breakfasts served in the cosy dining/TV lounge. Approximately one mile from station and town centre. Ideal base for exploring Hexham and its Abbey, Hadrian's Wall, Kielder, Beamish Museum and Gateshead Metro Centre. Totally non-smoking establishment. Open all year. Prices from £17. Brochure on request.

HEXHAM. Mrs E. Robson, 3 Woodlands, Hexham NE46 1HT (01434 603370). Large Edwardian house, central for visiting the Roman Wall and Kielder. Lots of golf courses in the area, from municipal to championship standard. Three minutes' walk from town centre, 20 minutes from Airport and Newcastle. One double room en suite from £18; one twin, two singles all with colour TV and tray service £16 per person per night. No smoking.

HEXHAM. Patricia M. Henderson, Riverside, Mickley, Stocksfield NE43 7DF (01661 842887).

NTB/ETB Listed. Spacious country house in large attractive gardens, reached by private level crossing. Peaceful riverside location for non-smoking country lovers, yet only 20 minutes from Hexham and Metro Centre. Close to A68 route to Scotland and the South. Ideal centre for visiting Roman Wall, Beamish, Northumberland coast and Durham Cathedral. Located half a mile from A695 past Thomas Bewick Museum, down quiet country lane. Take a stroll along the riverside path from the garden gate while your breakfast cooks on the wood stove, or plan your day using wall-chart, maps and literature. TV. Tea/coffee making facilities. Bed and Breakfast from £17. Proprietor holds award in Guest House Management.

HEXHAM. Mrs Ruby Keenleyside, Struthers Farm, Catton, Allendale, Hexham NE47 9LP (01434 683580). ☙☙ COMMENDED. Struthers Farm offers a warm welcome in the heart of England with many splendid local walks from the farm itself. Panoramic views. Double/twin rooms, en suite, central heating. Good farmhouse cooking. Ample safe parking. Come and share our home and enjoy beautiful countryside. Children welcome, pets by arrangement. Open all year. Bed and Breakfast from £16.50; Evening Meal from £8.50. Farm Holiday Bureau Member, Tourist Board inspected.

HEXHAM. Mrs E. Courage, Rye Hill Farm, Slaley, Hexham NE47 0AH (01434 673259; Fax: 01434 673608). ☙☙☙ COMMENDED. This is a 300-year-old stone farmhouse set in its own 30 acres of rural Tynedale. Rye Hill Farm offers you the freedom to enjoy the pleasures of Northumberland throughout the year while living comfortably in the pleasant family atmosphere of a cosy farmhouse adapted especially to receive holidaymakers. Family, double and single rooms, all with colour TV, hot-beverage facilities and bathrooms en-suite. Full English Breakfast, three-course Evening Meal (optional); table licence. There is even room for your caravan if you prefer not to live in. Well-mannered children and pets are more than welcome. Terms for Bed and Breakfast from £20 to £24. Brochure available. AA QQQ.

HEXHAM near. Mrs Doreen Cole, Hillcrest House, Barrasford, Hexham NE48 4BY (01434 681426). ☙☙☙ HIGHLY COMMENDED. Hillcrest House has been specifically extended to provide a high standard of accommodation with a homely, comfortable atmosphere. One family, one double, one twin and one single rooms, all with en-suite shower rooms, colour TV and tea/coffee making facilities. Evening Meal optional; packed lunches on request. Comfortable lounge; separate tables in diningroom. Residential licence. Situated seven miles from historic Hexham in beautiful North Tyne Valley. Ideal for touring Hadrian's Wall and within easy distance of Kielder, the Borders, Newcastle, and Gateshead Metro Centre. Car essential. Bed and Breakfast from £15 Single, £30 Double; Evening Meal £7.

KIELDER WATER by. The Pheasant Inn, Stannersburn, Falstone, Hexham NE48 1DD (01434 240382). ☙☙☙ COMMENDED. The Pheasant Inn is set in the Northumberland National Park and is everything a country inn should be. Originally a farm, it is nearly four centuries old, with stone walls and low beams. It became a staging post for mail and tax collection, but has since developed into a welcome and homely oasis to accommodate tourists and locals alike. The Barn and Hemmel now house 10 delightfully appointed bedrooms all of which have en suite facilities. There are two bars serving bar meals at lunchtime and in the evenings and the restaurant is open at night. Traditional, freshly prepared food. Please write, or telephone, for our full colour brochure.

PONTELAND near. Mr and Mrs Edward Trevelyan, Dalton House, Dalton, Newcastle-upon-Tyne NE18 0AA (01661 886225).

🐾🐾 We offer our visitors a warm welcome and a high standard of accommodation in this attractive Georgian house, situated in the peaceful little village of Dalton, near Ponteland on the A696. Ideal for touring Northumberland and exploring Hadrian's Wall, Border castles and glorious countryside and coastline. Newcastle, Morpeth and the Airport are within an easy 30-minute drive: this is a convenient place to stay out of town. Bed and Breakfast from £17.50 per person including bedtime drink; Evening Meal by arrangement from £10; light snacks £5. Excellent home cooking, using own produce when available. Children over 12 welcome. Sorry, no pets. Non-smokers preferred. Open May to October. Directions: four miles from Ponteland A696 follow signs to Dalton.

WARKWORTH. John and Edith Howliston, North Cottage, Birling, Warkworth NE65 0XS (01665 711263).

🐾🐾 *HIGHLY COMMENDED.* Situated on the outskirts of the historic coastal village of Warkworth, we are an ideal base from which to explore Northumberland with its superb beaches and castles. We have four comfortable, well furnished no-smoking rooms — two double and one twin-bedded rooms en suite, and one single with washbasin; all have colour TV. All bedrooms have hospitality trays, central heating and electric overblankets and all are on ground floor. There is of course a bathroom with shower, and a sitting-room with cheery gas fire and colour TV. A full breakfast is served in the diningroom and afternoon tea is served (free of charge) with home-made cakes/biscuits. Large well kept garden and water garden. Warkworth has its own castle, river, golf course and beautiful sandy beaches. Bed and Breakfast from £18. Weekly rates from £118. AA Recommended QQQ, RAC Acclaimed.

WARKWORTH. Mo and Brian Halliday, Beck 'n' Call Cottage, Warkworth NE65 0XS (01665 711653).

🐾🐾 *HIGHLY COMMENDED.* This traditional country cottage is set in beautiful terraced gardens with a stream and is only five minutes' walk to the village, castle, river walks and sandy beaches. The accommodation is comfortably furnished and includes two double rooms and one family room. All on ground floor with washbasins, shaver points, colour TV, tea/coffee making facilities and heating; en suite available. Residents' lounge. Warkworth makes an ideal base from which to explore rural Northumberland and the Borders with their unspoilt beauty and historic interest. Bed and Breakfast from £18. Children welcome, reduced rates. Non-smokers. Private parking. Colour brochure available. Open all year.

WARKWORTH. Mrs Sheila Percival, Roxbro House, 5 Castle Terrace, Warkworth NE65 0UP (01665 711416). 🐾 A small family guest house overlooking historic Warkworth Castle, and in the centre of this unspoilt village. Half a mile from sandy beach in a designated Area of Outstanding Natural Beauty. Central for touring Northumberland. Plenty of eating places within walking distance. The accommodation is comfortable and includes one family room and two double rooms. All have private shower and washbasin, are centrally heated and have locks on the doors. There is a lounge with TV, and tea/coffee is available. Open all year. Bed and Breakfast from £16, reduced rates for children. Non-smokers only.

WOOLER. Mr Terry Gilbert, Winton House, 39 Glendale Road, Wooler NE71 6DL (01668 281362).

🐾🐾 *COMMENDED.* Situated in a quiet street in Wooler, an attractive Edwardian house offering comfortable and very spacious accommodation. One twin and two double bedrooms, all with washbasins, TV and tea/coffee making facilities, shower room and separate luxury bathroom. Full English or vegetarian breakfast served in the guest dining room/lounge. Ideally situated for walking in the north Cheviot Hills or exploring the English and Scottish Borders with their historically rich mix of castles, abbeys and towns; Holy Island, the Farne Islands and miles of sandy beaches. Pony trekking, fishing, gliding and golf also available. Open March to October. Bed and Breakfast from £16. Non-smoking throughout.

WOOLER. Mrs J. Allan, Loreto Guest House, 1 Ryecroft Way, Wooler NE71 6BW (01668 281350). A

charming early Georgian house set in its own grounds, occupying a central position in the North Northumberland town of Wooler. For those who wish to explore old ruins, discover wildlife, sample superb beaches, walk through forests or over hills and moors, North Northumberland offers all of these in abundance. All rooms are tastefully decorated and have en suite facilities; guests' lounge with colour TV, cocktail bar. We are well known for our excellent cuisine and our elegant dining room with choice of menus at breakfast and evening meal offers charming surroundings for diners. Licensed. Please telephone, or write, for tariff and brochure.

NOTTINGHAMSHIRE

BURTON JOYCE. Mrs V. Baker, Willow House, 12 Willow Wong, Burton Joyce, Nottingham NG14 5FD (0115 931 2070). A large period house (1857) in quiet village location yet only four miles from city. Attractive, interesting accommodation with authentic Victorian ambience. Bright, clean rooms with tea/coffee facilities, TVs. Walking distance of beautiful stretch of River Trent (fishing). Ideally situated for Holme Pierrepont International Watersports Centre; golf course; Trent Bridge (cricket); Sherwood Forest (Robin Hood Centre) and the unspoiled historic town of Southwell with its Minster and Racecourse. Good local eating. Evening Meal by arrangement. Private parking. From £16 per person per night. Reduced rates for children. Please phone first for directions.

COTGRAVE. Mrs S.V.M. Herrick, Jerico Farm, Fosse Way, Cotgrave NG12 3HG (01949 81733).

🐾 🐾 *COMMENDED.* Jerico Farm is situated off the Fosse Way (A46) between Newark and Leicester, eight miles from Nottingham. Accommodation in attractive farmhouse comprises twin/double bedded rooms, one en-suite, all with washbasins, shaver points, tea/coffee making and heating. Guests have their own comfortable sitting/dining room with colour TV and cosy woodburner. Good farmhouse breakfast. Jerico overlooks the Nottinghamshire Wolds and is on the edge of the Vale of Belvoir, within easy reach of Nottingham City, its universities, sports venues and tourist sites. Non-smoking household. Open all year. Bed and Breakfast from £17. Please ring for brochure.

GONALSTON. Mr and Mrs R.C. Smith, Hall Farm, Gonalston NG14 7JA (01159 663112; Fax:

01159 9664844). 🐾 *COMMENDED.* This rambling old 17th century farmhouse stands in the centre of this unspoilt village surrounded by a beautiful cottage garden complete with tennis court and swimming pool. The Smiths have brought up their family here, and the reception rooms and bedrooms have a lived in feel to them — family photographs hang beside fine original paintings including those of Rosie Smith. Flagged and oak floors are covered with rugs and the polished carved furniture looks thoroughly at home with open fires and beamed ceilings. Although there is a formal dining room guests generally find their way to the large kitchen and eat next to the Aga. Three bedrooms, including one family room, with tea/coffee facilities. Children are welcome but sorry, we cannot accept pets or smoking upstairs. Please write or telephone for further details.

NOTTINGHAMSHIRE – ROBIN HOOD COUNTRY!

Sherwood Forest is now a country park and is one of Nottinghamshire's leading attractions. This county is rich in terms of its parks. There are others at Burntstump, Clumber, Holme Pierrepont and Rufford. Nottingham itself is a surprisingly attractive city.

MANSFIELD. John and Margaret Bennett, Bridleways Guest House and Holiday Homes, Newlands Road, Forest Town, Mansfield NG19 0HU (01623 635725).

Situated in glorious countryside and close to Sherwood Forest, Clumber Park, Newstead Abbey and Rufford Nature Reserve. John and Margaret Bennett invite you to enjoy the hospitality of their house on peaceful farmland. Our bed and breakfast offers wonderful value from £15 per person and we make sure the traditional meal gets your day off to a good start. Evening meals are available should you require them. Comfortable rooms, all en suite and with TV; guests' lounge with colour TV and tea/coffee making facilities. Alternatively, we have three static caravans with self-contained bedrooms, hot and cold water; a four-bedroomed detached house sleeping seven, and a cottage which is part of a barn conversion and has one bedroom plus lounge/bedsit which will sleep four. Ample safe parking. Children's play area. We look forward to making your holiday enjoyable.

MANSFIELD. Mrs L. Palmer, Boon Hills Farm, Nether Langwith, Mansfield NG20 9JQ (01623 743862).

This is a stone-built farmhouse, standing 300 yards back from A632 on edge of village. It is on a 155-acre mixed farm with dogs, cats, goats, chicks, calves. Situated on the edge of Sherwood Forest, six miles from Visitors' Centre, eight miles from M1, 10 miles from A1. Chatsworth House, Newstead Abbey, Hardwick Hall and Creswell Crags all within easy reach. Two double (one twin-bedded) rooms and one family room; bathroom; toilet; fitted carpets throughout. Open fires. Background central heating for comfort all year round. Large sittingroom/diningroom with colour TV. Children welcome, cot and babysitting. Pets allowed. Car essential — parking. Bed and Breakfast from £15 per night, which includes bedtime drink. Evening Meal available nearby. Non-smokers only. Rates reduced for children. Open March to October inclusive.

NEWARK. Ken and Margaret Berry, Lockwell House Guest House, Lockwell Hill, Farnsfield, Newark NG22 8JG (01623 883067).

Set in 25 acres with 10 acres of woodland and situated on the edge of Sherwood Forest near Rufford Park on the A614, we are within easy reach of Nottingham, Newark, Mansfield, Worksop and all local country parks and tourist attractions. Small family-run Bed and Breakfast offering friendly service and comfort. All bedrooms are en suite and have tea/coffee making facilities, hair dryers, etc. TV room. Full English breakfast. Tariff: Double room (twin/double bed) £36; Double room (single occupancy) £20; Family room (double and single beds) £50. Reductions for children. Brochure available.

NOTTINGHAM. Mrs J. Buck, Yew Tree Grange, 2 Nethergate, Clifton Village, Nottingham NG11 8NL (0115 984 7562).

Yew Tree Grange is a Georgian residence of great charm and character located five miles from the M1 Junction 24. The house is situated in the quiet rural setting of Clifton Village, only 10 minutes from the City Centre. Accommodation includes single, twin and family bedrooms, some with en suite facilities. There is ample car parking and a mature garden with duck pond. Ideally located for tourists visiting Robin Hood country or for businessmen stopping overnight. Bed and Breakfast from £18 per person per night with reduced rates for small children. Evening Meals by arrangement. A non-smoking establishment.

NOTTINGHAM/CLIFTON VILLAGE. Alan and Jane Haymes, Camelia House, 76 Village Road, Clifton Village, Nottingham NG11 8NE (0115 9211653). A quiet picturesque village only three miles from city centre, backing onto the River Trent with riverside wooded walks. Our new traditionally built house in mature setting is double glazed, has central heating and private parking. We offer double, twin and single rooms with colour TV and tea/coffee making facilities. Continental breakfast consisting of fruit juice, cereals, grapefruit, prunes, yoghurt, toast, jams, marmalade, warm rolls, cheeses, tea and coffee. Our rates are from £17.50 per night. We aim to provide a warm welcoming atmosphere at all times.

PLEASE SEND A STAMPED ADDRESSED ENVELOPE WITH ENQUIRIES

SOUTHWELL. Mrs Erica Henson, Archway House, Kirklington, Newark NG22 8NX (01636 812070;

Fax: 01636 812200). This atmospheric Edwardian country house is set in 40 acres of parkland with memorable views, gardens and woodland. Located between A1 and M1, three miles north of Southwell with its beautiful Minster and all-weather race course. Close to Sherwood Forest and a wealth of walks and golf courses. Accommodation comprises two double rooms, one with private bathroom, the other with shared bathroom; one twin-bedded room with en suite bath. No smoking in bedrooms. Colour TV and tea/coffee facilities in all rooms. Separate drawing room for guests' exclusive use. Bed and Breakfast from £17.50 to £19.50 pp; Dinner (if ordered in advance) £12.50. Children welcome. Tennis, croquet, snooker and four practice golf holes. Advance booking please.

STANTON-ON-THE-WOLDS. Mrs Val Moffat, Laurel Farm, Browns Lane, Stanton-on-the-Wolds NG12 5BL (0115 937 3488). Laurel Farm is an old farmhouse set in approximately four acres standing on a lane off the main A606. Rooms are spacious, all have shower and washbasin with three having full private facilities; all have colour TV and tea/coffee making. There are pet horses, sheep, cats and dogs and our own free range hens. Children are welcome in the large family room, at reduced rates. Babysitting free. Large garden with unusual plants, pond and bog area. Dogs housed in the stables. All day access to rooms. Evening meals by prior arrangement. Bed and Breakfast from £16 to £20. No smoking in the house.

UPPER BROUGHTON. Mrs Hilary Dowson, Sulney Fields, Colonel's Lane, Upper Broughton,

Melton Mowbray LE14 3BD (Tel & Fax: 01664 822204). Large country house in quiet position with magnificent views across the Vale of Belvoir. Easy access to Nottingham, Leicester, Loughborough and Melton Mowbray. Centrally placed for day trips to York, Cambridge, Warwick, Chatsworth and the Peak District. Spacious accommodation in twin/double rooms, most of which have private bathrooms and all have tea/coffee making facilities. Large sitting room with TV for guests' use. Bacon and sausages for breakfast come from the Award winning butcher in the village. Good pub/restaurant within walking distance which serves food every evening. Bed and Breakfast from £16 per person.

OXFORDSHIRE

BANBURY. Mrs E.J. Lee, The Mill Barn, Lower Tadmarton, Banbury OX15 5SU (01295 780349). Tadmarton is a small village three miles south-west of Banbury. The Mill, no longer working, was originally water-powered and the stream lies adjacent to the house. The Mill Barn has been tastefully converted, retaining many beams and exposed stone walls and with all the amenities a modern house can offer. Two spacious en-suite bedrooms, one downstairs, are available to guests in this comfortable family house. Base yourself here and visit Stratford, Oxford, Woodstock and the Cotswolds, knowing you are never further than an hour's drive away. Open all year round for Bed and Breakfast from £17.50. Reductions for children. Weekly terms available.

BANBURY. Mrs Rosemary Cannon, High Acres Farm, Great Bourton, Banbury OX17 1RL (01295 750217). New Farmhouse situated on edge of village off A423 Southam Road, three miles north of Banbury overlooking the beautiful Cherwell Valley. Ideally situated for touring Cotswolds, Stratford, Warwick, Oxford, Blenheim Palace. Pub in village serving evening meals Tuesdays to Saturdays. Very comfortable accommodation comprising one twin room, one family room (one double and one single bed). Tea/coffee facilities, hair dryers; central heating; shower room with electric shower; guests' sittingroom with colour TV. All rooms fully carpeted. Non-smoking. Parking. Bed and Breakfast from £16. Child under 10 sharing family room £10. Sorry, no pets. A warm welcome awaits you.

BLADON near. Tom and Carol Ellis, Wynford Guest House, 79 Main Road, Long Hanborough, Woodstock OX7 2JX (01993 881402; Fax: 01993 883661). Tourist Board Listed. Wynford Guest House is situated in the village of Long Hanborough only a mile from Bladon, final resting place of Sir Winston Churchill, and three miles from famous Woodstock and Blenheim Palace. The city of Oxford is twelve miles away and the Cotswolds are on our doorstep. We offer personal service, excellent food and comfortable accommodation consisting of a family room en-suite, with colour TV, and double and twin rooms; all have tea/coffee making facilities. Excellent pubs and restaurants less than five minutes' walk. Bed and Breakfast from £19; Evening Meal from £9. Open all year.

CHARLBURY. Mr and Mrs G. Widdows, Banbury Hill Farm, Enstone Road, Charlbury OX7 3JH (01608 810314; Fax: 01608 811891). Banbury Hill Farm offers Bed and Breakfast in Cotswold stone farmhouse with extensive views across Evenlode Valley. Comfortable rooms with tea/coffee and colour TVs. Ideal touring centre for Blenheim Palace, Oxford and Cotswolds. Ample parking. Terms: single from £16 to £25; double from £16 to £20 per person. Brochure available.

Banbury Hill Farm

COMBE. Mrs Rosemary Fox, Mayfield Cottage, West End, Combe, Witney OX8 8NP (01993 898298). ETB Listed *HIGHLY COMMENDED.* Guests are assured of a warm welcome in our home, a delightful Cotswold stone cottage with oak beams and inglenooks, yet providing all home comforts. Combe, a small unspoilt village, is an ideal base for touring the Cotswolds with Blenheim Palace and Woodstock only 10 minutes by car. There are lovely walks and many good pubs and restaurants in the area. Our accommodation comprises a single, a twin and a double room, all furnished in cottage style with bathroom exclusively for guests' use. There is also a comfortable lounge. Children over 12 years welcome. Sorry, no pets. Bed and Breakfast from £16.

FARINGDON (Oxon). Mr D. Barnard, Bowling Green Farm, Stanford Road, Faringdon, Oxfordshire SN7 8EZ (01367 240229; Fax: 01367 242568). ❀ ❀

Attractive 18th century period farmhouse offering 20th century comfort, situated in the Vale of White Horse, just one mile south of Faringdon on the A417. Easy access to the M4 Exit 13 for Heathrow Airport. An ideal place to stay for a day or longer. This is a working farm of cattle and horse breeding, poultry and ducks. Large twin-bedded/family room (en suite) on ground floor. All bedrooms have colour TV, tea/coffee making facilities and full central heating throughout. Ideal area for riding, golf, fishing and walking the Ridgeway. Interesting places to visit include Oxford, Bath, Windsor, Burford, Henley-on-Thames, Blenheim Palace and the Cotswolds. Open all year. Member of Farm Holiday Bureau.

FREELAND. Mrs B.B. Taphouse, Wrestlers Mead, 35 Wroslyn Road, Freeland, Oxford OX7 2HJ (01993 882003). A warm welcome awaits you at the home of the Taphouses. We are conveniently located for Blenheim Palace (10 minutes), Oxford (20 minutes), and the Cotswolds (25 minutes). Accommodation comprises one double and one single room, both with washbasins and at ground level. Our first floor family room has its own en-suite shower room with washbasin and toilet. The double and the family rooms each have a colour television. Cot, highchair and babysitting service available. Pets by arrangement. No hidden extras. Bed and Breakfast from £17.

HENLEY-ON-THAMES. Mrs Liz Roach, The Old Bakery, Skirmett, Near Henley-on-Thames RG9 6TD (01491 638309). This welcoming family house is situated on the site of an old bakery, seven miles from Henley-on-Thames and Marlow; half an hour from Heathrow and Oxford; one hour from London. It is in the Hambleden Valley in the beautiful Chilterns, with many excellent pubs selling good food. Riding school nearby; beautiful walking country. Two double rooms with TV, one twin-bedded and two single rooms; two bathrooms. Open all year. Parking for five cars (car essential). Children and pets welcome. Bed and Breakfast from £18 to £21 single; £38 to £42 double.

HENLEY-ON-THAMES. Mrs K. Bridekirk, The Laurels, 107 St. Marks Road, Henley-on-Thames RG9 1LP (01491 572982). A large comfortable house in a quiet location near town and River Thames. Very good for short breaks and visits to Oxford, Windsor and London, and river trips along the famous Henley Regatta course. Plenty of places to eat. Good area for walking. Easy to get to Heathrow. All rooms have colour TV, tea/coffee making facilities, washbasin. En suite available. Full central heating. Full English breakfast. Children under three years FREE, under 12 years half price. Singles from £20, double/twin from £35. Regret no dogs. Good parking facilities. Open all year.

OXFORDSHIRE – CHILTERNS, COTSWOLDS AND COLLEGES!
Many fine days can be spent studying Oxford's architecture – both old and new. Other interesting pastimes might include trips to Banbury and Europe's biggest cattle market, the Cotswold Wildlife Park near Burford, the Rollright Stones near Chipping Norton and the Vale of the White Horse at Uffington.

MILTON-UNDER-WYCHWOOD. Mrs Wendy Jones, Hillborough House, The Green, Milton-under-Wychwood OX7 6JH (01993 830501; Fax: 01993 832005). AA QQQQ Selected — Awarded Best Newcomer 1989. Elegant Victorian house set deep in the Evenlode Valley facing the village green in this delightful Cotswold village. The bedrooms are all en suite, warm and spacious; some are in an annexe of a cottage character across the courtyard from the main house. A guests' lounge with comfy sofas, and secluded, walled, lawned gardens make for a relaxing stay. Dinner may be arranged for you in our adjoining Willows Restaurant from Tuesday to Saturday. The Cotswolds are renowned for good walks and picturesque villages. Explore Shakespeare's Stratford, Warwick and Leamington Spa or the University City of Oxford. Tariff: Double £26 per person Tuesday to Saturday, £20 per person Sunday to Monday. Reductions for three nights or more.

MINSTER LOVELL. Mrs Katherine Brown, Hill Grove Farm, Crawley Road, Minster Lovell OX8 5NA (01993 703120; Fax: 01993 700528). 🐾🐾 *HIGHLY COMMENDED.* Hill Grove is a mixed family-run 300 acre working farm situated in an attractive rural setting overlooking the Windrush Valley. Ideally positioned for driving to Oxford, Blenheim Palace, Witney (Farm Museum) and Burford (renowned as the Gateway to the Cotswolds and for its splendid Wildlife Park). New golf course one mile. Hearty breakfasts, friendly atmosphere. One double/private shower, one twin/double en suite. Children welcome. Open all year except Christmas. Bed and Breakfast from £19. AA Listed.

OXFORD. Ascot House, 283 Iffley Road, Oxford OX4 4AQ (01865 240259/727669; Fax: 01865 727669). RAC Highly Acclaimed. Ascot House is a pretty Victorian house offering six beautifully refurbished en suite rooms affording every comfort to couples, families, business people and tourists. The River Thames and the University boathouses are within a five minute walk and a gentle 15 minute stroll along the towpath takes you into the centre of the city, via Christchurch Meadows and the Cathedral. The en suite rooms have colour TV, radio alarm, hair dryer, tea/coffee making facilities, fridge and direct-dial telephone. Single from £30, double from £40.

OXFORD. Mrs Gwen Absolom, The Old Post Office, 11 Church Road, Sandford-on-Thames, Oxford OX4 4XZ (01865 777213). A friendly welcome and comfortable accommodation await you in our centrally heated 17th century home. Situated in a Thameside village only four miles from the centre of Oxford (bus stop nearby); river and pub serving good food only five minutes' walk away. Accommodation offered in one double and one twin room, both en suite with colour TV and drinks making facilities; guests' sitting room. Regret no pets. No smoking. Bed and Breakfast from £17.50 per person.

OXFORD. Mr and Mrs L. Price, Arden Lodge, 34 Sunderland Avenue (off Banbury Road), Oxford OX2 8DX (01865 552076; 014020 68697). Modern detached house in select part of Oxford, within easy reach of Oxford Centre. Excellent position for Blenheim Palace and for touring Cotswolds, Stratford, Warwick, etc. Close to river, parks, country inns and golf course. Easy access to London. All rooms have tea/coffee making and private facilities. Parking. Bed and Breakfast from £20 per person per night.

OXFORD. Mr Stratford, The Bungalow, Cherwell Farm, Mill Lane, Old Marston, Oxford OX3 0QF (01865 557171). ETB Listed. Modern bungalow on five acres set in countryside but only three miles from the city centre. Offering comfortable accommodation and serving traditional breakfast. Colour TV, tea/coffee facilities in all rooms. Private parking. Non-smoking. Not on bus route. Bed and Breakfast from £18 to £22.50.

PLEASE SEND A STAMPED ADDRESSED ENVELOPE WITH ENQUIRIES

SOULDERN. Toddy and Clive Hamilton-Gould, Tower Fields, Tusmore Road, Near Souldern, Bicester OX6 9HY (01869 346554; Fax: 01869 345157). 🐾🐾 *COMMENDED.* Tower Fields is in an unspoilt

elevated position with outstanding views, situated half a mile from the village of Souldern. A recently renovated farmhouse and barn provide comfortable en-suite bedrooms on the ground floor, all with colour TV and tea/coffee making facilities. This is a working smallholding where you will see rare breeds of cattle, sheep, poultry and pigs. Full English breakfast using home produce is available. Stabling and garaging available on request. No smoking. Disabled guests accommodated. Three miles Junction 10 M40. Ideally situated Cotswolds, Silverstone, Birmingham, Oxford. Bed and Breakfast from £22. Full details on request.

STANTON HARCOURT. Mrs Margaret Clifton, "Staddle Stones", Linch Hill, Stanton Harcourt OX8 1BB (01865 882256). A chalet bungalow situated in a peaceful location on the outskirts of the village, with four acres of attractive surroundings including a carp pond; visitors are allowed to fish. A full breakfast is offered to satisfy the keenest of appetites. Disabled persons, children and dogs are welcome. In easy reach of the Cotswolds and Oxford. One double or family room en suite, two twin bedrooms with private bathrooms, also a comfortable TV lounge with tea/coffee available. Bed and Breakfast from £16.50.

TETSWORTH, near Thame. Julia Tanner, Little Acre, Tetsworth, Thame OX9 7AT (01844 281423).

A charming, secluded country house retreat, offering every comfort, set in 18 acres of private grounds, nestling under the Chilterns escarpment. Single, twin and double rooms, all with central heating, colour TV, tea/coffee making facilities; some with en suite facilities. Full English or Continental breakfast. A perfect place to relax and enjoy the local countryside in a quiet location, but only three minutes from Junction 6 on the M40. Children and well behaved family dog welcome. Lovely walking area (Oxfordshire Way and Ridgeway Path). Riding, fishing, gliding and excellent golf course nearby. Within easy reach of Blenheim Palace, Cotswold Wildlife Park, historic Oxford, etc. Little Acre offers a warm welcome and REAL VALUE FOR MONEY from just £13 per night. Reductions for weekly bookings and children. Highly recommended by previous guests. Plenty of good restaurants nearby. Open all year.

THAME, near Oxford. Mr and Mrs J. & G. Dean, Heath House, London Road, Milton Common, Thame OX9 2NR (01844 278904). A tastefully restored

Victorian farmhouse set in five acres with beautiful views to the Chilterns yet only three minutes from Junction 7 of M40 and 20 minutes' drive to Oxford's historic city centre. Bedrooms and bathrooms (some en suite) are decorated and furnished to a high specification; all bedrooms have tea/coffee making facilities, some have TV. The house is close to excellent golf courses and local pubs serve very good food. Enjoy a full English breakfast in beautiful surroundings. A friendly welcome is guaranteed. Sorry no smoking. Bed and Breakfast from £20.

WANTAGE. Mrs S. Mudway, Ormond Guest House, 23 Ormond Road, Wantage OX12 8EG (01235 762409). Victorian house five minutes' walk from market

square of Wantage in the Vale of the White Horse which is surrounded by beautiful downland. It is the birthplace of King Alfred who saw off the Vikings at Ashdown nearby. The Ridgeway Path, the oldest path in Britain, used since the Old Stone Age, runs two miles south of Wantage from Avebury to Ivanhoe Beacon (85 miles). The Ridgeway passes White Horse Hill and the Wayland Smithy (a megalithic long barrow) a few miles from Wantage. Car park. Tea/coffee making facilities and TV in all rooms; some en suite rooms. Bed and Breakfast from £16.

WITNEY. Mrs Elizabeth Simpson, Field View, Wood Green, Witney OX8 6DE (01993 705485). 🐾🐾 *HIGHLY COMMENDED.* Witney is famous for blankets, made here for over 300 years. Our house was built in 1959, of Cotswold stone. Set in two acres and situated on picturesque Wood Green, with football and cricket pitches to the rear, yet only ten minutes' walk from the centre of this lively, bustling market town. An ideal touring centre for Oxford University (12 miles), Blenheim Palace (eight miles), Cotswold Wildlife Park (eight miles) and country walks. Ample parking. Three delightful en suite bedrooms with central heating, tea/coffee making facilities and colour TV. No smoking. A peaceful setting and a warm, friendly atmosphere await you. Bed and full English Breakfast from £20.

WITNEY near. The Leather Bottel, East End, North Leigh, Near Witney OX8 6PY (01993 882174).

🐾 🐾 *COMMENDED.* Joe and Nena Purcell invite you to The Leather Bottel 16th century Inn situated in the quiet hamlet of East End near North Leigh, convenient for Blenheim Palace, Woodstock, Roman Villa, Oxford and the Cotswolds. Victorian conservatory restaurant, where you can enjoy our extensive home cooked bar snacks, vegetarian and à la carte menus, overlooking pretty gardens. Breathtaking countryside walks. Two double en suite bedrooms, one family room with own bathroom, one single bedroom, all with colour TV and tea/coffee making facilities. Bed and Breakfast £18 per person per night, £26 per night for single room. Children welcome. Open all year. Directions — follow signs to Roman Villa off A4095.

WOODSTOCK. Gorselands Farmhouse Auberge, Near Long Hanborough, Near Woodstock, Oxford OX8 6PU (01993 881895).

🐾 🐾 Situated in an idyllic peaceful location in the Oxfordshire countryside, Gorselands has its own grounds of one acre. This Cotswold stone farmhouse has exposed beams, flagstone floors, billiards room (full size table), guest lounge, dining conservatory and tennis court. En suite rooms, family room, double/twin rooms available. Large main bathroom with bath and shower. Near to Oxford, Blenheim Palace, East End Roman Villa, Cotswold villages. Children welcome. Bed and Breakfast from £17.50 per person; Evening Meal from £10.95. Licensed. RAC Listed; Elizabeth Gundrey Recommended.

WOODSTOCK. Mrs Kay Bradford, Hamilton House, 43 Hill Rise, Old Woodstock OX20 1AB (01993 812206). High quality Bed and Breakfast establishment with parking, overlooking Blenheim Park, Blenheim Palace and the town centre with good selection of restaurants, pubs and shops within walking distance. Accommodation offered — one twin-bedded room and two double rooms, all en suite with colour TV and tea making facilities. Pleasant dining room. Excellent selection of Continental and full English breakfast. Comfortable and relaxed atmosphere with informative and very hospitable hostess. Ideal base for Blenheim Palace, Bladon, the Cotswolds, Stratford-upon-Avon, Oxford and major airports. Access off A44 northern end of Woodstock, 200 yards from Rose and Crown pub. Children and pets welcome. Bed and Breakfast from £20.

Key to
Tourist Board Ratings

The Crown Scheme
(England, Scotland & Wales)

Covering hotels, motels, private hotels, guesthouses, inns, bed & breakfast, farmhouses. Every Crown classified place to stay is inspected annually. *The classification:* Listed then 1-5 Crown indicates the range of facilities and services. Higher quality standards are indicated by the terms APPROVED, COMMENDED, HIGHLY COMMENDED and DELUXE.

The Key Scheme
(also operates in Scotland using a Crown symbol)

Covering self-catering in cottages, bungalows, flats, houseboats, houses, chalets, etc. Every Key classified holiday home is inspected annually. *The classification:* 1-5 Key indicates the range of facilities and equipment. Higher quality standards are indicated by the terms APPROVED, COMMENDED, HIGHLY COMMENDED and DELUXE.

The Q Scheme
(England, Scotland & Wales)

Covering holiday, caravan, chalet and camping parks. Every Q rated park is inspected annually for its quality standards. The more √ in the Q – up to 5 – the higher the standard of what is provided.

SHROPSHIRE

BUCKNELL. Mrs Christine Price, The Hall, Bucknell SY7 0AA (01547 530249). 👒👒 *COMMENDED.*

You are assured of a warm welcome at The Hall, which is a Georgian farmhouse with spacious accommodation. The house and gardens are set in a secluded part of a small South Shropshire village, an ideal area for touring the Welsh Borderland. Offa's Dyke is on the doorstep and the historic towns of Shrewsbury, Hereford, Ludlow and Ironbridge are within easy reach as are the Church Stretton Hills and Wenlock Edge. Three bedrooms — one twin en-suite, two doubles (with washbasins). All have tea-making facilities and TV. Guest lounge. Ample parking. Bed and Breakfast from £17; Dinner £9. SAE, please, for details.

CHURCH STRETTON. Travellers Rest Inn, Upper Affcot (A49), Church Stretton SY6 6RL (01694 781275; Fax: 01694 781555). 👒👒 *APPROVED.* RAC Inn.

The Travellers Rest Inn is situated on the main A49 between Church Stretton and Craven Arms. Being privately owned by Fraser and Mauresia Allison, you can be assured of a good welcome, good food and good accommodation; together with good old-fashioned service, plus a smile, at no extra charge. The accommodation offered is fully centrally heated with four en suite rooms on the ground floor and six bedrooms on the first floor, all with washbasins and shaver points. Colour TVs are installed in all our rooms, together with tea/coffee making facilities. Children and pets welcome. Bed and Breakfast from £22 to £30; Evening Meal from £5.

CHURCH STRETTON. Mrs Isobel Burgoyne, Churchmoor Farm, Marshbrook, Church Stretton SY6 6PU (01694 781365).

Situated at the foothills of the Long Mynd, the farmhouse has panoramic views of all the hills of South Shropshire. Ideal for rambling and wildlife. Convenient to the A49 and for local places of interest. Homely atmosphere with personal attention. Two double rooms with own bathroom, tea/coffee facilities. Central heating. Bed and Breakfast from £15.

CHURCH STRETTON. Mrs Mary Jones, Acton Scott Farm, Acton Scott, Church Stretton SY6 6QN (01694 781260). 👒👒 *COMMENDED.*

Lovely 17th century farmhouse in peaceful village amidst the beautiful hills of South Shropshire, an area of outstanding natural beauty. The house is full of character and the rooms, which are all heated, are comfortable and spacious and have washbasins and beverage making facilities; en suite available. Colour TV lounge. We are a working farm, centrally situated for visiting Ironbridge, Shrewsbury and Ludlow, each being easily reached within half an hour. Visitors' touring and walking information available. No smoking. Bed and full English Breakfast from £15 per person. Farm Holiday Bureau member.

CHURCH STRETTON. Don and Rita Rogers, Belvedere Guest House, Burway Road, Church Stretton SY6 6DP (01694 722232). 👒👒👒 *COMMENDED.* A quiet, family-run guest house pleasantly situated on the slopes of Long Mynd, 200 yards from the centre of Church Stretton, yet only 200 yards from 6000 acres of National Trust hill country. Belvedere is an ideal centre for exploring the Welsh borders or for just enjoying the most beautiful county in England. All 12 rooms are centrally heated and have hairdryers, shaver points and tea making facilities. There are two lounges for guests' use (one with TV) and evening meals and packed lunches are available if required. Well-behaved pets are welcome. Bed and Breakfast from £22; Evening Meal £9.50. 50% reduction for children under 10, 10% reduction for weekly or party bookings. RAC Acclaimed. AA QQQQ.

CHURCH STRETTON. Mrs B. Norris, Court Farm, Gretton, Church Stretton SY6 7HU (01694 771219). ❦❦❦ *HIGHLY COMMENDED.* Large, stone

Tudor farmhouse in 325 acres of working farm. Situated in very rural surroundings just outside village of Cardington and within easy distance of most interesting places in Shropshire — Ironbridge Gorge, Shrewsbury and Ludlow being approximately 15 miles. Ideal situation for sightseeing, walking and relaxing. In the house, comfort is to the fore. Three large rooms upstairs, all en suite and with TV, tea/coffee making facilities and hair dryers. Downstairs we have separate lounge and diningroom; colour TV and log fires. High quality cuisine. NON-SMOKING HOUSEHOLD. Complimented by luxurious barn conversion consisting of double and twin en suite rooms. Bed and Breakfast from £21.50, Evening Meal from £13; bedtime drink included. RAC Acclaimed: "a place worth seeking". Farm Bureau Member.

CLUN. Mrs M. Jones, Llanhedric, Clun SY7 8NG (01588 640203). HETB Listed *COMMENDED.* **Working farm.** Mixed farm just two miles off the A488 road,

overlooking the picturesque Clun Valley, near the Welsh Border and Offa's Dyke. It is ideal for walking or exploring the many places of historic interest including Ludlow and Shrewsbury. Attractive beamed farmhouse with lawns and garden provides spacious accommodation, a friendly atmosphere and good food. One twin bedroom and two double rooms (one en suite), with washbasins and tea/coffee making facilities. Visitors' lounge with inglenook fireplace and separate dining room. Sorry, no dogs. Open Easter to October. Non smoking household. Bed and Breakfast from £15.00; Bed, Breakfast and Evening Meal from £23.00. Reductions for children.

CLUN. Mrs Miriam Ellison, New House Farm, Clun SY7 8NJ (01588 638314). ❦❦ *HIGHLY*

COMMENDED. AA QQQQ Selected. Isolated peaceful 18th century farmhouse set high in the Clun Hills near Welsh border. Hill farm in the Environmentally Sensitive Area of South Shropshire. Additional sheep hill farm which includes an Iron Age Hill Fort. Three major walking routes from the doorstep: Offa' Dyke, Shropshire Way and Kerry Ridgeway. Scenic views from large comfortable bedrooms, furnished to high standard with TV and tea/coffee making facilities. Twin room en suite, family room with adjacent bathroom and double room with shower room nearby. Packed lunches. Comprehensive selection of books. Our aim is to offer clean, comfortable accommodation with a friendly atmosphere in quiet peaceful surroundings. Bed and Breakfast from £20.

DORRINGTON. Ron and Jenny Repath, Meadowlands, Lodge Lane, Frodesley, Dorrington SY5 7HD (01694 731350). ETB Listed. Set in a quiet location seven miles south of Shrewsbury. Bedrooms overlook the Stretton Hills. The guest house lies on a no through road to a forested hill and is set in eight acres of gardens, paddocks and woodland. Guest accommodation in two double and a family bedroom. Large lounge with colour TV. Guests' bathroom. Children welcome and a cot is available. Itineraries can be arranged and maps and guide books borrowed. Central heating. Plenty of parking. Strictly no smoking. Brochure available. Drinks on arrival, evening drink. Bed and Breakfast from £15; Evening Meal by arrangement.

ELLESMERE. Mrs Stokes, Mereside Farm, Ellesmere SY12 0PA (01691 622404). An 18th century

farmhouse with warm, friendly atmosphere situated between the Llangollen Canal and The Mere — part of the Shropshire Lake District. Ideal for walking holidays or for touring North Wales, Shropshire and Cheshire. Ellesmere's shops and restaurants and the New Blackwater Meadow Marina is a few minutes walk. All bedrooms have tea/coffee making facilities and are non-smoking. Guests' sitting room with colour TV and open fire. All rooms recently refurbished and centrally heated. Full farmhouse breakfast with homemade sausages. Packed lunch/special diet on request. Stabling for guests' horses (by prior arrangement). Open all year. Bed and Breakfast from £16 per person.

FREE and REDUCED RATE Holiday Visits!
See our READERS' OFFER VOUCHER for details!

LUDLOW. Mrs Rachel Edwards, Haynall Villa, Little Hereford, Near Ludlow SY8 4BG (01584 711589). 🐾🐾 *COMMENDED.* 1820s farmhouse nestling in Teme Valley six miles from historic Ludlow, three-quarters of a mile from A456. Spacious bedrooms (one en suite) offer comfort, views to three counties, vanity units, tea/coffee making facilities. Guests' bathroom. Delicious farmhouse fayre (vegetarian and special diets). Relax in lounge with TV or in the attractive garden. Featured in Daily Telegraph. Children and pets welcome. Open all year except Christmas. Bed and Breakfast from £16; Evening Meal from £12.

LUDLOW. Mr and Mrs M.J. Hamson, Lower House Farm, Cleedownton, Ludlow SY8 3EH (01584 823648). Lower House Farm is a mellow 11th century stone house set in the picturesque Corve Valley six miles from Ludlow. John and Sheila Hamson will give you a very warm welcome to their clean and happy home. They have two double rooms and a twin-bedded/family room; all are en-suite and have tea/coffee making facilities and colour TV. Lounge and large garden with superb views of the surrounding countryside with its good walking. Ludlow, Tenbury Wells, Bridgnorth, Shrewsbury, Leominster and Worcester with all their charming history are within easy driving distance. Bed and Breakfast from £17 to £19. Telephone for further details.

LUDLOW. Malcolm and Margaret Lowe, Lower Hayton Grange, Lower Hayton, Ludlow SY8 2AQ (01584 861296; Fax: 01584 861371). Our beautiful home in the Corvedale Valley, which is designated an Area of Outstanding Natural Beauty, is three and a half miles from the medieval market town of Ludlow. The period house stands in grounds of four acres well away from busy roads and guests enjoy relaxing in our lovely gardens which include an attractive duck pond. We also have a swimming pool and all-weather tennis court. The accommodation is centrally heated, with tea/coffee facilities, colour TV and en suite. Dine in our magnificent conservatory and relax in our guest lounge. Plenty of off-road parking. Rates from £16.50 to £25 Bed and Breakfast. Evening Meal optional. Non-smoking house. We also offer two self catering cottages in grounds.

LUDLOW. Mrs Kath Lanman, "Red Roofs", Little Hereford, Near Ludlow SY8 4AT (01584 711439). 🐾🐾 "Red Roofs" is situated in the lovely Teme Valley overlooking glorious open countryside. Accommodation comprises one double ground floor room with big bay window looking out towards flower garden. Own colour TV and seating area; en suite luxury bathroom (suitable for disabled visitors). One double, twin or family room with washbasin and hospitality trays; adjacent private shower room. Central heating throughout. Ample parking. The historic town of Ludlow with its Norman Castle five miles, National Trust properties, Severn Valley Railway, Burford House and Gardens and Offa's Dyke nearby. Varied selection of hostelries, one within walking distance. Bed and Breakfast from £19 per person. AA QQQQ.

SHROPSHIRE – HISTORIC BORDER COUNTY!
The lonely Shropshire Hills – an "Area of Outstanding Natural Beauty" – are much favoured by walkers. Those seeking more traditional tourist activities would do well to visit the Acton Scott Working Museum, Ironbridge, Offa's Dyke, the black and white Tudor town of Shrewsbury or the market town of Bridgnorth.

LUDLOW. Clare and David Currant, Cordene, Coreley, Ludlow SY8 3AW (01584 890324). ♛♛

COMMENDED. B&B "PLUS". Relax in the peaceful setting of this former old rectory and farmhouse and enjoy a country break in the beautiful South Shropshire Hills close to Ludlow and Tenbury Wells. Convenient for Ironbridge Gorge Museum, Severn Valley Railway, Worcester, Hereford and the Welsh Border. Comfortable and spacious accommodation all en suite/private, mostly ground floor (single, twin and family bookings welcomed) with friendly and caring service PLUS use of visitors' own kitchen for preparation of snacks and light meals to give you extra freedom and flexibility. Ideally suited for wheelchair users and the less mobile. Sitting room with books, maps, games, TV and open fire. Central heating throughout. Packed lunches. Dogs by arrangement. Bed and Breakfast £21 per day. Discounts for children under 12 years and stays of four or more days. A "no smoking" house. Please write or phone for brochure.

LUDLOW near. Mrs P. Turner, The Brakes, Downton, Near Ludlow SY8 2LF (Tel and Fax: 01584 856485). ♛♛ *HIGHLY COMMENDED.* AA QQQ. Set in the

heart of beautiful rolling countryside only five miles from the picturesque historic town of Ludlow, The Brakes offers extremely comfortable accommodation with excellent cuisine. A period farmhouse, tastefully modernised, with central heating throughout; there are three double en suite bedrooms with colour TV and a charming lounge with log fire. Open March to October inclusive. The Brakes stands in three acres of grounds with a beautiful garden. Here is excellent walking country including Offa's Dyke and the Long Mynd not far away. Golf, riding and fishing are available. The area is steeped in history with many places of interest within easy reach. Bed and Breakfast £22.50; Dinner £17.50.

MINSTERLEY. Paul and Debbie Costello, Cricklewood Cottage, Plox Green, Minsterley SY5 0HT

(01743 791229). 🐾🐾 *HIGHLY COMMENDED.* AA QQQQ Selected. A delightful 18th century cottage at the foot of the Stiperstones Hills, retaining its original character with exposed beams, inglenook fireplace and traditional furnishings. The bedrooms are fully en suite with lovely views of the Shropshire countryside. Breakfast is served in the sun room, looking out to the hills, with an attractive blackboard menu. Especially inviting is the pretty cottage garden where guests can wander amongst many old-fashioned and unusual plants and stroll alongside the trout stream. Excellent restaurants/inns nearby — full details supplied to guests. Ideal for visiting Shrewsbury and Ironbridge. Private parking. No smoking. Bed and Breakfast from £19. Call for brochure.

MUCH WENLOCK. Mrs Jennifer Coldicott, Aldenham Weir, Muckley Cross, Near Much Wenlock

WV16 4RR (01746 714352). 🐾🐾 *COMMENDED.* A superb country house set in 11 acres of garden, woodlands and streams. We offer a warm friendly welcome and excellent accommodation in tastefully furnished double/twin and family rooms with en suite, colour TV and tea-making facilities. The Nest is our luxury suite; independent of the house it offers a little more privacy. The pine dining room opens out into a spacious conservatory for our guests' use. Aldenham Weir is ideally situated for visiting Ironbridge, Much Wenlock, the medieval town of Shrewsbury, Ludlow Castle and the Severn Valley Railway at Bridgnorth. Two and a half miles from Much Wenlock on the A458 heading for Bridgnorth. Bed and Breakfast £30 single room, £40 double/twin room. Brochure on request.

NEWPORT. Mrs Janice Park, Lane End Farm, Chetwynd, Newport TF10 8BN (01952 550337). 🐾🐾

COMMENDED. Be sure of a warm welcome at our interesting period farmhouse set amidst lovely countryside. Bedrooms with en suite facilities. Good woodland walks nearby. Located on A41 just two miles north of Newport; ideal touring location for visiting Ironbridge, Weston Park, Cosford, The Wrekin, Potteries, Chester, etc. We keep pedigree Suffolk and Rouge sheep — see the lambs in spring! Open all year. Children and pets welcome. Bed and Breakfast from £18; Dinner £11.

OSWESTRY. Mrs Margaret Jones, Ashfield Farm House, Maesbury, Near Oswestry SY10 8JH (01691 653589). 🐾🐾 *HIGHLY COMMENDED.* This warm and friendly old house was once a coach house and later a Georgian farmhouse originating in the 16th century. Full of warmth, charm and character set in large gardens and orchard just one mile from Oswestry, A5 and A483 roads. All the spacious rooms are fully equipped and have en suite or luxury bathrooms, decorated and furnished in a true country style with lovely views of Welsh mountains. Payphone and cot available. Log fires in winter. Lots of castles, mountains, lakes and valleys to explore. Chester, Shrewsbury and Llangollen about 30 minutes' drive. Good food, canal and boat hire only five minutes' walk. Good hospitality awaits you. Children and well behaved pets welcome. Bed and Breakfast from £18.50 per person per night. Special terms for short breaks. Details on request.

OSWESTRY near. Mrs Jill Plunkett, Rhoswiel Lodge, Weston Rhyn, Near Oswestry SY10 7TG (01691 777609). 🐾🐾 Victorian country house in delightful gardens beside the Shropshire Union/Llangollen Canal. We are easy to find — just 400 yards from the A5. A convenient place to stop overnight or better still as a centre to explore the Welsh hills, forests, lakes and castles to the west or the verdant, rural quietness of North Shropshire to the east. We enjoy where we live and would be disappointed should you not enjoy our area and our home — at a price of course! Bed and Breakfast from £17 to £20 per person. Double room is en suite and twin room has its own separate facilities.

SHREWSBURY. Mrs Pauline Williamson, Mickley House, Tern Hill, Market Drayton TF9 3QW (01630 638505). 🐾🐾 *HIGHLY COMMENDED.* Enjoy a traditional farmhouse welcome on our 125 acre farm with pedigree Limousin and Simmental cattle. Enjoy the pleasures of the Shropshire countryside, walking through Hawkstone Park with its unique follies, grottoes and caves. Historic Ironbridge, Shrewsbury, Chester and Wedgwood nearby. Gardeners' delight at Hodnet Hall, Dorothy Clive, Bridgmere and Stapley Water Gardens. Relax by the inglenook fireplace or stroll leisurely through the garden down to the brook and farm pools. Spacious and comfortable en suite bedrooms, two ground floor. Central heating, colour TV and hospitality trays. Terms from £20. Reduced rates for three nights or more. AA QQQQ Selected, Disabled Category 3.

SHREWSBURY. Anton Guest House, 1 Canon Street, Monkmoor, Shrewsbury SY2 5HG (01743

359275). ☙ *COMMENDED.* The Anton Guest House is an attractive corner-positioned Victorian house which stands on a main road just 10 minutes' stroll from both Shrewsbury town centre and the 10th century Abbey church. Family owned and run, offering a very friendly welcome to guests. Very tastefully decorated with each of the three bedrooms warm and comfortable (house has double glazing) and with tea/coffee making facilities and TVs. Breakfast is wholesome and delicious. The world famous Brother Cadfael books by the late Ellis Peters (now serialised for TV) are set in the area and visitors may be interested in retracing the intrepid monk's steps in the Brother Cadfael Walks. Open all year. Smoking banned throughout. Children welcome. No pets. Bed and Breakfast from £17 to £20.

SHREWSBURY. Mrs Janet Jones, Grove Farm, Preston Brockhurst, Shrewsbury SY4 5QA (01939

220223). ☙ *COMMENDED.* AA QQQ, RAC Acclaimed. This lovely 17th century farmhouse with a beautiful view, offers warmth and comfort to all guests. It is set in a little village on the A49, seven miles north of Shrewsbury. The house has a large lounge and dining room with fires and colour TV; four lovely bedrooms (one double/family, one twin both with showers en suite, one double, one single both with wash-basins) with easy chairs and tea/coffee trays. Guests' bathroom. Central heating throughout. Visitors are welcomed with tea and home-made cakes, and there is always a variety of delicious food offered for breakfast. Sorry, no smoking. No pets. Bed and Breakfast from £16.50. We look forward to welcoming you to our home. Reduced rates for children in family room. Short Breaks and weekly terms available.

SHREWSBURY near. Mrs Gwen Frost, Oakfields, Baschurch Road, Myddle, Shrewsbury SY4 3RX

(01939 290823). ☙ *COMMENDED.* Visiting Shropshire? Why not enjoy the warm welcome and home from home atmosphere at Oakfields, which is in a quiet, idyllic setting located in the picturesque village of Myddle made famous by Gough's "History of Myddle" written in 1700. All ground floor bedrooms, each tastefully decorated and equipped with colour TV, tea-making facilities, washbasin, hair dryers and shaver points; cot and high chair also available; guests' TV lounge. Central heating throughout. Large and pleasant garden for guests to enjoy. 15 minutes from Shrewsbury and Hawkstone Park and convenient for Ironbridge, Wales, Chester, etc. Golf and riding nearby. Extensive car park. No smoking. Bed and Breakfast from £16. Nearest main road A528, also straight road from A5.

STIPERSTONES. Roy and Sylvia Anderson, Tankerville Lodge, Stiperstones, Minsterley, Shrews-

bury SY5 0NB (01743 791401). ☙ *COMMENDED.* A cosy country house nestling below the Devil's Chair and Stiperstones nature reserve in the dramatic Shropshire Hills, Tankerville Lodge has won a reputation for its caring, friendly atmosphere and deliciously different food. Guests love the peaceful setting and the sweeping, unforgettable views the area offers. Rich in lore and legend, it's superb walking country and there's a strategic bonus: just 25 minutes from the Tudor delights of Shrewsbury, Tankerville Lodge is excellently placed for touring across the Welsh Border, too. So in addition to other Shropshire "musts" like historic Ironbridge, the Long Mynd and Ludlow, the lovely terraced gardens of Powis Castle and the beauty of Lake Vyrnwy are within easy reach. Bed and Breakfast from £15.95. AA Recommended QQ. Licensed. Pets welcome.

TELFORD. Mrs Mary Jones, Red House Farm, Longdon on Tern, Wellington, Telford TF6 6LE

(01952 770245). 🐦🐦 *COMMENDED.* Our Victorian farmhouse is on a mixed farm. Two double bedrooms have private facilities, one family room with separate bathroom, all large and comfortable. Excellent breakfast. Farm easily located, leave M54 Junction 6, follow A442, take B5063. Central for historic Shrewsbury, Ironbridge Gorge museums or modern Telford. Several local eating places. Open all year. Families most welcome, reductions for children. Pets also welcome. Bed and Breakfast from £17.

WEM, near Shrewsbury. Mrs B. Barnes, Foxleigh House, Foxleigh Drive, Wem SY4 5BP (01939

233528). 🐦🐦 *COMMENDED.* AA QQQQ. This elegant period country house of immense character is ideally placed for touring Roman Chester, Ironbridge and Wedgwood, where museums and visitor centres are plentiful. Moreover, it is within easy reach of the mountains of Snowdonia and National Trust castles and houses. Quietly situated yet convenient for Wem Station (Shrewsbury 12 minutes), Foxleigh is near to swimming pool, tennis club and sports centre; additionally, the house has its own croquet lawn. Parking. Accommodation comprises one large twin-bedded room with private bathroom, one family suite (sleeps four/six) with private bathroom; colour TV, tea/coffee facilities in both. Iron and hairdryer available. Both dining room and drawing room are beautifully appointed with classic period furniture — ideal for evening relaxation. Traditional English or Continental Breakfast; Dinner by arrangement from £11. Many good pubs and restaurants locally. From £18 per person nightly. Brochure from Mrs Barnes.

WHITCHURCH. Miss J. Gregory, Ash Hall, Ash Magna, Whitchurch SY13 4DL (01948 663151).

Tourist Board Listed *APPROVED.* **Working farm.** An early 18th-century house in the small North Shropshire village of Ash Magna. One-and-a-half miles from the A41 with easy access to Chester, Crewe, Shrewsbury, Wrexham, Llangollen: all 20 miles or less. Medium sized mixed farm with pedigree Friesians. The farmhouse has oak panelling in several rooms with a large oak staircase as a particular feature. Accommodation in two bedrooms, one with en-suite bathroom. Children are welcome and rates are reduced. Open all year.

FOR THE MUTUAL GUIDANCE OF GUEST AND HOST

Every year literally thousands of holidays, short-breaks and overnight stops are arranged through our guides, the vast majority without any problems at all. In a handful of cases, however, difficulties do arise about bookings, which often could have been prevented from the outset.

It is important to remember that when accommodation has been booked, both parties — guests and hosts — have entered into a form of contract. We hope that the following points will provide helpful guidance.

GUESTS: When enquiring about accommodation, be as precise as possible. Give exact dates, numbers in your party and the ages of any children. State the number and type of rooms wanted and also what catering you require — bed and breakfast, full board, etc. Make sure that the position about evening meals is clear — and about pets, reductions for children or any other special points.

Read our reviews carefully to ensure that the proprietors you are going to contact can supply what you want. Ask for a letter confirming all arrangements, if possible.

If you have to cancel, do so as soon as possible. Proprietors do have the right to retain deposits and under certain circumstances to charge for cancelled holidays if adequate notice is not given and they cannot re-let the accommodation.

HOSTS: Give details about your facilities and about any special conditions. Explain your deposit system clearly and arrangements for cancellations, charges, etc, and whether or not your terms include VAT.

If for any reason you are unable to fulfil an agreed booking without adequate notice, you may be under an obligation to arrange alternative suitable accommodation or to make some form of compensation.

While every effort is made to ensure accuracy, we regret that FHG Publications cannot accept responsibility for errors, omissions or misrepresentation in our entries or any consequences thereof. Prices in particular should be checked because we go to press early. We will follow up complaints but cannot act as arbiters or agents for either party.

SOMERSET
including Bath and North East Somerset, and North West Somerset

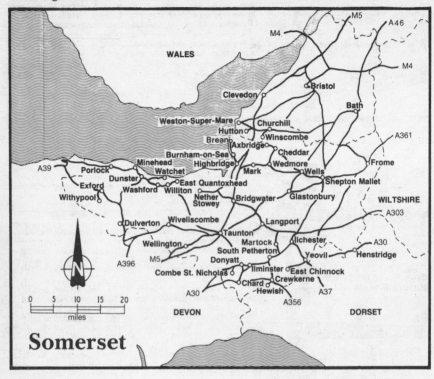

Somerset

ASH. Paterson and Sue Weir, Follys End, 6 Back Street, Ash, Martock TA12 6NY (01935 823073).

Set in an acre of peaceful gardens where ducks and geese idle beside the tranquil pond, Follys End welcomes you with its friendly relaxed atmosphere. All three rooms (two double, one twin) are attractively furnished in period style with central heating, colour TV, tea/coffee making, shaver points and washbasins; the twin room has en suite facilities. Guests are welcome to use the barbecue on summer evenings or improve their golf on the practice bunker and green. Ideal location for nearby National Trust properties, Somerset cider and Willow Craft Centres, Clark's Village Factory Shopping; Lyme Regis, the Dorset coast, Glastonbury, Wells, Cheddar, Stourhead all within easy reach. No smoking. Bed and Breakfast from £16 per person. B&B GB Approved.

ASHBRITTLE. Ann Heard, Lower Westcott Farm, Ashbrittle, Near Wellington TA21 0HZ (01398 361296). 👑 *COMMENDED.* On Devon/Somerset border,

230 acre family farm with Friesian herd, sheep, poultry and horses. Ideal for walking, touring Exmoor, Quantocks, both coasts and many National Trust properties. Pleasant farmhouse, tastefully modernised but with olde worlde charm, inglenook fireplaces and antique furniture. Set in large gardens with lawns and flower beds in peaceful scenic countryside. Two family bedrooms with private facilities and tea/coffee making; large lounge, separate dining room. Offering guests every comfort, noted for relaxed, friendly atmosphere and good home cooking. Bed and Breakfast from £15; Dinner £8 per person. Reductions for children. Brochure available.

AXBRIDGE near. Mrs S. Vincent, Hurdle House, Turnpike Road, Lower Weare, Near Axbridge BS26 2JF (01934 732491). Hurdle House is situated in the beautiful Cheddar Valley, on the A38, four-and-a-half miles from M5 Junction 22. It is within easy reach of Cheddar, Wells, Glastonbury, Weston-super-Mare. Ideal base for a touring holiday; also ideal overnight stop for travellers to Devon and Cornwall. There are two double bedrooms and one family room; bathroom, toilet; sittingroom, diningroom. Children welcome, cot, high chair and babysitting. Open January to November with central heating. Pets are allowed. Car is essential and there is parking space. Bed and Breakfast from £11.50. Rates reduced for children.

BATH. Mrs Maria Beckett, Cedar Lodge, 13 Lambridge, London Road, Bath BA1 6BJ (01225 423468). ♛♛ Within walking distance of historic city centre, this gracious detached Georgian house offers period elegance combined with modern comfort. Beautiful individually designed bedrooms, one with four-poster, one with half-tester bed and one twin-bedded room. All with TV and en suite/private facilities. Guests may relax in the lovely gardens or by the fire in the drawing room. Choice of breakfasts served with home-made preserves. Secure car parking. This is an ideal base for Bath, Avebury, Stonehenge, Salisbury, Wells, Longleat, Cotswolds, Wales and many other places of interest. Help given with planning your excursions. Children welcome. Sorry, no pets. Bed and Breakfast from £20 per person per night based on two people sharing.

TOGHILL HOUSE FARM

Warm and cosy 17th century farmhouse on working farm with outstanding views, yet only three miles north of the historical city of Bath. All rooms en suite with tea-making facilities and colour TV, or choose one of our luxury self-catering barn conversions which are equipped to a very high standard and include all linen.

Brochure – Tel: 01225 891261; Fax: 01225 892128

Jackie Bishop, Toghill House Farm, Freezing Hill, Wick BS15 5RT

♛♛ OAKLEIGH HOUSE

Your comfort is assured at Oakleigh House which is quietly situated only 10 minutes from the city centre. Combining Victorian elegance with today's comforts, Oakleigh gives your stay in Bath that extra special touch. All rooms have private bath/shower and WC, hairdryer, colour TV, clock radio and tea/coffee making facilities. Guests' lounge, telephone and private car park. Double or twin rooms with private bathroom and full English Breakfast £45–£60 per night. 10% reduction on a stay of five nights or more and reduced rates also for Senior Citizens. Winter Breaks available. RAC Highly Acclaimed.

Ms Jenny King, Oakleigh House, 19 Upper Oldfield Park, Bath BA2 3JX Tel: 01225 315698

BATH. Mrs Margaret Gentle, Ellsworth, Fosseway, Midsomer Norton, Bath BA3 4AU (01761 412305). Situated on the A367 Bath/Wells/Exeter Road, Ellsworth is eight miles from Bath and within easy reach of Bristol, Wells, Glastonbury, Cheddar and the heart of the West Country. The house is surrounded by an attractive garden, with plenty of garden furniture for relaxing. Ample parking space. There are three double/family rooms and one single room, all with colour TV, washbasins, shaver points, electric kettle for early morning tea or coffee. Two bathrooms. TV lounge. Central heating throughout. Good English Breakfast served. Open all year. Bed and Breakfast from £16. Reductions for children under 12.

Ashley Villa Hotel

26 Newbridge Road Bath BA1 3JZ

Tel: (01225) 421683

Fax: (01225) 313604

RAC HIGHLY ACCLAIMED

Comfortably furnished licensed hotel with relaxing informal atmosphere, situated close to the city centre. The hotel has its own car park, garden, patio and outdoor swimming pool. All 14 well appointed bedrooms have en-suite facilities, colour television, telephone, tea and coffee making and hairdrier. Residential bar and separate lounge. Ground floor rooms available. Warm welcome from resident owners. Most credit cards accepted. Short Breaks available.

BATH. Jill and Bunny Harvey, Della Rosa Guest House, 59 North Road, Combe Down, Bath BA2 5DF (01225 837193; Fax: 01225 835264). AA QQQ. Large Victorian home with rooms to suit every taste, plus a breakfast to satisfy your palate. Located one mile from the centre of Bath in quiet fresh air surroundings. Village pubs within walking distance. Plenty of off street parking. Bed and Breakfast from £15 per person.

BATH. The Old Malt House Hotel, Radford, Timsbury, Near Bath BA3 1QF (Tel & Fax: 01761 470106). ❀ ❀ ❀ *COMMENDED.* Between Bath and Wells in beautiful country surroundings, ideally situated for visiting many places of interest. A relaxing comfortable hotel, built in 1835 as a brewery malt house, now a hotel of character with interesting paintings, furnishings, etc., and with log fires in the colder months. Car park, gardens and lawns. Owned/managed by the same family for over 20 years. All 12 bedrooms (including two on the ground floor) have private facilities, colour TV, telephone and beverage trays. Extensive menus. Restaurant and bar meals served every evening. Full licence, wide choice including draught Bass. Bed and Breakfast from £27.50; Evening Dinner from £5. AA QQQ.

BATH. Mrs M.A. Cooper, Flaxley Villa, 9 New Bridge Hill, Bath BA1 3PW (01225 313237). ❀ Follow A4 through Bath to Queen Square, take top left hand exit and follow one mile to Weston. Comfortable Victorian house, five minutes from the town centre. All rooms with colour televisions, also showers and tea/coffee making facilities. En suite rooms available. Parking. Full English Breakfast. Terms from £18 per person.

The Bath Tasburgh Hotel

WARMINSTER ROAD, BATH BA2 6SH   TEL: 01225 425096   FAX: 01225 463842

A beautiful Victorian House built for a photographer to the Royal Family and set in over an acre of lovely gardens and grounds with breathtaking views. All rooms have ensuite bathrooms, tea/coffee facilities, colour TV, telephone, radio/alarm. The reception rooms are delightful and include a conservatory for guests. Private car park. A relaxed setting and a lovely place to stay.

ETB HIGHLY COMMENDED   AA QQQQ SELECTED

Personally managed by the resident owners – David and Susan Keeling

---

BATH. Marlborough House, 1 Marlborough Lane, Bath BA1 2NQ (01225 318175; Fax: 01225 466127). 👑👑 *COMMENDED*. Recently restored Victorian house in sunny position just five minutes' level walk to city centre and two minutes from Victoria Park and the Royal Crescent. Pretty en suite bedrooms, two with four-poster beds, all with colour TV, tea/coffee facilities and hair dryers. A non-smoking house with a friendly atmosphere. Private parking. Bed and Breakfast from £20 per person. Discount on stays of three nights or more; two night minimum stay at weekends. AA QQQQ.

BATH. Mrs Judith Goddard, Cherry Tree Villa, 7 Newbridge Hill, Bath BA1 3PW (01225 331671). 👑 Friendly Victorian home approximately one mile from centre of Bath, at the start of the A431. Very frequent bus service, or for those who enjoy walking, a stroll through Victoria Park will take you comfortably into the city. Bright comfortable bedrooms, all with washbasin, colour TV and tea/coffee making facilities. Full central heating and off-street parking. Bed and full English Breakfast from £16 per person per night. Children and pets welcome. Tourist Board registered. From city centre take main A4 Upper Bristol road, at Sportsman Pub take A431 and Cherry Tree Villa lies on the left hand side. Winner of an FHG Diploma awarded by readers.

FUN FOR ALL THE FAMILY IN SOMERSET

Cheddar Showcaves; Cricket St. Thomas Wildlife Park, Chard; Glastonbury Abbey; Haynes Sparkford Motor Museum; Peat Moors Visitors Centre, Westhay, near Glastonbury; Somerset Rural Life Museum, Glastonbury; Tropical Bird Gardens, Rode; West Somerset Railway, Minehead; Wookey Hole, near Wells.

BATH. Jane and John Shepherd, 21 Newbridge Road, Bath BA1 3HE (01225 314694).  Victorian house with friendly, family atmosphere one mile west of city centre on A4 by junction with A431. Very frequent bus service or pleasant walk (no steep hills) through Victoria Park or along the banks of the River Avon to rail and bus stations and city centre. Convenient for exploring Roman and Georgian Bath or easy access to Bristol, Wells, Glastonbury, Cheddar, Stonehenge, etc. All rooms have central heating, washbasins and shaver points. Tea/coffee making facilities. TV lounge. This is a house for non-smokers. We provide traditional English, vegetarian, vegan, gluten-free or dairy-free breakfasts. Bed and Breakfast from £17.

BATH. Mrs Peggy Hartley, Orchard Cottage, Dovers Lane, Bathford, Bath BA1 7SX (01225 858649).  COMMENDED. A detached cottage next to the village green in the conservation area of Bathford, some three miles east of Bath. In a quiet leafy lane leading to Browns Folly Wildlife Reserve affording outstanding views of surrounding countryside. Frequent bus service to Bath. Parking. Good 'pub food' in the village with many restaurants in Bath. The cottage was built around 1800 but has the modern features one now expects; en-suite, TV and coffee/tea facilities. Attractive walled garden. Guests have their own sitting-room. A choice of English, vegetarian or Continental breakfast. Children welcome. Dogs welcome by arrangement. Double or twin en-suite from £45. No smoking.

BATH. Geoff and Avril Kitching, Wentworth House Hotel, 106 Bloomfield Road, Bath BA2 2AP (01225 339193; Fax: 01225 310460).  Imposing Victorian Bath stone mansion (1887) standing in secluded gardens with stunning views of valley. Situated in quiet part of city with free car park. Walking distance Abbey, Baths. High standard of comfort. Licensed bar. Outdoor swimming pool, horse riding, golf nearby. Prices from £25 to £35 per person per night.

BATH. Mrs Chrissie Besley, The Old Red House, 37 Newbridge Road, Bath BA1 3HE (01225 330464; Fax: 01225 331661).  Welcome to our romantic Victorian "Gingerbread" house which is colourful, comfortable and warm; full of unexpected touches and intriguing little curiosities. The leaded and stained glass windows are now double glazed to ensure a peaceful night's stay. Each bedroom is individually furnished with canopied or king size bed, colour TV, complimentary beverages, radio alarm clock, hair dryer and either en suite shower or private bathroom. Generous four course breakfasts are served in a sunny conservatory. Waffles, pancakes or kippers are just a few alternatives to our famous hearty English grill. Dinner is available at the local riverside pub, just a short stroll away. We are non-smoking and have private parking. Prices range from £19.50 to £28 per person. Brochure on request.

BATH. Ron and Vanessa Pharo, Ashley House, 8 Pulteney Gardens, Bath BA2 4HG (01225 425027).  This charming, wisteria-clad, Victorian house in a quiet location is conveniently situated for all travellers to this beautiful city. We are a short level walk from the Roman Baths, Abbey, Pump Room and Sports Centre, and only 150 yards from the picturesque Kennet and Avon Canal where a stroll along the towpath will take you away from the crowds. All bedrooms have washbasins, shaver points, tea/coffee making facilities; some rooms have private shower and toilet; family rooms are available. Your breakfast is cooked to order and served with home-made marmalade. Double room £32 to £48. No smoking.

The Gainsborough Hotel

The Gainsborough Country House Hotel is situated in its own large attractive grounds, with 2 sun terraces, and is close to the lovely Botanical Gardens and Victoria Park. The hotel is both spacious and very comfortable, and provides a relaxed and informal atmosphere for guests. The Abbey, Roman Baths and Pump Room are all within walking distance. All of our 16 tastefully furnished bedrooms are ensuite, with colour TV, Satellite TV, tea/coffee facilities, telephones, hairdryers, etc. The hotel has a lounge and bar overlooking the lawns, and our own private car park. Highly recommended. Warm welcome from the friendly staff.

Singles £30-£40; Doubles £48-£65 (includes Full Breakfast &VAT)

Access, Visa, MasterCard, Eurocard, American Express all welcome.

Weston Lane · Bath · Avon · BA1 4AB
Tel: Bath (01225) 311380   Fax: (01225) 447411

WHEELBROOK MILL

A warm welcome and good food await you in this picturesque Mill nestling in a quiet valley overlooking the brook, fields and woodland just 15 minutes from Bath. The pretty en-suite, oak-beamed bedrooms are spacious, centrally heated, and furnished with antique pine, Laura Ashley linens and have all facilities. Guests can relax in the large garden or the cosy sitting room with its log fire, books, games and magazines in a friendly, informal family atmosphere.

Mrs S. Weeks, Wheelbrook Mill, Laverton, Near Bath BA3 6QY Telephone: 01373 830263

BATH. Mrs K.M. Addison, Bailbrook Lodge, 35/37 London Road West, Bath BA1 7HZ (01225 859090). 🌸🌸 *COMMENDED.* Bailbrook Lodge is a splendid Georgian hotel and with a warm welcome assured it makes an excellent base to tour the area. Its 12 bedrooms are elegantly furnished, all offering en suite bathrooms or showers, TV, coffee and tea making facilities; some with antique four-poster beds. Dining room and bar. Situated on the A4 London road, Bailbrook Lodge is just one and a half miles from Bath city centre and has ample car parking facilities. It is 100 yards from the A46 which leads to Junction 18 of the M4 and is also close to the beautiful villages of Castle Combe and Lacock. Price per person including full English breakfast is from £24 to £35. RAC Highly Acclaimed, AA QQQQ.

BATH. Jan and Bryan Wotley, The Albany Guest House, 24 Crescent Gardens, Bath BA1 2NB (01225 313339).

A warm welcome awaits you at our Victorian home, ideally placed to enjoy the delights of Bath — just five minutes' level walk from the city centre, Roman Baths, Abbey, etc. Our four attractively decorated bedrooms are equipped with colour TV, tea/coffee making facilities, washbasins and central heating. Enjoy a traditional English breakfast or try our delicious homemade vegetarian sausages! We happily cater for special dietary needs with prior notification. Many of our guests return again and again to enjoy the personal and unpretentious service we offer. Private parking. Non-smoking. Bed and Breakfast from £15 per person.

BATH. Marilyn and Colin Humphrey, Leighton House, 139 Wells Road, Bath BA2 3AL (01225 314769; Fax: 01225 443079). ETB ₩₩ AA QQQQQ

Premier Selected, RAC Highly Acclaimed, Ashley Courtenay Highly Recommended. Non-smoking. You are sure of a friendly welcome at this elegant detached Victorian house in large gardens overlooking Bath. 10 minutes' walk to city centre — even closer to bus/rail stations. Private car park. All rooms individually decorated, en suite bath and shower, TV, telephone, hair dryer, tea/coffee making facilities. Many with super king-size beds. Extensive à la carte breakfast with healthy options at this no smoking home. Double/twin £60 to £70 per night. 10% discount four nights April to September, two nights October to March. "Bath Together" offers attractive group discounts October to March. £5 off your bill on production of this advert.

BATH. Mr and Mrs Christopher Davies, Green Lane House, Hinton Charterhouse, Bath BA3 6BL (01225 723631). ₩₩

Five miles south of Bath in undulating countryside at the convergence of Somerset and Wiltshire lies the charming conservation village of Hinton Charterhouse. Green Lane House, originally three terraced 18th century Bath stone cottages, has been tastefully renovated and comfortably furnished. Traditional features such as exposed beams and open log fireplaces combine with the modern comforts introduced throughout the four distinctively decorated guest bedrooms, homely residents' lounge and dining room where full English breakfasts are cooked to order. Conveniently located within the village are two inns. An ideal centre for visiting Bath, Wells, Wookey, Cheddar, Glastonbury, Stourhead and Longleat. Bed and Breakfast from £18 per person in double/twin room to £24.50 per person in double/twin en suite room.

BATH. Jill and Rob Fradley, Sarnia, 19 Combe Park, Weston, Bath BA1 3NR (01225 424159). ₩₩

HIGHLY COMMENDED. Superb Bed and Breakfast in a large Victorian home. Come and sleep in our spacious bedrooms, individually decorated and freshly refurbished, all with TV, tea/coffee making facilities and central heating. They have new bathrooms and showers, en suite or private. Enjoy a four-course breakfast in our bright, sunny dining room; choose from English, Continental or vegetarian menus and sample our home made jams. We are non-smoking and have ample parking. Children are welcome, we even have a playroom! Prices from £20 per person, with reductions for children (under three years FREE). Our aim is to make you welcome and help you enjoy Bath and its surroundings. AA QQQQ Selected.

BATH. Mrs D. Strong, Wellsway Guest House, 51 Wellsway, Bath BA2 4RS (01225 423434). ₩ A comfortable Edwardian house with all bedrooms centrally heated; washbasins and colour televisions in the rooms. On bus route with buses to and from the city centre every few minutes or an eight minute walk down the hill. Alexandra Park, with magnificent views of the city, is five minutes' walk. Bath is ideal for a short or long holiday with many attractions in and around the city; Longleat, Wells and Bristol are all nearby. Parking available. Bed and Breakfast from £14, with a pot of tea to welcome you on arrival.

BATH. Mrs June E.A. Coward, Box Road Gardens, Box Road, Bathford, Bath BA1 7LR (01225 852071). Homely, comfortable country house in two acres, situated on A4 road three miles east of Bath City Centre. Easy access to M4, local beauty spots. Accommodation in twin, double and family rooms with central heating, vanity units, tea/coffee making facilities; TV. Some with shower en suite. Ample parking and good local "pub food". Open all year for Bed and Breakfast from £15 per person. This is a non-smoking house. Sorry, no pets. Phone June on **01225 852071** for further details.

BATH near. Mr and Mrs S.G. Morris, "Midstfields", Frome Road, Radstock, Near Bath, Somerset BA3 5UD (01761 434440). A large house standing in two acres of charming gardens. Play tennis or relax in the 40 foot long indoor heated swimming pool or sauna. Comfortable rooms include washbasins, TV and tea making facilities; one room now en suite. Good walking trails in the beautiful Somerset countryside. Bath and Wells 10 miles away. Full English breakfast. Pets and children welcome. Ample off road parking. Rates from £17 to £22 per person.

BATH. Mrs S.M. Johnson, Abercorn House, 38 St. James's Park, Bath BA1 2SU (01225 338162). A well restored Victorian residence in quiet cul-de-sac only a few minutes' walk from the City Centre and close to many museums and other attractions. Single, twin, double and family rooms available, all with washbasins, shaver points, central heating, tea/coffee facilities. Parking on premises. A non-smoking establishment. Fire Certificate. Terms from £15 to £19 per person.

BATH. Josie and Brian Surry, Dene Villa, 5 Newbridge Hill, Bath BA1 3PW (01225 427676). ♛♛ A friendly welcome is assured in our comfortable family home, with full central heating and parking facilities. It is situated one mile from Bath centre at the start of the A431, with buses passing, and close to the Royal United Hospital and the Caravan Park. Single, double, twin and family rooms, all en suite with colour TV; dining/sitting room with colour TV. Non-smoking rooms if required. Many people pay a return visit. Open all year. From £16 for Bed and full English Breakfast. Reduced rates for children.

BRIDGNORTH. Lower Clavelshay Farm, North Petherton, Bridgnorth TA6 6PY (01278 662347).

Working farm. Buzzards, badgers and beautiful countryside surround our traditional 17th century farmhouse on a 250 acre dairy farm. Peaceful with a relaxed "home from home" family atmosphere. Two double, one family rooms, all with tea making facilities. Small kitchen with cooker, fridge — useful for snacks, picnic lunches, etc. Sitting/dining room with beams, TV and log fire. Games, books, guide books and maps all freely available. Central heating. Ideally situated for exploring the Quantock Hills, Exmoor, Somerset Levels and coasts. Perfect for walking, riding, fishing or just relaxing. Children welcome — cot, high chair and babysitting available. Delicious home cooking from our produce where possible. Generous helpings. Discover why our guests keep returning!

BRIDGWATER. Mr and Mrs Fouracre, Oggshole Farmhouse, Broomfield, Bridgwater TA5 2EJ (01823 451689 or 0850 469220). All the fun of the farm.

Paradise for children and animal lovers at this charming 18th century farmhouse, nestling in the Quantock hills. With the emphasis on friendly, personal attention in a relaxing family atmosphere. Meet all the hand tame animals, join in with feeding. Pony rides for the children. We have two spacious, tastefully furnished rooms, both double/family rooms with washbasins and tea/coffee trays. TV lounge. Good home cooked meals optional. Easy access to M5 motorway. Convenient for walking, riding or fishing. Well behaved pets welcome. Stabling available. Phone for a brochure.

BRIDGWATER. Mr and Mrs Sally and Norman Hunt, West Town Farm, Greinton, Bridgwater TA7 9BW (01458 210277). ♛♛ *COMMENDED.* A warm wel-

come awaits you at West Town Farm, a comfortable 17th century country house in the village of Greinton. Ideally situated on the A361 Street-Taunton road for exploring the beauties of the Somerset countryside and within easy reach of coastal resorts. Breakfast is served in the flag-stoned diningroom and each bedroom has en-suite shower and toilet, tea/coffee making facilities and colour TV. Guest lounge with inglenook fireplace. Bed and Breakfast from £18 to £20. Reductions for children sharing. Open March to September. Car essential — parking. Non-smokers please.

BRIDGWATER near. Mrs F.S. Filsell, The Cedars, High Street, Othery, Near Bridgwater TA7 0QA (01823 698310). A warm welcome awaits guests at this

small Grade 3 Listed Georgian house in the centre of Othery village, well placed for touring and coarse fishing. Two twin and one double bedrooms with washbasins and tea/coffee making facilities; shower, bath, two toilets; diningroom; TV lounge; large garden, parking for six cars. Cot, high chair and babysitting available. Central heating. Car essential. Pets by arrangement. Glastonbury, Taunton only 10 miles away. Brendon, Quantock Hills 30 minutes; Dorset coast one hour's drive away. Bed and Breakfast from £30 per double/twin room. Reductions for children when sharing.

THE COTTAGE

A charming country cottage set in 2 acres of garden in an area of outstanding natural beauty and special interest close to rivers and canal where bird and wildlife flourish. A centre not only for the famous Somerset Levels but all of this historic County. We offer you privacy, comfort and tranquillity staying in antique four poster or twin bedded en suite rooms with TV and heating. Easy access with all rooms at ground level opening directly onto the gardens. Ample secure parking. Evening meals available by arrangement. English country cooking at its best using our own fresh vegetables, fruits, honey and free range eggs. Bed & Breakfast from £15 per person per night. Easy access junction 24 M5. Phone or write for brochure and map. No smoking in house please. Open all year.

Beverley and Victor Jenkins, The Cottage, Fordgate, Bridgwater TA7 0AP
Telephone: 01278 691908

BRISTOL. Downs View Guest House, 38 Upper Belgrave Road, Clifton, Bristol BS8 2XN (0117 9737046). ❀ *APPROVED.* RAC Approved. A well established, family-run Victorian guest house situated on the edge of Durdham Downs. All rooms have panoramic views over the city or the Downs. We are one and a half miles north of the city centre, just off Whiteladies Road where there are plenty of restaurants, shops and buses. We are within walking distance of Bristol Zoo and Clifton Suspension Bridge. All rooms have tea/coffee making facilities, washbasin, colour TV and central heating. There are four en suite rooms. We offer a varied menu including traditional English breakfast.

BRISTOL. Mr and Mrs J. & M. Horman, The Parsonage, Main Street, Farrington Gurney, Bristol BS18 5UB (01761 453553). A fine Grade II Listed building with a French influence. Built in the 17th century in its own grounds with ample secure parking, tea room and garden. Three large charming rooms retaining original features, two on ground floor suitable for disabled guests. All rooms have colour TV and complimentary tea trolley. Free laundry service. Special diets welcome. Standing at the foot of the Mendips The Parsonage is an ideal base for exploring Bath, Wells, Cheddar, Glastonbury and South Somerset. Close to airport and motorways. Relaxed home from home atmosphere.

BRISTOL near. Mrs Nicky Parsons, Langford Green Farm, Upper Langford, Near Bristol BS18 7DG (01934 852368). Dairy farm surrounded by fields, situated at the foot of the Mendip Hills. Picturesque farmhouse with lovely views from all rooms and a pleasant garden. Many local amenities including walking, horse riding, dry ski slope, pot-holing, fishing in Blagdon Lake, easy access to Weston-super-Mare, Wells, Cheddar Caves, Bath. M5 (exit 21) approximately 15-17 minutes. Bed and Breakfast from £14.50. Several local pubs with good eating facilities, one within walking distance. Two double bedrooms and one single with tea/coffee making facilities. Separate guests' lounge and diningroom; two bathrooms with showers. Children welcome. Open all year.

Terms quoted in this publication may be subject to increase if rises in costs necessitate

Brinsea Green Farm

Comfortable 18th century farmhouse on a 500 acre dairy, beef and sheep farm situated one and a half miles from village with views of the Mendip Hills. The farmhouse is located at the end of a quiet country lane surrounded by open fields. Easy access from M5 (approximately 12 to 15 minutes, Exit 21), and centrally situated between Bath, Bristol, Weston-super-Mare, Wells, Cheddar Caves and Blagdon Lake – fishing, dry ski slope, equestrian centre, golf course. The village has nine inns, many serving food. Bed and Breakfast with home-made marmalade and jams, offered to guests all year round. In keeping with their character, both sittingroom and diningroom have inglenook fireplaces. Three double bedrooms, two with en-suite hot drinks facilities. Bathroom with shower and separate toilet. Car essential – ample parking.

Mrs Delia Edwards,
Brinsea Green Farm,
Brinsea Lane, Congresbury,
Near Bristol BS19 5JN
Tel: Churchill (01934) 852278.

Stoneycroft House

Stock Lane, Langford, Bristol,
North Somerset BS18 7EX
Tel: 01934 852624   Mobile: 0973 737441
Proprietor: Mrs Griffin

Stoneycroft House is situated in the Wrington Valley, overlooking open farmland, close to the Mendip Hills and only 10 minutes from Bristol Airport. Superb four poster/family room with ensuite, twin room with ensuite and double room with adjacent bathroom. All rooms have colour TV, tea/coffee making facilities and excellent views. Enjoy your choice of breakfast in the beamed dining room with its Minster stone fireplace. Unlimited parking. Nearby attractions are the Cheddar Gorge, Wells Cathedral and the historic cities of Bath and Bristol. Sporting facilities and seaside nearby. Open all year round. Self-catering available. Please send for our brochure.

👑👑 **HIGHLY COMMENDED**

BURNHAM-ON-SEA. Mrs F. Alexander, Priors Mead, 23 Rectory Road, Burnham-on-Sea TA8 2BZ (01278 782116; Fax: 01278 782517; mobile 0860 573018). 👑👑 *APPROVED.* "Which?" Recommended. Peter and Fizz welcome guests to enjoy their enchanting Edwardian home set in half an acre of beautiful gardens with croquet and swimming pool. All three rooms have either twin or king-size beds, en suite/private facilities, washbasins, hospitality tray, colour TV, etc. Peaceful location, walk to the sea, town, golf and tennis clubs. Ideal touring base for Bristol, Bath, Wells, Glastonbury, Wookey Hole, Cheddar and Dunster. A no smoking home. Parking. Easy access to Junction 22 M5 for Wales, Devon and Cornwall. Bed and Breakfast from £15 to £17. Reductions for three nights.

CHARD. Doreen and Tony Botten, Watermead Guest House, 83 High Street, Chard TA20 1QT (01460 62834). AA Recommended QQQ. Situated in a private drive off the residential part of Chard High Street, this charming mid Victorian house has been sympathetically extended to provide clean and comfortable B&B accommodation together with friendly hospitality. Guest bedrooms are spacious and most have en suite facilities. All bedrooms have central heating, colour TV and courtesy tea/coffee making equipment. Full English breakfast with optional vegetarian choice is served every morning in our spacious dining room. Cot and high chair available. Pets are most welcome. Ample off-street parking. Open all year. Ideally situated for touring with numerous places to visit including the Crinkley Bottom TV Theme Park at Cricket St. Thomas. Bed and Breakfast from £18 per person per night; Evening meals available locally.

CHEDDAR near. Winston Manor Hotel, Bristol Road, Churchill, Near Cheddar BS19 5NL (01934 852348). 👑👑👑 *COMMENDED.* AA QQQ. This charming manor house stands in one and a half acres of secluded gardens overlooking the Mendip Hills. An ideal stop for visits to Bath, Wells, Longleat and Cheddar. Only a short drive from the beaches of Weston-super-Mare and Burnham-on-Sea. The proprietors Marion Sherrington and Jill Green offer a warm welcome to families, lone travellers and pets. All diets catered for, the cosy restaurant opens every evening. Bedrooms all en suite with tea/coffee making facilities and home made biscuits. The hotel is a member of Logis of Great Britain where hospitality wears a human face. Bed and English Breakfast from £25 per person.

CHEDDAR. Market Cross Hotel, Church Street, Cheddar BS27 3RA (01934 742264). 🏵🏵🏵

COMMENDED. This privately owned, licensed Regency Hotel is situated in the village of Cheddar, five minutes' walk from the famous Gorge, caves and Mendip Hills, making it an ideal centre for rambling, riding, caving, fishing, sightseeing. Wells, Glastonbury, Bath and Bristol are all within easy reach; the seaside is only 10 miles away. Seven bedrooms, some family, some en suite, are all centrally heated to ensure a comfortable stay. Log fires burn in the lounge during colder periods. A choice of excellent fresh home-cooked food and a desire to pleasure ensures our guests a happy stay at moderate prices. Bed and Breakfast from £20 to £22.50. Open all year. RAC Acclaimed. AA QQ. Excellent self catering apartments also available in adjacent Georgian house.

CHEDDAR. P.A. Phillips, The Forge, Cliff Street, Cheddar BS27 3PL (01934 742345). A non-smoking household, this is a comfortable old stone cottage complete with "TRADITIONAL WORKING FORGE". Set in the heart of the village with a five minute walk to famous Gorge and caves, pubs and restaurants. Accommodation comprises one double and one family bedrooms. *Includes Full English Breakfast (vegetarians catered for). *Tea/coffee making facilities in all rooms. *Guests' TV lounge. *Private parking and cycle lock-up. *Ramblers especially welcome. *Local maps and advice on walks available. *Lovely views from all rooms. Bed and Breakfast from £14.50, reduced rates for children.

CHEDDAR. Mrs Barbara Cook, The Poacher's Table, Cliff Street, Cheddar BS27 3PT (01934 742271). A friendly and warm welcome to all at our family-run guest house and licensed restaurant built in the 17th century and featuring many exposed oak beams. Situated at the foot of Cheddar Gorge, ideally placed to visit the many local places of interest including Bath, Wells, Glastonbury and Bristol. Three double en suite bedrooms and one twin standard bedroom, all have colour TV and tea/coffee making facilities; family rooms also available. Pets welcome. Bed and full English Breakfast from £14.50 per person per night. Evening Meal also available in our candlelit restaurant.

CREWEKERNE. Mr Gilmore, Manor Arms, North Perrott, Crewkerne TA18 7SG (Tel & Fax: 01460 72901). 🏵🏵 COMMENDED. AA QQQ. A lovely 16th century Grade II Listed inn, set in the conservation village of North Perrott and overlooking the village green. The Inn has been lovingly restored retaining much of its olde world charm. There is an inglenook fireplace, flagstone floors and oak beams. The guests' accommodation which consists of five well appointed en suite rooms, all with colour TVs and tea/coffee making facilities are situated in the Old Coach House which is behind the Inn away from the road. The Inn is renowned locally for its very high standard of home cooking both from the bar and restaurant menus. Bed and Breakfast from £21, low season breaks from £17.50 per person.

SOMERSET HAS IT ALL!

Peaceful thatched cottages, stately homes, sandy beaches, breathtaking caves, churches and cathedrals, romantic legends, heather-covered moorland — Somerset has something for everyone! Much of West Somerset lies within Exmoor National Park, and the county's many areas of upland make it ideal for a walking or nature-study holiday.

BROADVIEW GARDENS

ETB 👑👑👑 De Luxe &
AA QQQQQ Premier Selected
BOTH TOP QUALITY AWARDS

Unusual Colonial bungalow built in an era of quality. Carefully furnished with antiques. En suite rooms overlooking our beautiful 'NGS' acre of secluded, elevated gardens. Achieving top quality awards for comfort, cooking & friendliness. Quality traditional English home cooking. Rooms with easy chairs, col. T.V., Tea/Fac.C/H. Perfect touring base for country & garden lovers, antique enthusiasts, NT houses, moors & quaint old villages. Dorset coast 20 min. List of 50 places provided. A no smoking house. Open all year. B&B £23–£27. Dinner £12.50.

East Crewkerne, Nr Yeovil, Somerset
TA18 7AG (Dorset Border)
Mrs G. Swann   Tel: 01460 73424

DULVERTON. Mrs P.J. Vellacott, Springfield Farm, Ashwick Lane, Dulverton TA22 9QD (01398 323722). 👑👑 *COMMENDED.* At Springfield we offer you wonderful hospitality and delicious food. We farm 270 acres within the Exmoor National Park, rearing sheep and cattle. Peacefully situated one and a half miles' walk from Tarr Steps, four miles from Dulverton. Much wildlife including red deer can be seen on the farm. An ideal base for walking or touring Exmoor and North Devon coastal resorts. Riding and fishing nearby. One double with private WC and Shower, one twin en suite and one double en suite. Drinks making facilities in dining room. Guests' lounge with colour TV. Access to rooms at all times. Ample parking (garage by request). Children welcome. Pets by arrangement. No smoking in the house please. Bed and Breakfast from £17; Evening Meal £11.50. Reductions for children under 10 years and weekly bookings. FHB Member, West Country Tourist Board Member, Welcome Host.

DUNSTER. Mr and Mrs B.P. Lally, Exmoor House Hotel, 12 West Street, Dunster TA24 6SN (01643 821268). 👑👑👑 *HIGHLY COMMENDED.* An attractive Georgian building set in charming village of Dunster. AA and RAC Two Stars. AA Rosette for Culinary Skills. The rooms are bright and sunny in summer and centrally heated in winter. Bedrooms are en suite, with TV, radio and tea/coffee making facilities. Farm-fresh West Country produce is used to prepare varied and "different" menus, plus an extensive wine list. Home comforts, good food, and personal attention of a small hotel in relaxed informal atmosphere. Ideal for Exmoor and National Trust properties. An exclusively "no smoking" hotel. Bed and Breakfast from £26.50.

DUNSTER near. Mr and Mrs R. Brown, "Green Bay", Washford, Watchet TA23 0NN (01984 640303). 👑👑 *COMMENDED.* Small guesthouse close to Exmoor and sea. All rooms with private facilities, TV and tea/coffee trays. Good home cooking and friendly welcome assured. Bed and Breakfast from £15. Reduced rates for weekly stays.

EXFORD. Exmoor House Hotel and Restaurant, Exford TA24 7PY (01643 831304). ♛♛

APPROVED. Small, family-run Bed and Breakfast hotel over-looking the village green in the beautiful village of Exford and situated in the heart of the Exmoor National Park. Exford is an excellent base from which to enjoy riding, fishing, game shooting or just to explore the delights of the Moor. All our bedrooms have tea/coffee making facilities, colour TV, clock radios and offer en suite or private facilities. Children and pets welcome. There is a reading/residents' lounge. Please write or phone for our brochure.

EXMOOR. Merton Hotel, Western Lane, Minehead TA24 8BZ (01643 702375). Small friendly hotel in

a quiet area offering 10 en suite bedrooms, large oak-panelled dining room, lounge and bar area. Large car park. Approximately half a mile from town and sea front, ideal for exploring Exmoor and villages, walking or by car. Bed and Breakfast from £17 to £20 per night.

EXMOOR. Ann and Phillip Durbin, Cutthorne, Luckwell Bridge, Wheddon Cross TA24 7EW (Tel & Fax: 01643 831255). ♛♛♛ HIGHLY COMMENDED. Set

in the heart of Exmoor, one of the last truly unspoilt areas of the country, Cutthorne is a beautifully secluded country house dating from the 14th century. It is an ideal base for exploring the coast and countryside; good touring, walking and riding. Fly fishing is also available in our well-stocked trout pond. The house is spacious and comfortable with log fires and central heating. The three bedrooms have en suite bathrooms and the master bedroom has a four-poster bed. Candlelit dinners with traditional and vegetarian cooking and an excellent choice of breakfasts. Bed and Breakfast from £19.50. Dogs welcome. No smoking. Self catering accommodation also available.

EXMOOR. Abigail Humphrey, Highercombe Farm, Dulverton TA22 9PT (01398 323616). ♛

Highercombe Farm

COMMENDED. Relax and enjoy our special hospitality on a 450 acre working farm (including 100 acres of woodland), in an outstanding, peaceful situation on Exmoor. Off the beaten track yet only four miles from Dulverton. We are an ideal base for exploring coast and moor. There is an abundance of wildlife on the farm including wild red deer. We are happy to take you on a farm tour. The farmhouse enjoys spectacular views, central heating, large visitors' lounge and log fires. Pretty rooms with generous en suite bathrooms. Delicious farmhouse cooking, fresh produce, home-made marmalade, etc. Bed and Breakfast from £18; Dinner, Bed and Breakfast from £29. Private, well equipped self catering wing of farmhouse also available (4 KEYS COMMENDED).

EXMOOR NATIONAL PARK. Shelagh and Larry Maxwell, Little Brendon Hill, Wheddon Cross TA24 7BG (Tel & Fax: 01643 841556). ETB 🏵🏵 *HIGHLY COMMENDED.* AA QQQQ. Beautifully appointed farmhouse in the centre of the Exmoor National Park. Three lovely en suite bedrooms with colour TV and hospitality trays. Fully centrally heated, non-smoking. Cosy candlelit dinners, log fires and excellent food. A warm and friendly welcome awaits. Accommodation with full English breakfast from £17.50; four-course Dinner £12.50. Please ring for brochure.

FROME near. Mrs Molly Brown, The Lodge, Fairwood Farm, Standerwick, Near Frome BA11 2QA (01373 823515). The Lodge is situated in pleasant country surroundings with good walks and served by several good local inns. It is on the B3099 within quarter of a mile of the A36. Warminster is three miles and Bath 12 miles. All bedrooms are en suite with tea making facilities and colour TV. One has twin beds, two have double beds. Full breakfast is served and there is central heating throughout. Bed and Breakfast from £17.50 per person. Ample parking. Sorry no pets.

GLASTONBURY. Mrs J.M. Gillam, Wood Lane House, Butleigh, Glastonbury BA6 8TG (01458 850354). Charming old AA Listed house with lovely views over open countryside and woods. Quiet yet not isolated and only 200 yards from excellent village "local". Ideal touring centre for Cheddar, Wells, Bath and many beauty spots and only 20 miles from coast. Attractions include Butterfly Farm, Fleet Air Arm Museum, Rural Life Museum, cheese making, steam engines and many places of historic interest. Accommodation comprises three double rooms with well equipped en suite facilities; tea/coffee and TV on request. Comfortable and warm sitting/dining room. Open all year round except Christmas and New Year. Car essential. Parking. Bed and Breakfast £18.50. Half price for children.

GLASTONBURY. Mrs L. White, Bradley Batch, 64 Bath Road, Ashcott, Bridgwater TA7 9QJ (01458 210256). Tourist Board Listed. Cottage guest house, five miles from Glastonbury on A39; convenient for M5 Motorway (exit Junction 23). Three comfortable double rooms with washbasins; central heating; colour TV lounge; shower. Car park; attractive garden. Meals available in Inns nearby. Well behaved dogs welcome. Weekly terms, reductions for children on request. 30 minutes from Wells, Wookey and Cheddar, 20 minutes from Fleet Air Arm Museum, one hour to Bath, Exmoor or Dorset coast. Bed and Breakfast from £14.50; single occupancy from £15.50. Non smokers preferred. Send SAE or telephone for more information.

GLASTONBURY. Mrs D.P. Atkinson, Court Lodge, Butleigh, Glastonbury BA6 8SA (01458 850575). A warm welcome awaits at attractive, modernised 1850 Lodge with homely atmosphere. Set in picturesque garden on the edge of Butleigh, three miles from historic Glastonbury. Only a five minute walk to pub in village which serves lovely meals. Accommodation in one double, one twin and one single bedrooms; constant hot water, central heating. Bathroom adjacent to bedrooms. TV lounge. Tea/coffee served. Bed and Breakfast from £13.50; Evening Meal by arrangement. Children welcome at reduced rates.

GLASTONBURY. Mrs Dinah Gifford, Little Orchard, Ashwell Lane, Glastonbury BA6 8BG (01458 831620). This holiday accommodation is centrally positioned for touring the West Country, lying at the foot of historic Glastonbury Tor, with breathtaking views over the Vale of Avalon. Convenient for A361 Glastonbury to Shepton Mallet Road. Cheddar is ten miles away; Weston-super-Mare 18 miles; the "Lions of Longleat" 15 miles; and Wells Cathedral five miles. It is in the heart of the sheepskin and shoe-making industry — available at factory prices. Facilities for guests include colour TV lounge, central heating, hot & cold washbasins, and bathroom with shower. Car parking. Children welcome, cot. There will be a welcoming "cuppa" on your arrival at this friendly family home. Pay phone. Open all year. Bed and Breakfast from £14. Fire Certificate.

GLASTONBURY. Mrs Elizabeth Ruddle, Laverley House, West Pennard, Glastonbury BA8 8NE

(01749 890696). ww Tony and Liz look forward to welcoming you to their attractive and spacious Listed Georgian farmhouse with superb views, paddock and gardens, all set in a rural area. There are two double bedrooms with en-suite bathrooms and a family bedroom with private bathroom. Colour TV and hospitality trays in all bedrooms. We have a comfortable guests' lounge and diningroom and are happy to provide a cot and high chair for children. Fresh produce is served, traditionally cooked. A good area for touring; Wells six miles, Bath 20 miles. Many National Trust houses and gardens. Bed and Breakfast from £18.50. Please telephone for brochure.

GLASTONBURY. Mrs Mary Dodds, Twelve Hides, Quarry Lane, Butleigh, Glastonbury BA6 8TE

(01458 50380). A six acre smallholding with small pedigree Wensleydale flock (participation welcome), own handspinning. Four miles to Glastonbury and within easy reach of Bath, Cheddar Gorge, Wookey Caves, site of legendary Camelot, Wetlands, etc; yet peaceful and away from it all. Exceptional view across Vale of Avalon to Glastonbury Tor, Wells Cathedral and Mendip Hills. Overlooking picturesque Butleigh village, good pub food within walking distance. Accommodation comprises one double bedded room, two twin-bedded rooms (one with washbasin), all with tea/coffee making facilities. Guest bathroom with bath, WC and washbasin. Separate guest shower room with WC/washbasin. Traditional English Breakfast. Terms from £15.

GLASTONBURY near. Mrs M.A. Bell, New House Farm, Burtle Road, Westhay, Near Glastonbury

BA6 9TT (01458 860238). ww _HIGHLY COMMENDED._ Working dairy farm, situated on the Somerset Levels. Large Victorian Farmhouse offering comfortable accommodation, central for touring Wells, Cheddar, Bath, Burnham-on-Sea etc. Accommodation comprises one family room and one double room, each with en suite facilities, colour TV, tea/coffee facilities, hair dryer, clock radio, etc; lounge with colour TV, separate dining room and conservatory. Central heating throughout. Ample parking and warm welcome assured. Bed and full English Breakfast from £18 to £20; Evening Meal £10. Self catering also available. Directions: near Peat Moor Visitor Centre which is signposted from A39 and B3151.

GLASTONBURY near. Mrs Jan Hill, Pear Tree, 16 Manor Road, Catcott, Near Bridgwater TA7 9HF

(01278 722390). Family home offering comfortable accommodation pleasantly situated on the slopes of the Polden Hills overlooking the Somerset Levels. "Pear Tree" is a 17th century former farmhouse set in half an acre of gardens in the award-winning village of Catcott. Accommodation comprises one double and one twin-bedded room, both with washbasins, heating, shaver points and tea/coffee facilities. One bathroom with toilet and a separate toilet, both for use of guests. An ideal base for touring the history-rich county of Somerset. Glastonbury, Wells, Cheddar, Bath are all close by. Licensed. No smoking. Parking. Children welcome at reduced rates. Bed and Breakfast from £14.50 to £15.

GREINTON. Mrs M. Tingey, Greinton House, Near Bridgwater TA7 9BW (01458 210307). Greinton

is on the A361 between Taunton and Street where Clarks renowned factory shop village is located. The house is a beautiful Listed former rectory (dating back to the 16th century) with panelling and galleried hall, situated on the southern slopes of the Polden Hills, overlooking Sedgemoor. Accommodation can be arranged to suit individual requirements. There are two bathrooms, one luxury en suite and a shower room. All bedrooms have tea/coffee making facilities. Three sitting rooms; TV. Ample parking. There is a hard tennis court and a croquet lawn. The premises are not suitable for young children and no pets are allowed in the house. No smoking. In winter there is oil-fired central heating and log fires. Open all year for Bed and Breakfast from £20 nightly.

HENSTRIDGE. Fountain Inn Motel, High Street, Henstridge, Templecombe BA8 0RA (01963 362722). 👑👑 Friendly 17th century village inn situated just off the A30 serving real ale and an extensive menu seven days a week. Sited behind are six ground floor double bedrooms, all with shower and WC en suite, direct dial telephone, colour TV, beverage facilities, individual heating and easy parking. The motel lies in the Blackmore Vale and is an ideal touring base being close to the historic towns of Shaftesbury and Sherborne with many other attractions, gardens and sites to visit. Special rates for longer stays are available. Cot, extra bed and dogs by arrangement. One room with wheelchair access. Bed and Breakfast from £12.50 to £23.50. Evening Meal available.

HENSTRIDGE. Patricia and Brian Thompson, Quiet Corner Farm, Henstridge BA8 0RA (01963 363045; Fax:01963 363400). 👑👑 *COMMENDED.* Lovely

old stone farmhouse and barns, some converted to self catering cottages sleeping two/four, set in five acres beautiful garden and orchards with sheep and miniature Shetland ponies. The village, 'twixt Shaftesbury and Sherborne, has super pubs, two restaurants, shops and post office. Marvellous centre for touring Somerset, Dorset and Wiltshire with host of National Trust and other houses and gardens. Golf and fishing nearby. The spacious farmhouse is most comfortable with central heating throughout. Bedrooms with washbasins and tea making facilities; one en suite. Safe car parking. Payphone. Bed and Breakfast from £19. Reductions for children under 12 years. SAE, or telephone, for brochure. Special offer: Three days for price of two (subject to availability) October 1st to end May except Public Holidays.

HIGHBRIDGE near. Mrs B.M. Puddy, "Laurel Farm", Mark Causeway, Near Highbridge TA9 4PZ (01278 641216). 👑 *COMMENDED.* **Working farm.** Laurel Farm is over 200 years old with 120 acres and 70 milking cows, Friesian and Holstein. We are about two miles from MARK CHURCH and VILLAGE on the WELLS TO BURNHAM-ON-SEA B3139 road, two miles from M5 Junction 22. Ideal touring centre or halfway house. There is a large sittingroom with a colour TV, log fires September to May. CENTRAL HEATING, ELECTRIC BLANKETS. Washbasins in all bedrooms. Nicely decorated with fitted carpets throughout. Separate tables in dining room. Doubles, singles and family rooms, shower, two baths, three toilets. En suite available. Car essential/or bike. Undercover garages. OPEN ALL THE YEAR. RAC Commended.

ILMINSTER. Mrs G. Phillips, 'Hermitage', 29 Station Road, Ilminster TA19 9BE (01460 53028). Enjoy the friendly atmosphere of a lovely listed 17th century

house with beams and inglenook. Bedrooms, with four-posters, overlook two and a half acres of delightful gardens, woods and hills beyond. Twin or double rooms with washbasins. Lounge with log fire and colour TV. Tea or coffee with homemade biscuits on arrival. Full English breakfast. Traditional inns nearby for evening meals. Ideal touring centre for Quantock Hills, Wells, Glastonbury, Lyme Regis and many picturesque villages. Several National Trust properties, gardens and historic houses within a few miles. Ten miles from M5, half mile from A303. Bed and Breakfast from £15; reductions for children.

LANGPORT. Mrs E. Richardson, Wick Cottage, Wick, Langport TA10 0NW (01458 252788). Situated at the edge of Somerset Levels close to River Parrett, below wooded Wick Hill. Quiet hamlet in predominantly stock grazing agricultural setting. Stone cottage with modern facilities offering spacious double bedroom (en suite) and twin-bedded room (private bathroom). Tea/coffee making facilities. Guests' lounge with open fireplace and TV. Full English breakfast cooked on the Aga. Warm welcome assured. Ideal local fishing, cycling, crafts, RSPB. Easy reach high moors, north and south coasts, historic Bath, Wells, Dunster and National Trust properties. Terms: £17.50 per person for one night, £15 per person more than one night.

LANGPORT. Mrs S. Roberts, The White House, The Hill, Langport TA10 9QZ (01458 250892). Georgian house close to shops in conservation area with unbeatable views from terrace over Somerset Levels and River Parrett. Ideal walking country. Lovely garden and orchard; conservatory. One double and one twin-bedded room with washbasins; own bathroom. Close to M5, Dartmoor, Exmoor, Taunton and just a three quarter of an hour drive to Bath. Within easy reach for visiting Montacute House, Barrington Court, the famous East Lambrook Gardens and Kelways Nurseries — renowned for peonies and irises. Bed and Breakfast from £16 per person according to season.

MARTOCK. Mrs H. Turton, "Wychwood", 7 Bearley Road, Martock TA12 6PG (01935 825601).

👑👑 *HIGHLY COMMENDED.* Quality, comfortable accommodation. Excellent home cooking. In quiet position just off A303. Ideal touring location, close to Montacute House, Fleet Air Arm Museum, Tintinhull Gardens and eight other "classic" Gardens. Walk the Leland Trail through Camelot Country and the Legend of King Arthur. Yeovil 10 minutes, Sherborne 15 minutes; Glastonbury, Wells, Taunton and M5, Junction 25, under 30 minutes. TV, radio and tea/coffee making facilities in all bedrooms. Double rooms with en suite, twin with private bathroom. Comfortable residents' lounge, separate diningroom. Garden. Full central heating. Parking. No smoking. Bed and full English Breakfast from £18. Dinner £15. Open all year. AA QQQQ Selected, RAC Acclaimed, FHG Diploma Award. Credit cards accepted.

MINEHEAD near. Mrs Rosemary Tucker, West Luccombe Farm, Porlock, Near Minehead TA24 8HT (01643 862478). Working farm. West Luccombe is a working farm of 340 acres carrying beef cattle, sheep, arable. An ideal location for tourists needing bed and breakfast, with Porlock one mile, Minehead five miles and Horner quarter-of-a-mile. West Luccombe was originally a Manor House on the National Trust Estate and stands amidst lovely gardens, with a river running close to the grounds 100 yards away and surrounded by beautiful countryside of great interest to walkers. Accommodation comprises two double and one family bedrooms, all with washbasins and tea/coffee making facilities; bathroom, two toilets; sitting room with colour TV; dining room. Pets by arrangement. Children welcome at reduced rates. Open Easter to October. A car is essential and ample parking space is provided. Bed and Breakfast from £15 nightly; weekly rates quoted on request.

MINEHEAD near. Jane and Bryan Jackson, Hunters Moon, Exford, Near Minehead TA24 7PP

(01643 831695; Fax: 01643 831576). Hunters Moon in the heart of the Exmoor National Park on the edge of the village of Exford. Come and join us in our cosy bungalow smallholding set in five acres with glorious views, comfortable rooms with a large lounge to relax in plus a sun terrace to enjoy. Our dining room enjoys superb views across the Exe Valley to the moor beyond. Open all year including Christmas and New Year. Bed and Breakfast £16 per person per night; Evening Meal £10. Reductions for children. Seven nights for the price of six. Well behaved dogs are very welcome.

PORLOCK. Mrs Christine Fitzgerald, Seapoint, Upway, Redway, Porlock TA24 8QE (Tel & Fax:

01643 862289). 🐾🐾 *HIGHLY COMMENDED.* AA QQQ Recommended. A warm welcome awaits you at Seapoint, a comfortable Edwardian guesthouse with panoramic sea views and situated in Exmoor's wild heather moorland. The atmosphere at Seapoint is warm and friendly and relaxed with the added pleasure of open log fires. The luxurious bedrooms are all en suite and equipped with TV, etc. Dine by candlelight and enjoy our delicious traditional or vegetarian food together with a bottle of fine wine. We ensure that your stay is a memorable one and you will find that our tastefully furnished Edwardian house makes a perfect setting for that special occasion. Bed and Breakfast £20; Dinner £12.50.

PORLOCK. Mrs A.J. Richards, Ash Farm, Porlock, Near Minehead TA24 8JN (01643 862414). Ash Farm is situated two miles off the main Porlock to Lynmouth road (A39) and overlooks the sea. It is two-and-a-half miles from Porlock Weir, and eleven from Minehead and Lynmouth. Only 10 minutes to the tiny church of "Culbone", and Coleridge is reputed to have used the farmhouse which is 200 to 300 years old. The house has double, single and family bedrooms, all with washbasins; toilet; large sittingroom and diningroom. Open from Easter to October. Oare Church, Valley of Rocks, County Gate, Horner Valley and Dunkery Beacon are all within easy reach. Bed and Breakfast from £14 which includes bedtime drink. SAE please.

QUANTOCK HILLS. Susan Lilienthal, Parsonage Farm, Over Stowey, Bridgwater TA5 1HA (01278

733237). Traditional 17th century farmhouse and organic smallholding in quiet location in Quantock Hills with delightful walled gardens; orchard; and walks to explore. Delicious meals are prepared using the farm's produce — fresh eggs, home-made breads and jams — and served before an open fire. Three double bedrooms include colour TV and tea/coffee facilities, en suite available. Guests are invited to enjoy the gardens or relax in the log-fired sitting room. Spacious and welcoming, this is an ideal base for rambling and exploring the Quantock Hills, Exmoor, North Somerset Coast, as well as Glastonbury and Wells. No smoking. Bed and full Breakfast from £17, reductions for children. Optional Evening Meal £12.

FHG PUBLICATIONS LIMITED publish a large range of well-known accommodation guides. We will be happy to send you details or you can use the order form at the back of this book.

QUANTOCKS. Mrs N. Thompson, Plainsfield Court, Plainsfield, Over Stowey, Bridgwater TA5 1HH (01278 671292; Fax: 01278 671687). Plainsfield

Court is the 15th century ancestral home of the Blake family. The farmhouse, is a Listed building of historic interest set in the Quantock Hills, superbly located for walking, riding, fishing and all country pursuits. Magnificent views, walled garden and cider orchards; wild Red Deer are often seen grazing in the surrounding fields. Two stylish double bedrooms with private bathroom, TV, tea/coffee making facilities. Open log fires in the sitting room and ancient beamed dining room. Home cooked meals available. Bed and Breakfast from £20. Pets by arrangement, stabling available. No smoking in B&B. Self catering (The Granary) for four/six also available.

SHEPTON MALLET. Mrs M. White, Barrow Farm, North Wootton, Shepton Mallet BA4 4HL (01749 890245). Working farm. This farm accommodation is AA

QQQ Listed. Barrow is a dairy farm of 146 acres. The house is 15th century and of much character, situated quietly between Wells, Glastonbury and Shepton Mallet. It makes an excellent touring centre for visiting Somerset's beauty spots and historic places, for example, Cheddar, Bath, Wookey Hole and Longleat. Guest accommodation consists of two double rooms, one family room, one single room and one twin-bedded room, each with washbasin, TV and tea/coffee making facilities. Bathroom, two toilets; two lounges, one with colour TV; diningroom with separate tables. Guests can enjoy farmhouse fare in generous variety, home baking a speciality. Bed and Breakfast, with optional four course Dinner available. Car essential; ample parking. Children welcome; cot and babysitting available. Open all year except Christmas. Sorry, no pets. Bed and Breakfast from £15 to £16; Dinner, Bed and Breakfast from £140 weekly.

SHEPTON MALLET. Mr and Mrs J. Grattan, Park Farm House, Forum Lane, Bowlish, Shepton Mallet BA4 5JL (01749 343673; Fax: 01749 345279). A

17th century house, formerly a working farm, situated in a conservation area. The accommodation comprises one twin-bedded room (bathroom en suite) and a suite of a double bedroom and a twin bedroom with private bathroom. There is ample discreet car parking. Conveniently situated close to the ancient Cathedral City of Wells (four miles), Cheddar Gorge and Caves, the new Clarkes village at Street and Longleat within 12 miles. The Georgian city of Bath and Bristol are only 18 miles away. Shepton Mallet has good restaurants, many local pubs and easy access to the scenic Mendip Hills. Bed and Breakfast £16.50 per person per night: no single person supplement.

SOMERTON. Mrs Jennie Ruddle, Mathias House, High Street, Keinton Mandeville TA11 6DZ (Tel & Fax: 01458 223921). Luxury accommodation and a warm

welcome awaits you at this village property on the outskirts of a small Somerset village. Ideally situated for touring historic Glastonbury and Wells, four miles from Clarks Village, and famous Montacute House a mere 10 minutes' drive. Two double rooms, full bathroom, TV and welcome tray, all with the intent of making your stay as comfortable as possible. Good home cooking, evening meal optional. Guests' own sitting room. Strictly non-smokers. £18 per person per night.

TAUNTON. Mrs Chris Jordan, Waterpitts Farm, Broomfield, Quantock Hills, Bridgwater TA5 1AT (01823 451679). Tourist Board Listed. Quiet, friendly, secluded smallholding set in the beautiful Quantock Hills, six miles from Taunton and Bridgwater with good food and country pubs nearby. Ideally situated for most outdoor pursuits including walking, golfing, mountain biking, riding and fishing. Facilities on farm for cleaning; covered storage for bikes; stables for guests' horses. Large, safe parking area for cars. Animals on smallholding include free range ducks and chickens, sheep, cats and dogs. Accommodation comprises one family room and one double room. Central heating. No smoking. Bed and Breakfast from £15 per night. Children under 10 years half price.

TAUNTON. Mr and Mrs P.J. Painter, Blorenge House, 57 Staplegrove Road, Taunton TA1 1DG (Tel & Fax: 01823 283005). AA QQQQ Selected. Spacious Victorian residence set in large gardens with a swimming pool and large car park. Situated just five minutes' walking distance from Taunton town centre, railway and bus station. 21 comfortable bedrooms with washbasins, central heating, colour TV and tea making facilities. Four of the bedrooms have traditional four-poster beds, ideal for weekends away and honeymoon couples. Family and twin rooms are available. The majority of rooms have en suite facilities. Large dining room traditionally furnished; full English breakfast and continental breakfasts included in the price. Evening Meals available on request. Licensed bar. Please send for our colour brochure.

TAUNTON. Mrs Smy, Barn Close Nurseries, Taunton TA3 5DH (01823 443507). Bed and Breakfast or an ideal touring base for Somerset, Devon and Dorset. Just one mile from Junction 25 of the M5 motorway, two miles from Taunton on the A358. Pleasant gardens with heated swimming pool in season plus an all weather tennis court. Ample parking. A family home offering a warm welcome. Children and pets welcome. Central heating. Please write or telephone for further details.

TAUNTON. Tom and Rowena Kirk, Yallands Farmhouse, Staplegrove, Taunton TA2 6PZ (Tel & Fax: 01823 278979). A delightful 16th century Listed farmhouse which has become an oasis of "Old England" as the town has expanded over the former farmland. Quietly situated one and a half miles north-west of the town centre. Guests are assured of a warm welcome and individual attention. The en suite bedrooms are comfortable, well furnished and attractive with colour TV and tea/coffee making facilities. Ground floor single room available. Ideally situated between the Quantock and Blackdown Hills, with many places of interest within easy reach. A pub serving lunches and evening meals is within easy walking distance. Ample parking. Open all year. Brochure/tariff available.

TAUNTON. Mrs Dianne Besley, Prockters Farm, West Monkton, Taunton TA2 8QN (01823 412269). ✿✿ Prockters is a large 17th century oak-beamed farmhouse with open fireplace, only two miles from Taunton and M5 motorway. A cup of tea and a cake welcomes you on arrival at the family farmhouse, set at the foot of the Quantock Hills. All the bedrooms have washbasins, colour TV and tea-making facilities, including ground floor en-suite bedrooms suitable for disabled guests. Only five minutes from the M5, just off the A38 and A361. We are ideally situated to break your journey, or for a farmhouse holiday. Lovely walks and wild life parks and historic houses to see. Bed and Breakfast from £18. Reduction on a week's holiday. Children and pets welcome.

TAUNTON near. Mrs M. Summers, Warrescote, 2 Trendle Lane, Bicknoller, Taunton TA4 4EG (01984 656257). ETB Listed. Situated in this quiet picturesque friendly village at the foot of the Quantock Hills, the house stands in its own large garden just beyond the church. Easily accessible from the M5 motorway and the A39 Exmoor, Bath, Bristol and coast. Comfortable accommodation consisting of one twin bedroom and one single which easily converts to a twin, both with private bathroom and tea/coffee making facilities; lounge with TV. Well behaved pets welcome. Reduced rates for children. Bed and Breakfast from £13.

TAUNTON. Mrs Susan Honeyball, Manor Farm, Waterpitts, Broomfield, Bridgwater TA5 1AT (01823 451266). This 14th century farm house is situated in the folds of the beautiful Quantock Hills, six miles from Taunton and Bridgwater with good food and pubs. It is a working stud farm of 140 acres with a lovely lake and trout fishing available. Ideally situated for most outdoor pursuits including walking, golfing, mountain bikes, horse riding facilities, stables for guests' horses. Storage for bikes. Safe parking area for cars. Large garden. Accommodation itself comprises one double room with balcony and washbasin, one twin-bedded room; dining room with log fire. Children welcome, cot and babysitting available. Open all year. No smoking. Bed and Breakfast from £14; children under 10 years half price.

TAUNTON near. Mrs J. Greenway, Woodlands Farm, Bathealton, Near Taunton TA4 2AH (01984

623271). A warm, relaxed atmosphere, delicious food and comfortable accommodation are only some of the hallmarks of this cosy farmhouse which welcomes guests from June to September. Ideal for touring Somerset, Devon, Exmoor and the coast, there is also ample opportunity for simply relaxing on the farm or enjoying some carp fishing. Children welcomed at reduced rates. Family room en suite. Also available self-catering wing sleeping five. Bed and Breakfast, including bedtime drink and tea-making facilities, from £14 daily.

TAUNTON near. Anne and Bill Slipper, Strawbridges Farm, Churchstanton, Taunton TA3 7DP

(01823 601591). ᵿ ᵿ A non-working farm, Strawbridges is surrounded by unspoilt countryside on the Blackdown Hills, now designated an area of outstanding natural beauty, and offers a warm relaxed atmosphere. Accommodation comprises two double bedrooms with private facilities, two twin rooms and a single, all centrally heated, with washbasins, tea/coffee facilities and colour TVs. Guests have their own lounge and diningroom. Strawbridges is situated centrally between North and South Coasts, is ideal for touring and only six miles from Taunton. Directions: M5 Junction 26, take Wellington by-pass for one mile and left on Chard Road for approximately four miles. Bed and Breakfast from £15 to £18 per person.

TAUNTON near. Mrs Pam Parry, Pear Tree Cottage, Stapley Churchstanton, Taunton TA3 7QA

(Tel & Fax: 01823 601224). An old thatched country cottage halfway between Taunton and Honiton, set in the idyllic Blackdown Hills which has been designated an Area of Outstanding Natural Beauty. Picturesque countryside laced with winding lanes full of natural flora and fauna. Wildlife abounds. Three-quarters of an acre traditional cottage garden leading off to two and a half acres of meadow garden planted with specimen trees. Central for north/south coasts of Somerset, Dorset and Devon. Exmoor, Dartmoor, Bristol, Bath, etc within little more than an hour's drive. Many gardens and National Trust properties encompassed in day out. Double/single — own facilities, TV, tea/coffee. Dining/sitting room. Evening Meals available. Open all year.

TAUNTON near. Mrs Pamela Akers, Springfield House, Walford Cross, West Monkton, Taunton

TA2 8QW (01823 412116). ᵿ ᵿ *HIGHLY COMMENDED.* A country house set in grounds of two acres with a friendly relaxed atmosphere in quiet, tranquil surroundings. The bedrooms are all en suite and they, with a private sitting room, are in a newly converted annexe next to the house. All rooms have tea/coffee making facilities with complimentary tray, TV. Central heating. Toiletries supplied. There is an iron and board, hair dryers and telephone available. Ideal base for touring the area, excellent for walking, fishing and golf. Just five minutes' drive off M5 Junction 25 and Taunton centre. Signposted on A38. Set back up a private drive with private parking. Bed and Breakfast £18 per person (double occupancy), £25 single occupancy. Reductions on a week's holiday. AA QQQQ.

FREE and REDUCED RATE Holiday Visits!
See our READERS' OFFER VOUCHER for details!

TAUNTON/BRIDGWATER.Mrs Ann Comer, The Old Rectory, Thurloxton TA2 8RH (01823 412686).

👑 👑 Six miles from Taunton/Bridgwater, three miles from M5. Lovely old family house in rural village, overlooking Somerset Levels to Glastonbury and Cheddar. Set in very large, well-maintained gardens with putting green. Ideal for touring, fishing or just relaxing. Excellent accommodation with tea/coffee making facilities. TV lounge and separate dining room. Traditional English cooking. Rates are reduced for children. Open from Easter to October. Bed and Breakfast from £15 nightly, from £85 weekly. Write or phone for brochure.

WATCHET. Mrs Sarah Richmond, Hungerford Farm, Washford, Watchet TA23 0LA (01984 640285).

Hungerford Farm is a comfortable 13th century farmhouse on a 350-acre mixed farm, three-quarters of a mile from the West Somerset Steam Railway. Situated in beautiful countryside on the edge of the Brendon Hills and Exmoor National Park. Within easy reach of the North Devon coast, two and a half miles from the Bristol Channel and Quantock Hills. Marvellous country for walking, riding (STABLING FOR OWN HORSES AVAILABLE), and fishing on the reservoirs. Family room with TV and twin-bedded room; own bathroom, shower, toilet. Own lounge with TV and open fire. Children welcome at reduced rates, cot and high chair. Sorry, no pets. Bed and Breakfast from £16. Evening drink included. Open February to November.

WELLS. Mrs Janet Gould, Milton Manor Farm, Old Bristol Road, Upper Milton, Wells BA5 3AH (01749 673394). 👑 Working farm.

Manor Farm is a Grade II star Listed Elizabethan Manor House superbly situated on southern slopes of Mendip Hills one mile north from Wells. It is a beef farm of 130 acres. Three large rooms for visitors with hot and cold water, central heating and tea/coffee facilities. Full English breakfast with choice of menu served at separate tables in panelled dining room. Colour TV. Large peaceful garden with lovely view towards the sea. Ideal for walking on the Mendip Hills and exploring local places of historic interest. Access to house at all times. Fire Certificate held. AA listed QQQ. No smoking. Open January to December for Bed and Breakfast from £14.50 per person. Reductions for children and week-long stays. Brochure on request.

WELLS. Mrs Pat Higgs, Home Farm, Stoppers Lane, Coxley, Wells BA5 1QS (01749 672434). 👑 👑 COMMENDED. Pat Higgs offers a relaxed holiday, long or short stay welcome, in a peaceful spot just off the A39. We have seven bedrooms, some en suite. The rooms are well decorated and have TV and tea/coffee making facilities. We are in a very good touring area with Glastonbury, Wookey Hole Caves, Cheddar Gorge, National Trust properties and Bath all within easy reach, also many more places of interest. Good pubs and restaurants very close, within walking distance. Bed and Breakfast from £17 to £19 en suite. Directions: A39 between Wells and Glastonbury (one and a half miles from Wells, four miles Glastonbury). AA QQ Recommended. Please write or phone for brochure.

WELLS near. Mrs Betty Hares, Highcroft, Wells Road, Priddy, Wells BA5 3AU (01749 673446).

👑 COMMENDED. Set in 23 acres of rolling countryside, Highcroft is a new luxury, traditional, natural stone house, fully centrally heated and double glazed. It has two en-suite rooms and one with washbasin, all with tea/coffee making facilities. There is a separate TV lounge and diningroom. Situated in the Mendip Hills with delightful views, Highcroft is ideal for walking and touring. Four miles to Wells and Wookey Hole, six miles Cheddar. Trout fishing, golf, riding and swimming nearby. Bed and Breakfast from £17. Open all year.

WESTON-SUPER-MARE. Mrs Gillian F. Bowley, "Conifers", 63 Milton Road, Weston-Super-Mare BS23 2SP (01934 624404). 👑 👑 COMMENDED. A high quality Bed and Breakfast establishment situated on pleasant road into town centre (eight minutes' walk). Centrally heated house, lying back off the road, with private parking. Guests are accommodated in one double room, one double en-suite, one twin bedroom, all with colour TV and tea making facilities. Separate tables in a pleasant dining room. Many guests return year after year. Ideal centre for touring the many local attractions, Bath, Wells, Cheddar, etc. Open January to mid December for Bed and Breakfast from £16; singles taken £2 extra charge. Take A371, Junction 21 off M5. AA QQ Recommended.

WESTON-SUPER-MARE. Mrs Lynn Warren, Parasol Guest House, 49 Walliscote Road, Weston-super-Mare BS23 1EE (01934 636409) A warm welcome awaits you at our small but friendly Guest House, near beach; Tropicana, parks and town only 10 minutes' walk away. The Parasol is situated at the quiet end of town and on the flat. An ideal place for peace and quiet, but ideally situated for touring. Double, family and twin rooms available. We serve a hearty English breakfast. Bed and Breakfast from £16 per night, according to season. Bed, Breakfast and Evening Meal; weekly rates available. Free tea/coffee facilities and colour TVs in all rooms; all en suite. Please write or telephone for colour brochure.

ETB ♛♛♛ Commended

Resident hosts: Mr & Mrs D. Holt

"MOORLANDS"
Hutton, Near Weston-super-Mare
Tel: Bleadon (01934) 812283

Enjoy fine food and warm hospitality at this impressive late Georgian house set in landscaped gardens below the slopes of the Western Mendips. A wonderful touring centre, perfectly placed for visits to beaches, sites of special interest and historic buildings. Families with children particularly welcome; reduced terms and pony rides in our paddock. Good wholesome meals, with the emphasis on our own home-grown produce. Full central heating, open fire in comfortable lounge. Licensed. Open January to early November.

WESTON-SUPER-MARE. Mr and Mrs H. Wallington, Braeside Hotel, 2 Victoria Park, Weston-super-Mare BS23 2HZ (Tel & Fax: 01934 626642). ♛♛♛ COMMENDED. AA QQQQ Selected, RAC Highly Acclaimed. Our delightful family run Hotel is superbly situated close to the sea front, yet sufficiently far back from the hustle and bustle to enjoy a peaceful and relaxed holiday. Set in a cul-de-sac (with unrestricted parking) we are in a slightly elevated position with magnificent views over Weston Bay. All our nine bedrooms have bath/shower and toilet en suite; colour TV, coffee/tea making and are tastefully decorated, creating just the right atmosphere in which to relax after a busy day. Although we are a fairly small hotel guests can expect quality and service.

WESTON-SUPER-MARE. Mrs T.G. Moore, Purn House Farm, Bleadon, Weston-super-Mare BS24 0QE (01934 812324; Fax: 01934 811029). ♛♛ COMMENDED. 17th century creeper-clad house standing on a 700 acre mixed farm at the foot of Purn Hill where there are panoramic views of the Bristol Channel, Glastonbury Tor in the east to Exmoor and the Welsh Mountains in the west. The house contains some period furniture in day rooms. Tastefully decorated bedrooms — three double, one single, four family en suite rooms (one ground floor); modern conveniences; sitting room, dining room and games room for use of visitors. Excellent home cooking with traditional menus using home produce when possible. Special diets by arrangement. No pets. Open February to December. A car is not essential, though parking provided. Bed and Breakfast. Three day special breaks available. Fire Certificate held. Miles of sandy beaches a short distance at Uphill, Weston, Berrow and Brean. Fishing, golf, sailing available; also pony riding locally. En route for the West Mendip Way walk. Milking may be seen in the very modern milking parlour. SAE for brochure. AA Listed.

YEOVIL. Sue and Geoff Hector, Greystones Guest House, 152 Hendford Hill, Yeovil BA20 2RG (01935 26124). ♕ Close to showground, ski centre and Ninesprings beauty spot. Within walking distance of town. Accommodation comprises one single, two double, one triple family room, one twin en suite, two triple family rooms en suite, all have washbasin, colour TV, tea/coffee making facilities and central heating; three bathrooms. Parking available for seven cars. Open all year. Childen and pets welcome. Bed and Breakfast for one person (single) £18, for two people (twin/double) £32; en suite for one person £25, for two people (twin/double) £35.

STAFFORDSHIRE

ECCLESHALL. M. Hiscoe-James, Offley Grove Farm, Adbaston, Eccleshall ST20 0QB (01785 280205). ♕ *COMMENDED.* AA QQ Recommended, RAC Listed. You'll consider this a good find! Quality accommodation and excellent breakfasts. Small traditional mixed farm surrounded by beautiful countryside. The house is tastefully furnished and provides all home comforts. Whether you are planning to book here for a break in your journey, stay for a weekend or take your holidays here, you will find something to suit all tastes among the many local attractions. Situated on the Staffordshire/Shropshire borders we are convenient for Stoke-on-Trent, Ironbridge, Alton Towers, etc. Just 15 minutes from M6 and M54; midway between Eccleshall and Newport, four miles from the A519. Reductions for children. Play area for small children. Open all year. Bed and Breakfast from £15. Many guests return to enjoy our hospitality. Self catering cottages also available. Brochure on request.

ECCLESHALL. Mrs Sue Pimble, Cobblers Cottage, Kerry Lane, Eccleshall ST21 6EJ (01785 850116). ♕♕ A five minute walk from the centre of Eccleshall and just past the 12th century church is Cobblers Cottage, in a quiet lane within the conservation area. We offer three bedrooms (one double, one twin and one family), all en suite with colour TV, tea/coffee facilities and central heating. Eccleshall has seven pubs, five with restaurants for your evening meal. Five miles from Junction 14 of M6, Eccleshall is ideally situated for the Potteries, Wedgwood, Ironbridge, Alton Towers and other attractions. Children and pets welcome. Non-smoking establishment. Bed and Breakfast from £16 per person per night; £24 for single occupancy. Reduction for children sharing.

LEEK. Mrs Barbara White, Micklea Farm, Micklea Lane, Longsdon, Near Leek, Stoke-on-Trent ST9 9QA (01538 385006; Fax: 01538 382882). ETB Listed *APPROVED.* Quietly situated off A53 yet ideally located for touring the area, this delightful old stone house, boasting a warm friendly atmosphere and comfortable accommodation, is the perfect base for a family holiday. Open all year; two twin or double rooms and two single rooms; guest lounge with TV; large garden; ample parking. Children welcome. Visitors will enjoy pleasant canal and country park walks, fishing, golf, gliding and hang gliding. Alton Towers and the beautiful Peak District and Potteries are near at hand. Bed and Breakfast £16; Bed, Breakfast and Evening Meal £27 by arrangement. Further details on request.

WHEN MAKING ENQUIRIES PLEASE MENTION
FARM HOLIDAY GUIDES

NEWCASTLE-UNDER-LYME. Mary Hugh, The Old Hall, Poolside, Madeley, Near Crewe CW3 9DX

(01782 750209). Civic Trust Award. A Grade II Listed family-owned timbered house of great character and historic interest. Built between 1410 and 1420, predating its inscription "Walke knave what lookest at?" Situated in large attractive gardens with ornamental pool, tennis court and croquet lawn for visitors' use. Excellent accommodation; most rooms en suite; all with tea and coffee facilities, TV and central heating. Situated on A525, close to the Potteries and two of the largest garden centres in Europe — Bridgemere and Stapeley. Children over ten welcome at reduced rates. Bed and Breakfast from £19; Dinner £12; all meals by arrangement. Open all year. Grade II Listed.

The Old Hall, Madeley

STAFFORD near. Mrs Sue Busby, Littywood Farm, Bradley, Stafford ST18 9DW (01785 780234; Fax: 01785 780770). ♛♛ Littywod Farm is a beautiful

14th century double moated manor/farmhouse, secluded yet easily accessible from the M6. Set in its own grounds on the edge of Bradley village in beautiful countryside. One double-bedded room with en suite bathroom from £18.50 per person Bed and Breakfast, one twin-bedded room with washbasin (bathroom adjacent) from £17 per person Bed and Breakfast. Both rooms have tea/coffee making facilities and colour TV. Reductions for children. Open all year except Christmas and New Year.

STOKE-ON-TRENT. Mrs Diana Edwards, Balterley Hall Farm, Balterley, Crewe CW2 5QG (01270 820206). ETB ♛♛ *HIGHLY COMMENDED.* **Working farm.** AA Farmhouse QQQQ Selected. Balterley Hall is a 17th

century farmhouse situated on the Cheshire/Staffordshire border three miles from the M6 motorway, Exit 16. Take A500 towards Stoke-on-Trent, first exit to Audley, take A52/B5500 towards Balterley, keep going over motorway, past pub, then after three-quarters of a mile turn left, 500 yards on left. Many places of interest within easy reach, Wedgwood and Doulton Potteries, Alton Towers, Bridgemere Garden World and also historic towns of Nantwich and Chester. One family en suite, one double en suite (both with draped beds) and one single with washbasin. All are tastefully decorated and have colour TV and tea/coffee making facilities; separate bathroom. Open all year. Bed and Breakfast from £18 per night with reductions for children under 12 years.

BALTERLEY HALL.

STOKE-ON-TRENT. Mrs Anne Hodgson, The Hollies, Clay Lake, Endon, Stoke-on-Trent ST9 9DD (01782 503252). ♛♛ *COMMENDED.* Beautiful Victorian

house in quiet country setting off the B5051 convenient for the M6, Alton Towers, Staffordshire Moorlands and the Potteries. Five spacious comfortable bedrooms with en suite or private facilities, central heating, TV, tea/coffee makers. Children welcome sharing family room. Dogs by arrangement. Secluded garden, ample parking. Choice of breakfast with own preserves. No smoking, please. Bed and Breakfast from £18 with reductions for longer stays. Guests are assured of a warm friendly welcome. AA QQQ.

STAFFORDSHIRE – A STARK CONTRAST!

Staffordshire provides a stark contrast between rural and industrial landscapes. The former being represented by Cannock Chase and Dovedale, the latter by the Black Country and The Potteries. Of interest to the visitor might be the Staffordshire County Museum, Park Hall country park, the Watermills at Cheddleton, the Manifold Valley and the landscape gardens of Alton Towers.

STOKE-ON-TRENT (7 miles). Mrs I. Grey, The Old Vicarage, Leek Road, Endon, Stoke-on-Trent ST9 9BH (01782 503686).

Convenient stop-over for M6 travellers, Endon is a village on the Potteries to Leek road. North Staffordshire is an area of contrasts from unspoilt moorlands for motoring and walking to the Pottery towns with their wealth of history. Visit Alton Towers, the famous Pleasure Park; Gladstone Pottery Museum and City Museum, both award winners; Wedgwood, Royal Doulton, Spode etc, for visits and purchases. Accommodation is in a quiet situation and centrally heated with one double and two twin-bedded rooms, all with TV, tea/coffee making facilities; guests' lounge; two bathrooms and toilets; ample parking. Bed and Breakfast from £15 each, reduced rates for children. No smoking in the house, please.

SUFFOLK

BOXFORD. Mrs Janet Havard-Davies, Coxhill House, Boxford, Sudbury CO10 5JG (01787 210449).

Coxhill House is a delightful Suffolk country house situated on the top of Cox Hill overlooking the old wool village of Boxford with its Anglo-Saxon church and Elizabethan Grammar School. Nearby are the market towns of Sudbury (15 minutes), Hadleigh (10 minutes) and the picturesque village of Kersey (eight minutes). Within easy reach of Colchester, Ipswich, Harwich, Felixstowe, Dedham and Flatford Mill (Constable country), Cambridge and Lavenham. The accommodation comprises two twin-bedded rooms with en suite bathroom and one double bedded room with own facilities. Ample parking. Golf at Stoke-by-Nayland Golf Club by prior arrangement. Bed and Breakfast from £18.50 per person. No smoking.

BUNGAY/BECCLES. Mrs S. Cook, Butterley House, Leet Hill Farm, Yarmouth Road, Kirby Cane, Bungay NR35 2HJ (01508 518301).

A warm welcome awaits at this dairy/arable farm set in the heart of the Waveney Valley, with excellent rural views, situated between the historic towns of Beccles and Bungay, 15 minutes from Norwich, a 20-minute drive from the Suffolk/Norfolk coasts. Nearby is the famous Otter Trust at Earsham. Accommodation comprises one double/family room with en-suite facilities, one double with washbasin, one twin room; bathroom and two toilets. Guests have their own sittingroom with TV, separate diningroom. A full English breakfast is served. Evening Meal by arrangement. Farm produce used wherever possible. Car essential. No pets please. Reductions for children. Terms on request. Tourist Board registered.

BURY ST. EDMUNDS. Jenny Pearson, Hay Green Farm, Whepstead, Bury St. Edmunds IP29 4UD (01284 850567).

Hay Green Farm

Hay Green Farm, a typical Listed Suffolk farmhouse, is quietly situated off the A143 five miles south of Bury St. Edmunds, close to the National Trust property of Ickworth Park. Ideal base for exploring East Anglia, being close to the picturesque villages of Clare, Kersey, Long Melford and Lavenham to the south; Newmarket and Cambridge to the west. Accommodation comprises a family room, double room and single room, all with TV and tea making facilities. Open all year. As there are horses, sheep and other livestock on the farm, sorry no pets. Paddock and stabling available for horses. Bed and Breakfast from £20. Good evening meals in local pubs.

Terms quoted in this publication may be subject to increase if rises in costs necessitate

BURY ST. EDMUNDS. John Kemp, Gifford's Hall, Hartest, Near Bury St. Edmunds IP29 4EX (01284 830464; Fax: 01284 830229). ✿✿ *COMMENDED.* Gifford's Hall is a vineyard and small country living set in some of Suffolk's most beautiful and tranquil surroundings, midway between Bury, Lavenham and Sudbury. It is a listed Georgian farmhouse with large comfortable rooms including two twin and one double with en suite bathrooms. Guests have the use of the large drawing/TV/games room and breakfast is usually taken in the conservatory. You will be welcome to explore our 33 acres which includes 12 acres of vines and a winery, wild flower meadows grazed by rare breed sheep and pure breed free range hens, an acre rose garden, sweet peas and chrysanthemums, an organic vegetable garden and even a shop and tea room where you can enjoy a cream tea or taste the wines. Bed and Breakfast £36 double, £38 and £40 twin. Brochures on request.

CAVENDISH. The Red House, Stour Street, Cavendish, Sudbury CO10 8BH (Tel & Fax: 01787 280611). ✿✿ *HIGHLY COMMENDED.* Maureen and Brian Theaker extend a warm welcome to guests in their lovely 16th century Listed house, delightfully situated in one acre garden and overlooking unspoilt countryside. Attractive self-contained accommodation includes two twin bedrooms of character, one en suite and one with own facilities, offering every comfort including tea/coffee and homemade biscuits! Comfortable beamed sitting room with colour TV, radio and books adjoins both bedrooms. Breakfast room, guests' own entrance and private parking. Situated on A1092 half a mile from Cavendish village centre. Close to Bury St. Edmunds and many beautiful old Suffolk villages. Harwich one hour. Terms from £21.

CHEDISTON. Mrs Eileen Webb, Saskiavill, Chediston, Halesworth IP19 0AR (01986 873067). ✿✿✿ "Saskiavill" is set back from the road and stands in one and a half acres of garden. The spacious bungalow offers holidaymakers an ideal base for the fine city of Norwich, the coast and nearby Minsmere Bird Sanctuary. The village has many thatched cottages and an old church, and is only two miles from the market town of Halesworth. Convenient for golf courses, nature reserves, museums, Trust houses, gardens etc. One double, one family and one twin bedrooms, all with en-suite facilities; two bathrooms, two toilets; one room adapted for disabled visitors. TV lounge, sitting room, dining room. Children welcome at reduced rates, babysitting available. Sorry, no pets. Car essential, parking. Open all year for Evening Dinner/Meal, Bed and Breakfast or Bed and Breakfast. Varied menu with good home cooking, including home-made pastries, bread and preserves. Telephone or SAE for terms. Reductions for Senior Citizens out of season.

CLARE. Jean and Alastair Tuffill, "Cobwebs", 26 Nethergate Street, Clare, Near Sudbury CO10 8NP (01787 277539). ETB Listed. Situated in one of the loveliest parts of East Anglia, a friendly welcome awaits you at "Cobwebs" — this Grade II Listed beamed house dates back to the 14th century. Clare is an historic market town and the area abounds in history and ancient buildings — with many antique shops to explore. The house is within easy walking distance of the town centre and the delightful castle and country park. Good restaurants and pubs nearby for evening meals. Accommodation is provided in one twin and one single bedroom in the house, with bathroom, and an en-suite cottage (with twin beds) set within the delightful walled garden. All rooms have central heating, colour TV, handbasins and tea/coffee making facilities. Bed and Breakfast from £18 per person per night. Easy parking.

COLCHESTER. Ryegate House, Stoke-by-Nayland, Colchester CO6 4RA (01206 263679). ✿✿ *HIGHLY COMMENDED.* Situated on the B1068 within the Dedham Vale, in a quiet Suffolk village, Ryegate House is a modern property built in the style of a Suffolk farmhouse. It is only a few minutes' walk from the local shops, post office, pubs, restaurants and church and an ideal base for exploring Constable country. A warm welcome, good food and comfortable accommodation in a peaceful setting, with easy access to local historic market towns, golf courses and the east coast. Comfortable en suite bedrooms with colour TV, radio alarms, tea/coffee making facilities, shaver points and central heating. Children welcome. Parking for six cars. Open all year except Christmas. Bed and Breakfast from £23 to £26 per night single, double £34 to £39.

FRAMLINGHAM. Mrs Jennie Mann, Fiddlers Hall, Cransford, Near Framlingham, Woodbridge IP13 9PQ (01728 663729). Working farm, join in. Signposted on B1119, Fiddlers Hall is a 14th century, moated, oak-beamed farmhouse set in a beautiful and secluded position. It is two miles from Framlingham castle, 20 minutes' drive from Aldeburgh, Snape Maltings, Woodbridge and Southwold. A Grade II Listed building, it has lots of history and character. The bedrooms are spacious, one has en suite shower room, the other has a private bathroom. Use of lounge and colour TV. Plenty of parking space. Lots of farm animals kept. Traditional farmhouse cooking. Bed and Breakfast from £19.

FRAMLINGHAM. Brian and Phyllis Collett, Shimmens Pightle, Dennington Road, Framlingham, Woodbridge IP13 9JT (01728 724036). ETB Listed *COMMENDED*. Shimmens Pightle is situated in an acre of landscaped garden, surrounded by farmland, within a mile of the centre of Framlingham, with its famous castle and church. Ideally situated for the Heritage Coast, Snape Maltings, local vineyards, riding, etc. Cycles can be hired locally. Many good local eating places. Double and twin bedded rooms, with washbasins, on ground floor. Comfortable lounge with TV overlooking garden, central heating and log fires in winter. Morning tea and evening drinks offered. Sorry, no pets or smoking indoors. Bed and traditional English Breakfast, using local cured bacon and home made marmalade. Vegetarians also happily catered for. SAE please. Open all year. Self catering flats at Southwold also available.

FRAMLINGHAM. Mrs C. Jones, Bantry, Chapel Road, Saxtead, Woodbridge IP13 9RB (01728 685578). ♥ ♥♥ ♥ Bantry is situated in the picturesque village of Saxtead close to the historic castle town of Framlingham. Saxtead is best known for its working windmill beside the village green. Bantry is set in half an acre of gardens overlooking open countryside and three-quarters of a mile along Tannington Road on right hand side from Saxtead Windmill. We offer you accommodation in one of three purpose-built self-contained apartments, separate from the house. For secluded comfort each comprises an en suite bedroom leading through to its own private lounge/dining room with TV and drink making facilities. Bed and Breakfast from £19 per person. Bed, Breakfast and Evening Meal from £28.50 per person. Non-smoking.

FRAMLINGHAM near. Dominique Thomas, Birch Drive, Long Green, Bedfield, Woodbridge IP13 7JD (01728 628396). EATB Listed. Detached house in attractive setting with large natural pond and garden with its resident wildlife! Comfortable accommodation and relaxed atmosphere — a warm welcome all year round. A good central point from which to explore Suffolk with its castles, bird sanctuaries, beaches, harbours and rivers, etc. Accommodation comprises one double en suite (colour TV), one twin, and one double with own shower room and toilet — all with tea and coffee making facilities, central heating, electric blankets and fires. Spacious TV lounge. Ample parking. Bed and Breakfast from £16; Evening Meal by arrangement. Great value! Do come!

HITCHAM. Mrs Philippa McLardy, Hill Farmhouse, Bury Road, Hitcham IP7 7PT (01449 740651). Hill Farmhouse is "Which?" Recommended and has lovely views. Set in its own grounds of three acres. It is an ideal touring centre, close to Lavenham, Constable and Gainsborough country. The coast, Cambridge, Norwich, Ipswich and Colchester are within an hour's drive. Restaurant and three pubs serving food all within two miles. Accommodation is in the main farmhouse and adjoining oak-beamed Tudor cottage. Twin and double suites all have private or en-suite bathrooms, colour TV and tea/coffee making facilities. Pets by arrangement. Special diets catered for. Bed and Breakfast £17.50 for one to four nights, five nights or more £15.50 per night; Dinner £11. Tuesdays and Thursdays supper only (set menu) £6. Reductions for children. Closed November to beginning March.

SUFFOLK – CONSTABLE COUNTRY!

To be precise Dedham Vale is Constable Country and it is only one of Suffolk's attractions. The others include the country parks at Brandon and Clare Castle, Debenham, Lavenham, Newmarket, The Museum of East Anglian Life and the river port of Woodbridge.

LEVINGTON. Mrs Nancy Matthews, Redhouse, Bridge Road, Levington, Ipswich IP10 0LZ (01473

659670). Tourist Board Listed *APPROVED.* Spacious house, large garden with magnificent views over Orwell Estuary. On the edge of tiny village which sports a popular, charmingly thatched pub providing excellent evening meals from Wednesday to Saturday. Separate guest lounge/dining room with TV with all day access. Courtesy tray in bedrooms. Ideally situated for Constable country, the Heritage coast, the medieval wool villages, Suffolk Showground and Felixstowe. Lovely walks along the riverbank where many birds can be seen foraging on the waterline. Full English breakfast with free range eggs, fresh fruit in season. Special diets catered for. Bed and Breakfast from £17. Reductions for children sharing.

LOWESTOFT. The Bay Tree, 347 London Road South, Lowestoft NR33 0DY (01502 538252).

Beautifully maintained Victorian terrace house offering excellent accommodation at reasonable rates. You are guaranteed a relaxing stay at this small friendly guest house. All rooms are en suite with colour TV, room refreshments and radio alarm. Just three minutes from Lowestoft's award winning beach and five minutes from town centre, bus and rail stations. Breakfast is served in the tastefully furnished dining room. Ideally situated for bird watching, country walks, sea fishing and family entertainments with Minsmere, Southwold and Great Yarmouth all close by. Bed and Breakfast from £16.50 per person. Open all year. Please phone or write for details and brochure.

SAXMUNDHAM. Mr and Mrs D. Strachan, Rendham Hall, Rendham, Saxmundham IP17 2AW (Tel

and Fax: 01728 663440). Tourist Board Listed. A warm red brick Suffolk farmhouse with guests' rooms overlooking the dairy herd's grazing pasture and beyond over tranquil countryside. The bedrooms, one double en suite and one family, both with washbasins, are delightfully furnished and very peaceful. The guests' lounge and diningroom have been carefully renovated and are traditionally furnished. Just two miles from the A12, it is an ideal setting for touring the Heritage coastline from Southwold to Aldeburgh; also convenient for Norfolk Broads. We offer comfort and warm hospitality, as well as excellent food. Non-smokers preferred. Bed and Breakfast from £17 to £24.

SAXMUNDHAM. Margaret Gray, Park Farm, Sibton, Saxmundham IP17 2LZ (01728 668324). 🏵 🏵

COMMENDED. A friendly welcome, good food and comfortable accommodation await you at Park Farm. One double and one twin room for guests, each with washbasin, one twin with shower en suite. English breakfast and three-course dinner are prepared from our own, or very local, produce and all tastes and special diets gladly catered for. Ideally situated for enjoying the unspoiled Suffolk countryside. Open all year (closed Christmas and New Year). Children and pets welcome. Bed and Breakfast from £15; Evening Meal from £11.50.

PUBLISHER'S NOTE

SAXMUNDHAM. Mrs Ann Ratcliffe, Fir Tree Farm, Kelsale, Saxmundham IP17 2RH (01728 668356). A warm welcome awaits you at this Tudor farmhouse which has been modernised for your comfort, yet retains its olde worldе charm. Overlooking fields, gardens, pond with moorhens. Accommodation comprises a self-contained wing including a double bedroom, with extra single bed, sitting room with TV, tea-making facilities, own shower and toilet, shaver point. Breakfast is in the main part of the house (beams and inglenook) overlooking the conservatory. Mid-way Aldeburgh and Southwold, 10 minutes Minsmere Bird Sanctuary, Dunwich beach, Snape (Aldeburgh Music Festival) and sports centre with indoor heated swimming pool. Yoxford with its pottery, art gallery, pubs and restaurants one mile. Bed and Breakfast from £16 per person per night. Six berth caravan and self catering accommodation also available. SAE, or telephone, for further information.

SOUTHWOLD. Brenda Smith, Acton Lodge, 18 South Green, Southwold IP18 6HB (01502 723217). Acton Lodge is a unique Italianate/Gothic style red brick Victorian building with a turret. Situated on South Green, only 50 yards from the sea, it retains all its original splendour including marble fireplaces and exposed floorboards and has been lovingly restored, decorated and refurbished. The individually designed bedrooms are spacious and tastefully furnished with sofas or armchairs and offer superb views of the sea or marshes towards Walberswick and Dunwich. All rooms have washbasins, tea/coffee making facilities, TV, radio, shaver sockets and hair dryers. Comfortably furnished sitting room and well stocked library are available to our guests. Featured in "Which?" Good B&B Guide and "Period Living" Magazine. Brochure available.

STOWMARKET. Mrs Mary Noy, Red House Farm, Station Road, Haughley, Stowmarket IP14 3QP (01449 673323). 🐦🐦 *COMMENDED.* **Working farm.** Attractive farmhouse situated in the peaceful surroundings of mid Suffolk. Warm welcome and homely atmosphere. One and a half miles from A14 which makes an ideal base for exploring Suffolk, Norfolk, Cambridge, Constable Country and the coast. Central heating. Guests' lounge with TV and dining room. Tea/coffee making facilities in bedrooms. One twin, one double and one single, all en suite. Good local pubs and restaurants. Children over eight years old welcome. No pets or smoking. Open January to November. Terms from £17.50.

TUNSTALL. Mrs J. Pegrum, The Old Rectory, Tunstall, Woodbridge IP12 2JP (01728 688534). Relax at our home, set in two and a half acres of wooded grounds in Area of Outstanding Natural Beauty. Explore Heritage Coast and nearby towns of Woodbridge, Orford, Framlingham and Aldeburgh with delightful ancient houses and shops, castles, quays, etc. Only three miles from Snape Maltings Concert Hall. Many leisure activities can be enjoyed within immediate area — birdwatching at Minsmere and Havergate Island, river trips, swimming, golf, walking on nearby heaths and forests. Washbasins in all bedrooms. Lounge with colour TV. Non-smoking. Bed and Breakfast from £17 including early morning tea and bedtime drink. Evening Meal (tasty vegetarian) £8. Weekly terms.

If you've found
FARM HOLIDAY GUIDES
of service please tell your friends

WOODBRIDGE. Leslie and Jean Kelly, Grove House, 39 Grove Road, Woodbridge IP12 4LG (01394 382202). 👑👑👑 Grove House is conveniently situated on the main A12 at Woodbridge. There are excellent opportunities close by for bird-watching, walking, golf and fishing. We offer a warm welcome and excellent service. All our bedrooms are comfortably furnished and include colour TVs and welcome trays. Most bedrooms have en-suite facilities. We are also able to offer ground floor accommodation for the partially disabled. Separate lounge/bar. Ample car parking. Open all year. Superb à la carte breakfast menu. Bed and Breakfast from £19.50. Special rates for Short Break holidays. AA QQ. Brochure on request.

YOXFORD. Mrs S. Bloomfield, Priory Farm, Darsham, Near Saxmundham IP17 3QD (01728 668459). Comfortable 17th century farmhouse situated in peaceful Suffolk countryside and an ideal base from which to explore the Coast and Heathlands and numerous other local attractions. Excellent local pubs and restaurants nearby. Cycle hire is available from the farm. One double room and one twin-bedded room, each with private bathroom. Tea/coffee making facilities. Separate guests' dining and sitting rooms. Sorry, regret no pets or smokers. Prices from £18.50 per person per night.

SURREY

DORKING. The Waltons, 5 Rose Hill, Dorking RH4 2EG (Tel & Fax: 01306 883127). Tourist Board Listed. The Waltons is a listed house of historic interest situated in a conservation area. All the rooms are centrally heated with colour TV and tea/coffee facilties. Children are welcome, we can provide a cot and high chair. Evening meals and packed lunches are available if pre-booked, vegetarian diets are no problem. Smoking is discouraged but not totally forbidden in some areas. Prices for Bed and Breakfast start at £15, rising to £20 for a single with full English breakfast. Evening meals range between £6 for a snack or £10.50 for a three-course meal.

DORKING near. The Royal Oak, Holmbury St. Mary, Near Dorking RH5 6PF (01306 730120). A warm, comfortable, cheerful country inn with en suite rooms including tea making facilities, TV and hair dryer. Home cooked lunches, suppers and wholesome traditional breakfasts. Good wines and traditional beers. Situated on the village green in the heart of the Surrey countryside. Ideal for a peaceful break or an overnight business stop. Convenient for Gatwick and railway stations for London and the South Coast. Terms: £25 single, £38 double. AA QQQ.

DORKING. Mrs R.M. Treays, Steyning Cottage, Horsham Road, South Holmwood, Dorking RH5 4NE (01306 888481). Tourist Board Listed. Steyning Cottage is a private house just three miles south of Dorking and only twenty minutes' drive from Gatwick Airport, 45 minutes from Heathrow. We are within easy reach of fine historic houses such as Clandon Park and Polesden Lacey, and only a few minutes' walk from beautiful rambling country. We welcome walkers, families, business people and foreign guests. Babysitting offered. French spoken. One twin-bedded room, one single. Sittingroom with colour TV. Car parking. Adjacent taxi service offers reasonable rates. Bed and Breakfast from £15 to £20. Reductions for children under five. Evening Meal by arrangement from £8. Open all year.

DORKING. Mrs S. Plummer, Barn House, Mill Lane, Forest Green, Dorking RH5 5SJ (01306 621210; Fax: 01306 621224). Recently converted Victorian barn in area of outstanding natural beauty just south of the beautiful Surrey Hills, where there are many lovely walks and rides. The centrally heated rooms in this family home have bathrooms en suite, TV and tea/coffee making facilities. Full English breakfast served. Children, pets, horses welcome. Barn House provides a quiet country base from which to visit London or the South Coast and is within easy reach of Heathrow and Gatwick Airports. Car parking and transport can be arranged for Gatwick. Bed and Breakfast from £17.50 per person. Reductions for children under 12 years.

GATWICK. Rosemead Guest House, 19 Church Road, Horley RH6 7EY (01293 430546; Fax: 01293 430547). ETB Listed *COMMENDED.* AA QQQ. Gatwick Airport five minutes. Small, family-run, non-smoking guest house convenient for airport, shops, pubs and restaurants, local rail services to London and South Coast. Prices include full English breakfast between 7.30 and 9am — Continental before this time. Single £23, Double £35 to £45, Family £49 to £55. All bedrooms have washbasins, colour TV and tea/coffee making facilities; en suite available. Car parking. Credit cards accepted.

LINGFIELD. Mrs Vanessa Manwill, Stantons Hall Farm, Eastbourne Road, Blindley Heath, Lingfield RH7 6LG (01342 832401). Stantons Hall Farm is an 18th century farmhouse, set in 18 acres of farmland and adjacent to Blindley Heath Common. Family, double and single rooms, most with WC, shower and wash-hand basins en-suite. Separate bathroom. All rooms have colour TV, tea/coffee facilities and are centrally heated. There are plenty of parking spaces. We are conveniently situated within easy reach of M25 (London Orbital), Gatwick Airport (car parking for travellers) and Lingfield Park racecourse. Enjoy a traditional English breakfast in our large farmhouse kitchen. Bed and Breakfast from £18 per person, reductions for children sharing. Cot and high chair available. Well behaved dogs welcome by prior arrangement.

SURREY – LOVELY COUNTRYSIDE, CLOSE TO LONDON!

If you are staying in Surrey and only using it as a base for London you will be missing out. Try to find time to visit the Alice Holt Forrest, Leith Hill – the highest point in South-East England, Witley Common and the Downs at Epsom.

LINGFIELD. Mrs Vivienne Bundy, Oaklands, Felcourt, Lingfield RH7 6NF (01342 834705). Oaklands

is a spacious country house of considerable charm dating from the 17th century. It is set in its own grounds of one acre, about one mile from the small town of Lingfield, and three miles from East Grinstead, both with rail connections to London. It is convenient for Gatwick Airport and ideal as a stop-over or as a base to visit the many places of interest in south-east England. Dover and the Channel Ports are two hours' drive away whilst the major towns of London and Brighton are about one hour distant. One en-suite room; one double and one single bedrooms, with washbasins; two bathrooms, two toilets; sittingroom; diningroom. Cot, high chair, babysitting and reduced rates for children. Gas central heating. Open all year. Parking. Bed and Breakfast from £17. Evening Meal by arrangement.

OXTED. Pinehurst Grange Guest House, East Hill (A25), Oxted RH8 9AE (01883 716413). Victorian

ex-farmhouse offers one double, one twin and one single bedroom. All with washbasin, tea/coffee making facilities, colour TV; residents' dining room. Private parking. Close to all local amenities. Only 20 minutes' drive from Gatwick Airport and seven minutes' walk to the station with good trains to London/Croydon. Also close to local bus and taxi service. There are many famous historic houses nearby including "Chartwell", "Knole", "Hever Castle", and "Penshurst Place". Very handy for Lingfield Park racecourse. WALKERS NOTE: only one mile from North Downs Way. No smoking.

WALTON-ON-THAMES. Mrs Joan Spiteri, Beechtree Lodge, 7 Rydens Avenue, Walton-on-Thames KT12 3JB (01932 242738/886667). Tourist Board Listed. A comfortable Edwardian home situated in a quiet avenue, plenty of parking. Minutes from local shops and restaurants; station 10 minutes' walk, Waterloo 25 minutes. Easy access by bus to Heathrow and handy for Hampton Court, Chessington World of Adventure, Thorpe Park, Kempton and Sandown Exhibition Centres, Brooklands Aero/Motor Museum and glorious countryside. All rooms warm and comfortable with washbasins, colour TV, tea/coffee. Families catered for and business people welcome. French, Italian and Greek spoken. Coach trips can be booked. Bed and Breakfast from £16; family rates available. Sorry, no smoking. SEETB Approved and Listed.

Key to
Tourist Board Ratings

The Crown Scheme
(England, Scotland & Wales)

Covering hotels, motels, private hotels, guesthouses, inns, bed & breakfast, farmhouses. Every Crown classified place to stay is inspected annually. *The classification:* Listed then 1-5 Crown indicates the range of facilities and services. Higher quality standards are indicated by the terms APPROVED, COMMENDED, HIGHLY COMMENDED and DELUXE.

The Key Scheme
(also operates in Scotland using a Crown symbol)

Covering self-catering in cottages, bungalows, flats, houseboats, houses, chalets, etc. Every Key classified holiday home is inspected annually. *The classification:* 1-5 Key indicates the range of facilities and equipment. Higher quality standards are indicated by the terms APPROVED, COMMENDED, HIGHLY COMMENDED and DELUXE.

The Q Scheme
(England, Scotland & Wales)

Covering holiday, caravan, chalet and camping parks. Every Q rated park is inspected annually for its quality standards. The more √ in the Q – up to 5 – the higher the standard of what is provided.

SUSSEX

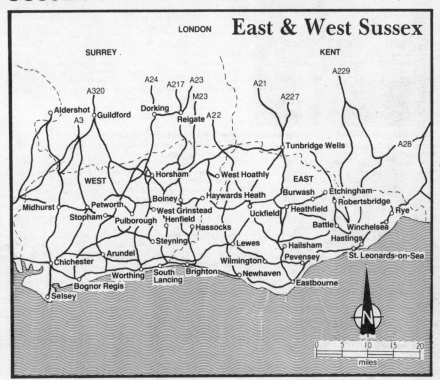

East & West Sussex

LONDON

SURREY

KENT

A229

A24 A217 A23

A320 M23

A21

Aldershot Dorking A227

A3 Guildford Reigate A22

Tunbridge Wells A28

Horsham West Hoathly

WEST EAST

Bolney Haywards Heath Burwash Etchingham

Midhurst Petworth West Grinstead Heathfield Robertsbridge

Stopham Henfield Uckfield Rye

Pulborough Hassocks Battle Winchelsea

Steyning Hastings

Chichester Arundel Lewes Hailsham St. Leonards-on-Sea

Wilmington Pevensey

Worthing South Brighton Newhaven

Bognor Regis Lancing Eastbourne

Selsey

N

0 5 10 15 20
miles

EAST SUSSEX

BATTLE. Mrs Fay Ramsden, Brakes Coppice Farm, Telham Lane, Battle TN33 0SJ (Tel & Fax: 01424 830347). Brakes Coppice Farmhouse is set in the midst of 70 acres of pasture and woodland with panoramic views to the sea five miles away. The house is modernised to a high standard and all bedrooms have en suite bath or shower rooms. A warm welcome and a hearty breakfast are provided by Fay Ramsden. The large towns of Hastings and Eastbourne are nearby and the surrounding area is famous as "1066 Country" with the Battle of Hastings actually having been fought within a mile of the farm. One double, one twin and one single bedrooms, all en suite with colour TV and tea/coffee making facilities; separate guests' lounge and dining room. No smoking or pets. Bed and Breakfast £30 single, £45 double. AA QQQQQ, RAC Highly Acclaimed.

BRIGHTON. Cavalaire House, 34 Upper Rock Gardens, Brighton BN2 1QF (01273 696899; Fax: 01273 600504). ♛ ♛ *COMMENDED.* AA QQQ, RAC Acclaimed. This family-run quality guest house is in an excellent position close to theatres, pier and town centre amenities. We offer a friendly atmosphere and a high standard of comfort and personal service. All rooms have colour TV, beverage trays, hair dryers and radio/clock alarms. Guests have unrestricted access with own keys. From £15 per person for a standard room; from £17 per person for room with shower; from £20 per person for a room with shower and WC. Discounts available for stays over two nights. Seventh night free on all weekly bookings. Open all year except Christmas.

BRIGHTON. Kempton House Hotel, 33/34 Marine Parade, Brighton BN2 1TR (01273 570248).

ww w COMMENDED. AA/RAC Highly Acclaimed. We are a private seafront Hotel offering a relaxed and friendly holiday or short break. Rooms available with magnificent views overlooking beach and pier. Rooms with full en-suite shower and toilet, central heating, tea/coffee facilities, self dial telephone, colour/Satellite TV, radio, hair dryer. Full English Breakfast served or Continental Breakfast in bed. Four-poster bed available overlooking sea. Residents' bar and sea-facing patio garden for your use. Ideally situated for business or pleasure. Please telephone for details. From only £22 per person per night Bed and Breakfast. Six nights for the price of five. Open all year.

BRIGHTON. Brighton Marina House Hotel, 8 Charlotte Street, Marine Parade, Brighton BN2 1AG (01273 605349 or 679484; Fax: 01273 605349).

w w w Your comfort and that of your children is our first concern. Cosy, clean, comfortable, caring, family-run, highly recommended, beautifully maintained, elegantly furnished, well equipped — we care for and cater to children's individual needs. Single, double, twin, triple and family bedrooms — standard and en suite with colour TV, tea/coffee making facilities, washbasin, radio, alarm, clock, telephone, hairdryer. Our own pets — fish, birds, cats. Near sea front and fun fair, central for Palace Pier, Royal Pavilion, Lanes (for antiques), tourist attractions, conference/exhibition halls and Marina. 24 hour access and check in/out. Bed and Breakfast from £15 to £27.50 per night. Please write or phone for further details.

BRIGHTON. Mr & Mrs P. Edwards, Four Seasons, 3 Upper Rock Gardens, Brighton BN2 1QE (01273 681496). A 200 year old Grade II Listed Guest House recently refurbished offering a warm and comfortable stay. Character rooms, some with sea views; all with central heating, colour TV, radio alarms, hospitality trays, showers and some with full en-suite. 100 yards to sea, close to Conference and Exhibition Centre, shops, Lanes and theatres. Excellent full English breakfast, vegetarian or Continental as preferred. All major credit cards accepted. Pets by arrangement. Children welcome (50% discount for children under 12 years sharing). Access at all times. Open all year. Prices from £15 per person.

BRIGHTON. Amblecliff Hotel, 35 Upper Rock Gardens, Brighton BN2 1QF (01273 681161; Fax: 01273 676945). w w w A NON-SMOKING HOTEL. AA QQQQ Selected, RAC Highly Acclaimed. This stylish hotel, highly recommended as the place to stay when in Brighton by a national newspaper and two television programmes, has been awarded the AA's coveted Select QQQQ, only given to two or three hotels in Brighton and the RAC's Highly Acclaimed for quality and customer satisfaction. Excellent location, close to the seafront, with historic Brighton, the Conference Centre, Royal Pavilion and the Marina only a stroll away. All double, twin and family rooms are en suite. Individually designed rooms with four poster and king size beds. Best in its price range, we believe you deserve an excellent service, comfortable accommodation and value for money. Bed and Breakfast from £19.00 to £28. Special offer — seven nights for the price of six!

EAST SUSSEX – A POPULAR DESTINATION!

Apart from its famous resorts East Sussex has many attractions, such as, Ashdown Forest, Ditchling Common Country Park, Lullington Heath Wildlife Refuge, the Medieval town of Rye and Hastings Country Park.

PasRins
Town House Hotel

A stylish Regency hotel at the heart of Brighton's culture, shopping, restaurants and antique trade. Our *organic* traditional English and vegetarian breakfasts are delicious. The comfortable bar serves interesting local beers and a fine selection of Scottish malt whisky, whilst our nearby French restaurant *'makes Angels dance on your tongue'*.

19 Charlotte Street, Brighton BN2 1AG
Telephone: 01273 601203 Fax: 01273 621973

WESTBOURNE HOTEL

Family run hotel situated a few minutes from seafront, palace Pier, Conference Centre, theatres and the Lanes. The hotel offers comfortable 3-crown accommodation with colour TV and hospitality tray in all the rooms, mostly en suite. There is a guests' lounge and licensed bar.
For your breakfast we offer a choice of menu – full English, Continental or vegetarian-style. Access at all times; open all year. AA Listed.

B&B per person for 1 night – £18.00–£28.00
B&B per person for 7 nights – £112.00–£160.00
46 Upper Rock Gardens, Brighton BN2 1QF
Telephone 01273 686920 AA QQQ ♛♛♛

Sea Breeze
PROBABLY BRIGHTON'S FRIENDLIEST GUEST HOUSE
"arrive as a guest, leave as a friend"

Sea Breeze is your home from home. All rooms are fully en-suite. Hospitality tray, radio alarm, colour TV with video and satellite channels. Rooms individually designed (have we your colour ?). Perhaps the family room. Brighton has much to offer: Entertainments, Shops, Pier, Lanes, Marina, Brighton Centre and the Sea. Sea Breeze's standards are very high. Friendship and a good time at Sea Breeze guaranteed. Own keys. Credit cards and cash accepted. Prices from £19.

12a Upper Rock Gardens, Brighton, East Sussex BN2 1QE
Tel: 01273 602608 Fax: 01273 607166

RECOMMENDED SHORT BREAK HOLIDAYS
IN BRITAIN
Introduced by John Carter, TV Holiday Expert and Journalist

Specifically designed to cater for the most rapidly growing sector of the holiday market in the UK. Illustrated details of hotels offering special 'Bargain Breaks' throughout the year.
Available from newsagents and bookshops for £4.25 or direct from the publishers for £4.80 including postage, UK only.

FHG PUBLICATIONS LTD
Abbey Mill Business Centre, Seedhill,
Paisley, Renfrewshire PA1 1TJ

BRIGHTON. Mrs M.A. Daughtery, Maon Hotel, 26 Upper Rock Gardens, Brighton BN2 1QE (01273 694400). This completely non-smoking Grade II Listed building is run by proprietors who are waiting with a warm and friendly welcome. Our standard of food has been highly commended by many guests who return year after year. Two minutes from the sea and within easy reach of conference and main town centres. All nine bedrooms are furnished to a high standard and have colour TV, hospitality trays, radio alarm clocks and hair dryers; most en suite. A lounge with colour TV is available for guests' convenience. Dining room. Full central heating. Access to rooms at all times. Terms from £19. Brochure on request with a SAE.

BRIGHTON/HOVE. Kingsway Hotel, 2 St. Aubyns, Hove BN3 2TB (01273 722068; Fax: 01273 778409). Tourist Board *COMMENDED.* This comfortable family hotel is conveniently situated opposite a modern leisure complex with a swimming pool and bowling alley. Close to all the lively attractions of Brighton; the Royal Pavilion, the Palace Pier and bustling shopping, theatres and restaurants. The hotel itself offers many sea view rooms and en suite facilities. All rooms have central heating, colour TV and tea/coffee making facilities. Bed and Breakfast £20 to £22 single or £40 to £45 double. Reductions for children.

BURWASH. Mrs E. Sirrell, Woodlands Farm, Burwash, Etchingham TN19 7LA (01435 882794). Working farm, join in. Woodlands Farm stands one third of a mile off the road surrounded by fields and woods. This peaceful and beautifully modernised 16th century farmhouse offers comfortable and friendly accommodation. Sitting/dining room; two bathrooms, one en suite, double or twin bedded rooms (one has four-poster bed) together with excellent farm fresh food. This is a farm of 55 acres with mixed animals, and is situated within easy reach of 20 or more places of interest to visit and half an hour from the coast. Open Easter to October. Central heating. Literature provided to help guests. Children welcome. Dogs allowed if sleeping in owners' car. Parking. Evening meal optional. Bed and Breakfast from £16.50. AA Listed. Telephone or SAE, please.

EASTBOURNE. Eric and Joanne Godfrey, Halcyon Private Hotel, 8 South Cliff, King Edwards Parade, Eastbourne BN20 7AF (01323 723710). Superbly situated on the sea front just west of the Wish Tower and Sun Lounge, overlooking the Western Lawns and quiet promenade walks. The Winter Gardens, Congress Theatre and Devonshire Park are approximately four minutes' walk away. All bedrooms have their own tea making facilities. The dining room has separate tables, meals are table d'hôte. Guests have access to the hotel and their rooms at all times. Ample unrestricted parking. Under personal suprvision. Dinner, Bed and Breakfast from £27. Brochure available.

EASTBOURNE. "Ambria House", 85 Pevensey Road, Eastbourne BN22 8AD (01323 642303). Relax in a friendly atmosphere with plentiful home cooking, vegetarians and diabetics welcome. Three minutes level walk to sea front, 10 minutes gentle stroll to our Arndale Shopping Centre and 15 minutes to our excellent theatres. Dotto trains for the less active enabling a trip along our beautiful three mile promenade, also good bus services to many places of interest. Bed and Breakfast from £15. Four-day Christmas Breaks. SAE please for brochure to **Amanda and Brian Bignell.**

EASTBOURNE. The Ellesmere Hotel, 11 Wilmington Square, Eastbourne BN21 4EA (01323 731463).

Ellesmere Hotel warmly welcomes and values all guests. We emphasise quality and individual service, comfort and hospitality at its best to ensure a pleasant and enjoyable stay, being a family-run Hotel. Situated in the most beautiful square in Eastbourne, a few yards from the sea front and Winter Gardens, there are splendid views from the hotel. Bedrooms are of a high standard offering en suite, remote control TV, radio, tea/coffee making facilities and hairdryers. Fully licensed bar lounge with colour TV. Lift to all floors. Full central heating and double glazing. Children welcome. Bed and Breakfast from £20, Half Board from £27. Weekly rates available. Brochure sent on request.

EASTBOURNE. Mr & Mrs J. Frost, "Sainvia", 19 Ceylon Place, Eastbourne BN21 3JE (01323 725943).

A warm welcome awaits you at "Sainvia". Three minutes from Pier, five minutes from a lovely shopping centre, approximately 10 minutes from theatres (walking). We are central for all your entertainment. Regular bus service to beautiful Beachy Head. All our rooms have colour TV and tea making facilities. Enjoy a drink in our comfortable bar. Open all year. Bed and Breakfast from £15.00. Special Christmas three-day Breaks available. Enquiries welcome.

EASTBOURNE. The Mayvere Guest House, 12 Cambridge Road, Eastbourne BN22 7BS (01323 729580). 👑👑 Just a few steps from the seafront and a short walk to the centre and all amenities, the bowling greens, Treasure Island for the children, the Redoubt Fortress with its historical museum, aquarium and tea rooms. All this and more at Mayvere, with its seven comfortable rooms and friendly caring atmosphere, with TV, washbasins and tea/coffee making facilities. Excellent food served at separate tables. Comfortable lounge. Licensed. Separate bath and shower rooms. Full central heating in winter. Bed and Breakfast from £13 to £15 per person. Optional Evening Dinner £5. Send SAE for colour brochure. Directions: A22 Eastbourne seafront (east) turn right at Seafront, pass Redoubt Fortress, turn right at Langham Hotel into Cambridge Road.

HAILSHAM near. David and Jill Hook, Longleys Farm Cottage, Harebeating Lane, Hailsham BN27 1ER (Tel & Fax: 01323 841227). Situated in quiet private country lane one mile north of the market town of Hailsham with its excellent amenities including modern sports centre and leisure pool, surrounded by footpaths across open farmland. Ideal for country lovers. Dogs and children welcome. The coast at Eastbourne, South Downs, Ashdown Forest and 1066 Country are all within easy access. The non-smoking accommodation comprises one single, one twin and one family room with en suite and tea-making facilities. Bed and Breakfast £15. Reductions for children.

HARTFIELD. Mrs G. Pring, Stairs Farmhouse, High Street, Hartfield TN7 4AB (01892 770793).

Tourist Board Listed *COMMENDED.* **Working farm.** Stairs Farmhouse dates from the 17th century, and has been carefully modernised whilst retaining various period features and has countryside views. Apart from a licensed Tea Room/ Restaurant and Farm Shop on site, there are three pubs serving both excellent bar snacks and restaurant meals, several shops, a church and Post Office all within easy walking distance. Also close to A.A. Milne's famous "Pooh Bridge", Hever Castle, Chartwell, Penshurst Place, Sheffield Park and the Bluebell Steam Railway. Gatwick/M25 30 minutes away. The accommodation consists of a family room, twin room and double room, all with pleasant views, colour TV and tea/coffee making facilities. Open all year. Bed and Breakfast from £20 double; from £25 single. Evening Meal, packed lunches, snacks, dinner by arrangement; vegetarian choice if required.

HASTINGS. Mr and Mrs R. Steele, Amberlene Guest House, 12 Cambridge Gardens, Hastings TN34 1EH (01424 439447). Hastings town centre, two minutes' walk from the beach, shops, entertainments, rail/bus stations and central car park. Single, double, twin and family rooms; some with en suite. Very clean, comfortable, well carpeted and decorated. All with central heating, colour TV, washbasins, power and shaver points. Guests have their own front door keys and access to rooms and facilities at all times. Bed and full four-course English Breakfast £13 to £17 per night (room only, £2 less), half price for children sharing. All prices include tea/coffee and biscuits in your room. Baby cots free. No extra charges. Sorry, no pets. Tourist Board registered. Also holiday flats available nearby.

HASTINGS. Mr and Mrs S. York, Westwood Farm, Stonestile Lane, Hastings TN35 4PG (01424 751038). Working farm. Farm with pet sheep, chickens, etc. Quiet rural location off country lane half a mile from B2093 approximately two miles fropm seafront and town centre. Golf course nearby. Central position for visiting places of interest to suit all ages. Elevated situation with outstanding views over Brede Valley. All bedrooms have washbasins, tea making facilities and TV; some en suite and two bedrooms on ground floor. Full English breakfast. Off-road parking. Bed and Breakfast from £15 to £25 per person for two persons sharing. Reduced rates for weekly booking. Also available six-berth self catering caravan — details on request.

HASTINGS. Mrs Afroditi G. Wall, Beechwood Hotel, 59 Baldslow Road, Hastings TN34 2EY (01424 420078). ✿✿ Beechwood is a typical example of late Victorian architecture with this atmosphere retained in the bedrooms, lounge, diningroom and bar. It is a small, family run hotel with full central heating, large south-facing garden and unrivalled views of Alexandra Park, situated in quiet surroundings adjacent to good bus routes or 15 minutes' walk to town centre, seafront or station. Off the A2101 and ideal for touring South East England. On and off the road parking. Tea/coffee making facilities on request. Open all year. Bed and English Breakfast from £15. Evening Dinner can be provided at £8. Bargain Breaks available. RAC Listed. Resident Proprietor: Afroditi G. Wall MHCIMA MRSH.

HASTINGS. Peter and Madeleine Mann, Grand Hotel, Grand Parade, St. Leonards-on-Sea, Hastings TN38 0DD (01424 428510). ✿✿✿ Seafront family-run hotel, recently renovated, with spacious lounge, licensed bar, central heating. Radio/room call/baby listening in all rooms. Some rooms ensuite; colour TV. Free access to clean, comfortable rooms at all times. Unrestricted parking and disabled parking. Non-smoking restaurant. In the heart of 1066 Country close to Battle Abbey, Bodiam and Hever Castles, Kipling's Batemans, and historic Cinque Ports of Rye and Winchelsea, plus Hastings Castle, caves, sealife centre, local golf courses, and leisure centres. Open all year. Bed and Breakfast from £12; Evening Meal from £8. Children welcome; half price sharing room. SAE to Resident Proprietors for further information.

HASTINGS near. Rosemarie Crouch, Highfield, Butchers Lane, Three Oaks, Hastings TN35 4NG (01424 814453). Clean friendly house in small country village betwen Hastings (five miles) and Rye (eight miles). One double room on ground floor with own adjoining lounge/dining room, one family room, both with private bath, shower and toilet, colour TV, tea/coffee making facilities. Central heating throughout. Ample parking in own grounds at rear of house. Strictly no smoking. Sorry no children under six years. Bed and Breakfast from £17 to £18. Reductions for children. Open April to October. From A259 Hastings/Rye Road signposted Three Oaks/Westfield. From A21 take A28 to Ashford/Tenterden. After two miles signposted Three Oaks.

HEATHFIELD. Mrs Angela Wardell, Yew Tree Cottage, Street End Lane, Broad Oak, Heathfield TN21 8SA (01435 864053). Yew Tree Cottage dates back to 1750 having been extensively modernised. Situated one mile east of Heathfield off the A265 and having glorious views over the Rother Valley. Close to the Sussex/Kent border making an ideal touring centre. South Coast and the historic towns of Battle, Rye and Hastings together with many other places of interest within easy reach; Dover two hours, Ashford one hour's drive. Many attractive eating houses in the vicinity. Accommodation comprises two double rooms (one with twin bed option) and one single. Tea-making facilities and TV. No pets. Ample parking. Open all year. Log fires. A warm welcome. Bed and Breakfast £17.50 per person.

Cleavers Lyng Country Hotel

10 minutes to several golf courses, 15 minutes to East Sussex National

For excellent home cooking in traditional English style, comfort and informality, this small family-run hotel in the heart of rural East Sussex is well recommended. Peacefully set in beautiful land-scaped gardens extending to 1.5 acres featuring a rockpool with waterfall. Adjacent to Herstmonceux Castle's West Gate, the house dates from 1577 as its oak beams and inglenook fireplace bear witness. This is an ideal retreat for a quiet sojourn away from urban clamour. The castles at Pevensey, Scot-ney, Bodiam and Hever are all within easy reach as are Battle Abbey, Kipling's House, Bateman's, Michelham Priory and the seaside resorts of Eastbourne, Bexhill and Hastings. Bedrooms are all fully ensuite and all have central heating and tea and coffee-making facilities with some having sep-arate siting area with colour television. On the ground floor there is an oak-beamed restaurant with a fully licensed bar, cosy residents' lounge with television and an outer hall with telephone and cloak-rooms. Peace, tranquillity and a warm welcome await you. Attraction: Badger Watch. Room rate from £22.50 p.p. upwards sharing double/twin room. No single rooms available however at certain times of the year we offer a reduced single occupancy rate for double/twin bedroom.

Church Road, Herstmonceux, East Sussex BN27 1QJ. Telephone: 01323 833131; Fax: 01323 833617

NINFIELD. The United Friends Inn, Alehouse and Restaurant, The Green, Ninfield TN33 9JL (01424 892462). Situated in a rural village half way between the resorts of Hastings, St Leonards and Eastbourne. Only four miles from Bexhill and five from Battle where William the Conquerer defeated King Harold on the slopes below the town, before building the abbey on this site. Bed and Breakfast £15 per person per night. For further details please contact proprietors: **Gerry and Shirley Fillingham.**

PEVENSEY BAY. Mrs Lin McKeever, Driftwood, 36 Eastbourne Road, Pevensey Bay BN24 6HJ

(01323 768530). A warm welcome awaits in our comfort-able family home. Situated in village centre with shops, pubs and restaurants at hand. Two minutes' walk to good clean beach (award winner 1996). One double and two family/twin bedrooms, all with TV, washbasins and drink making facili-ties. Guest lounge with TV. Central heating throughout. Private parking. No smoking. Good English breakfast. Peven-sey Castle one mile, Eastbourne four miles, Hastings 18 miles, Brighton 24 miles, Gatwick Airport 30 miles. Good train service to London. Lovely countryside close by. Open all year. £13 to £16 for Bed and Breakfast. Children (five plus) reduced rates. Off season breaks from £34 for three days.

POLEGATE. Mrs B. Drake, The Braes, 3 Filching Close, Wannock, Polegate BN26 5NU (01323 487181). Welcome to a relaxing holiday at The Braes, situated in a valley in the Sussex Downs where one can ramble for miles. Five miles from the seaside town of Eastbourne, plenty of interest within the area; Rudyard Kipling's home, Hertmonceaux Castle and Science Museum, Michelham Priory, etc. Two double and one single bedrooms; two bathrooms; lounge; dining room; kitchen where drinks can be made or sandwiches prepared. Garden and hard standing for cars. No smoking. No pets. Adults only. Terms from £15 per night. Discount for three nights or more. Open Easter to September 30th.

RYE. Mrs Dawn Keay, Aviemore Guest House, 28/30 Fishmarket Road, Rye TN31 7LP (Tel & Fax:

01797 223052). 🌸🌸 *APPROVED.* Guests are assured of a genuinely warm welcome and clean, comfortable accommo-dation at Aviemore, which overlooks the park and the River Rother, just two minutes' walk from the town centre. Four rooms have private shower and WC, four have shared facilities. Kenya tea/coffee. Fully licensed. Guests' lounge, dining room, TV. 24 hour access. Car park nearby. Excellent breakfasts, evening meals by prior arrangement. Credit cards accepted. Bed and Breakfast from £16 to £21.

RYE. Rita Cox, Four Seasons, 96 Udimore Road, Rye TN31 7DY (01797 224305). Four Seasons is

situated on Cadborough Cliff with spectacular views across the south facing garden to the Brede Valley, Rye and the sea. We offer excellent B&B in our attractive house which is decorated to reflect the changing seasons. Centrally heated rooms are en suite or have private facilities and have TV and hot drinks tray. Breakfasts are full English or vegetarian, with home-made preserves and local produce. Four Seasons is a short walk from the town centre, has private parking, is an excellent centre for touring East Sussex and Kent, and is convenient for the Channel Ports and Tunnel. Rates are £15 to £18 per person with special winter bargain breaks mid-November to February. Brochure on request.

FOUR SEASONS RYE

Cadborough Farm

Udimore Road, Rye, East Sussex
Tel: 01797 225426 Fax: 01797 224097

Jane Apperly

A lovely country house set in 24 acres with outstanding views towards the sea, overlooking Camber Castle and the medieval towns of Rye and Winchelsea. Spacious sunny bedrooms with ensuite facilities and sea views. Self contained suite with inner hall, bedroom, sitting room and bathroom. Colour TV, radio/alarm, hairdryer and hot drinks tray. Drawing room with log fire. Superb English, Continental and Vegetarian Breakfast. Ample parking. Short walk from town centre.

RYE. Norman and Agnes Bennett, Half House, 20 Military Road, Rye TN31 7NY (01797 223404).

Our house is delightful and full of character, overlooking Romney Marsh and a short walk from the centre of ancient Rye. We have three pretty bedrooms (one en-suite). All rooms have tea/coffee trays and TV. Breakfast is English or wholefood/vegetarian. Free bedtime drink; reduced rates for children and Senior Citizens. Non-smoking accommodation available. Parking is easy and our bicycles are available to guests. Rye is a good base for touring the South East — Canterbury, Royal Tunbridge Wells, Dover, Brighton are within an easy drive. Camber Sands with excellent beaches and new indoor leisure pools is three miles. Please send for brochure. Bed and Breakfast £15 to £20 per person.

THE HALF HOUSE, 20, MILITARY ROAD, RYE, SUSSEX.

RYE. Pat and Jeff Sullivin, Cliff Farm, Iden Lock, Rye TN31 7QE (Tel & Fax: 01797 280331, long ring please). Working farm. Our farmhouse is peacefully set in a quiet elevated position with extensive views over Romney Marsh. The ancient seaport town of Rye with its narrow cobbled street is two miles away. We are an ideal touring base although the town and immediate district have much to offer — golden beaches, quaint villages, castles, gardens etc. Comfortable guest bedrooms with washbasins and tea/coffee facilities; two toilets; own shower; dining-room and sittingroom. Home produce. Open March to October for Bed and Breakfast from £14.50 to £15. Reduced weekly rates. AA and RAC Recommended.

WHEN MAKING ENQUIRIES PLEASE MENTION
THIS *FHG* PUBLICATION

RYE. Mrs J.P. Hadfield, Jeake's House, Mermaid Street, Rye TN31 7ET (01797 222828). 👑👑

HIGHLY COMMENDED. This beautiful listed building, originally built as a wool store and later converted to a Baptist School, was built by Samuel Jeake in 1689. It stands in one of England's most famous streets, renowned for its cobblestoned charm and association with notorious gangs of smugglers. It was once the "deeply cherished" home of American author Conrad Aiken. Breakfast, traditional or vegetarian, is served in the 18th century galleried former chapel. Oak beamed and panelled bedrooms, overlooking the marsh and roof tops to the sea, are furnished with brass or mahogany bedsteads, linen sheets and lace. En-suite facilities. TV, telephones and hot drinks trays. Four poster honeymoon suite available. Residential licence. Terms from £20.50 to £29.50 per person.

RYE. Mrs Heather Coote, "Busti", Barnetts Hill, Peasmarsh, Rye TN31 6YJ (01797 230408).

Comfortable and clean accommodation in detached house on the edge of the rural village of Peasmarsh. Ideally located for touring both East Sussex and Kent and for visiting Bodiam Castle, the historic town of Rye, Great Dixter, Sissinghurst, Battle Abbey and many other seasonal attractions; lake fishing locally. Guest lounge/dining room with TV. Guests' shower/toilet. Bedrooms have tea/coffee making facilities. Central heating throughout. Hairdryer available. Friendly service and tourist advice provided. Full English breakfast or alternative. Ample off road parking. Bed and Breakfast from £15. No smoking in the house. Member of Rye and District Hotels and Caterers Association.

RYE near. The Corner House, Playden, Near Rye TN31 7UL (01797 280439).

We would like to welcome you to our cheerful friendly family home situated just one mile from Rye on the A268. We can offer you comfortable, attractive rooms with washbasin, central heating and hot drinks making facilities, double or twin beds. Guests' bathroom, shower and toilet. Spacious dining room/lounge with TV. Delicious English breakfast. Children welcome — family room available. We are ideally situated for you to visit the many historic and picturesque towns and places of interest in the surrounding Kent and Sussex countryside. Hastings, Battle, Canterbury, Dover, Folkestone, Tunbridge Wells, Tenterden, and of course Rye, are all within easy travelling distance. Prices from £16 per person.

RYE near. Nick & Ruth Wynn, Fiddlers Oast, Watermill Lane, Beckley, Near Rye TN31 6SH (Tel & Fax: 01797 252394; mobile 0836 621211). SETB

COMMENDED. Fiddlers Oast, near Rye with its cobbled streets and Mermaid Inn, close to the Kent border, is ideal for exploring 1066 country. If you like the countryside you will feel totally relaxed here in this beautiful wooded setting. Meander through the lanes on delightful walks, friendly pubs will tempt you with their local beers and gastronomic delights en route! Children, pets and well behaved adults welcome! All rooms en suite. 45 minutes from Le Shuttle. Find the Rose and Crown Pub in Beckley, take B2165 West for approximately 350 metres, turn left into Watermill Lane . . . now relax!

RYE near. David and Eliane Griffin, Kimblee, Main Street, Peasmarsh, Near Rye TN31 6UL (01797 230514 or 0831 841004 mobile). 👑👑 *COMMENDED.*

Friendly country house with views from all aspects. Rye five minutes' drive, beaches 15 minutes. Ample off road parking. Ideal base for visiting Kent and Sussex. Two large rooms with shower, toilet, washbasin en suite. Smaller room with en suite bathroom. Single room possible. All rooms have colour TV, radio alarm, tea/coffee facilities, hair dryers. Locally renowned pub/restaurant 250 metres. Generous English breakfast, vegetarian on request. Reduction for substantial Continental breakfast. French spoken. On A268 three miles from Rye in the direction of London. £18 to £19 per person. Reductions for three nights or more. Mid week breaks March to May: three nights for the price of two. Brochure on request.

SEAFORD. Mrs Roberts, Sunnyside, 23 Connaught Road, Seaford BN25 2PT (01323 895850). Comfortable farm house situated just 120 yards from Seaford, between Eastbourne and Brighton and three miles to Newhaven ferry and the South Downs Way. All bedrooms have washbasins, TV and tea/coffee making facilities. Please write or telephone for further details.

ST. LEONARDS-ON-SEA. Saint Matthews, 14 St. Matthews Drive, St. Leonards-on-Sea TN38 0TR

(01424 445590). Small, homely, comfortabe bed and breakfast accommodation in St. Leonards, near Silverhill. Adequate parking for guests. Three large bright rooms with central heating, washbasins, colour TV and tea/coffee making facilities. Full English or Continental breakfast. Evening meals available for five nights or more. TV lounge and diner for guests. Children welcome. Bed and Breakfast from £13. Short Break Packages available Spring and Autumn.

UCKFIELD. Mrs Fiona Brown, The Cottage, Chillies Lane, High Hurstwood, Near Uckfield TN22 4AA (Tel & Fax: 01825 732804). A pretty stone cottage in a quiet lane in a valley of outstanding natural beauty with beautiful views at the rear — on the edge of Ashdown Forest with its extensive views, open spaces and many walks. Many National Trust houses and gardens to visit locally and within easy reach of Tunbridge Wells and the South Coast. One twin/family room en suite, one twin and one single room, all have TV and tea/coffee facilities. Children welcome. Bed and Breakfast from £16 to £20 per person per night.

WINCHELSEA. A.N. Roche, The Strand House, Winchelsea, Near Rye TN36 4JT (Tel & Fax: 01797

226591). ❦ ❦ ❦ *COMMENDED.* Nestling beneath the cliff of the ancient medieval town of Winchelsea lies the 15th century Strand House. Full of atmosphere with oak beams and inglenook fireplaces, but with the comfort of en suite facilities, central heating, colour TV and hot drinks tray. Romantic four-poster bedroom available. A lounge with log fires in winter leads onto a pretty garden for your enjoyment in summer. A residential licence, payphone, and ample parking in the grounds make your visit relaxed and enjoyable. An ideal place to stay while you explore the many places of interest within easy reach. AA QQQQ Selected, RAC Acclaimed. Tariff from £20 to £29 per person. Visa/Mastercard/Eurocard accepted.

WEST SUSSEX

ARUNDEL. Swan Hotel, 27-29 High Street, Arundel BN18 9AG (01903 882314; Fax: 01903

883759). ❦ ❦ ❦ *HIGHLY COMMENDED.* RAC/AA Three Star. Situated in the heart of historic Arundel the Swan Hotel has been lovingly restored to its former Victorian splendour. Many of the hotel's original features, including English oak flooring and wall-panelling, are still very much in evidence creating a wonderful ambience throughout. Both table d'hôte and à la carte menus are available in the hotel's popular award-winning restaurant where local and seasonal produce is used extensively, and wines can be selected from the original 200 year old cellar. Local real ales can be sampled in the bar. All bedrooms have en suite bathroom, colour TV, hairdryer, telephone, tea/coffee making, room service. Prices from £30 per person per night including full English breakfast. Arundel is an enchanting place with its castle, Cathedral and parks; well placed for touring the lovely West Sussex countryside. All major credit cards accepted.

ARUNDEL near. Peter and Sarah Fuente, Mill Lane House, Slindon, Arundel BN18 0RP (01243 814440). Magnificent views to the coast. 18th century house with three acres of grounds, in pretty National Trust village on South Downs. Direct access to many miles of footpaths including South Downs Way; superb bird watching locally, at coastal harbours and Amberley Brooks. Easy reach Arundel Castle, Goodwood, Chichester with Roman Palace, Cathedral and Festival Theatre. Sandy beach six miles. Pubs within easy walking distance. Rooms en-suite and with TV; central heating and log fires in winter. One mile Junction A27/A29. Bed and Breakfast (double/twin room) £19.25 per person per night. Single occupancy and family rooms on request. Three course Evening Meals from £9.50 by arrangement. Weekly terms available.

ARUNDEL near. Mrs Angela Broughton, Bonhams House, Yapton BN18 0DX (01243 551301; Fax: 01243 586720). Beautiful period house with small gym and heated therapy pool. Horse-drawn carriage drives or riding lessons by arrangement. All rooms are furnished to a high standard (double, twin and family), and there is an elegant Victorian lounge. A full English breakfast is served; tea and coffee on request. Non smoking. Large car park. Open all year. Bed and Breakfast from £20.00 per person.

ARUNDEL near. Mrs Jocelyne Newman, Pindars, Lyminster BN17 7QF (01903 882628). ♛ *HIGHLY COMMENDED.* Charming country house with modern comfort, warm welcome, lovely garden, open air swimming pool. Three pretty bedrooms, two double (one en suite) and one twin-bedded; all have washbasins, colour TV, radio, tea/coffeetrays, hairdryers. Generous healthy breakfasts, delicious home cooking. Arundel is two miles northwards, the coast three miles south and we can direct you to stately homes, small villages, bird sanctuaries, South Downs walks, castles and cathedrals! Pindars is on the A284, turning off the A27 one mile east of Arundel, house on left one mile further. Non-smoking. Children over 10 years welcome. Bed and Breakfast from £16 per person. Evening meals can be provided. Full details on request.

BOGNOR REGIS. Mrs B.M. Hashfield, Taplow Cottage, 81 Nyewood Lane, Bognor Regis PO21 2UE (01243 821398). This cottage lies in a residential part, west of the town centre, 600 yards from the sea and shops. Proximity to many beaches and contrasting towns and countryside makes this an ideal touring centre. Chichester, Goodwood Racecourse, Arundel Castle, Brighton, Portsmouth and Southsea are but a few of the places of interest within easy reach. Accommodation comprises one double, one twin, and one family bedrooms, all with vanity units, tea/coffee making facilities and colour TVs. Lounge, dining-room; central heating throughout. The cottage is well appointed and the area is served by public transport. Parking space available. Dogs by arrangement. Bed and Breakfast only from £14 nightly. SAE, please.

"TAPLOW COTTAGE"

BOGNOR REGIS. Deborah S. Collinson, The Old Priory, 80 North Bersted Street, Bognor Regis PO22 9AQ (01243 863580; Fax: 01243 826597). A charming 17th century Priory restored to its former glory with a blend of historic charm. Situated in a picturesque rural village close to Bognor Regis, Chichester, Arundel, Goodwood, Fontwell and within easy access of Portsmouth, Brighton, Continental ferry port and all major commuting routes. Facilities include superb en suite rooms equipped to 4 star standard, four-poster water bed with jacuzzi bath, secluded outdoor swimming pool, Cordon Bleu cuisine, residential licence, open all year. Tariff from £20.

BURY. Mrs Jane Hare, Eedes Cottage, Bignor Park Road, Bury Gate, Pulborough RH20 1EZ (01798 831438). Eedes Cottage is situated in unspoilt countryside just north of the Downs, yet convenient for the A29 which is only half a mile away. There are interesting places to visit including Arundel, Petworth, Chichester and Bignor Roman Villa. There is very good walking and riding, and dogs are welcome. Accommodation comprises two twin bedded rooms and one double bedroom, all with colour TV. Also separate bathroom and toilet. Terms from £20 to include full English Breakfast.

CHICHESTER (Hambrook). Mrs Edna Bailey, 14 The Avenue, Hambrook, Chichester PO18 8TY (01243 573199). A genuinely warm welcome awaits you if you choose to stay with us. Our quiet and comfortable accommodation has two rooms — one twin and one double, both with TV and tea/coffee facilities. Shared bathroom. Central heating. Bed and full English Breakfast from £16 per person, reductions for children under 10 years. 10 minutes' drive to Chichester Cathedral and Festival Theatre, 20 minutes' drive to Portsmouth, Singleton Open Air Museum. We have a large garden. No smoking. Several good public houses and restaurants in the area.

CHICHESTER. Mrs Julie Newman and Mrs Jane Ashby, Abelands House, Merston, Chichester

PO20 6DY (01243 532675). Abelands House, former Victorian rectory, is set in two acres with views towards South Downs and open farmland. Conveniently situated two miles from Chichester, within easy reach of local unspoilt beaches and Goodwood. Light, spacious, centrally heated family, double and twin rooms with en suite or private bathroom. Tea and coffee making facilities, colour TV. Children welcome, cot and high chair available. Evening meals. Offering a friendly and relaxed atmosphere. For the romantic — four-poster bed. Strictly no smoking. Member of ETB. Brochure on request.

CHICHESTER. Mr R.S. Grocott, The Old Store Guest House, Stane Street, Halnaker, Chichester

PO18 0QL (Tel and Fax: 01243 531977). An impressive 18th century Grade II Listed house adjoining the Goodwood Estate. All bedrooms at The Old Store Guest House have en suite shower rooms, colour TV, tea/coffee making facilities, hair dryer and trouser press. A full English breakfast is served in a charming breakfast room. Guests' lounge and car park. Excellent pub/restaurant within walking distance. Well situated for Goodwood House and racecourse and Chichester Festival Theatre. Also close by are Petworth House, Arundel Castle, Fishbourne Roman Palace and at Portsmouth, Nelson's flag ship The Victory.

RAC Acclaimed

WATERHALL COUNTRY HOUSE

ETB ♛♛
Commended

Prestwood Lane, Ifield Wood, Near Crawley, West Sussex RH11 0LA
Tel: 01293 520002   Fax: 01293 539905

Surrounded by open countryside and yet only 5 minutes from Gatwick Airport, Waterhall Country House is an ideal place for an overnight stay. The house is attractively decorated and furnished and we provide a warm and friendly welcome to all our guests. We have a variety of rooms – all with en suite bath or shower, remote control colour TV and tea making facilities. There is an attractive guest lounge, and breakfast is served in the luxury dining room. Children are welcome. Holiday parking available.

Double/twin £40; Single £25; Family £50
Prices are per room and include full English or Continental Breakfast

---

GATWICK. Mrs Jane French, Caprice Guest House, Bonnetts Lane, Ifield, Crawley RH11 0NY

(01293 528620). ETB Listed *COMMENDED.* "Caprice" is a small, friendly, family-run Guest House offering quality accommodation at affordable prices. Situated in a rural country lane surrounded by open fields and farmland with extensive views over the countryside, yet only a short distance from several main line stations (London 45 minutes, Brighton 30 minutes) and only five minutes south of Gatwick Airport. Whether you are just flying out of Gatwick, working in the town or visiting family and friends, "Caprice" is ideal for that overnight stay or longer. All rooms have colour TV and tea/coffee facilities; en suites available. Prices from £25 to £30 single, £35 to £45 double/twin. Children very welcome (all ages).

Terms quoted in this publication may be subject to increase if rises in costs necessitate

HENFIELD. Mrs J.A. Pound, The Squirrels, Albourne Road, Woodmancote, Henfield BN5 9BH (01273 492761). The Squirrels is a country house with lovely large garden set in a secluded area convenient for south coast and downland touring. Brighton and Gatwick 20 minutes. Good food at pub five minutes' walk. One family, one double, one twin and one single rooms, all with colour TV, washbasin, central heating and tea/coffee making facilities. Ample parking space. A warm welcome awaits you. Open all year. Directions: from London take M25, M23, A23 towards Brighton, then B2118 to Albourne. Turn right onto B2116 Albourne/Henfield Road — Squirrels is approximately one and a half miles on left. Bed and Breakfast £16.

HENFIELD. Mrs J. Forbes, Little Oreham Farm, off Horne Lane, Near Woodsmill, Henfield BN5 9SB (01273 492931). Delightful old Sussex farmhouse situated in rural position down lane, adjacent to footpaths and nature reserve. One mile from Henfield village, eight miles from Brighton, convenient for Gatwick and Hickstead. Excellent base for visiting many gardens and places of interest in the area. The farmhouse is a Listed building of great character; oak-beamed sitting room with inglenook fireplace (log fires), and a pretty dining room. Three comfortable attractive bedrooms with en suite shower/bath; WC; colour TV; tea making facilities. Central heating throughout. Lovely garden with views of the Downs. Situated off Horne Lane, one minute from Woodsmill Countryside Centre. Winner of Kellog's award: "Best Bed and Breakfast" in the South East. You will enjoy a friendly welcome and pleasant holiday. Sorry, no children under 10. Bed and Breakfast from £17.50 per person. Evening Meals by arrangement. No smoking. Open all year.

HENFIELD. Mr and Mrs E. Wilkin, Great Wapses Farm, Henfield BN5 9BJ (01273 492544). Working farm. The Tudor/Georgian farmhouse is set in rural surroundings 10 miles north of Brighton, off the B2116 Albourne/Henfield road, with Hickstead nearby. There are horses on the farm. The three comfortable rooms (one with four-poster bed) all have own bathroom/shower en-suite, tea/coffee making facilities and TV. Hard tennis court. Children and well behaved dogs welcome. Open all year round for Bed and Breakfast from £22 single, from £36 double. Snacks usually available by arrangement. There is also an attractive self contained comfortable cottage. Sleeps two/four. Let on a weekly basis from £110 including electricity, TV, etc.

LITTLEHAMPTON. Mrs Mo Skelton, Bracken Lodge Guest House, 43 Church Street, Littlehampton BN17 5PU (01903 723174). ❀ ❀ ❀ *HIGHLY COMMENDED.* Category II Accessibility. Friendly atmosphere, first class service. Comfortable, character, detached non-smoking house near town centre, indoor swimming centre, sand dunes, promenade, amusements, golf course and River Arun. All bedrooms en suite, colour TV, drink making facilities, trouser press, iron and board, hair dryer, clock/radio. Ideal touring base. Explore a coast and countryside steeped in history. Private parking. Purpose built ground floor twin disabled suite. Spacious, comprehensive facilities ensuring accessibility and quality. Bed and Breakfast from £23. Weekly and short break terms available. Open all year.

PETWORTH. Phyl Folkes, "Drifters", Duncton, Petworth GU28 0JZ (01798 342706). Welcome to a quiet, friendly, comfortable house overlooking countryside. One double en suite, two twin and one single rooms. Duncton is three miles from Petworth on the A285 Chichester Road, South Downs Way close by and many interesting places to visit. Petworth House and Gardens, Roman Villa, Chichester Cathedral and Theatre, Goodwood House and racecourse, Wheld and Downland Museum and many more. TV and tea/coffee making facilities in all rooms. Sorry no young children and no smoking. Bed and Breakfast from £17 to £20 per person.

PULBOROUGH. The Barn Owls, London Road, Coldwaltham, Pulborough RH20 1LR (01798 872498). 🕊 🕊 🕊 Small country hotel specialising in gourmet home-cooked food using fresh local produce. Situated in a lovely country village location overlooking Amberley Wild Brooks which provide wonderful walks for you and your dog. Several open air attractions and gardens in the area also accept dogs. Two-night Breaks from £85. Bed and Breakfast (en suite) from £150 weekly. Bed and Breakfast from £24 per night. Ideal for touring South Downs and convenient for Arundel, Bognor and Chichester. Brochure available.

STEYNING. Mrs A. Shapland, Wappingthorn Farm, Horsham Road, Steyning BN44 3AA (01903 813236). Working farm. Delightful traditional farmhouse with oak-beamed lounge, open log fire and pretty dining room. Situated in rural position viewing "South Downs", four miles from seaside, seven miles Worthing, 12 miles Brighton, Gatwick and Hickstead convenient. Comfortable, attractive, spacious bedrooms with en suite shower/bath; WC; colour TV; tea/coffee making facilities. Lovely garden with heated swimming pool. Many footpaths surround the farm and old market town. Bed and Breakfast from £15. Evening meal and picnic baskets available. Children welcome. Babysitting possible. There is also a converted barn with two self contained cottages. Fully equipped, sleeps two/four, from £110 per week. Short breaks available. Open all year.

WASHINGTON. Judy Ward, Brook House, Old London Road, Washington RH20 4AL (01903 892142). Quiet village at the foot of the South Downs. Ideal base for both walking in the beautiful surrounding countryside or touring by car. Arundel, Amberley Wildbrooks, Chichester and Brighton are just some of the very many local places of interest. Six miles from the coast. Bed and full English breakfast in self-contained annexe. Family en suite room available. Tea and coffee making facilities. Guests have their own shower room/toilet, lounge with colour TV and fully equipped kitchen. Ample off the road parking. £16 per person per night. Special rates for children under 13 years. 10% discount for bookings of seven or more nights.

TYNE & WEAR

GATESHEAD. Mrs Joan Douglas, Dunster Lodge, Earls Drive, Low Fell, Gateshead NE9 6AB (0191 4879078). Detached property situated in a quiet area with large garden (excellent for children to play in) and ample parking. Accommodation comprises one double, two twin, one family and four single bedrooms, three of which are en suite, all have TV and tea/coffee making facilities. Ground floor accommodation available, suitable for disabled guests. Private residents' lounge. Children welcome, babysitting available. Dogs welcome. Ironing facilities. Near to Metro Centre, Newcastle and main motorways. Bed and Breakfast from £15 to £20; Evening Meal from £5 to £9.

**If you've found
FARM HOLIDAY GUIDES
of service please tell your friends**

WARWICKSHIRE

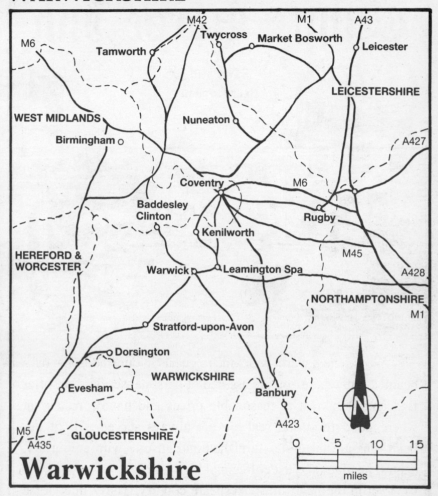

Warwickshire

COVENTRY near. **Mrs Barbara Chamberlain, Mill Farmhouse Country Residence, Mill Lane, Fillongley, Near Coventry CV7 8EE (01676 541898).**

❦ ❦ ❦ Experience the peace and tranquillity of our beautiful country home offering exceptional standards of comfort in idyllic surroundings. All rooms are centrally heated and immaculately furnished with comfortable new beds and hostess tray. Ample private car parking and gardens. No smoking. Tariff: Luxury double/twin en suite rooms with colour TV £40 to £45, single occupancy £25 including full English breakfast. 15 minutes NEC/Coventry, 30 minutes Birmingham, Stratford; convenient for Forest of Arden and Belfry Golf Courses. Special rates for lodgings — single and twin rooms.

COVENTRY near. Mrs Sandra Evans, Camp Farm, Hob Lane, Balsall Common, Near Coventry CV7 7GX (01676 533804).  Camp Farm is a farmhouse 150 to 200 years old. It is modernised but still retains its old world character. Nestling in the heart of England in Shakespeare country, within easy reach of Stratford-upon-Avon, Warwick, Kenilworth, Conventry with its famous Cathedral, and the National Exhibition Centre, Camp Farm offers a warm homely atmosphere and good English food, service and comfortable beds. The house is carpeted throughout. Dining room and sun lounge with colour TV. Bedrooms — five double, three family and five single, all have washbasins. Part of the house is suitable for disabled guests. Children welcome, cot, high chair, babysitting on request. Fire Certificate granted 1974. All terms quoted by letter or telephone.

FENNY COMPTON. Mrs D.J. Cotterill, The Granary, Fenny Compton, Leamington Spa CV33 0XE (01295 770214).  Modern hillside country house converted from old farm buildings in quiet situation and overlooking open farmland. Attractive garden borders Oxford Canal. Ground floor accommodation comprises three double centrally heated rooms, each having shower room with full facilities en-suite. Tea trays. Also guests' lounge/breakfast room. Bed and Breakfast only from £17 to £20 per person. Choice of good evening meals at local inns (nearest three minutes' walk). No facilities for children or pets, also non-smoking. The hamlet of Fenny Compton Wharf is on the A423, or may be reached from the B4100 via the villages of Northend and Fenny Compton. Ideal for touring Warwickshire, Oxfordshire, Northamptonshire and Cotswolds.

FENNY COMPTON. Mrs C.L. Fielder, Willow Cottage, Brook Street, Fenny Compton, Leamington Spa CV33 0YH (01295 770429). HETB Listed. A warm welcome awaits you in the centre of this attractive village near Oxfordshire/Northamptonshire borders. Character cottage with delightful garden and terrace in rural situation. Easy access to the Cotswolds and Shakespeare country and, for the businessman, to the NEC, Warwick, Leamington and Banbury. Very tasteful twin-bedded and single accommodation with own washing facilities, colour TV and radio. Family atmosphere. Dinner by previous arrangement from £9; Bed and Breakfast from £16.

FENNY COMPTON. Mrs Sylvia Hughes, The Grange, Fenny Compton, Leamington Spa CV33 0YB (01295 770361). The Georgian farmhouse and 450-acre working farm are pleasantly situated on the edge of the village, lying between the A423 and B4100, near the M40, with open views over beautiful and historic countryside, ideal for walking. We are within easy motoring distance for visiting Oxford, Stratford-upon-Avon, Warwick, Coventry, Sulgrave, the NAC and the NEC. Double, twin-bedded and single rooms are available. Good meals at local village inns. Bed and Breakfast from £16, with reductions for children.

AA QQQ

DRACHENFELS HOTEL ♔♔♔

25 Attleborough Road, Nuneaton CV11 4HZ

Near Coventry, Birmingham, Leicester and Tamworth. Just off the M6 motorway, the Drachenfels is a small private hotel, Licensed, with resident proprietor Mrs Doreen Ryder. The excellent bedroom accommodation includes colour TV, tea/coffee, radio/alarm, shaver socket and central heating; some ensuite. Overlooking playing fields, just five minutes' walk from the town centre. Nuneaton boasts a good shopping centre, pedestrianised, with seating, trees and fountains in the market place. A good base for touring, shopping or business. Bed and Breakfast from £15 per person. Small children free. **Telephone 01203 383030.**

PILLERTON HERSEY. Mrs Carolyn Howard, Docker's Barn Farm, Pillerton Hersey, Warwick CV35 0RL (Tel: 01926 640475; Fax: 01926 641747). Idyllically situated 18th century stone barn conversion surrounded by its own land, handy for Warwick, Stratford-upon-Avon, Cotswolds, NAC, NEC, Heritage Motor Centre and 6 miles from J12 M40. The house is full of character with antiques and interesting collections. The warm, attractive en suite bedrooms have tea/coffee trays and colour TV, and the four-poster suite has its own front door. Wildlife abounds and lovely walks lead from the barn, and we keep a few sheep, horses and poultry. If you are looking for total peace with friendly attentive service from £19 p.p., Docker's Barn is for you. No-smoking establishment.

LEAMINGSTON SPA. Marston House, Priors Marston, Near Leamington Spa CV23 8RP (01327 260297; Fax: 01327 262846). ♛ *COMMENDED.* Turn of the century well furnished family home situated in a pretty conservation village. Traditional English breakfasts are served and dinners with special diets are catered for. There are two pubs in the village. Bed and Breakfast accommodation (from £20 per person) consists of one double and a twin-bedded room, each with private bathroom. Large garden with a hard tennis court and croquet lawn. A warm welcome awaits you and help is available planning your visit to this area, with Stratford-on-Avon, Warwick Castle, Oxford, Blenheim Palace, Silverstone and Gaydon Car Museum all within easy reach.

LEAMINGTON SPA. David and Jean Selby, Coverdale Private Hotel, 8 Portland Street, Leamington Spa CV32 5HE (01926 330400; Fax: 01926 833388). 👑 👑 *COMMENDED.* Situated in a tree-lined avenue near the centre of Leamington Spa, Coverdale is a large attractive, detached house that has been carefully modernised. Very well furnished and centrally heated rooms all with direct-dial telephones, hospitality tray, colour TV, drinks makers and private bath or shower. A pleasant breakfast room and lounge. Car parking. Ideally located for touring the Heart of England — Warwick is two miles, Stratford-upon-Avon 10 miles, the National Agricultural Centre four miles and the NEC 14 miles. There are a number of good eating places within a quarter of a mile. AA Listed. Bed and full English Breakfast from £24. Reductions for children in family rooms.

LEAMINGTON SPA. Mrs Rebecca Gibbs, Hill Farm, Lewis Road, Radford Semele, Leamington Spa CV31 1UX (01926 337571). 👑 👑 *COMMENDED.* This friendly, comfortable farmhouse is set in 350 acres of mixed farmland in beautiful Shakespeare country, one mile from A425 on east of Leamington Spa. Pretty bedrooms with full facilities, some en-suite, all have TV. Excellent food. Guests' private bathroom, TV lounge and dining room. Children welcome, reduced rates. AA award winner. FHG Diploma. Bed and Breakfast from £16. Spacious five caravan site also available.

LEAMINGTON SPA. Miss Deborah Lea, Crandon House, Avon Dassett, Leamington Spa CV33 0AA (01295 770652). 👑 👑 *HIGHLY COMMENDED.* **Working farm.** Guests receive a specially warm welcome at our comfortable farmhouse offering an exceptionally high standard of accommodation. Set in 20 acres with beautiful views over unspoilt countryside this is a small working farm with rare breeds of cattle, sheep and poultry. Three attractive bedrooms with private facilities, tea/coffee making equipment and colour TV. Guests' dining room and sitting rooms, one with colour TV. Full central heating and log fire in chilly weather. Electric blankets available. Car essential, ample parking. Pets by arrangement. Peaceful and quiet yet offers easy access for touring the Heart of England, Warwick, Stratford-upon-Avon, the Cotswolds. Open all year. Bed and Breakfast from £18.50. Winter breaks available. Farm Holiday Bureau member. Write or ring for further details.

LIGHTHORNE, near Warwick. Mrs J. Stanton, Redlands Farm, Banbury Road, Lighthorne, Near Warwick CV35 0AH (01926 651241). 👑 👑 A beautifully restored 15th century farmhouse built of local stone, the Old Farmhouse is set in two acres of garden with its own swimming pool, well away from the main road, yet within easy travelling distance of Stratford and Warwick; two miles Junction 12 M40. Handy for the Cotswolds. Guest accommodation in one double (with bathroom), one single and one family bedrooms, all with tea making facilities; bathroom, beamed lounge with TV, dining room. Rooms are centrally heated and the farmhouse also has open fires. Bed and Breakfast from £17.50. Children welcome, facilities available and reduced rates. No pets. A car is recommended to make the most of your stay. AA QQQ.

WARWICKSHIRE – SHAKESPEARE'S COUNTY

Stratford-upon-Avon is the county's, and indeed one of the country's biggest attractions. Make time however to explore Northern Warwickshire and George Eliot Country around Nuneaton and "England's Historic Heartland" – the three very individual towns of Warwick, Royal Leamington Spa and Kenilworth, together with their surrounding villages.

RUGBY near. Mrs Helen Sharpe, Manor Farm, Willey, Near Rugby CV23 0SH (01455 553143). ♛ ♛

COMMENDED. Manor Farm is the well-kept secret that non-smokers return to repeatedly. Ideally placed, tucked into a rural village within the Midlands motorway network, it offers an oasis of peace and tranquillity yet is deceptively handy for town, city, universities, NEC, etc., avoiding the noise and aggravation of other venues. We are so easy to find and perfect for north, south, east, west travel. An abundance of good eating places surround us. Adults only. Our repeat bookings are our testimony.

STOURTON. Brook House, Stourton, Shipston-on-Stour CV36 5HQ (Tel and Fax: 01608 686281).

Mid 19th century farmhouse with lovely views on edge of quiet, unspoilt North Cotswold village. Furnished with antiques, the accommodation includes family room with en suite facilities, double room with bathroom, single room, guest sitting room and dining room. Parking. Stratford-upon-Avon, Stow-on-the-Wold, Oxford, Broadway, Kiftsgate and Hidcote Gardens all within easy distance. Open all year. Bed and Breakfast from £19. Dinner/supper available if booked in advance.

STRATFORD-UPON-AVON. Mrs Gillian Hutsby, Thornton Manor, Ettington, Stratford-upon-Avon CV37 7PN (01789 740210). ♛ ♛ **Working farm.** Enjoy

the peace and beautiful surroundings of this late 16th century manor house whilst taking a pleasant walk on the farm. The house is situated off the Warwick A429 road from Ettington, and is ideal for visiting Warwick, the Cotswolds and Stratford. Accommodation includes a comfortable lounge with a log fire and TV; two double bedrooms with en suite facilities and a twin-bedded room with private bathroom, all with tea/coffee making facilities. There is a kitchen for guests' use with tea/coffee making facilities, etc. Bed and Breakfast from approximately £18 per person per night.

STRATFORD-UPON-AVON. Highcroft, Banbury Road, Stratford-upon-Avon CV37 7NF (01789 296293). ♛ ♛ COMMENDED. AA QQQ. Highcroft visitors are assured of a warm welcome and an informal atmosphere, only two miles from Stratford on A422 in two acres of gardens surrounded by open countryside. We have two large rooms, double/family, adjacent to house with own access and suitable for disabled guests; one double in main house with the benefit of its own stairs (an adjoining room available for families). Both rooms enjoy en-suite facilities, central heating, colour TV and tea/coffee making facilities. Excellent country pubs nearby for eating out. Ideally situated for Cotswolds, Stratford, Warwick. Terms from £35 double room; discounts for children. Telephone for more details.

STRATFORD-UPON-AVON. Bill and Veronica Stevenson, "Dosthill Cottage", 2 The Green, Wilmcote, Stratford-upon-Avon CV37 9XJ (01789 266480).

✿ ✿ *COMMENDED*. One of the original properties situated in the centre of this Shakespearean village, overlooking Mary Arden's House and gardens. Walk three miles past 14 locks into Stratford-upon-Avon, take an easy drive to the NEC, Royal Show Ground or tour the Cotswolds. There are double and twin rooms, all with private facilities and TV. Non-smoking accommodation available. Car parking, garage if required. Bed and Breakfast from £20, family reductions.

STRATFORD-UPON-AVON. Mr Mathews, Thirkleby Guest House, 60 Evesham Road, Stratford-upon-Avon CV37 9BS (01789 298640). Detached period house set in delightful secluded garden. Twin room and single room, both with shower; double room. Parking. Within 10 minutes' walk of town. Bed and Breakfast from £17 to £19.

STRATFORD-UPON-AVON. Mrs E. Hunter, Hill House, Hampton Lucy, Warwick CV35 8AU (01789 840329). HETB Listed *COMMENDED*. Idyllically situated

midway between Stratford and Warwick, both of which are only five minutes away, this charming Georgian country house stands in two acres of private grounds and enjoys fine rural views. Traditionally furnished to a high standard, accommodation includes one double room with adjoining single, and one twin room with washbasin, each with private bathroom and tea/coffee making facilities; comfortable TV sittingroom with open fire and dining room where full breakfast is served. Ideal base for touring the Cotswolds, Oxford, Stratford, NEC or NAC. You will be assured of a very peaceful stay and warm hospitality. Bed and Breakfast from £20.

STRATFORD-UPON-AVON. Mrs A. Cross, Lemarquand, 186 Evesham Road, Stratford-upon-Avon CV37 9BS (01789 204164). Small homely accommodation, highly recommended, friendly atmosphere and personal attention. Providing full English Breakfast and

comfortable beds. All rooms centrally heated, with washbasins, some with private shower; tea/coffee making facilities and pleasant views. Separate tables in dining room. Parking on own private forecourt of house. Close to town centre, theatres, leisure centre, river and local places of interest including Shakespeare's birthplace and Anne Hathaway's Cottage; Warwick Castle and Cotswold villages are easily accessible and there are numerous golf courses for the golfing enthusiast. Local inns provide good food. Open all year.

STRATFORD-UPON-AVON. Allors, 62 Evesham Road, Stratford-upon-Avon CV37 9BA (01789 269982). ETB Listed *COMMENDED*. RAC Listed. Detached

house on the B439 Stratford/Evesham road, 15 minutes' walk from town centre. Well situated for visiting Royal Shakespeare Theatre, Stratford Racecourse, Shakespeare properties, Warwick Castle and the Cotswolds. We offer non-smokers comfortable centrally heated en suite accommodation. Each bedroom has its own sitting area with tea/coffee making facilities and colour TV. Pleasant dining room overlooking secluded garden. Private car parking. Bed and Breakfast from £18.50 per person. SPECIAL RATE FOR THREE NIGHT BREAKS THROUGHOUT THE YEAR.

WHEN MAKING ENQUIRIES PLEASE MENTION THIS *FHG* PUBLICATION

STRATFORD-UPON-AVON. Mrs J. Wakeham, Whitfield Farm, Ettington, Stratford-upon-Avon CV37 7PN (01789 740260). Working farm. Situated down its own private drive, off the A429, this 220-acre mixed farm (wheat, cows, sheep, geese, horses, hens) is ideal for a quiet and relaxing holiday. Convenient for visiting the Cotswolds, Warwick, Coventry, Stratford, Worcester. Near M40. Fully modernised centrally heated house with separate lounge having colour TV. Accommodation in one double room with washbasin, one double and one twin en-suite, all with tea/coffee making facilities. Parking. Open all year (except Christmas) for Bed and Breakfast from £14.50 per night. Home produced food served. Full English Breakfast. AA registered. SAE please.

STRATFORD-UPON-AVON. Mrs Marian J. Walters, Church Farm, Dorsington, Stratford-upon-Avon CV37 8AX (01789 720471 or 0831 504194 mobile; Fax: 01789 720830). ♥♥ *COMMENDED.* A friendly welcome awaits you throughout the year at our Georgian farmhouse with open fires and central heating. Stratford-upon-Avon, Warwick, NEC, Royal Showground and the Vale of Evesham are all within easy driving distance. Guests are free to explore the mixed working farm. Gliding, fishing, boating and horse riding are all nearby. Family, double and twin-bedded rooms with TV and tea/coffee making facilities, most en suite, some in converted stable block. Full Fire Certificate held. Children welcome at reduced rates. Bed and Breakfast from £16. Please write or telephone for further details.

STRATFORD-UPON-AVON. Mrs D.M. Hall, ''Acer House'', 44 Albany Road, Stratford-upon-Avon CV37 6PQ (01789 204962). Quality Bed and Breakfast, non-smoking establishment. Situated in a quiet road, within five minutes' walk from railway station and to town centre. Guest rooms overlook pleasant garden. Central heating, TV lounge. Enjoy a hearty English breakfast with choices, or Continental and vegetarian menus; early breakfasts on request. Double, twin, family and single rooms available. Tariff £14 to £17 per person Bed and Breakfast inclusive of tea/coffee making facilities. Street parking available. French spoken.

STRATFORD-UPON-AVON. John and Julia Downie, Holly Tree Cottage, Birmingham Road, Pathlow, Stratford-upon-Avon CV37 0ES (Tel & Fax: 01789 204461). Period cottage dating back to 17th century, with beams, antiques, tasteful furnishings and friendly atmosphere. Gardens with views over the countryside. Situated three miles north of Stratford towards Henley-in-Arden on A3400 (was A34), convenient for overnight stops or longer stays, and ideal for theatre visits. Excellent base for touring Shakespeare country, Heart of England, Cotswolds, Warwick Castle and Blenheim Palace. Well situated for National Exhibition Centre. Double, twin and family accommodation with en suite and private facilities; colour TV and tea/coffee in all rooms. Full English Breakfast. Restaurant and pub meals nearby. Bed and Breakfast from £19; reductions for children sharing. Telephone for information.

HOLLY TREE COTTAGE

STRATFORD-UPON-AVON. Mrs Karen Cauvin, Penshurst Guest House, 34 Evesham Place, Stratford-upon-Avon CV37 6HT (01789 205259; Fax: 01789 295322). ETB Listed *COMMENDED.* You'll get an exceptionally warm welcome at this prettily refurbished, totally non-smoking Victorian townhouse, five minutes' walk from the centre of town. Attention to detail is obvious and the proprietors, Karen and Yannick will go out of their way to make you feel at home. You'd like a lie-in while on holiday? No problem!! Delicious English or Continental breakfasts are served from 7.00 right up until 10.30 in the morning. Rooms have been individually decorated and are well-equipped with many little extras apart from the usual TV and beverages. Home-cooked evening meals by arrangement. Brochure available on request. Excellent value for money is obtained at Penhurst with prices ranging from £14 to £20 per person.

STRATFORD-UPON-AVON. Mrs R.M. Meadows, Monk's Barn Farm, Shipston Road, Stratford-upon-Avon CV37 8NA (01789 293714). Working farm. One-and-a-half miles south of Stratford-upon-Avon on the A3400 (formerly A34) is Monk's Barn, a 75 acre mixed farm welcoming visitors all year. Monk's Barn dates back to the 16th century and succeeds in combining real traditional character with first class amenities. One double room with washbasin and three twin/double rooms with en suite facilities (two on ground floor suitable for some disabled guests) and one single room. Visitors' lounge. Beautiful riverside walk to village. Bed and Breakfast from £15. Tea/coffee facilities and colour TVs in rooms. Sorry no pets. Non-smokers preferred. AA QQ. Details on request.

STRATFORD-UPON-AVON. Janet and Keith Cornwell, "Midway", 182 Evesham Road, Stratford-upon-Avon CV37 9BS (01789 204154). Relax, enjoy Stratford's attractions and surrounding area with us. Clean, centrally heated rooms — three double, one single, all en-suite, with colour TV, clock radio, tea/coffee facilities, tastefully and comfortably furnished. Superb English breakfast. Pleasant diningroom with separate tables. Keys provided, access at all times. Park your car on our forecourt and take a 10/15 minute walk to town centre, theatres, Anne Hathaway's Cottage or race course. Personal friendly service. Map and information on attractions provided in rooms. Fans in bedrooms during summer. Full Fire Certificate. Open all year. Sorry no dogs. Arthur Frommer recommended.

STRATFORD-UPON-AVON. Mrs Marguerite Allard, Windfall Guest House, 118 Alcester Road, Stratford-upon-Avon CV37 9DP (01789 266880). ☛ Stratford-upon-Avon is a very popular venue with tourists and this guest house, where fluent French is spoken, is within easy reach of the town centre and the famous Royal Shakespeare Theatre. Open all year. Mrs Allard provides special diets and will cater for an evening meal in special circumstances. Showers; central heating. Car parking. Babysitting. Situated on the A422 it is an ideal touring centre for Warwick Castle, the Cotswolds, Blenheim Palace and many places of historic and archaeological interest. Bed and Breakfast from £15 to £16. Reductions for children and Senior Citizens. Telephone bookings — arrive by 12.00am if possible.

STRATFORD-UPON-AVON. Judith Spencer, The Poplars, Mansell Farm, Newbold on Stour, Stratford-upon-Avon CV37 8BZ (01789 450540).

Tourist Board Listed *COMMENDED*. A warm welcome awaits you on our working dairy farm. Enjoy the views of the Cotswolds from our modern farmhouse which is in easy reach of Stratford, Warwick, Oxford and NEC. One family and one twin room, both en suite with TV and one single with washbasin. All have tea trays and central heating. Good food or walk to local hostelry. Open all year except Christmas and New Year. Children and pets welcome. Bed and Breakfast from £16 to £17.50. Brochure available on request.

STRATFORD-UPON-AVON. Ms Diana Tallis, Linhill, 35 Evesham Place, Stratford-upon-Avon CV37 6HT (01789 292879; Fax: 01789 414478). HETB Listed.

Linhill is a comfortable Victorian Guest House run by a friendly young family. It is situated only five minutes' walk from Stratford's town centre with its wide choice of fine restaurants and world famous Royal Shakespeare Theatres. Every bedroom at Linhill has central heating, colour TV, tea/coffee making facilities and washbasin. En suite facilities are also available, as are packed lunches and evening meals. Bicycle hire and babysitting facilities if desired. Leave the children with us and re-discover the delight of a candle-lit dinner in one of Stratford's inviting restaurants. Bed and Breakfast from £13 to £18; Evening Meal from £5 to £7.50. Reduced rates for Senior Citizens.

STRATFORD-UPON-AVON. Mrs Pat Short, Nando's Guest House, 18/20 Evesham Place, Stratford-upon-Avon CV37 6HT (Tel & Fax: 01789 204907).

A warm welcome awaits you at Nando's where Pat and Peter pride themselves on a high standard of cleanliness, good home cooking and a friendly atmosphere. Nando's is AA and RAC Acclaimed and a member of "Best Bed and Breakfast in the World" Association. It is ideally located only five minutes' walking distance from the town centre and famous Royal Shakespeare Theatre. It is also conveniently placed for the Cotswolds, Warwick Castle, Blenheim Palace and the National Exhibition Centre. Nando's has 21 rooms, 13 of which are en suite and four of these are located on the ground floor. All rooms are centrally heated, double glazed and have colour TV. Private parking is available. Room charges (including full English breakfast and VAT) start from £14 per person. Visa/Mastercard, Amex welcome.

STRATFORD-UPON-AVON near. Jane Weldon, Bridge House, Alderminster, Stratford-upon-Avon CV37 8NY (01789 450521; Fax: 01789 414681). *HIGHLY COMMENDED*. Set in the heart of Shakespeare's country our charming Georgian house with "Hayloft" dates from 1812 and has uninterrupted views across open countryside to the meandering River Stour and to the Cotswold Hills in the distance. Accommodation in either the Hayloft, the Blue and White Room or the Tulip Room. All have colour TV and tea/coffee facilities and have been recently stylishly redecorated, some have private facilities. Gardens. Alderminster is five miles south of Stratford-upon-Avon on the main Stratford to Oxford road (A3400) and Bridge House is the perfect place for a relaxing break. Bed and Breakfast from £20 per person per night to include full breakfast. Ample car parking. Licensed.

STRATFORD-UPON-AVON. Mrs K. Rosamund-Pepper, Barbette Guest House, 165 Evesham Road, Stratford-upon-Avon CV37 9BP (01789 297822). ✿✿ *COMMENDED*. Homely, friendly, Bed and Breakfast accommodation. Full English or Continental. Two family rooms (one with private facilities, the other with shower) will let either as doubles or twins, two single rooms and one double; separate bathroom. Washbasins, colour TV and drinks facilities in all rooms. TV lounge. Adequate car parking. Within walking distance of town centre and theatres; tours of the Shakespearian properties and Warwick Castle and numerous places of interest within easy drive. Bed and Breakfast from £16 per person per night. Senior Citizens off season reductions.

STRATFORD-UPON-AVON. Hampton Lodge, 38 Shipston Road, Stratford-upon-Avon CV37 7LP (Tel & Fax: 01789 299374). ✿✿ *COMMENDED*. Paul and Pru Williams welcome you to Hampton Lodge wich is situated within five minutes walking distance of the centre of this historic town and world famous theatre. The accommodation comprises cosy residents lounge, six comfortable rooms including two family, two double, one twin and one four-poster, all are en suite and have colour TV, tea/coffee trays and direct-dial telephones. Traditional English breakfasts are served in our large, relaxed conservatory overlooking attractive gardens and summer house. Ideal base for Cotswolds, Blenheim Palace, Warwick Castle, National Trust properties. Plentiful private parking. Prices from £18 per person per night.

TANWORTH IN ARDEN. Monica and Brian Palser, Mungunyah, Poolhead Lane, Tanworth in Arden,

Near Solihull B94 5EH (01564 742437). Monica and Brian Palser welcome you to their attractive home set in the peaceful Warwickshire countryside overlooking a golf course on the outskirts of the pretty village of Tanworth in Arden. It is centrally located for the National Exhibition Centre and major tourist attractions (Stratford-upon-Avon, Warwick Castle, National Trust Houses, etc) being only five minutes' drive from M42 Junction 3. They offer two twin-bedded rooms (one with washbasin), guests' private bathroom and sittingroom with TV. Tea/coffee making facilities plus hospitality tray on arrival and evening drink are included. Ample parking. Non-smokers please. Bed and Breakfast from £20 per person. Twin occupancy.

WARWICK. Mr and Mrs D. Clapp, The Croft, Haseley Knob, Warwick CV35 7NL (Tel & Fax: 01926

484447). ✿✿ *COMMENDED*. Join David and Pat on their four acre smallholding and share the friendly family atmosphere, the picturesque rural surroundings, home cooking and very comfortable accommodation. Bedrooms, most en-suite, have colour TV, tea/coffee making equipment. Ground floor en-suite bedrooms available. Dinners by arrangement. Bed and Full English Breakfast from £20. Centrally located for touring Warwick (Castle), Stratford (Shakespeare), Coventry (Cathedral), and Birmingham. Also ideal for the businessman visiting the National Exhibition Centre or Birmingham Airport, both about 15 minutes. No smoking inside. Ample parking. Mobile home available, also caravan parking. Large gardens. Open all year. RAC Acclaimed. French spoken.

WARWICK. Ian and Dawn Kitchen, The Old Rectory, Vicarage Lane, Sherbourne, Warwick CV35

8AB (01926 624562; Fax: 01926 624995). ✿✿✿ AA QQQQ Selected. A licensed Georgian country house, rich in beams, flagstones and inglenooks. Situated in a gem of an English village, half a mile from the M40 Junction 15. 14 elegantly appointed en suite bedrooms, thoughtfully provide all possible comforts. Some antique brass beds and some wonderful Victorian-style bathrooms. Try our Honeymoon Suite with hand-carved antique French bed and a spa bath. Choice of menu for breakfast and dinner in the oak and elm dining room. Ideally situated for Warwick Castle, Shakespeare's Stratford, the Cotswolds and many National Trust properties. NEC 20 minutes, Stoneleigh 10 minutes. Recommended by all major guides.

WHEN MAKING ENQUIRIES PLEASE MENTION
THIS *FHG* PUBLICATION

WARWICK. Mrs D.E. Bromilow, Woodside, Langley Road, Claverdon, Warwick CV35 8PJ (01926

842446). Woodside Guest House offers its guests something very special. Situated amidst acres of gardens and privately owned conservation woodland, it is perfect for families and those wishing to get away from traffic, yet is only 15 minutes from Warwick and Stratford-upon-Avon. Each of the large bedrooms have garden and woodland views and are comfortably and individually furnished providing tea and coffee making facilities (one en suite). Claverdon Village only five minutes away has a choice of pubs offering evening meals, alternatively dinner can be arranged at Woodside. Pets and children welcome. Open all year. Bed and Breakfast from £18. Reductions for children.

WEST MIDLANDS

BIRMINGHAM. Mrs Pamela E. Lendon, "Abberley", 51 Victoria Road, Acocks Green, Birmingham

B27 7YB (0121 707 2950). "Abberley" is a mid-Victorian house set among tall trees. Situated off the A41, midway between Birmingham and Solihull, about five miles from Birmingham International Airport and Station, National Exhibition Centre and New Convention Centre. Convenient for theatres in Birmingham, Coventry and Stratford-upon-Avon. Homely, welcoming atmosphere, with comfortable centrally-heated rooms, one with en-suite luxury bathroom including bidet. All rooms with washbasins, tea and coffee making facilities, radio and colour TV. Ample parking. If using us as a staging-post for holidays abroad we offer parking for your car while away. Bed and Breakfast from £20. Member Solihull Tourism Association.

PINEWAY GUEST HOUSE
Bed & Breakfast
5 Elmdon Road, Acocks Green,
Birmingham B27 6LJ
Tel: 0121 708 2177   Fax: 0121 628 3763
Proprietor: Dave McCoy.

Situated in a quiet, tree-lined cul-de-sac with free off-road parking, Pineway Guest House is the obvious choice for business and professional people seeking comfortable, convenient accommodation. Motorway links (M40, M42, M6 and M5) are close by, and the Guest House is near Birmingham Airport, the NEC, city centre, National Indoor Arena, Sea World and Solihull. Convenient for local transport, many restaurants (eg italian, Indian, Harry Ramsden's Fish & Chips, McDonalds etc) within easy walking distance.

Accommodation offers a high degree of comfort, with the convenience of guests always in mind. Three single bedrooms, two double rooms, one twin room and one large family room. Each has a washbasin, tea/coffee making facilities, shaver point and video and satellite-linked TV. All rooms centrally heated. bathrooms on each floor. Full Fire Certificate.

★ Good food always available – *Full English Breakfast* – flexible meal times ★
At the Pineways Guest House you can always be sure of a warm welcome.
Friendly, personal service is our first consideration.

BIRMINGHAM. Ian and Angela Kerr, Awentsbury Hotel, 21 Serpentine Road, Selly Park, Birmingham B29 7HU (0121-472 1258). ♛♛ A Victorian country house set in its own large garden. Close to buses, trains, Birmingham University, BBC Pebble Mill, Queen Elizabeth and Selly Oak Hospitals, and only two miles from the city centre. All rooms have colour TV, telephones, tea/coffee making facilities, washbasins and central heating. Some rooms ensuite, some with showers. TV lounge. Ample car parking. Open all year. Pets and children welcome. Reductions for children. AA and RAC Listed. Terms from £25 single room, from £39 twin room, inclusive of breakfast and VAT; Evening Meals if required. Light supper or bedtime drink at small charge.

SOLIHULL near. Mrs Kathleen Connolly, Holland Park Farm, Buckley Green, Henley in Arden, Near Solihull B95 5QF (01564 792625). ♛♛ A Georgian style farmhouse set in 300 acres of peaceful farmland, including the historic grounds of "The Mount" and other interesting walks. Three large en suite bedrooms (two with bath/shower, other with shower). Large garden with pond. Livestock includes cattle and sheep. Ideally situated in Shakespeare's country, within easy reach of Birmingham International Airport, NEC, NAC, Stratford-upon-Avon, Warwick and the Cotswolds. Open all year. Children and pets welcome. Bed and Breakfast from £18.

WILTSHIRE

BIDDESTONE, Near Bath. Elaine Sexton, Elm Farmhouse, The Green, Biddestone, Chippenham SN14 7DG (01249 713354). ♛♛ *COMMENDED.* A warm welcome is assured at Elm Farmhouse, a 17th century Cotswold stone property opposite the pond in the beautiful and peaceful village of Biddestone. Three traditionally decorated double bedrooms are offered with tea/coffee and colour TV provided. Two are en suite overlooking the pond and the other has a view of half acre walled garden. Two excellent pubs are also within walking distance. Biddestone is between the famous villages of Lacock and Castle Combe and is also close to Bath and Junction 17 of M4. There are many National Trust properties nearby. Children welcome. From £17.50 per person.

CALNE. Mrs Jean Henly, Lower Sands Farm, Calne SN11 8TR (01249 812402). Working farm. Very quiet and peaceful. Lovely garden to sit in and relax, one mile from centre of Calne, eight miles from M4. Good touring centre for Avebury, Lacock, Bath, Bowood, Salisbury or enjoy a quiet break whilst travelling. Accommodation in one single, one twin-bedded room, one room with double bed and additional single bed plus cot if required. Tea/coffee making in all rooms. Bathroom for use of guests. Three course cooked breakfast. Evening Meal can be provided, using own organically grown vegetables and fruit. Open all year. Bed and Breakfast from £16; Bed, Breakfast and Evening Meal from £22.

CHIPPENHAM near. Mrs Diana Barker, Manor Farm, Sopworth, Near Chippenham SN14 6PR (01454 238676). Working farm, join in. Manor Farm is a working mixed farm on the Beaufort estate near Badminton. The Jacobean farmhouse was updated in Georgian and Victorian times. It is very quietly situated in lovely countryside yet near many places of interest: Malmesbury, Tetbury and South Cotswolds, Berkeley Castle, Bristol, Bath, Castle Combe, Lacock Abbey, Avebury. Ideal overnight stop for travellers to South West. Junction 18, M4 six miles and close to Fosse Way and M5. Spacious comfortable rooms with heating and en-suite available. Lounge/diningroom with open fires in winter. Personal attention and a warm welcome. Bed and Breakfast from £12 to £25 per person.

CHIPPENHAM. Mrs K.M. Addison, The Old Rectory, Cantax Hill, Lacock, Chippenham SN15 2JZ (01249 730335). ✿✿ *COMMENDED.* Situated in the National Trust village of Lacock and standing in its own grounds with croquet, The Old Rectory offers easy access to a variety of interesting things for the visitor to see and do. Lacock Abbey, the home of Fox Talbot, is one of the few abbeys Henry VIII did not destroy, and a visit to the Fox Talbot Photographic Museum is well worthwhile. The village is centrally placed for touring such places as Bath, Avebury, Stonehenge, Salisbury and many other towns and villages. Pleasant drives and walks through the West Country. Elegant accommodation is offered with private bathroom to all bedrooms. Ample free parking space. Bed and Breakfast from £20 per person per night.

DEVIZES near. Rob and Jacqui Mattingly, The Old Coach House, 21 Church Street, Market Lavington, Devizes SN10 4DU (01380 812879). ✿✿ *COMMENDED.* A warm welcome awaits you at this delightful 18th century coaching house. Attractive rooms with en suite facilities and colour TV ensure your stay will be relaxed and comfortable. Whether you enjoy a traditional English breakfast or choose a speciality from the menu you can be sure it will be freshly prepared using the finest local ingredients. Situated a few miles south of Devizes it is a perfect location from which to explore the surrounding area. Bath, Salisbury, Stonehenge and many other places of interest are all within easy reach. Excellent for walking and cycling and ideal for Short Breaks. Children welcome but sorry no pets. Bed and Breakfast from £21 to £24. No smoking. AA QQQ.

FIGHELDEAN. Eddie and Judy Strefford, Vale House, Figheldean, Salisbury SP4 8JJ (01980 670713). ✿✿ *COMMENDED.* A detached family house in the centre of this quiet Wiltshire village on the River Avon. Stonehenge is two miles away and there is easy access to the Woodford Valley, Salisbury City and Salisbury Plain. This is an ideal centre to explore places of interest throughout Wiltshire, Bath and North East Somerset and West Hampshire. Accommodation available in one single and two twin rooms (one en suite); visitors' lounge and garden will be available throughout the day. All rooms have TV and tea/coffee facilities. Bed and Breakfast is from £14.50 to £16.50 (no single supplement). Reduced rates for children. Parking. Village pub meals nearby.

MALMESBURY. Mrs Doi Harwood, Winkworth Farm, Lea, Near Malmesbury SN16 9NH (01666 823267). Enjoy the warm, friendly atmosphere of our 17th century Cotswold stone farmhouse set in a delightful secluded walled garden. The house is very comfortable and beautifully decorated and has oak beams and log fires. There are two double rooms, one with private bathroom and the other en suite; both have a hospitality tray and TV. Winkworth Farm is ideally placed for a quiet holiday or as a base for touring. The village of Lea is just three miles from the ancient hilltop town of Malmesbury off the B4042, within easy reach of Cirencester, Cheltenham, Bath, Lacock and Westonbirt Arboretum. The farmhouse is about half a mile off the road, turning is opposite the village school. Children welcome. Non-smoking accommodation. Bed and Breakfast £18; Dinner by arrangement.

WILTSHIRE – "WHITE" HORSE COUNTY!

Many "White" horses adorn the Wiltshire chalk downs and the prehistoric theme continues with Stonehenge and Avebury. Also of interest are the landscape gardens at Studley, Chiselbury Camp, the Kennet and Avon canal with lock "staircase", Salisbury Plain, and the abandoned city Old Sarum.

MALMESBURY. Mrs Susan Barnes, Lovett Farm, Little Somerford, Chippenham SN15 5BP (01666 823268). 👑👑 *COMMENDED.* Situated in the beautiful Wiltshire countryside close to Malmesbury, England's oldest Borough, and within easy reach of the Cotswolds, Bath, Badminton, Avebury and Stonehenge. Our farmhouse, with delightful views, has full central heating. Guest accommodation in one double room and one twin room, both en suite, each offering tea/coffee making facilities, radio and colour TV. The lounge/dining room with a traditional log fire creates a warming atmosphere for our winter visitors who wish to enjoy an evening by the fireside. Enjoy a hearty farmhouse breakfast! Bed and Breakfast from £17. Reduced rates for children. Open all year. Farm Holiday Bureau member.

MALMESBURY. Mrs Edwards, Stonehill Farm, Charlton, Malmesbury SN16 9DY (01666 823310). ETB *Listed COMMENDED.* Superbly located on the edge of the Cotswolds in lush rolling countryside and only 15 minutes from the M4 Junction 16 or 17. John and Edna invite you to stay with them on their dairy farm in a relaxed friendly atmosphere where pets and children are welcome. The charming old farmhouse, originally built in 1483 and now modernised, offers an ideal centre from which to visit Bath, Avebury, Castle Combe and the beautiful Cotswold hills and villages. Three pretty rooms (one en suite) with comfortable beds and a delicious breakfast to start your day. AA QQ.

MALMESBURY. Mrs C.E. Weaver, Whychurch Farm, Malmesbury SN16 9JL (01666 822156). ETB **Listed** *COMMENDED.* **Working farm.** Situated on the edge of the Cotswolds in England's oldest borough, the 17th century farmhouse is on a family-run 500-acre dairy farm. A friendly and relaxed atmosphere awaits you in our comfortable and traditionally furnished home, including a hearty farmhouse breakfast. Separate guests' lounge, colour TV. Accommodation includes two twin and one double-bedded rooms, shower room with WC, and bathroom for guests' use. Two charming en suite ground floor conversions. The Cycling Touring Club welcome and Caravan Club Approved. Cream teas served and antiques for sale. Open all year. Bed and Breakfast from £15 to £17.50 nightly. Water sports, golf, fishing, horse riding are all close by.

MARLBOROUGH. Mrs Clarissa Roe, Clench Farmhouse, Malborough SN8 4NT (01672 810264). Attractive 18th century farmhouse set in its own grounds with lovely views. There are two double bedrooms beautifully furnished, one with its own bathroom and the other with a shower en suite. The house has a relaxed and happy atmosphere and a warm welcome awaits guests. Tennis court, heated pool and croquet lawn are all available. Three course dinner may be provided by prior arrangement. We are within easy reach of Stonehenge, Salisbury and Bath and close to the Avon and Kennet Canal. Children and pets welcome. Bed and Breakfast from £18; Dinner from £15.

MERE. Mrs Jean Smith, The Beeches, Chetcombe Road, Mere BA12 6AU (01747 860687). 👑 *COMMENDED.* A comfortable, old Toll House with interesting carved stairway and gallery, standing in beautiful garden at entrance to Early English village. Centrally situated for Bath, Wells, Salisbury, Bournemouth, New Forest and Sherborne. In close proximity to the famous Stourhead Gardens and Longleat House and Wildlife Park. We have two double and family rooms. The house is furnished to a very high standard, is centrally heated with TV, tea/coffee making facilities, washbasin and shaver points in all rooms, one room having en suite shower, the other room en suite bath and bidet. Large lounge. Large enclosed car park. Open all year. Bed and Breakfast from £17. Reductions for children.

MERE. Mrs Jane Hurd, Willowdown House, Wet Lane, Mere BA12 6BA (01747 860218). 18th
century farmhouse situated one mile from town centre, set in
four acres, surrounded by open fields and country footpaths.
Convenient for Stourhead Gardens, Shaftesbury, Salisbury
and Bath. There is a twin-bedded room with en suite bathroom and a double bedroom, both have TV, radio and
tea/coffee facilities. Open all year. Dinner by arrangement.
Bed and Breakfast £16 per person. Reductions for children,
who are very welcome.

**SALISBURY. Mrs K. Robinson, Michaelmas Cottage, Guilder Lane, Salisbury SP1 1HW (01722
329580/325335).** Two very pretty medieval cottages two
minutes from town centre, Old Chequers dating from the
14th century and Michaelmas Cottage from the 16th. Both
offer a warm welcome, good food and comfort in a non-
smoking environment. One double bedded room, oak-
beamed, in each house. Parking. Tea/coffee facilities and TV
in both. Excellent pub food and restaurants two/three
minutes away. This is a perfect centre for exploring Bath and
Winchester, each less than one hour away, as well as this
ancient beautiful city. Bed and Breakfast in both cottages £32
to £34 double. Enquire about special discounts.

**SALISBURY. Audrey Jerram, Chicklade Lodge, Chicklade, Hindon, Salisbury SP3 5SU (01747
820389).** Ideally situated for exploring this interesting area
— Salisbury, Stonehenge, Shaftesbury, Stourhead, Longleat,
Bath, Wells, Glastonbury, etc. This is a 19th century house of
character set amidst lovely countryside. Charming twin-bedded rooms with washbasins, shaver points and tea/coffee
making facilities. Pets welcome. Open all year. Painting
Holidays are also available, full details on request. Ample
parking space. Location: A303 nearby, about 28 miles west of
Andover. Going through Chicklade turn right at the small
cross road (signposted Hindon on left). Bed and Breakfast
from £15; optional Evening Meal.

**SALISBURY near. The Compasses Inn, Chicksgrove, Tisbury, Near Salisbury SP3 6NB (01722
714318).** A 14th century thatched Freehouse maintaining all
the olde worlde charm that is in keeping with its setting in the
depths of the Wiltshire countryside. The Inn, with its unique
oak-beamed and traditionally furnished bar, offers excellent
home cooked food, ales and wine. There are gardens at the
front and an enclosed children's play area to the rear. There
are two double en suite bedrooms and one twin-bedded
room with use of bathroom; separate lounge with tea/coffee
making facilities and a well stocked book case. All rooms are
comfortable, well appointed and centrally heated. Children
welcome. Open all year round. Prices per person per night for
Bed and full English Breakfast from £35 per night twin room,
£45 per night double room for two. Please write, or telephone
for brochure.

**SALISBURY. Violet and Victor Bath, "Beulah", 144 Britford Lane, Salisbury SP2 8AL (01722
333517). Tourist Board Listed.** "Beulah" is a pretty bungalow on the outskirts of Salisbury overlooking
meadows, 25 minutes' walk from the city centre, 16 minutes from Salisbury Cathedral with its beautiful
surrounding close and the tallest spire in England (404 ft). Situated at the end of a quiet lane, no passing
traffic. Within one hour by car of Stonehenge, Bournemouth, the New Forest and Southampton. A friendly
welcome awaits you. English or Continental breakfasts, all home made preserves. TV lounge, gas central
heating; TV, washbasins and tea/coffee making facilities in all bedrooms; bathroom and shower. Children
over three years welcome, reduced rates. Bed and Breakfast from £16. Open all year. Directions: bungalow at
end of lane (no through traffic), off A338 main road Salisbury to Bournemouth.

SALISBURY. Dawn and Alan Curnow, Hayburn Wyke Guest House, 72 Castle Road, Salisbury SP1 3RL (01722 412627). ❀ Hayburn Wyke is a Victorian house, situated adjacent to Victoria Park, half a mile from the city centre on the A345 Salisbury to Amesbury road. Salisbury and surrounding area has many places of interest to visit, including Salisbury Cathedral, Old Sarum, Wilton House and Stonehenge. Some bedrooms have en suite facilities, all have washbasins, televisions, and tea/coffee making equipment. Children are welcome at reduced rates. Sorry, no pets (guide dogs an exception). Private car parking for guests. Open all year. Bed and full English Breakfast from £15. AA QQQ and RAC Accredited.

SALISBURY. Mrs Suzi Lanham, Newton Farmhouse, Southampton Road, Whiteparish, Salisbury SP5 2QL (01794 884416). ❀❀ *COMMENDED.* Newton Farmhouse, bordering the New Forest and no longer a working farm, was originally part of the Trafalgar Estate gifted to Lord Nelson. All rooms (two with four- poster bed) are fully en suite and have colour TV and tea/coffee making facilities. The dining room has original flagstone floors, oak beams and huge open fireplace. The garden covers two acres and includes a swimming pool. Ideal location for Stonehenge, Salisbury, Wilton House, Broadlands, Beaulieu, Paultons Park, Winchester, Southampton and Bournemouth area, plus golfing, walking, cycling and horse riding nearby. Central heating. Children welcome. No pets. Evening meals by arrangement. AA QQQ Recommended.

SWINDON. County View Guest House, 31/33 County Road, Swindon SN1 2EG (01793 610434/ 618387; Fax: 01734 394100). This Victorian property is situated on the main road and is five minutes' walk from British Rail, coach station and Swindon town centre. County View is ideally placed for business and leisure visits in Swindon and Wiltshire area, with easy access to M4 Junctions 15 and 16. All rooms have TV, tea/coffee making facilities; most rooms are en suite and have shower rooms. Private parking. Open all year including Christmas. Breakfast cooked to guests' own requirements. Ground floor en-suite accommodation ideal for elderly and disabled visitors. Bed and Breakfast from £18 per person; Evening Meals available. Pilgrims Progress Commendation.

SWINDON near. Mrs Claire Read, Leighfield Lodge Farm, Cricklade, Near Swindon SN6 6RH (01666 860241). ❀❀ *COMMENDED.* Comfortable farmhouse half a mile from the main road. Ideal base for touring the Cotswolds and the Wiltshire Downs. Good food and a homely atmosphere. Choice of breakfast using home produced food where possible. Evening meal available with prior arrangement or local pub three miles away. Two double rooms both en suite with TV and tea/coffee making facilities. Ample parking. Children welcome. No pets. Open all year.

SWINDON near. Mrs Ruth Hibberd, Courtleigh House, 40 Draycot Road, Chiseldon, Swindon SN4 0LS (01793 740246). ❀❀ *COMMENDED.* Comfortable family home set in large garden with tennis court, enjoying downland views and ample parking. Situated one mile from M4 Junction 15 on edge of village, choice of nearby pubs for meals. Swindon four miles, Marlborough six miles. Convenient base for the prehistoric sites near Avebury, the downland Ridgeway path, for the Cotswolds and for the shops of Bath, Cheltenham and Oxford. Two twin-bedded, centrally heated rooms, both having own tea making facilities, one having colour TV and en suite bathroom. Children welcome. Bed and full English Breakfast from £17.50. Open all year.

YORKSHIRE

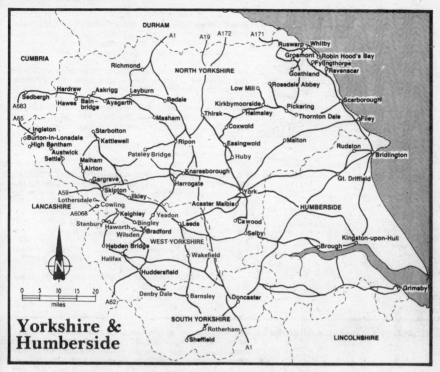

Yorkshire & Humberside

EAST YORKSHIRE

BRIDLINGTON. Mrs Pat Cowton, The Grange, Bempton Lane, Flamborough, Bridlington YO15 1AS (01262 850207). For a relaxing holiday come and stay in our Georgian farmhouse situated in 450 acres of stock and arable land on the outskirts of Flamborough village. Ideally situated for bird watching at RSPB Sanctuary at Bempton, sandy beaches, cliffs and coves on our Heritage Coast. Golf and sea fishing nearby. Children and pets welcome. Open all year except Christmas and New Year. Bed and Breakfast from £15.

POCKLINGTON near. Mrs A. Pearson, Meltonby Hall Farm, Meltonby, Near Pocklington YO4 2PW (01759 303214). Working farm, join in. Meltonby Hall Farm is in a small village at the foot of the Yorkshire Wolds, offering a relaxed and homely atmosphere. It provides a good base for historic York 13 miles, coast 30 miles, as well as the beautiful North Yorkshire Moors with their forest drives, also for stately homes. Pocklington with its magnificent water lilies is two and a half miles away. Gliding club nearby. Double and twin rooms with tea/coffee making facilities, cot and high chair if required; guests' own bathroom with electric shower; dining room/lounge. Own and local produce used and free range eggs. Central heating. Car essential, parking. Children welcome. Sorry, no pets. Open Easter to October. Bed and Breakfast from £14; Evening Meal available in nearby Pocklington. Reduced rates for children under 12 years. AA Recommended.

NORTH YORKSHIRE

AMPLEFORTH. Lin and Ray Beadnell, "Beadale Cottage", West End, Ampleforth YO6 4DX (01439 788383). Beadale Cottage is 200 years old. Ampleforth is on the southern slopes of the Hambleton Hills, within the National Park and on the edge of the North Yorkshire Moors ("Heartbeat country"). Rooms available, one single, one twin and one double. All are equipped with heating, washbasin and tea/coffee facilities. Guests have their own bathroom and toilets, their own sitting room/dining room which is equipped with TV, video. The cottage has an extensive garden in which guests are welcome to wander or just sit and admire the views. Bed and Breakfast £16 per person per night. Discount for longer stays. Good places to eat locally.

AMPLEFORTH. Mrs L.K. Chambers, The Old Summerhouse, East End, Ampleforth, York YO6 4DA (01439 788722). The original old stone summerhouse has been transformed into exclusive en suite accommodation for two guests only. Set in an attractive private garden, this very comfortable, tastefully furnished cottage ensures peace, privacy and almost everything you could need to make your holiday here memorable. The property lies within Ampleforth, well away from traffic. Very good evening meals available locally. Ryedale offers lovely countryside, abbeys and historic houses. So much to see and do (painting, walking) or just relax and forget the world — the choice is yours. NON-SMOKERS ONLY PLEASE. Brochure by request. Bed and Breakfast from £15.

BEDALE. Mrs D. Hodgson, Little Holtby, Leeming Bar, Northallerton DL7 9LH (01609 748762). 🐾🐾 *HIGHLY COMMENDED*. A period farmhouse with beautiful views at the gateway to the Yorkshire Dales, within easy distance of many places of great interest, just 100 yards off the A1 between Bedale and Richmond. Little Holtby has been restored and furnished to a high standard whilst still retaining its original character; polished wood floors, open fires and original beams in many of the rooms. All bedrooms have colour TV, tea/coffee making facilities and are centrally heated. One double bedroom (en-suite), two twin-bedded rooms with washbasins and one family room (en-suite). Bed and Breakfast from £17.50; Evening Meal available.

BEDALE. David and Thea Smith, Waterside, Glenaire, Crakehall, Bedale DL8 1HS (01677 422908). A warm and friendly welcome awaits you at Waterside where you can relax and enjoy the mature one acre gardens running down to the trout stream. As a holiday centre it is ideal for exploring by car or on foot the glories of the Yorkshire Dales and Moors . . . "The Gateway to Herriot Country" . . . Bed and Breakfast with private facilities £20 per person; reductions for longer stays. Evening Meal optional £12. Full details on request. Central heating, TV, tea and coffee facilities, radio in all rooms.

BEDALE. John and Freda Coppin, Richmond House, 6 Beech Close, Scruton, Northallerton DL7 0TU (01609 748369). Stay awhile at our detached house in a lovely rural village between Bedale and Northallerton. "WELCOME HOST" establishment. Only three miles from A1. Ideal stop-over for North/South travellers. One double room with colour TV, radio/alarm, tea/coffee making facilities, central heating, double glazing. Large luxury bathroom with shower, shaver point. Home cooked full English breakfast is served in our dining room/lounge. Private parking. Centrally located for touring Yorkshire Dales and Moors. York, Durham and coast all within one hour's drive. Bed and Breakfast from £13. Special reduced rates during July and August. Open April to October. Brochure available.

BEDALE. Mrs Sheila Dean, Hyperion House, 88 South End, Bedale DL8 2DS (01677 422334). 🐦🐦

HIGHLY COMMENDED. An attractive large detached house in the delightful market town of Bedale in lovely North Yorkshire. One large double bedroom with en suite bathroom, one double with adjacent private bathroom or can be shared with twin. Excellent well cooked varied breakfast of your choice (separate tables). Colour TV and tea/coffee in all rooms. Off street parking for four cars. Bar meals and restaurants in Bedale or surrounding villages. Ideal for holidays and north/south stopover. Enquire for Bargain Breaks. Bed and Breakfast £17 to £21, single in double £25. £20 deposit secures room. Completely non smoking, no pets.

BEDALE. Mrs Patricia Knox, Mill Close Farm, Patrick Brompton, Bedale DL8 1JY (01677 450257).

🐦🐦 *COMMENDED.* Mill Close is a working farm surrounded by beautiful rolling countryside at the foothills of the Yorkshire Dales and Herriot Country. Rooms are spacious and furnished to a very high standard. One double or family room; one twin room with tea/coffee making facilities. Guests' own sitting room with colour TV; diningroom; private bathrooms. Relaxing, peaceful atmosphere with large walled garden, summerhouse and pond. Open fires and central heating. Children welcome, cot available. Pets housed by arrangement. Enjoy wholesome farmhouse cooking using local produce, freshly prepared. Open Easter to October. Bed and Breakfast from £15 to £18; Evening Meal from £10. Please send for full colour brochure.

BEDALE near. Mrs J. Rudd, Tentrees, Exelby, Near Bedale DL8 2HF (01677 426541). Warm welcome

guaranteed in our modern dormer bungalow situated in the quiet hamlet of Exelby, two miles from Bedale and three-quarters of a mile from A1. Large garden with fishpond. One double/family room en suite, one single room both with tea/coffee facilities. Comfortable, homely rooms. Sitting room with TV, books, maps and guides. Ramblers and cyclists catered for — drying facilities. Vegetarian breakfast available (please ask). Central for Yorkshire Dales and Moors. Plenty of parking space. Nearest bus two miles away, lifts available. All non-smoking. Fishing, golf, tennis and horse riding nearby. No pets. Look forward to meeting you for a relaxing stay.

BEDALE. Mrs M. Keighley, Southfield, 96 South End, Bedale DL8 2DS (01677 423510). This is a quiet country town only five minutes from A1, so is ideal for breaking journey from South to Scotland. With the Dales immediate and the Lakes only one hour away, it is a good base for touring. Area attractions include Fountains Abbey, Ripon Cathedral, Harewood House, Bolton Castle, Lightwater Valley (as on TV) and many more. Two 18-hole golf courses and swimming, to keep husband and children happy. Marjorie will supply supper and babysitting free. Free off-road parking for four/five cars. One double, one single, twin and family bedrooms, all with washbasins. Bed and Breakfast £16. SAE please. Now open all year. "Which?" Recommended.

BEDALE. Bobbies XVIIth Century Cottage, Aiskew, Bedale DL8 1DD (01677 423385). Charming beamed cottage with old cottage gardens. Pretty rooms have washbasin, tea/coffee making, colour TV, razor points. Central heating. Gated car park. Same good value and friendly atmosphere in this our 19th year! Good base for "Herriot Country" and exploring Dales and Moors; only eight miles from Lightwater Valley Theme Park. From £16 per person per night.

BENTHAM. Mrs Shirley Metcalfe, Fowgill Park Farm, High Bentham, Near Lancaster LA2 7AH (015242 61630). 🐦🐦 *COMMENDED.* **Working farm.** Fowgill is a 200 acre stock rearing farm, situated in an elevated position and having magnificent views of the Dales and Fells. Only 20 minutes from M6 Junction 34. A good centre for touring the Dales, Lakes, coast and Forest of Bowland. Visit Ingleton with its waterfalls and caves only three miles away. Golf, fishing and horse riding nearby. Bedrooms have washbasins, shaver points and tea-making facilities, two bedrooms en suite. Comfortable beamed visitors' lounge to relax in with colour TV. Separate dining room. Bed and Breakfast from £14; Evening Meal optional £8.50. Reductions for children. Bedtime drink included in price. Brochure available.

BILSDALE. Brenda Johnson, Hill End Farm, Chop Gate, Bilsdale TS9 7JR (01439 798278). 🦢🦢

COMMENDED. Hill End Farm is recommended by "Which?" The Good Bed and Breakfast Guide. If you are looking for a comfortable peaceful break with beautiful views come and join us! Excellent walking country within the North Yorkshire National Park with way marked paths from the farm. Near to Captain Cook, Herriot and Heartbeat country. Guests' lounge with TV and open fire; dining room; two pretty en suite bedrooms. Bed and Breakfast £20. Children under 12 years half price.

COVERDALE. Mrs Julie A. Clarke, Middle Farm, Woodale, Leyburn DL8 4TY (01969 640271).

Middle Farm is a peacefully situated traditional Dales farmhouse, with adjoining stable block for guests accommodation. Situated on the unclassified road linking Wensleydale and Wharfedale. Ideal place to escape the 'madding crowd'. Good base for walking and touring any of the Dales' many beauty spots. Noted for excellent home cooking, offering Bed and Breakfast with optional Dinner. Two double and one twin-bedded rooms. Separate lounge, dining room. Some en-suite facilities, guests' privacy assured. Pets and children welcome. Ample private off-road parking. Open all year round. Brochure available on request. Directions — 5 miles Kettlewell, 10 miles Leyburn, unclassified road.

CROPTON/PICKERING. The New Inn, Cropton, Near Pickering YO18 8HH (01751 417330; Tel & Fax: 01751 417310). 🦢🦢🦢 COMMENDED.

Traditional country inn perched on the edge of the North Yorkshire Moors National Park. Warm and friendly with a high standard of food and accommodation. No smoking restaurant serving à la carte and table d'hôte, bar meals also served. Special two day Dinner, Bed and Breakfast breaks available. Home of the award winning Compton Brewery providing real ales at the bar and guided tours daily. Children welcome. Bed and Breakfast £25 per person.

EASINGWOLD. Mrs Christine Kirman, The Old Vicarage, Market Place, Easingwold YO6 3AL (01347 821015). 🦢🦢 COMMENDED.

This 18th century house sits in a corner of this quiet Geogian market town just off the A19 halfway between York and Thirsk. It provides an excellent touring centre for York, the Dales and the moors. The centrally heated "no smoking" accommodation comprises two twin, two double and one single bedrooms, all enjoying en suite facilities, colour TV, radio alarm and beverage tray. A large sitting room is available solely for guests and the private grounds include a croquet lawn and walled rose garden. Tea and Yorkshire biscuits await you on arrival. Bed and Breakfast from £21.

EASINGWOLD. Mrs Rachel Ritchie, The Old Rectory, Thormanby, Easingwold, York YO6 3NN (01845 501417). 🦢🦢

A warm welcome awaits you at this interesting Georgian rectory built in 1737 and furnished with many antiques including a four-poster bed. Three comfortable and very spacious bedrooms, two en suite, with tea/coffee making facilities; charming lounge with colour TV and open fire. Separate diningroom. Large mature garden. An excellent base for touring the Moors, Dales and York. This is the centre of "James Herriot" country with many historic houses and abbeys to visit in the area. Thormanby is a small village between Easingwold and Thirsk. Historic York is 17 miles away. Many delightful inns and restaurants serving good food locally. Bed and Breakfast from £13, reductions for children under 12 years. Reduced weekly rates. Ample private parking. SAE for brochure or telephone. Open all the year.

HARROGATE. P. Davidson, The Coppice, 9 Studley Road, Harrogate HG1 5JU (01423 569626; Fax: 01423 569005). 🌸🌸🌸 *COMMENDED.* A high

standard of clean and comfortable accommodation awaits you at The Coppice. Situated in a quiet road, we are convenient for the Conference Centre and all amenities in and around the town. All rooms are en-suite with colour TV, tea/coffee making facilities. An attractive, well maintained Victorian house, The Coppice offers a peaceful, pleasant and congenial atmosphere. To ensure your safety we have a Full Fire Certificate. Ideal for those visiting on business or pleasure. Bed and Breakfast Single £22; Double £40. Evening Meal from £12.

HARROGATE. Mr and Mrs P. Bell, Dene Court Guest House, 22 Franklin Road, Harrogate HG1 5EE (01423 509498). Friendly family-run guest house offering comfortable Bed and Breakfast accommodation. A good traditional English breakfast served, with a good choice for vegetarians too. Standard single, twin, double and family rooms available all with washbasins, tea/coffee facilities, radio/alarm clocks and central heating. TV in guest lounge, two bathrooms and third toilet. Private parking for three/four cars at rear of Victorian terrace house. Very close to town centre, exhibition halls, Valley Gardens, railway and bus station and other amenities. Bed and Breakfast from £15 per person; optional Evening Meal from £8. Reductions for children. Discount for weekly bookings.

HARROGATE. Mr Derek and Mrs Carol Vinter, Spring Lodge, 22 Spring Mount, Harrogate HG1 2HX (01423 506036). 🌸 Attractive Edwardian guest house

situated in a quiet cul-de-sac, yet close to all the amenities of Harrogate, Britain's floral spa town, with its elegant and outstanding architecture and gardens, antique shops and restaurants. Five minutes' walk from the International Conference and Exhibition Centre. Ideal for the business visitor or tourist, with the beautiful Yorkshire Dales within easy access. All year round a warm welcome awaits you from the resident proprietors. Accommodation comprises four double rooms, one triple and one single. En suite rooms available. Coffee and tea making facilities in all rooms. Dinner provided on request. Residential licence and no smoking. Bed and Breakfast from £16.

HARROGATE. Mrs M. Thomson, Knox Mill House, Knox Mill Lane, Harrogate HG3 2AE (01423 560650). 🌸🌸 *COMMENDED.* AA QQQ. A delightfully reno-

vated 200-year-old Millhouse, standing on the banks of a stream in a rural setting less than two miles from Harrogate's centre. Situated along a quiet country lane just off the A61 Ripon road, it is highly recommended for touring Yorkshire Dales and Moors, seeing York itself or for visiting conference and exhibition facilities in town. Inglenook fireplace and original oak beams give a 'farmhouse' atmosphere to the Residents' Lounge which faces south overlooking beautiful rolling meadow. All bedrooms are attractively furnished, some en suite, with complimentary tea/coffee making facilities, and there is ample private parking for residents. No smoking. Bed and Breakfast only (a wide choice of pubs, restaurants are close by) £20 per person. Brochure available.

HARROGATE. Mrs H.M. Phillips, Shutt Nook Farm, Chain Bar Lane, Killinghall, Harrogate HG3 2BS (01423 567562). Working farm. Shutt Nook Farm is a mixed 150 acre family-run farm, ideally situated for touring the Yorkshire Dales; the spa town of Harrogate is just three miles away and Ripley Castle, Fountains Abbey and the ancient city of York are all within easy reach. Good home cooking, colour TV. There are one double, one twin and one family bedrooms, all with washbasins; bathroom, toilet; sitting room, dining room. Sorry no pets. Open May to December. A car is recommended and there is parking. Bed and Breakfast. Reduced rates for children.

HARROGATE. Anne and Bob Joyner, Anro Guest House, 90 King's Road, Harrogate HG1 5JX (01423 503087). AA and RAC Listed. "Excellent!", "Exceptional value!", "Good food!", "Quiet!", "Never had it so good!" — just a few of the testimonials visitors have written in our book on leaving. Situated in a tree-lined avenue in a central position close to all amenities. Conference and Exhibition Centre two minutes' walk. Valley Gardens, town and local swimming baths close by. Our house is centrally heated, with tea/coffee making facilities and colour TV in all rooms, hot and cold throughout. Some rooms en-suite. Home cooking. Bed and Breakfast from £20. Four-course Dinner plus tea or coffee upon request £12. Ideal centre for touring Dales/Herriot country. Well recommended.

HARROGATE. Mrs Judy Barker, Brimham Guest House, Silverdale Close, Darley, Harrogate HG3  **2PQ (01423 780948).** The family-run guest house is situated in the centre of Darley, a quiet village in unspoilt Nidderdale. All rooms en suite and centrally heated with tea/coffee making facilities and views across the Dales. Full English breakfast served between 7am and 9.30am in the dining room; a TV lounge/conservatory is available for your relaxation. Off street parking. Central for visits to Harrogate, York, Skipton and Ripon, or just enjoying drives through the Dales and Moors where you will take in dramatic hillsides, green hills, picturesque villages, castles and abbeys. Children welcome. Bed and Breakfast from £15 (double room) to £20 (single room).

HARROGATE. Mrs C.E. Nelson, Nidderdale Lodge Farm, Fellbeck, Pateley Bridge, Harrogate HG3 5DR (01423 711677). ETB 🐾🐾 *COMMENDED.* Homely, comfortable, Christian accommodation. Spacious stone built bungalow in beautiful Nidderdale which is very central for touring the Yorkshire Dales; Pateley Bridge two miles, Harrogate 14 miles, Ripon nine miles. Museums, rocks, caves, fishing, bird watching, beautiful quiet walks, etc all near by. En suite rooms (one twin, two double), TV. Private lounge. Tea making facilities available. Choice of breakfast. Evening meals available one mile away. Ample parking space on this working farm. Open Easter to end of October.

HARROGATE. Mrs A. Wood, Field House, Clint, Near Harrogate HG3 3DS (01423 770638). Field House is situated five miles from Harrogate and a mile above the attractive village of Hampsthwaite commanding beautiful views over the Nidd Valley. Ideal for exploring the Dales and Moors, with ancient abbeys, castles and country houses. The market towns of Skipton, Ripon and Knaresborough and the historic City of York are within easy reach. Accommodation is in one twin and one double room with private bathroom. Private sittingroom with TV etc. Open all year. Car essential — private parking. Bed and Breakfast from £12.50 with Evening Meal readily available. A warm welcome guaranteed in a peaceful, friendly atmosphere. Telephone or SAE, please, for further details.

HAWES. Mrs M.A. Iveson, The Homestead, Hardraw, Hawes DL8 3LZ (01969 667003). A 17th  century house situated two miles out of Hawes in Hardraw village. Lovely big house with very large rooms — one bedroom with shower and washbasin, one family room with full bathroom. Central heating. Pub in village. Beautiful garden for relaxing in. Ideal for walkers on Pennine Way, also good fishing country. Children welcome, but sorry, no pets. Open all year. Bed and Breakfast from £16 per person.

HELMSLEY. Mrs Elizabeth Easton, Lockton House Farm, Bilsdale, Helmsley YO6 5NE (01439  **798303). Working farm, join in.** 16th century farmhouse on mixed family-run farm of 400 acres with sheep, cattle and ponies. Ideally situated for touring North Yorkshire Moors and the many other attractions of this area. There are peaceful panoramic views from the farm. Guest accommodation is in two double and one family rooms all with washbasins; lounge with colour TV. Good home cooking in abundance. One dog per family welcome. Open March to October. Bed and Breakfast from £14.50; Bed, Breakfast and Evening Meal from £24. Reduced rates for children.

NORTH YORKSHIRE – RICH IN TOURIST ATTRACTIONS!

Dales, moors, castles, abbeys, cathedrals – you name it and you're almost sure to find it in North Yorkshire. Leading attractions include Castle Howard, the moorlands walks at Goathland, the Waterfalls at Falling Foss, Skipton, Richmond, Wensleydale, Bridestones Moor, Ripon Cathedral, Whitby, Settle and, of course, York itself.

HELMSLEY. Mrs Margaret Wainwright, Sproxton Hall, Sproxton, Helmsley YO6 5EQ (01439 770225; Fax: 01439 771373). 👑👑 *HIGHLY COMMEN-*

DED. Enjoy the peaceful atmosphere, magnificent views and comfort of Sproxton Hall, a 17th century Listed farmhouse on a 300-acre family farm. A haven of peace and tranquillity, lovingly and tastefully furbished with antiques and co-ordinating fabrics giving the warm, cosy, elegance of a country home. Set amidst idyllic countryside, one and a half miles from Helmsley. Excellent base for touring North Yorkshire Moors, Dales, Coast, National Trust properties and York. One double room en suite, one twin room with private bathroom, double and twin with shared luxury shower room. Colour TV, central heating, drinks facilities, washbasins and razor points in all rooms. Laundry facilities. "A non-smoking household". No children under 10 years. Bed and Breakfast from £18.50 per person. Brochures available. Five self catering award-winning cottages also available.

HELMSLEY. Mrs J. Milburn, Barn Close Farm, Rievaulx, Helmsley YO6 5LH (01439 798321). 👑👑👑 *COMMENDED.* **Working farm.** Farming family offer

homely accommodation on mixed farm in beautiful surroundings near Rievaulx Abbey. Ideal for touring, pony trekking; good walking terrain! Home-made bread, own home produced meat, poultry, free range eggs — in fact Mrs Milburn's excellent cooking was praised in "Daily Telegraph". En suite double and one family bedrooms; bathroom; toilets; sitting room and dining room. Children are welcome, cot, high chair and babysitting available. Sorry, no pets. Open all year round. Open log fires. Storage heaters in bedrooms. Car essential — parking. Bed and Breakfast from £20 to £22; Dinner £10. Reduced rates for children under 10 sharing parents' room. Farm Holiday Bureau Member.

HELMSLEY. Mrs Sally Robinson, Valley View Farm, Old Byland, Helmsley, York YO6 5LG (01439 798221). 👑👑 *HIGHLY COMMENDED.* **Working farm.**

Stylish, well appointed farmhouse accommodation twixt the Moors and Dale, within the North York Moors National Park, outstanding views across beautiful countryside. Relax in rural peace and tranquillity in warm, spacious en suite rooms each with tea/coffee making facilities, colour TV and central heating. Residents' lounge furnished traditionally; welcoming open fires. Dining room where substantial breakfasts and old-fashioned leisurely farmhouse dinners are served. Licensed. Vegetarian meals on request. Open all year. Guests' comfort is the main priority. Bed and Breakfast £25; Dinner, Bed and Breakfast from £37. Please phone for brochure. Three superb self catering cottages sleeping two/four or six also available.

HELMSLEY. Mrs C. Swift, Stilworth House, 1 Church Street, Helmsley YO6 5AD (01439 771072).

👑👑 *COMMENDED.* Helmsley is beautifully situated for touring the North York Moors National Park, East Coast, York, "Herriot" and "Heartbeat" country. There is a wealth of footpaths and bridleways to explore. Stilworth House overlooks All Saints Church to the front and Helmsley Castle to the rear. A warm welcome awaits you in the comfortable relaxed atmosphere of this elegant Georgian town house just off the market square. Highly recommended for good food. All rooms are en-suite, with tea/coffee making facilities, colour TV, radio alarms, hair dryer, central heating. Private gardens and car park. Bed and Breakfast from £20 per person per night. Please telephone, or write, for colour brochure.

HORTON-IN-RIBBLESDALE. Marilyn Pilkington, Middle Studfold Farm, Horton-in-Ribblesdale, Settle BD24 0ER (01729 860236). 🏆 *HIGHLY COMMEN-*

DED. 18th century Dales farmhouse superbly situated in the lower slopes of Pen-y-ghent (one of the famed "Three Peaks") and overlooking the lovely valley of Upper Ribblesdale, Middle Studfold provides an ideal base for exploring the Yorkshire Dales National Park. A homely lounge with real log fire makes for the cosiest of evenings whilst hearty dinners, with fine wines if desired, are enjoyed in the oak beamed dining room to round off another perfect day. The visitors' book is testimony to the excellence of the cuisine — breakfast especially! Facilities include free "taxi" service to Horton and the scenic Settle to Carlisle railway and early breakfast for "Three Peakers". Our quiet location, with private approach road offers ample parking. Bed and Breakfast from £15; Dinner from £7. Child reductions. Residential licence. Pets by arrangement.

INGLETON. Allan and Louise Bruns, Ferncliffe Guest House, Ingleton, Carnforth LA6 3HJ (015242 42405). 🏆🏆 *COMMENDED.* A spacious late Victorian

house refurbished by present owners Allan and Louise with the comfort of their guests in mind. All rooms are en suite with TV and tea/coffee trays. Dinner by owner chef should not be missed. Ferncliffe House stands on the edge of the village of Ingleton known as the beauty spot of the north with its waterfalls, glens and walks and Ingleborough Hill as a back drop. All this makes an ideal base for touring the Dales. Bed and Breakfast £22; Dinner £12.50. Weekly and Short Break prices on request. AA QQQQ, RAC Acclaimed, Les Routiers. Ring or write for brochure.

INGLETON. Mrs Claire Faraday, Langber End Farm, Ingleton, Via Carnforth LA6 3DT (015242

41776). Quietly situated one and a half miles out of Ingleton. The house is centrally heated and has one double, one twin and one single bedrooms, all with washbasins, shaver points and tea-making facilities; one room en-suite. Comfortable sittingroom with access at all times. A good four-course breakfast is served; vegetarian and special diets catered for. Good pubs and restaurants in the area serve Evening Meals at reasonable prices. Good centre for touring Lakes, Dales and coast. No smoking in the house. Bed and Breakfast from £13 (£15 en-suite).

INGLETON. Carol Brennand, Nutstile Farm, Ingleton, Via Carnforth LA6 3DT (015242 41752). Tourist Board Listed *COMMENDED.* Surrounded by the

outstanding beauty of the Yorkshire Dales, Nutstile is a typical working farm providing first class accommodation. The mountains, caves and waterfalls of Ingleton are immediately accessible, the Lake District also close by. Try a leisurely ride on the scenic Settle-Carlisle railway. Three bedrooms (all with views) with washbasin and tea/coffee facilities, en suite available. Guests' lounge with TV. Children welcome. Open all year. No smoking. Bed and Breakfast from £15 to £17.

NUTSTILE

INGLETON. Mrs Mollie Bell, Langber Country Guest House, Ingleton, via Carnforth LA6 3DT (015242 41587). 🏆🏆 Ingleton, "Beauty Spot of the North" in the Dales National Park area. Renowned for waterfalls, glens, underground caves, magnificent scenery and Ingleborough Mountain (2,373 feet), an excellent centre for touring Lakes, Dales and coast. Golf, fishing, swimming and tennis in vicinity; pony trekking a few miles away. Guests are warmly welcomed to "Langber", a detached country guest house with beautiful views and 82 acres of gardens, terrace and fields. Lambs and sheep kept. Ample parking space available. Three family, three double/twin and one single bedrooms, all with washbasins, some en-suite. Bathroom and two toilets. Sunny comfortable lounge and separate diningroom. Central heating; fire precautions. Babysitting offered. Open all year except Christmas. Fire Certificate granted. AA and RAC Listed. Bed and Breakfast from £15.50; Bed, Breakfast and Evening Meal from £21.50. Reductions for children under 13 sharing parents' room.

PLEASE SEND A STAMPED ADDRESSED ENVELOPE WITH ENQUIRIES

KEIGHLEY. Joe and Joyce Sawley, The Hawthorns, Ickornshaw, Cowling, Keighley BD22 0DH (01535 633299 or 0831 720796). Tourist Board Listed.

"HILTON"! But have you stayed at the "HAWTHORNS", set in its own grounds just off the beaten track in the lovely hamlet of Ickornshaw. Ample parking, heated outdoor swimming pool (weather permitting). Ideally situated for Skipton, Yorkshire Dales, Haworth and the Bronte country. Marvellous centre for touring or walking. Colour TV and tea/coffee facilities in all bedrooms; en suite rooms. Recommended for home cooking and a "BIG" farmhouse breakfast. Guests are assured of a warm, friendly, "at home" atmosphere. Situated three miles from Crosshills just off the A6068 road at Cowling. Bed and Breakfast from £15. SAE for further details.

KETTLEWELL-WITH-STARBOTTON. Tim and Marie Louise Rathmell, Hilltop Country Guest House, Starbotton, Near Skipton BD23 5HY (01756 760321).

🐾🐾 *HIGHLY COMMENDED.* AA QQQQQ Premier Selected. Superbly situated Country Guest House with beckside gardens overlooking unspoilt village in the heart of the Yorkshire Dales National Park. The immaculate bedrooms have bath or shower en suite, TV and tea tray. In the sitting room there is a log fire and plenty of books. The bar is well stocked and often lively. Dinner is served on Fridays and Saturdays and for parties of six or more. And by day, Hilltop is perfectly situated for fell and riverside walks and for touring some of England's loveliest countryside. To quote the BTA "This delightful house . . . offers the warmth and hospitality of a house party . . ." Please telephone for booking or brochure.

LEYBURN. Mrs H.M. Richardson, Sunnyridge, Argill Farm, Harmby, Leyburn DL8 5HQ (01969 622478).

Situated on a smallholding in Wensleydale, Sunnyridge is a spacious bungalow in an outstanding position. Magnificent views are enjoyed from every room. In the midst of the Yorkshire Dales, it is an ideal centre for touring the many places of interest — ancient and modern. Visitors also enjoy hiking, golf, pony trekking plus Lightwater Valley Theme Park. Accommodation is all on the ground floor and comprises one double or twin-bedded room with washbasin, one family room with/without en suite shower room; bathroom/toilet; guest lounge with TV. Tea making facilities. Evening Meal optional. Children welcome, pets by arrangement. Parking. Prices from £14.

LEYBURN. Barbara and Barrie Martin, The Old Star, West Witton, Leyburn DL8 4LU (01969 622949).

Formerly a 17th century coaching inn, now a family-run guest house. You are always welcome at the Old Star. The building still retains many original features. Comfortable lounge with oak beams and log fire. Dinner available if ordered in advance. Bedrooms mostly en suite with central heating and tea/coffee facilities. In the heart of the Yorkshire Dales National Park we are ideally situated for walking and touring the Dales. Large car park. Open all year except Christmas. Bed and Breakfast from £15 to £18 with special breaks available.

LITTON. Lyn and Bryan Morgan, Park Bottom, Litton, Near Skipton BD23 5QJ (01756 770235).

A modern house built in traditional style, using stone from the miners' cottages originally on the site. It is set in a peaceful, unspoilt hamlet in Littondale, the "secret dale" in the heart of the Yorkshire Dales, away from the crowds yet an ideal centre for walking and touring. Bedrooms are en suite, with tea/coffee facilities. There is a large garden and private parking. Bed and Breakfast £18 to £23 with discounts for longer stays, special package deals and family rates. The excellent Queen's Arms Inn, 100 yards away, serves meals and real ale in a traditional bar.

MALHAM. Sparth House Hotel, Malham, Skipton BD23 4DA (01729 830315). Malham is an ideal base for the Yorkshire Dales, and several of the National Park's major attractions are only a short walk away. York, the Settle — Carlisle Railway, Bronte country and the Lake District are easy days out. Sparth House has an enviable reputation for imaginative freshly prepared meals — you should not miss Dinner! The accommodation is attractive and comfortable. All rooms have tea/coffee facilities and most have high quality en-suite bathrooms and colour TV. One ground floor bedroom is equipped for disabled guests. Two lounges (one for non-smokers) and a well stocked bar complete this delightful country hotel. Bed and Breakfast from £18.50; Evening Meal £13.50.

MALHAM (near Skipton). Keith and Patricia Dyball, Malham Cafe, The Green, Malham, Near Skipton BD23 4DB (01729 830348). 🐌 17th century building situated in the centre of Malham village offering three olde worlde en-suite bedrooms with colour TV and tea/coffee making facilities. Homely atmosphere and a true Yorkshire welcome. Residential licence. Bed and Breakfast from £18. Reduced rates for children. Pets welcome. Ideally situated for touring the popular Yorkshire Dales and National Park. Skipton nearby, also the interesting old village of Gargrave. Within easy reach of Harrogate, York and Bronte country. Lovely walking countryside.

MALTON. Mrs Ann Hopkinson, The Brow, 25 York Road, Malton YO17 0AX (01653 693402). The Brow is a large house with beautiful views. It was the home of the Walker family who owned the oldest of the five breweries for which Malton was famous. Captain Walker of Whitby (to whom Captain Cook was apprenticed) was a member of the same Walker family. A visit to The Brow should not be missed. A warm welcome awaits you here with TV and tea/coffee making facilities in all rooms. Children welcome, reduced rates. Bed and Breakfast from £14 to £25.

MALTON. Mrs C.R. Neuff, North's Farm, 2 Westgate, Rillington, Malton YO17 8LN (01944 758620). A warm welcome awaits you at this non working early 19th century farmhouse with beamed lounge and open fire. Accommodation comprises one twin-bedded room and one single. Open all year it is suitable as a one night stop for walkers or cyclists or as a base for a wide range of visits and activities including the Wolds Way, the North York Moors, the East Coast and the ancient walled city of York. Coastliner buses stop outside and off road parking is available. Spinning and rug weaving (on Scandinavian peg loom) courses are available on request. Bed and Breakfast from £12. Visa/Access cards accepted.

MASHAM. Mrs R. Robinson, Lamb Hill Farm, Lamb Hill, Masham, Ripon HG4 4DJ (01765 689274). 🐌🐌 *COMMENDED.* **Working farm.** A warm welcome awaits you in our genuine old farmhouse on a working farm situated off the A6108 between West Tanfield and Masham. Accommodation comprises large, comfortable bedrooms with private bathrooms. We are centrally situated for exploring "Herriot" and "Heartbeat" country. Many National Trust properties within easy reach. Excellent opportunities for eating out within a two mile radius. York 45 minutes, Durham one hour. Children over eight years welcome. Open all year. Bed and Breakfast from £16.

MIDDLESBOROUGH. Mr Richmond, Red Hall, Great Broughton, Middlesborough TS9 7ET (Tel & Fax: 01642 712300). Elegant 17th century Grade II Listed building offers the charm of the small country house. Our family-run business with spacious, centrally heated, en suite bedrooms provides personal service in a warm and friendly atmosphere. Join us in our lovely Queen Anne country house set in tranquil meadows and woodland at the foot of the rugged North Yorkshire Moors National Park. Let us plan your visit for you and see the unique drama the area has to offer. Horse riding and stabling available at Red Hall and there are excellent walks nearby. From £22.50 Bed and Breakfast per night for four nights, £18.50 per night thereafter; single person supplement. Dinner by arrangement.

MYTON-ON-SWALE. Mrs Jean Hammond, Plump House Farm, Myton-on-Swale, Helperby, York YO6 2RA (Tel & Fax: 01423 360650). 👑 👑 Plump House Farm is a working sheep farm in the small agricultural hamlet of Myton-on-Swale on the banks of the River Swale ideally placed for visiting all parts of North Yorkshire — England's largest county. We have two en suite letting rooms (one double/twin and one family) with central heating, TV and tea/coffee making facilities. Guests can relax in the large comfortable lounge with open fire and colour TV. Meals are served in the dining room. Full traditional English breakfast. Evening dinner is available every evening except Wednesday. Bed and Breakfast from £15; Dinner, Bed and Breakfast from £21. Brochure on request.

PICKERING. Mrs Livesey, Sands Farm Country Hotel, Wilton, Pickering YO18 7JY (01751 474405). Enjoy a relaxing holiday in a friendly atmosphere where food, rooms and service are of the highest standard. Laura Ashley style bedrooms, with flowers, colour TV and tea-making facilities; all en-suite and some with four-poster beds. Full English Breakfast; tea-trays in front of a log fire. Many sporting facilities and places of interest nearby — we are happy to suggest many places to visit. NO SMOKING. No children under 10 years. No dogs. Terms from £17.50 per person per night. Special low fat diets on request. Private parking. Special low season breaks. Self catering cottages also available, set in 15 acres. Write or phone for full details.

PICKERING. Stan and Hilary Langton, Vivers Mill, Mill Lane, Pickering YO18 8DJ (01751 473640). Vivers Mill is an ancient watermill situated in peaceful surroundings, quarter mile south of Pickering Market Place on Pickering Beck. The Mill is a listed building constructed of stone, brick and pantiles, part of which possibly dates back to the 13th century. The building with its characteristic beamed ceilings has been renovated and most of the machinery is being preserved (including the water wheel and millstones). Pickering is an excellent centre from which to explore the North York Moors National Park, Ryedale and the spectacular Heritage Coast. It is the terminal station for the preserved North York Moors Railway and is only 26 miles from historic York. Visitors are assured of a friendly welcome with nourishing, traditional breakfasts. Large lounge and six comfortable en suite bedrooms with tea/coffee making facilities. Bed and Breakfast £23 daily. Reductions for family room. Pets welcome.

PICKERING. Mrs G. Smith, Eden House, 120 Eastgate, Pickering YO18 7DW (01751 472289; Fax: 01751 477024). 👑 👑 *COMMENDED.* Charming Yorkshire cottage, offering B&B accommodation. All rooms have TV, radio, tea/coffee, central heating, washbasin, dressing gowns, etc; en suite available. Parking. Situated on the outskirts, only three minutes from the main town and the Moors, coast, York, "Heartbeat" country are all very near. Optional dinner if booked in advance using own produce when available. Open all year except Christmas. Bed and Breakfast from £17. Off peak rates available. Booking advisable — very popular.

PICKERING. Judy and Keith Russell, Heathcote House, 100 Eastgate, Pickering YO18 7DW (01751

476991). ww *COMMENDED.* Our early Victorian house with original arched fireplaces, mahogany staircase and galleried landing has five comfortably furnished bedrooms (double or twin) each with en suite facilities, hostess tray, colour TV, hair dryer, radio alarm and toiletries to make you stay care-free. Enjoy our personal attention in a relaxed, friendly, NON-SMOKING atmosphere. Pickering is central for York, Castle Howard, Eden Camp, North York Moors National Park and Whitby with lots of castles, abbeys, pretty villages and beautiful countryside in between. Bed and Breakfast from £19.50 per person per night. Optional Dinners £12. Secluded parking. Mastercard/Visa accepted.

---

ww Highly Commended

BRIDGEFOOT GUEST HOUSE
Thornton Le Dale, Pickering,
North Yorkshire YO18 7RR
Telephone 01751 474749

Bridgefoot House is situated in the village of Thornton-le-Dale, by the trout stream in a wall-enclosed garden next to the thatched cottage. Ideal touring base for the moors, east coast, countryside, forestry and York. Centrally heated throughout, open fires in season. Family room; several double and twin-bedded rooms; ground floor double (most rooms en-suite), tea and coffee facilities, shaver points, electric blankets. Colour TV. Guest lounge; diningroom. Bed and Breakfast from £17.50 (en-suite from £19.50). Registered with ETB. Car parking. Open Easter to November. Contact **Mr and Mrs B. Askin** for brochure.

PICKERING. Mrs Ella Bowes, Banavie, Roxby Road, Thornton-le-Dale, Pickering YO18 7SX (01751

474616). ww *COMMENDED.* Banavie is a large stone built semi-detached house set in Thornton-le-Dale, one of the prettiest villages in Yorkshire with a stream flowing through the centre. Situated in an attractive part of the village, it is ideal for touring coast, moors, forest, Scarborough, Castle Howard, Flamingo Park, Eden Camp. A real Yorkshire breakfast is served by Mrs Bowes herself which provides a good start to the day. Two restaurants and three inns in village for meals. Three double bedrooms, one en suite, all with washbasins, shaver points, colour TV and tea/coffee making facilities (own keys); bathroom and toilet; dining room; lounge with colour TV, central heating. Children welcome; cot, high chair, babysitting and reduced rates. Pets accepted. Car park. Open all year. Bed and Breakfast (including tea and biscuits at bedtime) from £14. SAE please.

RAVENSCAR. Mrs Joan Greenfield, Smuggler's Rock Country Guest House, Ravenscar YO13 0ER

(01723 870044). ww Smuggler's Rock is a stone built Georgian Farmhouse between Whitby and Scarborough with panoramic views over surrounding North Yorkshire National Park and sea. The farmhouse has a homely and relaxed atmosphere. Home cooking is served in our old world dining room and there is an open fire and colour TV in our beautiful open-beamed lounge. All bedrooms have private facilities, bedroom TV available. We have a residential licence and our own car park. This is an ideal country holiday area, with many picturesque seaside villages on the Heritage Coast, and beautiful Dales just a few miles inland. AA QQQ. Reasonable prices; please send for brochure. Also a self catering cottage available.

Terms quoted in this publication may be subject to increase if rises in costs necessitate

RICHMOND. Mrs L. Brooks, Holmedale, Dalton, Richmond DL11 7HX (01833 621236). ♛

COMMENDED. Holmedale is a Georgian house set in a quiet village midway between Richmond and Barnard Castle. Seven miles from Scotch Corner and ideally situated for touring Swaledale, Wensleydale and Teesdale. One double and one family room, both with washbasins and central heating. Comfortable sittingroom with open fire when necessary. Good plain home cooking with plentiful Yorkshire helpings. Tea/coffee making facilities available. Bed and Breakfast from £13.50 per person; Bed, Breakfast and Evening Meal from £22, single room from £15.

RICHMOND. Mrs Dorothy Wardle, Greenbank Farm, Ravensworth, Richmond DL11 7HB (01325 718334). This 170-acre farm, both arable and livestock, is four miles west of Scotch Corner on the A66, midway between the historic towns of Richmond and Barnard Castle, and within easy reach of Teesdale, Swaledale and Wensleydale. Only an hour's drive from the Lake District. The farm is one mile outside the village of Ravensworth, with plenty of good eating places within easy reach. Guests' own lounge, diningroom; two double rooms and one en suite room, one family room. All bedrooms have washbasins, tea/coffee facilities, heating and electric blankets. Children welcome; play area with swings, slides, trampoline, etc. Sorry, no pets. Car essential. Bed and Breakfast from £12.50 includes light supper/bedtime drink. Evening Meals available. Reductions for children and Senior Citizens. Open all year. Luxury mobile home available.

RICHMOND. Mrs Diana Greenwood, Walburn Hall, Downholme, Richmond DL11 6AF (Tel & Fax: 01748 822152). ♛♛ *HIGHLY COMMENDED.* Walburn Hall

is one of the few remaining fortified farmhouses in England. Dating from the 14/16th centuries it has an enclosed cobbled courtyard and terraced gardens. Accommodation for guests includes two bedrooms (one double/twin, one double/family) both with en suite bathrooms. Rooms have tea/coffee making facilities and there is a guests' lounge and dining room with beamed ceilings and stone fireplaces with log fires. Your stay at Walburn Hall offers you the opportunity to visit places of historic interest — Richmond, Bolton and Middleham Castles and numerous Abbeys. Children welcome, but sorry no pets. Non-smoking. Bed and Breakfast from £20 per person. Open March to November.

RICHMOND. Helen and Colin Lowes, Wilson House, Barningham, Richmond DL11 7EB (01833 621218). ♛♛ *COMMENDED.* Wilson House is ideally situ-

ated enjoying magnificent views over open countryside. Located one mile from A66, this is an ideal base for exploring the Yorkshire and Durham Dales and the Lake District; Durham City, Newcastle and the Beamish Museum are all within one hour's drive. The historic towns of Richmond and Barnard Castle are both under 10 miles away and offer castle, museums, galleries, antiques, shops and sports facilities. This charming farmhouse is tastefully decorated, clean, comfortable and centrally heated throughout. Accommodation comprises double and twin rooms en-suite with colour TV and tea/coffee facilities, guests' lounge with colour TV. Non-smoking accommodation available. We offer good farmhouse cooking, Evening Meal by arrangement. Bed and Breakfast from £16; Evening Meal from £10. Children welcome at reduced rates.

RIPON. Mrs S. Gordon, St. George's Court, Old Home Farm, High Grantley, Ripon HG4 3EU (01765 620618). At beautifully situated St. George's Court sleep in

our renovated cow byre and dairy. Modern comfort with old world charm. Five bedrooms — three double, one twin and one family suite, all with private bathrooms, colour TV and tea making facilities. Each room has superb views over farmland and woods. All rooms on ground level. Peace and tranquillity is our password. We are 200 yards from any road. We have a third of an acre pond where wildlife and flora are encouraged to flourish. Breakfast in our 17th century farmhouse, before a log fire. Only fresh local food cooked to a very high standard. A warm and friendly welcome guaranteed. Open all year. Children and dogs welcome.

RIPON. Mrs Dorothy Poulter, Avenue Farm, Bramley Grange, Ilton Road, Grewelthorpe, Ripon HG4 3DN (01765 658348). Small dairy farm with scenic countryside views, very peaceful and quiet yet within easy reach of Ripon, York, Fountains Abbey and gateway to the Yorkshire Dales, Emmerdale Farm and Herriot country. Easy access to the A1. Golf, fishing and pony trekking nearby. Or why not visit Masham for a tour of Theakston Brewery and its famous Old Peculier. Avenue Farm guarantees a warm welcome with a cup of tea on arrival and bedtime drink. Bed and Breakfast from £12.50 to £13.50 per night.

RIPON near. Peter and Irene Foster, Lime Tree Farm, Hutts Lane, Grewelthorpe, Near Ripon HG4

3DA (01765 658450). 🌺 🌺 🌺 Working farm, join in. Secluded Dales farm near Ripon where horses are bred; ideal for touring and visiting Yorkshire's many attractions. The farmhouse is almost 200 years old with exposed beams, oak panelling and open fires, clipped rugs, grandfather clocks, etc., plus central heating throughout. All bedrooms are en suite and have colour TV and tea/coffee making facilities. The dining room has separate tables and guests have their own lounge with access to books and games. Full English breakfast, good traditional home cooking with four-course evening meal. Open all year. Bed and Breakfast from £17.50; Evening Meal £12.50. Brochure on request.

RIPON. Abbey Nordale Hotel, 1 & 2 North Parade, North Road, Ripon HG4 1ES (01765 603557). A small friendly hotel with the accent on high standards of food and service. We have two single, four double, five twin and two family rooms, half of which have en suite facilities. All have tea/coffee facilities and TV and are comfortable and well furnished. A good Yorkshire breakfast starts the day and after sightseeing in our lovely countryside or merely passing through Ripon or visiting the many sites of historic interest. Evening meals are available either in the hotel or in the town. All food is freshly cooked. Places to visit include the Dales, Fountains Abbey, Newby Hall, Richmond, Lightwater Valley Theme Park and many more. Private car park. Prices from £18 to £24 for Bed and Breakfast.

ROBIN HOOD'S BAY. Mrs G. Hogdson, Low Farm, Fylingthorpe, Whitby YO22 4QF (01947

880366). Robin Hood's Bay, where the North York Moors roll down to the sea. A real Yorkshire welcome awaits you in our traditional Georgian farmhouse. We offer guests a large south facing family room with washbasins and central heating, comfortably furnished in country style. Exclusive use of spacious lounge with period oak furniture and a large fireplace built of local stone. A working farm in beautiful countryside, we are ideal for walking, riding or cycling, with Whitby five miles, Scarborough 14 miles or "Heartbeat" country 10 miles.

ROBIN HOOD'S BAY. David and Angela Pattinson, Hogarth Hall, Boggle Hole Road, Robin Hood's

Bay, Near Whitby YO22 4QQ (01947 880547). Hogarth Hall is a newly built farmhouse set in 145 acres of habitat, situated at the top of the valley with wonderful views of sea, farmland, moors and sky. Experience the wonder of glorious sunrises and sunsets, June being the loveliest month for these. Bring your binoculars to study the wildlife all around. All rooms are en suite with whirlpool baths and showers, and TV. Tea/coffee making facilities available. There is a large lounge for relaxing and enjoying these views and we also have a sauna. Scarborough 15 miles, Whitby nine miles, York 40 miles, Durham 60 miles, Hornsea 50 miles. Please write, or telephone, for further details.

ROBIN HOOD'S BAY. Mrs B. Reynolds, Gilders Green, Raw, Robin Hood's Bay, Whitby YO22 4PP (01947 880025). Comfortable accommodation in 17th century farm cottage on a sheep-rearing and stock farm. Pleasantly situated in the hamlet of Raw, overlooking Robin Hood's Bay and close to the Moors, it is ideal for walking and touring. One mile from the A171, it is within easy reach of Whitby, Scarborough and many more places of interest. There is one family room, with children welcome. Bed and Breakfast from £15, with bedtime drink included. Open Easter to October. Also available, self catering house in village.

ROBIN HOOD'S BAY. Mrs Margaret Saynor, Rounton House, Mount Pleasant South, Robin Hood's Bay, Whitby YO22 4RQ (01947 880341). Margaret and Neville Saynor warmly welcome guests to share their lovely home, a Victorian house on a quiet road above the old village. Robin Hood's Bay is a beautiful, historic village on the Cleveland Way, five miles Whitby, 17 miles Scarborough. An excellent centre with four pubs, ideal base for sightseeing, walking, cycling, North Yorks Moors and "Aidensfield" with a fascinating rocky beach. All rooms have washbasins, colour TV and tea/coffee making facilities. Off road parking, garden and summer house. Sorry, non-smoking throughout. Bed and Breakfast from £15 to £19.

WHEN MAKING ENQUIRIES PLEASE MENTION
FARM HOLIDAY GUIDES

SALTBURN. Mrs Stevenson, Fox Inn, Roxby, Staithes, Saltburn TS13 5EB (01947 840335). Pets welcome, children by appointment! Your pets are welcome "free of charge" in our small family-run village Inn situated just two miles from beaches where your dogs can run free. We also have our own four acre exercise field. We are within the North York Moors and "Heartbeat" country is only a 10 minutes' drive away. If you are looking for a quiet relaxing break, away from the crowds, this is the place for you. Bed and Breakfast from £16; Evening Meals available. There is also a self-contained, fully equipped static caravan (sleeps six) for long or short lets where, again, your pets are welcome. Please contact us for any further details.

The Premier Hotel   Maureen and Ron Jacques, 66 Esplanade,
Scarborough, North Yorkshire YO11 2UZ. Tel: 01723 501062

This lovely Victorian licensed Hotel overlooking the sea and coastline has all the warmth and hospitality of a bygone era. It is conveniently situated for all Scarborough's attractions and is near the Italian, Rose and Holbeck Gardens; also convenient for the historic city of York, North York Moors, Whitby, and many stately homes in the area.
The Premier has a high reputation for its standards of food and service, specialising in traditional English cuisine using the very best local produce. Peaceful, relaxing atmosphere; lift to comfortable bedrooms, some with magnificent sea views and all with private facilities en suite, colour TV, tea tray, clock radio and hairdryer. Private car park.
AA, RAC Highly Acclaimed. PETS VERY WELCOME!

SCARBOROUGH. Mr Mark Radford, The White House, 2 South End Close, Burniston, Scarborough YO13 0JL (01723 870018). The White House is set in a quiet location off the Scarborough to Whitby Road in the small rural village of Burniston. It is an ideal place to enjoy the many amenities of nearby Scarborough and to explore the North Yorkshire Moors and spectacular Heritage Coastline. You may sample peace and relaxation in a friendly country house atmosphere all year round. A luxury suite of rooms comprising double bedroom with king-size bed, private bathroom and sitting room is at your disposal and breakfast is served in the conservatory overlooking the gardens. Non smokers only. Terms from £20 per person per night.

SCARBOROUGH. Sue and Tony Hewit, Harmony Country Lodge, Limestone Road, Burniston, Scarborough YO13 0DG (01723 870276). DISTINCTIVELY DIFFERENT HARMONY COUNTRY LODGE is a peaceful and relaxing retreat, octagonal in design and set in two acres of private grounds overlooking the National Park and sea. An ideal centre for walking or touring. Three miles from Scarborough and within easy reach of Whitby, York and the beautiful North Yorkshire countryside. Comfortable standard or en suite centrally heated rooms with colour TV, all with superb views. Attractive dining room, guest lounge and relaxing conservatory. Traditional English breakfast, optional evening meal including vegetarian. Fragrant massage available. Bed and Breakfast from £18.50. Non smoking, licensed, private parking facilities. Personal service and warm, friendly Yorkshire hospitality. Spacious six-berth caravan also available for self-catering holidays. Open all year. Please telephone or write for brochure.

SCARBOROUGH. Sue Batty, Wheatcroft Motel, 156 Filey Road, Scarborough YO11 3AA (01723 374613). Privately run, purpose-built Motel with resident proprietors, who are proud of their establishment's reputation for cleanliness and standard of facilities. All rooms, majority non-smoking, are en suite with colour TV, direct-dial telephone and tea and coffee facilities. Central heating is under guests' direct control. Full English breakfast is served in new dining room, alternatively Continental breakfast is served directly into the rooms via specially constructed hatches, ensuring total privacy and flexibility. Own large, private car park and conveniently situated on the South Cliff (A165). Room and choice of breakfast from £17. Reductions for children. RAC Listed. Roy Castle Good Air Award. Open most of the year.

SELBY. Jean Leake, Hazeldene Guest House, 32-34 Brook St, Doncaster Road, Selby YO8 0AR (01757 704809). ETB ♥ APPROVED. Hazeldene is an attractive Victorian town house close to the centre of Selby, an historic Yorkshire market town. Being equidistant, twixt London and Edinburgh, we are a popular stop-off point to break the journey overnight. Selby lies six miles north of Junction 34, M62; eight miles east of A1, and only 13 miles south of York. Each year more and more tourists come to recognise the value of Selby as a base for the Yorkshire coast, dales and moors, all of which are accessible in approximately one hour's motoring. Bed and Breakfast from £16 to £20 (some rooms en suite), including bedtime drink. Private parking. Non-smoking. AA and RAC Approved.

SKIPTON. Mrs Christine Clarkson, Bondcroft Farm, Embsay, Skipton BD23 6SF (01756 793371).

Tourist Board Listed. Bondcroft Farm is a working sheep and beef farm in the beautiful area of the Yorkshire Dales National Park with excellent walks and car drives. Mrs Clarkson is an excellent cook and the family make everyone welcome. All rooms have washbasin, TV and tea making facilities. We offer a peaceful holiday but you are only 10 minutes from the market town of Skipton (street market). Embsay has three village pubs serving very good food. Yorkshire Dales Railway is an attraction. Brochure available.

SKIPTON. Mrs Heather Simpson, Low Skibeden Farmhouse, Skibeden Road, Skipton BD23 6AB (01756 793849; Mobile 0831 126473). ETB ♥♥

COMMENDED. "Welcome Host", "Which?". Detached 16th century farmhouse in private grounds one mile east of Skipton off the A59/A65 gateway to the Dales, eg Bolton Abbey — Malham, Settle. Luxury bed and breakfast with fireside treats in the lounge. All rooms are quiet, spacious, have panoramic views, washbasins, tea facilities and electric overblankets. Central heating October to May. All guests are warmly welcomed and served tea/coffee and cakes on arrival, bedtime beverages are served from 9.30pm. Breakfast is served from 7am to 8.45am in the dining room. No smoking. No pets and no children under 12 years. Safe parking. New arrivals before 10pm. Quality and value guaranteed. Bed and Breakfast from £16 to £17.50 per person per night; two piece toilet en suite room from £18 per person per night; full en suites from £20 per person per night; single occupancy from £25 to £32. A deposit secures a room. Open all year.

• RED HALL •

Ingleby Road, Great Broughton, Stokesley TS9 7ET

Tel/Fax 01642 712300

Red Hall offers the welcoming calm and elegance of the small country house. Our family-run business with spacious centrally heated bedrooms and large en suite bathrooms provides personal service in a friendly, inviting atmosphere. Join us here in our lovely Queen Anne 17th century Grade II Listed country home set in tranquil meadows and woodland at the foot of the rugged North Yorkshire Moors National Park. Your visit to Red Hall will give you access to some of England's most dramatic and beautiful scenery, superb in autumn and winter. **From £22.50 per night bed and breakfast (for 4 nights); £18.50 per night thereafter. Single supplements. Dinner by arrangement. Open all year.**

THIRSK. Mrs T. Williamson, Thornborough House Farm, South Kilvington, Thirsk YO7 2NP (01845 522103). ♥♥ COMMENDED. Working farm. Ideally positioned farmhouse, one and a half miles north of Thirsk on the fringe of the North Yorkshire Moors, 35 minutes from the Pennine Dales and beautiful, historic York itself. Guests can be assured of a traditional warm Yorkshire welcome in comfortable, homely accommodation. Three bedrooms, two en-suite. Tasty home cooking, special diets catered for. Children and pets welcome. A perfect centre for walking and touring the beautiful surrounding area. Golf course half a mile, fishing and riding available locally. Open all year, Bed and Breakfast from £14 per person. Reductions for children, and for Senior Citizens — out of high season. Evening Meals can be provided.

THIRSK. Joyce Ashbridge, Mount Grace Farm, Cold Kirby, Thirsk YO7 2HL (01845 597389). 🏵 🏵

COMMENDED. A warm welcome awaits you on working farm surrounded by beautiful open countryside with magnificent views. Ideal location for touring or exploring the many walks in the area. Luxury en suite bedrooms with tea/coffee facilities. Spacious guests' lounge with colour TV. Garden. Enjoy delicious, generous helpings of farmhouse fayre cooked in our Aga. Children welcome. No smoking. Bed and Breakfast from £18. Weekly rates available. Open all year except Christmas.

THIRSK. Mrs Julie Bailes, Glen Free, Holme-on-Swale, Sinderby, Near Thirsk YO7 4JE (01845 567331). Glen Free is an old Lodge Bungalow set in a very peaceful situation, but still only one mile from A1 motorway (off the B6267 Masham/Thirsk road). Approximately seven miles from Ripon, Thirsk, Bedale, York and Harrogate 40 minutes approximately. One double, one twin rooms with central heating, tea making facilities and TV. Children welcome. All rooms ground floor. Golf, fishing, swimming and riding available locally. Ideal for touring the Dales and Herriot country. Bed and Breakfast fron £13 per person.

THIRSK. Mrs Lynda Dolan, Fourways Guest House, Town End, Thirsk YO7 1PY (01845 522601). 🏵 🏵 APPROVED. FOURWAYS is a comfortable family home with the advantage of being only two minutes' walk from the Town Centre and James Herriot's veterinary practice. Ideal for touring North Yorkshire Moors and Yorkshire Dales. All rooms have colour TV, tea/coffee facilities, washbasins; some rooms have en-suite facilities. Traditional English Breakfast with Evening Meal available if booked in advance. Licensed. Open all year. Ample parking provided. Bed and Breakfast from £15 per person with reductions for children. Evening Meal from £6.50.

THORNTON LE DALE. Mrs Sandra M. Pickering, "Nabgate", Wilton Road, Thornton le Dale, Pickering YO18 7QP (01751 474279). 🏵 APPROVED.

Situated at the eastern end of this beautiful village "Nabgate" was built at the turn of the century. Accommodation comprises three double rooms, one being en suite, all with washbasins, shaver points, TV, tea making facilities. Bathroom, toilet. Central heating. Dining room/lounge with Sky TV. Keys provided for access at all times. Car park. Children and pets welcome. Thornton le Dale has three pubs all providing meals, also cafes and fish and chip shop. Situated in the North Yorkshire Moors National Park it is an ideal base for East Coast resorts, Steam Railway, Flamingoland, Castle Howard, York and "Heartbeat" village. Open all year. Bed and Breakfast from £14. Welcome Host and Hygiene Certificate held.

THORNTON-LE-DALE. Mrs S. Wardell, Tangalwood, Roxby Road, Thornton-le-Dale, Pickering YO18 7SX (01751 474688). Tangalwood is a large detached family house providing a warm welcome, clean comfortable accommodation and good food. Situated in a quiet part of this picturesque village, which is in a good central position for Moors ("Heartbeat" country), coast, North Yorkshire Moors Railway, Flamingo Park Zoo and forest drives, mountain biking and walking. Good facilities for meals provided in the village. Accommodation in one twin room en suite and two doubles (one with washbasin), all with tea/coffee making facilities and TV; bathroom, two toilets and washroom; diningroom; central heating. Open Easter to October for Bed and Breakfast from £13.50 each. Private car park.

THORNTON LE DALE. Mrs Ella Bowes, Banavie, Roxby Road, Thornton-le-Dale, Pickering YO18 7SX (01751 474616). ❀❀ COMMENDED. Banavie is a large stone built semi-detached house set in Thornton-le-Dale, one of the prettiest villages in Yorkshire with a stream flowing through the centre. Situated in an attractive part of the village, it is ideal for touring coast, moors, forest, Scarborough, Castle Howard, Flamingo Park, Eden Camp. A real Yorkshire breakfast is served by Mrs Bowes herself which provides a good start to the day. Two restaurants and three inns in village for meals. Three double bedrooms, one en suite, all with washbasins, shaver points, colour TV and tea-making facilities; bathroom and toilet. Dining room, lounge with colour TV, central heating. Children welcome; cot, high chair, babysitting and reduced rates. Pets accepted. Own door keys. Car park. Open all year. Bed and Breakfast (including tea and biscuits at bedtime) from £14. SAE, please.

THRESHFIELD. Long Ashes Inn, Threshfield, Grassington, Near Skipton (01756 752434). This is a charming traditional old Dales Inn set in the heart of picturesque Wharfedale in the Yorkshire Dales National Park. The Inn has recently been sympathetically refurbished to a very high standard and offers de luxe accommodation. All rooms have en suite bathrooms, central heating, TV, tea and coffee making facilities. This is a tranquil retreat in an idyllic setting, perfect for exploring the Dales. There is a wide range of hand-pulled ales and freshly prepared food, as well as a heated indoor pool, sauna, squash courts, etc., adjacent for use by residents.

WHITBY. Netherby House, 90 Coach Road, Sleights, Whitby YO22 5EQ (01947 810211). ❀❀❀ COMMENDED. Netherby House is a Victorian house in two and a half acres of garden literally on the edge of the North Yorkshire Moors National Park. "Heartbeat" country is just up the road and the whole area is one of stunning natural beauty. The coast and fishing port of Whitby are three and a half miles away. Bed and Breakfast from £17.50. There is a varied dinner menu and times of meals are flexible. Guests are also welcome to use the games room and small gym. Four-poster bed available. All bedrooms are en suite. Private off-road parking available. Special bargain breaks available.

WHITBY near. Mrs G. Watson, The Bungalow, 63 Coach Road, Sleights, Whitby YO22 5BT (01947 810464). Be sure of a warm Yorkshire welcome at this large, comfortable, well appointed bungalow in the picturesque village of Sleights, just three miles from historic Whitby, half an hour's drive from Scarborough, close to North Yorkshire Moors National Park, Moors Railway, River Esk for fishing and boating; bowling nearby. Superb area for walkers. We offer one double and one twin room, both large, with en suite bathrooms, colour TV and tea/coffee making equipment. Central heating. Large lounge, separate diningroom. Substantial breakfast. Large parking area. Suitable for disabled. Bed and Breakfast from £17.50 to £18.50. Open Easter to October. Car not essential, near bus route.

WHITBY. Jim and Mu Wilkinson, High Whins, Tranmire, Whitby YO21 2BW (01947 840546). ❀ Situated on the side of a peaceful pastoral valley in the heart of the North Yorkshire National Park. Apart from the moorland and woodland that decorate our area we have the sea just down the road with good beaches at Sandsend and Runswick Bay. Staithes and Whitby are within easy reach. Good walking country with numerous public footpaths and bridle paths. Real food (home made bread a speciality), Real hospitality, Real people. All bedrooms have washbasins, tea/coffee facilities and central heating. Guests' sitting room with TV and separate dining room. Flexible meal times. Unrestricted access. Bed and Breakfast; optional evening meal. Brochure on request.

WHITBY. Mrs Avril Mortimer, Hollins Farm, Glaisdale, Whitby YO21 2PZ (01947 87516). Hollins Farm is 10 miles from Whitby, surrounded by beautiful countryside and moorland, with lots of lovely walks. Moors Steam Railway, Pickering market town with castle, National Park Centre at Danby are places of interest nearby, as also Whitby, Staithes, Robin Hood's Bay and other coastal villages to visit; choice of pony trekking and fishing. The 16th century farmhouse provides comfortable accommodation comprising one large family or double room with washbasin and TV, sleeps four/five, also twin room, both with tea-making facilities and storage heaters; bathroom; sitting/diningroom with colour TV. Conservatory. In winter peat and log fires are cosy. Cot and high chair. Access to rooms at all times. Camping facilities available. Phone or send SAE for terms.

WHITBY near. Mrs Pat Beale, Ryedale House, Coach Road, Sleights, Near Whitby YO22 5EQ (01947 810534). Welcoming non-smoking Yorkshire house of charm and character at the foot of the Moors, National Park and "Heartbeat" country, three and a half miles from Whitby. Rich in history, magnificent scenery, picturesque harbours, cliffs, beaches, scenic railways, superb walking. Three double/twin beautifully appointed bedrooms with private facilities. Guests' lounge and dining room (separate tables) with breathtaking views over Eskdale. Enjoy our large sun terrace and gardens, relax, we're ready to pamper you! Long established for delicious Yorkshire fare; extensive breakfast and snacks menus, picnics (traditional and vegetarian). Recommended local inns and restaurants. Parking, near public transport. Regret no pets. Bed and Breakfast £16 to £18 per person, minimum two nights. Weekly reductions, special Spring and October breaks. Tourist Board Member.

WHITBY near. Mrs M. Bradshaw, Hawthorn Farm, Ellerby, Hinderwell, Whitby TS13 5JD (01947 840228). A pleasant farmhouse situated on the B1266 road, link road between A171 moors road and A174 coast road. Set in the beautiful North Yorkshire National Park, two miles from Runswick Bay, it makes an ideal base for all Yorkshire beauty spots and places of interest. Whitby is only seven miles away. Hawthorn Farm has central heating, dining room cum sitting room with colour TV, two double bedrooms (twin beds), shower room with washbasin and toilet. Tea/coffee making facilities. Bed and Breakfast from £12.50 per night. Sorry, no pets.

YORK. Joan and Bill Wharton, Linden Lodge, 6 Nunthorpe Avenue, Scarcroft Road, York YO2 1PF (01904 620107; Fax; 01904 620985). 🏵🏵 *COMMENDED.* Under the personal supervision of the owners, this small, friendly hotel is situated in a quiet cul-de-sac with easy access from A64. Only ten minutes' walk to the city centre, railway station, racecourse and many places of historic interest. Double, twin, family and single rooms all with washbasin, razor points and tea/coffee making facilities; en suite facilities available; large lounge with TV. Colour TV in most rooms. Licensed. Full Fire Certificate. Highly recommended. Bed and good English Breakfast from £18.50. AA and RAC inspected. Member of York Hotel and Guest House Association. Low off season rates available.

YORK. Mr Roy Dodd, Charlton House, 1 Charlton Street, Bishopthorpe Road, York YO2 1JN (01904 626961). Charlton House, built 1913, is a well established Guest House within easy walking distance of the rail and bus stations, City Centre, Minster, Castle Museum, Viking Centre and Racecourse. Personally managed to a high standard, it offers "Yorkshire hospitality" at its very best. Full English breakfast in a relaxed and friendly atmosphere, with no restrictions. Single, twin, double, family en suite spacious rooms with TV, tea/coffee facilities. Ground floor en suite bedroom available. Double glazed and centrally heated. Close to local shops, good restaurants and children's play-park. Enclosed garden. Parking facilities. No smoking. Open all year. Bed and Breakfast from £15 per person. Reduced rates for children. Highly recommended.

YORK. Mr N. Douthwaite, The Bedford Hotel, 108/110 Bootham, York YO3 7DG (01904 624412). 🏵🏵 *COMMENDED.* Family-run licensed hotel with guaranteed space in private car park. Short walk along historic Bootham to the Minster and city centre. 15 rooms en-suite with colour TV and tea/coffee making facilities. Full central heating. Children welcome. Sorry no pets. Bed and Breakfast from £22 per person per night. AA Listed QQQ. RAC Acclaimed.

YORK. Mrs Barbara Curtis, Cumbria House, 2 Vyner Street, Haxby Road, York YO3 7HS (01904 636817). ETB Listed *COMMENDED.* **AA QQQ.** A warm and friendly welcome awaits you at Cumbria House — an elegant, tastefully decorated Victorian guest house, where comfort and quality is assured. We are convenient for the city, being only 12 minutes' walk from York's historic Minster and yet within minutes of the northern by-pass (A1237). A launderette, post office and children's park are close by. All rooms have colour TV, radio alarms and tea/coffee facilities. Most are en suite or have certain private facilities. Central heating. Fire Certificate. Guests' car park. Full English breakfast or vegetarian alternative. £15 to £18 per person. "You arrive as guests but leave as friends".

THE GREEN GUEST HOUSE

31 BEWLAY ST., BISHOPTHORPE ROAD, YORK YO2 1JT
Telephone: (01904) 652509

Norma and Ted welcome you to their small Non-Smoking Guest House and offer you a full English or Vegetarian breakfast. Open all year with en suite rooms available. Colour TV and hospitality tray in all rooms. Only 10 minutes' walk to city centre. Evening meal on request. Children welcome at reduced rate. Bargain Breaks from November to March. A warm welcome awaits you with tea and biscuits on arrival. Bed and Breakfast from £15. Proprietors: Norma and Ted Long.

Member Yorkshire and Humberside Tourist Board 👑 Commended

YORK. Mrs K. Rhodes, Beckside House, Bolton Percy, York YO5 7AQ (01904 744246). Beckside House is in the centre of a very small, peaceful village (no through traffic), eight miles south of York and some three miles from Tadcaster. Accommodation is in one very comfortable twin-bedded room, with private bathroom, in a self-contained ground floor wing with own entrance. Central heating; cot available; colour TV; tea/coffee making facilities. Many delightful country walks locally, yet very convenient for York and touring the Dales, North York Moors and coast. Bed and Breakfast from £15; Evening Meal available if required. No smoking.

YORK. Mrs R. Foster, Brookland House, Hull Road, Donnington, York YO1 5LW (01904 489548). Private house situated on A1079 to Hull, where a warm welcome awaits you. Beautifully appointed and spacious double rooms and small single. No smoking. Enjoy full English breakfast whilst overlooking our delightful garden. A five minute walk to pub serving evening meals; park and ride nearby. Private parking. Within easy reach of Yorkshire Dales, North Yorkshire Moors and coastal resorts. Bed and Breakfast from £15.

YORK. Mrs S. Hare, Chimneys, 18 Bootham Crescent, Bootham, York YO3 7AH (01904 644334). Beautifully decorated house less than five minutes' walk from the city centre, on the north side of York on the A19. All rooms have central heating and washbasins, tea/coffee making facilities and colour TV. Access to rooms at all times. Enjoy breakfast in our olde worlde dining room. You will feel cosy and relaxed in between your sightseeing around historic York. We will guarantee you the wonderful Yorkshire welcome that is world-famous. Open all year. Bargain Winter Breaks for three nights or more. Sorry, no pets. Ample parking. Ground floor rooms and toilet available. Family-run thus ensuring personal attention. No smoking establishment.

HOLLY HOUSE

Broad Lane, Appleton Roebuck, York YO5 7DS
Eunice and Bill Whitehead – Tel: 01904 744314
Fax: 01904 744546

Situated in open countryside close to York, this attractive house offers quiet relaxation. It is an ideal base for touring the Yorkshire Dales, Moors, Wolds and Coast. Holly House has five bedrooms (three en-suite) including one family room, a sitting room and separate TV lounge; central heating throughout; a heated indoor swimming pool and jacuzzi; pleasant gardens, ample parking and laundry facilities will enhance your stay at Holly House. All bedrooms non-smoking: vegetarians can be catered for. Terms from £20.00

Eunice and Bill Whitehead
Telephone: 01904 744314

YORK. Mav and Maureen Davidson, "Oaklands" Guest House, 351 Strensall Road, Old Earswick, York YO3 9SW (01904 768443). ❧ ❧ COMMENDED. A warm welcome awaits you at our attractive family house set in open countryside, yet only three miles from York with easy access to the A64, A1 and A1237. Ideally situated for City, Coast, Dales and Moors. Our comfortable bedrooms are centrally heated with vanity unit, colour TV, razor point, tea-making equipment and radio alarms. En-suite facilities available. A more than ample Breakfast is served in a light, airy dining room. Your hosts, Maureen and Mav, look forward to seeing you. Bed and full English Breakfast from £16. Discounts available. Open all year. No pets. Smoking in garden only.

YORK. Mr and Mrs G. Steel, Alder Carr House, York Road, Barmby Moor, York YO4 5HU (01759 380566; mobile 0585 277740). ❧ ❧ A spacious country house situated between the villages of Wilberfoss and Barmby Moor, set in 10 acres of grounds and enjoying lovely views of the Yorkshire Wolds. Close to the historic city of York, Castle Howard, the Moors, etc., also the unspoilt and uncrowded delights of the Wolds, and the free museums of Hull. A gliding club and the National Collection of Water Lilies are only three miles away. All bedrooms are en suite or with private bathroom. They are spacious and tastefully furnished; centrally heated and with TV and tea/coffee making facilities. An excellent range of local restaurants and village pubs offer evening meals. Open all year. Bed and full farmhouse Breakfast from £17 single, £32 double with en suite or private facilities.

YORK. Mrs J.W. Harrison, Fairthorne, 356 Strensall Road, Earswick, York YO3 9SW (01904 768609). ❧ ❧ COMMENDED. John and Joan Harrison invite you for a restful holiday in a peaceful country setting — a dormer bungalow with central heating, TV, shaver points, tea making facilities and en suite in bedrooms; TV lounge and dining room. Pleasant family atmosphere. Situated three miles north of York, within easy reach of East Coast and Yorkshire Moors and near golf course. Bus stop 50 yards if required. Bed and Breakfast from £15 per night. Reductions for children. Private car park and large garden. Open all year.

YORK. Carolyn and Ian McNabb, The Hazelwood, 24-25 Portland Street, Gillygate, York YO3 7EH (01904 626548; Fax: 01904 628032). 🐾🐾 *COMMEN-*

DED. AA QQQQ Selected, RAC Acclaimed. Non-smoking. Situated in the centre of York only 400 yards from York Minster yet in an extremely quiet location and with private car park the Hazelwood is an elegant Victorian townhouse offering excellent value for money. Our comfortable bed-rooms (some with four-poster beds) are mostly en suite and all have colour TV, hairdryer, radio alarm and tea/coffee making facilities. Relax in our secluded garden or in our peaceful guests' lounge with its range of books and where tea and coffee are always available. Our quality breakfasts cater for all tastes including vegetarian. Bed and Breakfast from £16.

YORK. Mrs Margaret Munday, Cornmill Lodge, 120 Haxby Road, York YO3 7JP (01904 620566).

🐾🐾 *COMMENDED.* The Cornmill Lodge is a deceptively large Victorian town house situated 12 minutes' walk from York Minster and city centre. We are AA and ETB Inspected. The beautifully refurbished house offers colour TVs, tea/coffee trays, clock radios; most rooms are en suite. A hearty full breakfast is served though we offer a vegetarian alternative. We have central heating, tourist information, full Fire Certificate and a guests' car park. A bank, post office and launderette are close by. Bed and Breakfast from £16 to £20 per person depending on type of room and season.

YORK. Four Poster Lodge Hotel, 68/70 Heslington Road, off Barbican Road, York YO1 5AU (01904

651170). 🐾🐾🐾 *COMMENDED.* RAC Highly Acclaimed, AA QQQ. Four Poster Lodge, imaginatively named and unique in its conception, is a Victorian house lovingly restored and furnished. We are almost a whisper away from historic York with all its fascinations — the Castle, the Shambles, the Viking Centre — invitingly close. When on holiday dream of the exciting days to come, and plan the tasks ahead amidst the lush covers of a four-poster bed. En suite facilities, hair dryers, colour TV, radio and hospitality trays. Licensed. Car park. Bed and hearty English Breakfast from £25 to £27 per person. Brochure available.

YORK. Gordon and Trudi Smith, Rosedale Guest House, Wetherby Road, Rufforth, York YO2 3QB (01904 738297). 🐾 *COMMENDED.* Rufforth is a delight-

ful village situated three and a half miles west from the historic city of York, ideally situated for touring Yorkshire Moors and Dales. Rosedale offers you the comfort of a family guest house; all our rooms are furnished to a high standard, some with en suite facilities, and for the comfort of our guests we provide tea/coffee making facilities and TV in all bedrooms. Guest lounge. Full central heating. Private parking. Children welcome, reduced rates available. Low season rates available. Open all year. Bed and full English Breakfast from £16.

YORK. Mrs Susan Sturdy, Glenville Guest House, 132 East Parade, York YO3 7YG (01904 425370). 🐾🐾 Susan and Bob invite you to enjoy Yorkshire hospitality in a warm, friendly, family guest house. This Victorian house is quietly situated in a residential area of York yet only 12 minutes' walk to the city centre, 'bar' walls and Minster. York University is quite near. Central heating, colour TV, coffee making facilities. Cot available. Some rooms en suite or have private showers. Open all year. We offer Bed and full English Breakfast from £13. Child reductions. No smoking in some bedrooms.

YORK. Feversham Lodge, 1 Feversham Crescent, York YO3 7HQ (01904 623882). 🌑🌑 Bob and Jill

Peacock, the proprietors of Feversham Lodge, offer you a warm welcome and a pleasant stay in York. Conveniently situated for the Yorkshire Moors and "Herriot" country, yet only ten minutes' walk from the Minster and city centre. Frequent bus service almost from the door to the city, bus and rail stations. The Lodge was converted from a 19th century manse in 1981 and retains much of its grandeur. Some rooms en suite. Central heating. Diningroom, TV lounge. Colour TV in bedrooms. Car park. Full Fire Certificate. Tea/coffee making facilities. Bed and Breakfast from £16 to £20. Enjoy your stay with us.

YORK. Mrs Diana S. Tindall, Newton Guest House, Neville Street, Haxby Road, York YO3 7NP

(01904 635627). Diana and John offer all their guests a friendly and warm welcome to their Victorian end townhouse, a few minutes' walk from city centre, York's beautiful Minster, city walls and museums. Situated near an attractive park with good bowling greens. York is an ideal base for touring Yorkshire Moors, Dales and coastline. One bedroom (private facilities outside), all other rooms en suite and have colour TV, tea/coffee making tray. Full central heating, Fire Certificate. Private car park. Personal attention. We are a non-smoking house.

YORK. Pauleda House Hotel, 123 Clifton, York YO3 6BL (01904 634745; Tel & Fax: 01904

621327). Enjoy superb accommodation centrally situated only minutes away from all the historic attractions. A warm and friendly welcome awaits you at Pauleda, a small family-run hotel offering excellent value for money. All rooms are en suite and tastefully equipped, some with four-poster beds, colour TV with satellite, tea/coffee tray, etc. Car park. Bed and Breakfast from £20 to £35.

YORK. Mr Mike Cundall, Orillia House, 89 The Village, Stockton on Forest, York YO3 9UP (01904

400600). 🌑🌑 A warm welcome awaits you at Orillia House, conveniently situated in the centre of the village, three miles north east of York, one mile from A64. The house dates back to the 17th century and has been restored to offer a high standard of comfort with modern facilities yet retaining its original charm and character. All rooms have private facilities, colour TV and tea/coffee making facilities. Our local pub provides excellent evening meals. We also have our own private car park. Bed and Breakfast from £17. Telephone for our brochure.

NORTH YORKSHIRE – RICH IN TOURIST ATTRACTIONS!

Dales, moors, castles, abbeys, cathedrals – you name it and you're almost sure to find it in North Yorkshire. Leading attractions include Castle Howard, the moorlands walks at Goathland, the Waterfalls at Falling Foss, Skipton, Richmond, Wensleydale, Bridestones Moor, Ripon Cathedral, Whitby, Settle and, of course, York itself.

YORK. Mrs Lorna Edmondson, The Lodge, 302 Strensall Road, Earswick, York YO3 9SW (01904 761387). 🐛🐛 *COMMENDED.* The best for less, where guests become friends. This "no smoking" house surrounded by open fields is only three miles north of York. Large, well kept gardens where guests can sit and children play in safety. The upper floor of this modern house has two exceptionally large en suite bedrooms, shower room and toilet. Twin room on ground floor near main bathroom for those who cannot manage stairs. Full English Breakfast with own free range eggs. We understand the needs of "allergy" diets and cater willingly for all others. Bed and Breakfast from only £17 with reductions for children.

YORK. Mr and Mrs C. Steele, Avimore House Hotel, 78 Stockton Lane, York YO3 0BS (01904 425556). 🐛🐛 *COMMENDED.* An Edwardian house situated in a pleasant, quiet, tree-lined avenue, on the East side of the city, now a small, comfortable, friendly family-run hotel, with double, twin, family and single rooms. All rooms en-suite with hairdryers, colour TV, clock radios and tea/coffee making facilities. Residents' lounge. Private parking. Fire Certificate. RAC Acclaimed. Bed and full English Breakfast, twin/double from £16 — £24; single £18 — £25 per person per night. Reduced rates for children. Autumn/Spring Breaks from £32 (minimum two nights).

YORK. Keith Jackman, Dairy Guesthouse, 3 Scarcroft Road, York YO2 1ND (01904 639367). Beautifully appointed Victorian townhouse that was once the local dairy! Well equipped cottage-style rooms that include colour TV, CD players, hair dryers and hot drinks facilities. Some en suite rooms, one four-poster room. Informal and relaxed, non smoking environment. Offers traditional or vegetarian menu. Bed and Breakfast from £17 per person. Please write or phone for a colour brochure or reservation.

GUESTHOUSE
Traditional and Wholefood

YORK. Mont-Clare Guest House, 32 Claremont Terrace, Gillygate, York YO3 7EJ (01904 627054; Fax: 01904 651011). 🐛🐛🐛 Take advantage and enjoy the convenience of City Centre accommodation in a quiet location close to magnificent York Minster. A warm and friendly welcome awaits you at the Mont-Clare. All rooms are en-suite, tastefully decorated, with colour TV (Satellite), Radio Alarm, Direct Dial Telephone, Hairdryer, Tea/Coffee Tray, Shoe Cleaning, etc. All of York's attractions are within walking distance and we are ideally situated for the Yorkshire Dales, Moors and numerous Stately Homes. Fire and Hygiene Certificates. Cleanliness, good food, pleasant surroundings and friendliness are our priorities. Private car park. Open all year. Reduced rates for weekly stay. Bed and Breakfast from £17.50 per person per night.

YORK. Stanley House, Stanley Street, York YO3 7NW (01904 637111). 🐛🐛 *COMMENDED.* Stanley House is situated just 10 minutes' walk from Britain's most beautiful and fascinating city. Our aim is to provide you with comfort and a friendly base from which you can discover the history and ancient charm of York. All rooms have en-suite facilities with colour TV and courtesy tray. There is off street car parking and payphone for guests' use. We are open all year except Christmas and Boxing Day. Sorry, no smoking or pets. Bed and Breakfast from £16.

YORK. Mrs Jackie Cundall, Wellgarth House, Wetherby Road, Rufforth, York YO2 3QB (01904

738592 or 738595). ✿✿ AA Listed. FHG Diploma. A warm welcome awaits you at Wellgarth House, ideally situated in Rufforth (B1224) three miles from York, one mile from the Ring Road (A1237) and convenient for "Park and Ride" into York City. This country guest house offers a high standard of accommodation with en suite Bed and Breakfast from £16. All rooms have complimentary tea/coffee making, colour TV with Sky. Rooms with four-poster or king-size beds also available. Excellent local pub just two minutes' walk away which serves lunches and dinners. Large private car park. Telephone or write for brochure. Access/Visa accepted.

YORK. Mrs Susan Viscovich, The Manor at Acaster Malbis, Acaster Malbis, York YO2 1UL (Tel &

Fax: 01904 706723). ✿✿✿ *HIGHLY COMMENDED.* Atmospheric Manor in rural tranquillity with our own private lake set in five and a half acres of beautiful mature grounds. Preservation orders on all trees with abundant bird life. Fish in the lake, cycle or walk, bring your own boat for river cruising. Close to racecourse and only 10 minutes' car journey from the city or take the leisurely river bus (Easter to October). Conveniently situated to take advantage of the Dales, Moors, Wolds and splendid coastline. Find us via A64 exiting for Copmanthorpe, York, Thirsk, Harrogate or Bishopthorpe (Sim Balk Lane). 10 centrally heated en suite bedrooms with direct-dial phones, hair dryers, TV, courtesy tray; dining room with open coal fire. Licensed. Optional Evening Meal. Bed and Breakfast from £22.50 to £28 per person per night. For details SAE or telephone. See our Colour Advertisement on the Outside Back Cover of this guide.

YORK. Mrs J.Y. Tree, Inglewood Guest House, 7 Clifton Green, York YO3 6LH (01904 653523).

✿✿✿ The Inglewood Guest House has a warm and friendly atmosphere where guests will really feel at home. The bedrooms all have colour TV and some have en suite bathrooms. Open all year with central heating. Breakfast is an enjoyable experience in our pleasant dining room with dark wooden tables and chairs. Helpful information is given on where to go and what to see. It is an ideal centre for exploring York and making day excursions to many market towns and attractive villages around York. Places of historic interest also to visit. Children are welcome. Sorry, no pets. A car is not essential, but there is parking. Bed and Breakfast from £17.50; reductions for children.

YORK. Mr D.G. Tree, Clifton Green Hotel, 8 Clifton Green, York YO3 6LH (01904 623597). ✿✿✿ Small, elegant hotel, privately owned and managed. Attractive location overlooking Clifton Green. Just 10 minutes' walk to the city centre and York Minster. Spacious bedrooms, some with en-suite bathrooms and all with colour televisions. Children welcome. Private car parking. Bed and Breakfast from £17.50. Reductions for children and Senior Citizens. Bargain Short Breaks between November and March. AA and RAC Listed.

YORK near. Mrs Jean A. Tomlinson, Wheelgate Guest House, 7 Kirkgate, Sherburn-in-Elmet, Near York LS25 6BH (01977 682231). Wheelgate Guest House is set in the attractive village of Sherburn-in-Elmet, only 20 minutes' drive from York, Selby or Leeds. Easy access to M62 and M1 motorways and an ideal stop when travelling north/south. Sherburn is easily accessible, only three miles off the A1 on the B1222 road. The house is olde worlde, set in attractive gardens; central heating throughout; guests' lounge; washbasins, tea/coffee making facilities, colour TV in all rooms. Superb home cooking; Evening Meals and packed lunches available. Car parking. Children and pets welcome. Open all year. Licensed. Terms on request.

SOUTH YORKSHIRE

DONCASTER. Canda Lodge, Hampolebalk Lane, Skellow, Doncaster DN6 8LF (01302 724028). Delightful individually designed house built of York stone. Ideal half way stopover for London or Scotland, good access for A1 north and south; other places that can be reached within an hour are Manchester, Nottingham, Sheffield, Leeds, Hull, Wakefield, Rotherham, Ripon; there is a good road to beautiful York. All rooms have remote-control colour TV, trouser press, tea trays, direct-dial telephone. Double en suite £38, without £35; single en suite £35, without £26. Most of our rooms are chalets in the grounds at the rear of the property as is our car park; a courtesy car is available to Doncaster Races on request. A homely and friendly welcome awaits you from your hosts Phil and Lorraine Toomey.

HOLMFIRTH (Penistone). Mrs Ann Unitt, Aldermans Head Manor, Hartcliffe Hill Road, Langsett, Stocksbridge, Sheffield S30 5GY (Tel and Fax: 01226 766209). 👑👑👑 *HIGHLY COMMENDED.* Award-winning Licensed Guest House. Set in 50 acres of dramatic country-side, the Manor enjoys panoramic views across the Langsett, Midhopestones reservoirs and the Peak District moorland beyond. Seven centuries ago the monks of Kirkstead Abbey owned the farm, and today the welcoming atmosphere of peace and tranquillity still prevails — just right for relaxing and unwinding. Four bedrooms, some en suite, TV and tea/coffee making facilities in all rooms; full central heating. Home cooking with local produce. Bed and Breakfast from £22.50. Ideal centre for walking and exploring the Derbyshire and Yorkshire countryside. A non smoking household. Brochure on request.

WEST YORKSHIRE

PONTEFRACT/WENTBRIDGE. Mrs I. Goodworth, The Corner Cafe, Wentbridge, Pontefract WF8 3JJ (01977 620316). Tourist Board Listed. A sixteenth century cottage featuring oak beams and a lovely secluded garden with plenty of car parking space, set in a small village but within easy reach of main roads (a quarter-of-a-mile A1). Accommodation includes two single, one double, one twin with private bathroom and two family rooms en suite, all with washbasins, TV, tea and coffee making facilities and full central heating. Non-smoking accommodation available. Two family rooms en suite in annexe. This picturesque village has three very nice old Inns and restaurants where evening meals or snacks can be obtained. Children welcome. Terms from £18. Open all year round, except Christmas.

ISLE OF WIGHT

CARISBROOKE. Mrs V.A. Skeats, The Mount, 1 Calbourne Road, Carisbrooke, Near Newport PO30 5AP (01983 522173/524359). "The Mount" is superbly situated in the charming village of Carisbrooke, overlooking Carisbrooke Castle. Ideally located for all amenities. Delightful lanes and downs for walking. Information/requirements of maps and details on local activities can be provided. Rooms are comfortably furnished with washbasins/razor points. Own keys. Private car park. Lock-up cycle shelter. Children welcome. We offer homely accommodation in a Victorian house with personal service. Bed and Breakfast from £15. Reductions for children. Any day bookings accepted. For further details, please write or telephone.

CARISBROOKE. Mrs P. Chick, Plaish Farm, Carisbrooke, Newport PO30 3HU (01983 520397). *Southern Tourist Board COMMENDED.* Family-run arable/stock farm in lea of historic Carisbrooke Castle. Two spacious double en suite bedrooms with tea/coffee and colour TV. Ideal walking, touring, cycling.

FRESHWATER. Mr and Mrs Reynolds, Brookside Forge Hotel, Brookside Road, Freshwater PO40 9ER (01983 754644). 🐾 🐾🐾 A substantial detached property recently converted and extended to meet the hotel requirements of today. Ideally located for the beautiful West Wight countryside and the three coastal bays of Freshwater, Colwell and Totland. All bedrooms are en suite and have colour TV, tea/coffee making facilities and hair dryers. Lounge has colour TV and is available at all times. We serve an excellent standard of cuisine and enjoy an enviable reputation on the Island. Terraced lawns with sun chairs, games lawn and patio provide a peaceful haven after your day's activities. Bed and Breakfast from £19.50 per night; Bed, Breakfast and three-course Evening Meal from £27.45 per night. Reduced rates for groups and off season rates. We also have a self catering bungalow with two bedrooms sleeping four to six persons. From £200 per week. Brochure available.

RYDE. Mr David D. Wood, Seaward Guest House, 14/16 George Street, Ryde PO33 2EW (Tel & Fax: 01983 563168). ETB Listed *COMMENDED.* Seaward is a friendly, family-run, 200 year old guest house. All rooms have colour TV, tea/coffee facilities, washbasins and razor points. Some en suite rooms available. Telephone, hair dryer and ironing facilities available for guests' use. Mini bus for collection from ferries or island tours. An excellent base from which to tour the island, with bus, train stations and ferry/hovercraft terminals, as well as shops and sea front, within three minutes' walk. Open all year. Special rates for Senior Citizens. Full English, Continental or Vegetarian breakfast. Bed and Breakfast from £14; Bed, Breakfast and Evening Meal from £20.

ISLE OF WIGHT – A SHORT SAIL AWAY!

Just across The Solent, The Isle of Wight offers many attractions, such as Alum Bay, the Roman villa at Brading, The Country Park at Robin Hill and Yafford Mill Museum. Don't miss the coloured sands either!

SANDOWN. Cliffways Hotel, 39 Ranelagh Road, Sandown PO36 8NT (01983 403659). 🌸🌸🌸

COMMENDED. The Cliffways offers eight suites of quality accommodation. Charming and very select bed and breakfast hotel. All bedrooms have comfortable sitting area, remote control colour TV with satellite channel, clock/radio, full hot drinks making facilities. Special lounge with bar; central heating throughout. Parking. Central beach, theatre, railway and all other amenities. Prices from £16.50. Send for brochure from **Mrs S. Bax.**

SHANKLIN. Denise and Martin Nickless, Keats Cottage Hotel and Tea Rooms, 76 High Street, Shanklin Old Village PO37 6NJ (01983 866351). The rear part of the building forms "Eglantine Cottage" where John Keats stayed in 1819 writing "Otho the Great" and other works. George Morland, the landscape artist, stayed in 1789 and Thomas Morton, dramatist, in 1798. If it was good enough for them, then it's even better for you! Keats Cottage is situated next to the old village, in the High Street of Shanklin. A small family-run, licensed hotel, centrally heated. TV lounge with log fire. Tea making facilities and washbasin in all rooms; en suite rooms available. An 18 jet aqua spa bath available. Children welcome. Open all year. A five minute walk through tree-lined Chine Avenue to the sandy beach. Bed and Breakfast at 1992 prices: Low Season from £13.50 to High Season £19.50; Evening Meals optional. Reductions for children. "One night or more — that's what we're here for". Mini Breaks welcome. Holiday insurance available. Credit cards accepted.

SHANKLIN. Pete and Barbara Tubbs, Hazelwood Hotel, 14 Clarence Road, Shanklin PO37 7BH (Tel & Fax: 01983 862824). 🌸🌸🌸 After leaving the ferry, follow signs for Shanklin, take A3055 into Shanklin, take a right off Arthurs Hill. Guests of all ages can enjoy the freedom of our family-run hotel with its home from home atmosphere and great value for money. Good home cooking with a choice of menu at dinner, served in our lovely diningroom. We have a large TV lounge and most rooms are en-suite. TV in all rooms. Tea/coffee making facilities are provided at no extra cost and we are fully centrally heated. We give reductions for children and over 55's. Hazelwood is set in spacious grounds in a quiet tree-lined road close to the sea, station, shops and the famous cliff path. Car parking available. Bed and Breakfast from £16 to £19.50. Evening Meal available. All major credit cards accepted.

TOTLAND. Frenchman's Cove Country Hotel, Alum Bay Old Road, Totland PO39 0HZ (01983 752227; Fax: 01983 755125). 🌸🌸🌸 Our delightful family-run country hotel is set amongst National Trust downland, not far from the Needles and safe sandy beaches. Ideal for ramblers, bird watchers, cyclists and those that enjoy the countryside. Cots and high chairs are available. Most rooms are en suite, all with colour TV and tea/coffee making facilities. Guests can relax in the cosy bar or in the attractive lounge. Also available is the Coach House, a delightfully appointed apartment (ETB 3 KEYS) for two adults and two children. Please contact Sue and Chris Boatfield for further details. AA QQ.

If you've found
FARM HOLIDAY GUIDES
of service please tell your friends

Full Board • Bed & Breakfast • Self-Catering

Campus Holidays

How about a University holiday this year, or perhaps you'd fancy a College?

If you are interested, you'll be joining thousands of non-students who have discovered the delights of the Campus as a value-for-money holiday destination.

For 1997 around 100,000 places are available during the summer and even during term-time many campuses can offer holiday facilities. The various establishments have organised themselves into two marketing groups, both of which will be more than happy to provide you with brochures and information on request.

THE BRITISH UNIVERSITIES ACCOMMODATION CONSORTIUM (BUAC)

First in the field, the members of BUAC can now offer accommodation at over 60 venues nationwide for individual and family holidays, for conferences and study vacations. From Aberdeen to Exeter, from Aberystwyth to Norwich, you will find comfortable and modern accommodation at affordable prices. *Further details from: Carole Formon, BUAC Ltd., University Park, Nottingham NG7 2RD (0115 950 4571).*

THE HIGHER EDUCATION ACCOMMODATION CONSORTIUM (HEAC)

Representing a wider range of institutions as the name suggests, HEAC now has over 70 members with around 30,000 beds available throughout Britain, in seaside, rural and city centre locations.

For further information you should contact: HEAC Ltd., 36 Collegiate Crescent, Sheffield S10 2BP (0114 268 3759).

Here are just a few different possibilities for Campus Holidays for 1997.

EDINBURGH & LOTHIANS, EDINBURGH. Vickie Allan, Conference Office, Heriot Watt University, Riccarton, Edinburgh EH14 4AS (0131-451 3115). Year round accommodation. The en suite year round bedrooms are mainly for conference delegates but there is often availability, especially at weekends. Student accommodation is available during vacations although booking is recommended during the Edinburgh Festival.

SCOTLAND

ABERDEENSHIRE

ABERDEEN. John and Beth Fraser, Abbian Guest House, 148 Crown Street, Aberdeen AB11 6HS (Tel & Fax: 01224 575826). STB 🐝🐝 *COMMENDED.*

John and Beth Fraser give a friendly family welcome at this Victorian, terraced city centre town house. It is the ideal starting point for exploring Royal Deeside and the Grampian Region with its unique Whisky and Castle Trails. Situated within 400 yards of Union Street, the main shopping area, it is convenient for the cinemas and varied night life of this popular Granite City. The bus and rail stations and the sea ferry terminal where the 1997 Tall Ships Race begins are nearby. The popular Duthie Park, with its magnificent Winter Gardens open all year, is also easily accessible. Totally refurbished in 1995/6, all bedrooms have en suite facilities and teletext TV. There is a free video, cassette and book library for guests.

ABERDEEN. Skala Guest House, 2 Springbank Place, Aberdeen AB11 6LW (01224 572260). STB *COMMENDED.* Personally-run accommodation in quiet location five minutes' walk from city centre. Convenient for shopping, dining out, local parks, walks and sightseeing. All rooms have central heating, washbasins, colour TV and tea/coffee making facilities. An ideal base from which to visit Royal Deeside and the Highlands, castles and distilleries. Bed and Breakfast from £16 per person.

ABERDEEN. Roselodge Guest House, 3 Springbank Terrace, Aberdeen AB1 2LS (01224 586794). STB Listed *COMMENDED.* Terraced house situated in the city centre, ideal for shops, bus/rail station, theatre and park. Accommodation comprises two double, two twin and one family bedrooms; two bathrooms. Car parking. Bed and Breakfast from £18 single, £15 double. Special rates for children. Open January to December. Please write or telephone for further details.

ABERDEEN. Mrs D. Ramsay, Klibreck Guest House, 410 Great Western Road, Aberdeen AB10 6NR (01224 316115). 🐝 *COMMENDED.* AA QQ, RAC Listed. Personally run, comfortable guest house on main city bus route and very conveniently situated for touring Royal Deeside, Donside and all other areas of Grampian. All rooms are non-smoking and are equipped with tea/coffee facilities and colour TV. Ground floor rooms available. Brochure.

ABOYNE. Migvie House, Migvie, By Tarland, Aboyne AB34 4XL (Tel & Fax: 013398 81313).

🐝🐝🐝 *HIGHLY COMMENDED.* Amidst a small Highland estate in Royal Deeside our peaceful old farmhouse provides a delightful base to explore the serenity and grandeur in this land of unspoilt beauty, with its romantic castles, famous distilleries and numerous sporting pursuits. Lovingly restored to create an atmosphere of warmth and comfort. Our three charming bedrooms are all en suite. We have a sitting room with log fires and meals are taken around our huge farmhouse table. Bed and Breakfast £20 per person per night. Evening Meal £13 by arrangement. No smoking.

ABOYNE. Charleston Hotel, Ballater Road, Aboyne AB3 5HY (013398 86475). Comfortable family-run hotel superbly situated in village within easy reach of a host of wonderful golf courses and outdoor leisure activities. Open all year. Family parties, disabled/handicapped guests most welcome. A self catering cottage in the hotel grounds sleeps six with everything laid on including heating, linen and bedding. "BIG" Aberdeen Angus steaks, wild salmon and home made meals our speciality — "Best on Deeside". Real ales at their best. Mamie and Cliff extend a warm welcome to patrons old and new, young and otherwise (special meal rates for reduced portions). Come and enjoy stupendous scenery and countryside.

BRAEMAR. Maria and Mike Franklin, Callater Lodge Hotel, 9 Glenshee Road, Braemar AB35 5YQ (Tel & Fax: 013397 41275). STB ❀ ❀ ❀ COMMENDED. AA QQQQ Selected, Les Routiers. Located in the charming Highland town of Braemar, famous for its Highland Gathering and Games, Callater Lodge is a small, comfortable, welcoming family-run hotel. Only nine miles from Balmoral Castle, it provides an excellent base for exploring the beautiful hills and valleys of Royal Deeside. Eight miles from Glenshee, one Scotland's largest ski centres, Braemar is a great base for outdoor activities such as ski-ing, fishing, climbing, walking, etc. It has large grounds which contain two self catering units. All six bedrooms are en suite; residents' lounge, drying room, licensed, parking. Bed and Breakfast from £24 per person.

HUNTLY. Mrs B. Barclay, Elmbank, Richmond Road, Huntly AB54 5BA (01466 792809). ❀ HIGHLY COMMENDED. Gracious Victorian house. Private garden and parking. Newly refurbished providing cosy en suite bedrooms. Residents' lounge. Good food. Peaceful and friendly. Open January to December. Prices from £20. Please write or telephone for further details.

INSCH by. Mrs Grant, Earlsfield Farm, Kennethmont, By Insch AB52 6GQ (Tel & Fax: 01464 831473). ❀ ❀ COMMENDED. Arable farm within one mile of Leith Hall (National Trust for Scotland) and close to Castle and Whisky Trails. Beautiful countryside. Ideal hill walking. The accommodation comprises one family, one double and one single bedrooms, two rooms sharing bathroom, one with en suite facilities. Children welcome. Bed and Breakfast from £16 single, £14 double per person; with Evening Meal from £22 (booked in advance). Open January to December.

INVERURIE. Mrs Shena McGhie, Fridayhill, Kinmuck, Inverurie AB51 0LY (Tel & Fax: 01651 882252). STB ❀ ❀ HIGHLY COMMENDED. Fridayhill is a lovely Scandinavian style house in three-quarters of an acre of attractive gardens set amidst farm country, about four miles from Inverurie, seven miles from Dyce Airport, Aberdeen on Grampians "Castle Trail". Convenient for Newmachar Golf Course, hill walking, horse riding and beaches. Double bedroom with en suite dressing room and shower room. Private sitting room with colour TV, tea/coffee making facilities and central heating. Non smoking household. Sorry, no pets. Bed and Breakfast from £18 per person.

GRAMPIAN REGION – RICH IN CHOICES.

Whether you are looking for castles to visit, mountains to climb, beaches to lie on or rivers to fish Grampian Region will satisfy all of these and many more demands. Try and visit Crathes Castle, Tomintoul, Elgin, Pitmedden House, Cullen Bay, Culbin Forest and it hardly needs to be said, the granite city of Aberdeen itself.

STONEHAVEN. Mrs C. Pollock, Ormesby Guest House, 24 Dunnottar Avenue, Stonehaven AB39 2JJ (01569 763840). Quiet family-run guest house offering Bed and Breakfast accommodation in clean comfortable bedrooms, all with colour TV and tea/coffee facilities. Accommodation consists of one family/double room with en suite facilities, one double and one twin rooms with washbasin; bath, shower and two toilets. Non-smoking. Parking available. Harbour, town centre, bowling green, swimming pool, tennis courts and golf courses all within walking distance. Stonehaven is just 15 miles south of Aberdeen and makes an ideal base for touring Royal Deeside. Prices from £16 to £18 per person per night.

ANGUS

BRECHIN. Mrs Margaret Stewart, Doniford, 26 Airlie Street, Brechin DD9 6JX (01356 622361).

ẅ ẅ *HIGHLY COMMENDED.* AA QQQQ Selected. 19th century detached villa in quiet residential area of town within easy reach of Angus Glens and coast, Glamis Castle, Pictish Stones at Aberlemno and an hour's drive to Aberdeen and Royal Deeside and over the Tay Bridge to St. Andrews. Central to many golf courses and hill walking and fishing available locally. Accommodation comprises one double/ twin room en suite and one twin room en suite, both tastefully decorated and furnished, having clock radios, electric blankets, colour TV and tea/coffee facilities. Large garden and plenty parking. All home cooking and baking; home-made preserves served. A warm welcome is extended to all guests. Bed and Breakfast from £17.50; Dinner (optional) from £9.

Key to
Tourist Board Ratings

The Crown Scheme
(England, Scotland & Wales)

Covering hotels, motels, private hotels, guesthouses, inns, bed & breakfast, farmhouses. Every Crown classified place to stay is inspected annually. *The classification:* Listed then 1-5 Crown indicates the range of facilities and services. Higher quality standards are indicated by the terms APPROVED, COMMENDED, HIGHLY COMMENDED and DELUXE.

The Key Scheme
(also operates in Scotland using a Crown symbol)

Covering self-catering in cottages, bungalows, flats, houseboats, houses, chalets, etc. Every Key classified holiday home is inspected annually. *The classification:* 1-5 Key indicates the range of facilities and equipment. Higher quality standards are indicated by the terms APPROVED, COMMENDED, HIGHLY COMMENDED and DELUXE.

The Q Scheme
(England, Scotland & Wales)

Covering holiday, caravan, chalet and camping parks. Every Q rated park is inspected annually for its quality standards. The more √ in the Q – up to 5 – the higher the standard of what is provided.

ARGYLL

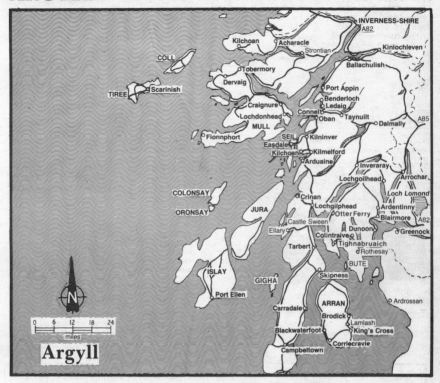

ACHARACLE. Mrs Learmouth, Belmont, Acharacle PH36 4JT (01967 431266). Good food and a warm welcome await you at Belmont, a converted manse situated in a beautiful lochside position with uninterrupted views of Loch Shiel, and the mountains of Moidart, this is an ideal centre for walking, touring, sea and loch fishing, sailing — or just relaxing on nearby beaches. Convenient for trips to the Inner Hebridean Islands — or exploring the historic countryside. All bedrooms are tastefully furnished with en suite facilities or washbasins and have central heating and tea/coffee making facilities. Lounge open all day. Rates from £16; Dinner £11.

ACHARACLE. Mrs Ruby MacNaughton, Carm Cottage, Monument Park, Strontian, Acharacle PH36 4HZ (01967 402112 evening; 01967 402268 daytime). Modern bungalow ideally situated overlooking Loch Sunart, just five minutes' walk from Strontian village centre with shops and hotels where excellent food is served. Strontian is a central place to stop to tour Ardnamurchan which is the most westerly point on the British mainland. Home to a wonderful array of wildlife, walks, fishing, also day trips to Mull and Iona can be arranged. One double en suite, one double and one twin rooms with TV and tea making facilities. Pets by arrangement. Open April to October. From £15 per person per night including full Scottish breakfast.

BALLACHULISH (near Glencoe). Mr and Mrs J.A. MacLeod, Lyn-Leven Guest House, Ballachulish PA39 4JW (01855 811392; Fax: 01855 811600).

♛ ♛ ♛ COMMENDED. Lyn-Leven, a superior licensed guest house overlooking Loch Leven, with every comfort, in the beautiful Highlands of Scotland, situated one mile from historic Glencoe village. Four double, two twin and two family bedrooms, all rooms en suite; sitting room and dining room. Central heating. Excellent and varied home cooking served daily. Children welcome at reduced rates. An ideal location for touring. Fishing, walking and climbing in the vicinity. The house, open all year, is suitable for disabled guests. Car not essential but private car park provided. Dinner, Bed and Breakfast from £17 to £19.50 per person. AA QQQQ Selected, RAC Acclaimed.

CRAIGNURE. Pennygate Lodge Guest House, Craignure PA65 6AY (01680812 333/444). ♛ ♛ ♛

COMMENDED. Georgian house in four and a half acres of landscaped garden with magnificent views of Sound of Mull, 500 yards from ferry point. Eight bedrooms, four en suite, all with tea/coffee making facilities. Delicious home cooking. Children welcome. No dogs. Parking; car hire arranged. Bed and Breakfast from £16 to £28; Dinner optional.

CRAIG VILLA GUEST HOUSE

Dalmally, Argyll PA33 1AX Tel: 01838 200255

Craig Villa stands in its own grounds of 1½ acres and was built in 1878 as a substantial farmhouse. Now, extensively modernised and tastefully decorated it presents a relaxed and homely atmosphere. It has a spacious Georgian lounge and the dining room offers outstanding views of idyllic mountain scenery. It is fully centrally heated, all rooms have private facilities and tea-makers and two have four-poster beds for that romantic occasion. An ideal centre from which to explore Argyll's wildlife and its scenic and historic attractions. B&B from £19 per person.

A warm and sincere welcome awaits you from Margaret and Tony Cressey.

♛ ♛ ♛ COMMENDED

DUNOON. Mr and Mrs A. Jones, Rosscairn Hotel, Hunter Street, Kirn, Dunoon PA23 8JR (Tel & Fax: 01369 704344). STB ♛ ♛ ♛ **COMMENDED.** RAC Acclaimed. Superb accommodation and the warmest of welcomes await you at Rosscairn. Our Victorian house hotel is set within mature gardens with ample private parking and is adjacent to Cowal Golf Course. We have seven en suite bedrooms, all non smoking with tea making facilities. After an excellent meal in our spacious non-smoking dining room, relax in one of the two TV/video lounges. There is full central heating for all season comfort. The area has a wealth of natural beauty with opportunities for forest walks, fishing, pony trekking, bowling and golf nearby. Bed and Breakfast from £19; Dinner, Bed and Breakfast from £25 per person. Free colour brochure available.

Terms quoted in this publication may be subject to increase if rises in costs necessitate

DUNOON. Mrs M. Kohls, Ashgrove Guest House, Wyndham Road, Innellan, Dunoon PA23 7SH **(01369 830306; Fax: 01369 830776).** Ashgrove Guest House in the village of Innellan, four miles south of Dunoon, is ideal for a quiet restful holiday. In four acres of grounds Ashgrove has ponies, goats, hens, ducks, geese and other small animals. Guests can enjoy leisurely woodland walks, boat or coach trips, or simply relax in the secluded gardens with outstanding views over the Firth of Clyde. For the more energetic visitors golf, tennis, bowls, fishing, pony trekking are all nearby. The shore is only minutes away. Ashgrove is a family run guesthouse with a friendly, informal atmosphere. All rooms have en suite shower, WC and washbasin, colour TV, tea/coffee making facilities. Dogs and other pets welcome. Open all year. Bed and Breakfast from £17 daily. Reductions for children and Senior Citizens.

ISLE OF COLL. Achmore Guest House, Isle of Coll PA78 6TE (01879 230430). A comfortable guest house where you and your pets will receive a warm welcome, excellent home cooking, vegetarian and special diets no problem! Not only can you hire a boat, bikes and golf clubs but you can even indulge in scuba diving. Open from January to December with cosy well appointed rooms. Please write or telephone for further information.

KINLOCHLEVEN. Elsie Robertson, Edencoille, Garbhien road, Kinlochleven PA40 4SE (01855 **831358).** COMMENDED. A warm welcome and excellent home cooking at our family-run Bed and Breakfast. All rooms centrally heated and have tea/coffee facilities, colour TV and hair dryers. Perfect base for touring, fishing, ski-ing, climbing, walking or relaxing. We are situated opposite the Mamores which are famous for their 12 Munroes which are within five minutes' walk from Edencoille. Bed and Breakfast £15 per person; Evening Dinner £9 per person. Extensive menu.

OBAN. Donra Holiday Properties. , and COMMENDED. Offers the best of both worlds — town and country. Comfortable self catering properties in Oban sleeping two to six persons, or relax at Torlin House with tastefully decorated en suite rooms. Also our properties on the Isle of Luing offer a tranquil and beautiful location for quality relaxation. Wildlife abounds, and there is a richness of Celtic and Norse myths to explore. Ideal for water sports enthusiasts while ensuring a sanctuary of calm for those of a less vigorous temperament. Boat trips and bicycles available. Open all year. Self catering from £150 to £295 per week; Bed and Breakfast from £15 to £22. Reductions for three nights or more. Details from **Mrs S. Russell, Torlin, Glencruitten Road, Oban PA34 4EP (01631 64339).**

OBAN. Mr and Mrs Eccleson, Braeside, Soroba Road, Oban PA34 4SA (01631 563303). Braeside is a small friendly Bed and Breakfast on the outskirts of Oban. It is set in its own grounds with private parking. Accommodation comprises two double rooms, one en suite and one twin-bedded room, all rooms are heated and have tea/coffee facilities and TV. Pets are welcome by arrangement but advise we are a non smoking establishment. Oban is considered to be the Gateway to the Highlands and is a good base for visiting surrounding areas as well as boats sailing to the neighbouring islands.

OBAN. Mr and Mrs I. Donn, Palace Hotel, Oban PA34 5SB (01631 562294). A small family hotel offering personal supervision situated on Oban's main street with a panoramic view over the Bay. The Palace is an ideal base for a real Highland holiday. By boat you can visit the Islands of Kerrera, Coll, Tiree, Lismore, Mull and Iona, and by road Glencoe, Ben Nevis and Inveraray. Please write or telephone for brochure.

Kathmore   A gentle walk from the town centre and all main bus, train and ferry terminals, KATHMORE offers a superb base from which to explore the beautful town of Oban and capture the breathtaking beauty of the West Highalnds. Our rooms, most ensuite, are tastefully furnished and all equipped with colour TV, tea/coffee tray, hairdryer, etc. Spacious private car park. Open all year. Restricted licence. The Mull of Kintyre, Loch Ness, Glencoe, Mull and Iona, and much more all close by. Your hosts, Keith and Morven are on hand to offer their local knowledge so you will never be short of places to go and things to do. Our only rule, Happy Holiday Folks. STB listed Commended. Bed & Breakfast £14-£20, Dinner £9.

Mrs Morvern Wardhaugh, Kathmore, Soroba Road, Oban PA34 4JF. Telephone 01631 562104.

OBAN. Mrs E.M. Giles, The Old Manse, Dalriach Road, Oban PA34 5JE (01631 564886). 🌢🌢🌢 *COMMENDED.* Detached Victorian house in quiet location yet close to town centre and only 10 minutes walk from ferries to Mull, Colonsay, Islay and Tiree. Close to swimming pool, bowling green and tennis courts. Also available in the area are golf, sailing, horse riding and hill walking. Panoramic sea views, pleasant secluded garden and safe parking. Real home cooking, friendly family atmosphere. The accommodation comprises two double and one twin bedrooms all with shower rooms, WC, washbasins, TV and tea making facilities. Central heating. Hairdryer, drying, iron and payphone available. Please send for our brochure.

OBAN. Mrs J. Waugh, Foxholes Hotel, Cologin, Lerags, Oban PA34 4SE (01631 564982). 🌢🌢🌢 *HIGHLY COMMENDED.* Enjoy peace and tranquillity at Foxholes, situated in its own grounds in a quiet glen, three miles from Oban. We have magnificent views of surrounding countryside, all bedrooms en suite, colour TV, tea/coffee making facilities. Enjoy our superb six-course table d'hôte menu and large selection of wines. Send for colour brochure and tariff. Bed and Breakfast from £25. Please write or telephone for further information.

OBAN. Mrs C. MacDonald, Bracker, Polvinister Road, Oban PA34 5TN (01631 564302). ♛♛

COMMENDED. Bracker is a modern bungalow built in 1975 and extended recently to cater for visitors. We have three guest rooms — two double and one twin-bedded, all en suite with TV and tea/coffee making facilities. Small TV lounge and dining room. Private parking. The house is situated in a beautiful quiet residential area of Oban and is within walking distance of the town (approximately eight to 10 minutes) and the golf course. Friendly hospitality and comfortable accommodation. Bed and Breakfast £16 to £18. Non-smoking.

OBAN. John and Maureen Simons (MHCIMA), Braeside Guest House, Kilmore, Near Oban PA34 4QR (01631 770243). STB ♛♛♛ COMMENDED. Beauti-

Braeside

fully set overlooking Loch Feochan, superb views of local hills. Three miles south of Oban on the A816 this family-run guest house provides excellent home-cooked foods and fine wines in comfortable surroundings. Ideal base for touring, walking, trips to the Isles, etc. Non-smoking. All rooms on ground floor and tastefully decorated. Private parking. Satellite TV. Extended stay, early and late season reductions. Please write or telephone for further information.

OBAN. Mr and Mrs E. Hughes, "Sgeir-Mhaol" Guest House, Soroba Road, Oban PA34 4JF (01631 562650). Family-run guest house situated only an approxi-

mate five minutes' walk from town centre, bus/rail stations, main ferry terminal for sailings to the islands of Mull, Iona, Staffa, Coll, Tiree and Colonsay. Bedrooms comprise double, twin and family, all colour co-ordinated and furnished to a high standard with colour TV, tea/coffee makers, etc and most with en-suite facilities. The lounge and diningroom overlook a pleasant garden and, like the bedrooms, are on the ground floor. There is a spacious private car park within the grounds. Open all year. The area has a wealth of natural beauty with opportunities for walks, golf, fishing, sailing, pony trekking and a sports complex where swimming, tennis, squash and bowling are available. Oban is an excellent base for day trips by coach or car to many places including Campbeltown, Fort William, Glencoe, etc., or for a day's sailing to the Islands. Dinner, Bed and Breakfast from £23; Bed and Breakfast from £15.

OBAN. Tony and Carol Ridley, Briarbank, Glencruitten Road, Oban PA34 4DN (01631 566549). ♛♛♛ COMMENDED. AA QQQ, RAC Acclaimed. Peace,

privacy, good food, friendly service, bright comfortable rooms with views to the Soroba hills. All of these are provided at Briarbank. A traditional, detached Highland house set in landscaped gardens where guests may wander at will. Country and hill walks are freely accessible yet Oban town centre and ferries are just five minutes' walk away. Start your day with a substantial Scottish or Continental breakfast, then perhaps choose dinner from our comprehensive menu. Just three double rooms with en suite facilities, two with four-poster beds, ensure that our guests enjoy the personal attention that helps to make a holiday. Brochure on request.

TAYNUILT. Mrs M. McLellan, "Manish", Brochroy, Taynuilt PA35 1JQ (01866 822572).

Detached villa situated close to Loch Etive amidst superb mountain and loch scenery. Taynuilt is a friendly village with numerous points of interest and two hotels. Excellent loch and sea fishing; sea cruises, woodland, mountain and coastal walks can all be enjoyed in the area. Well located for Oban and ferries to Inner and Outer Hebrides. Sealife Centre 20 minutes' drive away. Ceilidhs held weekly in village hall. Twin room with separate bathroom; Double room with en suite; Family room with en suite. Bed and Breakfast £16. Children half price. TV and tea/coffee facilities.

ALANDON
Taynuilt, Argyll PA35 1JH
Tel. 01866 822280 Mrs Anne P. Kennedy

Bed and Breakfast accommodation offered in one double bedroom, one twin-bedded ensuite room and one family ensuite room. Lovely golf course in village 100 yards from 'Alandon'. Cruise on Loch Etive. Plenty of eating places in the area. Only 12 miles from Oban, handy stop if sailing to islands. Children and pets welcome. Bed and Breakfast from £13 to £17 per person per night. Non-smoking accommodation if required. Fishing boats for hire, early breakfasts available. Directions: off A85 at Taynuilt village, drive half a mile approximately, house well signed.

Other specialised

FHG PUBLICATIONS

* Recommended SHORT BREAK HOLIDAYS IN BRITAIN £4.25

* Recommended COUNTRY HOTELS OF BRITAIN £4.25

* PETS WELCOME! £4.50

* BED AND BREAKFAST IN BRITAIN £3.50

Published annually. Please add 50p postage (U.K. only)
when ordering from the publishers:

FHG PUBLICATIONS LTD
Abbey Mill Business Centre, Seedhill,
Paisley, Renfrewshire PA1 1TJ

AYRSHIRE

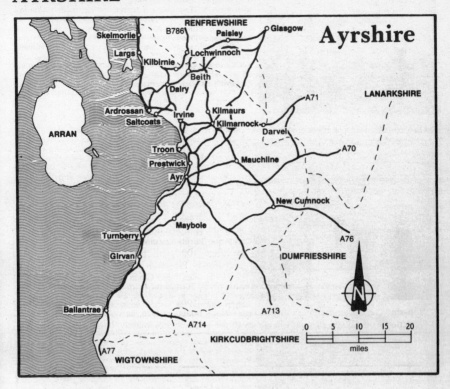

AYR. **Peter and Julia Clark, Eglinton Guest House, 23 Eglinton Terrace, Ayr KA7 1JJ (01292 264623).** 👑 👑 *COMMENDED.* Situated within a part of Ayr steeped in history, within a few minutes' walk of the beach, town centre and many other amenities and entertainment for which Ayr is popular. There are sea and fishing trips available from Ayr Harbour, or a cruise "Doon the Water" on the "Waverley"; golf, swimming pool, cycling, tennis, sailing, windsurfing, walking etc all available nearby; Prestwick Airport only three miles away. We have family, double and single rooms, all with washbasins, colour TV and tea/coffee making facilities. En suite facilities and cots available on request. We are open all year round. Please send for our brochure for further information.

BEITH. **Mrs Jane Gillan, Shotts Farm, Beith KA15 1LB (01505 502273). STB Listed** *COMMENDED.* Comfortable friendly accommodation is offered on this 160 acre dairy farm situated one and a half miles from the A736 Glasgow to Irvine road; well placed to visit golf courses, country parks, leisure centre or local pottery, also ideal for the ferry to Arran or Millport and for many good shopping centres all around. A high standard of cleanliness is assured by Mrs Gillan who is a first class cook holding many awards, food being served in the diningroom with its beautiful picture windows. Three comfortable bedrooms (double, family and twin), all with tea-making facilities, central heating and electric blankets. Two bathrooms with shower; sittingroom with colour TV. Children welcome. Bed and Breakfast from £11. Dinner can be arranged. AA QQ.

DARVEL. Mrs J. Seton, Auchenbart Farm, Darvel, Near Priestland KA17 0LS (01560 320392). 🐚

COMMENDED. **Working farm.** Auchenbart Farmhouse is situated in an elevated position overlooking the Irvine Valley. A pleasant house offering comfortable and quiet accommodation of a high standard. One family and one double (cot available) rooms, both with washbasins, tea/coffee making facilities and electric blankets. Bathroom with shower. Guests' sittingroom with colour TV. Heating throughout. Access to Auchenbart is at the east end of Darvel, one mile off the A71 to Edinburgh. We are central for Kilmarnock, Prestwick and Glasgow. Reductions for children. Car essential. Pets welcome. Open Easter till end of October. Bed and Breakfast from £16 per person per night.

GALSTON. Mrs Bone, Auchencloigh Farm, Galston KA4 3NP (01563 820567). STB COMMENDED.

AA QQQ Recommended, Welcome Host. Auchencloigh is situated in the heart of Ayrshire countryside. The tranquil setting of this 18th century spacious farmhouse, set in mature gardens, offers guests old and new a warm and relaxing atmosphere after a day spent visiting the many attractions in Ayrshire. The accommodation consists of two twin rooms and one double room, each with central heating, TV, radio, tea/coffee making facilities. This house has been lived in by the same farming family for five generations. We are an ideal centre for touring the south west, or a round or two of golf on our superb local courses. Open January to December. Brochure available.

KILMARNOCK. Mrs Agnes Hawkshaw, Aulton Farm, Kilmaurs, Kilmarnock KA3 2PQ (01563 538208). Tourist Board Listed COMMENDED. AA QQQ.

Aulton Farmhouse is 200 years old and built of yellow sandstone. It is situated in the open countryside and has been totally refurbished inside with new decor throughout. Relax in our cosy lounge with colour TV; tea/coffee making facilities in each room. Guests are assured of a good Scottish breakfast and tea on arrival. Located only 10 minutes from Prestwick Airport and 25 minutes from Glasgow; ideal for the West Coast of Scotland and a gateway to the Highlands; Royal Troon Golf Course only 10 minutes away. Bed and Breakfast from £14 per person. Children half price.

KILMARNOCK. Mrs Mary Howie, Hill House Farm, Grassyards Road, Kilmarnock KA3 6HG (01563 523370). 🐚 🐚 🐚 🐚 COMMENDED. Working dairy farm, in

beautiful open countryside, offering warm welcome and home cooking. Two miles east of Kilmarnock and one mile from A77 with easy access to Glasgow, Ayrshire coast, Arran and Burns' country. Sport and Leisure with skating, swimming pools, theatre etc. within easy reach. Three large comfortable bedrooms (one ensuite) with washbasins and tea/coffee facilities; bathroom and toilet; lounge, diningroom. Central heating. Excellent walking country and ideal base for touring and for golf. Bed and Breakfast from £15 (including light supper). Self-catering cottages available. Brochure on request.

KILMARNOCK near. Mr and Mrs P. Gibson, Busbiehill Guest House, Knockentiber, Near Kilmarnock KA2 0DJ (01563 532985). This homely country guest house is situated in the heart of Burns' Country and also handy for touring Loch Lomond, the Trossachs, Edinburgh and the Clyde coast. Golf course nearby. Two single rooms; four family suites; two double rooms with bathroom; tea making facilities. Sittingroom, two dining rooms. Children welcome; cot, high chair and swing available. Car essential; parking space. Sorry, no pets. Open all year. Bed and Breakfast from £11 to £12 per night. Evening Meal available at £4. Fully licensed. 10% discount for Senior Citizens.

KILMARNOCK. Mrs M.S. Love, Muirhouse Farm, Gatehead, Kilmarnock KA2 0BT (01563 523975). 🐚 🐚 COMMENDED. Muirhouse is situated approximately two miles south west of Kilmarnock, adjacent to Gatehead village which is on the A759 Kilmarnock to Troon road. It is a family-run 170 acre dairy/arable farm. Easy access to Ayrshire coast, Burns Country, Culzean Castle and Glasgow (Burrell Collection). Ample facilities available for all outdoor sports, plus two modern indoor sports complexes nearby. Traditional stone-built comfortable farmhouse with central heating. One family room en suite, one double room en suite and one twin-bedded room with private bathroom; all have tea-making facilities and radio alarms. Sitting room with TV; dining room. Children welcome, cot available. Car essential. Bed and Breakfast from £15 to £18. Reductions for children and for weekly bookings. SAE, please, for further details.

KILMARNOCK. Mrs Anna Steel, Laigh Langmuir Farm, Kilmaurs, Kilmarnock KA3 2NU (01563

538270). 🐝🐝 *COMMENDED.* Laigh Langmuir is an attractive stone-built farmhouse in lovely surroundings just outside Kilmaurs village. Easily accessible from Glasgow and the South. Perfect stop-over for the Highlands, or stay and golf at Troon or visit the island of Arran, Loch Lomond or South West Scotland. Relax in the evening by a log fire and in the morning enjoy a real farmhouse breakfast made from our own produce, home baking and preserves. All bedrooms have central heating, washbasins, electric blankets, hair dryers and tea-making facilities; one room with en-suite facilities. Children very welcome. Cot, high chair and baby-sitting available. Bed and Breakfast from £14. A Scottish Farmhouse of the Year Award Winner. Telephone or write for further details.

LARGS. Mrs M. Watson, South Whittlieburn Farm, Brisbane Glen, Largs KA30 8SN (01475

675881). 🐝🐝 *HIGHLY COMMENDED.* **Working farm.** AA QQQQ Selected, RAC Listed, chosen by "Which?" Best Bed and Breakfast, Welcome Host. Why not try our superb farmhouse accommodation? With lovely peaceful panoramic views, we are two miles north east of the popular tourist resort of Largs, which is only five minutes' drive away. Also near the ferries for the Islands of Arran, Bute, Cumbrae and Dunoon. Enjoy day trips to Loch Lomond, Inveraray or Culzean Castle; 45 minutes from Glasgow or Ayr. Golf, horse riding, fishing, sailing, diving, shooting, hill walking nearby. All rooms have TV, washbasins, tea/coffee facilities, central heating, hair dryers, radio alarms, toiletries etc; en suite available. TV lounge. Payphone. Large car park. No smoking in bedrooms or dining room. Packed lunches and vegetarian meals can be provided. Bed and Breakfast from £16.50.
Reduced rates for children under 11 years. Open all year. Certified caravan and camping site on farm with electric hook-ups, toilet, shower, hot and cold washbasins etc. From £5 per night. Enormous delicious breakfasts and warm friendly hospitality from Mary Watson. Highly recommended!

LARGS. Mr and Mrs Capocchi, Ardmore, 16 Aubery Crescent, Largs KA30 8PR (01475 672516).

Ardmore is situated in a Victorian terrace on the seafront with stunning views across to the Islands of Cumbrae, Bute and Arran. We are in a peaceful and select part of Largs within walking distance of the shopping centre, the pier, the Vikingar Museum with its theatre and swimming complex. You may also enjoy golf, bowling, fishing or sailing the Clyde on one of the many steamers. Tastefully decorated bedrooms with tea/coffee making facilities, comfortable TV lounge and dining room. Private car parking. Indeed Ardmore is your ideal base to explore this beautiful part of the West of Scotland. Open April to mid-October. Bed and Breakfast £16.

MAUCHLINE. Mrs J. Clark, Auchenlongford, Sorn, Machuline KA5 6JF (01290 550761). The farm is situated in the hills above the picturesque village of Sorn, with its Castle set on a promontory above the River Ayr, and nearby its 17th century church. It is only 19 miles east from the A74 and 20 miles inland from the town of Ayr. Accommodation can be from a choice of three attractive, furnished bedrooms and there is also a large well appointed residents' lounge. Full Scottish breakfast is served with home made jams and marmalade; traditional High Tea and/or Dinners are also available on request. Bed and Breakfast £15; Bed, Breakfast and Evening Meal £25. Brochure available.

MUIRKIRK. Mr and Mrs P. Pape, West Glenbuck Farm, Glenbuck, Muirkirk KA18 3SB (01290

661285). Non working farmhouse set in a beautiful Ayrshire glen overlooking a brown trout loch. Great area for bird watching, hill walking, fishing, falconry and golf. We are situated on the A70 between Douglas and Muirkirk, within easy reach of Ayr, Glasgow and Edinburgh. Our accommodation consists of one twin, one double and one family room plus cot, bathroom and shower; guests' lounge with TV, tea/coffee facilities. All bedrooms are centrally heated. We also run Falconry Courses from our premises with our own Hawks and Falcons, or you can bring your own birds and enjoy a few days Hawking. Dog kennels available. Bed and Breakfast £15 per night; Bed, Breakfast and Evening Meal £20. Falconry Course prices on application.

BERWICKSHIRE

DUNS. Mrs W.M. Kenworthy, St. Albans, Clouds, Duns TD11 3BB (01361 883285 — free call

diversion may be in operation). ✿ ✿ *HIGHLY COMMEN-DED.* Recommended in "Staying Off The Beaten Track". Pleasant Georgian house with secluded south-facing garden. Magnificent views over small country town to Cheviot Hills. Excellent centre for touring. Very quiet location but only three minutes from town centre. Open all year. Colour TV, tea/coffee making facilities, towelling bath robes and hot water bottles in all bedrooms. Private bathroom available. Excellent varied breakfast served in gracious surroundings. Bed and Breakfast from £16. Credit cards accepted. Directions:- Clouds is a lane running parallel to and to the North of Newtown Street where the police station and county offices are situated.

DUNS. Mrs G.E. Burrough, Harelawside Farm, Grants House, Duns TD11 3RP (01361 850380).

Working farm. A 550 acre family farm situated in the picturesque Lammermuir foothills very close to St. Abb's Head Nature Reserve and the East Coast fishing villages — ideal for a Borders holiday. The farmhouse has an outstanding view of the wooded Eyewater Valley. It has electric central heating for chilly evenings. Traditional farmhouse cooking. Children welcome. Regretfully we cannot take dogs in the house and would appreciate no smoking. Open all year. Bed and Breakfast from £15 to £19 per person per night. Evening meals available in the village. Brochure available.

DUMFRIESSHIRE

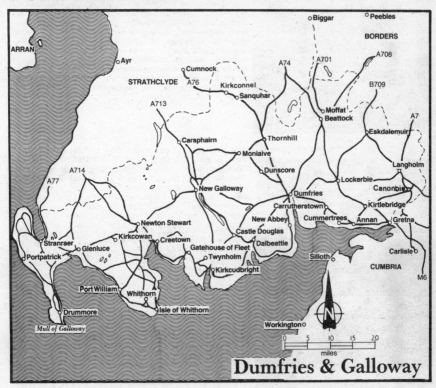

Dumfries & Galloway

CANONBIE. Mrs Steele, North Lodge, Canonbie DG14 0TA (013873 71409). A warm welcome awaits you at this small family-run guest house situated approximately one mile south of the village of Canonbie, on the tourist route A7 to Edinburgh. Canonbie village is renowned for its fishing — private fishing on the "Willow Pool" can be arranged. NORTH LODGE is a 19th century cottage set in beautiful gardens and was recently extended to include five double/twin bedrooms, four en suite, the other has private facilities. The ground floor en suite room is suitable for the disabled traveller (Grade 1 classification). Within easy reach of Hadrian's Wall, the Lake District, Carlisle, Dumfries, Moffat, Keilder Dam, Hawick, Gretna and many more interesting places. An ideal touring base. Breaks available. Please telephone for further details.

LOCKERBIE. Bob and Majorie Rae, Nether Boreland Farm, Boreland, Lockerbie DG11 2LL (Tel & Fax: 01576 610248). 🐾 🐾 *HIGHLY COMMENDED.* Farmhouse situated seven miles from M74 at Lockerbie. Sample Scottish hospitality, peaceful friendly surroundings and hearty breakfasts with our own free-range eggs and home-made preserves. The spacious, comfortable farmhouse has one double and one twin en suite bedrooms and one double with private bathroom; all have TV, tea/coffee trays, hair dryers and clock radios. Enjoy our many golf courses, local fishing, pony trekking or leisurely sightseeing. Open April to October. Bed and Breakfast from £19 to £21. Please telephone or fax for more details.

FREE and REDUCED RATE Holiday Visits!
See our READERS' OFFER VOUCHER for details!

LOCKERBIE. Mrs Marion Cornthwaite, Balgray Home Farm, Lockerbie DG11 2JT (01576 610244; 0378 551959 mobile).

A large working hill farm off the beaten track yet only three miles from Lockerbie and the M74. Central heating, own sitting/dining room with TV and games, etc. Tea/coffee making facilities, towels, hairdryers and other extras. Access at all times. Large garden for relaxation or ball games. See the farm, enjoy walks, there's plenty to see and do in the area. A substantial breakfast, evening meals by arrangement; all home made, though plenty of good eating places locally. Reductions for children under 12 years. Well behaved pets welcome. Bed and Breakfast from £14; Dinner if requested. A warm welcome awaits you!

LOCKERBIE. Mrs Cecilia Hislop, Carik Cottage, Waterbeck, Lockerbie DG11 3EU (01461 600652).

Tourist Board Listed HIGHLY COMMENDED. Bed and Breakfast accommodation set in peaceful village of Waterbeck with beautiful views where you can see our Belted Galloways. Twin or double tastefully decorated rooms, some with en suite, all with tea/coffee making facilities, central heating, visitors' lounge. Ideal for touring south west Scotland and Cumbria or an overnight stop between North and South. 10 miles north of Gretna, seven miles south of Lockerbie, situated three miles from A74(M), exit Junction 20 onto B722 east, turning left at Post Office in Eaglesfield. We are first cottage in Waterbeck Village. Bed and Breakfast from £15; Dinner (booked in advance) £7. Three night Dinner, Bed and Breakfast £65.

MOFFAT. Mr Terence Hull, Alton House, Moffat DG10 9LB (01683 220903; mobile 0850 129105).

Alton is an historic country house situated in several acres of secluded grounds at the end of a long private lane. The property is a former home of Chiefs of the Clan Moffat and is of considerable historic and architectural interest. The present property dates from circa 1650 and has evolved over several centuries. It contains many period features including elegant public rooms, marble fireplaces, fine plasterwork and woodwork with period furnishings throughout and has wonderful views. All bedrooms have washbasins, TV, tea making facilities and welcome tray; en suite available. There is full central heating. Bed and Breakfast from £15.

MOFFAT. Mr and Mrs W. Gray, Barnhill Springs Country Guest House, Moffat DG10 9QS (01683 220580). 🐾🐾 *COMMENDED.* AA Listed. Barnhill Springs is an early Victorian country mansion standing in its own grounds overlooking Upper Annandale. Situated half-a-mile from the A74, the house and its surroundings retain an air of remote peacefulness. Internally it has been decorated and furnished to an exceptionally high standard of comfort. Open fire in lounge. Accommodation includes family, double, twin and single rooms, some en suite. Children welcome. Pets welcome free of charge. Open all year. Bed and Breakfast from £18.50; Evening Meal (optional) from £12.50.

MOFFAT. Mr Gary Hall, The Lodge, Sidmount Avenue, Moffat DG10 9BS (01683 20440). The Lodge is a late Victorian stone house situated in a quiet cul-de-sac, about a quarter of a mile from the centre of Moffat. Surrounded by superb lawned gardens with fine mature trees, there is a splendid view spanning the valley. Ample parking space. Selection of twin, single and double bedrooms and a family suite with two rooms. Children welcome, cot and high chair available. Tea making facilities and colour TV in all bedrooms. Comfortable lounge; large diningroom. Two bathrooms, one with shower. Central heating in all rooms. Spacious garden which is perfect for ball games and croquet. Open all year. Local attractions include golf, putting, boating, fishing, riding, tennis, bowls. Numerous castles, abbeys, forests and hills within easy reach. Bed and Breakfast from £14. Reduced rates for children.

MOFFAT. Mrs Jean McKenzie, "Hidden Corner", Beattock Road, Moffat DG10 9SE (01683 220243). Hidden Corner stands in an acre of ground only half a mile from the A74 and half a mile from Moffat. An ideal base for exploring the Borders and South West Scotland; Edinburgh, Glasgow, The East and West Coasts are within one hour's drive. Accommodation comprises two double and one twin-bedded rooms, all with washbasins, shaver points; bath/shower room; lounge with TV; dining room. Open all year. Ample parking. Bed and Breakfast £14 to £18. Also self-catering caravan available.

MOFFAT. Mr and Mrs A. Armstrong, Boleskine, 4 Well Road, Moffat DG10 9AS (01683 220601). 🐾 🐾 *HIGHLY COMMENDED.* A fine Victorian town house in a quiet street offering comfortable accommodation only two minutes' walk from town centre. All rooms are centrally heated, have washbasins, colour TV, tea/coffee making facilities, electric blankets and hair dryer. En suite rooms available, including twin room on ground floor. Private parking. Ideal stopover, or base for walking or touring. Open all year. Bed and Breakfast from £15. No single supplement. AA QQQ. Directions: from High Street turn into Well Street beside Spar grocery, at end of Well Street turn right into Well Road. Also self-catering cottage available.

MOFFAT. Burnock Water, Haywood Road, Moffat DG10 9BU (01683 221329). 🐾 🐾 *COMMENDED.*

David & Sheila Barclay offer a warm welcome to Burnock Water, a comfortable Victorian family house set in large secluded garden where you can relax and unwind in peaceful surroundings overlooking the Moffat hills. Approximately half a mile from town centre. There are three double/twin, two family bedrooms, three en suite. Children welcome, cot available. Pets welcome. Ample parking. Ideal base for touring. Glasgow/Edinburgh one hour's drive. Bed and Breakfast from £17 single, £15 per person double/twin. Evening Meal available. Open January to December.

SANQUHAR. Neil and Anne Miller, Drumbringan Guest House, 53 Castle Street, Sanquhar DG4 6AB (01659 50409). Drumbringan has a comfortable

residents lounge. Home cooking is served and our table licence allows you to enjoy alcoholic refreshments with your meal. Rooms have tea/coffee facilities, washbasin and TV; some rooms en suite. Drumlanrig Castle and Wanlockhead Mining Museum are both nearby. There are many interesting places within easy driving distance including Culzean Castle and Threave Gardens. A pick up service can be arranged for Southern Upland Way walkers. Salmon and sea trout fishing on the River Nith — tickets arranged; golf available locally. Bed and Breakfast from £14.50, weekly from £95; Dinner, Bed and Breakfast from £21.50, weekly from £140. Brochure available.

THORNHILL. Mrs Hill, Drumcruilton, Thornhill DG3 5BG (01848 500210). 🐾 🐾 *HIGHLY COMMENDED.* **Working farm.** A fine country farmhouse on a working

stock farm in an outstanding scenic location within easy reach of Glasgow and Edinburgh. The area abounds with places to visit. Fishing, shooting, walking and golf locally. A welcome comfortable stay is assured with excellent local food. Three double/twin rooms; one en suite, two private facilities. Bed and Breakfast £21 single, £19 to £21 per person double/twin. Evening Meal available. Brochure available on request.

DUMFRIES AND GALLOWAY REGION – BURNS' COUNTRY.

A fair sprinkling of castles, the Solway Firth coast and, of course, Burns' Country makes this region an interesting tourist destination. Other attractions include the Grey Mare's Tail, Galloway Forest Park, Caerlaverock and Clatteringshaws deer museum.

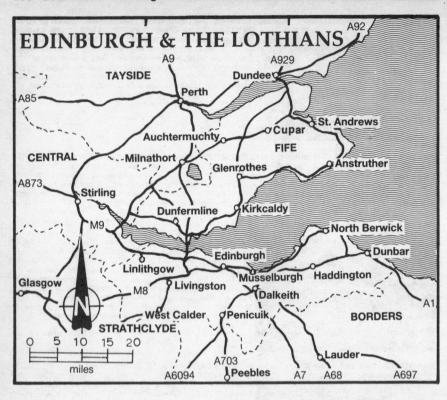

EDINBURGH & THE LOTHIANS

BATHGATE near. Mrs F. Gibb, Tarrareoch Farm, Station Road, Armadale, Near Bathgate EH48 3BJ (01501 730404). This 17th century farmhouse is situated two miles from M8 Junction 4, which is midway between Glasgow and Edinburgh. This peaceful location overlooks panoramic views of the countryside. All rooms are on the ground floor, ideal for disabled visitors, and have central heating, colour TV and tea/coffee making facilities. We are within easy reach of golf, fishing, cycling (15 mile cycle track runs along back of property). Ample security parking. Open January to December.

EAST CALDER (near Edinburgh). Mrs Jan Dick, Overshiel Farm, East Calder EH53 0HT (01506

880469; Fax: 01506 883006). ♥♥ *COMMENDED.* Working farm in a peaceful country setting yet only six miles west of Edinburgh. Easy access into city centre by car, bus or train (station one and a quarter miles). Comfortable rooms (one double, one twin, one family) look onto a large attractive garden. All have colour TV, washbasins, tea/coffee making facilities and two are en suite. Ample private parking. Sorry no smoking. Excellent local pubs and restaurants. Bed and Breakfast from £16.

EDINBURGH. Angus Beag Guest House, 5 Windsor Street, Edinburgh EH7 5LA (0131-556 1905). City centre Georgian guest house close to all amenities. 10 minutes Princes Street, adjacent Playhouse Theatre, bus and railway stations. All rooms have washbasins, shower, TV, tea/coffee facilities; one en suite. Delicious full Scottish breakfast available. Terms from £19 per person per night.

EDINBURGH. Norah Alexander, Tiree Guest House, 26 Craigmillar Park, Edinburgh EH16 5PS (0131-667 7477; Fax: 0131-662 1608). STB Listed COMMENDED. AA QQ. Terraced Victorian villa situated on main bus route to city centre, 10 minutes from historic High Street and Princes Street. All rooms have tea/coffee making and colour TV. Private parking. Full Scottish breakfast.

EDINBURGH. Villa San Monique, 4 Wilton Road, Edinburgh EH16 5NY (0131-667 1403; Fax: 0131-662 1608). Lovely Victorian villa situated in a quiet residential area, one and a half miles south of the city centre, just off the main bus route into town. The bedrooms are generally large and well equipped. We have basic accommodation as well as en suite. Private parking. Open April to October.

EDINBURGH. Vickie Allan, Conference Office, Heriot Watt University, Riccarton, Edinburgh EH14 4AS (0131-451 3115). Year round accommodation. The en suite year round bedrooms are mainly for conference delegates but there is often availability, especially at weekends. Student accommodation is available during vacations although advance booking is recommended during the Edinburgh Festival. The University is well sited just off the City Bypass. The bypass links with the M8, M9 and A1 giving convenient access from all directions. There is ample free car parking on site. The campus enjoys a beautiful rural location just six miles from the City Centre. On site facilities include a bank, general store, bookshop, sportscentre, hairdressing salon and medical centre.

EDINBURGH. Alan and Angela Vidler, Rowan House, 13 Glenorchy Terrace, Edinburgh EH9 2DQ (0131-667 2463). ✿ COMMENDED. Quietly located in one of Edinburgh's loveliest areas, Rowan House is an elegant Victorian home tastefully and comfortably furnished. Some rooms en-suite. Complimentary tea/coffee and biscuits available. Children welcome at reduced rates. Leave your car here and travel into town by bus, good service into the centre only 10 minutes away. Conveniently located for roads A701, A772, A7 main roads from the south (turn left at Brights Crescent, off Mayfield Gardens). You will receive a warm welcome and attentive service. Bed and Breakfast from £19 per person. Breakfast choice includes porridge and freshly baked scones.

LOTHIAN REGION – THE CAPITAL ATTRACTION.

Although your first stop will probably be Edinburgh – and with every justification – you should endeavour to get out of town and visit the likes of South Queensferry, the Bass Rock, Haddington and Preston Mill.

EDINBURGH. Mrs Maureen Sandilands, Sandilands House, 25 Queensferry Road, Edinburgh EH4 3HB (Tel & Fax: 0131-332 2057). 👑 👑 👑 *COMMENDED.*

Sandilands House is ideally located five minutes from Edinburgh's city centre by bus with its own guests' private parking. A distinctive and attractive detached bungalow in its own gardens with excellent bus service to the city centre or a short walk to the city's West End; also near to Murrayfield Stadium. Enjoy the friendly welome and relax in the well furnished and tastefully decorated accommodation with en suite facilities. All rooms are equipped with central heating, colour TV, hair dryer, tea/coffee making facilities, etc. Full Scottish breakfast is included. Family rooms available and discounts of 50% apply for children under 12 years sharing with adults. Open all season. Terms from £38 to £58 for en suite double/twin room or from £30 to £40 for single occupancy.

EDINBURGH. Mr and Mrs John and Rita Veitch, Dunstane House Hotel, 4 West Coates, Edinburgh EH12 5JQ (0131-337 6169). 👑 👑 *COMMENDED.*

A beautiful detached mansion of historic and architectural interest, set in delightful gardens. Handy for town centre, good bus service, railway station, golf courses and 15 minutes by car to airport, five minutes to Princes Street. A friendly welcome awaits you at this private, family-run hotel, open all year. Rooms are comfortable and spacious and are either fully en suite or with private shower and washbasin, each having tea/coffee making facilities, shaver/hairdryer points, radio and colour TV. Family and single rooms available. Licensed residents' bar. Private, secluded car park. Bed and Breakfast from £25 to £36 per person. AA QQ.

EDINBURGH. The Ivy Guest House, 7 Mayfield Gardens, Edinburgh EH9 2AX (0131-667 3411). STB 👑 👑 *COMMENDED.*

AA QQQ Recommended, RAC Acclaimed. Bed and Breakfast in a comfortable Victorian villa. Open all year round. Private car park. Close to city centre and all its cultural attractions with excellent public transport and taxi services available on the door step. Many local sports facilities (booking assistance available). All rooms have central heating, washbasins, colour TV and tea/coffee making facilities. Choice of en suite or standard rooms, all power showers. Public phone. Large selection of eating establishments nearby. A substantial Scottish breakfast and warm welcome is assured, courtesy of Don and Dolly Green. Terms from £17 per person per night.

EDINBURGH. Mrs Rhoda Mitchell, Hopetoun Guest House, 15 Mayfield Road, Edinburgh EH9 2NG (0131-667 7691). 👑 *COMMENDED.* AA QQ. "Which?" Good Bed and Breakfast Guide. COMPLETELY NON-SMOKING.

Hopetoun is a small, friendly, family-run guest house situated close to Edinburgh University, one and a half miles south of Princes Street, and with an excellent bus service to the city centre. Very comfortable accommodation is offered in a completely smoke-free environment. Having only three guest bedrooms, and now offering private facilities, the owner prides herself in ensuring a friendly, informal atmosphere. All rooms have central heating, washbasins, colour TV and tea/coffee making facilities. Parking is also available. Bed and Breakfast from £17 to £30.

EDINBURGH. Mrs Marie C. Murray, Arlington Guest House, 23 Minto Street, Edinburgh EH9 1RQ (0131-667 3967; Fax: 0131-662 9605). Modernised Georgian villa, conveniently situated on the A7, with most bedrooms to the rear of the house. There are 10 very comfortable rooms — single, family and double/twin, all with colour TV and tea/coffee making facilities. Many rooms are en-suite, some have shower only. Private parking. Children welcome, reduced rates. Pets accepted. Bed and Breakfast from £17.

EDINBURGH. Mrs Catherine Kelly, Highland Park Guest House, 16 Kilmaurs Terrace, Edinburgh

EH16 5DR (0131-667 9204). *COMMENDED.* Friendly family run Guest House situated in quiet area off Dalkeith Road (A68/A7). Unrestricted street parking. Close to Royal Commonwealth Swimming Pool, Cameron Toll Shopping Centre, Holyrood Park and local golf course with shops and launderette easily accessible. Excellent bus service to city centre (one and a half miles). Accommodation comprises two family, two twin and two single bedrooms, all with wash-basin, tea/coffee making facilities and colour TV, central heating. Open all year except Christmas. Terms for Bed and Breakfast from £15 to £21. Reductions for children sharing with two adults.

EDINBURGH. Mardale Guest House, 11 Hartington Place, Edinburgh EH10 4LF (0131-229 2693).

COMMENDED. Elegant Victorian villa situated in central but quiet residential cul-de-sac. Theatres, restaurants and city centre are all within easy reach whether by foot or by use of the excellent bus service. The extremely comfortable bedrooms are individually decorated with care and flair and have washbasins, TV, tea/coffee facilities, hair dryer and telephone, some en suite available. Choice of breakfast is served at individual tables in the cosy lounge/dining room. Visitors' comments include "A cosy, friendly amd most beautiful home", "Excellent 10/10". AA QQQ Recommended.

EDINBURGH. Mrs H. Donaldson, "Invermark", 60 Polwarth Terrace, Edinburgh EH11 1NJ (0131-

337 1066). *COMMENDED.* "Invermark" is a Georgian semi-detached villa situated in quiet surburbs on the main bus route into the city and only five minutes by car. Edinburgh bypass — Lothianburn Junction — two miles — left Balcarres Street, right Myreside Road — Grays Loan — right into Polwarth Terrace. Edinburgh is one of Europe's most splendid cities, famous for its dramatic beauty, historic interest, extensive shopping and dining facilities. There is a park to the rear of the house. Accommodation consists of one single, one twin and one family rooms (with tea/coffee making facilities); TV lounge/diningroom; toilet; bathroom/shower. Non-smoking accommodation available. Friendly atmosphere. Children and dogs welcome. Bed and Breakfast from £17. Reductions for children.

EDINBURGH. Classic Guest House, 50 Mayfield Road, Edinburgh EH9 2NH (0131-667 5847; Fax: 0131-662 1016). *HIGHLY COMMENDED.* Good value Bed and Breakfast accommodation is offered at this friendly, well-run guest house. All bedrooms are tastefully decorated and thoughtfully equipped and have shower en suite, hair dryer, garment press, TV and welcome tray. Conveniently located for bypass and city centre, so come and explore this historic city. Breakfast is served at individual tables in the large dining room. The Classic proudly displays a collection of certificates such as "Welcome Host", Customers Come First, Guest Courtesy and Health and Hygiene. TOTALLY NON-SMOKING. AA Selected. Bed and Breakfast from £18 to £28. Brochure.

Don't miss the SPECIAL ENTRY OFFERS for visits to the
Edinburgh Crystal Visitors Centre **near Penicuik and**
Myreton Motor Museum **at Aberlady.**
See your READERS' OFFER VOUCHER for details.

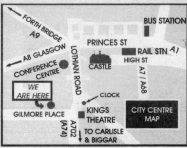

EDINBURGH (14 miles). Mrs Janet Burke, Patieshill Farm, Carlops, Penicuik EH26 9ND (01968

660551). ꝡ ꝡ COMMENDED. This is a working hill sheep and cattle farm set in the midst of the Pentland Hills with panoramic views of the surrounding countryside yet only 20 minutes' drive from the city of Edinburgh. It is situated near the main A702 Edinburgh — Carlisle road close to the village of Carlops. Accommodation, all in separate guest wing, consists of two double and one twin-bedded rooms, all with full en suite facilities. Each room has tea/coffee making facilities, central heating and TV. This is an ideal base for many activities including fishing, golf, ski-ing, hill walking and pony trekking. A very warm and friendly welcome is extended to all guests. Bed and Breakfast from £18 with reductions for children.

INVERESK. 16 Carberry Road, Inveresk, Musselburgh EH21 7TN (0131-665 2107). A lovely Victorian

stone detached house situated in a quiet conservation village seven miles east of Edinburgh, overlooking fields and close to a lovely river walk and seaside with harbour. Buses from door to city, very close to sports centre with swimming pool and within easy distance of many golf courses. Spacious accommodation comprises one family room and two double rooms, all have central heating, colour TV and tea/coffee making facilities. Two large, fully equipped bathrooms adjacent. Parking in quiet side road or in garden if required by arrangement. Full cooked breakfast included from £18 per person per night; reduction for children.

LINLITHGOW. Mr and Mrs R. Inglis, Thornton, Edinburgh Road, Linlithgow EH49 6AA (01506

844216). STB ꝡ ꝡ HIGHLY COMMENDED. Comfortable family-run Victorian house with original features retained. Centrally situated in a peaceful location near the Union Canal in historic Linlithgow, only five minutes' walk from town centre, Linlithgow Palace and railway station. This is a real home-from-home offering quality accommodation and friendly personal attention in a relaxing atmosphere. One double and one twin room, both en suite and furnished to high standards with colour TV etc. Ample off-street parking and large garden. Excellent base for visiting Edinburgh, Stirling, Glasgow and Central Scotland; Edinburgh Airport 10 miles. Open all year except Christmas and New Year. Early booking advisable.

LINLITHGOW. Mrs Mary Mitchell, The Cedars, 135 High Street, Linlithgow EH49 7EJ (01506 845952). Small comfortable house with double, twin and single bedrooms, all with washbasin and tea/coffee making facilities. Lounge for guests' use. Historic Linlithgow, birthplace of Mary, Queen of Scots, is an ideal location for visiting the many attractions in Central Scotland. Good rail and bus links to Edinburgh, Glasgow, Stirling, etc. 11 miles from Edinburgh Airport, nine miles from the Forth Bridge. Bed and Breakfast from £16 per person per night. Reductions for children under 10 years. Pets by arrangement.

LIVINGSTON (West Lothian). Ms M. Easdale, 3 Cedric Rise, Dedridge East, Livingston EH54 6JR (Tel & Fax: 01506 413095). Open all year except Christmas and New Year, with central heating, a friendly welcome is assured in this New Town accommodation situated 15 miles from Edinburgh, one of Europe's most splendid cities. Easy access to the motorway for visitors touring north or south. Fife, Borders, Trossachs, Loch Lomond, country parks in Lothian and Central regions, recreation park at Falkirk, all within easy driving distance. Four golf courses in the surrounding area. Accommodation comprises one twin-bedded, one single, one room with double and single beds and a triple bedded room (these rooms are located on the first and second floors). Tea/coffee making facilities and TV in all bedrooms. Bathroom with shower, two toilets; shared sitting/diningroom. Children welcome, but sorry, no pets. Parking nearby. Bed and Breakfast from £15; reductions for children under 10 years.

**Terms quoted in this publication may be subject to increase
if rises in costs necessitate**

MUSSELBURGH. Mrs J.R.M. Dewar, "Glenesk", Delta Place, Smeaton Grove, Inveresk, Mussel-burgh EH21 7TP (0131-665 3217). Quietly situated in the picturesque and historic village of Inveresk, "Glenesk" is a spacious detached villa convenient for all the scenic beauties, beaches and sporting activities of the East Coast. Seven miles from the centre of Edinburgh and a mile from the busy shopping centre of Musselburgh. All bedrooms have private shower ·rooms or bathrooms, colour TV and tea-making facilities. The ground floor accommodation includes a bed-room and a comfortable lounge for guests. Bed and Breakfast from £18 per person per night. Free parking. No signs displayed — conservation area. SAE please.

NORTH BERWICK. "Craigview", 5 Beach Road, North Berwick EH39 4AB (01620 892257). Margaret and Willie Mitchell — British Institute of Innkeep-ing, Welcome Host, AA QQ Recommended, RAC Caradon. "Craigview" is situated in the centre of North Berwick with views over the West Bay, the Harbour and the Firth of Forth. Overlooking a sandy beach and 100 yards from the West Links Golf Course it is ideally placed for both activity and leisure breaks in and around North Berwick including bird-watching, historic castles, golf courses, boat trips, good restaurant and excellent sports facilities. Good train and bus links. Private facilities, four-poster beds, central heating, colour TV, tea/coffee and biscuits, hi-power hairdryers, irons and ironing boards. Full cooked breakfast with alternative healthy or vegetarian options. Open all year. Bed and Break-fast £20 to £25 single, £16 to £20 double. No smoking. Also self catering flat. Brochure available.

PATHHEAD. Mrs Margaret Winthrop, "Fairshiels", Blackshiels, Pathhead EH37 5SX (01875 833665). We are situated on the A68, three miles south of Pathhead at the picturesque village of Fala. The house is an 18th century coaching inn (Listed building). All bedrooms have washbasins and tea/coffee making facilities; one is en suite. The rooms are comfortably furnished. We are within easy reach of Edinburgh and the Scottish Borders. A warm welcome is extended to all our guests — our aim is to make your stay a pleasant one. Cost is from £14 per person; children two years to 12 years £8, under two years FREE.

FOR THE MUTUAL GUIDANCE OF GUEST AND HOST

Every year literally thousands of holidays, short-breaks and overnight stops are arranged through our guides, the vast majority without any problems at all. In a handful of cases, however, difficulties do arise about bookings, which often could have been prevented from the outset.

It is important to remember that when accommodation has been booked, both parties — guests and hosts — have entered into a form of contract. We hope that the following points will provide helpful guidance.

GUESTS: When enquiring about accommodation, be as precise as possible. Give exact dates, numbers in your party and the ages of any children. State the number and type of rooms wanted and also what catering you require — bed and breakfast, full board, etc. Make sure that the position about evening meals is clear — and about pets, reductions for children or any other special points.

Read our reviews carefully to ensure that the proprietors you are going to contact can supply what you want. Ask for a letter confirming all arrangements, if possible.

If you have to cancel, do so as soon as possible. Proprietors do have the right to retain deposits and under certain circumstances to charge for cancelled holidays if adequate notice is not given and they cannot re-let the accommodation.

HOSTS: Give details about your facilities and about any special conditions. Explain your deposit system clearly and arrangements for cancellations, charges, etc, and whether or not your terms include VAT.

If for any reason you are unable to fulfil an agreed booking without adequate notice, you may be under an obligation to arrange alternative suitable accommodation or to make some form of compensation.

While every effort is made to ensure accuracy, we regret that FHG Publications cannot accept responsibility for errors, omissions or misrepresentation in our entries or any consequences thereof. Prices in particular should be checked because we go to press early. We will follow up complaints but cannot act as arbiters or agents for either party.

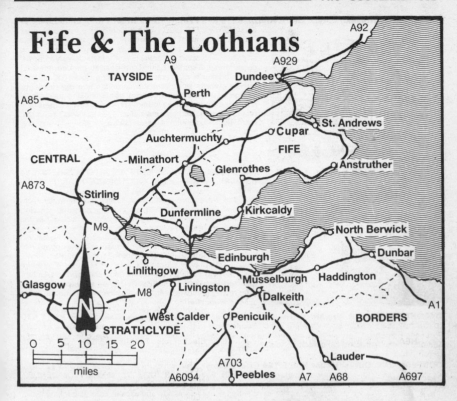

Fife & The Lothians

ABERDOUR. Cedar Inn, 20 Shore Road, Aberdour KY3 0TR (01383 860310). A true Scottish welcome awaits you in this cosy Inn. Close to beaches, golf course, bowling green and a marina. Enjoy boat trips near by or hop on a train to Edinburgh to see the sights of the capital as the train station is just a two minutes' walk from the Cedar Inn. The historic sights of Aberdour are also well worth visiting. The Inn has seven well appointed rooms, three are en suite and one is a nice sized family room. Dinner, Bed and Breakfast prices available on request.

AUCHTERMUCHTY. The Forest Hills Hotel, Auchtermuchty KY14 7AP (Tel & Fax: 01337 828318). STB ✿ ✿ ✿ COMMENDED. This Inn is situated at the village square of the olde worlde village of Auchtermuchty. Since the Inn was established in 1738 it has been a resting place for the traveller. Nowadays the bedrooms have been upgraded with all modern comforts including en suite. Comfortable lounges and cocktail bar, the oak beamed candlelit restaurant serves à la carte and flambé cooking. For further information please telephone. Edinburgh 28 miles, Dundee 18 miles. AA, Les Routiers, The Independents.

PLEASE SEND A STAMPED ADDRESSED ENVELOPE WITH ENQUIRIES

CRAIL. Mr A. Strachan, Caiplie Guest House, 53 High Street, Crail KY10 3RA (01333 450564). 🏴

COMMENDED. AA QQQ, Taste of Scotland. Situated 10 miles from St. Andrews, the historic and picturesque fishing village of Crail has one of the prettiest harbours to be found anywhere in Scotland. Caiplie is a comfortable very informal guest house. Centrally heated throughout, the bedrooms all have radio alarms, tea/coffee making facilities, electric blankets, washbasins and shaver points and the residents' lounge has colour TV. Excellent home cooking using local produce provides great breakfasts and superb dinners and there is a restricted licence which allows residents to complement their meal with a good choice of wines, beers and spirits.

CUPAR by. Mrs Gill Donald, Todhall House, Dairsie, By Cupar KY15 4RQ (Tel & Fax: 01334 656344). 🏴🏴🏴 HIGHLY COMMENDED. AA PREMIER

SELECTED QQQQQ. Traditional Scottish country home surrounded by superb scenery and only seven miles from historic St. Andrews. Ideally situated for pursuing sporting activities and exploring the many places of interest in the Kingdom of Fife and beyond. There is something for everyone! Guests enjoy comfortable bedrooms en suite, an elegant guests' lounge, traditional food and the opportunity to relax and unwind. On site facilities include ample parking, a walled garden, outdoor swimming pool and golf practice net. This is a home for non-smokers. Open April to October. Bed and Breakfast from £22; Dinner by arrangement. Children over 12 years welcome. Contact Gill Donald for a brochure/booking.

DALGETY BAY. Mr & Mrs Mead, The Coach House, 1 Hopeward Mews, Dalgety Bay KY11 5TB (01383 823584). STB Listed COMMENDED. Comfortable family bungalow with beautiful views of River Forth and Edinburgh. Large waterfront gardens with access to Fife Coastal Path. One twin, one double/family and one single bedrooms. No smoking. No pets. Bed and Breakfast from £17.00 per person. Open January to December.

DUNFERMLINE. Davaar House Hotel, 126 Grieve Street, Dunfermline KY12 8DW (01383 721886/736463; Fax: 01383 623633). 🏴🏴🏴 COMMENDED.

Very comfortable hotel personally run by Jim and Doreen ensures warm hospitality and excellent home cooking. Edinburgh within 20 minutes' drive over the River Forth, passing the historic Railway Bridge. St. Andrews 45 minutes' drive. Numerous excellent local golf courses. Knockhill Racing Circuit five miles away, exciting race meetings — test your skill at the driving school. Open January to December. Bed and Breakfast from £24; Dinner, Bed and Breakfast from £44.

FALKLAND. Mrs C. Wilson, The Red House, Freuchie, Falkland KY15 7EZ (01337 857555). Built in 1736, this traditional house is situated in a lovely village in the rural heart of the Kingdom. Less than one hour's drive from Edinburgh, Stirling and Pitlochry and a stone's throw from St. Andrews, Perth and Dundee. Golfers love it here — over 50 courses within a 30 mile radius including Ladybank, Carnoustie and the Old Course. National Trust properties, especially Falkland Palace convenient, as are clean beaches, sports facilities, entertainment, crafts and shops. Start your day with a wholesome breakfast served in the conservatory overlooking our beautiful mature gardens. Come and savour Scottish hospitality at its best.

LETHAM. Mrs Susan Jackson, Lindifferon Farm, Letham KY15 7RX (Tel & Fax: 01337 810230).

Working farm. A warm welcome awaits you at Lindifferon, a working arable/beef/sheep farm situated in the beautiful Howe of Fife within easy reach of Perth, St. Andrews, Dundee and Edinburgh. An ideal base for touring and golfing. This spacious, tastefully decorated farmhouse with traditional furniture has one double and one family room with large seating areas, tea/coffee making facilities, hair dryers. Home baking. Central heating. Open from Easter to October. Bed and Breakfast from £18.

LEVEN by. Mrs Audrey Hamilton, Duniface Farm, By Leven KY8 5RH (01333 350272). Working

farm. Situated on the A915 between Windygates and Leven, Duniface is well placed for exploring historic Fife, playing the numerous golf courses and visiting the endless places of interest within the county and in the surrounding shires; St. Andrews 25 minutes' drive, Forth Road Bridge 30 minutes' drive. The elegant, spacious Victorian farmhouse with its lovely gardens is particularly beautiful, a place where comfort combined with hospitality, relaxed atmosphere and personal attention is assured. Open all year.

NEWBURGH. Mrs Kathleen Baird, East Clunie Farmhouse, Easter Clunie, Newburgh KY14 6EJ

(01337 840218). 🏵 🏵 *COMMENDED.* David and Kathleen Baird warmly welcome you to their 18th century centrally heated farmhouse on a working farm. Home baking and tea on arrival. Relax in the splendid walled garden, enjoy panoramic views of the River Tay. Surrounding countryside provides a wealth of scenic walks. Ideal touring base for Fife and Perthshire. Golf courses nearby. Children over three years welcome. Bed and Breakfast from £15 to £17. Open April to October.

ST. ANDREWS. Mrs Anne Duncan, Spinkstown Farmhouse, St. Andrews KY16 8PN (01334 473475). Only two miles from St. Andrews on the picturesque A917 coast road to Crail, Spinkstown is a uniquely designed farmhouse with views of the sea and surrounding countryside. Bright and spacious, it is furnished to a high standard. Accommodation consists of double and twin rooms, all with en suite facilities; diningroom and lounge with colour TV. Substantial farmhouse breakfast to set you up for the day, evening meals by arrangement only. The famous Old Course, historic St. Andrews and several National Trust properties are all within easy reach, as well as swimming, tennis, putting, bowls, horse riding, country parks, nature reserves, beaches and coastal walks. Plenty of parking available. Bed and Breakfast from £18; Evening Meal £11. AA Selected.

FIFE REGION – THE KINGDOM PERSISTS!

Sandwiched between the Firth of Forth and the Firth of Tay, Fife Region has much to commend it to the tourist. The home of golf at St Andrews, the restored National Trust village of Culross, Falkland Palace, the Fife Folk Museum and the East Neuk, a delightful stretch of coastline, where days can be spent exploring.

GLASGOW and District

AIRDRIE. Mrs Elsie Hunter, Easter Glentore Farm, Slamannan Road, Greengairs, By Airdrie ML6 7TJ (01236 830243). 👑👑 *HIGHLY COMMENDED.* Best B&B Award Winner. Come and enjoy peace and quiet with a warm, friendly, homely relaxed atmosphere (home from home) with good traditional food and hospitality. Working farm with 18th century ground floor farmhouse offering one double/twin en suite, two double rooms with washbasins; guests' own bathroom. Tea/coffee facilities with homemade shortbread and radio alarms in all rooms. Central heating throughout. Lounge with colour TV, separate dining room. Evening tray with home baking. Telephone on request. Excellent touring base — Glasgow and Stirling 15 miles, Edinburgh 28 miles, Airdrie, Cumbernauld and Falkirk all 10 minutes' drive, Strathclyde Leisure Park 13 miles. Museums, sports and parks too numerous to mention nearby. Non-smoking only. Bed and Breakfast from £18, single supplement £5. Evening meal optional £10. Reductions for long stays. Open all year.

GLASGOW. Mr Douglas Rogen, Kirklee Hotel, 11 Kensington Gate, Glasgow G12 9LG (0141-334 5555; Fax: 0141-339 3828). 👑👑 *HIGHLY COMMENDED.* The Kirklee is set in Glasgow's West End Conservation Area and is an Edwardian townhouse. The character of the building has been retained and there is an extensive collection of paintings, drawings and etchings. As we are away from the main roads all our rooms are quiet. The hotel wins many awards for its gardens and there is a private park facing the hotel which can be used by hotel guests. All rooms have en suite bathrooms, TVs, telephones and much more. The hotel is only a short walk from many restuarants and bars in the centre of the "West End".

HOLLY HOUSE

54 IBROX TERRACE
GLASGOW G51 2TB

STB Listed COMMENDED

Situated in an Early Victorian tree-lined terrace in the City Centre south area Holly House offers spacious rooms with ensuite facility. Room rates include breakfast.

Glasgow Airport and the City Centre are only a short drive away; Ibrox Underground Station two minutes' walk. Other local places of interest include the Burrell Collection in Pollok Park, Pollok House, Bellahouston Park and the Ibrox Football Stadium. SECC 10 minutes.

ROOM RATES: *Singles £20–£25   Twins/Doubles £36–£50*

TEL: 0141-427 5609   MOBILE: 0850 223500

Mr Peter Divers

Member of 'Harry James Appreciation Society' – Ask for details.

GLASGOW. Park Hotel, 960 Sauchiehall Street, Glasgow G3 7TH (0141-337 3000). Small, comfortable and friendly Hotel situated near town centre, good bus service. Only 10 minutes into town for bus and railway stations plus the Royal Concert Hall, Exhibition and Conference Centre, not forgetting our modern variety theatres with all the well known popular artistes appearing there. The Hotel is only five minutes' walk to Kelvingrove Park with its tennis courts and bowling greens; the Botanic Gardens with all its splendour is worth a visit — 10 minutes from hotel by bus. Heating, colour TV, biscuits/tea/coffee facilities in all bedrooms. Bed and Breakfast from £15 to £17.50 per person per night.

INVERNESS-SHIRE

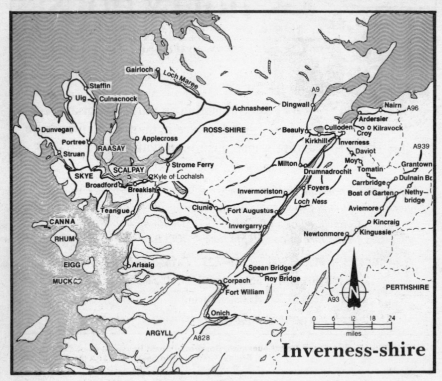

Inverness-shire

CARR-BRIDGE. Lynn and Dave Benge, The Pines Country House, Duthil, Carr-Bridge PH23 3ND (01479 841220). Relax and enjoy our Highland hospitality, offering you personal service in a friendly family atmosphere. Situated in the peaceful surroundings of a pine forest, two miles from the village of Carr-Bridge, we are open all year. All rooms en suite with TV and tea/coffee facilities, central heating throughout. Enjoy our home cooking with traditional or vegetarian meals. Special diets can be arranged. Children and pets are welcome. This is an ideal base for birdwatching, fishing, golf, hill walking, pony trekking, ski-ing plus lots more. A car is essential, parking available. Bed and Breakfast from £16 daily; Dinner, Bed and Breakfast from £150 weekly.

CULLODEN MOOR. Mrs Margaret Campbell, Bay View, Westhill, By Inverness IV1 2BP (01463 790386). 👑 👑 *COMMENDED.* Bay View is set in a rural area on famous Culloden Moor, offering comfortable homely accommodation in one twin-bedded room with en suite shower, one double room en suite and one double room with private washbasin and toilet; bathroom and shower. An excellent touring base for the Highlands of Scotland and many famous historic sites. All home made food, local produce used. Bed and Breakfast from £16.

Kilravock Castle

CROY, INVERNESS IV1 2PJ, SCOTLAND
Telephone Croy (01667) 493258

Experience the best in Christian hospitality in this 15th century castle, commended for good, hearty Scottish home cooking and a warm and homely welcome. Most of the rooms are ensuite, all have washbasins and tea/coffee making facilities. Home to the Roses of Kilravock since 1460, the castle is full of historical interest and Bonnie Prince Charlie was entertained here in 1746. Today, the Castle is run as a non-denominational guest house, Grace is said before breakfast and dinner and a short Bible reading and comment follows. Enjoy the nature trails, sporting facilities, fishing or just relax in our beautiful gardens. You'll want to come back! Open to residents from May 17th to October 4th 1997. Reductions for weekly stays and for children sharing parents' accommodation. Dinner, Bed and Breakfast reservations only please. The castle is unlicensed and we ask guests to refrain from smoking. Please send a stamp for a colour brochure and tariff.

DAVIOT. Torguish House, Daviot, Inverness (01463 772208). Torguish House, once the local manse and childhood home of the late author Alistair MacLean of "Guns of Navarone" fame, has now been converted into a very homely Guest House, with generous rooms, most en suite. All rooms have TV and tea/coffee facilities. Guests' lounge. Ample parking, large garden and play area for children. Pets welcome. Bed and Breakfast £16 to £18. Reductions for children. The STEADING has recently been converted into self catering cottage sleeping 2/4 with extra bed settee in lounge. Fully equipped kitchen and bathroom. Lighting included in the rent, all other electricity by £1 coin meter. Cot and high chair available. Rent £110 to £195 (one bedroom) and £150 to £295 (two bedrooms) per week.

DULNAIN BRIDGE. Cheryl and Tim Shouesmith, Rosegrove Guest House, Skye of Curr, Dulnain Bridge, Grantown-on-Spey PH26 3PA (01479 851335). ☙ ☙ *COMMENDED.* Situated close to the famous Heather Centre, in the beautiful Spey Valley, 10 miles from Aviemore. Ideal for birdwatching, walking, fishing, golfing and exploring the mountains and glens of the Scottish Highlands. The food is something special, venison, salmon and Scotch beef. After dinner relax by the log fire enjoying the view over the valley to the Cairngorms. Accommodation is in double, twin, single and family rooms, some en-suite. Rosegrove is a holiday for the whole family, children and pets are welcome and there is ample parking. Open New Year. Bed and Breakfast from £15.50; Dinner, Bed and Breakfast from £24. Weekly terms available.

FORT WILLIAM. Patricia Jordan, "Beinn Ard", Argyll Road, Fort William PH33 6LF (01397 704760). ☙ ☙ *COMMENDED.* Situated in a quiet street in an elevated position just above the town with panoramic views of Loch Linnhe and surrounding hills. Only five minutes' walk from town centre, pier and station. This is a most attractive wooden house which has recently been extended and renovated to a high standard. We offer our guests a pleasant informal and comfortable base from which to view the magnificent local scenery and experience the many attractions Fort William has to offer. One family room en suite, one double room en suite, one twin room and two single rooms; all have colour TV and tea/coffee making facilities. Open 28th December to end October. Skiers welcome. Bed and Breakfast from £15 to £18.

Highland Folk Museum offer FREE entry for child when accompanied by full-paying adult. For more details see our READERS' OFFER VOUCHER.

FORT WILLIAM. Mr F. Henderson, Ashburn House, Achintore Road, Fort William PH33 6RQ (Tel & Fax: 01397 706000). 🐾🐾 *DE LUXE.* Luxury Victorian

house, personally run, specialising in Bed and Breakfast. 500 yards from town in private grounds on the shores of Loch Linnhe. Parking, central heating. Five double and two single bedrooms, all en suite. Choice of traditional Scottish breakfast. No smoking. TV, hospitality tray. Credit cards accepted. AA QQQQQ. Bed and Breakfast from £25 to £30 per person. Open February to November.

FORT WILLIAM. 6 Caberfeidh, Fassifern Road, Fort William PH33 6BE. A warm Scottish welcome

awaits you at No 6 Caberfeidh in the heart of the Highlands and of course Ben Nevis for the more energetic with its breathtaking views. You are four minutes from the railway and bus station and two minutes from the High Street. A full Scottish breakfast is included in the price. Tea/coffee making facilities and colour satellite TV in all rooms. En suite rooms available, also four-poster room with en suite corner bath. For further details please contact **Jim or Wilma McCourt on 01397 703756.**

FORT WILLIAM. Glenmoidart, Fassifern Road, Fort William PH33 6LJ (Tel & Fax: 01397 705790).

🐾🐾 *COMMENDED.* Glenmoidart is a fine Victorian house restored to a very high standard. Centrally situated in an elevated position above the town centre with magnificent views of Loch Linnhe and the mountains beyond. Fort William is ideally located for various attractions all year round, a good base for touring or for many outdoor sports — walking, climbing, mountain biking, golfing and ski-ing. We have one double room en suite and a double and twin room standard. All have TV, washbasins and tea/coffee making facilities. We offer a choice of Continental or cooked breakfast from £15 to £22. Private parking at rear of house on Cameron Road. Non smoking.

FORT WILLIAM. Mrs Mary MacLean, Innishfree, Lochyside, Fort William PH33 7NX (01397 705471). 🐾🐾 *HIGHLY COMMENDED.* Set against the back-

ground of Ben Nevis, this spacious Bed and Breakfast house offers a high level of service. Just two miles from the town centre and three miles from Glen Nevis. Visitors are guaranteed a warm friendly welcome and excellent accommodation. All rooms have en suite facilitiesand also offer remote control colour TV and tea/coffee making facilities. Breakfast is served in the conservatory, which is overlooked by panoramic views. Enthusiastic advice on pursuits and activities are given. Access to private car park is available. This house has a no-smoking policy and pets are not allowed. Open all year. Prices range from £16 to £20.

FORT WILLIAM. Mrs Campbell, The Grange, Grange Road, Fort William PH33 6JF (01397 705516).

Overlooking Loch Linnhe, set in its own grounds, The Grange is a totally renovated Victorian house 10 minutes' walk from the town centre and seafood restaurant, etc. Each bedroom having its own character is en suite. Awarded the highest grade for quality by the AA and Scottish Tourist Board, the dining room and lounge with open fires and loch view provide the perfect start and end to your day. A large varied menu for breakfast; vegetarians catered for. No smoking. Private parking. Bed and Breakfast from £28 to £33 per person.

FORT WILLIAM. Mrs Catherine Smith, Ben View Guest House, Belford Road, Fort William PH33 6ER (01397 702966). 🌸🌸 *COMMENDED.* Family-run guest house on A82 Glasgow/Fort William/Inverness road, five minutes' walk from town centre, bus and rail stations, town gardens and sports centres. Bedrooms have en suite facilities, central heating, tea/coffee makers, radio and colour TV. There are two comfortable lounges and spacious diningroom. Car parking available within grounds. Excellent touring area. Full fire precautions. Member of Tourist Board and Automobile Association. Bed and full Scottish Breakfast £17 to £21 per person. AA QQQQ.

FORT WILLIAM. Mr A. & Mrs P. McQueen, Stronchreggan View Guest House, Achintore Road, Fort

William PH33 6RW (01397 704644). Our guest house is on the A82, one mile south of Fort William, overlooking Loch Linnhe with views to the Argour Hills. Accommodation offers an excellent guest lounge, full central heating, washbasins in all bedrooms, three toilets, two showers and one bathroom. Parking within grounds. Fort William is a good touring centre with Isle of Skye, Oban and Inverness, etc all within easy reach. Bed and Breakfast from £14 to £15.

FORT WILLIAM. Mrs A. Grant, Glen Shiel Guest House, Achintore Road, Fort William PH33 6RW

(01397 702271). 🌸🌸🌸 *HIGHLY COMMENDED.* Modern purpose built guest house situated near the shore of Loch Linnhe with panoramic views of the surrounding mountains. Accommodation comprises three en suite double bedrooms, one twin-bedded room and one family room (to suit three adults), all with colour TV and tea making facilities. Non smoking. Large car park. Garden. Bed and Breakfast from £15. Directions: on the A82 one and a half miles south of Fort William.

FORT WILLIAM near. Mrs F.A. Nisbet, Dailanna Guest House, Kinlocheil, Near Fort William PH33

7NP (01397 722253). 🌸🌸 *COMMENDED.* Dailanna is a small family run guest house situated in an elevated position overlooking Locheil in the grounds of Altdarroch Farm. It is nine miles west of Fort William on the road to the Isles and is ideally situated as a base for touring Lochaber and surrounding area. Good food a speciality — farm cream and eggs, roast beef, lamb, chicken, pork and salmon and trout when available. All bedrooms are en suite and have electric blankets, shaver points and tea/coffee making facilities. Guests have use of two lounges, one non-smoking, both with colour TV and picture window looking onto Locheil. Car park. Guests return year after year. Dinner, Bed and Breakfast from £27.50; Bed and Breakfast from £17.50. Weekly Dinner, Bed and Breakfast from £185. SAE please.

GLENFINNAN. Sue and Gilbert Scott, Craigag Lodge, Glenfinnan, Fort William PH37 4LT (01397

722240). STB Listed *APPROVED.* Craigag Lodge is an old shooting lodge set amongst superb mountain scenery and is very quiet and peaceful, being well away from the main road up a private drive. All rooms have washbasins, electric blankets and tea/coffee facilities. Excellent home cooking with an extensive menu including traditional Scottish fare. No children under five years. Non smokers only. Bed and Breakfast from £17.50; Dinner from £10. One mile from the famous Glenfinnan Monument to Bonnie Prince Charlie. Ideal location for walking and wild life, also touring the North West Highlands. We also have a tame Red Deer!

PLEASE ENCLOSE A STAMPED ADDRESSED ENVELOPE WITH ENQUIRIES

INVERGARRY. Caroline Francis, Drynachan Cottage, Invergarry PH35 4HL (01809 501225). STB

COMMENDED. A friendly welcome awaits you all year round at our 17th century Highland cottage, visited by Bonnie Prince Charlie in 1746, idyllically situated in the Great Glen. All rooms are either en suite (bath and shower) or with washbasins, together with comfortable seating, central heating and tea/coffee making. There is a cosy sitting room with log fire, colour TV and comfortable armchairs and a separate dining room where breakfast and home cooked evening meals are served. There is also a large garden and ample parking. Drynachan is ideal for touring, hillwalking and cycling; outdoor activities packages are also available.

INVERGARRY. Mrs Buswell, 1/2/3 Nursery Cottages, Invergarry PH35 4HL (01809 501297).

Traditional Highland village stone cottage. One double, one family, one single rooms; private facilities in family room. Dinner by prior arrangement. Good home cooking, all rooms on ground floor with washbasin, central heating. Colour TV, hospitality tray, electric blankets in winter and traditional wood burning fire. One of the Highland's most central locations for visitor attractions and scenic tours. Loch Ness and Fort Augustus seven miles, ski slopes 20 miles, Fort William 25 miles, Isle of Skye, etc 50 miles. Glen Garry, Glen Quoich and Kinloch Mourn close by. Open all year. Ample off street parking. Brochure on request.

INVERGARRY (by Spean Bridge). Mrs F. Jamieson, Lilac Cottage, South Laggan, Invergarry, by Spean Bridge PH34 4EA (01809 501410). Tourist Board Listed *COMMENDED.*

Comfortable accommodation in country cottage with central heating and double glazing. One double, one twin and one family bedrooms, all with washbasins and tea/coffee making facilities. Guests' lounge with colour TV and video. Situated on the A82 in the heart of the Great Glen just one hour from Skye Bridge with Inverness 50 miles, Fort William 23 miles, Spean Bridge 14 miles and Invergarry three miles. Visit Mallaig or Oban and see beautiful Glen Garry and Loch Hourn. Plenty to do and see — near the Great Glen cycle route, the Gondola at Aonach Mor, forest walks; climb Ben Nevis, go fishing, hunt for the Loch Ness Monster or look for red deer. A friendly welcome on your return. Ample car parking. Open all year.

INVERNESS. Mrs Joan Hendry, 'Tamarue', 70A Ballifeary Road, Inverness IV3 5PF (01463 239724). *COMMENDED.*

Comfortable Bed and Breakfast base whilst you tour the many beauty spots and places of interest in the Highlands, or if you are simply passing through. Guests are accommodated in one double with private facilities and one double and one twin; all rooms overlook attractive garden to rear and have washbasins and tea-making facilities; central heating; TV lounge; separate shower for visitors' use. Near to riverside walks, golf course and Loch Ness cruises; 10 minutes' walk to Eden Court Theatre and 15 minutes to shops, restaurants, bus and railway station. Ample parking. Long established reputation for cleanliness and attractive surroundings. Completely non-smoking house. Bed and Breakfast from £13, no VAT.

INVERNESS. Miss Storrar, Abb Cottage, 11 Douglas Row, Inverness IV1 1RE (01463 233486). A historic Listed terraced cottage in a quiet, central riverside street. No smoking policy throughout. Three twin bedrooms have washbasins, shaver points; lounge/dining room has books, puzzles, games, tourist information and timetables, etc. All ground floor rooms are wheelchair accessible, one step only at front door. Evening meals by arrangement, vegetarians and special diets catered for. Packed breakfasts are provided for early departures. Sorry no children under 12 years and no pets.

INVERNESS. Mrs A. MacLean, Waternish, 15 Clachnaharry Road, Inverness IV3 6QH (01463 230520). *COMMENDED.* Delightful bungalow in beautiful setting overlooking Moray Firth and Black Isle. On main A862 road to Beauly, and just five minutes to Inverness town centre. Ideal touring centre for North and West. Canal cruises five minutes' walk away, lovely walks by banks of Caledonian Canal. Golf course is also nearby, and Loch Ness is just 15 minutes' drive. Accommodation comprises three double/twin rooms, one ensuite, all with tea/coffee making facilities. Comfortable TV lounge, full Scottish breakfast. Private car park. Open March to October. Bed and Breakfast from £13.

INVERNESS. Mrs F. McKendrick, Lyndale Guest House, 2 Ballifeary Road, Inverness IV3 5PJ (01463 231529).

Lyndale Guest House, adjacent to the A82 on entering Inverness from Loch Ness, is delightfully situated in an exclusive residential area close to the River Ness and within eight minutes' walk from town centre. Eden Court Theatre and Restaurant 200 yards, the municipal golf course and Loch Ness Cruise departure point five minutes' walk. Standing in private grounds Lyndale is well appointed, with an attractive diningroom; all bedrooms with colour TV and tea/coffee facilities; several en suite. Guests have full use of amenities of the house all day. Private parking in grounds. Bed and Breakfast from £15; en suite £20.

INVERNESS. Mrs E. MacKenzie, The Whins, 114 Kenneth Street, Inverness IV3 5QG (01463 236215). Comfortable, homely accommodation awaits you here 10 minutes' walking distance from town centre, bus and railway stations, Inverness being an excellent touring base for North, West and East bus and rail journeys. Bedrooms have TV and tea-making facilities, washbasins and heating off-season. Bathroom has a shared shower and toilet. Pensioners welcome at slightly reduced rate. Two double/twin rooms from £13 per person per night. Write or phone for full details.

INVERNESS. Mrs Marion Singer, Balvonie Cottage, Drumossie Hill, Inverness IV1 2BB (Tel & Fax: 01463 230677).

Situated downhill from the Drumossie Hotel (two miles approximately south east of Inverness). Guests are accommodated in a charming fully en suite spacious bedsittingroom (twin) convertible to a family bedroom (twin and double) with colour TV, tea/coffee making, etc. Graded Superior by international operator. From Balvonie Cottage, an attractive residence between two farms, guests enjoy panoramic views of mountains and firths with all the advantages of town nearby. Ideal touring centre for Loch Ness and convenient for Culloden Battlefield Visitor Centre. Bed and Breakfast from £16.50 or three night breaks from £15 per person per night (May and October) in this non-smoking residence. Tariff including single and family occupancy rates and illustrated brochure on application. Loan video £5 (returnable). NB accommodation unsuitable for very young children.

KINCRAIG/INSH. Ian and Pamela Grant, Greenfield Croft, Insh PH21 1NT (01540 661010). ♛♛

HIGHLY COMMENDED. Nestled on the edge of Insh village, with panoramic views over Insh Marshes Bird Reserve to the Monadhliath Mountains. A working croft set in quiet, peaceful countryside, ideal for all outdoor pursuits including birdwatching, climbing, shooting, gliding, fishing, mountaineering, pony trekking, riding, golf, cycling, mountain biking, downhill and cross-country ski-ing and watersports. There are many forest trails from the doorstep, rivers, glens and mountains to explore. Relax in the evening by our cosy log fire. Double and twin rooms available, all with en suite shower room. Bed and Breakfast from £15. Dinner by arrangement from £11. Reduced weekly rates.

KINGUSSIE. Mrs J. Stewart, Inverton House, Kingussie PH2 1NR (01540 661866).

Inverton House is in a secluded setting 600 yards off the main A9 (signposted) on the outskirts of Kingussie, situated between Kingussie and Newtonmore. An excellent stopover for people travelling north or south. This is an area full of historic interest, and with recreational facilities including golf, fishing, pony trekking, sailing and Sports Centre at Aviemore all within easy reach. A warm welcome, good food with generous portions and every comfort is offered to guests all year. Accommodation comprises one family, one double and one single bedrooms; bathroom with shower, two toilets. TV lounge and diningroom. Heating throughout. Bed and Breakfast from £12.50 with coffee and tea available at no extra cost. Evening Dinner optional. Reductions for children. Parking space.

Terms quoted in this publication may be subject to increase if rises in costs necessitate

MALLAIG. Jill and Tom Smith, Springbank, East Bay, Mallaig PH41 4QF (01687 462459). ✿

APPROVED. Overlooking Harbour and the Sound of Sleat to Skye. Five minutes walk from railway station at the end of the world famous West Highland Line. The house is fully centrally heated and double glazed. Evening dinner available by arrangement. Children and pets welcome. Please telephone for our brochure.

NAIRN. Mrs B. Fraser, Sandown House, Sandown Farm Lane, Nairn IV12 5NE (01667 454745). STB

Listed COMMENDED. Situated on the outskirts of Nairn offering comfortable B&B accommodation. Double, twin, family and single rooms available, all have washbasin and are centrally heated. Visitors are welcome to make themselves at home in our very comfortable TV lounge or if you are feeling more energetic a swim in our indoor swimming pool. Tea/coffee facilities available. Ample off street parking. Enjoy the tranquillity of the countryside while being only five minutes' drive to town centre. Two championship golf courses and beautiful clean sandy beaches nearby. Bed and Breakfast from £14 to £16.

ROY BRIDGE. Mr and Mrs M. Vallely, Stronlossit Hotel, Roy Bridge PH31 4AG (01397 712253).

Nine fully appointed bedrooms with en suite shower and toilet rooms, TV and tea maker. Lounge bar with log fire. Excellent food — full breakfast, à la carte evening meals. Bar meals service. Ideal centre for touring the Scottish Highlands. Bed and Breakfast from £27 to £32 per night. Discounts available for three nights or more. All major credit cards accepted. Please telephone for our brochure.

SMITHTON. Mrs M.B. Mansfield, 3A Resaurie, Smithton, By Inverness IV1 2NH (01463 791714).

✿ ✿ COMMENDED. Three miles east of Inverness. Views across open farmland to Moray Firth, Ross-shire hills. Double with en suite facilities. Double and twin with shared bathroom. Non-smoking. Car parking. Home baking. High Tea £6. Evening Meal from £12. Public transport nearby. Bed and Breakfast from £15.

SPEAN BRIDGE. Springburn Farmhouse, Stronaba, Spean Bridge PH34 4DX (01397 712707). STB

HIGHLY COMMENDED. Springburn Farm house is situated in its own grounds, just outside the picturesque village of Spean Bridge. All bedrooms have private facilities, colour TV, hair dryers and tea makers plus magnificent views. The farmhouse is under personal family management and offers visitors a friendly, country atmosphere in which to relax after a days' travelling with a view to remind you that this is one of the most beautiful parts of Britain. No smoking. No dogs. Price from £16 to £20 per person.

PLEASE SEND A STAMPED ADDRESSED ENVELOPE WITH ENQUIRIES

SPEAN BRIDGE. Coinachan Guest House, Spean Bridge PH34 4EG (01397 712417). 👑👑👑 COMMENDED. Peaceful rural location overlooking Commando Memorial, enjoying magnificent open hill views. Perfect base for touring, walking, fishing or just relaxing. All of our three non-smoking en suite bedrooms are bright and comfortable, equipped with tea/coffee making facilities and adjustable central heating. We serve a choice of traditional breakfasts and offer an evening meal (four courses), home cooking using fresh ingredients, bring your own wine. Guests' lounge area with TV, wide selections of local information and books for reference. A warm welcome and personal attention provides a cosy and informal atmosphere. Open all year.

TOMATIN. Mhorag and Tony Lucock, Glenan Lodge (Licensed), Tomatin (01808 511217; Fax: 01808 511356). The Glenan Lodge is a typical Scottish Lodge situated in the midst of the Monadhliath Mountains in the valley of the Findhorn River, yet only one mile from the A9. It offers typical Scottish hospitality, home cooking, warmth and comfort. The 10 bedrooms all have central heating, tea making facilities and washbasins; some have en suite facilities. There is a large comfortable lounge and a homely dining room. The licensed bar is well stocked with local malts for the guests. Glenan Lodge caters for the angler, birdwatcher, hillwalker, stalker and tourist alike whether passing through or using as a base. Open all year round. Bed and Breakfast from £16; Dinner £9.50 (optional). Fishing is available at a modest price on our own two mile private beat.

LANARKSHIRE

CALDERBANK. Mrs Betty Gaines, Calderhouse, 13 Main Street, Calderbank ML6 9SG (01236 769077). Calderhouse is situated five minutes from the M8 motorway, 12 miles from Glasgow and 30 miles from Edinburgh, close to Strathclyde Park and various other attractions. A very spacious Victorian sandstone house which is over 100 years old and has been tastefully refurbished over the last three years. Twin en suite room, family room and singles, all with shower and washbasins, TV and tea making facilities. Guest lounge with TV. Ample parking. Bed and Breakfast from £18 per person. Reduced rates for children.

CARNWATH. Mrs M. Armstrong, Dunsyre Mains, Dunsyre, Carnwath ML11 8NG (01899 810251). 👑 COMMENDED. If you want a holiday to remember, Dunsyre Mains is the place. You can relax in quiet pleasant countryside, admire the animals and become friends with the Border collies, yet be close enough to visit the holiday attractions of Edinburgh, the Scottish Borders and New Lanark. Convenient for five golf courses. End the day with an evening meal made from home produce, then finish with coffee around the log fire. Make your holiday a lasting memory. Children and pets welcome. Open all year. Bed and Breakfast £16; Evening Meal from £9. Reduced rates for children.

LANARK. Mrs Margaret Kirby, Walston Mansion Farmhouse, Walston, Carnwath, Lanark ML11 8NF (Tel & Fax: 0189-981 0338). 👑 👑 👑 *COMMENDED.*

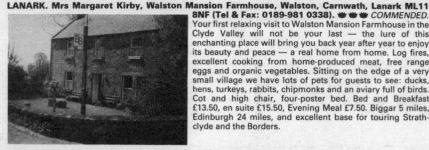

Your first relaxing visit to Walston Mansion Farmhouse in the Clyde Valley will not be your last — the lure of this enchanting place will bring you back year after year to enjoy its beauty and peace — a real home from home. Log fires, excellent cooking from home-produced meat, free range eggs and organic vegetables. Sitting on the edge of a very small village we have lots of pets for guests to see: ducks, hens, turkeys, rabbits, chipmonks and an aviary full of birds. Cot and high chair, four-poster bed. Bed and Breakfast £13.50, en suite £15.50, Evening Meal £7.50. Biggar 5 miles, Edinburgh 24 miles, and excellent base for touring Strathclyde and the Borders.

LESMAHAGOW. Mrs Hamilton, Kerse Farm, Lesmahagow ML11 0HX (01555 894545; Fax: 01555 894646). STB *HIGHLY COMMENDED.* The farm is situated in quiet peaceful surroundings yet only five minutes from Junction 10 on M74. It is an ideal base for touring in the south of Scotland. Accommodation is in two twin bedrooms, both have washbasins and tea/coffee making facilities. Guests bathroom with bath, shower, WC and washbasin. Sorry no pets. It is a no smoking house. Bed and Breakfast from £18.

MORAY
including Morayshire and part of Banffshire

ELGIN. Mrs Lorna Smith, Gladhill Farm, Garmouth, Elgin IV32 7NN (0134 3870331). A warm friendly atmosphere awaits you on our family farm, situated on the Moray Coast only 15 minutes' walk from the sea. We grow barley and have cows, sheep, hens, goats and a dog. Children welcome. The accommodation comprises two double, one twin and one single bedrooms. Relax in our comfortable lounge with colour TV and log fires on cooler nights. Enjoy good home cooking. We are an ideal base for visiting the Whisky and Castle Trails, for touring Moray beaches and golf courses. Well situated for walkers and bird watchers, and within 10 minutes' of beautiful sandy beaches. Open April to September. Please send SAE for terms and further details.

ELGIN. Mr W.G. Ross, The Bungalow, 7 New Elgin Road, Elgin IV30 3BE (01343 542035). 👑 *COMMENDED.* Family-run guest house, 15 minutes' walk from town centre, five minutes from railway station. Convenient for touring, six to 10 miles to beaches, Whisky Trail and historic Castle Trail near by. Links and inland golf courses and river or loch fishing available locally. There are one single, one double and one twin-bedded rooms, two with shared bathroom, all with TV. Open January to December. Children and pets welcome. Central heating. Bed and Breakfast from £12.50. Please write, or telephone, for further details.

**WHEN MAKING ENQUIRIES PLEASE MENTION
THIS *FHG* PUBLICATION**

FORRES. John and Louise Cousens, Neptune Guest House and Verdant Restaurant, 22/24 Tolbooth Streeet, Forres IV30 0PH (01309 674387).

🏵🏵🏵 *COMMENDED.* Neptune Guest House is a 17th century modernised Scottish townhouse offering every modern convenience in traditional surroundings. It is situated in a quiet location just off Forres town centre within easy walking distance of all local amenities. All rooms are beautifully appointed and have colour TV, tea/coffee making facilities, radio alarms and washbasins; some rooms also have en suite bathrooms. Children and pets are welcome, and we accept all major credit cards. We also boast a fully licensed restaurant specialising in vegetarian and vegan cuisine which offers a range of meals and snacks throughout the day and into the evening.

TOMINTOUL. Mrs Elma Turner, Findron Farm, Braemar Road, Tomintoul AB37 9ER (01807 580382).

🏵🏵🏵 *HIGHLY COMMENDED.* Farmhouse on Tomintoul to Braemar road, one mile from Tomintoul. An ideal base for touring, walking and the Malt Whisky Trail. Two double bedrooms, one family room; two rooms en suite, one with private bathroom. Central heating, tea making facilities. Private parking. Bed and Breakfast £13 to £16 single/double; with Evening Meal £19 to £22. Open January to December.

PEEBLESSHIRE

PEEBLES. Mrs A. Waddell, Lyne Farm, Peebles EH45 8NR (01721 740255).

🏵🏵🏵🏵 A warm welcome is assured at Lyne Farm situated in an area of scenic beauty. Located only four miles on the A72 from the picturesque town of Peebles. Guests can walk around the farm, relax in walled garden or go hill walking up the Black Meldon. The tastefully decorated Georgian Farmhouse accommodation consists of one twin room and two double rooms with tea/coffee making facilities; two bathrooms; dining room and sitting room for guests. Also available, spacious cottage which sleeps two to eight persons. Traquair House, Kailzie, Neidpath Castle and Dawyck Botanical Gardens within a few miles. Bed and Breakfast from £15 to £17 per person, reductions for children.

PERTH & KINROSS

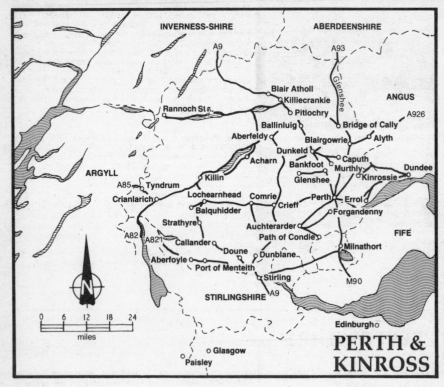

INVERNESS-SHIRE ABERDEENSHIRE

A9 A93

Blair Atholl
Killiecrankie ANGUS
Rannoch Sta. Pitlochry A926
Ballinluig Bridge of Cally
Aberfeldy Blairgowrie Alyth
Dunkeld Caputh
Acharn Bankfoot Murthly Dundee
ARGYLL Killin Glenshee Kinrossie
A85 Tyndrum
Crianlarich Lochearnhead Comrie Perth Errol
Balquhidder Crieff Forgandenny
Strathyre Auchterarder
A82 A821 Callander Path of Condie FIFE
Doune Dunblane Milnathort
Aberfoyle Port of Menteith
Stirling M90
STIRLINGSHIRE A9

0 6 12 18 24
miles

Edinburgh

PERTH & KINROSS

Glasgow
Paisley

ABERFELDY. Mrs Sharp, Laigh of Cluny Steading, Edradynate, Aberfeldy PH15 2JU (Tel & Fax: 01887 840469). Laigh of Cluny Steading has been renovated to high standards with magnificent views over the River Tay offering comfortable Bed and Breakfast accommodation with the option for evening meal. Accommodation comprises one family room with one double and two single beds, colour TV, tea/coffee making facilities, radio alarm, shower en suite. Bed and Breakfast from £16 to £20; Evening Meal £12 extra per person. Private gardens and ample parking. We have our own salmon and trout fishing locally. Perthshire in winter is spectacular — why not try a Winter Break? Self catering accommodation is also available.

BRIDGE OF CALLY. Mrs Josephine MacLaren, Blackcraig Castle, Bridge of Cally PH10 7PX (01250 886251 or 0131-551 1863). A beautiful castle of architectural interest situated in spacious grounds. Free trout fishing on own stretch of River Ardle. Pony trekking can be arranged. Excellent centre for hill walking, golf and touring — Braemar, Pitlochry (Festival Theatre), Crieff, Dunkeld, etc., Glamis Castle within easy reach by car. Four double, two twin, two family and two single bedrooms, eight with washbasins; two bathrooms, three toilets. Cot, high chair. Dogs welcome free of charge. Car essential, free parking. Open for guests from July to early September. £20.50 per person per night includes full breakfast plus tea/coffee and home baking served at 10pm in the beautiful drawing room which has a log fire. Reduced rates for children under 14 years. Enquiries November to end June to **1 Inverleith Place, Edinburgh EH3 5QE.**

Blackcraig Castle, Bridge of Cally, Perthshire

CRIANLARICH. Daisey Ferries, The Lodge House, Crianlarich FK20 8RU (01838 300276). ♛ ♛ ♛

HIGHLY COMMENDED. AA Commended. Situated just west of Crianlarich on the A82, The Lodge offers good quality accommodation in five en suite rooms, plus a two-roomed chalet adjacent, all enjoying magnificent views of the local countryside. The emphasis in our dining room is on good home cooking, using local produce as far as possible. Dinner is normally a set menu but alternatives are always available. Vegetarians are catered for and other special needs by arrangement. Pack lunches available. We have a restricted licence and apart from the bar area the house is non-smoking. Well behaved pets are welcome by arrangement.

CRIANLARICH. Mr & Mrs A. Chisholm, Tigh Na Struith, The Riverside Guest House, Crianlarich FK20 8RU (01838 300235). Voted the Best Guest House in

Britain by the British Guild of Travel Writers in 1984, this superbly sited Guest House comprises six bedrooms, each with unrestricted views of the Crianlarich Mountains. The three-acre garden leads down to the River Fillan, a tributary of the River Tay. Personally run by the owners, Janice and Sandy Chisholm, Tigh Na Struith allows visitors the chance to relax and enjoy rural Scotland at its best. To this end, each bedroom is centrally heated, double glazed, with colour TV and tea/coffee making facilities. Open March to November. Bed and Breakfast from £16 per person.

INCHTURE. "The Orchard", Easter Ballindean, Inchture PH14 9QS (01828 686318). Attractive

south-facing country cottage offering comfortable Bed and Breakfast accommodation in peaceful location with panoramic views overlooking the Tay Valley, only a mile from the A9 Perth to Dundee dual carriageway. Accommodation comprises one double, one twin, one family and one single bedrooms, all with tea/coffee making facilities; some en suite with TV. Lounge. Breakfast is served in a relaxed and spacious conservatory overlooking the tranquil garden and Fife hills beyond. Bed and Breakfast from £17 to £20. Reductions for children under 12 years. Private parking. The Orchard is an ideal base for walking, fishing or golf being only 40 minutes from at least 12 golf courses including St. Andrews, Carnoustie, Rosemount and Gleneagles.

KINROSS. The Innkeeper, The Innkeepers Cottage, 32 Muirs, Kinross KY13 7AS (Tel & Fax: 01577 862270). Kinross, known as "The Crossroads of Scotland",

is ideal for business or pleasure, having all of Scotland's major towns and cities (not to mention 130 golf courses) within driving distance. The cottage itself which dates back to the Battle of Waterloo in 1815 is simply idyllic and well situated in this popular ancient market town. It is the home of the keeper of the award-nominated Muirs Inn situated opposite, where breakfast is partaken every morning and which has been welcoming guests for many years. Bed and Breakfast from £15 per person. The standard of both the comfort provided and the food served is simply superb as the visitors' book confirms.

PERTH near. Mrs Mary Jackson, Sunnylea, Methven PH1 3RF (01764 683354). Comfortable cottage with large garden, adjacent A85, three and a half miles to Methven, seven miles Crieff. One large twin room with sitting area. Private bathroom adjacent. Tea/coffee facilities and fridge. Electric blankets, remote control TV; central heating, double glazing; use of laundry in outbuilding. Ample parking on premises. Ideal for touring, fishing, golf, walks; trout fishing on private loch can be arranged. No smoking. All ground floor. Bed and Breakfast from £15 to £17 per person. Discount for full week. April to October. Also self catering apartment for two with all facilities available all year.

KIRKMICHAEL by. Malcolm & Jacky Catterall, "Tulloch", Enochdhu, By Kirkmichael PH10 7DY

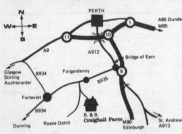

(01250 881404). STB *COMMENDED*. Peace and quiet guaranteed in this friendly, family-run, former farmhouse situated on the A924 Braemar/Kirkmichael Road from Pitlochry. We have three bedrooms — one double en suite and two with washbasins. There are lots of walks and wildlife and birds to be seen from the house. We are members of the RSPB and can show you where many sites of interest are. We are central (geographically) to the Highlands and within an hour or two you can drive to most towns and cities in Scotland. Ideal base for walking or touring. Bed and Breakfast £15; three-course Dinner if required £9.

PERTH. Mrs Mary Fotheringham, Craighall Farmhouse, Forgandenny, Near Bridge of Earn, Perth PH2 9DF (01738 812415). 🌷🌷 *COMMENDED*. **Working**

farm. Come and stay in a modern and warm farmhouse with a cheerful, friendly atmosphere situated in lovely Earn Valley, half a mile west of village of Forgandenny on B935 and only six miles south of Perth. True Highland hospitality and large choice for breakfast served in diningroom overlooking fields where a variety of cattle, sheep and lambs graze. Farm produce used. Open all year, the 1000 acre arable and stock farm is within easy reach of Stirling, Edinburgh, St. Andrews, Glasgow and Pitlochry. Fishing, golf, tennis, swimming locally. Hill walking amid lovely scenery. Rooms with private facilities, others all en suite. Tea making facilities. Sittingroom. Cot and reduced rates for children. Sorry, no pets. Central heating. Car not essential, parking. Bed and Breakfast from £16.50. Mid-week bookings taken. AA/RAC Acclaimed.

PERTH. Mrs Irene Millar, Blackcraigs Farmhouse, Scone PH2 7PJ (01821 640204). 🌷 *COMMENDED*. **Working farm.** Relax in a homely atmosphere at

Blackcraigs farmhouse where a warm, friendly welcome is assured. Peace and tranquillity with panoramic views. Tastefully decorated bedrooms and large lounge to relax in. All rooms have colour TV and tea/coffee making facilities. Large garden and ample parking. Bed and Breakfast £16 to £18. Open all year. Murrayshall Golf Course is only one and a half miles away, an 18-hole course with a driving range and indoor school. The Fair City of Perth with its charm and many amenities is four miles to the west. Perthshire is renowned the world over for the splendour of Highland scenery, historic towns and atmospheric villages. Come and see!

PITLOCHRY. Dalshian House, Old Perth Road, Pitlochry PH16 5JS (01796 472173). 🌷🌷🌷 *COMMENDED*. Quiet, secluded and set in its own parklands only one and a half miles south of Pitlochry, Dalshian House is an early 19th century farmhouse built in 1812. The original public rooms are elegantly furnished and the spacious bedrooms retain their original character. Four double, one twin and two family bedrooms, all en suite with colour TV and welcome tea/coffee tray. The resident owners Malcolm and Althea Carr have created an atmosphere of comfort and quality with a reputation for good food. Bed and Breakfast from £20.50 to £24 per person; Dinner, Bed and Breakfast from £30.50 to £34. Pets welcome. Brochure available.

TAYSIDE REGION – RIVERS, HILLS AND FERTILE PLAINS.

The land to the north of the Tay will provide many interesting days and many lasting memories. Make sure you visit Pitlochry, Dunkeld, Glamis, Montrose, Edzell, Ben Lawers, and Scotland's former capital, Perth.

PITLOCHRY. Mrs Ruth MacPherson-MacDougall, Dalnasgadh House, Killiecrankie, By Pitlochry

PH16 5LN (01796 473237). Attractive country house in grounds of two acres amidst magnificent Highland scenery. Close to National Trust Centre in Pass of Killiecrankie, historic Blair Castle nearby. Only seven minutes from Pitlochry with its famous Festival Theatre. Easy touring distance to Queen's View, Loch Tummel, Balmoral, Braemar, Glamis Castle, Scone Palace and Aviemore. Centrally heated throughout. Lounge with colour TV. All bedrooms have washbasins, shaver points, electric blankets and tea/coffee making facilities. Convenient toilets, showers, bathroom. Sorry no pets. No smoking. Open Easter to October. AA and RAC Listed. Fire Certificate Awarded. Write, telephone or just call in to enquire about terms.

PITLOCHRY. Mrs Barbara Bright, Craig Dubh Cottage, Manse Road, Moulin, Pitlochry PH16 5EP

(01796 472058). We invite you to come and stay with us for Bed and Breakfast in our family home which is in the historic conservation village of Moulin, one mile from Pitlochry. Set in one and a half acres of garden, our accommodation comprises one twin room (ground floor) en suite £14.50 per person per night, one double room (with washbasin) £13.50 per person per night, two single rooms £13.50 per night. Disabled guests can be accommodated and most diets catered for on request. All rooms have tea/coffee making facilities and electric blankets. There is a TV lounge. Cot is available. Dogs are welcome. Public transport can be met by arrangement. Open mid-April to mid-October. Come to the heart of the Highlands and relax with us.

PORT OF MENTEITH. Mrs C. Tough, Collymoon Pendicle, Port of Menteith, By Kippen FK8 3JY (01360 850222). 🐾 *COMMENDED.* This large modern bungalow which sits off the B8034 is an ideal base for touring the Trossachs, Aberfoyle, Callander and Loch Lomond. Sample good home cooking in the newly built sun lounge with panoramic views of the Campsie Hills to the south. Next door is the family farm where you are free to wander and walk along the banks of the River Forth where salmon and brown trout fishing is available. Golf, putting, hill walking, pony trekking all within eight miles. Trout fishing on Lake of Menteith three miles away. Accommodation comprises one family, one double and one single bedrooms, all with tea making facilities, washbasins and shaver points. Cot and high chair provided. Bathroom, toilet and shower facilities. Separate residents' lounge with colour TV. Central heating. Ample parking. Open Easter to October. Sorry no pets. Bed and Breakfast from £15; Evening Dinner £10 per person. Reduced rates for children. Member AA.

STANLEY. Mrs Ann Guthrie, Newmill Farm, Stanley PH1 4QD (01738 828281). 🐾 🐾 🐾 *COMMEN-*

DED. This 330 acre farm is situated on the A9, six miles north of Perth. Accommodation comprises twin room, double room and family rooms, most en suite; lounge, sittingroom, dining room; bathroom, shower room and toilet. Bed and Breakfast from £17; Evening Meal on request. The warm welcome and supper of excellent home baking is inclusive. Reductions and facilities for children. Pets accepted. The numerous castles and historic ruins around Perth are testimony to Scotland's turbulent past. Situated in the area known as "The Gateway to the Highlands" the farm is ideally placed for those seeking some of the best unspoilt scenery in Western Europe. Many famous golf courses and trout rivers in the Perth area.

STRATHYRE. Mrs Catherine B. Reid, Coire Buidhe, Strathyre FK18 8NA (01877 384288). Tourist

Board Listed *APPROVED.* Run by the longest established hosts in Strathyre, Coire Buidhe sits in the beautiful valley of Strathyre, nine miles from Callander. An excellent base for touring Loch Lomond, Trossachs, Stirling, Edinburgh, with both east and west coasts within easy reach. Two single, two twin, two double (one with en suite bathroom), two family rooms, all with heaters, washbasins, electric blankets, shaver points and tea making facilities; two showers, bathroom, three toilets. Sitting and dining rooms. Open all year. Parking. Regret no dogs. Children welcome at reduced terms; cot, high chair and babysitting offered. All water sports and shooting available plus trekking, tennis, hill walking, golf and putting. Bed and Breakfast from £14; Dinner from £10. All food personally prepared; home baking. Special diets catered for. Well recommended. Full Fire Certificate. Reduced weekly terms.

TROSSACHS. Mrs Valerie Jones, Trossachs Old Manse, Brig O' Turk FK17 8HX (01877 376250).

This fine old Victorian house is situated by Loch Achray in the lovely mountain scenery of the Queen Elizabeth Forest Park. The area is ideal for walking and we can provide rowing or fishing on the loch. Valerie and Peter Jones offer a warm personal welcome. The spacious and comfortable bedrooms have tea/coffee and full en suite facilities. Enjoy eating in our oak panelled dining room and relaxing in the elegant lounge with its fine decorative plasterwork. Open all year. Bed and Breakfast from £20 per person. Three course Dinner (by arrangement) £12. Enquire for special weekly rates. No smoking.

RENFREWSHIRE

JOHNSTONE. Mrs Capper, Auchans Farm, Johnstone PA6 7EE (01505 320131). Family-run working farm with large farmhouse offering Bed and Breakfast accommodation. All bedrooms are centrally heated and have colour TV and tea/coffee making facilities. Only five minutes from Glasgow Airport; convenient for City Centre and for touring Burns Country, Loch Lomond, Trossachs, etc. Excellent salmon and trout fishing on River Gryffe close by, permits available. Children welcome. Parking. Open all year. Bed and Breakfast from £15 to £18 per person per night.

LOCHWINNOCH. Mrs Janet Blair, East Kerse Farm, Lochwinnoch PA12 4DU (01505 502400). An

attractive farmhouse with sun lounge and panoramic views over Kilbirnie Loch. A warm welcome awaits you on this 200 acre family-run dairy farm situated just off the A760 Lochwinnoch to Largs road and just 15 minutes from Glasgow Airport. Close by are Muirshiel Country Park, RSPB Centre and canoeing at Lochwinnoch; Burns Country within easy reach; Kelburn Country Park; many golf courses; fishing in the Maich Burn and Kilbirnie Loch. Accommodation comprises one double room, one twin and one single bedroom. Home baking. Bed and Breakfast from £11.

ROSS-SHIRE

BALINTORE. Mrs J. Palfreman, Rowchoish, East Street, Balintore, Near Tain IV20 1UE (01862 832422). Welcome Host Award. Bed and Breakfast in Balintore overlooking the Moray Firth, north-east of Inverness. Comfortable homely accommodation in one double and one twin room with tea-making facilities; separate shower and toilet. Visitors' lounge. Packed lunches available. Guests can enjoy sea angling, golf and riding in the area, plus the unique Dolphin Watch. Bed and Breakfast £14.50 per person per night. Longer stay reductions. Brochure on request.

GAIRLOCH. Mrs V. Mullaney, Wayside, Strath, Gairloch IV21 2BZ (01445 712008). Set amidst the spectacular scenery of the Scottish Highlands, in the lovely village of Gairloch overlooking Gairloch Bay. Ideally situated for walking, touring, fishing and sandy beaches; six miles away is the world famous National Trust's Inverewe Gardens. Wayside provides central heating, tea/coffee making facilities, TV and wash-basins in all rooms — two double and one twin-bedded. Bed and Breakfast from £13.50 to £15 per person. A warm welcome awaits you.

TAIN. Mrs K.M. Roberts, Carringtons, Morangie Road, Tain IV19 1PY (01862 892635). STB ♥ ♥

COMMENDED. Welcome Host. Situated two/three minutes' walk from town centre, Carringtons is an attractive Victorian house with magnificent views over Dornoch Firth. Family, double, twin, single rooms available; some en suite, all with tea/coffee facilities, colour TV, shaver points, hair dryers. Public telephone available. Guest lounge with colour TV. Extensive breakfast menu. Washing/drying facilities. Reduced rates for children and under two year olds FREE- cot and babysitting service available. Tain has numerous hotels and restaurants serving food and drink, boasts its own golf course and is close to other courses. Excellent spot for touring; West Coast, Ullapool, John O'Groats, Inverness are within a day's reach. Tariff from £13 per person per night.

ROXBURGHSHIRE

HAWICK. Mrs Sheila Shell, Wiltonburn Farm, Hawick TD9 7LL (01450 372414; mobile 0374 192551).

Wiltonburn is a friendly, working, mixed farm situated in a sheltered valley and surrounded by fields, hills and a small stream. Relax in the garden, or use the local facilities, including fishing, riding, swimming, golf, squash, tennis or hill walking. An ideal base for visiting castles, museums and stately homes or for buying knitwear. Farm shop selling designer cashmere knitwear, costume jewellery; art gallery, small gifts. Good selection of eating places nearby. Open all year. Family room en suite, shower available. Two bathrooms. TV lounge and garden with furniture and barbecue. Dogs by arrangement. Cot available. Listed "Commended". Bed and full Scottish Breakfast from £15. Self catering unit available.

SELKIRKSHIRE

GALASHIELS. Sheila Berguis, Overlangshaw Farm, Langshaw, Galashiels TD1 2PE (01896 860244). ♥ *COMMENDED.*

Situated only four miles from Galashiels and Melrose. A welcoming, centrally heated home amidst rolling hills and shady woods. Delicious Scottish cooking with emphasis on quality home produce and preserves. Children welcome, cot available. Also dogs by arrangement. Roomy bedrooms — one family with private bathroom, one double with en suite shower room. Southern Upland Way nearby. Open all year. Bed and Breakfast from £17 to £20. FHB Member.

STIRLING

including Stirlingshire and Falkirk County

FINTRY. Mrs M. Mundell, Craigton Farm, Denny Road, Fintry G63 0XQ (0136-086 0426). One mile from the beautiful village of Fintry, this new farmhouse sits on the banks of the Endrick Water. The house looks onto the Campsie Fells and the Fintry Hills which we farm. There are two comfortable bedrooms, bathroom, large TV lounge. Local amenities include trout fishing and scenic hill and river walks. Ideal centre for touring Loch Lomond, Trossachs, Callander, Stirling (all 20 minutes by car); Glasgow 35 minutes; Perth, Loch Tay, Lochearnhead, Crieff, Edinburgh all within one hour by car. A cup of tea and a very warm welcome greets guests on arrival. Bed and Breakfast from £15.

SUTHERLAND

DORNOCH. Mrs Audrey Hellier, Achandean, Meadows Road, Dornoch IV25 3SF (Tel & Fax: 01862 810413). ♥♥ COMMENDED. Warm welcome assured in our superb Bungalow set in half an acre. Secluded picturesque garden. Large bedrooms, en suite and private facilities. All have colour TV, tea/coffee facilities. Pleasant lounge, separate dining room. Very central. Relaxing, fishing, sandy beach, Championship golf course, others nearby. Loch Fleet Bird Sanctuary, Dunrobin Castle. One hour's drive above Inverness. Excellent for touring Northern Highlands with its magnificent wildlife, spectacular lochs, mountains and waterfalls; all within a day trip or less of our home. Disabled or handicapped people welcome. Full cooked breakfast. Weekly rates. Come as a guest, welcome back as a friend! Please telephone/fax for our brochure.

DORNOCH. Mallin House Hotel, Church Street, Dornoch IV25 3LP (01862 810335; Fax: 01862 810810; E-mail mallin.house.hotel@zetnet.co.uk). MALLINGERER! Such a person is the Bunkered Duffer who prefers to Feign an Indisposition and to Hold Back in the Comfortable Surroundings of the Mallin House Hotel rather than brave the Formidable Hazards of Royal Dornoch. Amid the Welcoming Comforts of the Friendly and Hospitable bar and restaurant at the Mallin, this individual enjoys to the full a fine selection of Single Malt Whiskies, First Class Wines and a Memorable Choice of Food, thus avoiding the Infamous traps awaiting the Unwary, the Unlucky and the Unskilled at our marvellous old links course. Why don't you, too, take the easy way out and join the Bunkered Duffer and his chums at the bar of the Mallin? Special golfing rates available up to the end of June and from September to the end of October. Special weekend breaks are also available at £125 per person full board. The Mallin House Hotel, the place for True Mallingerers, is only one minute away from the Royal Dornoch Clubhouse and within an hour of a dozen of the finest links and upland courses in Scotland. For more information contact Malcolm or Linda Holden.

WIGTOWNSHIRE

NEWTON STEWART. Miss K.R. Wallace, Kiloran, 6 Auchendoon Road, Newton Stewart DG8 6HD (01671 402818). Spacious, luxury bungalow set in secluded landscaped garden, with panoramic views of Galloway Hills, in quiet area of Newton Stewart. Enjoy comfortable accommodation on one level in two double bedrooms (one twin-bedded); bathroom with shower; cloakroom with WC. Soap and towels supplied. Lounge (colour TV), dining room where good home cooking is served (menu changed daily). Central heating. Children over 10 years welcome. Dogs allowed, but not in house. Ideal centre for touring Galloway. Safe, sandy beaches 12 miles. Within easy reach of hill walking, golf, riding and trekking. Terms on request. SAE, please, for Evening Dinner, Bed and Breakfast or Bed and Breakfast only. For Auchendoon Road, turn at Dashwood Square to Princess Road, then second on right. Ample parking available.

SCOTTISH ISLANDS

ISLE OF ARRAN

LAMLASH. June, Jeannette and Ken Price, Aldersyde Hotel, Lamlash KA27 8LU (01770 600219 or 600732). Small family-run hotel with outstanding sea views over to Holy Island. Ideal location for golf, walking, fishing, sailing. Live music in lounge bar in season. Discounts given for party bookings, long stays or out of season. Home cooking. Bed and Breakfast £15; Bed, Breakfast and Evening Meal £20. Please write or telephone for further information.

WHITING BAY. Burlington Hotel, Shore Road, Whiting Bay KA27 8PZ (01770 700255; Fax: 01374 595327). Experience traditional Scottish hospitality in this sea-front Edwardian hotel situated opposite stairs to the sandy beach. Recently refurbished, the bedrooms have private facilities, hospitality trays, hair dryers and colour TV. The Burlington Restaurant offers varied table d'hôte and à la carte menus in a stylish relaxed atmosphere. Comfortable residents' lounge with outstanding views of the Bay, Holy Isle and the Ayrshire coast. Arrangements can be made for pony trekking, sailing, golf, paragliding, boat trips and guided tours of the island. Children and pets welcome.

**If you've found
FARM HOLIDAY GUIDES
of service please tell your friends**

ISLE OF MULL

CRAIGNURE. Chronicle, Craignure PA65 6AY (01680 812364). John and Ingrid would like to

welcome you to their home. Chronicle is convenient for the ferry from Oban and makes a good base from which to explore the delights of Mull. Iona, Staffa and Ulva each have their own magic. The scenery is beautiful, the wildlife is plentiful. Torosay Castle and Gardens are a short walk away, while Duart Castle (home of the MacLean chief) makes a good excursion. Both our rooms are en suite, on the ground floor and have their own entrances. Cyclists and walkers are welcome. Vegetarians can be catered for. We are a non-smoking home.

SHETLAND ISLES

BRAE. Mrs E. Wood, Westayre Bed and Breakfast, Muckle Roe, Brae ZE2 9QW (01806 522 368).

👑👑 *HIGHLY COMMENDED.* A warm welcome awaits you at our working croft on the picturesque island of Muckle Roe, where we have breeding sheep, pet lambs, ducks and cats. The island is joined to the mainland by a small bridge and is an ideal place for children. The accommodation is of a high standard and has en suite facilities and guests can enjoy good home cooking and baking. In the evening sit by the open peat fire and enjoy the views looking out over Swarbacks Minn. Spectacular cliff scenery and clean safe sandy beaches, bird watching and hill walking and also central for touring North Mainland and North Isles. Bed and Breakfast £16; Dinner, Bed and Breakfast £24.

ISLE OF SKYE

LUIB, by Broadford. Harvey and Gill Willett, Laimhrig, Luib, By Broadford IV49 9AN (01471 822686). With its own access to the sea and magnificent views of the Red Cuillin Hills and the islands of Raasay and Scalpay, this centrally situated bungalow on the shores of Loch Ainort is perfect for exploring Skye. Walking, climbing, bird watching, sailing and golf are popular pastimes in this peaceful area. Explore at will or let us help you plan your days to gain the most from your visit. Bed and Breakfast (English or Continental) from £11.50. Three-day breaks (Bed, Breakfast and Evening Meal) from £58. Vegetarians welcome. Sorry, no smoking.

PORTREE by. Mrs M. MacKenzie, Caberfeidh, 2 Heatherfield, Penifiler, By Portree IV51 9NE (01478 612820). This farmhouse is situated on a croft three miles from Portree on the Isle of Skye. It is in a beautiful setting beside the sea, overlooking Portree Bay, and with views of the Old Man of Storr and the magnificent Cuillins. Two double, one single and one family bedrooms; bathroom, two toilets; sittingroom; diningroom. Children welcome, babysitting available. Pets permitted. Central heating. Car essential, parking. Open from April to October for Bed and Breakfast from £14. Reduced rates for children. Further details gladly sent on request.

UIG. Mrs G.J. Wilson, Garybuie Guest House, 4 Balmeanach, Glennhinnisdal, Snizort IV51 9UX (01470 542310). Tourist Board Listed *APPROVED.* Situ-

ated in the glen by the side of the River Hinnisdal. Turn off A856 at Hinnisdal Bridge, over cattle grid to telephone box next to house. Accommodation can be provided in two family rooms, one double, one twin, one single. Warm family house, home cooking. Dinner on request. Tea/coffee trays and TV all rooms. Lounge. 10 minutes Uig ferry to Outer Hebrides. River fishing, walking Trotternish Ridge, scenic area. From £14 to £15 for Bed and Breakfast; Evening Dinner £10. Brochure available, please ring.

'Garybuie'

WALES

NORTH WALES (formerly Clwyd and Gwynedd)
Aberconwy & Colwyn, Anglesey, Denbighshire, Flintshire, Gwynedd and Wrexham

ABERDARON. Mrs V. Bate, Bryn Mor, Aberdaron LL53 8BS (01758 760344). Bryn Mor is a family run Guest House. Full English breakfast, evening meal optional. Comfortable lounge and separate diningroom. Access to rooms at all times. TV and tea making facilities in all rooms. Bathroom and shower facilities. The house overlooks the Bay a few minutes from village and beach. Ample parking space in our own grounds. Bryn Mor is situated in the village of Aberdaron at the tip of the Lleyn Peninsula. Around the Bay are numerous walks with panoramic views, also fishing, sailing and golf in the locality. Assuring you of our best endeavours to make your holiday a pleasant one. Sorry, no pets. Bed and Breakfast £14.50; Bed, Breakfast and Evening Meal £21.

ANGLESEY. Mrs Gwen McCreadie, Deri Isaf, Dulas Bay, Anglesey LL70 9DX (01248 410536). ♛♛♛ Beautiful Victorian country house standing in 20 acres of woodland, garden and fields, surrounded by lovely countryside, overlooking the bay. Easily accessible, excellent base for touring the island and exploring the coastline with its many lovely beaches. Local amenities include golf, swimming pool and sports centre. Pony for riding. Accommodation of a very high standard in two family rooms and one double all en suite. Guests' own sittingroom with TV, video, etc. Separate diningroom. Full central heating. Pets welcome; horse stabling available. Car advisable. Bed and Breakfast from £18; Bed, Breakfast and Evening Meal from £25. Reductions for children. Holder of FHG Diploma. Call **01248 370125** Student Services.

ANGLESEY. Mrs Ritson, "Ger-y-Coed", Gaerwen, Anglesey LL60 6BS (01248 421297). ♛♛ *HIGHLY COMMENDED.* Homely guest house situated six miles from Bangor on main Holyhead road (A5). Comfortably furnished. Tea/coffee making facilities, washbasins, shaver points and colour TVs in all rooms. Some rooms en-suite. Sky TV in lounge. Nice garden, with off-road parking. Good and plentiful food. Double, twin and family rooms available. Central heating. Open all year. Close to all amenities and ferry. Ideal for touring and discovering Snowdonia. Warm welcome assured. Bed and Breakfast from £16. Evening Meals by arrangement. Access and Visa accepted. Full Fire Certificate.

ANGLESEY. Mrs Kirkland, "Carreg Goch", Llanedwen, Llanfairpwll, Anglesey LL61 6EZ (01248 430315). 👑 *HIGHLY COMMENDED.* "Carreg Goch" is quietly situated in the south of Anglesey and is set well back off the A4080 in four acres of gardens and paddock. Easy access to the coast, National Trust properties, Snowdonia and many places of interest makes it a convenient centre. Two centrally heated ground floor rooms have washbasins and tea making facilities. There is a shared guest bathroom/shower but two separate toilets. Both rooms have French windows opening onto a private patio and garden with magnificent views of Snowdonia. Separate guest sitting room with colour TV. Bed and Breakfast £16. Weekly rates available.

BALA. Mrs G. Jones, Erw Feurig Farm, Cefnddwysarn, Bala LL23 7LL (01678 530262). 👑👑 *HIGHLY COMMENDED.* Welsh Tourist Board Farm Guest House Award Holder. Beautifully situated facing the Berwyn Mountains, Erw Feurig offers extremely comfortable and spacious accommodation in family, double and twin bedrooms; two en-suite rooms and one ground floor room; all with tea/coffee making facilities. Own keys and central heating. Excellent breakfast served and dinner available by prior arrangement. Colour TV in separate lounge. Private coarse fishing on the farm. Ideal centre for walking, touring and seaside. Picturesque market town of Bala three and a half miles away. Plenty of pubs, restaurants and shops. Bed and Breakfast from £15; Dinner £8.50 by prior arrangement.

BALA. Lesley Andrews, Bronwylfa Guest House, Llandderfel, Bala LL23 7HG (01678 530207). 👑👑 *DE LUXE.* AA QQQ, RAC Highly Acclaimed. Welcome Host trained. Bronwylfa is a large stone manor house with coach house situated in quiet picturesque surroundings with beautiful views of the Berwyn Mountains and River Dee. Two large double en suite rooms, one family room with private facilities and one twin en suite in the Coach House, all with colour TV, tea/coffee making facilities, hair dryers etc. Large car park. Relax and unwind in beautiful Victorian conservatory with a large selection of maps and books on walks and places of interest. Central for touring Mid and North Wales with Snowdonia National Park, watersports, walking, fishing, golf, Little Trains, waterfalls, lakes and rivers all within easy reach. Bed and Breakfast from £17 to £22 per person. Reduced rates for children sharing parent's room. Situated on the edge of farmland, six miles west off A5 or four miles east from Bala after village.

BALA. Brynllech Isaf, Llanuwchllyn LL23 7SU (01678 540374). Quiet, comfortable Bed and Breakfast off the beaten track in Snowdonia National Park near Bala Lake. Superb views. Ideal base for walking and touring. Accommodation comprises one twin bedroom and one single bedroom (or two full size bunk beds if required) on first floor with own private bathroom and sitting room with TV on ground floor. Tea/coffee making facilities and drying facilities. Central heating. Car park, garden and own entrance. Open all year. Bed and Breakfast from £14 per person. Reductions for children under 16 years. Phone for directions.

BALA. Mrs G.A. Evans, Pant-y-Ceubren, Llanuwchllyn, Bala LL23 7DD (01678 540252). Working farm. Comfortable beamed farmhouse, dating back to 1648, overlooking the village of Llanuwchllyn where the Berwyn, Aran and Arenig meet at the southern tip of Bala Lake. Wonderfully peaceful area for the country lover; walking, wildlife, unsurpassed panoramic views, yet conveniently situated for the nearby town of Bala with its attractive new leisure centre and the interesting little town of Dolgellau; Machynlleth with the Alternative Technology Centre is well worth a visit. Lovely beaches at nearby Barmouth, Tywyn and Aberdovey. One double and one family bedrooms, bathroom. Tea/coffee making facilities. Full Welsh breakfast using home produce. SAE, please, for terms.

BALA. Glynn and Wenda Jones, Frondderw, Bala LL23 7YD (01678 520301). 🐦🐦🐦 *COMMENDED.*

A period mansion situated in own grounds overlooking Bala town and Lake, with views of the Berwyn Mountains. Ideally situated for walking, sailing, golfing and general sightseeing around North and Mid Wales. Accommodation consists of eight bedrooms, four with en-suite facilities and two with showers. All bedrooms have washbasins, central heating, tea/coffee making facilities. Guests' lounge. Separate TV lounge, colour TV. Residential licence. Free parking. Sorry, NO PETS. Open March to November inclusive. Bed and Breakfast from £15 to £21 daily per person. Optional three course Dinner £9, including tea/coffee. Home cooked meals. Special diets catered for by prior arrangement. Weekly terms. AA QQ, WTB Welcome Host.

BALA. Mrs S.E. Edwards, Bryn Melyn Farm, Rhyduchaf, Bala LL23 7SD (01678 520376). 🐦 *COMMENDED.* Situated one and a half miles from Bala, near the foot of the Arrenig Mountain, Bryn Melyn offers a warm welcome and beautiful views of the surrounding countryside. Accommodation is in three double/twin bedrooms, all with central heating. There is a TV lounge to relax in after a delicious, wholesome, home cooked four-course evening meal. Bala is set in Snowdonia National Park on the shores of a lake, and the area offers plenty of variety for holidaymakers. A genuine Welsh welcome is extended to all visitors. Winner of British Farm Holiday Award 1988. Bed and Breakfast from £14.50; Bed, Breakfast and Evening Meal from £23. Weekly terms £148. No smoking.

BALA near. Mrs J. Best, Cwm Hwylfod, Cefn-Ddwysarn, Bala LL23 7LN (01678 530310). 🐦 *COMMENDED.* **Working farm.** Remote, peaceful 400-year-old farmhouse on working sheep farm. Beautiful countryside and wonderful views. Two double rooms, one large family room, all with washbasins and tea making facilities. Two bathrooms, clothes washing and drying machines. Guests' lounge with colour TV. Full central heating. Cot, high chair available. Parking space. All meals are home cooked. Special diets catered for. Ideal centre for touring, walking, fishing, pony trekking and watersports. Bala Lake 10 minutes by car. Snowdon and many beaches can be reached in 40 minutes. Bed and Breakfast from £14 to £16; Evening Meal (optional) from £10. Reductions for long stays and children under 10 years. Brochure available. Children most welcome.

Cwm Hwylfod

BARMOUTH. Mrs Lesley Amison, Fronoleu Hall, Llanaber Road, Barmouth LL42 1YT (01341 280491). 🐦🐦 If you are planning a holiday in Wales you could do no better than stay in this gracious house with unrivalled views across Cardigan Bay to the Cader Idris range and the Lleyn Peninsula. A warm personal welcome, good food, spacious en suite rooms with colour TV and tea/coffee making facilities, beach access and ample parking combine to make Fronoleu Hall the perfect base. We are ideally situated for the beach, touring in Snowdonia or walking in the Rhinogs or the Cader Idris. We offer help and advice in planning walks and tours, and pledge our best efforts to make your stay a happy one. Bed and Breakfast from £15 to £22; Evening Meal £9. Directions: one mile north of Barmouth on the coast side of the main road to Harlech just after a layby.

BARMOUTH. Doreen and David Iliffe, Ty'n y Coed Guest House, Caerdeon, Barmouth LL42 1TL (01341 430228). WTB Listed *COMMENDED.* 18th century farmhouse set in 16 acres of hilly woodland over which guests are free to roam. Comfortable bedrooms, each with washbasin and tea/coffee making facilities. Homely, peaceful atmosphere. Log fires in the lounge and dining room when chilly. Oil-fired central heating. Ample parking. Non-smoking throughout. Six guests maximum. Good food, special diets catered for. Bed and Breakfast £13; Evening Dinner (optional) £10. Reductions for children. Special Offer: Dinner, Bed and Breakfast for a full week only £140.

BEAUMARIS. Mrs E. Roberts, Plas Cichle, Beaumaris, Anglesey LL58 8PS (Tel & Fax: 01248 810488). 🐾🐾 *HIGHLY COMMENDED.* Welcome Host Gold Award, Farmhouse Award. We welcome you to Plas Cichle, a large period farmhouse set in 200 acres, one and a half miles from the historic town of Beaumaris and the Menai Straits. Accommodation is offered in spacious, comfortable rooms, most are en suite, all have hospitality tray, colour TV and hair dryers. Most have panoramic views over to Snowdonia. Start your day in our elegant dining room and enjoy a hearty breakfast. Relax in the comfortable guest lounge, sit out in the garden or stroll around the farm to see the animals. Plas Cichle is an ideal base from which to explore Anglesey and Snowdonia. Many guests return year after year. Come along and find out why! Bed and Breakfast from £20. Open February to November. Brochure available.

BETWS-Y-COED. Mrs Florence Jones, Maes Gwyn Farm, Pentrefoelas, Betws-y-Coed LL24 0LR (01690 770668). WTB Listed *HIGHLY COMMENDED.* Maes Gwyn is a mixed farm of 90-97 hectares, situated in lovely quiet countryside, about one mile from the A5, six miles from the famous Betws-y-Coed. The sea and Snowdonia Mountains about 20 miles. Very good centre for touring North Wales, many well-known places of interest. Houses dates back to 1665. It has one double and one family bedrooms with washbasins and tea/coffee making facilities; bathroom with shower, toilet; lounge with colour TV and diningroom. Children and Senior Citizens are welcome at reduced rates and pets are permitted. Car essential, ample parking provided. Good home cooking. Six miles to bus/railway terminal. Open May/November for Bed and Breakfast from £14. SAE, please, for details.

BETWS-Y-COED. Mrs E. Jones, Maes-y-Garnedd Farm, Capel Garmon, Llanrwst, Betws-y-Coed (01690 710428). Tourist Board Listed *APPROVED.* **Working farm.** This 140-acre mixed farm is superbly situated on the Rooftop of Wales as Capel Garmon has been called, and the Snowdonia Range, known to the Welsh as the "Eyri", visible from the land. Two miles from A5. Surrounding area provides beautiful country scenery and walks. Safe, sandy beaches at Llandudno and Colwyn Bay. Salmon and trout fishing (permit required). Mrs Jones serves excellent home produced meals with generous portions including Welsh lamb and roast beef. Gluten-free and coeliacs' wheat-free diets can be arranged. Packed lunches, with flask of coffee or tea. One double and one family bedrooms with washbasins; bathroom, toilet; sittingroom, dining room. Children welcome; cot, high chair and babysitting available. Regret, no pets. Car essential, ample parking. Open all year. Bed and Breakfast; Evening Meal optional. SAE brings prompt reply with details of terms. Reductions for children. Bala Lakes, Bodnant Gardens, Ffestiniog Railway, slate quarries, Trefriw Woollen Mills nearby. Member of AA.

BETWS-Y-COED. Mrs E.A. Jones, Pant Glas, Padoc, Pentrefoelas Road, Betws-y-Coed LL24 0PG (01690 770248). WTB Listed. Peaceful and quiet, but with a friendly atmosphere, this beef and sheep farm of 181 acres, with scenic views, is situated five miles from Betws-y-Coed. Ideal for touring, within easy reach of Snowdon, Bodnant Gardens, Caernarfon Castle, Llandudno, Black Rock Sands, Ffestiniog Railway, Llechwedd Slate Mines, Swallow and Conwy Falls and woollen mills. Accommodation comprises two double and one twin bedrooms, all with washbasins and tea/coffee making facilities; bath and shower, two toilets. Use of colour TV lounge. Sorry no pets. Car essential, parking for three/four cars. Evening Meal, Bed and Breakfast from £17.50 to £19; Bed and Breakfast from £12.50 to £13.50. Open Easter to November.

BETWS-Y-COED. Jim and Lilian Boughton, Bron Celyn Guest House, Llanrwst Road, Betws-y-Coed LL24 0HD (01690 710333; Fax: 01690 710111). 🐾🐾🐾 *HIGHLY COMMENDED.* A warm welcome awaits you at this delightful Guest House overlooking the Gwydyr Forest and Llugwy/Conwy Valleys and village of Betws-y-Coed in Snowdonia National Park. Ideal centre for touring, walking, climbing, fishing and golf. Also excellent overnight stop for Holyhead ferries. Easy walk into village and close to Conwy/Swallow Falls and Fairy Glen. Most rooms en-suite. All with colour TV and beverage makers. Full central heating, lounge. Garden, car park. Open all year. Full hearty breakfast, packed meals, snacks, Evening Meals. Special diets catered for. Bed and Breakfast from £16 to £20. Reduced rates for children under 12 years.

BETWS-Y-COED. Summer Hill Non-Smokers' Guest House, Coedcynhelier Road, Betws-y-Coed LL24 0BL (01690 710306). 🐾🐾 *COMMENDED.* Especially for the non-smoker, Summer Hill is delightfully situated in a quiet, sunny location overlooking the River Llugwy and Fir Tree Island; 150 yards from main road, shops and restaurants. Seven comfortable bedrooms (four en suite), washbasins and tea/coffee making facilities. Residents' lounge with colour TV. Singles, children and pets welcome. Flasks filled, packed lunches provided, evening meals bookable in advance. Vegetarians, special diets catered for. Private car parking. Betws-y-Coed is the gateway to Snowdonia, with spectacular mountains, forests and rivers. Golf, fishing, gardens, castles all accessible. Bed and Breakfast from £15; Evening Meal from £8.50. Reductions for children.

BETWS-Y-COED. Mr and Mrs M. Fakhri, Bryn Bella Guest House, Llanrwst Road, Betws-y-Coed

LL24 0HD (01690 710627). ♛♛♛ *HIGHLY COMMEN-DED.* Bryn Bella is a small Victorian guest house noted for its caring and friendly atmosphere, situated in a quiet elevated position overlooking Betws-y-Coed, in the Snowdonia National Park. Four recently refurbished rooms (three with en-suite), each having tea/coffee making facilities and colour TV. Guest lounge and patio from which to enjoy the glorious views. Private parking. Superb breakfast; packed lunches on request. Ideal centre for touring, climbing, riding, fishing and golf and within easy reach of Holyhead Ferry. Bed and Breakfast from £16. Reduced rates for children sharing parents' room. Special off-peak weekly rates. Open all year.

"The Country House in the Village!"

Fron Heulog Country House
Betws-y-Coed, North Wales LL24 0BL
Tel/Fax: 01690 710736
Jean & Peter Whittingham welcome house guests

Betws-y-Coed – "Heart of Snowdonia"

We invite you to visit our home where you will enjoy real hospitality. Fron Heulog is an elegant Victorian stone-built house, facing south in quiet, peaceful, wooded riverside scenery, which offer deluxe accommodation, completely non-smoking, with full facility bedrooms, ensuite bathrooms, spacious lounges, a pleasant dining room and private parking. Sorry, no pets. Highly recommended for friendly atmosphere, warmth, comfort and hostess' home cooking. Full central heating. In Betws-y-Coed, in the heart of the wonderfully picturesque Snowdonia National Park – with so much to see and do – Fron Heulog is an ideal touring and walking centre. Bed and Breakfast from £18-£26.

WTB ♛♛♛ Highly Commended. Guest House Award.
More home than hotel! Welcome – Croeso!

BETWS-Y-COED. Mrs Joyce Melling, Mount Pleasant, Betws-y-Coed LL24 0BN (01690 710502).

WTB Welcome Home *COMMENDED.* AA QQ. A warm Welsh welcome awaits you at our Victorian stone-built house only a few minutes' walk from the centre of Betws-y-Coed, yet overlooking open fields and woodland. Our comfortable centrally heated rooms all provide tea/coffee facilities, colour TV, washbasins, and some have en suite facilities. Enjoy a hearty breakfast at individual tables in our light and airy breakfast room, where you can choose between a vegetarian or more traditional breakfast. Walkers are welcome and packed lunches are available on request. We welcome children over 12 years, but regret we are unable to take pets. Some off-road parking available. Totally non-smoking. Bed and Breakfast from £15 per person per night.

BETWS-Y-COED near. Mrs Eleanore Roberts, Awelon, Plas Isa, Llanrwst LL26 0EE (01492

640047). ♛ Awelon once formed part of the estate of William Salisbury, translator of the New Testament into Welsh in the 16th century. With three-foot thick outer walls, it has now been modernised and is an attractive small guest house. Three bedrooms (one en suite) with colour TV and teamakers; cosy lounge; central heating ensures a comfy stay. Private parking. Llanrwst, a busy market town at the centre of the beautiful Conway Valley, is close to Snowdonia, Bodnant Gardens and North Wales coast. A warm Welsh welcome awaits all guests. Bed and Breakfast from £14.50 to £17. Dinner optional. All home cooking. Children and pets welcome.

PLEASE SEND A STAMPED ADDRESSED ENVELOPE WITH ENQUIRIES

AA
★★★
RAC

plas hall hotel & Restaurant

COMMENDED

Snowdonia National Park

Standing in its own gardens offering PEACE and SECLUSION on the banks of the River Lledr off the main A470 road, this magnificent stone built hall is ideally placed for the tourist, walker, fisherman or golfer.

All bedrooms are ensuite, with colour TV, telephone, clock radio and central heating. Licensed bar and superb restaurant. Bed and Breakfast from £19.95, Evening Meal from £10. 2 day Breaks DBB from £47.95. Write or phone for colour brochure B.M.Williams.

Plas Hall Hotel & Restaurant, Dolywyddelan, near Betws-y-Coed, Gwynedd LL25 0PJ. Telephone: 01690 750206. Fax: 01690 750526.

BLAENAU FFESTINIOG. Mrs G.E. Hughes, Bryn Celynog Farm, Cwm Prysor, Trawsfynydd, Blaenau Ffestiniog LL41 4TR (01766 540378). A true Welsh welcome awaits you on this working beef/sheep farm surrounded by beautiful scenery in the centre of Snowdonia National Park. Choice of spacious twin, double or family bedrooms, all with washbasins and tea/coffee facilities, one room en suite. Guest bathroom. Lounge with colour TV, open fire. Reputation for excellent food and friendliness. Bed and Breakfast from £17 to £18.50. SAE please.

CAERNARVON. Mrs S. Williams, Tal Menai Guest House, Bangor Road, Caernarvon LL55 1TP (01286 672160). ⚜ ⚜ Victorian house standing in its own grounds off the A487 to Bangor (about one mile from Caernarfon Castle), Tal Menai enjoys panoramic views over Menai Straits and Anglesey. It is an ideal centre for touring Snowdonia. Off the road private parking. Twin and double rooms, all en suite, colour TV, tea/coffee making facilities and central heating. Access to house at all times. Packed lunches available and special diets catered for. Special terms for four nights stay and out of season bookings. Sorry no pets and no smoking. From £17 per person.

CAERNARVON. Mrs B. Cartwright, Tan Dinas, Llanddeiniolen, Caernarvon LL55 3AR (01248 670098). Tourist Board Listed. A modernised stone farmhouse situated in a picturesque, secluded, yet very central location and surrounded by typical Welsh scenic beauty, with a pleasant garden sloping down to a small stream running alongside the woods. Guests have their own private and centrally heated lounge and diningroom. The area is ideal for touring, all types of fishing, walking and pony trekking if required. Caernarvon, Bangor, Anglesey and Snowdon itself are all within very easy reach. Take the B4366 out of Caernarvon. One mile through Bethel, come to the "Gors Bach Inn". Turn into lane by side of inn, travel on for half a mile. Children welcome, cot, high chair, babysitting available. Car essential — parking. Open March to October with central heating and open fires. Pets accepted. Bed and Breakfast from £15; Evening meal optional. Reductions for children.

CAERNARFON. Mrs V. Edwards, Chatham Farmhouse, Llandwrog, Caernarfon LL54 5TG (01286

831257). 🐾🐾 *HIGHLY COMMENDED.* Croeso, welcome to our peaceful 18th century guesthouse situated four miles from Caernarfon, two miles from Dinas Dingle beach, very near good bird watching area. All Snowdonia's attractions within easy reach. Enjoy lazy breakfasts that include free-range eggs from our own hens. Wholesome evening meals include vegetables organically grown in our own garden. Tea-making facilities in all the cosy rooms (two en suite, one with private bathroom). Rooms have central heating, dining room has a wood burning stove. Guests' TV lounge. Children welcome, sorry no pets. Bed and Breakfast £17; Evening Meal £10. Looking forward to meeting you.

CAPEL CURIG. Alison Cousins, Bryn Glo Tea Room and Guest House, Capel Curig, Betws-y-Coed

LL24 0DT (01690 720215/312). Small family business, attractively situated in mountain village in Snowdonia National Park, easily located near A5 trunk road. Clean, comfortable accommodation in refurbished Welsh cottage. Genuine home cooking, special diets catered for. Convenient for visits to walking and climbing areas, castles, beaches and numerous places of interest including Snowdon. "Taste of Wales member". Tea/coffee facilities. Central heating. Private parking. Open all year. Bed and Breakfast from £15.

CHESTER near. Mrs Christine Whale, Brookside House, Brookside Lane, Northop Hall, Mold CH7

6HN (01244 821146). 🐾🐾 Relax and enjoy the hospitality of our recently refurbished 18th century Welsh stone cottage. The home-from-home accommodation offers a double, twin or family room with private bathroom upon request. All rooms have colour TV and tea making facilities. Within a short walk the village has an excellent restaurant and two pubs (one of which serves bar meals). Suitable for touring North Wales, Chester and Liverpool or just a short break away from it all. Bed and Breakfast from £17.

CHESTER near. Mrs J. Major, The Mount, Higher Kinnerton, Near Chester CH4 9BQ (01244

660275). Large family house in beautiful gardens with tennis court and croquet lawn. A quiet location on the edge of the village just off the A55. All rooms are decorated to a high standard, have tea/coffee making facilities, TV and either private or en suite bath. Guests have use of all facilities. Good home cooking using produce from our large vegetable garden. Historic Chester, National Trust properties, gardens and coast of North Wales on the doorstep; Liverpool and Manchester within 45 minutes' drive. Open all year. From £35 double, £20 single, with reduction for three nights or more. Evening Dinner £12. Details on request.

CONWY. Mrs E. Wagstaff, Pinewood Towers Country Guest House, Sychnant Pass Road, Conwy LL32 8BZ (01492 592459). Victorian Country House with residential licence set in 10 acres, gardens, woods and paddocks on Conwy mountainside situated in the Snowdonia National Park. Tea/coffee making facilities and washbasins in all rooms. Plentiful home cooked food. Reduction for children sharing, children under five years not accepted. Dogs in owners' rooms or kennels available if required. Ideal for real country lovers and people liking peace and quiet — yet not isolated. Open April to September. Stamp for brochure please.

CONWY. Mr and Mrs W. Hansel, Llys Gwilym Guest House, 3 Mountain Road, Cadnant Park, Conwy LL32 8PU (01492 592351). 🐾 *COMMENDED.* Just a few minutes' walk to Conwy Castle, town, quayside and close to the Conwy Valley and all Snowdonia. Quietly located at the foot of Conwy Mountain and adjacent to the Sychnant Pass. Bill and Barbara offer you a warm and friendly welcome. There are seven letting bedrooms comprising singles, double, twin and family; all have washbasins, colour TV and tea/coffee making facilities. There is also a homely residents' lounge with books and games etc. A hearty breakfast is one of our features with other meals by arrangement. Special off season price Bed, Breakfast and Evening Meal £18 per person.

CONWY. Glan Heulog Guest House, Llanrwst Road, Conwy LL32 8LT (01492 593845). ♥ ♥ ♥ AA

QQQ. Spacious Victorian house, close to historic walled town of Conwy and its castle. All rooms have TV and tea/coffee facilities. There is off-street parking, en suite facilities are available and we have a large lounge for guests with games and books available and a residential licence. There is a large garden with good views. We are conveniently situated for Snowdonia National Park, Anglesey, Bodnant Gardens and other well-known attractions. Our guests say "great rooms", "excellent service", "wonderful meals", "charming hosts", "lovely warm welcome", "best place I've stayed", "we will be back". Book early to avoid disappointment. Bed and Breakfast from £13.

CONWY. Mrs Michele Harpur, Caerlyr Hall, Conwy Old Road, Dwygyfylchi LL34 6SW (01492 623518). ♥ ♥ ♥ ♥ HIGHLY COMMENDED. A charming

country house, once the summer home of the Victorian MP Picton, Caerlyr Hall is nestled at the foothills of Snowdonia National Park overlooking Penmaenmawr Golf Course with the finest views in North Wales. Guests never tire of the breathtaking sea and mountain views. Delightful and spacious en suite bedrooms with original stained glass windows, colour TV, hospitality tray and trouser press. Converted from the master's library our lounge with its vaulted ceiling and open fire is an ideal room to relax in. Our extensive breakfast menu is enjoyed in our beautiful dining room or on our sun terrace. Bed and Breakfast from £20 per person.

CORWEN. Bob and Kit Buckland, Corwen Court Private Hotel, London Road, Corwen LL21 0DP (01490 412854). ♥ ♥ COMMENDED. Situated on the main A5, this converted old police station and courthouse has six prisoners' cells turned into single bedrooms. Hot and cold in each, with a bathroom to service three on the first floor and a shower room for three on the ground floor. All double bedrooms have bathrooms en suite. The dining room in the old courthouse is where the local magistrates presided, and the comfortable lounge spreads over the rest of the court. Central heating throughout and colour TV in the lounge. Fire Certificate. Bed and Breakfast from £13 to £14; Evening Meal £7. Children and pets welcome. AA listed. Convenient base for touring North Wales.

CRICCIETH. Mrs A. Reynolds, Glyn-y-Coed Hotel, Porthmadoc Road, Criccieth LL52 0HL (01766 522870; Fax: 01766 523341). ♥ ♥ ♥ HIGHLY COMMENDED. Lovely Victorian family run hotel overlooking sea, mountains, Criccieth and Harlech Castles. Fully centrally heated, cosy bar, parking in our grounds. Special diets catered for, highly recommended home cooking. Separate tables in our pretty pink restaurant. All bedrooms are en-suite with colour TV, tea/coffee making facilities. Fire Certificate. Moderate rates, from £19 for Bed and Breakfast. Good reductions for children. One ground floor bedroom with facilities available. Self catering accommodation also available. Les Routiers, AA, RAC. SAE please. Brochure sent with pleasure.

DOLGELLAU. Mrs G.D. Evans, "Y Goedlan", Brithdir, Dolgellau LL40 2RN (Tel and Fax: 01341 423131). ♥ COMMENDED. Guests are welcome at "Y

Goedlan" from February to October. This old Vicarage with adjoining farm offers peaceful accommodation in pleasant rural surroundings. Three miles from Dolgellau on the B4416 road, good position for interesting walks (Torrent, 400 yards from the house), beaches, mountains, narrow gauge railways and pony trekking. All bedrooms are large and spacious; one double, one twin and one family room, all with colour TV, tea/coffee facilities and washbasins; bathroom, two toilets; shower; lounge with colour TV; separate tables in dining room. Reduced rates for children under 10 years. Central heating. Car essential, parking. Comfort, cleanliness and personal attention assured, with a good hearty breakfast; Bed and Breakfast from £15.

DOLGELLAU. Mr and Mrs J.S. Bamford, Ivy House, Finsbury Square, Dolgellau LL40 1RF (01341

422535). ♛ ♛ ♛ A country town Guest House offering a welcoming atmosphere and good food. Guest accommodation consists of six double rooms, three with en suite toilet facilities, all with TV and tea/coffee making. In the evening the dining room is open to non-residents as well as residents offering an extensive menu of HOME MADE FOOD including many vegetarian dishes. There is a bar in the cellar. The lounge has tourist information literature and there are maps available to borrow. Dolgellau is an ideal touring and walking centre in the Snowdonia National Park. Bed and Breakfast from £18.

DYFFRYN ARDUDWY. Mrs A. Jones, Byrdir Farm, Dyffryn Ardudwy LL44 2EA (01341 247200).

♛ ♛ ♛ *HIGHLY COMMENDED.* Dragon Awarded, Welsh stone farmhouse in peaceful setting in Snowdonia National Park with coastline in front, mountains to rear. Woods, streams, beaches, lovely walks, golf, swimming pools, fishing, riding nearby. Double and family bedrooms (three en suite); sitting room with colour TV; dining room. Children welcome at reduced rates. Bed and Breakfast from £17 to £19 per person. Open March to September.

FAIRBOURNE. John and Ann Waterhouse, Einion House, Friog, Fairbourne LL38 2NX (01341

250644). ♛ ♛ ♛ *COMMENDED.* Lovely old house between mountains and sea, set in beautiful scenery. Comfortable rooms, double, twin or single, en suite available. Reputation for good home cooking — vegetarians catered for. All rooms with colour TVs, clock/radios, hairdryers, teamakers, sea or mountain views. Separate dining tables. Guests' TV lounge. Restaurant and residential licence. Wonderful sunsets, marvellous walking — maps and Land Rover lifts available. Pony trekking, fishing and bird watching. Good centre for Narrow Gauge Railways. Castle within easy reach. Safe sandy beach few minutes' walk from house. Children and dogs welcome. Bed and Breakfast from £17; optional three-course Dinner £9. Weekly terms.

FFESTINIOG. Mrs R. Lethbridge, Morannedd Guest House, Ffestiniog LL41 4LG (01766 762734).

Snowdonia guest house enjoying spectacular views over Vale of Ffestiniog and Moelwyn. Most bedrooms are en suite and all have tea making facilities. Landscaped gardens for sitting and admiring the views also offer plant swapping opportunities. The dining room with log fire, exposed beams and mountains views complement the delicious home cooked food including many local dishes. Excellent choice for vegetarians. Ideal base for touring, walking, beaches, National Trust properties and other tourist attractions including slate caverns, Portmeirion, Ffestiniog and other narrow gauge railways. Non-smoking. Group rates. Optional packed lunches and dinner. Spring, Autumn and Christmas Breaks. Brochure available.

LLANBERIS. Dolafon Hotel, High Street, Llanberis LL55 4SU (01286 870993). ❦❦ A small family-run NON SMOKING HOTEL, all rooms are en suite with colour TV and tea/coffee making facilities. We have a small licensed restaurant and bar which offers a varied menu including home made Welsh dishes and a good vegetarian selection. DOLAFON is situated on the main street of Llanberis and is separated from the road by a large lawned garden bordered by mature trees and a small mountain stream offering ample secluded private parking. Llanberis has many places of interest, the slate museum, Dinorwic Hydro Electric Power Station, Dolbardarn Castle and nearby Caernarfon and Beaumaris Castles. Bed and Breakfast from £16.

LLANDUDNO. Mrs Ruth Hodkinson, Cranleigh, Great Orme's Road, West Shore, Llandudno LL30 2AR (01492 877688). A comfortable, late Victorian private residence and family home situated on the quieter West Shore of Llandudno. Only yards from beach and magnificent Great Orme Mountain. Parking: no problem. Town centre is a short pleasant walk away. Many places of interest in surrounding area, and opportunities for sports and recreational activities. Excellent home cooked food. Two en suite rooms available, both with views of sea and mountains. Conforms to high standards of S.I. 1991/474. Most highly recommended.

LLANDUDNO. Mrs T. Williams, Roselea, Deganwy Avenue, Llandudno (01492 876279). Situated a few minutes from sea front and shops, entertainments, etc. Near to ski slope and Great Orme Tram. Access to house at all times with own front door and bedroom keys. TV lounge. Children welcome; small dogs welcome by arrangement. Car park. Bed and Breakfast £13 per person per night. Please write or telephone for further details.

LLANDUDNO. White Lodge Hotel, Central Promenade, Llandudno LL30 1AT (01492 877713). ❦ ❦ ❦ *HIGHLY COMMENDED.* Have a holiday to remember at the family-run White Lodge Hotel, set on the Promenade in beautiful Llandudno. Comfortable lounge with bay views, dining room with separate tables and superb food from our chef. All rooms en suite with colour TV and tea making facilities. Central heating. Parking for all guests' cars. The perfect base for touring scenic Snowdonia. Bed and Breakfast from £21 per person. AA/RAC two star.

LLANFACHRAETH. Mrs Joyce A. Roberts, Penyrorsedd Farm, Llanfachraeth, Holyhead LL65 4YB (01407 730630). Member of Welsh Tourist Board. A 17th century 400 acre working farm just off the A5025 outside the village of Llanfachraeth, ideally situated for overnight stops, when travelling to Ireland. The farm is two miles from sandy beach with other beaches close by. The farmhouse is full of character and has a home from home atmosphere. Traditional English breakfast served to guests' own requirements. Central heating. Accommodation comprises double en suite, double room and twin room with private bathroom. Separate lounge with TV. Reductions for children; travelling cot available. Open all year. Bed and Breakfast from £17. Further details gladly provided on application.

LLANFAIRFECHAN. Mrs K.M. Coleman, Plas Heulog, Mount Road, Llanfairfechan LL33 0HA (Tel & Fax: 01248 680019). ❦ ❦ *COMMENDED.* Situated in the Snowdonia region, Plas Heulog gives breathtaking views of both sea and mountains. It offers total seclusion in its nine acres of woodland, yet it is easily accessible from the A55 Expressway and main line station. Sailing, windsurfing, jet ski-ing, golf, bowls, riding, sea and freshwater fishing are all within easy reach as well as several nature reserves. Centrally heated double and twin en suite bedrooms are situated in modern chalets above main house, with provision for making tea and coffee. Breakfast is taken in the main house where a spacious lounge is available for guests' use. Facilities include drying room, secure bicycle storage and ample parking. Wales Tourist Board Approved for walkers and cyclists.

LLANGOLLEN. Mrs Janet Jones, The Cottage, Carrog, Corwen LL21 9AP (01490 430255). Dating from the 17th century The Cottage is idyllically situated in the Dee Valley, eight miles west of Llangollen and one mile from the A5. Bed and Breakfast is offered in one double and one twin room each with TV, tea/coffee and private facilities. Guests are welcome to use all the house and large gardens. Ideal position for exploring the north of the principality with its many attractions or simply relax and enjoy the peace and tranquillity of the immediate locality. Bed and Breakfast from £16 per person. Please telephone for further information.

LLANGOLLEN. Mrs A. Dennis, Oaklands Guest House, Llangollen Road, Trevor, Llangollen LL20

7TG (01978 820152). 🌸🌸 Situated in the beautiful Vale of Llangollen, Oaklands is a charming Victorian house set in lovely gardens. All rooms are warm, spacious and comfortably furnished, with tea-making facilities, washbasins, and very comfortable beds. Guests' television lounge. Nearby are places of interest such as Telford's Aqueduct (as filmed in "Treasure Hunt"), Llangollen Steam Railway, swimming baths, and National Trust properties at Chirk and Erddig. Ideal base for touring, golf, climbing, pony trekking, walking Offa's Dyke or on Berwyn Mountains. On bus route to Chester and coast. Bed and hearty English Breakfast from £15. Seven nights Bed and Breakfast from £78 per person; three nights Bed and Breakfast from £42 per person. Families welcome at reduced rates. Sorry, no pets. Ample parking. Open all year.

LLANNERCH-Y-MEDD (Anglesey). Mrs J. Bown, Drws-y-Coed, Llanerch-y-Medd, Anglesey LL71

8AD (01248 470473). 🌸🌸🌸 *DELUXE*. Drws-y-Coed, a beautifully appointed farmhouse on 550 acres of beef, sheep and arable farmland, is set in beautiful wooded countryside with panoramic views of Snowdonia, near to picturesque Bodafon Mountain. Centrally located for beaches, fishing, golf, riding, leisure centres. Tarmac drives. A warm welcome awaits our guests who are accommodated in beautifully decorated and furnished bedrooms, all en suite with colour TV, tea-making facilities and clock radios. Full central heating. Spacious lounge with log fire. Dining room with separate tables; delicious meals. Games room. Lovely walks in vicinity. WTB Rural Tourism Award. Farm Holiday Guide Diploma Award. Reductions for children. Bed and Breakfast from £20 to £23 (Evening Meal optional). Non-smoking establishment. Open all year. Brochure available.

LLANRWST. Mr Michael John Bucknall, Pickwicks Hotel, Bridge Street, Llanrwst LL26 0ET (01492

PICKWICKS

640275). 🌸🌸 A 400 year old, family-run guest house/tearoom, oak beamed and retaining its "olde worlde" character, whilst offering modern facilities: central heating, en suite rooms, tea/coffee makers, etc. Centrally situated in Llanrwst, a small market town nestling in the beautiful Conwy Valley, an ideal base for exploring Snowdonia, lakes, forests, coastal resorts and popular local attractions. Friendly and informal, a haven for walking and climbing enthusiasts with drying area, storage for equipment and comfortable lounge for relaxation. Parking. Packed lunches, evening meals available (with vegetarian options). Open all year. Bed and Breakfast from £14.50.

LLANSILIN. Mrs G. Jones, Lloran Ganol Farm, Llansilin, Oswestry SY10 7OX (01691 791287).

WTB 🌸 Working farm, join in. A friendly welcome is assured at this modern farm set in 300 acres in Welsh valley. A busy working farm of dairy, sheep and cattle, it has surrounding garden and lawns. Fly fishing, rough shooting and horse riding locally. Tastefully furnished farmhouse has two double bedrooms (one double, one twin), each with washbasin, colour TV and tea/coffee making facilities; modern bathroom. Large lounge and dining room; colour TV. English Breakfast and Evening Meal. Bed and Breakfast from £12.50; Dinner, Bed and Breakfast from £24. Weekly self catering from £80.

MACHYNLLETH. Mrs Lynwen Edwards, Bryn Sion Farm, Cwm Cywarch, Dinas Mawddwy, Machynlleth SY20 9JG (01650 531251). A very warm welcome awaits you when you visit Bryn Sion Farm which is situated in the quiet, unspoilt valley of Cywarch at the foot of Arran Fawddwy (3,000ft), within easy reach of the beach. Fishing and shooting available on farm. Bryn Sion is a mixed farm of 700 acres offering a variety of good farmhouse meals and bedtime tea/coffee. Log fire in sittingroom in the evenings. Two double rooms, both with tea making facilities, shaving points, washbasin; bathroom. Car essential — parking. Open April to November for Bed and Breakfast at £15 per person. SAE, please, with enquiries.

NEFYN. Mrs E. Jones, "Terfyn", Morfa Nefyn, Pwllheli LL53 6BA (01758 721332). Detached house situated in quiet seaside village, only seven miles from Pwllheli, popular market town. Beach and 18 hole golf course 10 minutes' walk away. Accommodation available in family, double, twin and single rooms. House is centrally heated and double glazed. Open all year except family holidays. Children welcome. Private parking. Sorry, no pets. Bed and Breakfast from £14; children up to five free, over five £6.

PENGWERN. Gwyndaf and Jane Lloyd Rowlands, Pengwern, Saron, Llanwnda, Caernarfon LL54 5UH (Tel & Fax: 01286 831500; Mobile: 0378 411780). ♥♥♥ *DE LUXE.* Charming spacious farmhouse of character, situated between mountains and sea. Unobstructed views of Snowdonia. Well appointed bedrooms, all en suite. Set in 130 acres of land which runs down to Foryd Bay. Jane has a cookery diploma and provides excellent meals with farmhouse fresh food, including home-produced beef and lamb. Excellent access. Children welcome. Open February to November. Bed and Breakfast from £20 to £25; Evening Meal from £12.

PORTHMADOG. Tyddyn Du Farm Holidays (FHG), Gellilydan, Near Ffestiniog LL41 4RB (01766 590281). ♥♥♥ *HIGHLY COMMENDED.* AA QQQQ. Enchanting old world farmhouse, set amidst spectacular scenery in the heart of the Snowdonia National Park, with a friendly, relaxed atmosphere. One superb private ground floor cottage suite. Delicious candle-light dinners with excellent farmhouse cuisine. Working sheep farm — feed the ducks on our mill pond, bottle feed pet lambs and fuss over Polly the pony. Excellent central base. Stamp please for brochure. Weekly Dinner, Bed and Breakfast from £160–£200. Bed and Breakfast from £16–£20. Stamp for brochure please to **Mrs Paula Williams**.

Terms quoted in this publication may be subject to increase if rises in costs necessitate

RHOS-ON-SEA, near Llandudno. Mr and Mrs Mike Willington, Sunnydowns Hotel, 66 Abbey Road, Rhos-on-Sea, Near Llandudno LL28 4NU (01492 544256; Fax: 01492 543223). ❦ ❦ ❦ ❦ A family-run

hotel. All rooms en suite with colour TV, video and Satellite channels, clock radio, tea/coffee facilities, hair dryer, mini-bar refrigerator, direct dial telephone and central heating. Hotel facilities also include bar, pool room, restaurant, sauna and car park. Situated just a five minute walk from Rhos-on-Sea Golf Club and with four more Championship courses close by. Telephone or Fax for brochure and special group terms.

RUTHIN. Mrs Anna V. Meadway, Firgrove, Llanfwrog, Ruthin LL15 2LL (01824 702677). ❦ *HIGHLY COMMENDED.* A Listed Georgian country house set in one and a half acres of mature gardens with panoramic views of the Vale of Clwyd, Firgrove is situated one and a half miles from the medieval market town of Ruthin on the B5105, conveniently centred for visiting Chester and Snowdonia, only one and a half hours from Manchester Airport and Holyhead, the Irish Ferry Port. We offer Bed and Breakfast in comfortable surroundings with two tastefully decorated double rooms in the house sharing one bathroom and an attached ground floor cottage offering full en suite facilities. All rooms have colour TV and tea/coffee facilities. Please ring for further details.

RUTHIN. Mrs S.M. Edwards, Cygnet, Llangynhafal, Near Denbigh LL16 4LN (Tel & Fax: 01824 790322). ❦ ❦ ❦ *DE LUXE.* Welcome Host. No smoking.

Cygnet is situated below the Clwydian hills close to 15th century church and inn hosting Welsh singing (Saturday evenings). Magnificent views of the Vale of Clwyd, ideal for visiting Snowdonia, Llangollen, Chester, Ruthin four miles, Denbigh six miles. All bedrooms have tea/coffee facilities, colour TV, central heating and en suite bathrooms. Children welcome, cots and high chairs available. Dogs by arrangement. Accessible to wheelchair user with an assistant, ground floor bedrooms available. Discount for two nights or more. Christmas and New Year Breaks. Open all year. Bed and Breakfast from £20; Evening Meal by prior arrangement £15 with free wine. Colour brochure available.

RUTHIN. Mrs B. Quinn, Berllan Bach, Ffordd Las, Llandyrnog, Ruthin LL16 4LR (01824 790732 or 01374 128494). ❦ ❦ ❦ This 18th century cottage nestles

at the foot of the Clwydian Hills. En suite bedrooms with French windows opening onto individual patios to give our guests freedom and privacy. The "Olde Worlde" sittingroom with inglenook and beamed ceiling and a bright conservatory are available for your pleasure. Situated equidistant between the medieval towns of Ruthin and Denbigh with castles and medieval banquets. While evening meals are available there are country pubs and restaurants within one and a half miles. Ideally situated for touring with Chester and Snowdonia Park less than 25 miles away and Caernarfon and Conwy Castles reached in less than one hour. Children and pets warmly welcomed. Bed and Breakfast from £17.50 to £20. Further details on request. FHG Diploma Winner.

ST. ASAPH. Mrs N. Price, Plas Penucha, Caerwys, Mold CH7 5BH (01352 720210). ❦ ❦ ❦ *HIGHLY*

COMMENDED. One family has owned this unique farmhouse for over 400 years. Over the centuries it has been altered and modernised, but always with the aim of retaining its sense of history and serenity. Extensive gardens overlook the Clwydian Hills. A spacious lounge has large library, grand piano and Elizabethan panelling. Full central heating. There are four bedrooms, two en suite, all with washbasins, shaver points, hairdryers and tea/coffee making facilities. Two miles from A55 expressway — 30 minutes Chester and North Wales Coast — one hour Snowdonia. Open all year. Bed and Breakfast £17.50; Evening Meal from £10.50. Discounts available. Brochure on request.

ST. ASAPH. Mrs Eirlys Jones, Rhewl Farm, Waen, St. Asaph LL17 0DT (01745 582287). 🐾🐾

COMMENDED. Enjoy Welsh hospitality on our 180 acre farm, conveniently situated three-quarters of a mile from A55 expressway in peaceful and beautiful setting. Comfortable bedrooms with radiators and tea/coffee making facilities. Double room has en suite facilities, twin and family rooms have washbasins. Spacious lounge with inglenook fireplace and colour TV. Convenient for Chester, coast and Snowdonia. Free fishing. Reductions for children. Bed and Breakfast from £15 to £16.50. This is a non-smoking household. Welcome Host Certificate. Please send SAE for brochure.

TREFRIW. Mrs B. Cole, Glandwr, Trefriw, Near Llanrwst LL27 0JP (01492 640 431). Large country

house on the outskirts of Trefriw Village overlooking the Conway River and its Valley, with beautiful views towards the Clwydian Hills. Good touring area; Llanrwst, Betws-y-Coed and Swallow Falls five miles away. Fishing, walking, golfing and pony trekking all close by. Comfortable rooms, lounge with TV, dining room. Good home cooking using local produce whenever possible. Parking. Bed and Breakfast from £16; Dinner if required.

TREFRIW. Arthur and Ann Eaton, Crafnant Guest House, Trefriw LL27 0JH (01492 640809). Quality

accommodation and service can be enjoyed at Crafnant, an elegant Victorian residence in the charming village of Trefriw, Conwy Valley. The village is known for its Woollen Mill, Roman Spa, fishing, lakes and forest walks. The RSPB Nature Reserve, Snowdon, Bodnant Gardens and other attractions are within easy reach. Five en suite double/twin rooms with drinks tray and TV. Bed and Breakfast from £15 to £16; children up to 12 years £8. Special discount — book seven nights, pay only for six. Non-smoking, private parking. Open all year except Christmas and Boxing Days.

TYWYN. Gweniona Pugh, Tanycoed Ucha, Abergynolwyn, Tywyn LL36 9UP (01654 782228).

Tourist Board *COMMENDED.* Welcome Host. Enjoy a quiet break on a traditional Welsh farm in this tranquil rural setting close to Dolgoch Falls, with Talyllyn Narrow Gauge Railway running through our land. Over 100 years old, the farmhouse has been modernised for comfort. Tea/coffee facilities in bedrooms. Log fires when cold and wet. Home cooking. Children and pets welcome. Open March to November. Bed and Breakfast from £13.50 to £14.50.

WREXHAM. Mrs M.A. Smith, Aldersey Guest House, 25 Hightown Road, Wrexham LL13 8EB (01978 365687). 🐾 *HIGHLY COMMENDED.* A warm

friendly welcome awaits you at this small family-run guest house situated minutes from the town centre, an ideal base for exploring the Welsh and English borderlands. The historic city of Chester and the beauty of the Vale of Llangollen are within easy travelling distance. Full central heating, TV lounge, tea and coffee making facilities. One double bedroom, a spacious twin/family room and three single rooms, all with washbasins and shaver points. Three bath/shower rooms with toilets. Large parking area. Bed and Breakfast £15 to £17 per person per night.

DYFED
Cardiganshire, Carmarthenshire and Pembrokeshire

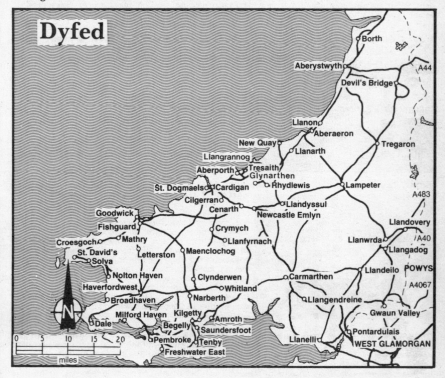

ABERYSTWYTH. Sarah and Lester Ward, Sinclair Guest House, 43 Portland Street, Aberystwyth SY23 2DX (Tel & Fax: 01970 615158). ♛ ♛ ♛ *HIGHLY COMMENDED.* Centrally situated in a peaceful tree-lined street close to the seafront and shopping and convenient for the University and the National Library of Wales. Sinclair is a late Victorian terraced house of character with three spacious en suite bedrooms individually designed and decorated and equipped to the highest standard. A comfortable sitting room leads through to the dining room and conservatory which overlooks our maturing town garden. If you are looking for somewhere with personal service, that is relaxing, clean and totally smoke-free, Bed and Breakfast is £22.50 per person.

ABERYSTWYTH. Mrs E. Jones, Ael-y-Bryn Guest House, Capel Bangor, Aberystwyth SY23 3LR (01970 880681). ♛ *HIGHLY COMMENDED.* Small family-run guest house situated 100 yards off the A44 road, five miles east of Aberystwyth. It has lovely views overlooking the Rheidol Valley and is an ideal base from which to explore the beautiful beaches of Dyfed and many other places of interest. All rooms have washbasin, TV, radio and tea/coffee facilities; dining room with separate tables; TV lounge. Central heating. Bed and Breakfast from £15 to £17 each per night. Evening Meal by prior arrangement. There is safe parking within the grounds. Sorry no pets. No smoking. SAE for brochure.

ABERYSTWYTH. Mrs F.J. Rowlands, Tycam Farm, Capel Bangor, Aberystwyth SY23 3NA (01970 84662). ✿ ✿ Peaceful dairy and sheep farm situated seven and a half miles from Aberystwyth and just two and a half miles off A44 road. Accommodation comprises one double bedroom and one family room en suite; lounge and diningroom with separate tables and colour TV. Central heating. Perfect centre for walking, sightseeing, bird watching, fishing, golf, swimming and many beaches within easy reach. Ample car parking. Bed and Breakfast from £15 to £17.50 per person. Reduction for children over five years sharing parents' room.

BLAENFFOS. Castellan House, Blaenffos, Boncath SA37 0HZ (01239 841644). ✿ ✿ ✿ Castellan

nestles on the edge of the Preseli Hills with spectacular panoramic views and our own valley with badger setts, fox and buzzard lairs. We are 10 minutes from Cardigan market town and Cardigan Bay, home of the famous bottle nose dolphins. We have salmon, sewin and trout fishing within five miles, several golf courses within 10 miles, beaches rivalling the Mediterranean, National Trust walks; riding available on premises plus delightful tea rooms, gardens and antique shop. Quality ground floor bedrooms with own front door, en suite, central heating, TV, tea making facilities. Pets welcome. Bed and Breakfast from £17 per person; optional Evening Meal £12. Reductions for children. RAC Acclaimed.

BROAD HAVEN near. Sandra Davies, Barley Villa, Walwyn's Castle, Near Broad Haven, Haverfordwest SA62 3EB (01437 781254). WTB ✿ ✿ *COMMEN-*

DED. Situated in peaceful, attractive countryside, our comfortable modern house overlooks a small nature reserve and is an ideal base for touring Pembrokeshire's beautiful coastline and sandy bays, suitable for sailing, surfing and swimming. Visit the bird islands famous for puffins, Manx shearwaters, kittiwakes and many other species. We have one double room and one twin en suite room with tea/coffee making facilities; spacious lounge/dining room has TV, board games and coal fire on chilly evenings. Comfort, cleanliness and personal attention assured. Substantial breakfasts; packed lunches; special diets catered for. Off road parking. Bed and Breakfast from £14.50 to £16. Six berth caravan also available for hire.

CARDIGAN. Audrey and Terry Smith, Talywerydd, Penbryn, Sarnau SA44 6QY (01239 810322). ✿ ✿ *HIGHLY COMMENDED.* A warm welcome awaits you at Talywerydd which was built in the year 1893. We are situated eight miles from the small market town of Cardigan and 28 miles from Aberystwyth on the beautiful Cardigan coast featuring magnificent sea and country views. Talywerydd is approximately one mile from Penbryn Beach which is owned by the National Trust. Two double and one twin rooms. All rooms have colour TV along with tea making facilities and washbasins. Comfortable sitting room with log fire and TV. Guests are invited to use our heated swimming pool which is adjacent to our touring caravan site. Bed and Breakfast from £16 per person including en suite. Children welcome, reductions available. Directions: from Cardigan take second Penbryn turning, from Aberystwyth take second Penbryn turn off main A487.

CARMARTHEN. Ken and Pam Moore, Troedyrhiw Country Guest House, Llanfynydd, Carmarthen SA32 7TQ (01558 668792). ✿ ✿ Troedyrhiw is a traditional Welsh farmhouse offering genuine hospitality with excellent food and luxurious accommodation. Bed and Breakfast only £19 per person. The guest house has eight acres of grounds which guests are welcome to wander, meet our friendly Jacob sheep and walk round our vineyard. Situated on the edge of a lovely West Wales village this is ideal country for walking or just relaxing and enjoying the sights with castles, coasts and crafts all within easy reach. We have special Short Break bargains and also a holiday cottage sleeping four. Please contact Pam Moore for our brochure.

CARMARTHEN. Mrs Margaret Thomas, Plas Farm, Llangynog, Carmarthen SA33 5DB (01267 211492). ❦❦ *COMMENDED.* Welcome Host. Situated six miles west of Carmarthen town along the A40 towards St. Clears. Quiet location, ideal touring base. Working farm run by the Thomas family for the past 100 years. Very spacious, comfortable farmhouse. En suite rooms available, all with tea/coffee making facilities, colour TV and full central heating. TV lounge. Evening meals available at local country inn nearby. Good golf course minutes away. Plas is en route to Fishguard and Pembroke Ferries. Bed and Breakfast from £15 per person. Children under 16 years sharing family room half price. Special mid-week breaks available. A warm welcome assured.

FISHGUARD near. Heathfield Mansion, Letterston, Near Fishguard SA62 5EG (01348 840263).

WTB ❦❦❦ *HIGHLY COMMENDED.* A Grade II Listed Georgian country house in 16 acres of pasture and woodland, Heathfield is the home of former Welsh rugby international, Clive Rees and his wife Angelica. This is an ideal location for the appreciation of Pembrokeshire's many natural attractions. There is excellent golf, riding and trout fishing in the vicinity and the coast is only a few minutes' drive away. The accommodation is very comfortable and two of the three bedrooms have en suite bathrooms. The cuisine and wines are well above average. This is a most refreshing venue for a tranquil and wholesome holiday. Bed and Breakfast from £18 per person; Dinner by prior arrangement.

HAVERFORDWEST. Joyce Canton, Nolton Haven Farm, Nolton Haven, Haverfordwest SA62 1NS

(01437 710263). The farmhouse is beside the beach on a 200 acre mixed farm, with cattle, calves and lots of show ponies. It has a large lounge which is open to guests all day, as are all the bedrooms. Single, double and family rooms, two family rooms ensuite, four other bathrooms. Pets and children most welcome, babysitting free of charge. 50 yards to the beach, 75 yards to the local inn/restaurant. Pony trekking, surfing, fishing, excellent cliff walks, boating and canoeing all available nearby. Riding holidays, and short breaks all year, a speciality. Colour brochure on request.

HAVERFORDWEST. Mrs M.E. Davies, Cuckoo Mill Farm, Pelcomb Bridge, St. David's Road,

Haverfordwest SA62 6EA (01437 762139). Tourist Board Listed. Working farm. This farm is situated in central Pembrokeshire, two miles out of Haverfordwest on St. David's Road. It is within easy reach of many beaches and coastline walks. Peaceful country walks on the farm, also a small trout stream. Children are welcome at reduced rates and cot, high chair and babysitting provided. The house is cosy with open fires and welcomes guests from January to December. Car is not essential, but parking available. Home-produced dairy products; poultry and meats all home-cooked. Mealtimes arranged to suit guests. Well appointed, warm, comfortable bedrooms with washbasins and tea making facilities. Pets permitted. Evening Dinner/Meal, Bed and Breakfast or Bed and Breakfast only. Rates also reduced for Senior Citizens.

LAMPETER. Mrs Eleanor Marsden-Davies, Brynog Mansion, Felinfach, Lampeter SA48 8AQ

(01570 470266). ❦❦ *HIGHLY COMMENDED.* Enjoy a relaxing holiday in the friendly atmosphere of this spacious 250 year old country mansion. Brynog is a 170 acre grazing farm situated in the beautiful Vale of Aeron, midway between Lampeter market town and the unique Aberaeron seaside resort, just 10 minutes by car. The mansion is approached by a three-quarter-mile rhododendron-lined drive. Spacious en suite bedrooms with bathroom or shower, other room with washbasin, near bathroom. Tea making facilities on request. Central heating and a welcoming woodburner in cold weather. Full Welsh breakfast provided, served in the grand old well-furnished dining room. There is a spacious comfortable lounge with TV. Rough shooting, private fishing, bird-watching and riverside walk nearby. Children over six years welcome. Sorry, no dogs. Bed and Breakfast from £16.50 to £18. Tourist Board "Welcome Host" Award.

PLEASE SEND A STAMPED ADDRESSED ENVELOPE WITH ENQUIRIES

LAMPETER. Mrs J.P. Driver, Penwern Old Mills, Cribyn, Lampeter SA48 7QH (01570 470762). A

former rural woollen mill set in a quiet valley alongside a small stream. Penwern, after its demise in 1953 when it subsequently lay derelict for 20 years, is now enjoying a new lease of life. Renovated and converted to living accommodation, the Old Mill now offers a comfortable, interesting and relaxing base from which to enjoy your sojourn in Mid Wales. Double, single and twin rooms. Cot and high chair available. Trout lakes nearby. Bed and Breakfast £13 per person; optional Evening Meal £6. Reduced rates for children and weekly bookings. Totally non-smoking.

LLANDYSUL. Mrs Joan Austwick, Pellorwel, Bwlchygroes, Llandysul SA44 5JU (01239 851 226).

WTB Listed *HIGHLY COMMENDED*. A friendly welcome awaits you in the homely atmosphere of this charming Victorian-style house. Situated in beautiful mid-Wales countryside near the Teifi River Valley and market towns of Llandysul and Newcastle Emlyn. We are ten miles from the sandy beaches of Cardigan Bay. Meals are lovingly prepared and varied, with home-grown produce used abundantly. The bedrooms consist of double room with four-poster bed, twin room and two single rooms. We like to welcome our guests as we would our family and have no house rules other than "Please close the gate". Brochure available. Bed and Breakfast from £13.50, Evening Meal from £8.50. Directions: Five miles north Llandysul on A486 opposite telephone box.

PEMBROKE. Mrs Sheila Lewis, Poyerston Farm, Cosheston, Pembroke SA72 4SJ (01646 651347; mobile 0402 391013). ♛ ♛ *HIGHLY COMMENDED*.

Working farm. AA QQQQ Selected, Taste of Wales member, Farm Holiday Bureau Member. Welcome Host. Enjoy a relaxed holiday and warm hospitality at our old farmhouse set in 300 acres of picturesque, unspoilt countryside, two miles east of Pembroke, six miles Tenby. Centrally situated on a dairy farm where home cooking is assured. Ideal base for exploring National Park, beaches and coastal walks, lily ponds, Carew Castle and local inns near by. Relax in our Victorian conservatory; comfortable lounge with colour TV, separate dining room; double and family bedrooms tastefully decorated and having en suite facilities, beverage trays, full central heating. Sorry, no pets. Regret no smoking in farmhouse. Ample parking. Bed and Breakfast and Evening Meal or Bed and Breakfast only. Three miles to B&I ferry to Ireland. Brochure on request.

PEMBROKE. Mrs Ruth Smith, Chapel Farm, Castlemartin, Pembroke SA71 5HW (01646 661312).

WTB Listed *HIGHLY COMMENDED*. Chapel Farm offers comfortable accommodation for a relaxing holiday. The 260 acre dairy farm is a mile from the coast in Pembrokeshire Coast National Park and has splendid views out to sea. The large bedrooms are equipped with radios and tea making facilities. The TV lounge with its inglenook fireplace has a grand piano for guests to enjoy. Good tasty farmhouse food is prepared; packed lunches on request. The long distance footpath passes the farm and within five miles are wild surfing beaches, quiet bathing coves, fishing and fishing. Bed and Breakfast from £16; Dinner, Bed and Breakfast from £150 to £160 per week. Reductions for children sharing.

SAUNDERSFOOT. Mrs Joy Holgate, Carne Mountain Farm, Reynalton, Kilgetty SA68 0PD (01834 860546). WTB Listed *COMMENDED.* **Working farm.** A warm welcome awaits you at our lovely 200 year old farmhouse set amidst the peace and tranquillity of the beautiful Pembrokeshire countryside. Distant views of Preseli Hills, yet only three and a half miles from Saundersfoot. Pretty, picturesque bedrooms with colour TV, washbasins, tea/coffee tray, central heating. Separate dining room with interesting plate collection, books and maps. Delicious traditional or light farmhouse breakfast; vegetarians very welcome. Let the strain and stress slip away as you enjoy the peaceful atmosphere and friendly farmyard animals. Bed and Breakfast from £14. Welcome Host and Farmhouse Award. Quality six-berth caravan also available in pretty, peaceful setting from £90 per week. SAE please.

SOLVA. Mrs Julia Hann, Min-yr-Afon, Y Gribin, Solva, Haverfordwest SA62 6UY (01437 721752). Charming cottage/self-contained annexe, surrounded by flowers. Tucked away in a peaceful hamlet with the River Solva winding its way down to the harbour. Restaurants, coastal path, pubs and shops are just a short walk away. The Annexe is suitable for partially disabled guests. All on ground floor is en suite. Twin bedroom, lounge/kitchen for refreshments, fridge/microwave, with an upstairs en suite double bedroom. A full choice breakfast is served in the low beamed dining room in the cottage next door. Upstairs is a double room with its sloping ceiling and chintzy decor. Refreshment tray, TV and washbasin. From £14 per person per night. "Which?" Recommended.

TENBY. Emilio a ~~ ~~ *HIGHLY COM...* and a half miles) in Pemb... just a few minutes' walk. South... and sheltered bays is ideal for s... interesting walks along the coastal path... Italy" at Pen Mar, our friendly fully licensed... tables, a well stocked bar, table d'hôte and... Continental cuisine. Recommended by Guild of M... and Breakfast £17 to £22. Some rooms en suite. Priva...

New Hedges, Tenby SA70 8TL (01834 842435). ...between Tenby (one mile) and Saundersfoot (one ...ews of Carmarthen Bay. Waterwynch Bay is ...coastline, unspoiled beaches, golden sands ...ding, golfing or touring. There are many ...ng atmosphere awaits offering "a touch of ...We have a pleasant diningroom with separate ...enus offering a wide choice of English and ...ers. Open all year. Reductions for children. Bed ...park. All credit cards accepted.

TREGARON. Will and Jacky Davies, Neuaddlas Guest House, Tregaron, SY25 6LG (01974 298905). ~~ ~~ ~~ *HIGHLY COMMENDED.* AA QQQ. Enjoy the timeless beauty of Mid-Wales. The Guest House stands in own grounds overlooking Cors Caron Nature Reserve and under the shadow of Cambrian Mountains. An ideal touring centre with places of interest, quiet country walks and local beauty spots. Open all year, specialising in mid- and weekend breaks for yourself and groups. Some en-suite rooms, all rooms with tea/coffee facilities and washbasins. Traditional food; special diets catered for. For enquiries or brochure write or phone. FHG Diploma winner.

POWYS

BRECON. Mrs Marion Meredith, Lodge Farm, Talgarth, Brecon LD3 0DP (01874 711244). ✿✿✿

HIGHLY COMMENDED. Welcome to the "Lodge", a working family farm nestling in the Black Mountains in the eastern section of the Brecon Beacons National Park, one and a half miles from Talgarth off A479. Hay-on-Wye/Brecon eight miles, Llangorse Lake four miles. The house enjoys mountain views and is set in a large garden where guests are welcome to relax. This 18th century house with original oak beams offers quality en suite rooms with tea making facilities; lounge with TV, dining room with separate tables, original inglenook fireplace and flagstone floor. Freshly prepared "real food", including vegetarian choice using local and home grown produce, is a speciality. A non-smoking establishment. Bed and Breakfast from £18 to £19 per person; Evening Meal from £11.

BRECON. Mrs Pamela Boxhall, The Old Mill, Felinfach, Brecon LD3 0UB (01874 625385). ✿✿

HIGHLY COMMENDED. Peacefully situated in its own grounds in the village of Felinfach just 50 metres off A470 Brecon to Hereford Road. The Old Mill has a wealth of character with original features being retained. Friendly atmosphere, large garden. One double with bathroom and two en suite twin-bedded rooms; TV lounge, tea/coffee facilities. Within easy reach of Brecon Beacons, Black Mountains, Hay-on-Wye. Pony trekking nearby. Local pubs within walking distance. Packed lunches by arrangement. Children welcome. Terms: double from £15 per person, twin en suite from £16 per person, single from £16 to £18. Reductions for weekly stays.

BRECON. Beacons Guest House, 16 Bridge Street, Brecon LD3 8AH. ✿✿✿ COMMENDED.

Experience the friendly atmosphere at this Georgian guest house. Comfortably furnished and well equipped rooms (most with en suite facilities). Private parking. Cosy bar, spacious dining room and residents' lounge. Guests can book an excellent Aga-cooked evening meal prepared with care from fresh local produce — "Taste of Wales" recommended. The Beacons is situated just two minutes' walk from the centre of Brecon with its muesums, Cathedral, Castle, canal and River Usk. At the centre of the National Park surrounded by magnificent scenery and wonderful walking country. Bargain Breaks from £49. Ring **Peter or Barbara 01874 623339.**

BRECON near. Gwyn and Hazel Davies, Caebetran Farm, Felinfach, Brecon LD3 0UL (01874 754460). ✿✿✿ HIGHLY COMMENDED. **Working farm, join in.** "Welcome Host". A warm welcome, a cup of tea and home-made cakes await you when you arrive at Caebetran.

Visitors are welcome to see the cattle and sheep on the farm. There are breathtaking views of the Brecon Beacons and the Black Mountains and just across a field is a 400 acre Common, ideal for walking, bird watching or just relaxing. Ponies and sheep graze undisturbed, while buzzards soar above you. The farmhouse dates back to the 17th century and has been recently modernised to give the quality and comfort visitors expect today. There are many extras in the rooms to give that special feel to your holiday. The rooms are all en suite and have colour TV and tea making facilities. Comfortable lounge with colour TV for guests' use. Caebetran is an ideal base for exploring this beautiful unspoilt part of the country with pony trekking, walking, birdwatching, wildlife, hang gliding and so much more. For more details, a brochure and terms please write or telephone. "Arrive as visitors and leave as friends".

BUILTH WELLS. Mrs Linda Williams, Old Vicarage, Erwood, Builth Wells LD2 3SZ (01982 560680).

Secluded position in own grounds where guests can relax and enjoy the magnificent views across the Wye Valley to Black Mountains. The house retains its former character with stone mullion windows, pine backed floors, high ceilings and spacious double aspect rooms. Three attractively decorated bedrooms with central heating, beverages, washbasins, period furniture, Victorian patchwork bedcover, comfy easy chairs all adding to the comfort. Private TV lounge with wood burner, literature, information, indoor games. Separate dining room and tables. Bathroom, separate WC for guests' use only. Close to walks, fishing, Elan Valley, Hay-on-Wye, Brecon Beacons, canoeing, trekking, spa and Border towns. Traditional evening meals available by prior arrangement.

BUILTH WELLS. Derek Johnson, Halcyon House, Cilmery, Builth Wells LD2 3NU (Tel & Fax: 01982 552838).

"Relaxed atmosphere", "Superb", "The ambience", "Delicious breakfast", and that's the visitors' book! Tranquil with panoramic southerly views. Short Breaks specialist. Centrally situated for touring the "secret" heart of Wales, Severn Bridge, Cardiff, Worcester and West/South Wales. Beaches within one and a half hours. Silver service breakfast. All rooms remote control colour TV, tea/coffee making, central heating. Billiard room. Shower and jacuzzi bathrooms. Conference facility for 30. Dormitory accommodation available. Adjacent inn/restaurant. Nearby (two miles) golf, fishing, riding, bowls, tennis, swimming, theatre, sports centre, Wales Showground. Under one hour to Hay-on-Wye, Hereford, Brecon Beacons and Elan Valley Reservoirs. Convenient for railway station (200 yards) and bus services. Terms from £16 for Bed and Breakfast.

BUILTH WELLS. C. Davies, Gwern-y-Mynach, Llanafan Fawr, Builth Wells LD2 3PN (01597 860256). Gwern-y-Mynach Farm is a mixed sheep and dairy working farm near Builth Wells in mid-Powys where golf, rugby, bowls, cricket and a new sports hall are all available. Our house is centrally heated throughout. Guest accommodation comprises one single room and one double room with bathroom en suite. Situated in a lovely area, ideal for walking, enjoying the open mountains and watching the Red Kites in flight. Close to the farm in the forest we have Greenwood chair making, steam bending, coracle making which attract people from overseas to the classes. Please write, or telephone, for further information and tariff.

BUILTH WELLS near. Mrs Margaret Davies, The Court Farm, Aberedw, Near Builth Wells LD2 3UP (01982 560277). NON SMOKERS PLEASE. We welcome

guests into our home, on a family-run livestock farm, situated away from traffic in a peaceful, picturesque valley surrounded by hills which overlook the River Wye. Lovely walking, wildlife area, central to Hay-on-Wye, Brecon Beacons, Elan Valley and very convenient for Royal Welsh Showground. We offer comfort, care and homeliness in our spacious stone-built farmhouse with traditional cooking using home produced food. All bedrooms have washbasins, shaver points, adjustable heating and electric blankets. Lounge with TV. Bed and Breakfast from £15 per person per night; Dinner from £8 (by arrangement).

CARNO. Mrs G. Bound, Pentre Uchaf, Carno SY17 5JP (01686 420663). 🐑🐑 A warm Welsh

welcome awaits you at our family run sheep and beef rearing farm. Situated half a mile from Carno village off the A470 coast road, set in an elevated position overlooking glorious countryside with panoramic scenery. A traditional stone farmhouse, central heating throughout. Lounge with oak beams, inglenook fireplace, log fires, colour TV, video; dining room. Double bedroom (en suite, shaver point), twin-bedded room. Bathroom. Both bedrooms have colour TV and drinks tray. Children welcome; cot. Ideal base for touring, golfing, shooting, walking, cycling, quad bikes, pony trekking, fishing; 30 miles from sea. Bed and Breakfast from £13. Brochure available.

PLEASE SEND A STAMPED ADDRESSED ENVELOPE WITH ENQUIRIES

CRICKHOWELL. Mrs Priscilla Llewelyn, White Hall, Glangrwyney, Crickhowell NP8 1EW (01873 811155 or 840267). 🐦🐦 Open all the year round, White

Hall is well placed for riding and walking in the Brecon Beacons and Black Mountains and is situated just two miles from Crickhowell and near the market towns of Abergavenny and Hay-on-Wye. Accommodation in double-bedded and twin-bedded rooms, some en-suite, with TV and tea-making facilities. One single room. All bedrooms are very comfortably furnished, with central heating, and there is a sitting-room with colour TV for guests' use. Newspapers are delivered and there is an extensive library of books. Bed and Breakfast from £15, small single £13. Reduced rates for stays of three nights or more and for party bookings by arrangement. Village inn nearby for meals, and there are restaurants at Crickhowell.

GLADESTRY. Mrs M.E. Hughes, Stonehouse Farm, Gladestry, Kington, Herefordshire HR5 3NU (01544 370651). Working farm. Large Georgian farmhouse, modernised whilst retaining its character, situated on Welsh border with Offa's Dyke footpath going through its 380 acres of mixed farming. Beautiful unspoiled area for walking. Many places of interest within easy driving distance such as Elan Valley Dams, Devil's Bridge, Llangorse Lake, Kington golf course. Guests are accommodated in one double and one twin-bedded rooms, with washbasins; bathroom, two toilets; sitting and dining room. TV. Homely informal atmosphere with home produced food and home cooking. Vegetarian meals on request. Children and dogs welcome. Babysitting available. Bed and Breakfast from £14; Evening Meal by arrangement.

HAY-ON-WYE. Peter and Olwen Roberts, York House, Cusop, Hay-on-Wye HR3 5QX (01497 820705). From January to December enjoy a relaxing holi-

day in this elegant Victorian guest house, quietly situated on the B4348, five minutes' walk from Hay-on-Wye, the famous "town of books". Accommodation comprises four comfortable bedrooms all with en suite facilities. Dining room and separate lounge. All rooms are furnished and equipped to a very high standard including TV and overlook beautiful one-acre gardens towards the mountains. Full English Breakfast served, packed lunches and evening meals by arrangement; complimentary hot bedtime drinks. Large private car park. Secure cycle shed. Heated drying room. Hay is an ideal walking base and a good centre for touring the lovely Border country. Bed and Breakfast from £22. Further details from resident proprietors. AA Listed QQQ, RAC Highly Acclaimed. No smoking indoors.

LLANDRINDOD WELLS. Greenway Manor Hotel, Crossgates, Llandrindod Wells LD1 6RF (01597 851230; Fax: 01597 851912). 🐦🐦🐦🐦 *HIGHLY*

COMMENDED. Built in the early 1900's the imposing Mock Tudor building is set in approximately 12 acres of garden and woodland and has one mile of private fishing. A family-run residence boasting a 50-seater restaurant, residents' lounge, coffee/reading room and large lounge bar. All bedrooms have en suite facilities, colour TV with Sky, radio alarms, telephones and beverage trays. There are also facilities for disabled visitors. Llandrindod Wells approximately three miles away and the beautiful Elan Valley dams and reservoirs only 10 minutes' drive away it is the perfect base for all country pursuits. Open all year. Colour brochure available. Heart of Wales membr, Taste of Wales member, Welcome Host.

Greenway Manor Hotel

LLANDRINDOD WELLS. The Park Motel, Crossgates, Llandrindod Wells LD1 6RF (Tel & Fax: 01597 851201). 🐦🐦 *COMMENDED.* Set in three acres, amidst

beautiful mid Wales countryside yet conveniently situated on the A44. The centrally heated units are available for Bed and Breakfast or self catering. Each unit has a twin-bedded room, shower room with toilet and a fully fitted kitchenette. The dining area converts to a double bed. Equipped with colour TV, tea/coffee making facilities. The Motel has several advantages over a conventional hotel or bed and breakfast accommodation, being completely self contained with a front and back door giving the freedom to come and go as you please. Fully licensed restaurant open all day, offering a good selection of reasonably priced meals, including vegetarian or take away. Pets welcome. Bed and Breakfast £18 to £23 per night. Self catering £25 to £37 per night. Three-course meals and coffee from £9.

Terms quoted in this publication may be subject to increase if rises in costs necessitate

LLANIDLOES. Mrs Janet Evans, Dyffryn Glyn, Llanidloes SY18 6NE (01686 412129). Dyffryn is

centrally situated in an Area of Natural Beauty two miles from the friendly market town of Llanidloes, one mile from Clywedog Lake with its spectacular views where sailing, fishing, birdwatching and walking can be pursued. Ideal area for touring. Accommodation comprises one en suite room and one twin-bedded room with washbasin and use of bathroom; both rooms have towels and tea making facilities. Visitors' own sitting room with TV, separate dining room. Ample parking. Bed and Breakfast from £15.

LLANIDLOES. Jean Bailey, Glangwy, Llangurig, Llanidloes SY18 6RS (01686 440697). Local river

stone ((Wye) built house offering comfortable Bed and Breakfast accommodation in beautiful countryside. Traditional English breakfast served with all home cooked evening meals; special diets catered for, vegetarians included. Accommodation comprises two double (can be used as family rooms as single bed also in each) and one twin bedrooms with washbasins, tea/coffee facilities and storage heaters (all beds have electric underblankets); bathroom, separate shower room; dining room (separate tables per party); lounge with colour TV. Pets welcome. Parking. Central for touring and local walks. Bed and Breakfast £14 per person; reductions for children under nine years.

LLANWRTHWL. Dyffryn Farm, Llanwrthwl, Llandrindod Wells LD1 6NU (01597 811017). Situated in

the picturesque upper Wye Valley, dating from the 17th century, this stone farmhouse with exposed beams offers relaxing accommodation — one double room with en suite shower room,another double and one twin room. Shared bathroom. Large lounge in converted hayloft. Pleasant gardens. Close to the Elan Valley with its magnificent dams and lakes. Wonderful walking country. Kite country. Near RSPB reserve. Ideal for quiet retreat. Bed and Breakfast from £16.50; dinner by prior arrangement. No smoking. One mile off A470 three miles south of Rhayader. Keep to right through village, right at T-junction on hill, quarter of a mile along.

**MACHYNLLETH. Jill and Barry Stevens, Yr Hen Felin, Abercegir, Machynlleth SY20 8NR (01650

511868).** ♛ ♛ *HIGHLY COMMENDED.* Peace and relaxation can be enjoyed at "The Old Mill", set on the banks of the River Gwydol, where you can watch the trout from your bedroom window. The walking and scenery are some of the finest in Wales and the coast with its fine sandy beaches can be reached in 20 minutes by car. Heavily beamed throughout with original stripped pine floors the character of our converted stone watermill, circa 1820, has been enhanced with antique furniture and an interesting collection of china and clocks. Our double and two twin-bedded rooms all have en suite facilities and there is a large comfortable guests' sitting room with TV. The Mill is NOT suitable for smokers. Traditional or vegetarian breakfasts. Bed and Breakfast £19 per person per night. Brochure available.

MACHYNLLETH. Mrs E.O. Harris, Cefn Coch Uchaf, Cemmaes Road, Machynlleth SY20 8LH (01650 511552). WTB Merit Award. 16th century farmhouse in the Welsh hills. Excellent country for bird watching, walking, golfing and fishing. Easy access to beaches. Good home cooking — vegetarians catered for. One en suite bedroom available. Central heating. Bed and Breakfast from £15; Evening Meal £7.50. Open April to October. Children and pets welcome. Babysitting offered.

WHEN MAKING ENQUIRIES PLEASE MENTION
FARM HOLIDAY GUIDES

NEWTOWN. Mrs Vi Madeley, Greenfields, Kerry, Newtown SY16 4LH (01686 670596; Fax: 01686 670354). ☙ ☙ ☙ A warm welcome awaits you at Greenfields. All rooms are tastefully decorated and are spacious in size, each having panoramic views of the rolling Kerry hills. There is a good choice of breakfast menu and evening meals can be provided by prior arrangement; packed lunches are also available. Licensed for residents. Accommodation available in one double and one twin-bedded rooms, both en suite, and one twin-bedded room with private facilities (twin rooms let as singles if required). The dining room has individual tables, the guests' lounge has colour TV and open log fire when the weather requires. Excellent off road parking. Bed and Breakfast from £17.50 to £18 per person; Evening Meal £4.50 to £10. Brochure available.

RHAYADER. Mrs Lena Powell, Gigrin Farm, South Road, Rhayader LD6 5BL (01597 810243). WTB Listed. Gigrin is a 17th century longhouse, retaining original oak beams and cosy atmosphere. Peacefully situated overlooking the Wye Valley and half a mile from the market town of Rhayader with its numerous inns and new leisure centre. The spectacular Elan Valley dams, which supply Birmingham with water — home of the Red Kite — are three miles away. The sea is only an hour's drive away over the Cambrian Mountains to Aberystwyth. A two mile Nature Trail on the farm; Red Kite feeding station November to March. The farmhouse is centrally heated and guests have shared use of a bathroom with shower. There are two bedrooms, each with double bed, washbasins and hospitality trays. Residents' sittingroom and dining room. Bed and Breakfast from £15. No smoking. Restaurant nearby (200 yards) for Evening Meals. Children welcome. Self catering accommodation also available. Brochure on request.

See also Colour Display Advertisement **TALGARTH. Mrs Bronwen Prosser, Upper Genfford Guest House, Talgarth LD3 0EN (01874 711360).** The cottages are situated amongst the most spectacular scenery of the Brecon Beacons National Park. An excellent location for walking and exploring the Brecon Beacons, Black Mountains and Wye Valley. An Area of Outstanding Natural Beauty, rich in historic and archaeological interest. The cottages are beautifully furnished with fitted carpets, oil-fired Rayburn, oak-beamed lounges, antique furniture, open log fires, Calor gas heaters and colour TVs. In Bed and Breakfast cottage bedrooms are en suite with colour TV and beverage trays. Tea and home made cakes served on arrival at both cottages. Pets welcome. Linen provided. A warm friendly welcome awaits you. Children enjoy our friendly pony "Topsy". Bed and Breakfast from £16. Weekend breaks available. Highly recommended. Self catering available from £100 to £150 per week. Caravan also for hire. Mrs Prosser has been nominated one of the top 20 proprietors for the AA Landlady of the Year Competition 1996 and is also one of the only two winners from Wales of the FHG Diploma 1995/6.

TALGARTH near. Mrs Ann Powell, Penyrheol, Pengenffordd, Near Talgarth, Brecon LD3 0EY (01874 711409). Family-run modern farmhouse with full central heating comprising two comfortable rooms with washbasins. This is an ideal place for keen walkers, situated between the Black Mountains and Llangorse Lake. Close to many sporting facilities including gliding, trekking, water sports, sailing, fishing and many more. A warm welcome is offered to all guests. Prices on application.

WELSHPOOL. Mrs Jane Jones, Trefnant Hall, Berriew, Welshpool SY21 8AS (01686 640262). ☙ ☙ ☙ Trefnant Hall offers a warm welcome in a Grade II Listed farmhouse built in 1742. All rooms are comfortably furnished with tea/coffee making facilities, colour TV and are en-suite. This sheep and beef farm is set in beautiful peaceful countryside away from the busy roads with superb views and gardens. Powis Castle and gardens are just two miles away with the market town of Welshpool close by. An ideal centre for exploring mid-Wales with the seaside less than an hour away. Bed and Breakfast from £17.

SOUTH WALES (formerly Glamorgan and Gwent)

Blaenau Gwent, Bridgend, Caerphilly, Cardiff, Merthyr Tydfil, Monmouthshire, Neath & Port Talbot, Newport, Rhondda Cynon Taff, Swansea, Torfaen, and Vale of Glamorgan

BLAINA. Mr J.W. Chandler, Lamb House, Westside, Blaina NP3 3DB (01495 290179). ♛♛ Lamb House nestles amongst trees in its own well kept gardens with private off-road parking. Set in the Upper Gwent Valleys, close to all major tourist attractions in South Wales. Activities in the area include walking, fishing, golfing, boating, etc. Accommodation comprises two double en suite rooms on ground floor suitable for partially disabled guests and one twin/double room on first floor with washbasin; all rooms have radio alarms. Tea/coffee available at all times. TV lounge, separate dining room. No smoking in bedrooms. Full central heating throughout. Local public house for excellent food only a five minute walk. Children welcome but sorry, no pets. Bed and Breakfast from £15 per person per night.

CARDIFF. Austins Hotel, 11 Coldstream Terrace, City Centre, Cardiff CF1 8LJ (01222 377148). ♛♛ Situated in the centre of Cardiff, 300 yards from the Castle. Five single and six twin-bedded rooms, five with full en-suite facilities, all with washbasins, shaver points, fixed heating, colour TV and tea/coffee making facilities. Full English Breakfast. Only 10 minutes' walk from central bus and train stations. Fire Certificate held. Warm welcome offered to all. Bed and Breakfast from £16 single, £28 twin. Reduced rates for children and Senior Citizens.

CARDIFF. Mrs Sarah Nicholls, Preste Gaarden Hotel, 181 Cathedral Road, Cardiff CF1 9PN (01222 228607). ♛♛ *COMMENDED.* "Welcome Host". This spacious Victorian family home offers olde worlde charm with modern amenities, including en suite facilities in most rooms. You will immediately feel relaxed by the warm welcome given by Sarah. Situated in the heart of the City, close to the Castle, museums, shops and an international array of restaurants and only 100 yards from Sophia Gardens offering walking, fishing and horse riding. Bed and Breakfast from £16 to £25 per person includes tea/coffee and biscuits in your room. Well established and independently recommended.

CHEPSTOW. The Coach and Horses Inn, Welsh Street, Chepstow NP6 5LN (01291 622626). Chepstow's first traditional pub. Take advantage of your stay here by visiting the Chepstow Racecourse (just two miles) or simply by enjoying the Welsh countryside; Offa's Dyke Walk nearby. Accommodation comprises seven bedrooms; ample bath and toilet facilities. Restaurant, licensed. Children welcome. Sorry, no pets. Bed and Breakfast accommodation offered (breakfast served between 7am and 9am). CAMRA Gwent Pub of the Year 1992. Real Ale Festival yearly — live music, darts, quiz.

COWBRIDGE near. Mrs Sue Beer, Plas Llanmihangel, Llanmihangel, Near Cowbridge CF7 7LQ (01446 774610). Plas Llanmihangel is the finest medieval manor house in the beautiful Vale of Glamorgan. We offer a genuine warmth of welcome, delightful accommodation, first class food and service in our wonderful home. The baronial hall, great log fires, the ancient tower and acres of beautiful historic gardens intrigue all who stay in this fascinating house. Its long history and continuous occupation have created a spectacular building in romantic surroundings unchanged since the 16th century. A great opportunity to experience the ambience and charm of a past age. Three double rooms. Bed and Breakfast £25. High quality home cooked evening meal on request.

GOWER. Mrs Anne Main, Tallizmand, Llanmadoc, Gower SA3 1DE (01792 386373). ♛♛♛

HIGHLY COMMENDED. Located near the splendid Gower coastline surrounded by beautiful countryside. Miles of unspoilt beaches, pine woods and salt marshes. Ideal for walking, surfing, bird watching and wild flowers. Tallizmand has tastefully furnished en suite bedrooms with tea/coffee making facilities; TV lounge. Home cooking, packed lunches, vegetarians catered for. Ample parking. Bed and Breakfast from £16; Evening Meal available.

GOWER. Mrs C.W. Ashton, Fairfield Cottage, Knelston, Gower SA3 1AR (01792 391013). Fairfield

Cottage is an 18th century Gower cottage set in attractive gardens in the hamlet of Knelston. Approximately 12 miles west of Swansea with its marina, theatres and excellent shopping and entertainment facilities. The Cottage has comfortable lounge with wood fires set in an inglenook fireplace, pretty double bedrooms with washbasins, tea/coffee making facilities and full central heating. Home cooking is to a high standard with locally produced vegetables and fruit when in season. Elizabeth Gundry recommended. There is also ample parking. Sorry no dogs unless prepared to leave in cars. No smoking. Bed and Breakfast £16/£17 per person; Dinner £11. Brochure available.

GOWER PENINSULA. Mrs M. Valerie Evans, The Old Rectory, Reynoldston, Swansea SA3 1AD

(01792 390129). A warm welcome awaits visitors to our home in this beautiful peninsula. The village is 12 miles west of Swansea and the area offers lovely coast and hill walks, wild flowers, birdwatching, pony trekking, golf and sea activities. We offer comfort, peace and quiet, a lovely secluded garden and good food grown in own garden or locally. Tea/coffee facilities in all bedrooms. Central heating. Open most of the year. Bed and Breakfast £18; Evening Meals to order £10. Non-smokers preferred.

MONMOUTH near. Tresco Guest House, Redbrook, Near Monmouth (01600 712325). Situated in the Wye Valley. Evening meals available including local Wye salmon. Packed lunches. Special rates for children. Ground floor bedrooms have views of flower gardens. Ample parking. Bed and breakfast from £14.50.

**FHG PUBLICATIONS LIMITED publish a large range of well-known
accommodation guides. We will be happy to send you details or you can use
the order form at the back of this book.**

MONMOUTH. Rosemary and Derek Ringer, Church Farm Guest House, Mitchel Troy, Monmouth NP5 4HZ (01600 712176). 👑👑 *COMMENDED.* AA QQQ.

A spacious and homely 16th century former farmhouse with oak beams and inglenook fireplaces, set in large attractive garden with stream. An excellent base for visiting the Wye Valley, Forest of Dean and Black Mountains. All bedrooms have washbasins, tea/coffee making facilities and central heating; most are en suite. Own car park. Terrace, barbecue. Colour TV. Non-smoking. Bed and Breakfast from £17 to £20 per person, Evening Meals by arrangement. We also offer a programme of guided and self-guided walking holidays and short breaks. Separate "Wysk Walks" brochure on request.

NEATH. Mr S. Brown, Green Lantern Guest House, Hawdref Ganol Farm, Cimla, Neath SA12 9SL (01639 631884). 👑👑👑 *HIGHLY COMMENDED.* AA

QQQQQ West Glamorgan's only AA Premier Selected Guest House. Family run 18th century luxury centrally heated farmhouse with beautiful scenic views over open countryside. Close to Afan Argoed and Margam Parks; one mile from birthplace of Sir Richard Burton. Ideal for walking, cycling, horse riding from farm. Perfect base for touring South Wales Valleys and the beautiful Gower Coast. Large guest room with inglenook fireplace and TV; colour TV and tea/coffee facilities in all rooms. En suite available. Reductions for children. Pets welcome. Please telephone for colour brochure.

NEWPORT. Mr and Mrs R. Evans, "Westwood Villa Guest House", 59 Risca Road, Crosskeys, Newport NP1 7BT (01495 270336). 👑👑👑 *HIGHLY*

COMMENDED. Six miles M4; close Newport, Cardiff, Wye Valley. Brecon Beacons one hour's drive, Ebbw Vale 20 minutes. Scenic drives, walks, sport and leisure entertainment. Guest House has central heating and is double glazed. Single, double and family rooms available, en suite rooms can be supplied, all with colour TV, washbasin, tea/coffee making facilities, radio alarm clocks; two bathrooms. Tasty home cooking; evening meals. Licensed bar. Garden and play area. Children, contractors and pets very welcome. Set in beautiful valleys with outstanding scenery "Westwood Villa", originally a manse, offers beautiful accommodation with that personal touch which makes all the difference and a holiday to remember. Bed and Breakfast from £22 single, £38 double. Bar meals from £5 served 6pm to 9pm. A warm welcome from hosts Robert and Maureen awaits guests. Visa accepted.

NEWPORT near. West Usk Lighthouse, St. Brides, Near Newport NP1 9SF (01633 810126/ 815860). 👑👑 Unique opportunity to stay in a 170-year-old

lighthouse, recently converted into a wonderful guest house. All rooms wedge-shaped and equipped with colour TV and tea/coffee making facilities. Ideal for bird watching, fishing and golf. Walks along deserted seashore to nearest pub/restaurant. Relaxation floating — the ultimate in deep relaxation — and champagne breakfast are optional extras. Only 10 minutes from Junction 28 of M4 and half an hour's drive from Cardiff. Definitely lots to do and see in the area — an experience not to be missed. Terms from £18 per person per night. Full tariff on request.

If you've found
FARM HOLIDAY GUIDES
of service please tell your friends

SOUTHGATE/GOWER/SWANSEA. Mrs Joyce Churchill, Heatherlands, 1 Hael Lane, Southgate, Gower, Swansea SA3 2AP (01792 233256). 👑👑

HIGHLY COMMENDED. Delightfully situated Heatherlands is an immaculate non-smoking residence. Pretty garden, 100 yards from cliffs and sea, spectacular scenery, lovely walks to Pobble and Three Cliff Bays, golf course 500 yards away (18 holes). Three double bedrooms, one a twin, washbasins, shaver points, one bedroom en suite, the other two each with private bathroom; tea/coffee making facilities. Dining room with separate tables, TV lounge for guests' use. Open all year. Bed and Breakfast from £18 per person. Children over eight years welcome. Single person occupying double room supplement £3 to £5. Parking. Excellent breakfast. Warm welcome.

ST. BRIDES WENTLOOG (Near Newport). Mr David W. Bushell, Chapel Guest House, Church Road, St. Brides Wentloog, Near Newport NP1 9SN (01633 681018). 👑👑 *COMMENDED.* Comfortable accommodation in a converted chapel situated in a village between Newport/Cardiff, near Tredegar House. Restaurant and inn adjacent, car park available. Guest lounge with TV and pool/snooker table. Single, double and twin rooms en suite or private bathroom. Beverage trays, TV, shaver points in all rooms. From £17. Children under three years FREE, three to 12 year olds half price sharing parents' room. Pets by arrangement. Leave M4 at Junction 28, take A48 towards Newport, at roundabout take third left exit signposted St. Brides, B4239. Drive to centre of village, turn right into Church Road and left into Church House Inn car park; the guest house is on the left and a warm welcome awaits.

TINTERN. Anne and Peter Howe, Valley House, Raglan Road, Tintern, Near Chepstow NP6 6TH (01291 689652). 👑👑 *COMMENDED.*

Valley House is a fine Georgian residence situated in the tranquil Angidy Valley 800 yards from the A466 Chepstow to Monmouth road and within a mile of Tintern Abbey. Numerous walks through picturesque woods and valleys right from our doorstep. The accommodation is of a very high standard; all rooms are en suite, have tea/coffee making facilities and colour TV. The guests' lounge has a wealth of exposed beams and a working range whilst the dining room has an arched stone ceiling. Numerous places to eat nearby. Bed and Breakfast from £19 per person. Open all year. Non-smoking preferred. AA QQQ, RAC Acclaimed.

Key to Tourist Board Ratings

The Crown Scheme
(England, Scotland & Wales)

Covering hotels, motels, private hotels, guesthouses, inns, bed & breakfast, farmhouses. Every Crown classified place to stay is inspected annually. *The classification:* Listed then 1-5 Crown indicates the range of facilities and services. Higher quality standards are indicated by the terms APPROVED, COMMENDED, HIGHLY COMMENDED and DELUXE.

The Key Scheme
(also operates in Scotland using a Crown symbol)

Covering self-catering in cottages, bungalows, flats, houseboats, houses, chalets, etc. Every Key classified holiday home is inspected annually. *The classification:* 1-5 Key indicates the range of facilities and equipment. Higher quality standards are indicated by the terms APPROVED, COMMENDED, HIGHLY COMMENDED and DELUXE.

The Q Scheme
(England, Scotland & Wales)

Covering holiday, caravan, chalet and camping parks. Every Q rated park is inspected annually for its quality standards. The more √ in the Q – up to 5 – the higher the standard of what is provided.

NORTHERN IRELAND

ANTRIM

BALLINTOY. Mrs Rita McFall, Ballintoy House, 9 Main Street, Ballintoy (012657 62317). Two and a

half storey Listed Georgian building situated in the village of Ballintoy. Within walking distance of Carrick-a-Rede Rope Bridge and one and a half miles to Whitepark Bay. Boat trips and fishing from Ballintoy harbour. Accommodation comprises one double, one twin and one single bedrooms, two en suite, one with washbasin, all with tea/coffee facilities. TV lounge. Central heating. Three course breakfast served. Friendly atmosphere. Bed and Breakfast from £12 (en suite extra).

BALLYCASTLE. Mrs Oonagh McHenry, Torr Brae, 77 Torr Road, Torr Head, Ballycastle BT54 6RQ

(012657 69625). A warm and friendly welcome awaits you at Torr Brae with its spectacular view as shown of Torr Head with the Mull of Kintyre visible in the background. Torr Head is an ideal location for exploring the Causeway Coast and the famous Glens of Antrim. This homely farmhouse offers large en suite rooms fully centrally heated and having tea/coffee making facilities. Residents' TV lounge. Choice of breakfast. Stunning country walks, sea fishing, golfing and tennis nearby. Private parking. Children welcome, reduced rates available if sharing. Bed and Breakfast from £15 to £18. Vouchers accepted.

BUSHMILLS. Mrs E. Rankin, Ballyholme Farm, 198 Ballybogey Road, Bushmills (012657 31793).

Modern dairy farmhouse situated three miles from Portrush and Bushmills. One double and one twin bedroom, both with washbasins. Visitors' lounge with TV. Home cooking. Supper provided as required. Central heating. Children welcome. No smoking. Old fashioned cottage with interesting antique artefacts nearby. Bed and Breakfast from £14.

**Terms quoted in this publication may be subject to increase
if rises in costs necessitate**

COUNTY DOWN

ANNALONG. Mrs Caroline Gordon, Dairy Farm, 52A Majors Hill, Annalong, Newry BT34 4QR

(013967 68433). Modern bungalow on working dairy farm situated at the foot of the beautiful Mourne Mountains; 500 metre walk to village and harbour. Silent Valley two miles, Annalong is midway between Newcastle and the fishing port of Kilkeel. Ideal base for sightseeing, hill walking, fishing and bowls. Bungalow offers three bedrooms — one double, one family and one twin, all en suite with colour TV and tea/coffee making facilities. Evening meal arrangement with the Harbour Restaurant. Open all year.

BALLYNAHINCH. Mrs Sally Murphy, "Bushymead Country House", 86 Drumaness Road, Ballynahinch BT24 8LT (01238 561171). "Bushymead Country

House" is built in classical style and is a family run Bed and Breakfast establishment offering comfort, cleanliness and personal attention — guaranteed. We are situated in the centre of County Down on the A24 (Belfast to Newcastle route), close to Belfast, Lisburn, Downpatrick, Ards Peninsula and on the doorstep to Newcastle and the Mourne Mountains. Close to all tourist attractions — museums, forest, parks, golf, fishing, nature reserves, National Trust properties. All rooms have TV and tea/coffee making facilities. Winner of Best for Guests Award, Welcome Host Award, Irish Hospitality Award, N.I.T.B. Guest House Award, Food Hygiene Certificate, 706/2 City and Guilds Full Catering Advanced Bakery. Bed and Breakfast from £13 to £20. Special Break rates.

PORTAFERRY. Barholm, 11 The Strand, Portaferry BT22 1PF (012477 29598; Fax: 012477

29784). Modern low cost accommodation on the shore of Strangford Lough (an Area of Special Scientific Interest). Barholm, newly opened in 1994, provides comfortable accommodation in beautiful surroundings, strategically situated near the ferry terminal and boat jetties and only 200 yards from the town centre. Services provided include family rooms, modern fully fitted kitchen facilities, dining room and lounge, etc. Large groups catered for by prior arrangement. Study/lecture room available. Car parking, cycle store, utility and drying rooms. Portaferry has a lot to offer both the serious sportsman and the casual traveller seeking relaxation. Pets welcome. Bed linen and towels are provided. Tariff: £9.95 Self Catering, £13.40 Bed and Breakfast, £24 Full Board. Please write, or telephone, for full colour brochure.

FOR THE MUTUAL GUIDANCE OF GUEST AND HOST

Every year literally thousands of holidays, short-breaks and overnight stops are arranged through our guides, the vast majority without any problems at all. In a handful of cases, however, difficulties do arise about bookings, which often could have been prevented from the outset.

It is important to remember that when accommodation has been booked, both parties — guests and hosts — have entered into a form of contract. We hope that the following points will provide helpful guidance.

GUESTS: When enquiring about accommodation, be as precise as possible. Give exact dates, numbers in your party and the ages of any children. State the number and type of rooms wanted and also what catering you require — bed and breakfast, full board, etc. Make sure that the position about evening meals is clear — and about pets, reductions for children or any other special points.

Read our reviews carefully to ensure that the proprietors you are going to contact can supply what you want. Ask for a letter confirming all arrangements, if possible.

If you have to cancel, do so as soon as possible. Proprietors do have the right to retain deposits and under certain circumstances to charge for cancelled holidays if adequate notice is not given and they cannot re-let the accommodation.

HOSTS: Give details about your facilities and about any special conditions. Explain your deposit system clearly and arrangements for cancellations, charges, etc, and whether or not your terms include VAT.

If for any reason you are unable to fulfil an agreed booking without adequate notice, you may be under an obligation to arrange alternative suitable accommodation or to make some form of compensation.

While every effort is made to ensure accuracy, we regret that FHG Publications cannot accept responsibility for errors, omissions or misrepresentation in our entries or any consequences thereof. Prices in particular should be checked because we go to press early. We will follow up complaints but cannot act as arbiters or agents for either party.

FERMANAGH

BLANEY. Mrs Hanna E. Bruce, Lough Erne House, St. Catherine's, Blaney, Enniskillin BT93 7AY

(013656 41216). Family guesthouse in rural setting on the shores of Lower Lough Erne. Convenient for all tourist amenities, boating marina adjacent, fishing available. Accommodation offered in one double, one single and one family bedrooms. Open all year. Meals available. Enniskillen 10 miles on A46 to Belleek. Vouchers accepted.

BROOKEBOROUGH. Norfolk House, Killykeeran, Brookeborough BT94 4AQ (013655 31681).

Family-run country house situated in a peaceful area, ideal for walking and cycling and fishing is within walking distance. A warm welcome awaits you and a great breakfast is served. We are situated off the main Belfast Road, one mile Maguiresbridge, one mile Brookeborough, nine miles Enniskillen and close to all amenities. The accommodation comprises one double with en suite, one family with en suite, one twin-bedded room and one single bedroom, all with washbasin. Separate luxury guest room with oak beams and colour TV; separate dining room. Children welcome, reduced rates. Private parking. Open all year. Bed and Breakfast £14.

EDERNEY. Mrs E. McCord, Greenwood Lodge, Erne Drive, Ederney BT93 0EF (013656 31366). On

the outskirts of a peaceful village this comfortable family-run guesthouse has en suite rooms with tea/coffee facilities, central heating and TV; several on ground floor. Convenient for fishing, boating, golf, pony trekking and touring the Lakelands, Donegal and Omagh areas. Situated near Kesh, Castle Archdale, Necarne Equestrian Centre, Lakeland Airport and Belleek Pottery. Plenty of parking. Open all year.

KILLADEAS. Mr and Mrs J. Williams, Rossfad House, Kesh Road, Killadeas (01365 388505).

Rossfad is a Georgian country house with spacious grounds adjoining Lower Lough Erne. Between Enniskillen and Castle Archdale, it is conveniently situated for ferry crossings to Devenish and White Island as well as good restaurants and a variety of sporting activities including boating, golf and pony trekking. The south facing rooms, one double (en suite) and one family room, all have views of the lake. Central heating. Children welcome. Open all year. Bed and Breakfast from £12.50. Please write or telephone for further information.

**If you've found
FARM HOLIDAY GUIDES
of service please tell your friends**

MAGUIRESBRIDGE. Mr Aubrey and Mrs Wendy Bothwell, Derryvree House, 200 Belfast Road, Maguiresbridge BT94 4LD (013655 31251). NITB APPROVED.

A warm and friendly welcome awaits you at Derryvree House, where guests can relax and enjoy a memorable family holiday at competitive rates. Situated on main Belfast/Enniskillen road. Large lounge with colour TV and turf fire. Central heating throughout. Spacious bedrooms, all with washbasins and one room en suite. Tea/coffee making facilities. Children welcome. Packed lunches available. Enjoy good home cooking in our breakfast room. Trout fishing within walking distance at Colebrooke River. Convenient to Upper and Lower Lough Erne, Ardhowen Theatre and National Trust properties. Ideally located for touring Fermanagh's lakes and mountains. Open all year. Bed and Breakfast from £14 to £16 per person.

LONDONDERRY

COLERAINE. Mrs Heather Torrens, "Heathfield", 31 Drumcroone Road, Garvagh, Coleraine BT51 4EB (02665 58245).

Winner of A.I.B. Agr-Tourism Farm Guest House 1995. 17th century farmhouse of great character and warmth set in large garden. Working beef and sheep farm. Ideally situated for business guest or holiday. From your peaceful rural base discover our many local attractions, Causeway Coast, etc; golf, horse riding and fishing nearby. En suite bedrooms. Tea/coffee facilities, TV, hair dryers, etc. Guest lounge with piano and log fire. Farm house hospitality and home cooking. Access/Visa accepted. On A29 Garvagh to Coleraine Road. Open all year. Bed and Breakfast from £16.

COLERAINE. Dartries House, 50 Gortycavan Road, Articlave, Coleraine BT51 4JY (Tel & Fax: 01265 848312).

Country house on a working farm situated on an elevated site giving panoramic views of the River Bann and coastal towns of Portstewart and Castlerock. An excellent base for walking or touring the scenic north coast. Accommodation comprises one double and two twin-bedded rooms, one room en suite, all with washbasins. Sample the home baking when you arrive. Central heating. Children welcome. Directions: drive along the Castlerock Road, two and a half miles from Coleraine, turn left onto the Gortycavan Road. Bed and Breakfast from £16 (en suite extra). Weekend and mid-week breaks available.

REPUBLIC OF IRELAND

CLARE

QUILTY. Mrs T. Donnellan, "Fionnuaire", Mullagh, Quilty (Tel & Fax: 00 353 65 87179). Working dairy farm in quiet location with sweeping views of scenic countryside and Atlantic Ocean. Fitted games and leisure room. Also available, guided walks, cycle tours (bicycle hire arranged). Guests welcome to participate in farm work. Music in village pubs within walking distance. Families especially welcome. Children catered for — farm pets and pony; play area. Bed and Breakfast per person with en suite room £16, without en suite £14. Evening Meal £12. Reductions for children sharing with parents 50% discount. Self catering accommodation also available. Brochure and full tariff on request.

KERRY

ABBEYDORNEY, Near Tralee. Mrs Mary O'Connor, The Abbey Tavern, Abbeydorney (00 353 66 35145). Country village pub ideal for touring Ring of Kerry and Dingle Peninsula, five miles from sandy beaches. Five bedrooms, two en suite. Situated near Tralee, Killarney and Ballybunion Golf Courses. Children welcome. Bed and Breakfast is £13. Licensed. Bar snacks available. Four-bedroomed self catering house and apartments also available. Please write or telephone for further details.

KILLARNEY. Eden Villa Farm, Loreto Road, Killarney (064 31138; from UK 00 353 64 31138). Lovely old country house in extensive gardens in peaceful farmland surroundings overlooking the lakes, mountains and Killarney town. One mile from Glen Eagle Hotel Complex, the National Park with forest and nature walks, pony trekking, boating and fishing nearby. Two double bedrooms and two single ones, electric blankets on beds. Bathroom with shower and two toilets. Lounge cum dining room. Tea on arrival to welcome you and also night snacks up to 10.30pm. Car essential. Three miles to Killarney town.

TIPPERARY

LIMERICK near. Mrs Mary Sheary, "Eagles Nest", Greenhills, Bird Hill, Co. Tipperary, Via Limerick (00-353 61 379178). Working farm. "Eagles Nest" farmhouse is situated one kilometre off the N7 in peaceful surroundings in an area of great scenic beauty. Killaloe, three kilometres, is well known for its water sports and scenery. There are many country pubs within easy reach. Matt the Thrasher situated in the village of Birdhill is well known for its fine food and drink. Good golf and pitch and putt courses nearby. The farm is mainly a dairy farm but we also have a Charolais breeding herd. There are many pets on the farm. Guests may wander freely on the farmland. Supervised pony rides for children. Good old fashioned cooking with ample portions, all freshly prepared, with own organic produce used. No microwave cooking. Choice of breakfast menu. Complimentary tea/coffee, scones and home made jam on arrival. Bed and Breakfast £10.50; Evening Dinner £10; Evening Meal £6. Open all year. 50% reduction for children.

SPECIAL WELCOME SUPPLEMENT

Are you looking for a guest house where smoking is banned, a farmhouse that is equipped for the disabled, or a hotel that will cater for your special diet? If so, you should find this new supplement useful. Its three sections, NON-SMOKERS, DISABLED, and SPECIAL DIETS, list accommodation where these particular needs are served. Brief details of the accommodation are provided in this section; for a full description you should turn to the appropriate place in the main section of the book.

NON-SMOKERS

LONDON, CHISWICK. Mrs A. Louis, 18 Silver Crescent, Chiswick, London W4 5SE (0181-994 6265). Situated two minutes from Gunnersbury Underground station, M4 and A4. Central heating and colour TV in all rooms. Non-smokers preferred.
LONDON, HIGHGATE/CROUCH END. Penny and Laurence Solomons, The Parkland Walk Guest House, 12 Hornsey Rise Gardens, London N19 3PR (0171-263 3228; Fax: 0171-831 9489; email@parkwalk.demon.co.uk). Friendly Bed and Breakfast in pretty, comfortable Victorian family house. Smoking banned throughout the house. Bed and Breakfast from £25 nightly.

BEDFORDSHIRE, SANDY. Mrs. Joan M. Strong, Orchard Cottage, 1 High Street, Wrestlingworth, Near Sandy SG19 2EW (01767 631355). 🐦 *COMMENDED*. Picturesque 16th Century thatched cottage with modern extension, situated in a quiet, country location. Reduced terms for children. No smoking establishment.

CAMBRIDGESHIRE, ELY. Mrs Margaret Sicard, The Laurels, 104 Victoria Street, Littleport, Ely CB6 1LZ (01353 861972; 0850 199299 mobile). Spacious attractive Victorian house situated on the Norfolk/Suffolk/Cambridge borders. Non-smoking guests only please.
CAMBRIDGESHIRE, HEMINGFORD GREY. Maureen and Tony Webster, The Willow Guest House, 45 High Street, Hemingford Grey, St. Ives, Cambs PE18 9BJ (01480 494748). Large private guest house in centre of this picturesque village. Family, twin, double and single rooms available. All bedrooms en suite and non-smoking. Sorry no pets.
CAMBRIDGESHIRE, HOUGHTON. Robin and Marion Seaman, The Elms, Banks End, Wyton PE17 2AA (01480 453523). 🐦 🐦 *COMMENDED*. Edwardian house with cottage garden. All rooms en-suite or with vanity units. No pets. No smoking.

CHESHIRE, SANDBACH. Mrs Helen Wood, Arclid Grange, Arclid Green, Sandbach CW11 0SZ (01270 764750). Some of our rooms are strictly non-smoking. Please confirm when booking. ETB Category 3 Disabled.
CHESHIRE, TARPORLEY. Mrs. Sutcliffe, Roughlow Farm, Willington, Tarporley CW6 0PG (Tel/Fax: 01829 751199). 🐦 🐦 *COMMENDED*. 18th Century sandstone farmhouse in outstanding position with magnificent views to Shropshire and Wales. Non smoking accommodation available. Ideal touring base. Recommended by Which? Good Bed and Breakfast Guide.

CORNWALL, CAMBORNE. Mrs Christine Peerless, Highdowns (formerly Cargenwen Farm), Blackrock, Praze-an-Beeble, Camborne TR14 9PD (01209 831442). Set on a hillside with extensive country views towards St. Ives Bay. A non-smoking household offering Bed and Breakfast and optional Evening Meal.

CORNWALL, FALMOUTH. Celia and Ian Carruthers, Harbour House, 1 Harbour Terrace, Falmouth TR11 2AN (01326 311344). Enjoy quality Bed and Breakfast accommodation with some of the most fantastic harbour views in Cornwall. We welcome guests for long or short stays, especially non-smokers. Please call for brochure.

CORNWALL, PENZANCE. Mr and Mrs G.W. Buswell, Penalva Private Hotel, Alexandra Road, Penzance TR18 4LZ (01736 69060). 👑👑👑 *APPROVED*. AA QQQ.Non-smoking hotel — immaculate fresh interior — excellent position close to amenities. Total ban on smoking on premises. Open all year. Highly recommended.

CORNWALL, PENZANCE. Mrs L. Sunderland, Kerris Manor Farm, Kerris, Penzance TR19 6UY (01736 731198). Come and share our lovely old farmhouse where you are assured of a friendly welcome, a comfy bed and good food. Sorry — no smoking.

CORNWALL, ST. AGNES. Cleaderscroft Hotel, 16 British Road, St. Agnes TR5 0TZ (01872 552349). Heart of village. Mature gardens. Children's play area. Lounge, Bar, Dining and Games rooms. Private parking. Non-smokers welcomed. Bed and Breakfast from £19.50.

CORNWALL, TRURO. Marcorrie Hotel, 20 Falmouth Road, Truro TR1 2HX (01872 77374; Fax: 01872 41666). 👑👑👑 *APPROVED*. Victorian town house in conservation area, five minutes' walk from the city centre and cathedral. Non-smokers welcome.

CORNWALL, TRURO. Mrs Shirley Wakeling, Rock Cottage, Blackwater, Truro TR4 8EU (01872 560252). 👑👑👑 *HIGHLY COMMENDED*. AA QQQQ Selected. RAC Acclaimed. 18th century beamed cottage, two double rooms and one twin, all en suite. Haven for non-smokers. Dinner by arrangement. A la carte menu. Open all year.

CUMBRIA, AMBLESIDE. Linda & Alan Bleasdale, Borwick Lodge, Outgate, Hawkshead, Ambleside LA22 0PU (015394 36332). 👑👑 *HIGHLY COMMENDED*. Charming 17th century country house. Peaceful perfection. AWARD-WINNING accommodation. Prize winning home-made breads. Non-smoking throughout.

CUMBRIA, BOWNESS-ON-WINDERMERE. Mrs Susan Lewthwaite, Beech Tops, Meadowcroft Lane, Storrs Park, Bowness-on-Windermere LA23 3JJ (015394 45453). Modern detached house near lake offers first class, spacious accommodation in double/twin/family suites. Sorry, no smoking.

CUMBRIA, CARLISLE. Ellen & John McLaughlin, "The Warren Guest House", 368 Warwick Road, Carlisle CA1 2RU (01228 33663). 👑👑👑 *COMMENDED*. AA QQQ. RAC Listed. Ideal touring base. 6 en suite bedrooms. A warm welcome awaits non-smokers.

CUMBRIA, CONISTON. Mr and Mrs R. Newport, Brigg House, Torver, Coniston LA21 8AY (015394 41592). 👑👑 *HIGHLY COMMENDED*. Explore the Lake District from our tranquil early 19th century country house. Lots of activities nearby or just simply relax and enjoy the scenery. Pets welcome. A completely "no smoking" establishment.

CUMBRIA, ENNERDALE. Mrs Elizabeth Loxham, Beckfoot, Ennerdale, Cleator CA23 3AU (01946 861235). Comfortable no smoking guest house overlooking Lake. Superb home cooking. Breakfast menu. Please phone for leaflet.

CUMBRIA, HAWKSHEAD. Linda & Alan Bleasdale, Borwick Lodge, Outgate, Hawkshead, Ambleside LA22 0PU (015394 36332). 👑👑 *HIGHLY COMMENDED*. Charming 17th century country house. Peaceful perfection. AWARD-WINNING accommodation. Prize winning home-made breads. No smoking throughout.

CUMBRIA, KENDAL. Mrs. Judith Keep, 'West Mount', 39 Milnthorpe Road, Kendal LA9 5QG (01539 724621). Friendly, non smoking, centrally heated Victorian guest house on southern outskirts of Kendal. Open all year.

CUMBRIA, KENDAL.Mrs Val Sunter, Higher House Farm, Oxenholme Lane, Natland, Kendal LA9 7QH (015395 61177). 👑👑👑 *COMMENDED*. AA QQQQ Selected. 17th century farmhouse offers comfortable bed and breakfast accommodation in tranquil village. TV, hair dryer, and tea/coffee making facilities in all bedrooms. Pets welcome. NO SMOKING.

CUMBRIA, KENDAL. Eileen and Brian Kettle, Holmfield, 41 Kendal Green, Kendal LA9 5PP (01539 720790). ETB Listed *DE LUXE*. Bed and Breakfast in style in elegant Edwardian house. Completely non-smoking. From £19 per person. Short listed for ETB B&B of the year.

CUMBRIA, KESWICK. Mrs Sharon Helling, Beckside Guest House, 5 Wordsworth Street, Keswick CA12 4HU (017687 73093). 👑👑 *COMMENDED*. AA QQQ, RAC Highly Acclaimed. Small very comfortable guest house for non-smokers situated close to town centre and convenient for the shops, Fitz Park, pool, Lake, walking and touring.

CUMBRIA, KESWICK. Gladys & David Birtwistle, Kalgurli Guest House, 33 Helvellyn Street, Keswick CA12 4EP (017687 72935). 👑👑 *COMMENDED*. Be assured of a warm and friendly welcome at this comfortable non-smoking four-bedroomed guest house. Ideal location for touring and walking. Children welcome.

CUMBRIA, KESWICK. Mr & Mrs J.M. Pepper, Beckstones Farm, Thornthwaite, Keswick CA12 5SQ (017687 78510). 👑👑 *COMMENDED*. Comfortable, Georgian farmhouse situated in peaceful surroundings. Regret no pets. No children under five years. No smoking in dining room.

CUMBRIA, KESWICK. AnneMarie and Ian Townsend, Latrigg House, St. Herbert Street, Keswick CA12 4DF (017687 73068). 👑👑 An attractive detached Victorian house situated in a quiet area, only a few minutes' walk from the town centre and Lake, offering a no smoking environment for the well-being and safety of guests.

CUMBRIA, KESWICK. Mr. Jack Jenkins, Bay Tree, Wordsworth Street, Keswick CA12 4HU (017687 73313). 👑👑 Small family-run licensed guesthouse. Non-smoking.

CUMBRIA, KESWICK. Mr Picken, Lynwood House, 35 Helvellyn, Keswick CA12 4EP (017687 72398). Fantastic scenery. Fabulous fell walking. Five minutes from town centre. Five more to Lake Derwentwater. Free from smoke. Full Fire Certificate. Full breakfast menu. Bed and Breakfast from £15 per person per night.

CUMBRIA, KESWICK. David and Margaret Raine, Clarence House, 14 Eskin Street, Keswick CA12 4DQ (017687 73186). 👻 👻 👻 *COMMENDED*. AA QQQ. A lovely Victorian house ideally situated for the Lake, parks and market square. A warm welcome and hearty breakfast await you. Non smoking. Brochure sent on request.

CUMBRIA, KESWICK. Mr and Mrs J.A. McMullan, Jenkin Hill Cottage, Thornthwaite, Keswick CA12 5SG (017687 78443). 👻 👻 *HIGHLY COMMENDED*. Each room is tastefully decorated and furnished with matching en-suite shower rooms. Tea/coffee making facilities, colour TV, central heating are available in all the rooms. We have a no smoking policy throughout.

CUMBRIA, KESWICK. M. Bamber & H. Yates, Brienz Guest House, 3 Greta Street, Keswick CA12 4HS (017687 71049). **Tourist Board Listed** *COMMENDED*. High standards of comfort and cuisine. Special diets catered for. Open February to mid-December. No smoking.

CUMBRIA, KESWICK. Alan & Jean Redfern, Heatherlea, 26 Blencathra Street, Keswick CA12 4HP (017687 72430). Charming and friendly guesthouse personally run by the owners. Non-smokers only please. AA QQQ.

CUMBRIA, LAKESIDE/NEWBY BRIDGE. Brian and Sylvia Slingsby, Landing Cottage, Newby Bridge, Ulverston LA12 8AS (015395 31719). 👻 👻 We extend a warm welcome to all our new and returning guests — offering good home cooking, packed lunches and complimentary pot of tea/coffee on arrival. Car parking. Open all year. Brochure available.

CUMBRIA, MUNGRISDALE. Mike and Penny Sutton, Bannerdale View, Mungrisdale, Near Penrith CA11 0XR (017687 79691). Centrally heated 17th century Lakeland cottage. Idyllic, peaceful mountain and riverside location. Superb breakfasts. Non smokers only.

CUMBRIA, PENRITH. Mrs Jean Raynor, Blue Swallow Guest House, 11 Victoria Road, Penrith CA11 8HR (01768 866335). 👻 👻 *COMMENDED*. Resident proprietors Jean and Mel Raynor look forward to welcoming you whether you are on holiday, just breaking a long journey or in the area for business — you'll be made to feel at home. Non-smokers welcome.

CUMBRIA, PENRITH. Mrs S.E. Bray, Norcroft Guest House, Graham Street, Penrith CA11 9LQ (01768 862365). 👻 👻 👻 *COMMENDED*. Victorian house in quiet area. Large and comfortable en-suite bedrooms. No smoking in bedrooms and diningroom.

CUMBRIA, PENRITH. Angela and Ivor Davies, Woodland House Hotel, Wordsworth Street, Penrith CA11 7QY (01768 864177; Fax: 01768 890152). 👻 👻 👻 *COMMENDED*. Small, friendly and elegant licensed private hotel situated at the foot of Beacon Hill and only five minutes from centre of town. Hotel is NO SMOKING throughout.

CUMBRIA, TROUTBECK. Gwen and Peter Parfitt, Hill Crest, Troutbeck, Penrith CA11 0SH (017684 83935). A unique warm and friendly Lakeland home, with non smoking lounge/dining room, where children and dogs are welcome. En suite rooms available.

CUMBRIA, WINDERMERE. Mrs S. Garside, Boston House, 4 The Terrace, Windermere LA23 1AJ (015394 43654). 👻 👻 👻 *COMMENDED*. Delightful Victorian Gothic building. Hearty breakfasts; superb home-cooked dinners. Restaurant/residential licence. Romantic four-poster beds. Private parking. Brochure on request.

CUMBRIA, WINDERMERE. Barry and Gill Pearson, Broadlands Guest House, 19 Broad Street, Windermere LA23 2AB (Tel & Fax: 015394 46532). 👻 👻 *COMMENDED*. Ideal base for the Lake District being only 300 yards from train/coach station. Double, twin and family rooms all en suite. Open all year. No smoking in lounge and diningroom.

CUMBRIA, WINDERMERE. Bob and Maureen Theobald, Oldfield House, Oldfield Road, Windermere LA23 2BY (015394 88445; Fax: 015394 43250). 👻 👻 *COMMENDED*. AA QQQ, RAC Acclaimed. Friendly, informal atmosphere in traditionally-built Lakeland stone residence. A quiet central location. Non smoking establishment.

CUMBRIA, WINDERMERE. Mrs P.A. Wood, The Haven, 10 Birch Street, Windermere LA23 1EG (015394 44017). AA QQ. The Haven is a comfortable Victorian guest house, conveniently located in the attractive village of Windermere. Open all year. Vegetarians catered for. Parking. Reductions for children. No smoking. Brochure on request.

CUMBRIA, WINDERMERE. Mick & Angela Brown, Haisthorpe Guest House, Holly Road, Windermere LA23 2AF (Tel/Fax: 015394 43445). 👻 👻 *COMMENDED*. Comfortable family house situated in a quiet part of Windermere yet close to the village centre and local amenities. Special breaks October to June. No smoking in bedrooms. AA QQQ, RAC Highly Acclaimed.

CUMBRIA, WINDERMERE. Mrs L. Christopherson, Villa Lodge, Cross Street, Windermere LA23 1AE (Tel & Fax: 015394 43318). 👻 👻 *COMMENDED*. AA QQQ. Extremely comfortable non-smoking accommodation in peaceful area overlooking Windermere village. Open all year. Non-smokers welcomed.

DERBYSHIRE, ASHBOURNE. Mrs E.J. Harrison, Little Park Farm, Mappleton, Ashbourne DE6 2BR (01335 350 341). 👻 *COMMENDED*. Oak beamed listed farmhouse offering two double and one twin-bedded rooms. Open Easter to end October. Non smoking establishment. SAE for details.

DERBYSHIRE, ASHBOURNE. Mr and Mrs A. Kingston, Old Boothby Farm, The Green, Ashbourne DE6 1EE (01335 342044). Bed and Breakfast accommodation in an idyllic location, the "Gateway to the Peak District". Handy for visiting Alton Towers, Dovedale, Buxton, etc. Non-smoking accommodation available.

DERBYSHIRE, ASHOVER. Mrs Ann Brookes, The Red Lion Inn, Ashover S45 0EW (01246 590271). A picturesque Tudor Inn in the very historic, pretty village of Ashover. Recently refurbished, with an extensive menu of cooked foods. Activities nearby — fishing, shooting (clays), riding and country walks.

DERBYSHIRE, BAKEWELL. Mrs Jenny Spafford, Barleycorn Croft, Sheldon, Near Bakewell DE45 1QS (01629 813636). Converted barn accommodating 2, 3 or 4 people in twin and/or double rooms making a private apartment with independent access and key. Non-smokers welcomed — see main section.

DERBYSHIRE, BAKEWELL. Mrs Julia Finney, Mandale House, Haddon Grove, Bakewell DE45 1JF (01629 812416). ☙☙ Relax in the warm and friendly atmosphere of our peaceful farmhouse situated in the edge of Lathkill Dale. Completely non-smoking. Telephone for brochure.

DERBYSHIRE, BAKEWELL near. Mr and Mrs R.H. Tyler, Sheldon House, Chapel Street, Monyash, Near Bakewell DE45 1JJ (01629 813067). 18th century listed building in Peak District. One double room with private bathroom and three doubles en-suite available. No smoking in bedrooms and public rooms.

DERBYSHIRE, BUXTON. Maria and Roger Hyde, Braemar, 10 Compton Road, Buxton SK17 9DN (01298 78050). Accommodation comprises comfortable double and twin rooms fully en-suite with colour TV and tea/coffee making facilities. Non-smokers preferred. Diets catered for.

DERBYSHIRE, HATHERSAGE. Mrs Jean Wilcockson, Hillfoot Farm, Castleton Road, Hathersage, Near Sheffield S30 1AH (01433 651673). Tourist Board Listed *COMMENDED.* Welcome Host. Newly built accommodation offering comfortable, well appointed en suite rooms. Current Fire Certificate held. Non smokers please.

DERBYSHIRE, TIDESWELL. Mr D.C. Pinnegar, "Poppies", Bank Square, Tideswell, Buxton SK17 8LA (01298 871083). Situated in attractive Derbyshire village. Bed, Breakfast and Evening Meal available. No smoking in bedrooms or dining room.

DERBYSHIRE, TIDESWELL. Mrs Pat Harris, Laurel House, The Green, Litton, Near Buxton SK17 8QP (01298 871971). ☙☙ *COMMENDED.* Overlooking the village green. One double with en-suite facilities and a twin room with washbasin and private use of bathroom and toilet; tea/coffee making facilities in both. Private lounge. No smoking.

DEVON, ASHBURTON.Mrs Anne Torr, Middle Leat, Holne, Near Ashburton TQ13 7SJ (01364 631413). Very comfortable accommodation with wonderful views. Sorry, no smoking in the house. SAE for details or telephone for brochure.

DEVON, BAMPTON. Elaine Goodwin, Lodfin Farm, Morebath, Tiverton EX16 9DD (Tel & Fax: 01398 331400) Beautiful 17th century farmhouse situated on the edge of Exmoor nestling in a secluded valley. Children and pets welcome. Open all year.

DEVON, BIDEFORD. Jenny and Barry Jones, The Pines at Eastleigh, Near Bideford EX39 4PA (01271 860561; E-mail Barry@barpines.demon.co.uk). ☙☙☙ *HIGHLY COMMENDED.* Georgian house overlooking Bideford and the sea at Hartland Point and Lundy Island. Bed, Breakfast and optional Evening Meal. Short Breaks available. No smoking.

DEVON, BUCKFASTLEIGH. Mrs Rosie Palmer, Wellpark Farm, Dean Prior, Buckfastleigh TQ11 0LY (01364 643775). ETB Listed *HIGHLY COMMENDED.* Set on the edge of Dartmoor near Buckfast Abbey, a warm and friendly welcome is extended to all our guests. Very comfortable rooms. Reductions for children and weekly bookings.

DEVON, CLOVELLY. Mrs J. Johns, Dyke Green Farm, Clovelly, Near Bideford EX39 5RU (01237 431699 or 431279). Tastefully converted barn offering beautiful accommodation. Ideal base for Devon and Cornwall. No smoking in bedrooms.

DEVON, COLEBROOKE. Mrs V.K. Hill, Birchmans Farm, Colebrooke, Crediton EX17 5DN (01363 82393). ☙☙ *COMMENDED.* **Working farm.** We are situated seven miles from Crediton in peaceful countryside with unspoilt views. All rooms en suite. No smoking in bedrooms please.

DEVON, CROYDE BAY. Chris and Roslyn Gedling, West Winds Guest House, Moor Lane, Croyde Bay EX33 1PA (01271 890489). ☙☙☙ AA QQQ Recommended. Small guest house located by picturesque water's edge. Comfortable, relaxing atmosphere. Open all year. No smoking in dining room, lounge and some bedrooms.

DEVON, LYNTON. Mrs Helen Christian, Woodlands, Lynbridge Road, Lynton EX35 6AX (01598 752324). ☙☙☙ *COMMENDED.* Ideal base for exploring Exmoor and the stunning coastal scenery. Private parking. Licensed, cosy lounge. Non-smoking. Delicious home cooking.

DEVON, OKEHAMPTON. Mrs E.G. Arney, The Old Rectory, Bratton Clovelly, Okehampton EX20 4LA (01837 871382). Thoroughly modernised property ideally situated for touring Devon and Cornwall. A warm welcome, friendly atmosphere and personal attention. Pets welcome.

DEVON, PLYMOUTH near. Slade Barn, Netton, Noss Mayo, Near Plymouth PL8 1HA (01752 872235). WCTB COMMENDED. Sandy Cherrington assures you of a warm welcome to Slade Barn. All rooms have central heating, TV/radio and hair dryers. Tea/coffee on request. Indoor pool, games room, tennis court and private gardens. Plenty of parking. Open all year.

DEVON, SEATON near. The Bulstone, Higher Bulstone, Branscombe, Near Seaton EX12 3BL (01297 680486). A relaxed and pleasant stay is offered at The Bulstone all year round from the new proprietors Judith and Kevin Monaghan. Hotel caters for families with children under 12 years. No smoking. Brochure available.

DEVON, TAVISTOCK. Mrs Rose Bacon, April Cottage, Mount Tavy Road, Tavistock PL19 9JB (01822 613280). ☙☙ *HIGHLY COMMENDED.* Victorian cottage situated on riverside two minutes from town centre. Superb accommodation with excellent food. No smoking in bedrooms.

DEVON, TORQUAY near. Mrs R. Wilkinson, Deane Thatch Accommodation, Deane Thatch, Stoke-in-Teignhead, Near Torquay TQ12 4QU (Tel & Fax: 01626 873724). ☙☙ *COMMENDED.* Bed and Breakfast offered in charming thatched Devonshire cob cottage. Open all year. Non-smoking.

DEVON, UMBERLEIGH. Ms Carolyn Billington, Westacott, Townsend, Chittlehampton, Umberleigh EX37 9PU (01769 540463). Centrally heated 300-year-old former bakery now offering Bed and Breakfast accommodation. Non-smokers only. Self catering also available.

DEVON, WHIDDON DOWN. Mrs Elizabeth Knox, Tor View, Whiddon Down, Okehampton EX20 2PR (01647 231447). Ideal base for exploring Dartmoor. All accommodation on ground floor. TV lounge. Sorry, no smoking, no pets.

DEVON, WOOLFARDISWORTHY. Chris and Keith Merton, Ford Mill, Woolfardisworthy, Near Bideford EX39 5RF (Tel & Fax: 01409 241289). 16th century farmhouse set in nine acre meadows with duck pond. Midway between Bideford and Bude. Children and pets welcome.

DORSET, BOURNEMOUTH. Bournecliff House, 31 Grand Avenue, Southbourne, Bournemouth BH6 3SY (01202 426455). Enjoy a happy holiday in the comfort of our small family hotel. Open all year. Off-season bargain breaks. Non-smokers appreciated. Please telephone for further details.

DORSET, BOURNEMOUTH. Gervis Court Hotel, 38 Gervis Road, East Cliff, Bournemouth BH1 3DH (01202 556871). ✿ ✿ Late Victorian detached hotel set in its own attractive gardens with ample parking space. Non smoking accommodation available. Ask about special activity breaks.

DORSET, BOURNEMOUTH. Alison & Adrian Homa, Bay View Hotel, Southbourne Overcliffe Drive, Bournemouth BH6 3QB (01202 429315; Mobile: 0585 488150; Fax: 01202 424385). ✿ ✿ ✿ COMMENDED. 14 en suite bedrooms. Non-smoking accommodation available. Write or phone for brochure.

DORSET, DORCHESTER. Mr and Mrs Michael Eaton, The Dower House, Bradford Peverell, Dorchester DT2 9SF (01305 266125). Warm welcome in Grade II Listed village house. Tea and home made cakes on arrival. No smoking.

DORSET, DORCHESTER. Michael and Jane Deller, Churchview Guest House, Winterbourne Abbas, Near Dorchester DT2 9LS (01305 889296). ✿ ✿ ✿ COMMENDED. Beautiful 17th Century Non Smoking licensed Guest House set in the heart of West Dorset. Character bedrooms, delightful period dining room, two lounges and a bar. Pets welcome. AA QQQ.

DORSET, DORCHESTER near. Mr Howell, Appletrees, 23 Affpuddle, Dorchester DT2 7HH (01929 471300). '60's character home with one double, two single and one twin-bedded room with TV and tea making facilities. Use of kitchen if required. Non smoking accommodation available.

DORSET, LULWORTH COVE. Jenny and John Aldridge, The Orchard, West Road, West Lulworth BH20 5RY (01929 400592). Peaceful off-road position in large garden with mature fruit trees. Short step from coastal paths and beaches. Non-smokers welcome. Open all year.

DORSET, LYME REGIS. Mrs S.G. Taylor, Buckland Farm, Raymonds Hill, Near Axminster EX13 5SZ (01297 33222). Smallholding of five acres, three miles from Lyme Regis and Charmouth offering Bed and Breakfast accommodation. No smoking in bedrooms. SAE for details.

DORSET, LYME REGIS. Jenny & Ivan Harding, Coverdale Guesthouse, Woodmead Road, Lyme Regis DT7 3AB (01297 442882). ✿ ✿ Friendly, well established guesthouse situated in a quiet residential area. No smoking please. Write or phone for brochure.

DORSET, POOLE. Mrs Margaret Gregory, Ashton Lodge, 10 Oakley Hill, Wimborne Minster BH21 1QH (01202 883423; Fax: 01202 886180). ✿ ✿ COMMENDED. Warm, friendly greeting awaits guests. Accommodation includes en-suite bedrooms. Full English Breakfasts. We welcome non-smokers.

DORSET, SHERBORNE. Mrs Pauline Tizzard, Venn Farm, Milborne Port, Sherborne DT9 5RA (01963 250598). AA QQ Recommended. Attractively furnished accommodation situated in beautiful wooded parkland within walking distance of local village inn. Open all year.

DORSET, WAREHAM. Mr and Mrs Axford, Sunnyleigh, Hyde, Wareham BH20 7NT (01929 471822). Situated in the quiet hamlet of Hyde five miles west of Wareham. Accommodation comprises double and twin bedrooms. Open all year. No smoking.

DORSET, WEYMOUTH near. Mrs Joyce Norman, Dingle Dell, Osmington, Near Weymouth DT3 6EW (01305 832378). Tourist Board HIGHLY COMMENDED. This family home of mellow local stone is set in a large garden full of roses and apple trees in quiet corner of Hardy's Wessex. Two spacious, attractively furnished bedrooms (one en suite) available. Open March to October. No smoking please.

DORSET, WIMBORNE. Mrs Eveline Stimpson, Acacia House, 2 Oakley Road, Wimborne Minster BH21 1QJ (01202 883958; Fax: 01202 881943). Warm welcome, very high standard of decor and quality English Breakfast served. No smoking throughout the house.

DURHAM, TEESDALE. Mrs M. Rabbitts, Glendale, Cotherstone, Barnard Castle DL12 9UH (01833 650384). ✿ ✿ HIGHLY COMMENDED. Beautiful house situated in superb open countryside. En suite double rooms with TV etc. No smoking. No children under 10. Brochure on request.

ESSEX, COLCHESTER. Mrs Wendy Anderson, The Old Manse, 15 Roman Road, Colchester CO1 1UR (01206 545154). A friendly welcome to this elegant and spacious town centre Victorian family home. Accommodation completely non-smoking.

ESSEX, KELVEDON. Mr & Mrs R. Bunting, Highfields Farm, Kelvedon CO5 9BJ (01376 570334). ✿ ✿ COMMENDED. Peaceful overnight stop on the way to Harwich or as a base to visit historic Colchester and Constable country. Three twin rooms, all with en suite facilities. No smoking.

GLOUCESTERSHIRE, AMBERLEY. The Dial Cottage, Amberley, Near Stroud GL5 5AL (01453 872563). We are well positioned to explore Cheltenham, Bath, Cirencester and Tetbury. Children welcome. Non-smoking and sorry, no pets.

GLOUCESTERSHIRE, CHELTENHAM near. Mr and Mrs Rooke, Frogfurlong Cottage, Frogfurlong Lane, Down Hatherley GL2 9QE (01452 730430). Exclusive accommodation for one couple. The 18th century cottage is surrounded by fields. No smoking.

GLOUCESTERSHIRE, CHEW MAGNA. Mrs Judi Hasell, Woodbarn Farm, Denny Lane, Chew Magna, Bristol BS18 8SZ (01275 332599). Woodbarn Farm is a working farm five minutes from Chew Valley Lake and is central for touring. Open March to December (closed Christmas). Children welcome. Non smokers preferred. Brochure on request.

GLOUCESTERSHIRE, MINSTERWORTH. Mrs S. Carter, Severn Bank, Minsterworth GL2 8JH (01452 750357). 👜 A fine country house standing in its own six acre grounds on the bank of the River Severn. Non-smoking bedrooms.

GLOUCESTERSHIRE, PAINSWICK. Jean Hernen, Brookhouse Mill Cottage, Tibbiwell Lane, Painswick GL6 6YA (Tel & Fax: 01452 812854). Beautiful 17th century cottage in an area of outstanding natural beauty. Indoor swimming pool. Plenty of parking. Brochure available.

GLOUCESTERSHIRE, RANDWICK. Mr and Mrs Taylor, Court Farm, Randwick, Stroud GL6 6HH (01453 764210; Fax: 01453 766428). 17th century beamed farmhouse, centre of hillside village of Randwick on Cotswold Escarpment. Convenient overnight stop, good base for touring. No smoking in public rooms.

GLOUCESTERSHIRE, STOW-ON-THE-WOLD. Mrs F.J. Adams, Aston House, Broadwell, Moreton-in-Marsh GL56 0TJ (01451 830475). (Formerly at Banks Farm, Oddington). Stone chalet bungalow in peaceful village overlooking fields. Bed & good English Breakfast, bedtime drink. No smoking in public areas. Car essential — parking. ETB Listed *COMMENDED.*

GLOUCESTERSHIRE, WOODCHESTER. Mrs Wendy Swait, Inschdene, Atcombe Road, South Woodchester, Stroud GL5 5EW (01453 873254). Comfortable family house with magnificent views across the valley, set in an acre of garden. No smoking in the house.

HAMPSHIRE, BARTON-ON-SEA.Mrs J. Copeland, Laurel Lodge, 48 Western Avenue, Barton-on-Sea BH25 7PZ (01425 618309). ETB 👜👜👜 AA QQQQ Selected, RAC Acclaimed. A superb area in all seasons for that special break. Scenic clifftop walks, beaches, golf, sailing, riding and the delights of the nearby historic New Forest. Open all year.

HAMPSHIRE, BURLEY. Mrs Gina Russell, Charlwood, Longmead Road, Burley BH24 4BY (01425 403242). Situated in the midst of beautiful New Forest. Ideal walking/touring base. No smoking on premises.

HAMPSHIRE, FRITHAM (New Forest). John and Penny Hankinson, Fritham Farm, Fritham, Lyndhurst SO43 7HH (Tel & Fax: 01703 812333). 👜👜 *COMMENDED.* AA QQQQ Selected. Lovely farmhouse on working farm in the heart of the New Forest. All rooms are en suite. No smoking.

HAMPSHIRE, LYMINGTON. Jane and Mike Finch, "Dolphins", 6 Emsworth Road, Lymington SO41 9BL (01590 676108 or 679545; Fax: 01590 688275). Very quiet central position, just five minutes' walk from railway/bus stations. Non-smoking. Open all year. Please write or telephone for brochure. Access/Visa/Mastercard accepted.

HAMPSHIRE, NEW FOREST. Mrs Pauline Harris, Little Heathers, 13 Whitemoor Road, Brockenhurst SO42 7QG (01590 623512). Warm welcome for all non-smokers. Ground floor bedrooms with limited wheelchair use. Special diets can be catered for.

HAMPSHIRE, NEW FOREST. Mrs M. Stone, Heathlands, Lepe Road, Langley SO4 1YT (01703 892517). New Forest bungalow near Beaulieu, offering Bed and Breakfast in comfortable rooms for non-smoking couples only.

HAMPSHIRE, NEW FOREST. Mrs J. Pearce, St. Ursula, 30 Hobart Road, New Milton BH25 6EG (01425 613515). 👜👜👜 Ideal base for visiting New Forest. Comfortable accommodation. Children and pets welcome. No smoking in bedrooms. Smoke detectors installed.

HAMPSHIRE, SOUTHSEA. Mr and Mrs Willett, Oakleigh Guest House, 48 Festing Grove, Southsea PO4 9QD (01705 812276). Southern Tourist Board Listed. Small family-run guest house two minutes' from sea. Double, twin, family or single rooms available. Open all year including Christmas and Easter.

HAMPSHIRE, WINCHESTER.Mrs S. Buchanan, "Acacia", 44 Kilham Lane, Winchester SO22 5PT (01962 852259; 0585 462993 mobile). 👜👜 *COMMENDED.* Accommodation consists of one double and two twin bedrooms, all of which have en-suite or private bathroom, plus tea and coffee making facilities. Off street parking. Non-smokers only.

HAMPSHIRE, WINCHESTER. Susan and Richard Pell, The Lilacs, 1 Harestock Close, off Andover Road North, Winchester SO22 6NP (01962 884122). A non-smoking family home offering an excellent English Breakfast, including vegetarian meals. Country views.

HAMPSHIRE, WINCHESTER. Mrs Ann Regan, "Leckhampton", 62 Kilham Lane, Winchester SO22 5QD (01962 852831). AA QQQQ. Peacefully situated along a quiet, rural lane just five minutes' drive from City Centre. All areas non-smoking.

HEREFORD & WORCESTER, BROADWAY. Mr Allen, "Tudor Cottage", 56 High Street, Broadway WR12 7DT (01386 852674). 👜👜 AA QQQQ Selected. Traditional 17th century Cotswold stone cottage, an ideal base for touring. All bedrooms are en suite and equipped with modern comforts.

HEREFORD & WORCESTER, CLIFTON UPON TEME. The Threshing Barn, Harpley, Clifton upon Teme WR6 6HG (Tel & Fax: 01886 853578). Luxury period barn offering olde world charm with delightful bedrooms, all with private facilties, peacefully yet conveniently situated. B&B from £19.50 per person.

HEREFORD & WORCESTER, ROSS-ON-WYE. Mrs M.E. Drzymalska, Thatch Close, Llangrove, Ross-On-Wye HR9 6EL (01989 770300). 👜👜 *COMMENDED.* Traditional farmhouse offering Bed and Breakfast, evening meal optional, using mainly home grown produce. Non-smokers only.

HEREFORD & WORCESTER, VOWCHURCH. The Old Vicarage, Vowchurch HR2 0QD (Tel & Fax: 01981 550357). Attractive en suite single/family/double rooms. Quality breakfasts. Dinners by arrangement. Warm hospitality guaranteed in one-time home of Lewis Carroll's brother. Completely non smoking.

HEREFORD & WORCESTER, WINFORTON. Mrs Jackie Kingdon, Winforton Court, Winforton HR3 6EA (01544 328498). Set in old world gardens close to the Black Mountains. Luxurious drawing room, open fires and good books. We appreciate non-smoking visitors.

KENT, CANTERBURY. The White House, 6 St. Peters Lane, Canterbury CT1 2BP (01227 761836). ❤ ❤ ❤ A warm welcome awaits you in this family-run, spacious Regency house within the old city walls. Open all year. No smoking.

KENT, CANTERBURY. Peter and Majorie McEwan, Four Oaks, Swan Lane, Edenbridge TN8 6BA (01732 863556; Fax: 01732 867022). Friendly and comfortable accommodation convenient for the M25. Double en suite and single rooms available. Close to pub for evening meals. No smoking.

KENT, CANTERBURY near. Tracy Childs, Beech Bank, Duckpitt Lane, Waltham, Near Canterbury CT4 5QA (01227 700302). ❤ ❤ AA QQQ. 15th century Tudor style coach house surrounded by magnificent views with landscaped garden. Luxury bedrooms. No smoking.

KENT, FOLKESTONE/ASHFORD. Duncan and Alison Taylor, Boldens Wood, Stowting, Near Ashford TN25 6AP (01303 812011). Friendly atmosphere and good food at comfortable smallholding. No smoking throughout. Enjoy wandering through private, secluded woodland and downland. Nature lovers delight. Come and relax.

KENT, HAWKHURST. Mrs Susan Woodard, Southgate, Little Fowlers, Rye Road, Hawkhurst, near Cranbrook TN18 5DA (01580 752526). ❤ ❤ *COMMENDED*. AA QQQ Recommended. Historic old country house welcomes you to this beautiful part of England. No smoking throughout. Choice of breakfast. Bed and Breakfast from £20.

KENT, MAIDSTONE.Mrs Burbridge, Waterkant Guest House, Moat Road, Headcorn, Ashford TN27 9NT (01622 890154). Small guest house offering a warm and friendly welcome to all our visitors, many of whom return year after year. No smoking in the diningroom.

LANCASHIRE, BLACKPOOL. Ronald and Elsie Platt, Sunnyside and Holmesdale Guest House, 25/27 High Street, Blackpool FY1 2BN (01253 23781). Two minutes from North Station, promenade, all shows and amenities. No smoking. Bed and Breakfast; Evening Meal optional.

LANCASHIRE, BLACKPOOL NORTH SHORE. Mildred & Ken Robinson, The Birchley Hotel, 64 Holmfield Road, Blackpool FY2 9RT (01253 354174). Totally "No Smoking" you are assured of a warm welcome in a friendly relaxed "Smoke Free" atmosphere, personal attention and a service often promised but rarely obtained these days. Telephone for brochure.

LANCASHIRE, LYTHAM ST. ANNES. Mr M.J. Doran, Willow Trees, 89 Heyhouses Lane, Lytham St. Annes FY8 3RN (01253 727235). Warm welcome awaits you in this comfortable detached house with pleasant gardens. No smoking in the house please.

LANCASHIRE, ROCHDALE. Mrs J.M. Neave, Leaches Farm, Ashworth Valley, Rochdale OL11 5UN (01706 41116/7 or 228520). Beautiful 17th century farmhouse with unrestricted views over Lancashire, Cheshire and Derbyshire. Non-smokers preferred.

LEICESTERSHIRE, MELTON MOWBRAY. Mrs Brenda Bailey, Church Cottage, Holwell, Melton Mowbray LE14 4SZ (01664 444255). 18th century listed building in the heart of the Leicestershire countryside. No smoking in bedrooms. Excellent food and accommodation.

LEICESTERSHIRE, MELTON MOWBRAY. Mrs R.S. Whittard, Elms Farm, Long Clawson, Melton Mowbray LE14 4NG (Tel and Fax: 01664 822395). A warm welcome awaits you in this non-smoking 17th century farmhouse situated in the beautiful Vale of Belvoir. Open all year except Christmas.

LINCOLNSHIRE, HORNCASTLE. Michael and Jill Swan, The Old Rectory, Fulletby, Near Horncastle LN9 6JX (Tel & Fax: 01507 533533). Country house, idyllic situation, nestling in Wolds. Superior Bed and Breakfast en suite. Non smoking establishment.

LINCOLNSHIRE, LINCOLN. Mr David Benson, Mayfield Guest House, 213 Yarborough Road, Lincoln LN1 3NQ (01522 533732). ❤ ❤ *COMMENDED*. Small, friendly Victorian guest house with private enclosed parking. Quality bed and breakfast at a comfortable price. A completely non-smoking establishment.

LINCOLNSHIRE, LINCOLN. Hilary and Tony Raley, Tinley Cottage, Broxholme, Near Saxilby, Lincoln LN1 2NG (01522 704001). ❤ ❤ *HIGHLY COMMENDED*. An old world beamed cottage set in peaceful hamlet only 10 minutes' drive from the centre of the historic city of Lincoln. The perfect base for visiting many places of interest. A non smoking home.

NORFOLK, AYLSHAM. David Newman & Hazel Stringer, Old Pump House, Holman Road, Aylsham NR11 6BY (01263 733789). ❤ ❤ *HIGHLY COMMENDED*. Creature comforts, home cooking, modern facilities. 1750's house near church and market place. Breakfast in pine-shuttered sitting room overlooking peaceful garden. Dinner by arrangement October to May. No smoking.

NORFOLK, GILLINGHAM. Mr and Mrs Craggs, Windle Hill House, Gillingham, Beccles NR34 0EF (01502 677392; Fax: 01502 678293). Attractive Listed 18th century house set in extensive gardens and paddocks. All rooms centrally heated. Dogs by arrangement. Children over ten welcome. Open January to December. No smoking in bedrooms.

NORFOLK, HORSEY CORNER. The Old Chapel, Horsey Corner NR29 4EH (01493 393498). ETB Listed *COMMENDED*. Strolls to beach and Broads. Non smoking throughout. Double, twin, en suite rooms from £15 B&B. Evening meal available.

NORFOLK, NORWICH. Mr Brian and Mrs Diane Curtis, Rosedale Guest House, 145 Earlham Road, Norwich NR2 3RG (01603 453743). Friendly Victorian guest house. Full English Breakfast served. Vegetarians catered for. Non-smoking breakfast room.

NORFOLK, NORWICH. Mrs Daphne Vivian-Neal, Welbeck House, Brooke, Near Norwich NR15 1AT (01508 550292). Ideal for exploring the Broads and the Norfolk and Suffolk coasts. Open January to November. No smoking throughout.

NORFOLK, RACKHEATH. Julie Simpson, Barn Court, Back Lane, Rackheath NR13 6NW (01603 782536). Friendly and spacious accommodation in a traditional Norfolk barn conversion built around a courtyard. Accommodation includes a double en suite with a four-poster. All bedrooms are non smoking.

NORFOLK, RACKHEATH. Mr and Mrs R. Lebbell, Manor Barn House, Back Lane, Rackheath NR13 6NN (01603 783543). 👹👹 *COMMENDED.* A family home with lovely gardens in quiet surroundings. Accommodation includes double rooms with central heating, tea/coffee facilities, TV and own bathroom. Open all year for Bed and Breakfast. Non-smoking.

NORFOLK, THETFORD/WATTON. Kevin and Yvonne Fickling, Rose Cottage, Butters Hall Lane, Thompson, Thetford IP24 1QQ (01953 488104). A spacious and comfortable house in an acre of ground. No smoking throughout.

NORFOLK, WALSINGHAM. Mrs Pile, The Old Rectory, Waterden, Walsingham NR22 6AT (01328 823298). This charming rectory is situated in peaceful rural surroundings on the Holkham Estate, ideally positioned for exploring. There are three well appointed en suite rooms and a warm welcome awaits all year. This is a non smoking house.

NORTHUMBERLAND, HEXHAM. Mrs D.A. Theobald, Dukeslea, 32 Shaws Park, Hexham NE46 3BJ (01434 602947). 👹👹 *HIGHLY COMMENDED.* AA QQQ Recommended. Open all year. Totally non-smoking establishment. Reduced rates for children and stays of four or more nights.

NORTHUMBERLAND, HEXHAM. Patricia M. Henderson, Riverside, Mickley, Stocksfield NE43 7DF (01661 842887). ETB Listed. Spacious country house in large attractive gardens in peaceful riverside location for non-smoking countryside lovers yet only 20 minutes from Hexham and Metro Centre.

NORTHUMBERLAND, HEXHAM. Mrs E. Courage, Rye Hill Farm, Slaley, Hexham NE47 0AH (01434 673259). 👹👹👹 *COMMENDED.* Cosy 300-year-old farmhouse set in 30 acres of rural Tynedale. No smoking accommodation.

NORTHUMBERLAND, PONTELAND. Mr and Mrs Edward Trevelyan, Dalton House, Dalton, Ponteland NE18 0AA (01661 886225). 👹👹 Warm welcome extended, high standard of accommodation offered in this attractive Georgian house. No smoking in bedrooms or public rooms.

NORTHUMBERLAND, WARKWORTH. Mrs Sheila Percival, Roxbro House, 5 Castle Terrace, Warkworth NE65 0UP (01665 711416). Completely non-smoking establishment overlooking castle. Bed and Breakfast. Open all year.

NORTHUMBERLAND, WOOLER. Mr Terry Gilbert, Winton House, 39 Glendale Road, Wooler NE71 6DL (01668 281362). Ideally situated for exploring the north Cheviot hills and the English and Scottish borders with their mix of castles, abbeys and towns. Pony trekking, fishing, gliding and golf all available.

NOTTINGHAMSHIRE, NOTTINGHAM. Mrs J. Buck, Yew Tree Grange, 2 Nethergate, Clifton Village, Nottingham NG11 8NL (0115 9847562). Georgian residence of great charm and character located ten minutes from the City Centre. No smoking.

NOTTINGHAMSHIRE, STANTON-ON-THE-WOLDS. Mrs Val Moffat, Laurel Farm, Browns Lane, Stanton-on-the-Wolds, Nottingham NG12 5BL (0115 9373488). An old farmhouse in approximately four acres on a lane off the main A606. Spacious rooms all have colour TV and tea/coffee facilities. Children welcome, babysitting FREE. Large garden. No smoking in the house.

OXFORDSHIRE, SOULDERN. Toddy and Clive Hamilton-Gould, Tower Fields, Tusmore Road, Near Souldern, Bicester OX6 9HY (01869 346554). 👹👹 *COMMENDED.* Recently renovated farmhouse. Full English Breakfast using home produce when available. No smoking.

OXFORDSHIRE, THAME. Mr and Mrs Dean, Heath House, London Road, Milton Common, Thame OX9 2NR (01844 278904). A tastefully restored Victorian farmhouse set in five acres with beautiful views to the Chilterns. A friendly welcome is guaranteed. Sorry, no smoking.

OXFORDSHIRE, WITNEY. Mrs Elizabeth Simpson, Field View, Wood Green, Witney OX8 6DE (01993 705485). 👹👹 *HIGHLY COMMENDED.* Set in two acres and situated on picturesque Wood Green, yet only ten minutes from the centre of town. No smoking.

SHROPSHIRE, CLUN. Mrs Jones, Llanhedric, Clun, Craven Arms SY7 8NG (01588 640203). Working farm. Attractive old stone house with lawns and garden overlooking the picturesque Clun Valley, near the Welsh border and Offa's Dyke. Spacious accommodation, friendly atmosphere and good food.

SHROPSHIRE, FRODESLEY. Ron and Jenny Repath, Meadowlands, Frodesley, Dorrington SY5 7HD (01694 731350). ETB Listed. Set in quiet location seven miles south of Shrewsbury. Children welcome. Itineraries can be arranged and maps and guide books borrowed. Strictly no smoking. Brochure available.

SHROPSHIRE, LUDLOW. Mrs P. Turner, The Brakes, Downton, Near Ludlow SY8 2LF (01584 856485). 👹👹 *HIGHLY COMMENDED.* Extremely comfortable accommodation with excellent cuisine. A period farmhouse tastefully modernised with central heating throughout. Non-smokers are very welcome.

SHROPSHIRE, LUDLOW. Mr and Mrs Lowe, Lower Hayton Grange, Lower Hayton, Ludlow SY8 2AQ (01584 861296; Fax: 01584 861371). Centrally heated accommodation with tea/coffee facilities, colour TV and en suite facilities. Guest lounge. Conservatory. A non smoking house.

SHROPSHIRE, LUDLOW. Mrs Kathy Lanman, "Red Roofs", Little Hereford, Near Ludlow SY8 4AT (01584 711439). 👹👹 AA QQQQ Situated in the lovely Teme Valley overlooking glorious open countryside. Central heating throughout. Ample parking. Hospitality trays. Non-smoking accommodation available.

SHROPSHIRE, MINSTERLEY. Paul and Debbie Costello, Cricklewood Cottage, Plox Green, Minsterley SY5 0HT (01743 791229). ✿✿ *HIGHLY COMMENDED.* Delightful 18th century cottage at foot of Stiperstones Hills. All rooms en suite. Pretty cottage garden with trout stream. No smoking.

SHROPSHIRE, SHREWSBURY. Mrs Gwen Frost, Oakfields, Baschurch Road, Myddle, Shrewsbury SY4 3RX (01939 290823). ✿ *COMMENDED.* Situated in a quiet, idyllic setting in the picturesque village of Myddle. 15 minutes from Shrewsbury and Hawkstone Park. A non-smoking establishment.

SHROPSHIRE, SHREWSBURY. Anton Guest House, 1 Canon Street, Monkmoor, Shrewsbury SY2 5HG (01743 359275). ✿✿ *COMMENDED.* Tony and Anne Sandford offer a very friendly welcome to guests at their completely non-smoking home. Special diets can be accommodated by arrangement.

SOMERSET, BATH. Marrilyn and Colin Humphrey, Leighton House, 139 Wells Road, Bath BA2 8AL (01225 814761; Fax: 01225 448079). ✿✿ *HIGHLY COMMENDED.* AA QQQQQ Premier Selected, RAC Highly Acclaimed, Ashley Courtenay Highly Recommended. You are sure of a friendly welcome at this non smoking elegant detached Victorian house situated just 10 minutes' walk from Bath city centre. Brochure.

SOMERSET, BATH. Mrs Peggy Hartley, Orchard Cottage, Dovers Lane, Bathford, Bath BA1 7SX (01225 858649). ✿✿ *COMMENDED.* Detached cottage situated next to the village green. Attractive walled garden. No smoking.

SOMERSET, BATH. The Old Malt House Hotel, Radford, Timsbury, Near Bath BA3 1QF (01761 470106). ✿✿✿ *COMMENDED.* Between Bath and Wells, ideally situated for touring. No smoking in the dining room.

SOMERSET, BATH. Jill and Rob Fradley, "Sarnia", 19 Combe Park, Bath BA1 3NR (01225 424159). Welcome to our lovely Victorian home, rooms individually decorated, with all facilities. Ample parking, main bus route to city. No smoking please.

SOMERSET, BATH. Jan and Bryan Wotley, The Albany Guest House, 24 Crescent Gardens, Bath BA1 2NB (01225 313339). Non smoking accommodation at our friendly Victorian home. Just five minutes' walk from city centre.

SOMERSET, BATH. Ron and Vanessa Pharo, Ashley House, 8 Pulteney Gardens, Bath BA2 4HG (01225 425027). ✿ Charming Victorian house in quiet location conveniently situated for all travellers to this beautiful city. Non-smoking establishment.

SOMERSET, BATH. Mrs Chrissie Besley, The Old Red House, 37 Newbridge Road, Bath BA1 3HE (01225 330464). Tourist Board *HIGHLY COMMENDED.* Our romantic "Gingerbread House" has stained glass windows. The cosy double bedrooms have canopied beds, colour TVs, showers, etc. Breakfast in sunny conservatory. Private parking. This is a non-smoking house.

SOMERSET, BURNHAM-ON-SEA. Peter and Fizz Alexander, Priors Mead, 23 Rectory Road, Burnham-on-Sea TA8 2BZ (01278 782116). "Which?" Recommended, enchanting Edwardian home with beautiful grounds, swimming pool and croquet. Peaceful quality accommodation. Walk to sea and golf. Touring area. Sorry no smoking.

SOMERSET, CHEDDAR. P.A. Phillips, The Forge, Cliff Street, Cheddar BS27 3PL (01934 742345). Non-smoking comfortable old stone cottage with traditional working forge set in the heart of the village. Lovely views. Ramblers especially welcome.

SOMERSET, CHEDDAR near. Winston Manor Hotel, Bristol Road, Churchill, Near Cheddar BS19 5NL (01934 852348). Charming manor house standing in one and a half acres of secluded gardens overlooking the Mendip Hills. The hotel is a member of Logis of Great Britain where hospitality wears a human face.

SOMERSET, CREWKERNE. Mr Gilmore, Manor Arms, North Perrott, Crewkerne TA18 7SG (Tel & Fax: 01460 72901). ✿✿ *COMMENDED.* Lovely 16th century grade II Listed inn set in conservation village. Five well appointed en suite bedrooms. Renowned locally for very high standard of home cooking from both bar and restaurant. No smoking.

SOMERSET, DUNSTER. Mr and Mrs Lally, Exmoor House Hotel, 12 West Street, Dunster TA24 6SN (01643 821268). ✿✿✿ *HIGHLY COMMENDED.* Attractive Georgian building set in the charming village of Dunster. Ideal for Exmoor and National Trust properties. No smoking throughout the hotel.

SOMERSET, GLASTONBURY. Mrs L. White, Bradley Batch, 64 Bath Road, Ashcott, Bridgwater TA7 9QJ (01458 210256). Cottage guest house, five miles from Glastonbury. Bed and Breakfast. Meals available from local Inn. Vegetarian breakfast can be provided. Non-smokers preferred.

SOMERSET, GREINTON. Sally and Norman Hunt, West Town Farm, Greinton, Bridgwater TA7 9BW (01458 210277). ✿✿ *COMMENDED.* Bed and Breakfast accommodation. Open March to September. Non-smokers only please.

SOMERSET, MARTOCK. Mrs H. Turton, "Wychwood", 7 Bearley Road, Martock TA12 6PG (01935 825601). ✿✿ *HIGHLY COMMENDED.* Quality accommodation. RAC Acclaimed, AA QQQQ Selected, FHG Diploma. Credit cards accepted. Visit South Somerset's classic gardens. Non-smokers welcomed.

SOMERSET, NETHER STOWEY. Susan Lilienthal, Parsonage Farm, Over Stowey, Bridgwater TA5 8HA (01278 733237). Traditional farmhouse and organic smallholding, lovely location in picturesque Quantock Hills village. Delightful gardens. Comfortable spacious home with log fires. Delicious meals. No smoking throughout.

SOMERSET, TAUNTON. Mrs Chris Jordan, Waterpitts Farm, Broomfield, Quantock Hills, Bridgwater TA5 1AT (01823 451679). Tourist Board Listed. Quiet, friendly, secluded smallholding set in the beautiful Quantock Hills. Central heating in all rooms. No smoking.

SOMERSET, TAUNTON. Tom and Rowena Kirk, Yallands Farmhouse, Staplegrove, Taunton TA2 6PZ (Tel & Fax: 01823 278979). Delightful 16th century farmhouse one and a half miles from town centre, offering comfortable and attractive en suite accommodation. Warm welcome and friendly atmosphere. No smoking in bedrooms.

SOMERSET, WELLS. Mrs. Janet Gould, Milton Manor Farm, Old Bristol Road, Upper Milton, Wells BA5 3AH (01749 673394). ✿ Working farm. Grade II star Listed Elizabethan Manor House offering no smoking accomodation. Ideal for walking on the Mendip Hills and exploring local places of historic interest. Brochure on request. AA listed QQQ.

STAFFORDSHIRE, ECCLESHALL. Mrs Sue Pimble, Cobblers Cottage, Kerry Lane, Eccleshall ST21 6EJ (01785 850116). 🌸🌸 A five minute walk from the centre of Eccleshall situated within the conservation area. Children and pets welcome but we are non-smoking.

STAFFORDSHIRE, STOKE-ON-TRENT. Mrs I. Grey, The Old Vicarage, Leek Road, Stoke-on-Trent ST9 9BH (01782 503686). Convenient stopover for M6 travellers. Accommodation is centrally heated with one double and two twin-bedded rooms. Children welcome. Ample parking. No smoking in the house please.

SUFFOLK, BOXFORD. Mrs Janet Havard-Davies, Coxhill House, Boxford, Sudbury CO10 5JG (01787 210449). Delightful Suffolk country house situated on the top of Cox Hill overlooking Boxford and near the market towns of Sudbury, Hadleigh and within easy reach of Colchester, Ipswich, Harwich, Felixstowe and Cambridge. Ample parking.

SUFFOLK, CLARE. Jean and Alastair Tuffill, "Cobwebs", 26 Nethergate Street, Clare, Near Sudbury CO10 8NP (01787 277539). A friendly welcome awaits you at this Grade II Listed beamed house. Within walking distance of town centre, the delightful castle and country park. Non-smokers very welcome.

SUFFOLK, WOODBRIDGE. Mrs J. Pegrum, The Old Rectory, Tunstall, Woodbridge IP12 2JP (01728 688534). Non-smoking vegetarian accommodation in pleasant surroundings. Washbasins in all bedrooms. Lounge. Bed and breakfast from £17, Evening Meal £8. Weekly terms.

SURREY, DORKING. Mrs. M. L. Walton, The Waltons, 5 Rose Hill, Dorking RH4 2EG (Tel/Fax: 01306 883127). Listed house of historical interest situated in a conservation area. Vegetarian meals available. Smoking is discouraged but not totally forbidden in some areas.

SURREY, DORKING near. The Royal Oak, Holmbury St. Mary, Near Dorking RH5 6PF (01403 741537). A warm comfortable Inn with en-suite, home cooked lunches, suppers and wholesome traditional breakfasts. Good cask conditioned beers and fine wines. Non-smokers are very welcome.

SUSSEX (EAST), HASTINGS. Rosemarie Crouch, Highfield, Butchers Lane, Three Oaks, Hastings TN35 4NG (01424 814453). Clean friendly house in small country village. Non-smoking throughout. Bed and Breakfast with private bathroom.

SUSSEX (EAST), HASTINGS. Mrs Afroditi G. Wall, Beechwood Hotel, 59 Baldslow Road, Hastings TN34 2EY (01424 420078). 🌸🌸 Small family run hotel. Open all year. Ideal for touring. Bargain Breaks available. Non-smokers preferred.

SUSSEX (EAST), RYE. Mrs Heather Coote, "Busti", Barnetts Hill, Peasmarsh, Rye TN31 6YJ (01797 230408). Bed and Breakfast in country area. One double, one twin bedded room. No smoking in the house.

SUSSEX (EAST), WINCHELSEA. A.N. Roche, The Strand Hotel, Winchelsea, Near Rye TN36 4JT (Tel & Fax: 01797 226276). 🌸🌸🌸 *COMMENDED.* AA QQQQ Selected, RAC Acclaimed. Nestling beneath the cliff of the ancient medieval town of Winchelsea lies the 15th century Strand Hotel. An ideal place to stay while exploring many places of interest nearby.

SUSSEX (WEST), ARUNDEL near. Mrs Jocelyne Newman, Pindars, Lyminster BN17 7QF (01903 882628). 🌸 *HIGHLY COMMENDED.* Charming country house with modern comfort, warm welcome, lovely garden with open air swimming pool. Delicious home cooking. Non-smoking.

SUSSEX (WEST), LITTLEHAMPTON. Mrs Mo Skelton, Bracken Lodge Guest House, 43 Church Street, Littlehampton BN17 5PU (01903 723174). 🌸🌸🌸 *HIGHLY COMMENDED.* Friendly atmosphere, first class service. No smoking throughout the house. All rooms en suite. Ideal touring base. Staying on business or for pleasure, a warm welcome awaits you throughout the year.

WARWICKSHIRE, LEAMINGTON SPA. Marston House, Priors Marston, Near Leamington Spa CV23 8RP (01327 260297; Fax: 01327 26846). A warm welcome awaits guests at this well furnished family home, situated in pretty conservation village. No smoking.

WARWICKSHIRE, LIGHTHORNE. Mrs J. Stanton, Redlands Farm, Banbury Road, Near Warwick CV35 0AH (01926 651241). 🌸🌸 AA QQQ Farmhouse set in two acres of garden with its own swimming pool. Children welcome, facilities available and reduced rates. No pets. Non-smoking rooms available.

WARWICKSHIRE, STRATFORD-UPON-AVON. Mrs S.E. Hunter, Hill House, Hampton Lucy, Warwick CV35 8AU (01789 840329). HETB Listed *COMMENDED.* Idyllically situated midway between Stratford and Warwick, this charming Georgian country house stands in two acres of private grounds. You will be assured of a very peaceful stay and warm hospitality.

WARWICKSHIRE, STRATFORD-UPON-AVON. Mrs R.M. Meadows, Monk's Barn Farm, Shipston Road, Stratford-Upon-Avon CV37 8NA (01789 293714). AA QQ Bed and Breakfast. Non-smokers preferred and guests are particularly requested not to smoke in public rooms.

WARWICKSHIRE, STRATFORD-UPON-AVON. Mrs Karen Cauvin, Penshurst Guest House, 34 Evesham Place, Stratford-upon-Avon CV37 6HT (01789 205259). Prettily refurbished Victorian townhouse. Town centre five minutes' walk. Bed and Breakfast from £13.50. Totally non-smoking establishment.

WARWICKSHIRE, TANWORTH IN ARDEN. Monica and Brian Palser, Mungunyah, Poolhead Lane, Tanworth in Arden B94 5EH (01564 742437). Set in peaceful Warwickshire countryside overlooking golf course on the outskirts of the pretty village of Tanworth in Arden. Two twin-bedded rooms. Tea/coffee making facilities plus hospitality tray on arrival and evening drink are included. Ample parking. Non-smokers please.

WARWICKSHIRE, WARWICK near. Carolyn Howard, Willowbrook Farmhouse, Lighthorne Road, Kineton, Near Warwick CV35 0JL (01926 640475; Fax: 01926 641747). 👑👑 Very comfortable house and small farm in rolling countryside, handy for Stratford, Warwick and the Cotswolds. No smoking.

WILTSHIRE, DEVIZES near. The Old Coach House, 21 Church Street, Market Lavington, Devizes SN10 4DU (01380 812879). 👑👑 *COMMENDED.* This completely non-smoking house also offers guests the option of a vegetarian breakfast.

WILTSHIRE, MALMESBURY. Mrs C.E. Weaver, Whychurch Farm, Whychurch Hill, Malmesbury SN16 9JL (01666 822156). ETB Listed *COMMENDED.* **Working farm.** 17th century farmhouse situated on a family-run 200-acre dairy farm. Open all year. No smoking in bedrooms or bathrooms.

WILTSHIRE, SALISBURY. Mr and Mrs V. Bath, "Beulah", 144 Britford Lane, Salisbury SP2 8AL (01722 333517). Bed and Breakfast accommodation offered in pretty bungalow on outskirts of Salisbury. Totally non-smoking establishment.

YORKSHIRE (NORTH), CROPTON/PICKERING. Mrs Sandra P. Lee, The New Inn, Cropton, Near Pickering YO18 8HH (01751 417330) 👑👑👑 *COMMENDED.* Traditional, informal, family-run village inn. No smoking in conservatory or Victorian restaurant.

YORKSHIRE (NORTH), EASINGWOLD. Mrs Christine Kirman, The Old Vicarage, Market Place, Easingwold, York YO6 3AL (01347 821015). 👑👑 *COMMENDED.* Situated in this quiet Georgian market town half way between Thirsk and York. Excellent touring centre for York, the Dales and the Moors. No smoking throughout.

YORKSHIRE (NORTH), HARROGATE. Carol and Derek Vinter, Spring Lodge, 22 Spring Mount, Harrogate HG1 2HX (01423 506036). 👑 All year round a warm welcome awaits you from the resident proprietors. Tea and coffee making facilities in all rooms. Dinner provided on request. Residential licence, no smoking.

YORKSHIRE (NORTH), KETTLEWELL-WITH-STARBOTTON. Mr and Mrs Rathmell, Hilltop Country Guest House, Starbotton, Near Skipton BD23 5HY (01756 760321). 👑👑👑 *HIGHLY COMMENDED.* Guests at Hilltop are requested not to smoke in any of the bedrooms or in the dining room.

YORKSHIRE (NORTH), MALHAM. Sparth House Hotel, Malham, Skipton BD23 4DA (01729 830315). Country hotel of charm and individuality. All bedrooms no smoking. Separate no smoking lounge.

YORKSHIRE (NORTH), PICKERING. Judy and Keith Russell, Heathcote House, 100 Eastgate, Pickering YO18 7DW (01751 476991). 👑👑 *COMMENDED.* Early Victorian house with original features. Enjoy our personal attention in relaxed, friendly NON-SMOKING atmosphere.

YORKSHIRE (NORTH), SCARBOROUGH. Sue and Tony Hewitt, Harmony Country Lodge, Limestone Road, Burniston, Scarborough YO13 0DG (01723 870276). Relaxing octagonal retreat, superb views overlooking National Park and sea. Licensed, private parking, completely non-smoking. Warm and friendly.

YORKSHIRE (NORTH), SKIPTON. Mrs Heather Simpson, Low Skibeden Farmhouse, Skibeden Road, Skipton BD23 6AB (01756 793849). 16th century farmhouse set in private grounds. Open all year. Plenty of parking. No pets. No smoking. No children under 12 years.

YORKSHIRE (NORTH), THIRSK. Joyce Ashbridge, Mount Grace Farm, Cold Kirby, Thirsk YO7 2HL (01845 597389). 👑👑 *COMMENDED.* A warm welcome awaits you on working farm, surrounded by beautiful open countryside, ideal touring location. Open all year except Christmas. No smoking.

YORKSHIRE (NORTH), WHITBY near. Mrs Pat Beale, Ryedale House, Coach Road, Sleights, Near Whitby YO22 5EQ (01947 810534). Friendly Yorkshire house of charm and character at the foot of the moors and amid magnificent scenery. Totally non-smoking accommodation — always country-fresh and clean.

YORKSHIRE (NORTH), YORK. Roy Dodd, Charlton House, 1 Charlton Street, Bishopthorpe Road, York YO2 1JN (01904 626961). Well established guest house within easy walking distance of bus and rail stations, City Centre, Minster, Castle Museum, Viking Centre and Racecourse. Close to local shops, good restaurants and childrens' playpark.

YORKSHIRE (NORTH), YORK. Mrs R.M. Foster, Brookland House, Hull Road, Dunnington, York YO1 5LW (01904 489548). Excellent location on the edge of York. Park and Ride nearby. Spacious double rooms. Private parking. No smoking. Public house five minutes' walk. Evening meals.

YORKSHIRE (NORTH), YORK. Four Poster Lodge Hotel, 68/70 Heslington Road, off Barbican Road, York YO1 5AU (01904 651170). 👑👑 *COMMENDED.* RAC Acclaimed, AA QQQ. Victorian house lovingly restored and furnished. Close to historic York with all its fascinations. En suite four-poster bedrooms. Licensed. Non-smokers welcomed.

YORKSHIRE (NORTH), YORK. Ian and Carolyn McNabb, The Hazelwood, 24-25 Portland Street, Gillygate, York YO3 7EH (01904 626548; Fax: 01904 628032). 👑👑 *COMMENDED.* AA QQQQ Selected. Only 400 yards from York Minster, yet in extremely quiet location. Non smoking, quality accommodation with private car park. Comfortable en suite bedrooms. Quality breakfasts catering for all tastes, including vegetarian.

YORKSHIRE (NORTH), YORK. Mr D.R. Dawson, Stanley House, Stanley Street, York YO3 7NW (01904 637111). 👑👑 *COMMENDED.* All rooms have en-suite facilities with colour television and courtesy tray. Off street parking and a pay phone. Sorry, no pets or smoking.

YORKSHIRE (NORTH), YORK. Mr Whitehead, Holly House, Broad Lane, Appleton Roebuck, York YO5 7DS (01904 744314). Approximately seven miles from York centre. Conveniently placed for Yorkshire Dales, Moors, Wolds and coast. All bedrooms non-smoking.

YORKSHIRE (SOUTH), HOLMFIRTH/PENISTONE. Mrs Ann Unitt, Aldermans Head Manor, Hart-cliffe Hill Road, Langsett, Stocksbridge, Sheffield S30 5GY (01226 766209). 👑👑👑 *HIGHLY COMMENDED.* A non-smoking establishment. Monks once farmed on the site of this historic farmhouse. Spectacular views yet close to Penistone, Holmfirth, Huddersfield, Sheffield and Manchester.

ISLE OF WIGHT, SHANKLIN. Denise and Martin Nickless, Keats Cottage Hotel and Tea Rooms, 76 High Street, Shanklin Old Village PO37 6NJ (01983 866351). A small family-run, licensed hotel, centrally heated. TV lounge with log fire. Children welcome. Open all year.

SCOTLAND

ANGUS, BRECHIN. Mrs Margaret Stewart, Doniford, 26 Airlie Street, Brechin DD9 6JX (01356 622361). 👑👑 *HIGHLY COMMENDED.* AA QQQQ Selected. 19th century detached villa in quiet residential area of town. All home cooking and baking. A warm welcome is extended to all guests. No smoking.

ARGYLL, OBAN. Mr and Mrs Eccleston, Braeside, Soroba Road, Oban PA34 4SA (01631 563303). A small friendly B&B on the outskirts of Oban set in its own grounds. All rooms are heated and have tea/coffee facilities and TV. Pets welcome by arrangement. We are a non-smoking establishment.

ARGYLL, OBAN. Mrs. Giles, The Old Manse Guest House, Dalriach Road, Oban PA34 5VE (01631 564886). Detached Victorian house in quiet location offering no smoking accommodation. Real home cooking, friendly family atmosphere.

AYRSHIRE, KILMARNOCK. Mrs Agnes Hawkshaw, Aulton Farm, Kilmaurs, Kilmarnock KA3 2PQ (01563 538208). 200 year old farmhouse ideally situated for the West Coast of Scotland and a footpath to the Highlands. Only 10 minutes from Prestwick Airport and 25 minutes from Glasgow. Guests are assured of a good Scottish welcome.

AYRSHIRE, LARGS. Mrs Mary Watson, South Whittlieburn Farm, Brisbane Glen, Largs KA30 8SH (01475 675881). STB 👑👑 *HIGHLY COMMENDED.* AA QQQQ Selected. Chosen by Which? Bed and Breakfast, Welcome Host. Superb farmhouse accommodation, two miles from popular tourist resort of Largs. Warm friendly hospitality, enormous delicious breakfast. Highly recommended. No smoking in bedrooms or dining room.

DUMFRIESSHIRE, LOCKERBIE. Mrs Cecilia Hislop, Carik Cottage, Waterbeck, Lockerbie DG11 3EU (01461 600652). Tourist Board Listed *HIGHLY COMMENDED.* Set in peaceful village of Waterbeck with beautiful views. Twin or double rooms, some en suite. Ideal for touring South West Scotland, Cumbria or as an overnight stop.

DUMFRIESSHIRE, MOFFAT. Mr Terence Hull, Alton House, Moffat DG10 9LB (01683 220903; mobile 0850 129105). Historic country house situated in several acres of secluded grounds at the end of a long private lane. Bed and breakfast from £15. En suite available.

EDINBURGH & LOTHIANS, EDINBURGH. Mrs Maureen Sandilands, Sandilands House, 25 Queens-ferry Road, Edinburgh EH4 3HB (0131-332 2057). 👑👑👑 A distinctive and attractive detached bungalow in its own gardens with excellent bus service to the city centre. Open all season. Family rooms available.

EDINBURGH & LOTHIANS, EDINBURGH. Mrs Janet Burke, Patieshill Farm, Carlops, Penicuik EH26 9ND (01968 660551). 👑👑 *COMMENDED.* Working hill sheep and cattle farm set in the midst of the Pentland Hills offering Bed and Breakfast. No smoking.

EDINBURGH & LOTHIANS, EDINBURGH. Mrs H. Donaldson, "Invermark", 60 Polwarth Terrace, Edinburgh EH11 1NJ (0131-337 1066). 👑 *COMMENDED.* Non-smoking accommodation five minutes' drive from city centre. Reductions for children.

EDINBURGH & LOTHIANS, EDINBURGH. Mrs. Rhoda Mitchell, Hopetoun Guest House, 15 May-field Road, Edinburgh EH9 2NG (0131 667 7691). 👑 *COMMENDED.* Completely smoke-free environment situated close to Edinburgh University. Personal attention in a friendly, informal atmosphere. AA QQ, Which? Good Bed & Breakfast Guide.

EDINBURGH & LOTHIANS, LINLITHGOW. Mr and Mrs R. Inglis, Thornton, Edinburgh Road, Linlithgow EH49 6AA (01506 844216). Family-run Victorian house in peaceful location near town centre. Both rooms en suite. Off-street parking, friendly relaxed non smoking home.

GLASGOW, AIRDRIE BY. Mrs Hunter, Easter Glentore Farm, Slamannan Road, Greengairs, By Airdrie ML6 7TJ (01236 830243). 👑👑 *HIGHLY COMMENDED.* Best B&B Award Winner. Non-smoking only. Scottish hosts offering quality accommodation in 18th century ground floor farmhouse with panoramic views.

INVERNESS-SHIRE, CARRBRIDGE. Lynn and Dave Benge. The Pines Country Guest House, Duthil, Carrbridge PH23 3ND (01479 841220). Relax and enjoy our Highland hospitality, woodland setting. All rooms en-suite. Traditional or vegetarian home cooking. Non-smokers welcomed. Bed and Breakfast from £16 daily; Dinner, Bed and Breakfast from £150 weekly.

INVERNESS-SHIRE, INVERNESS. Mrs Joan Hendry, 'Tamarue', 70A Ballifeary Road, Inverness IV3 5PF (01463 239724). ✿ *COMMENDED.* Comfortable Bed and Breakfast base while you tour the many beauty spots of the Highlands. Completely non-smoking house.

INVERNESS-SHIRE, INVERNESS by. Mr M.B. Mansfield, 3A Resaurie, Smithton, By Inverness IV1 2NH (01463 791714). ✿ ✿ *COMMENDED.* Three miles east of Inverness with views across open farmland to the Moray Firth and Ross-shire hills. Home baking. Non-smoking. Ample parking.

ISLE OF MULL, CRAIGNURE. Mr John Cable, Chronicle, Craignure PA65 6AY (01680 812364). Non-smoking Bed and Breakfast. Two rooms en suite on ground floor (one step only). Vegetarians catered for. Close to ferry. Cyclists welcome.

SUTHERLAND, DORNOCH. Achandean, Meadows Road, Dornoch IV25 3SF (Tel & Fax: 01862 810413). We are mainly non-smoking. Bedroom and dining room are no smoking areas. Smoking permitted in lounge only.

WALES

NORTH WALES, BALA. Mrs Fran Burn, Brynllech Isaf, Llanuwchllyn LL23 7SU (01678 540374). Quiet, comfortable B&B off the beaten track in Snowdonia National Park near Bala Lake. Ideal base for walking and touring. Central heating. Tea/coffee making facilities and drying facilities. Car park. Open all year.

NORTH WALES, BALA. Mr T.G. Jones, Frondderw Private Hotel, Stryd-y-Fron, Bala LL23 7YD (01678 520301). ✿ ✿ *COMMENDED.* Delightful period mansion, five minutes from Bala. Non-smoking areas available. Open March to November inclusive. AA QQ. WTB Welcome Host.

NORTH WALES, BEAUMARIS. Mrs. E. Roberts, Plas Cichle, Beaumaris, Anglesey LL58 8PS (Tel/Fax: 01248 810488). ✿ ✿ *HIGHLY COMMENDED.* Large period farmhouse in 200 acres. Ideal touring base. No smoking accommodation. Welcome Host Gold Award, Farmhouse Award.

NORTH WALES, BETWS-Y-COED. Mr J.H. Whittingham, Fron Heulog, Betws-y-Coed LL24 0BL (01690 710736). ✿ ✿ *HIGHLY COMMENDED.* Guest House Award. "The Country House in the Village!" We invite you to visit our home where you will enjoy real hospitality. A completly non-smoking house. "More home than hotel!" Welcome! Croeso!

NORTH WALES, BETWS-Y-COED. Mrs Joyce Melling, Mount Pleasant, Betws-y-Coed LL24 0BN (01690 710502). WTB Welcome Home *COMMENDED.* AA QQ. A warm Welsh welcome awaits you at our Victorian stone built house. Vegetarian breakfast available. Some off road parking. Totally non-smoking.

NORTH WALES, BETWS-Y-COED. Summer Hill Non-Smokers' Guest House, Betws-y-Coed LL24 0BL (01690 710306). ✿ ✿ *COMMENDED.* Especially for the non-smoker, Summer Hill is delightfully situated in a quiet sunny location. Bed, Breakfast and Evening Meals offered.

NORTH WALES, CAERNARFON. Sylvette Williams, Tal Menai Guest House, Bangor Road, Caernarfon LL55 1TP (01286 672160). ✿ ✿ Victorian house standing in its own grounds off the A487. An ideal centre for touring Snowdonia. Access to house at all times. No smoking.

NORTH WALES, CAPEL CURIG. Mrs Alison Cousins, Bryn Glo Tea Room and Guest House, Capel Curig, Betws-y-Coed LL24 0DT (01690 720215/720312). ✿ Centrally situated in Snowdonia National Park by A5 trunk road. Private parking. Open all year. All rooms non smoking.

NORTH WALES, CONWY. Mrs. Michele Harpur, Caerlyr Hall, Conwy Old Road, Dwygyfylchi, Conwy LL34 6SW (01492 623518). ✿ ✿ ✿ *HIGHLY COMMENDED.* Deluxe, en suite, no smoking accommodation with the finest views in North Wales. Extensive breakfast menu, special diets catered for.

NORTH WALES, ST. ASAPH. Mrs Jones, Rhewl Farm, Waen, St. Asaph LL17 0DT (01745 582287). ✿ ✿ *COMMENDED.* 18th century farmhouse on 180 acre farm in peaceful setting. Comfortable bedrooms double en suite, family/twin. Spacious lounge with inglenook fireplace, colour TV. Coast six miles, three-quarters of a mile to A55. Excellent breakfasts.

NORTH WALES, ST. ASAPH. Mrs N. Price, Plas Penucha, Caerwys, Mold CH7 5BH (01352 720210). ✿ ✿ *HIGHLY COMMENDED.* Bed and Breakfast, Evening Meal available. No smoking in bedrooms and discouraged in the rest of the house.

NORTH WALES, TREFRIW. Ann and Arthur Eaton, Crafnant Guest House, Trefriw LL27 0JH (01492 640809). Totally non-smoking Victorian country home in charming village setting. Five en suite double/twin rooms with drinks tray and TV. Traditional/vegetarian menu. Private parking.

DYFED, ABERYSTWYTH. Sarah and Lester Ward, Sinclair Guest House, 43 Portland Street, Aberystwyth SY23 2DX (Tel & Fax: 01970 615158). ✿ ✿ *HIGHLY COMMENDED.* Immaculate en suite accommodation in totally smoke free guest house.

DYFED, BROAD HAVEN. Sandra Davies, Barley Villa, Walwyns Castle, Broad Haven, Haverfordwest SA2 3EB (01437 781254). ✿ ✿ *COMMENDED.* Comfort, cleanliness and personal attention assured. Substantial breakfasts; special diets catered for. Ample off road parking. Non-smoking accommodation available.

DYFED, LAMPETER. Mrs J.P. Driver, Penwern Old Mills, Cribyn, Lampeter SA48 7QH (01570 470762). Formerly a rural woollen mill set in a quiet valley alongside a small stream. Idyllic surroundings. Comfortable lounge. Double, single, twin rooms, cot. Washbasins in all rooms. High chair available. Non-smoking.

DYFED, LLANDYSUL. Mrs Joan Austwick, Pellorwel, Bwlchygroes, Llandysul SA44 5JU (01239 851226). Homely atmosphere created in this Victorian-style house. A non-smoking establishment.

DYFED, PEMBROKE. Mrs Sheila Lewis, Poyerston Farm, Cosheston, Pembroke SA72 4SJ (01646 651347; mobile 0402 391013). ❦❦❦ *HIGHLY COMMENDED.* **Working farm.** AA QQQQ Selected, Taste of Wales Member, Farm Holiday Bureau Member. Enjoy a relaxed holiday and warm hospitality at our old farmhouse. En suite rooms available. Full central heating. Sorry no pets and regret no smoking.

POWYS, BRECON. Mrs Marion Meredith, Lodge Farm, Talgarth, Brecon LD3 0DP (01874 711244). ❦❦❦ *HIGHLY COMMENDED.* 18th century house with original oak beams offers quality en-suite rooms with tea making facilities. Lounge with TV. A non-smoking establishment.

POWYS, BUILTH WELLS near. Mrs Margaret Davies, The Court Farm, Aberedw, Near Builth Wells LD2 3UP (01982 560277). We welcome guests into our home on a family-run livestock farm. All bedrooms have washbasins, shaver points, etc. Lounge with TV. Non-smokers please.

POWYS, CARNO. Mrs G. Bound, Pentre Uchaf, Carno SY17 5JP (01686 420663). ❦❦ A warm Welsh welcome awaits guests at our family-run farm situated half a mile from Carno village off the A470 coast road. An ideal base for touring. Children welcome. Brochure available.

POWYS, HAY-ON-WYE. Peter and Olwen Roberts, York House, Cusop, Hay-on-Wye HR3 5QX (01497 820705). Totally non-smoking, elegant, quiet Victorian Guest House on the edge of Hay-on-Wye (town of books). Excellent touring and walking centre. No smoking indoors.

POWYS, LLANWRTHWL. Dyffryn Farm, Llanwrthwl, Llandrindod Wells LD1 6NU (01597 811017). In picturesque upper Wye Valley. 17th century stone farmhouse with exposed beams offers relaxing accommodation in peaceful surroundings.

POWYS, WELSHPOOL. Mrs Jane Jones, Trefnant Hall, Berriew, Welshpool SY21 8AS (01686 640262). ❦❦❦ Warm welcome in Grade II Listed farmhouse. All rooms en-suite with tea/coffee making facilities and colour TV. No smoking.

SOUTH WALES, BLAINA. Mr J.W. Chandler, Lamb House, Westside, Blaina NP3 3DB (01495 290179). ❦❦ Set in the Upper Gwent Valleys close to all major tourist attractions in South Wales. Children welcome. No smoking in bedrooms.

SOUTH WALES, GOWER PENINSULA. Mrs M. Valerie Evans, The Old Rectory, Reynoldston, Swansea SA3 1AD (01792 390129). A warm welcome awaits visitors to our home in this beautiful peninsula. Non-smoking household. Visitors asked to refrain from smoking in the house. Bed and Breakfast £18; Evening Meal available, £10.

SOUTH WALES, NEWPORT near. Mrs D. Sheahan, The West Usk Lighthouse, St. Brides, Near Newport NP1 9SF (01633 810126/815860; Fax: 01633 815582). ❦❦ A real lighthouse with superb accommodation in peaceful and serene surroundings. Great hospitality. Distinctly different. Non-smokers very welcome.

SOUTH WALES, ST. BRIDES WENTLOOG. Mr. David W. Bushell, Chapel Guest House, Church Road, St. Brides Wentloog, Near Newport NP1 9SN (01633 681018). ❦❦ *COMMENDED.* Comfortable, non smoking accommodation in a converted chapel situated in a village between Newport and Cardiff. Children under three years FREE.

SOUTH WALES, TINTERN. Anne and Peter Howe, Valley House, Raglan Road, Tintern, Near Chepstow NP6 6TH (01291 689652). ❦❦ *COMMENDED.* Accommodation of a very high standard in a fine Georgian residence. Open all year. Non-smoking preferred.

DISABLED

LONDON, HYDE PARK. Mr R.S. Bhasin, Barry House Hotel, 12 Sussex Place, Hyde Park, London W2 2TP (0171-723 7340/0994; Fax: 0171-723 9775). ☙ *APPROVED.* Family-run Bed and Breakfast. Rooms en suite with colour TV, telephones and tea/coffee making facilities. Disabled guests welcome.

CAMBRIDGESHIRE, CAMBRIDGE. Paul & Alison Tweddell, Dykelands Guest House, 157 Mowbray Road, Cambridge CB1 4SA (Tel: 01223 244300; Fax: 01223 566741). ☙ Detached guest house with ground floor rooms suitable for disabled guests. Ideal touring base to discover the secrets of the Cambridgeshire countryside. Access and Visa welcome. AA QQ.

CAMBRIDGESHIRE, ELY. Mrs Margaret Sicard, The Laurels, 104 Victoria Street, Littleport, Ely CB6 1LZ (01353 861972; 0850 199299 mobile). Attractive, non-smoking, Victorian house 200 yards from the Great Ouse River. Central heating, tea/coffee making facilities, colour TV and radio in rooms. Suitable for partially disabled visitors.

CHESHIRE, BALTERLEY. Mrs Joanne Hollins, Green Farm, Deans Lane, Balterley, Near Crewe CW2 5QJ (01270 820214). ☙ ☙ **Working farm.** Jo and Pete Hollins offer guests a friendly welcome to their home on a 145-acre farm in quiet and peaceful surroundings on the Cheshire/Staffordshire border — an excellent stopover. Children and pets welcome. Accommodation suitable for disabled visitors.

CHESHIRE, SANDBACH. Mrs Helen Wood, Arclid Grange, Sandbach CW11 0SZ (Tel: 01270 764750; Fax: 01270 759255). Category 3 Accessible Scheme. Three of our rooms are on the ground floor. Easy access to car park by ramp. No steps into the house.

CORNWALL, TRURO. Marcorrie Hotel, 20 Falmouth Road, Truro TR1 2HX (01872 77374; Fax: 01872 41666). ☙ ☙ ☙ *APPROVED.* Victorian town house in conservation area, five minutes' walk from city centre and cathedral. All rooms are en suite and have central heating, colour TV, tea making facilities and telephone. Accommodation suitable for disabled visitors. Open all year.

CUMBRIA, CARLISLE. Ellen & John McLaughlin, The Warren Guest House, 368 Warwick Road, Carlisle CA1 2RU (01228 33663). ☙ ☙ ☙ *COMMENDED.* AA QQQ, RAC Listed. Ideal touring base. Six en suite bedrooms, two on ground floor leading out into patio area. A warm welcome awaits you.

CUMBRIA, PENRITH. Mr S.E. Bray, Norcroft Guest House, Graham Street, Penrith CA11 9LQ (01768 62365). ☙ ☙ ☙ *COMMENDED.* This spacious Victorian house, set in a quiet location and with en-suite ground floor twin room, is ideal for disabled guests.

DERBYSHIRE, BAKEWELL. Mrs Julia Finney, Mandale House, Haddon Grove, Bakewell DE45 1JF (01629 812416). ☙ ☙ Peaceful farmhouse offers bedrooms with colour TV and tea-making facility. Two rooms on the ground floor with en suite facilities suitable for disabled guests.

DERBYSHIRE, CASTLETON. Mrs B. Johnson, Myrtle Cottage, Market Place, Castleton, Near Sheffield S30 2WQ (01433 620787). Accommodation includes ground floor en-suite bedrooms with level access from car park. Disabled visitors welcome.

DEVON, ASHBURTON. Mrs Anne Torr, Middle Leat, Holne, Near Ashburton TQ13 7SJ (01364 631413). A warm welcome and relaxed friendly atmosphere assured in very peaceful surroundings. Accommodation in three ground floor bedrooms, suitable for disabled visitors.

DEVON, BIDEFORD. Jenny and Barry Jones, The Pines at Eastleigh, Eastleigh, Near Bideford EX39 4PA (01271 860561; E-mail Barry@barpines.demon.co.uk). ☙ ☙ ☙ *HIGHLY COMMENDED.* AA QQQQ Selected, RAC Highly Acclaimed. Georgian house in seven acres with glorious views overlooking Bideford and the sea at Hartland Point and Lundy Island. Disabled visitors can be accommodated. Short Breaks available.

DEVON, ILFRACOMBE. Sunnymeade Country House Hotel, Dean Cross, West Down, Ilfracombe EX34 8NT (01271 863668). ☙ ☙ ☙ A charming country house hotel in its own large gardens set in the rolling Devonshire countryside. 10 pretty en suite bedrooms; some on the ground floor for those less mobile guests.

DEVON, WHIDDON DOWN. Mrs Elizabeth Knox, Tor View, Whiddon Down, Okehampton EX20 2PR (01647 231447). Ideal base for exploring Dartmoor. All accommodation on ground floor. TV lounge. Sorry, no smoking.

DORSET, BRIDPORT. Ann and Dan Walker MHCIMA, Britmead House, West Bay Road, Bridport DT6 4EG (01308 422941). ☙ ☙ *HIGHLY COMMENDED.* AA QQQQ Selected, RAC Acclaimed. Facilities offered include one full en suite ground floor twin bedroom, limited wheelchair use. Optional Dinner. Open all year.

DORSET, LYME REGIS. Mr and Mrs C.S. Ansell, Providence House, Lyme Road, Uplyme, Lyme Regis DT7 3TH (01297 445704). Small Regency guest house beautifully renovated. All rooms either en-suite or with private facilities; ground floor room with adjoining bathroom suitable for partially disabled visitors.

DORSET, LYME REGIS. Mrs S.G. Taylor, Buckland Farm, Raymonds Hill, Near Axminster EX13 5SZ (01297 33222). Smallholding of five acres, three miles from Lyme Regis and Charmouth. En suite accommodation with shower available on ground floor suitable for disabled visitors.

ESSEX, COLCHESTER. Mrs Wendy Anderson, The Old Manse, 15 Roman Road, Colchester CO1 1UR (01206 545154). This elegant and spacious town centre Victorian home provides one ground floor double bedded room with separate toilet/shower suitable for partially disabled visitors.

HAMPSHIRE, NEW FOREST. Mrs Pauline Harris, Little Heathers, 13 Whitemoor Road, Brocken-hurst SO42 7QG (01590 623512). Warm welcome for all non-smokers. Ground floor bedrooms with limited wheelchair use. Special diets can be catered for.

HAMPSHIRE, NEW FOREST. Mrs J. Pearce, "St. Ursula", 30 Hobart Road, New Milton BH25 6EG (01425 613515). ✿✿✿ Ideal base for visiting New Forest. Comfortable accommodation includes downstairs twin bedroom with en-suite shower and wheelchair ramp access. Children and pets welcome. Smoke detectors fitted.

HAMPSHIRE, NEW FOREST. Mrs M. Stone, Heathlands, Lepe Road, Langley SO45 1YT (01703 892517). Comfortable accommodation in a large bungalow. All rooms have washbasins, central heating, tea-making facilities and colour TV. There is a shower room and WC. Suitable for disabled guests.

HAMPSHIRE, WINCHESTER. Mrs Ann Regan, "Leckhampton", 62 Kilham Lane, Winchester SO22 5QD (01962 852831). AA QQQQ Peaceful country home set in large garden overlooking countryside. Ground floor rooms available for less mobile guests.

KENT, DYMCHURCH. Caroline Rasmussen, Wenvoe House, 88 Dymchurch Road, St. Mary's Bay, Romney Marsh TN29 0QR (01303 874426). Family run Guest House situated on the sea front. All rooms have tea/coffee making facilities. En-suite chalets available. Disabled guests welcome.

LANCASHIRE, BLACKPOOL. Ronald and Elsie Platt, Sunnyside and Holmesdale Guest House, 25/27 High Street, Blackpool FY1 2BN (01253 23781). Two minutes from North Station. Friendly atmosphere awaits guests. Bed and Breakfast; optional Evening Meal. Handicapped and slightly disabled visitors welcome.

NORFOLK, GREAT YARMOUTH. Mr and Mrs Brian and Diana Kimber, Anglia House, 56 Wellesley Road, Great Yarmouth NR30 1EX (01493 844395). Our reputation and good name have been built on service, a friendly atmosphere and fine food with a choice of menu. Partially disabled guests can be accommodated. Ground floor en suite.

NORFOLK, HORSEY CORNER. The Old Chapel, Horsey Corner NR29 4EH (01439 393498). ETB Listed COMMENDED. Category 3 National Accessible Scheme for Wheelchair Users. Minutes to beach and Broads. Non smoking throughout. Double, twin, en suite rooms, all on ground floor. Evening meal available.

NORFOLK, RACKHEATH. Julie Simpson, Barn Court, Back Lane, Rackheath NR13 6NW (01603 782536). Friendly and spacious accommodation in a traditional Norfolk barn conversion built around a courtyard. All accommodation on ground floor.

NORFOLK, RACKHEATH. Mr and Mrs R. Lebbell, Manor Barn House, Back Lane, Rackheath, Norwich NR13 6NN (01603 783543). ✿✿ COMMENDED. Family home with lovely gardens in quiet surroundings. Open all year for bed and breakfast. Accommodation available for disabled visitors.

OXFORDSHIRE, SOULDERN. Mrs C. Hamilton-Gould, Tower Fields, Tusmore Road, Near Souldern, Bicester OX6 9HY (01869 346554; Fax: 01869 345157). ✿✿ COMMENDED. A recently renovated farmhouse and barn. All bedrooms on the ground floor (not designed for wheelchairs).

SHROPSHIRE, LUDLOW. Mrs Kathy Lanman, "Red Roofs", Little Hereford, Near Ludlow SY8 4AT (01584 711439). ✿✿ Situated in the lovely Teme Valley overlooking glorious open countryside. Ample parking. Accommodation suitable for disabled guests. AA QQQQ.

SHROPSHIRE, SHREWSBURY. Gwen Frost, Oakfields, Baschurch Road, Myddle, Near Shrewsbury SY4 3RX (01939 290823). ✿ COMMENDED. Situated in a quiet, idyllic setting. All bedrooms are on the ground floor, suitable for less mobile guests, and have colour TV, tea making facilities, radio, washbasin, hairdryer and shaver point. Central heating throughout.

SOMERSET, CREWKERNE. Mr Gilmore, Manor Arms, North Perrott, Crewkerne TA18 7SG (Tel & Fax: 01460 72901). ✿✿ COMMENDED. AA QQQ. Lovely 16th century Grade II Listed inn set in the conservation village of North Perrott. Five well appointed en suite rooms situated in the old coach house which is behind the inn. Disabled guests accommodated.

SOMERSET, DUNSTER. Mr and Mrs Lally, Exmoor House Hotel, 12 West Street, Dunster TA24 6SN (01643 821268). ✿✿✿ HIGHLY COMMENDED. Attractive Georgian building set in the charming village of Dunster. Ground floor bedroom suitable for disabled guests.

SOMERSET, TAUNTON. Mrs Diane Besley, Prockters Farm, West Monkton, Taunton TA2 8QN (01823 412269). ✿✿ Large 17th century oak-beamed farmhouse only two miles from Taunton and M5 motorway. All bedrooms have washbasins, colour TV and tea making facilities. Ground floor en-suite bedrooms suitable for disabled guests.

SUFFOLK, HALESWORTH. Mrs Eileen Webb, Saskiavill, Chediston, Halesworth IP19 0AR (01986 873067). ♨ ♨ ♨ Spacious bungalow offers an ideal base for the fine city of Norwich. One room adapted for disabled visitors. Telephone or SAE for terms.

SUSSEX (EAST), HASTINGS. Mrs Afroditi G. Wall, Beechwood Hotel, 59 Baldslow Road, Hastings TN34 2EY (01424 420078). ♨ ♨ Small family-run hotel. Open all year. Ideal for touring. Bargain Breaks available. Some accommodation suitable for disabled guests.

SUSSEX (WEST), ARUNDEL. Peter and Sarah Fuente, Mill Lane House, Slindon, Arundel BN18 0RP (01243 814440). ♨ ♨ Rooms en-suite and with TV; central heating and log fires in winter. Special unit for disabled guests available.

SUSSEX (WEST), LITTLEHAMPTON. Mrs Mo Skelton, Bracken Lodge Guest House, 43 Church Street, Littlehampton BN17 5PU (01903 723174). ♨ ♨ ♨ *HIGHLY COMMENDED.* Purpose built, ground floor, twin bedded room. En suite with wheel in shower, good WC lateral transfer, wheelchair accessible washbasin. Private patio overlooking garden. Spacious comprehensive facilities ensuring accessibility and quality.

WARWICKSHIRE, STRATFORD-UPON-AVON. Mrs Karen Cauvin, Penshurst Guest House, 34 Evesham Place, Stratford-upon-Avon CV37 6HT (01789 205259) Prettily refurbished Victorian townhouse. One ground floor en suite room specially adapted for disabled guests. ETB Category 2 Accessibility symbol awarded.

WILTSHIRE, SWINDON. County View Guest House, 31/33 County Road, Swindon SN1 2EG (01793 610434/618387). Situated on the main road and five minutes' walk from rail and coach stations and the town centre. Ground floor rooms available, suitable for less mobile guests.

YORKSHIRE (NORTH), MALHAM. Sparth House Hotel, Malham, Skipton BD23 4DA (01729 830315). Relaxing country Hotel in heart of Yorkshire Dales. One ground floor en-suite bedroom equipped for disabled guests. Tourist Board Accessible Scheme Category 3.

YORKSHIRE (NORTH), WHITBY near. Mrs G. Watson, The Bungalow, 63 Coach Road, Sleights, Whitby YO22 5BT (01947 810464). Large bungalow, ample parking. One double room and one twin, both en suite, TV and tea making facilities. Disabled guests welcome.

YORKSHIRE (NORTH), YORK. Carolyn and Ian McNabb, The Hazlewood, 24-25 Portland Street, Gillygate, York YO3 7EH (Tel: 01904 626548; Fax: 01904 628032). ♨ ♨ *COMMENDED.* AA QQQQ Selected. NON SMOKING. Situated in extremely quiet location, 400 yards from York Minster, with private car park and comfortable en suite bedrooms. Quality breakfasts catering for all tastes including vegetarian.

SCOTLAND

ARGYLL, OBAN. Mrs Giles, The Old Manse Guest House, Dalriach Road, Oban PA34 5JE (01631 564886). Detached Victorian house in quiet location yet close to town centre, just a 10 minute walk from ferries to Mull, Colonsay, Islay and Tiree. Central heating. Disabled guests welcome.

AYRSHIRE, KILMARNOCK. Mrs Agnes Hawkshaw, Aulton Farm, Kilmaurs, Kilmarnock KA3 2PQ (01563 538208). Tourist Board Listed *COMMENDED.* AA QQQ. 200 year old farmhouse situated only 10 minutes from Prestwick Airport and 25 minutes from Glasgow; ideal for touring the West Coast of Scotland and a footpath to the Highlands. Disabled visitors welcome.

DUMFRIESSHIRE, CANONBIE. Mrs Steele, North Lodge, Canonbie DG14 0TA (01387 371409). A warm welcome awaits you at this 19th century cottage set in beautiful gardens. A ground floor en suite bedroom is available, suitable for the disabled traveller. Grade 1 Classification awarded by the STB.

DUMFRIESSHIRE, LOCKERBIE. Mrs Cecilia Hislop, Carik Cottage, Waterbeck, Lockerbie DG11 3EU (01461 600 652). Tourist Board Listed *HIGHLY COMMENDED.* All rooms have central heating and tea/coffee making facilities. Three steps up to front door, but all rooms are on ground level. May be suitable for disabled guests.

DUMFRIESSHIRE, MOFFAT. David and Sheila Barclay, Burnock Water, Haywood Road, Moffat DG10 9BU (01683 221329). ♨ ♨ *COMMENDED.* Comfortable Victorian family house set in large, secluded garden. Disabled access. Tranquil, scenic surroundings.

DUMFRIESSHIRE, MOFFAT. Mr Terence Hull, Alton House, Moffat DG10 9LB (01683 220903; mobile: 0850 129105). Historic country house situated in several acres of secluded grounds. All bedrooms have washbasins, tea making facilities and welcome tray. Full central heating.

EDINBURGH & LOTHIANS, EDINBURGH. Mrs Janet Burke, Patieshill Farm, Carlops, Penicuik EH26 9ND (01968 660551). ♨ ♨ *COMMENDED.* A very warm and friendly welcome is extended to all guests. Ground floor accommodation available.

EDINBURGH & LOTHIANS, LINLITHGOW. Mr and Mrs R. Inglis, Thornton, Edinburgh Road, Linlithgow EH69 6AA (01506 844216). Family-run Victorian house in peaceful location near town centre. Both our en suite rooms are on ground floor — no steps. Off-street parking. Friendly, relaxed non-smoking home.

INVERNESS-SHIRE, INVERNESS. Abb Cottage, 11 Douglas Row, Inverness IV1 1RE (01463 233486). All ground floor rooms are wheelchair accessible, one step only at front door. Vegetarians welcome, special diets catered for.

PERTHSHIRE, PITLOCHRY. Mrs Barbara Bright, Craig Dubh Cottage, Manse Road, Moulin, Pitlochry PH16 5EP (01796 472058). One ground floor twin room, en suite, no steps. Car can be parked at door for easy access.

SUTHERLAND, DORNOCH. Achandean, Meadows Road, Dornoch IV25 3SF (Tel & Fax: 01862 810413). We have large comfortable ground floor rooms with good wide doors and ramp for easy access into bungalow.

ISLE OF MULL, CRAIGNURE. Mr John Cable, Chronicle, Craignure PA65 6AY (01680 812364). Non-smoking B&B. Two rooms en suite on ground floor (one step only). Vegetarians catered for. Close to ferry. Cyclists welcome.

WALES

DYFED, SOLVA. Mrs Julia Hann, Min Yr Afon, Y Gribin, Solva SA62 6UY (01437 721752). Set in a peaceful hamlet, easy access to harbour, shops, restaurants, pubs. Annexe suitable for partially disabled guests. All on ground floor. Twin en suite, kitchen, lounge. Upstairs double en suite.

NORTH WALES, BALA. Mr T. Glynn Jones, Frondderw Private Hotel, Stryd-y-Fron, Bala LL23 7YD (01678 520301). ✿ ✿ ✿ *COMMENDED.* One downstairs double bedroom en suite available for the mobile partially disabled or elderly guests. Bed and Breakfast; optional Evening Meal. AA QQ. WTB Welcome Host.

SOUTH WALES, BLAINA. Mr J.W. Chandler, Lamb House, Westside, Blaina NP3 3DB (01495 290179). ✿ ✿ Set in the Upper Gwent Valleys close to all major tourist attractions. Accommodation includes two double en suite rooms on ground floor suitable for partially disabled guests.

SPECIAL DIETS

LONDON, HIGHGATE/CROUCH END. Mr and Mrs L. Solomons, The Parkland Walk Guest House, 12 Hornsey Rise Gardens, London N19 3PR (0171-263 3228; Fax: 0171-831 9489). Value for money Bed and Breakfast in pretty, comfortable Victorian house. Special diets catered for by arrangement. Brochure available. Email@parkwalk.demon.co.uk).

LONDON, HYDE PARK. Mr R.S. Bhasin, Barry House Hotel, 12 Sussex Place, Hyde Park, London W2 2TP (0171-723 7340/0994; Fax 0171-723 9775). ♛ *APPROVED.* Family-run guest house situated close to many tourist attractions. Vegetarian breakfast available if ordered.

CAMBRIDGESHIRE, ELY. Mrs Margaret Sicard, The Laurels, 104 Victoria Street, Littleport, Ely CB6 1LZ (01353 861972). Spacious attractive Victorian house. Ideal base for sightseeing. Special diets available.

CORNWALL, CAMBORNE. Mrs Christine Peerless, Highdowns, Blackrock, Praze-an-Beeble, Camborne TR14 9PD (01209 831442). Set on hillside with extensive country views towards St. Ives Bay. Bed and Breakfast; optional evening meal. Special and vegetarian diets catered for.

CORNWALL, FALMOUTH. Celia and Ian Carruthers, Harbour House, 1 Harbour Terrace, Falmouth TR11 2AN (01326 311344). Enjoy quality Bed and Breakfast accommodation with some of the most fantastic harbour views in Cornwall. Delicious home cooking with generous and varied menus. Special diets catered for.

CORNWALL, LOOE. Mrs Jean Henly, Bucklawren Farm, St. Martin-by-Looe PL13 1NZ (01503 240738; Fax: 01503 240481). ♛ ♛ ♛ *HIGHLY COMMENDED.* **Working farm.** Situated deep on unspoilt countryside yet only one mile from the beach, two and a half miles from Looe. Excellent accommodation with en suite rooms and farmhouse cooking; special diets can be catered for. Open March to October. Brochure.

CORNWALL, MITCHELL. Mr F.L. Blaiklock, Mitchell Farm, Mitchell TR8 5AX (01872 510657). Comfortable, homely farmhouse making an ideal base for touring both the North and South Coast resorts. Catering policy is to use fresh, natural foods; we specialise in organic farming with Soil Association Symbol; special diets catered for.

CORNWALL, PENZANCE. Mr and Mrs G.W. Buswell, Penalva Private Hotel, Alexandra Road, Penzance TR18 4LZ (01736 69060). ♛ ♛ ♛ *APPROVED.* AA QQQ. Victorian hotel set in a wide tree-lined boulevard. Special diets catered for by prior arrangement. Highly recommended.

CORNWALL, TINTAGEL. Kate and Peter West, Chilcotts, Bossiney, Tintagel PL34 0AY (01840 770324). Friendly, old, listed cottage with beamed ceilings. Vegetarian, vegan, wholefood or special diet breakfasts.

CORNWALL, TRURO. Marcorrie Hotel, 20 Falmouth Road, Truro TR1 2HX (01872 77374; Fax: 01872 41666). ♛ ♛ ♛ *APPROVED.* Victorian town house just five minutes' walk from city centre and cathedral. All rooms en suite. Special diets can be catered for. Open all year.

CUMBRIA, AMBLESIDE. Mr D. Sowerbutts, 2 Swiss Villas, Vicarage Road, Ambleside LA22 9AE (015394 32691). A full English Breakfast or vegetarian meal available. We are open all year round and you are sure of a friendly welcome and good home cooking.

CUMBRIA, CARLISLE. Ellen & John McLaughlin, The Warren Guest House, 368 Warwick Road, Carlisle CA1 2RU (01228 33663). ♛ ♛ ♛ *COMMENDED.* AA QQQ, RAC Listed. Six en suite bedrooms. Ideal touring base. Special diets catered for.

CUMBRIA, KENDAL. Mrs V.T. Sunter, Higher House Farm, Oxenholme Lane, Natland LA9 7QH (015395 61177). ♛ ♛ ♛ *COMMENDED.* AA QQQQ Selected. 17th century beamed farmhouse offers comfortable bed and breakfast accommodation in tranquil village. Self catering accommodation also available. No smoking. Pets welcome.

CUMBRIA, KENDAL. Eileen and Brian Kettle, Holmfield, 41 Kendal Green, Kendal LA9 5PP (Tel & Fax: 01539 720790). ETB Listed *DE LUXE.* Bed and Breakfast. Special diets catered for on request. Non-smoking establishment. From £19 per person. Short-listed for ETB B&B of the year.

CUMBRIA, KESWICK. Gladys & David Birtwistle, Kalgurli Guest House, 33 Helvellyn Street, Keswick CA12 4EP (017687 72935). ♛ ♛ *COMMENDED.* Be assured of a warm and friendly welcome. Excellent grilled breakfast served between 8am and 9am, menu choice, vegetarians catered for; packed lunches available. Children welcome.

CUMBRIA, KESWICK. Alan & Jean Redfern, Heatherlea, 26 Blencathra Street, Keswick CA12 4HP (017687 72430). **Tourist Board Listed** *COMMENDED.* This charming "no-smoking" guest house offers all guests a friendly welcome. Home cooking is a speciality, with a full breakfast menu and optional four course evening meal. Special diets catered for if prior notice is given. AA QQQ.

CUMBRIA, KESWICK. AnneMarie and Ian Townsend, Latrigg House, St. Herbert Street, Keswick CA12 4DF (017687 73068). ♛ ♛ We promise a very warm welcome, good food, comfort and hospitality (vegetarian and vegan meals provided if required).

CUMBRIA, PENRITH. Mr S.E. Bray, Norcroft Guest House, Graham Street, Penrith CA11 9LQ (01768 862365). ♛ ♛ ♛ *COMMENDED.* Victorian house in quiet area. Bed and Breakfast. Evening Meal available. Vegetarians catered for by prior arrangement.

CUMBRIA, PENRITH. Angela and Ivor Davies, Woodland House Hotel, Wordsworth Street, Penrith CA11 7QY (01768 864177; Fax: 01768 890152). ♛ ♛ ♛ *COMMENDED.* Licensed hotel situated at foot of Beacon Hill. Special diets catered for by prior arrangement.

CUMBRIA, TROUTBECK. Gwen and Peter Parfitt, Hill Crest, Troutbeck, Penrith CA11 0SH (017684 83935). A unique warm and friendly Lakeland home with vegetarian and healthy eating menus, where children and dogs are welcome. En suite rooms available.

CUMBRIA, WINDERMERE. Mick & Angela Brown, Haisthorpe Guest House, Holly Road, Windermere LA23 2AF (Tel/Fax: 015394 43445). ✿✿ *COMMENDED.* AA QQQ, RAC Acclaimed. Comfortable family-run house situated in a quiet part of Windermere yet close to the village centre and local amenities. Ideal location for touring the Lakes. Special diets catered for.

CUMBRIA, WINDERMERE. Barry and Gill Pearson, Broadlands Guest House, 19 Broad Street, Windermere LA23 2AB (015394 46532). ✿✿ *COMMENDED.* A warm welcome awaits guests at Broadlands, close to all amenities and an ideal base for the Lake District. Substantial full English Breakfast or vegetarian Breakfast provided on request.

CUMBRIA, WINDERMERE. Mrs Christopherson, Villa Lodge, Cross Street, Windermere LA23 1AE (015394 43318). ✿✿ *COMMENDED.* AA QQQ. Extremely comfortable accommodation in peaceful area overlooking Windermere village. Access to rooms at all times. Vegetarian/Special diets catered for.

CUMBRIA, WINDERMERE. Mr Brian Fear, Cambridge House, 9 Oak Street, Windermere LA23 1EN (015394 43846). ETB Listed *COMMENDED.* A traditional Lakeland guest house situated in Windermere village centre, convenient for all amenities. Modern, comfortable rooms with en-suite facilities. Full English, Continental or vegetarian breakfast is provided.

DERBYSHIRE, BAKEWELL. Mrs Julia Finney, Mardale House, Haddon Grove, Bakewell DE45 1JF (01629 812416). ✿✿ Vegetarians catered for, other special diets by arrangement.

DERBYSHIRE, BUXTON. Maria and Roger Hyde, Braemar, 10 Compton Road, Buxton SK17 9DN (01298 78050). Accommodation comprises comfortable, fully en suite double and twin rooms with colour TV and tea/coffee making facilities. Non-smokers preferred. Diets catered for.

DERBYSHIRE, HATHERSAGE. Mrs Jean Wilcockson, Hillfoot Farm, Castleton Road, Hathersage, Near Sheffield S30 1AH (01433 651673). Tourist Board Listed *COMMENDED.* Welcome Host. Newly built accommodation onto exisiting farmhouse offering comfortable, well appointed en suite rooms. Excellent home cooked food including vegetarian meals. Open all year.

DERBYSHIRE, TIDESWELL. Mr D.C. Pinnegar, Poppies, Bank Square, Tideswell, Buxton SK17 8LA (01298 871083). Comfortable accommodation. Restaurant. Vegetarians/vegans, diabetics catered for, other diets by arrangement.

DERBYSHIRE, TIDESWELL. Mrs Pat Harris, Laurel House, The Green, Litton, Near Buxton SK17 8QP (01298 871971). ✿✿ *COMMENDED.* Overlooking the village green. One double with en-suite facilities, and a twin room with washbasin and private use of bathroom and toilet. Tea/coffee making facilities in both. Private lounge. Special diets catered for.

DEVON, ASHBURTON. Mrs Anne Torr, Middle Leat, Holne, Near Ashburton TQ13 7SJ (01364 631413). Comfortable accommodation with wonderful views. Full English Breakfast, vegetarians/vegans welcome. Special diets catered for.

DEVON, BIDEFORD. Jenny and Barry Jones, The Pines at Eastleigh, Eastleigh, Near Bideford EX39 4PA (01271 860561; E-mail Barry@barpines.demon.co.uk). ✿✿✿ *HIGHLY COMMENDED.* AA QQQQ Selected, RAC Highly Acclaimed. Georgian house in seven acres with glorious views overlooking Bideford and the sea at Hartland Point and Lundy Island. Generous farmhouse style cooking, catering for all diets.

DEVON, COLEBROOKE. Mrs V.K. Hill, Birchmans Farm, Colebrooke, Crediton EX17 5DN (01363 82393). ✿✿ *COMMENDED.* **Working farm.** We are seven miles from Crediton in a peaceful part of the countryside with unspoilt views. All rooms en suite with tea/coffee making facilities. Evening meal available if required; vegetarians catered for.

DEVON, CREDITON. Mr and Mrs R. Barrie-Smith, Great Leigh Farm, Crediton EX17 3QQ (01647 24297). This outstandingly comfortable accommodation is fully centrally heated. Children welcome. Special diets catered for if prior notice is given. Bed and Breakfast £15, Bed, Breakfast and Evening Meal £21. Children half price.

DEVON, ILFRACOMBE. Sunnymeade Country House Hotel, Dean Cross, West Down, Ilfracombe EX34 8NT (01271 863668). ✿✿✿ A charming country house hotel in it own large gardens set in the rolling Devonshire countryside. There is always a vegetarian choice on the menu and any special diets can be accommodated.

DEVON, LYNTON. Woodlands, Lynbridge Road, Lynton EX35 6AX (01598 752324). ✿✿✿ *COMMENDED.* Ideal base for exploring Exmoor and the stunning coastal scenery. Private parking, licensed, cosy lounge, log fire and central heating. Vegetarians catered for.

DEVON, OKEHAMPTON. Mrs E.G. Arney, The Old Rectory, Bratton Clovelly, Okehampton EX20 4LA (01837 871382). Ideal centre for visiting Devon and Cornwall. Comfortable accommodation and good food.

DEVON, TAVISTOCK. Mrs Rose Bacon, "April Cottage", Mount Tavy Road, Tavistock PL19 9JB (01822 613280). ✿✿ *HIGHLY COMMENDED.* Extremely comfortable accommodation. En-suite facilities, colour TV, radios, tea/coffee. Special diets/vegetarians catered for.

DEVON, TORQUAY near. Mrs R. Wilkinson, Deane Thatch Accommodation, Deane Thatch, Stoke-in-Teignhead, Near Torquay TQ12 4QU (01626 873724). ✿✿ *COMMENDED.* Bed and Breakfast offered in charming thatched Devonshire cob cottage. Open all year. Special diets catered for, vegetarians welcome.

DEVON, UMBERLEIGH. Ms. Carolyn Billington, Westacott, Townsend, Chittlehampton, Umberleigh EX37 9PU (01769 540463). Centrally heated 300 year old former bakery now offering Bed and Breakfast accommodation. Special diets can be catered for.

DEVON, WOOLFARDISWORTHY. Chris and Keith Merton, Ford Mill, Woolfardisworthy, Near Bideford EX39 5RF (Tel & Fax: 01409 241289). 16th century farmhouse mentioned in the Domesday Book set in nine acre meadow with duck pond bordering Torridge River. Relaxed dining room with versatile cuisine and daily home made bread.

DORSET, BOURNEMOUTH. Bournecliff House, 31 Grand Avenue, Southbourne, Bournemouth BH6 3SY (01202 426455). Enjoy a happy holiday in the comfort of our small family guest house offering excellent food with friendly personal service. Optional evening meal. Vegetarians catered for.

DORSET, BOURNEMOUTH. Mayfield Private Hotel, 46 Frances Road, Bournemouth BH1 3SA (01202 551839). ♥♥ Sandra and Mike Barling welcome you to this AA Listed hotel offering a high standard of comfort and comfort. Most diets and vegetarians can be catered for with prior notice.

DORSET, BOURNEMOUTH. Alison & Adrian Homa, Bay View Hotel, Southbourne Overcliffe Drive, Bournemouth BH6 3QB (01202 429315; Mobile: 0585 488150; Fax: 01202 424385). ♥♥♥ COMMENDED. 14 en suite bedrooms. Special diets catered for by arrangement. Write or phone for brochure.

DORSET, DORCHESTER. Mr and Mrs Michael Eaton, The Dower House, Bradford Peverell, Dorchester DT2 9SF (01305 266125). Relaxing old village house. Home baking a speciality. "Special"/ vegetarian breakfasts provided.

DORSET, DORCHESTER near. Mr Howell, Appletrees, 23 Affpuddle, Dorchester DT2 7HH (01929 471300). Ideal stopover for Devon/Cornwall (A35 2km); cyclists and walkers especially welcome. One double, twoi single and one twin-bedded rooms. Use of kitchen if required. Special diets catered for.

DORSET, LULWORTH COVE. Mrs J.M. Aldridge, The Orchard, West Road, West Lulworth, Near Wareham BH20 5RY (01929 400592). Modern family home in peaceful off-road position. Home produce, eggs, etc used when possible; vegetarians and vegans catered for. Open all year.

DORSET, LYME REGIS. Mr and Mrs C.S. Ansell, Providence House, Lyme Road, Uplyme, Lyme Regis DT7 3TH (01297 445704). Set in the lovely village of Uplyme, one mile from Lyme Regis. The meals are special and all diets catered for.

DORSET, LYME REGIS. Mrs S.G. Taylor, Buckland Farm, Raymonds Hill, Near Axminster EX13 5SZ (01297 33222). Smallholding of five acres, three miles from Lyme Regis and Charmouth. Full English breakfast served, special diets catered for. SAE for details.

DORSET, WIMBORNE. Mrs Eveline Stimpson, Acacia House, 2 Oakley Road, Wimborne Minster BH21 1QJ (01202 883958; Fax: 01202 881943). ♥♥ HIGHLY COMMENDED. Warm welcome, very high standard of decor and quality English breakfast served; special diets catered for.

ESSEX, COLCHESTER. Mrs Wendy Anderson, The Old Manse, 15 Roman Road, Colchester CO1 1UR (01206 545154). A friendly welcome to this elegant spacious town centre Victorian home. Most special diets catered for.

GLOUCESTERSHIRE, AMBERLEY near Stroud. The Dial Cottage, Amberley, Near Stroud G15 5AL (01453 872563). Tastefully decorated rooms, en suite, and all modern facilities. Non-smoking. Bed and Breakfast from £25 per person. Special Diets catered for.

GLOUCESTERSHIRE, RANDWICK. Mr and Mrs J.E. Taylor, Court Farm, Randwick, Stroud GL6 6HH (01453 764210; Fax: 01453 766428). 17th century beamed farmhouse with beautiful views over Stroud valleys. Much of our food produced organically; special diets catered for.

HAMPSHIRE, BARTON-ON-SEA. Mrs J. Copeland, Laurel Lodge, 48 Western Avenue, Barton-on-Sea BH25 7PZ (01425 618309). ♥♥♥ AA QQQQ Selected, RAC Acclaimed. A superb area in all seasons for that special break. Scenic clifftops walks, beaches, golf, sailing, riding and the delights of the nearby historic New Forest. Open all year.

HAMPSHIRE, BURLEY. Mrs Gina Russell, Charlwood, Longmead Road, Burley BH24 4BY (01425 403242). Situated in an ideal walking and touring area. Riding and golf nearby. Bed and Breakfast. Vegetarian/special diets catered for.

HAMPSHIRE, NEW FOREST. Mrs Pauline Harris, Little Heathers, 13 Whitemoor Road, Brockenhurst SO42 7QG (01590 623512). A warm welcome for all non-smokers. Ground floor bedrooms with limited wheelchair use. Special diets can be catered for. Brochure.

HAMPSHIRE, SOUTHSEA. Mr and Mrs Willett, Oakleigh Guest House, 48 Festing Grove, Southsea PO4 9QD (01705 812276). Southern Tourist Board Listed. Small family-run guesthouse two minutes from sea. Double, twin, family or single rooms available. Central heating. Children welcome. Open all year. Special diets catered for.

HAMPSHIRE, WINCHESTER. Mrs S. Buchanan, Acacia, 44 Kilham Lane, Winchester SO22 5PT (01962 852259; 0585 462993 mobile). ♥♥ COMMENDED. Accommodation consists of one double and two twin bedrooms, all of which have en-suite or private bathroom, plus tea and coffee making facilities. Off street parking. Excellent choice of breakfast.

HAMPSHIRE, WINCHESTER. Mrs Ann Regan, "Leckhampton", 62 Kilham Lane, Winchester SO22 5QD (01962 852831). ♥♥ Peaceful country home set in large secluded garden overlooking open countryside. Special diets catered for by prior arrangement.

HAMPSHIRE, WINCHESTER. Susan and Richard Pell, The Lilacs, 1 Harestock Close, off Andover Road North, Winchester SO22 6NP (01962 884122). A non-smoking family home offering an excellent English Breakfast, including vegetarian meals. Country views.

HEREFORD & WORCESTER, ROSS-ON-WYE. Mrs M.E. Drzymalska, Thatch Close, Llangrove, Ross-On-Wye HR9 6EL (01989 770300). ☙☙ COMMENDED. Breakfast and optional evening meal prepared using home grown produce. Vegetarian and diabetic meals arranged.

HEREFORD & WORCESTER, WINFORTON. Mrs Jackie Kingdon, Winforton Court, Winforton HR3 6EA (01544 328498). A warm welcome and country hospitality at its best awaits you at 16th century Winforton Court set in its old world gardens close to the Black Mountains. Special diets are catered for.

KENT, CANTERBURY. Mr and Mrs Martin, The Tanner of Wingham Restaurant, 44 High Street, Wingham, Canterbury CT3 1AB (01227 720532). Family run restaurant with bed and breakfast accommodation. Relax and enjoy evening meals from our monthly changing menu — which includes the largest selection of vegetarian and vegan options in East Kent.

KENT, CANTERBURY. The White House, 6 St. Peters Lane, Canterbury CT1 2BP (01227 761836). ☙☙☙ Spacious Regency house within city walls. Excellent base for sight-seeing. Vegetarian breakfast on request.

KENT, CANTERBURY. Mr and Mrs P.W. Harris, London Guest House, 14 London Road, Canterbury CT2 8LR (01227 765860). SEETB Listed COMMENDED. Victorian Listed house situated within easy walking distance of many places of interest. Bed and Breakfast. Home cooking. Special and vegetarian diets catered for.

KENT, DYMCHURCH. Mrs Caroline Rasmussen, Wenvoe House, 88 Dymchurch Road, St. Mary's Bay, Romney Marsh TN29 0QR (01303 874426). This family-run guest house is ideal for a relaxing break. En-suite chalets available. All bedrooms have tea and coffee facilities. Vegetarians catered for.

KENT, MAIDSTONE. Mrs D. Burbridge, Waterkant Guest House, Moat Road, Headcorn, Ashford TN27 9NT (01622 890154). ☙ Small guest house offering a warm and friendly welcome. Special diets catered for.

LANCASHIRE, BLACKPOOL. Elsie and Ron Platt, Sunnyside and Holmesdale Guest House, 25/27 High Street, Blackpool FY1 2BN (01253 23781). Two minutes from North Station. Friendly atmosphere awaits guests. Bed and Breakfast; optional Evening Meal. Special diets catered for.

LANCASHIRE, LYTHAM ST. ANNES. Mr M.J. Doran, Willow Trees, 89 Heyhouses Lane, Lytham St. Annes FY8 3RN (01253 727235). Accommodation is quietly situated and centrally heated. Ample parking. Children welcome, reduced rates. Vegetarian diets catered for.

LEICESTERSHIRE, MELTON MOWBRAY. Mrs R.S. Whittard, Elms Farm, Long Clawson, Melton Mowbray LE14 4NG (01664 822395). Warm welcome awaits you in this 17th century farmhouse offering superb cooking — vegetarian and special diets catered for by prior arrangement.

NORFOLK, GREAT YARMOUTH. Mr and Mrs Brian and Diana Kimber, Anglia House, 56 Wellesley Road, Great Yarmouth NR30 1EX (01493 844395). Warm and friendly atmosphere. Three minutes from beach, pier and town centre. Licensed bar. Tea making facilities. Vegetarian and vegan diets catered for.

NORFOLK, HORSEY CORNER. The Old Chapel, Horsey Corner NR29 4EH (01493 393498). ETB Listed COMMENDED. Strolls to the beach and Broads. Non smoking throughout. Double, twin, en suite rooms. Evening meal available. We cater for any special dietary requirements.

NORFOLK, KING'S LYNN. Mrs Joan Bastone, Maranatha Guest House, 115 Gaywood Road, King's Lynn PE30 2PU (01553 774596). ☙☙ APPROVED. Friendly, small establishment close to town centre. Ideal for business travellers or holidaymakers alike. Special diets catered for.

NORFOLK, RACKHEATH. Julie Simpson, Barn Court, Back Lane, Rackheath NR13 6NW (01603 782536). Friendly and spacious accommodation in a traditional Norfolk barn conversion built around a courtyard. Vegetarian breakfasts catered for.

NORTHUMBERLAND, ALLENDALE. Mrs E. Finn, Thornley House, Allendale NE47 9NH (01434 683255). ☙☙☙ HIGHLY COMMENDED. Beautiful country house. Vegetarian meals available and guests may bring their own wine.

NORTHUMBERLAND, HEXHAM. Mrs E. Courage, Rye Hill Farm, Slaley, Hexham NE47 0AH (01434 673259). ☙☙☙ COMMENDED. 300-year-old farmhouse set in 30 acres of rural Tynedale. Special diets catered for by prior arrangement. Brochure available.

NORTHUMBERLAND, PONTELAND. Mr and Mrs Edward Trevelyan, Dalton House, Dalton, Ponteland NE18 0AA (01661 886225). ☙☙ Bed and Breakfast, optional Evening Meal. Excellent home cooking, using own home and organically grown produce when available. Vegetarian meals on request.

NOTTINGHAMSHIRE, NOTTINGHAM. Mrs J. Buck, Yew Tree Grange, 2 Nethergate, Clifton Village, Nottingham NG11 8NL (0115 9847562). Situated in a quiet, rural setting only ten minutes from the City Centre. Special diets catered for.

SHROPSHIRE, CLUN. Mrs M. Jones, Llanhedric, Clun, Craven Arms SY7 8NG (01588 640203). Attractive old stone house with lawns and garden, spacious accommodation. Open Easter to October. Sorry, no dogs.

SHROPSHIRE, LUDLOW. Mrs P. Turner, The Brakes, Downton, Near Ludlow SY8 2LF (01584 856485). ♚♚ *HIGHLY COMMENDED*. A period farmhouse, tastefully modernised; three double en-suite rooms. Excellent cuisine. Vegetarians catered for on request.

SHROPSHIRE, SHREWSBURY. Gwen Frost, Oakfields, Baschurch Road, Myddle, Near Shrewsbury SY4 3RX (01939 290823). ♚ *COMMENDED*. Situated in a quiet, idyllic setting in the picturesque village of Myddle. Golf and riding nearby. Pleasant garden for guests to enjoy. Extensive car park. Special diets catered for.

SHROPSHIRE, SHREWSBURY. Anton Guest House, 1 Canon Street, Monkmoor, Shrewsbury SY2 5HG (01743 359275). ♚ *COMMENDED*. Tony and Anne Sandford offer a very friendly welcome to guests at their completely non-smoking home. Special diets can be accommodated by arrangement.

SOMERSET, BATH. Jan and Bryan Wotley, The Albany Guest House, 24 Crescent Gardens, Upper Bristol Road, Bath BA1 2NB (01225 313339). Welcoming accommodation at our Victorian home, just five minutes from city centre. Vegetarians, vegans and special diets happily catered for.

SOMERSET, BATH. The Old Malt House Hotel, Radford, Timsbury, Near Bath BA3 1QF (01761 470106). ♚♚ *COMMENDED*. Between Bath and Wells, ideal for touring. Good choice for vegetarians always available, other diets by arrangement.

SOMERSET, BATH. Mrs Chrissie Besley, The Old Red House, 37 Newbridge Road, Bath BA1 3HE (01225 330464). HIGHLY RECOMMENDED. Our romantic Victorian "Gingerbread House" has stained glass windows. The cosy double bedrooms have canopied beds, colour TVs, showers, etc. Breakfast features multi-choice menu with wholesome/vegetarian dishes.

SOMERSET, CHEDDAR. P.A. Phillips, The Forge, Cliff Street, Cheddar BS27 3PL (01934 742345). Comfortable old stone cottage set in the heart of the village. Full English breakfast; vegetarian/vegan breakfasts on request.

SOMERSET, CHEDDAR near. Winston Manor Hotel, Bristol Road, Churchill, Near Cheddar BS19 5NL (01934 852348). Charming manor house in one and a half acres of secluded gardens overlooking the Mendip Hills. An ideal stop for visits to Bath, Wells, Longleat and Cheddar. All diets catered for; cosy restaurant open every evening.

SOMERSET, DUNSTER. Mr and Mrs Lally, Exmoor House Hotel, 12 West Street, Dunster TA24 6SN (01643 821268). ♚♚ *HIGHLY COMMENDED*. Attractive Georgian building set in village of Dunster. Farm-fresh West Country produce used to prepare varied and "different" menus; AA Rosette for Culinary Skills; special diets catered for. Extensive wine list.

SOMERSET, NETHER STOWEY. Susan Lilienthal, Parsonage Farm, Over Stowey, Bridgwater TA5 1HA (01278 733237). Parsonage Farm is an organic smallholding in the Quantock Hills. Meals are prepared using the farm's produce and delicious vegetarian fare is our speciality.

SOMERSET, TAUNTON. Mrs Chris Jordan, Waterpitts Farm, Broomfield, Quantock Hills, Bridgwater TA5 1AT (01823 451679). Tourist Board Listed. Bed and Breakfast accommodation in beautiful part of the Quantock Hills. Ideal for riding, mountain biking, walking, fishing or golf. Good public houses nearby. For more information please phone.

STAFFORDSHIRE, ECCLESHALL. Mrs Sue Pimble, Cobblers Cottage, Kerry Lane, Eccleshall ST21 6EJ (01785 850116). ♚♚ Eccleshall is ideally situated for the Potteries, Alton Towers and other attractions. Children and pets welcome. Special diets can be accommodated. Non-smoking.

SUFFOLK, WOODBRIDGE. Mrs J. Pegrum, The Old Rectory, Tunstall, Woodbridge IP21 2JP (01728 688534). Non-smoking vegetarian accommodation in pleasant surroundings. Washbasins in all bedrooms. Lounge. Bed and Breakfast from £17, Evening Meal £8. Weekly terms.

SURREY, DORKING. Mrs. M. L. Walton, The Waltons, 5 Rose Hill, Dorking RH4 2EG (Tel & Fax: 01306 883127). A listed house of historical interest situated in a conservation area. Evening meals and packed lunches are available if pre-booked, vegetarian diets are no problem.

SURREY, DORKING. The Royal Oak, Holmbury St Mary, Near Dorking RH5 6PF (01306 730120). A warm, comfortable, cheerful country Inn with en-suite facilities, home cooked lunches, suppers and wholesome traditional breakfasts. Always a vegetarian option, and special diets are catered for. Good cask conditioned beers and fine wines.

SUSSEX (EAST), BRIGHTON. Mrs A. Edwards, Four Seasons, 3 Upper Rock Gardens, Brighton BN2 1QE (01273 681496). ♚♚ Charming 200 year old guesthouse. Open all year. Vegetarians catered for.

SUSSEX (EAST), HASTINGS. Mrs Afroditi G. Wall, Beechwood Hotel, 59 Baldslow Road, Hastings TN34 2EY (01424 420078). ♚♚ Small family run hotel. Open all year. Ideal for touring. Bargain Breaks available. Special diets catered for.

SUSSEX (EAST), RYE. Mrs P.M. Hadfield, Jeake's House, Mermaid Street, Rye TN31 7ET (01797 222828). ♚♚ *HIGHLY COMMENDED*. Beautiful Listed building standing in one of England's most famous streets. Traditional or vegetarian breakfast served.

SUSSEX (EAST), WINCHELSEA. A.N. Roche, The Strand House, Winchelsea, Near Rye TN36 4JT (Tel & Fax: 01797 226276). ♚♚♚ *COMMENDED*. AA QQQQ Selected, RAC Acclaimed. Full of atmosphere with oak beams and inglenook fireplaces but with the comfort of all modern facilities. Residential licence. Ample parking. Special diets catered for.

SUSSEX (WEST), LITTLEHAMPTON. Mrs Mo Skelton, Bracken Lodge Guest House, 43 Church Street, Littlehampton BN17 5PU (01903 723174). ✿ ✿ ✿ *HIGHLY COMMENDED.* A warm welcome awaits you whatever your dietary needs may be. Telephone to discuss your preferred menu so you can enjoy the pleasure of a quality stay. Comprehensive breakfast choice.

WARWICKSHIRE, KINETON. Mrs C. Howard, Willowbrook Farmhouse, Lighthorne Road, Kineton, Near Warwick CV35 0JL (01926 640475; Fax: 01926 641747). ✿ ✿ Very comfortable house and small farm situated in rolling countryside. Bed and Breakfast. Low-fat, diabetic and vegetarian diets catered for.

WARWICKSHIRE, STRATFORD-UPON-AVON. Mrs Karen Cauvin, Penshurst Guest House, 34 Evesham Place, Stratford-upon-Avon CV37 6HT (01789 205259; Fax: 01789 295322). Prettily refurbished Victorian townhouse. Town centre five minutes' walk. Will cater for any special diet, including vegetarian.

WILTSHIRE, DEVIZES. Mr and Mrs R. Mattingly, The Old Coach House, 21 Church Street, Market Lavington, Devizes SN10 4DU (01380 812879). ✿ ✿ *COMMENDED.* This completely non-smoking house offers guests the option of a vegetarian breakfast.

WILTSHIRE, MARLBOROUGH. Mrs P. Roe, Clench Farmhouse, Near Marlborough SN8 4NT (01672 810264). Attractive 18th century farmhouse set in own grounds with lovely views. Three-course dinner by prior arrangement. Special diets catered for.

WILTSHIRE, SWINDON. County View Guest House, 31/33 County Road, Swindon SN1 2EG (01793 610434/618387). Victorian property situated on main road, five minutes' walk stations and town centre. Bed and Breakfast; Evening Meal available. We cater for vegetarians.

YORKSHIRE (NORTH), HELMSLEY. Mrs. C. Swift, Stilworth House, 1 Church Street, Helmsley YO6 5AD (01439 771072. ✿ ✿ *COMMENDED.* Beautifully situated accommodation. Ideal touring base. Highly recommended for good food, we cater for special diets. Telephone or write for brochure.

YORKSHIRE (NORTH), KETTLEWELL-WITH-STARBOTTON. Mr and Mrs M.L. Rathmell, Hilltop Country Guest House, Starbotton, Near Skipton BD23 5HY (01756 760321). ✿ ✿ ✿ *HIGHLY COMMENDED.* Vegetarian meals are available but advance notice is requested.

YORKSHIRE (NORTH), PICKERING. The New Inn, Cropton, Near Pickering YO18 8HH (01751 417330; Fax: 01751 417310). Warm and friendly inn with high standard of food and accommodation. No smoking restaurant serving à la carte and table d'hôte.

YORKSHIRE (NORTH), SKIPTON. Mr D.W. Oates, Sparth House Hotel, Malham, Skipton BD23 4DA (01729 830315). Country hotel. Delightful Yorkshire Dales village. Imaginative, home-cooked meals. Vegetarian — no problem, by arrangement. For other diets — please ask. Bed and Breakfast reasonable rates.

YORKSHIRE (NORTH), WHITBY. Mrs Pat Beale, Ryedale House, Coach Road, Sleights, Near Whitby YO22 5EQ (01947 810534). Any diet catered for, vegetarian and wholefoods always available. Please state any special needs when booking.

YORKSHIRE (NORTH), WOODALE IN COVERDALE. Mrs J.A. Clarke, Middle Farm, Woodale, Coverdale, Leyburn DL8 4TY (01969 640271). Two double and one twin bedded rooms, some en suite facilities. Pets and children welcome. Ample parking. Open all year. Special diets catered for.

YORKSHIRE (NORTH), YORK. Norma and Ted Long, The Green Guest House, 31 Bewlay Street, Bishopthorpe Road, York YO2 1JT (01904 652509). ✿ Choice of vegetarian/wholefood or traditional English breakfast offered at this environmentally-friendly guesthouse.

YORKSHIRE (NORTH), YORK. Four Poster Lodge Hotel, 68/70 Heslington Road, off Barbican Road, York YO1 5AU (01904 651170). ✿ ✿ *COMMENDED.* RAC Acclaimed, AA QQQ. Victorian house lovingly restored and furnished. Almost a whisper away from historic York with all its fascinations. En suite four-poster bedrooms. Licensed. Special diets catered for.

YORKSHIRE (NORTH), YORK. Ian & Caroline McNabb, The Hazelwood, 24-25 Portland Street, Gillygate, York YO3 7EH (01904 626548; Fax: 01904 628032). ✿ *COMMENDED.* AA QQQQ Selected. Non-smoking, quality accommodation only 400 yards from York Minster, yet in extremely quiet location. Private car park and comfortable en suite bedrooms. Quality breakfast catering for all tastes including vegetarian.

YORKSHIRE (NORTH), YORK. Mr and Mrs Whitehead, Holly House, Broad Lane, Appleton Roebuck, York YO5 7DS (01904 744314; Fax: 01904 744546). Approximately seven miles from York centre, conveniently placed for Yorkshire Dales, Moors, Wolds and Coast. Special diets and vegetarians catered for.

ISLE OF WIGHT, SHANKLIN. Denise and Martin Nickless, Keats Cottage Hotel and Tea Rooms, 76 High Street, Shanklin Old Village PO37 6NJ (01983 866351). Small, family-run, licensed hotel, centrally heated. Open all year. Children welcome. Mini breaks welcome.

SCOTLAND

ARGYLL, OBAN. Mrs Giles, The Old Manse Guest House, Dalriach Road, Oban PA34 5JE (01631 564886). Detached Victorian house in quiet location, yet close to town centre, only 10 minutes from ferries to Mull, Colonsay, Islay and Tiree. Real home cooking, friendly family atmosphere.

AYRSHIRE, KILMARNOCK. Mrs Agnes Hawkshaw, Aulton Farm, Kilmaurs, Kilmarnock KA3 2PQ (01563 538208). Tourist Board Listed COMMENDED. AA QQQ. 200 year old farmhouse situated only 10 minutes from Prestwick Airport and 25 minutes from Glasgow. Guests are assured of a good Scottish breakfast and tea on arrival. Special diets can also be catered for.

AYRSHIRE, LARGS. Mrs Mary Watson, South Whittieburn Farm, Brisbane Glen, Largs KA30 8SH (01475 675881). STB ❦❦ HIGHLY COMMENDED. AA QQQQ Selected, Chosen by "Which?" Best Bed and Breakfast, Welcome Host. Superb farm house accommodation two miles from popular tourist resort of Largs. Warm, friendly hospitality. Enormous, delicious breakfasts. Vegetarian/Special diets catered for. Highly recommended.

DUMFRIESSHIRE, MOFFAT. Mr Terence Hull, Alton House, Moffat DG10 9LB (01683 220903; mobile: 0850 129105). Historic country house situated in secluded grounds. All bedrooms have washbasins, TV, tea making facilities and welcome tray.

EDINBURGH & LOTHIANS, EDINBURGH. Mrs Janet Burke, Patieshill Farm, Carlops, Penicuik EH26 9ND (01968 660551). ❦❦ COMMENDED. A very warm and friendly welcome is extended to all guests. Special diets catered for by arrangement.

EDINBURGH & LOTHIANS, EDINBURGH. Mrs Maureen Sandilands, Sandilands House, 25 Queensferry Road, Edinburgh EH4 3HB (0131-332 2057). ❦❦❦ Enjoy the friendly welcome and relax in the well furnished and tastefully decorated accommodation near Murrayfield Stadium. Full Scottish breakfast and special diets catered for. Children welcome. Open all season.

EDINBURGH & LOTHIANS, LINLITHGOW. Mr and Mrs R. Inglis, Thornton, Edinburgh Road, Linlithgow EH49 6AA (01506 844216). Family-run Victorian house in peaceful location near town centre. Both our rooms are en suite. Vegetarians and special diet breakfasts are available. Friendly relaxed non-smoking home.

INVERNESS-SHIRE, CARR-BRIDGE. Lynn and Dave Benge, The Pines Country House, Duthil, Carr-Bridge PH23 3ND (01479 841220). Relax and enjoy our Highland hospitality, woodland setting, all rooms en suite. Traditional or vegetarian home cooking. Children/pets welcomed. Bed and Breakfast from £16 daily; Dinner, Bed and Breakfast from £150 weekly.

INVERNESS-SHIRE, INVERNESS. Abb Cottage, 11 Douglas Row, Inverness IV1 1RE (01463 233486). All ground floor rooms are wheelchair accessible, one step only at front door. Vegetarians welcome, special diets catered for.

MORAY, FORRES. Verdant Restaurant and Neptune Guest House, 22/24 Tolbooth Street, Forres IV36 0PH (01309 674387). Fully licensed restaurant specialising in Vegetarian and Vegan cuisine which offers a range of meals and snacks throughout the day and into the evening.

PERTHSHIRE, PITLOCHRY. Mrs Barbara Bright, Craig Dubh Cottage, Manse Road, Moulin PH16 5EP (01796 472058). Family home always providing a wide choice of breakfast. Most diets catered for. Please ask on booking.

PERTHSHIRE, STRATHYRE. Mrs Catherine B. Reid, Coire Buidhe, Strathyre FK18 8NA (01877 384288). Open all year. All food personally prepared. Home baking. Special diets catered for. Well recommended. Full Fire Certificate.

ISLE OF MULL, CRAIGNURE. Mr John Cable, Chronicle, Craignure PA65 6AY (01680 812364). Non-smoking B&B. Two rooms en suite on ground floor (one step only). Vegetarians catered for. Close to ferry. Cyclists welcome.

WALES

NORTH WALES, BALA. Mr T.Glynn Jones, Frondderw Private Hotel, Stryd-y-Fron, Bala LL23 7YD (01678 520301). ❦❦❦ COMMENDED. Bed, Breakfast and Evening Meal available. Special diets can be catered for if advance notice is given. AA QQ, WTB Welcome Host.

NORTH WALES, BETWS-Y-COED. Mrs Joyce Melling, Mount Pleasant, Betws-Y-Coed LL24 0BN (01690 710502). WTB Welcome Home COMMENDED. AA QQ. A warm Welsh welcome awaits you at our Victorian stone-built house. We welcome children over 12, but regret we are unable to take pets. Totally non-smoking. Diets/vegetarians catered for.

NORTH WALES, CAPEL CURIG. Mrs Alison Cousins, Bryn Glo Tea Room and Guest House, Capel Curig, Betws-y-Coed LL24 0DT (01690 720215/720312). ❦ Centrally situated in Snowdonia National Park by A5 trunk road. Vegetarian, diabetic or other special diets provided on prior request. Open all year.

NORTH WALES, CONWY. Mrs. Michele Harpur, Caerlyr Hall, Conwy Old Road, Dwygyfylchi, Conwy LL34 6SW (01492 623518). ❦❦❦❦ HIGHLY COMMENDED. Historic country house with the finest views in North Wales. Deluxe en suite accommodation with extensive breakfast menu, catering for special diets.

NORTH WALES, CRICCIETH. Mrs S.A. Reynolds, Glyn-y-Coed Hotel, Porthmadoc Road, Criccieth LL52 0HL (01766 522870; Fax: 01766 523341). ❦❦❦ *HIGHLY COMMENDED.* Lovely Victorian, family-run hotel and self catering accommodation overlooking the sea. Vegetarian, diabetic, low-fat and low-cholesterol diets catered for. Ground floor bedroom suitable for disabled guests.

NORTH WALES, FAIRBOURNE. John and Ann Waterhouse, Einion House, Friog, Fairbourne LL38 2NX (01341 250644). ❦❦❦ *COMMENDED.* Lovely old house, five minutes' walk from sea; mountain walks start just across the road. Bed and Breakfast; Evening Meal optional. Diabetic diets and vegetarians catered for. En suites available.

NORTH WALES, TREFRIW. Ann and Arthur Eaton, Crafnant Guest House, Trefriw LL27 0JH (01492 640809). Totally non-smoking Victorian country home in charming village setting. Five en suite double/twin rooms with drinks tray and TV. Traditional/vegetarian menu. Private parking.

DYFED, BROAD HAVEN near. Mrs Sandra Davies, Barley Villa, Walwyns Castle, Near Broad Haven, Haverfordwest SA62 3EB (01437 781254). ❦❦ *COMMENDED.* Comfort, cleanliness and personal attention assured. Substantial breakfasts; special diets catered for. Ample off road parking.

DYFED, LLANDYSUL. Mrs Joan Austwick, Pellorwel, Bwlchygroes, Llandysul SA44 5JU (01239 851226). WTB Listed *HIGHLY COMMENDED.* Homely atmosphere created in this Victorian-style house. Meals are lovingly prepared and varied, with home-grown produce used abundantly. We cater for vegetarians. Brochure available.

DYFED, TENBY. Mr E. Romeo, Pen Mar Guest House, New Hedges, Tenby SA70 8TL (01834 842435). ❦❦❦ *HIGHLY COMMENDED.* Table d'hôte, à la carte menus offer a wide choice of English and Continental cuisine; vegetarian, low fat, diabetic diets catered for.

POWYS, BRECON. Mrs Marion Meredith, Lodge Farm, Talgarth, Brecon LD3 0DP (01874 711244). ❦❦❦ *HIGHLY COMMENDED.* Freshly prepared "real food" including vegetarian, using local and home grown produce, is a speciality. A non-smoking establishment.

POWYS, HAY-ON-WYE. Peter and Olwen Roberts, York House, Cusop, Hay-on-Wye HR3 5QX (01497 820705). Elegant quiet Victorian guesthouse on the edge of Hay-on-Wye (town of books). Excellent touring and walking centre. Imaginative vegetarian meals available on request.

SOUTH WALES, BLAINA. Mr J.W. Chandler, Lamb House, Westside, Blaina NP3 3DB (01495 290179). ❦❦ Set in the Upper Gwent Valleys close to all major tourist attractions. Full central heating. Children welcome: Special diets catered for.

SOUTH WALES, GOWER PENINSULA. Mrs M. Valerie Evans, The Old Rectory, Reynoldston, Swansea SA3 1AD (01792 390129). A warm welcome awaits visitors to our home in this beautiful peninsula. Special diets catered for happily. Open most of the year. B&B £18, dinner £10.

SOUTH WALES, NEWPORT near. West Usk Lighthouse, St. Brides, Near Newport NP1 9SF (01633 810126/815860 Fax: 01633 815582). ❦❦ A real lighthouse with superb accommodation in peaceful and serene surroundings. Great hospitality which is distinctly different and deeply relaxing. Special diets catered for.

ONE FOR YOUR FRIEND 1997

FHG Publications have a large range of attractive holiday accommodation guides for all kinds of holiday opportunities throughout Britain. They also make useful gifts at any time of year. Our guides are available in most bookshops and larger newsagents but we will be happy to post you a copy direct if you have any difficulty. We will also post abroad but have to charge separately for post or freight. The inclusive cost of posting and packing the guides to you or your friends in the UK is as follows:

**Farm Holiday Guide
ENGLAND, WALES and IRELAND**
Board, Self-catering, Caravans/Camping,
Activity Holidays.   **£5.50**

Farm Holiday Guide SCOTLAND
All kinds of holiday accommodation.   **£4.00**

**SELF-CATERING HOLIDAYS
IN BRITAIN**
Over 1000 addresses throughout for
Self-catering and caravans in Britain. **£5.00**

BRITAIN'S BEST HOLIDAYS
A quick-reference general guide
for all kinds of holidays.   **£4.00**

**The FHG Guide to CARAVAN &
CAMPING HOLIDAYS**
Caravans for hire, sites and
holiday parks and centres.   **£4.00**

BED AND BREAKFAST STOPS
Over 1000 friendly and comfortable
overnight stops. Non-smoking, The
Disabled and Special Diets
Supplements.   **£5.50**

**CHILDREN WELCOME! FAMILY
HOLIDAY & ATTRACTIONS GUIDE**
Family holidays with details of
amenities for children and babies.   **£5.00**

SCOTTISH WELCOME
Introduced by Katie Woods.
A new guide to holiday accommodation
and attractions in Scotland.   **£4.80**

**Recommended SHORT BREAK
HOLIDAYS IN BRITAIN**
'Approved' accommodation for
quality bargain breaks. Introduced by
John Carter.   **£4.80**

**Recommended COUNTRY HOTELS
OF BRITAIN**
Including Country Houses, for
the discriminating.   **£4.80**

**Recommended WAYSIDE AND
COUNTRY INNS OF BRITAIN**
Pubs, Inns and small hotels.   **£4.80**

**PGA GOLF GUIDE
Where to play. Where to stay**
Over 2000 golf courses in Britain with
convenient accommodation. Endorsed
by the PGA. Holiday Golf in France,
Portugal, Spain and USA.   **£9.80**

PETS WELCOME!
The unique guide for holidays for
pet owners and their pets.   **£5.50**

BED AND BREAKFAST IN BRITAIN
Over 1000 choices for touring and
holidays throughout Britain.
Airports and Ferries Supplement.   **£4.00**

**THE FRENCH FARM AND VILLAGE
HOLIDAY GUIDE**
The official guide to self-catering
holidays in the 'Gîtes de France'.   **£9.80**

Tick your choice and send your order and payment to FHG PUBLICATIONS, ABBEY MILL BUSINESS CENTRE, SEEDHILL, PAISLEY PA1 1TJ (TEL: 0141-887 0428. FAX: 0141-889 7204). **Deduct** 10% for 2/3 titles or copies; 20% for 4 or more.

Send to: NAME ....

ADDRESS ....

....

.... POST CODE ....

I enclose Cheque/Postal Order for £ ....

SIGNATURE .... DATE ....

Please complete the following to help us improve the service we provide. How did you find out about our guides:

☐ Press   ☐ Magazines   ☐ TV   ☐ Radio   ☐ Family/Friend   ☐ Other.